INSOLVENCY WITHIN MULTINATIONAL ENTERPRISE GROUPS

Insolvency within Multinational Enterprise Groups

IRIT MEVORACH

School of Law, University of Nottingham

OXFORD

UNIVERSITY PRESS

OXFORD

UNIVERSITY PRESS

Great Clarendon Street, Oxford, OX2 6DP
United Kingdom

Oxford University Press is a department of the University of Oxford.
It furthers the University's objective of excellence in research, scholarship,
and education by publishing worldwide. Oxford is a registered trade mark of
Oxford University Press in the UK and in certain other countries

Crown copyright material is reproduced under Class Licence
Number C01P0000148 with the permission of OPSI
and the Queen's Printer for Scotland

Published in the United States of America by Oxford University Press
198 Madison Avenue, New York, NY 10016, United States of America

British Library Cataloguing in Publication Data
Data available

ISBN 978-0-19-954472-1

Contents

Acknowledgements

This work is an expansion of my Ph.D. thesis submitted in 2006 to the University of London. I would therefore like first to express my profound gratitude to Professor Ian F. Fletcher (UCL) who was my Ph.D. supervisor. His expert guidance has been invaluable, and I can still always rely on his vast knowledge and advice.

Other people have also played a part in the conception and realization of this book. Particular thanks go to those who read and commented on drafts of the book: Dr. Sandra Frisby, Professor Paul Torremans, Professor James Fawcett, Professor Harry Rajak, Professor Jay Westbrook, and Professor Phillip Blumberg. I owe a special debt to Professor Niamh Maloney for her all-round encouragement and support. I am also grateful for research assistance to Stuart Stock and Natalie Eliades.

Other people assisted me indirectly by giving their support or kindly sharing their views with me on multinational groups in insolvency. In particular I would like to thank Catherine Burton, Christine McCreath, Suzan Johnston, Ralph Mabey, Bruce Leonard, Neil Cooper, Ron Harmer, Mahesh Uttamchandani, Dr Dalia Even-Lahav and my colleagues at Lipa Meir & Co.

Finally, I owe much to Carmel, Roni and Amit for their unconditional support and patience during the time I spent working on this book. Roni's message on the white board above my desk—"Mummy I hope you write well in the book"—has been a great comfort in time of need.

Dr Irit Mevorach
University of Nottingham,
November 2008

Abbreviations

ALI	American Law Institute
ADB	Asian Development Bank
BCCI	Bank of Credit and Commerce International
COMI	Centre of Main Interests
DIP	Debtor in Possession
EBRD	European Bank for Reconstruction and Development
EC	European Community
ECJ	European Court of Justice
EEIG	European Economic Interest Grouping
EU	European Union
IMF	International Monetary Fund
MEG	Multinational Enterprise Group
NAFTA	North American Free Trade Agreement
OECD	Organization for Economic Co-operation and Development
SE	Societus Europaea
SPE	Societus Privata Europaea
SPV	Special Purpose Vehicle
UNCITRAL	United Nations Commission on International Trade Law
UNCTAD	United Nations Conference on Trade and Development

Table of Cases

GERMANY

HUNGARY

ITALY

IRELAND

ISRAEL

LUXEMBURG

NEW ZEALAND

UNITED KINGDOM

UNITED STATES

ECJ CASES

Table of Statutes and Other Instruments

PORTUGAL

SOUTH AFRICA

UNITED KINGDOM

UNITED STATES

EC LEGISLATION

UNITED NATIONS

Introduction

The book deals with multinational enterprise groups (MEGs[1]) and the event of their financial distress. This includes issues pertaining to the international insolvency proceedings of several MEG members or the insolvency of a single affiliate member of a MEG.[2]

The insolvency of companies brings forth complex issues such as the possibility of reorganizing the business or opting for liquidation, the availability of assets for distribution, how to divide the insolvency estate among the company's stakeholders which may be in different positions. The foreign elements involved in failures of multinational enterprises add further to this complexity as assets, creditors, or activities of the debtor are spread among different jurisdictions. The value of the debtor's estate may be undermined by the lack of cooperation among jurisdictions, especially when reorganization is sought. Foreign creditors may be in a vulnerable position compared to 'local' ones, costs may be significant if multiple proceedings are taking place, supervising a global operation by an insolvency representative may demand considerable expertise, and so forth. All of these issues reach a yet further level of complexity where the multinational enterprise is comprised of a group of debtors with separate legal personalities. Although separate legal persons are usually subject to separate insolvency proceedings the economic reality of the enterprise may suggest that it would benefit from a global group-wide perspective in its insolvency. Additional issues related to the multi-element nature of groups, such as group liability and vulnerable intra-group transactions, may also arise in the course of such insolvencies.

---

[1] The meaning of the term MEG will be discussed in chapter 1. Essentially, a broad meaning to the term will be proposed so that various types of connections between various types of entities will be included (that is, not only traditional corporate groups of the parent-subsidiary type of relationship but also, for example, franchisors and franchisees). The book, though, will focus on companies.

[2] International insolvency may be defined as the management of the general financial default of a multinational enterprise (see J. L. Westbrook, 'A Global Solution to Multinational Default' (2000) 98 Mich. L. Rev. 2276, 2279). 'Insolvency' or 'bankruptcy' refers to collective proceedings for the adjustment or collection of debts on behalf of all creditors and other interested parties. In certain legal regimes (such as the English, New Zealand, Australian, and Canadian regimes) the term 'bankruptcy' is reserved for liquidation of individual debtors, yet under the US and French insolvency regimes 'bankruptcy' is used also for corporations (see I.F. Fletcher, *Insolvency in Private International Law* (Oxford University Press, Oxford 2005, supplement 2007), 25–6). This book refers to the terms interchangeably and focuses on insolvency of legal persons (the insolvency of MEG members).

The book sets out to offer a framework for critically analysing means of treating insolvencies within MEGs. This is first and foremost comprised of two pillars supporting the issue. One relates to the group aspect of the phenomenon and the other to the multinational (cross-border) aspect of its insolvency. The book attempts to identify certain consistencies and prevailing principles in regard to these two problems, across legal regimes on national and international levels, and their legitimizing arguments. These 'master principles' are then placed at the core of the proposed framework. In the rest of the work the principles are put to the test in light of what insolvency law strives to achieve in the context of MEGs. In that, the proposed framework takes into account the inter-action between these legal areas when employed to assess possible measures in the case of insolvency within MEGs. That is, when considering a particular tool the framework enables us to ask not only whether this tool is supportive of insolvency law goals but also at the same time where it stands in regard to company law theory (in the context of the group problem) and conflict of laws theory (in the context of insolvency). The proposed framework is further assisted by a new nomenclature proposed in this work for easy classification of different types of MEGs and their specific insolvency scenario.

The reasons for taking such a multi-tiered approach are twofold. First, it is necessary to appreciate the effects of certain tools for MEG insolvency on the fundamental principles of the relevant areas of the law inherent to this issue, mainly insolvency, company law, and private international law. The framework will not be comprehensive if taking a narrow perspective based only on the insolvency angle. The intersection between the relevant areas should also be appreciated. The framework will further suffer from over-generalization if it fails to take into account the diversified scene in which MEGs live and die—the different types of MEGs, their inter-connections and managerial patterns, as well as the specific insolvency scenario.

Second, it is hypothesized that for 'laws of MEG insolvency' to be meaningful they should both enable the pursuit of desirable values and be feasible in terms of the possibility of their acceptance and adoption by a wide number of countries. As the MEG is international its default may generate proceedings in different legal regimes. If only a few legal regimes implement any such laws while others refrain from modernizing laws in this direction, it may result in an increase in jurisdictional clashes as well as cases where a MEG case ends up in a jurisdiction lacking the desired rules for MEG insolvencies. Therefore, considering approaches across jurisdictions to reveal common grounds in the relevant areas, while also ascertaining whether they are grounded on legitimate values, and then construing a framework for analysing tools for MEG insolvencies accordingly, can result in 'attractive' suggestions. Thus, measures for MEG insolvency which are consistent with the framework are likely to be acceptable on a wide basis. The book, therefore, does not focus on a particular legal system when considering approaches to the above problems. Rather, it takes a universal perspective to these issues.

However, the book does not solely aim to provide a useful theoretical framework to the case of insolvency within MEGs. Thus, it attempts to describe in detail a desired approach to MEG insolvencies also in terms of rules and procedures that can be applied in such cases. It seeks to consider various 'linking tools' for insolvency within MEGs (i.e. legal means which may link between the entities comprising the MEG in the course of their insolvency—across the group and/or across borders) and identify those measures which are beneficial in light of the suggested framework and its underlying 'master principles'. In this regard, relevant legal means existing in national laws are examined while discussing their competence as desirable measures on a universal basis. These may be primarily designed as means to link between group members in a domestic insolvency case, yet the book considers the applicability of such measures in the international case. This also requires examination of 'global measures' for dealing with cross-border insolvency. Here too, the book considers available linking measures even where these may have been designed for single debtors (linking between debtors' elements spread among different jurisdictions, such as its creditors, branches, etc) in terms of their applicability to the MEG case, and compatibility with the suggested framework. In general, the book does not focus on a particular legal regime. Rather, it considers various 'linking tools' available under different legal systems (either domestic or within regional or international frameworks). The problems and the desirability of possible solutions are exemplified by referring to recent MEG insolvency cases which may have been subjected to different cross-border insolvency regimes. To the extent there are shortcomings in current regimes (in regard to their applicability to the MEG case), the book attempts to propose improvements or refinements to current approaches, as well as new measures.

The issue of enterprise groups in general and the event of their collapse in particular has been to a large extent neglected thus far in legal regimes, even though their importance is growing and their magnitude is sometimes profound with the capability to affect wide groups of stakeholders. This state of affairs is undergoing change these days. It is more 'active' at present in current considerations of reform. In particular, UNCITRAL Working Group V (Insolvency Law) is currently addressing the matter.[3] The work of the Working Group will be considered throughout the book. This book is therefore timely in providing means for evaluation and consideration of rules and procedures for treatment of MEG insolvencies. It could be utilized in developing and modernizing current regimes in this area of the law. Crucially, the approach proposed in this book may assist considerations by national systems of adoptions of any proposals promoted by international organizations. Clearly, the adoption of such rules in practice is essential for a framework to become operative and practical.

---

[3] See n 96 chapter 1.

Structure

The work comprises three distinct parts. Part I provides the relevant background and deals with the main problems underlying the issue of MEG insolvencies, the problem of groups, and the problem of cross-border insolvency. Chapter 1 discusses the phenomenon of MEGs, various legal structures that may constitute a MEG, and discusses the meaning of the term MEG for the purpose of this work (i.e. which sorts of structures and 'linkages' among entities should be considered as MEGs in the context of insolvency). Chapters 2 and 3 discuss the two 'pillars' of MEG insolvency and provide the basic platform for the framework mentioned above. Specifically, chapter 2 discusses different areas of the law where the group problem arises, the basic tension between entity and enterprise law, the economic essence of legal separateness, and legal regimes' approach to the problem. Chapter 3 discusses the main schools of thought in international insolvency—mainly the universality–territoriality dilemma, as well as the application of these theories in practice—examining different frameworks and models for cross-border insolvency and international initiatives at harmonization of insolvency laws.

As aforementioned, assessing the problem of insolvency within MEGs is done in light of insolvency goals, while also taking into account the nature of MEGs and the diversified scene of its types of operation, as well as the insolvency scenarios. Part II is devoted to offering these further aspects to accompany the framework suggested in the previous part. Chapter 4 attempts to identify shared key objectives and tasks of insolvency systems which are also desirable on the policy level. Based on existing theories of insolvency law the chapter considers what could be perceived as key values of insolvency systems and their corresponding tasks. It then shows that such objectives are also widely accepted among different legal regimes, primarily referring to key insolvency objectives as stressed in the UNCITRAL Legislative Guide on Insolvency Law.[4] Chapter 5 attempts to delineate a set of prototypical scenarios of MEG organizational structures combined with relevant insolvency scenarios, which bear significance to the application of the framework mentioned above to possible rules and procedures for MEG insolvencies.

Part III is devoted to the examination of possible solutions for insolvency within MEGs. That is, using the framework proposed in the previous two parts, it considers measures for MEG insolvencies and the extent to which they fit with key principles relevant to the problem of groups and the problem of cross-border insolvency while referring to the prototypical scenarios proposed above. As the driving force for adopting various measures is the pursuance of insolvency goals, the chapters in this part are arranged according to the key goals which were

----

[4] See n 137 chapter 3.

identified in Part II of the book. Chapter 6 focuses on the administration of MEG insolvencies and examines 'linking tools' which could enhance preservation of the estate, wealth maximization, and rescues. Chapter 7 focuses on pursuing fairness in distribution and procedural fairness. It examines the compatibility of the tools proposed in chapter 6 in light of these goals as well as additional features which should be adopted in order for the 'law of MEG insolvency' to achieve substantive and procedural fairness. Chapter 8 focuses on the possibility of the tools proposed in previous chapters to generate certain and predictable rules, and considers additional measures which could enhance these goals. Chapter 9 focuses on the issue of group opportunism and examines the desirability of imposing various remedies in the course of insolvency within MEGs which could combat misbehaviour and enhance fairness in distribution.

A summary and conclusion follows with certain additional observations and concluding thoughts.

PART I

THE CONTEXT OF INSOLVENCY WITHIN MULTINATIONAL ENTERPRISE GROUPS—THE PHENOMENON AND KEY PROBLEMS

1

The Phenomenon of the Multinational Enterprise Group

1.1 Introduction

This work focuses on multinational enterprise groups (MEGs) in insolvency. Hence, it is important at first to appreciate the phenomenon of MEGs in general: the economic significance of these business organizations and their considerable power in the modern world. Clearly, if the phenomenon is widespread, the need to address issues of law pertaining to its operations (and in our case—its default) is more crucial. This may be true either in case there is a multitude of MEGs operating worldwide, or if, regardless of their numbers, each MEG tends to be large and thus its operation or collapse may affect a large body of stakeholders and the community at large.

It is also fundamental to consider at the outset what exactly 'MEG' means for the purpose of addressing the problem of its default. In other words, which sort of enterprises will be the subject of this work? Different definitions are attributed to enterprise groups in different legal systems. There may even be differences of definition and meaning among different areas of the law within the same system. Sometimes the law does not provide any definition of a group at all. It will be crucial for the purposes of this study to address this question, and propose some guidance as to what should be the subject matter of an approach to insolvency within MEGs. For this purpose, it is necessary to consider various potential legal and organizational forms of what can be regarded as a MEG.

This chapter aims to address these issues. It starts by briefly reviewing the historical background of the multinational enterprise and the use of the group device in this regard. It describes the various reasons for the emergence of the MEG and its growth into what became a significant phenomenon in world business. It will point out the way in which such enterprises are expanding their businesses across borders using subsidiaries or other separate business units to achieve their economic goals. It then delineates the various forms such enterprises may use when they embark on a multinational venture, and finally suggests what should constitute a MEG for the purposes of addressing insolvencies within MEGs.

1.2 The MEG as a Key Player in World Business

1.2.1 Introduction

Multinational enterprises operating through group structures are essentially enterprises comprising two or more companies (or other forms of undertaking) which are linked in such a way that they may be regarded as 'related entities' and which operate in a transnational setting (i.e. a group consisting of entities from at least two different countries). The next section will elaborate on the various legal structures of MEGs and further discuss what will constitute a MEG—mainly, what is the sort of linkage needed in order to formulate the group for the purposes of this work, and what would constitute the international dimension of such groups. For now, however, it will suffice to suggest that the MEG is a combination of the group business form (i.e. a business comprising separate legal units which are together linked in some way), mainly the corporate group,[1] and the multinational enterprise (i.e. the enterprise operating in more than one country). Accordingly, the growth of the MEG phenomenon has been the result of developments at its two core axes: the rise of the multinational enterprise and the emergence of the corporate group business pattern. As will be shown here, at some point these two axes coincided in that the multinational enterprise adopted the group structure as a major form for its operation, thus coagulating the MEG as a major force in world business.

1.2.2 The emergence of corporate groups

In the evolutionary process corporate groups represent an advanced stage of development, building upon the now established concepts of the corporate separate personality and limited liability. Thus, corporate groups exploit the concept of a company's distinct personality which is detached from the identity of its shareholding members. Moreover, they normally rely on the limit of the holding company's liability for the subsidiaries' debts to the amount it has paid or have agreed to pay to the company for its shares.[2] It appears that corporate groups first surfaced in the US. It was not until 1889–93 that states within the US began enacting statutes granting powers to corporations to acquire and hold shares of other corporations.[3] Before that, the action of purchasing stock of another corporation was seen as an improper expansion of the restricted corporate purpose. There was also a general anti-corporate feeling in the US during the nineteenth

---

[1] This may also include groups linked by contract, as will be discussed herewith.

[2] See further on the application of the corporate personality and limited liability notions in the group context in chapter 2.

[3] See P.I. Blumberg, *The Multinational Challenge to Corporation Law: the Search for a New Corporate Personality* (Oxford University Press, Oxford 1993) [hereinafter: Blumberg, *The Multinational Challenge*] ch. 3.

century, stemming from the antagonism towards monopolies, particularly where the purchase represented not merely an investment, but an attempt to gain control of the other corporation and perhaps to achieve monopoly power over the market as well.[4] With the new rules that gradually dropped all restrictions on acquiring the shares of other companies, corporate groups soon grew to occupy a commanding role in American industry.[5]

It is more difficult to track the entry of corporate groups onto the English scene, since there was not an equivalent rule in English law regarding ownership by companies.[6] However, the period of the 1920s and the 1930s has been indicated as the point of entry of groups into the conscious jurisprudence of UK company law.[7] There is less information on the emergence of corporate groups in other European countries, though it is clear that the civil law systems' tendency was towards permitting and even encouraging various sorts of group relationships.[8] Corporate groups had significant dominating power in Japan in the pre-war period, though later on they have changed their typical structures to comply with the prohibition imposed by the US on the operation of pure holding companies (whose principal activity is to control the business of other Japanese companies).[9]

1.2.3 The phenomenon of the multinational enterprise

It can be argued that the multinational enterprise should be traced back to several hundred years earlier, however not in its modern form, when a genuine international division of production by firms was presented.[10] This phenomenon of control over the production of goods and services in foreign countries originated with the establishment in the sixteenth century of the great European colonial trading companies.[11] Initially, this worldwide business was achieved via trade relations. In time, big companies exerted a growing degree of control through independent foreign agencies. Finally, multinational enterprises in their modern sense began to appear in the nineteenth century with the growth of world trade and industrial production, and the simultaneous

---

[4] Ibid.

[5] Ibid.

[6] See D. Milman, 'Groups of Companies: The Path towards Discrete Regulation', in *Regulating Enterprise* D. Milman (ed.) (Hart Publishing, Oxford 1999) 218, 220.

[7] T Hadden, 'Inside Corporate Groups' (1984) 12 Int. J. of Soc. of Law 271.

[8] See T. Hadden, 'Regulating Corporate Groups: An International Perspective', in J. McCahery, S. Picciotto and C. Scott (eds.), *Corporate Control and Accountability* (Oxford University Press, Oxford 1993) 343, 350–51.

[9] Ibid, 352. See further on typical corporate group structures in Japan in section 1.3.3.

[10] See P.T. Muchlinski, *Multinational Enterprises and the Law*, 2nd edn (Oxford University Press, Oxford 2007) [hereinafter: Muchlinski, *Multinational Enterprises*] 8–9.

[11] See I. Wallerstein, *The Modern World-system* vol i and ii (Academic Press, New York 1974, 1980). See also V. Bornschier and H. Stamm, 'Transnational Corporations', in S. Wheeler (ed.) *The Law of the Business Enterprise* (Oxford University Press, Oxford 1994) 340.

growing importance of technological know-how.[12] The pressure to find affiliates increased, due to the need to open up new attractive markets and to secure
access to raw materials. Independent agents still played a major role in this
regard, but as they were often unreliable they were replaced more and more by
directly controlled affiliates.[13]

In fact, various theoretical explanations regarding the establishment and continued growth of the multinational enterprise were suggested by economists over
time. Initially it was suggested that ownership advantages were the driving force
behind multinational enterprises. According to this view enterprises expanded
beyond their national seat of operations primarily to be able to expand market
power.[14] Later on, another explanation linked the expansion of firms abroad
to the development sequence of their products, suggesting that enterprises use
foreign markets to seek new opportunities for profit and to remain competitive.[15]
Yet another view explained the motivation for expansion into foreign markets as
derived from minimizing transaction costs. According to this theory, internalization of activities (that is, the vertical and horizontal integration of operations)
increases efficiency.[16] Another approach concentrated on location advantages.
Namely, that the choice of the enterprise to expand to foreign markets depends
on the advantages that host countries may or may not offer, such as the market
size or local protective measures (access to cheap labour may also be an incentive to expand into particular markets). This approach is closely related to the
classical theory of trade.[17] Later, it was suggested that the development of the
multinational enterprise should be explained as a combination of those different

---

[12] M. Wilkins, *The Emergence of Multinational Enterprises: American Business Abroad from the Colonial Era to 1914* (Harvard University Press, Cambridge MA 1970) Part Two.

[13] See ibid. See also V. Bornschier and H. Stamm, 'Transnational Corporations' in S. Wheeler (ed.) *The Law of the Business Enterprise* (Oxford University Press, Oxford 1994) 340.

[14] See the 'monopolistic' approach illustrated in the work of Hymer (see, for example, S. Hymer, *The International Operations of National Firms: Study of Foreign Direct Investment* (MIT Press, Cambridge MA 1976); S. Hymer and R. Rawthorn, 'Multinational Corporations and International Oligopoly: The Non-American Challenge' in Kindleberger (ed.), *The International Corporation* (MIT Press, Cambridge MA 1970) 57). See also S. Wheeler 'The Business Enterprise: A Socio-Legal Introduction', in S. Wheeler (ed.), *The Law of the Business Enterprise* (Oxford University Press, Oxford 1994) 36–7; V. Bornschier and H. Stamm, 'Transnational Corporations', in S. Wheeler (ed.), *The Law of the Business Enterprise* (Oxford University Press, Oxford 1994) 334–5.

[15] Known as the 'product cycle' model developed by Professor Vernon (see R. Vernon, *Sovereignty at Bay: The Multinational Spread of U.S. Enterprises* (Longman, Harlow 1971); R. Vernon, *The Economic and Political Consequences of Multinational Enterprise,* 2nd edn (Harvard University Press, Cambridge MA 1973)). The model has lost its relevance since the mid-70s, in particular it was not thought to work as an explanation for the behaviour of established multinational enterprises or the expansion of non-US enterprises abroad (see in the writings of Professor Vernon himself (R. Vernon, 'The product cycle hypothesis in a new international environment' (1979) 41 Oxford Bull. Econ. & Stat. 255)).

[16] See, for example, P.I. Buckley and M. Casson, *The Future of Multinational Enterprise* (Holmes & Meier, New York 1991) 2.

[17] See, for example, J.H. Dunning, *Explaining International Production* (Allen & Unwin, London 1988) 22–3.

approaches into an 'eclectic paradigm', which combines ownership, location, and internalization factors.[18]

1.2.4 The use of affiliates by multinational enterprises

The corporate group legal structure helps to achieve some of the above goals.[19] Thus, ownership advantages (i.e. expansion of market power) can be achieved through the process of acquiring existing corporations, resulting in a corporate group structure.[20] Transaction costs can be minimized by operating an integrated corporate group,[21] in which for instance a subsidiary can serve as a supplier of required goods, rather than third party companies, ultimately internalizing the activities of the enterprise. The enterprise can exploit 'location advantages' by placing a local subsidiary in the foreign market that will be subject, as a legal person, to the foreign jurisdiction.[22] Sometimes it is a regulatory requirement of the foreign jurisdiction that local businesses be conducted through separate subsidiaries. In addition, the multinational group device may be used for various other reasons and purposes. For instance, though the integrated multinational enterprise structure helps businesses to achieve market power, companies may also be motivated to invest in foreign subsidiaries merely for the purpose of diversifying investment (and reducing risk).[23] Tax advantages are often cited as a main driving force for conducting businesses via groups.[24] The limited liability notion in particular (applied to groups) enables businesses to ring-fence risks and to isolate potential liabilities. This could be particularly opportune when the enterprise considers embarking on a new hazardous activity.[25]

---

[18] See J.H. Dunning, *Industrial Production and the Multinational Enterprise* (Allen & Unwin, London 1981); J. Black and J.H. Dunning (eds.), *International Capital Movements* (Macmillan, London 1982).

[19] Though, there are other legal factors that may influence the growth of multinational enterprises (for a thorough discussion of the role of legal factors in the growth of multinational enterprises, see Muchlinski, Multinational Enterprises (n 10 above) 33–43).

[20] See O.E. Williamson, 'Organization Form, Residual Claimants and Corporate Control' (1983) 26 J. L. & Econ. 351, 362; O.E. Williamson, 'The Modern Corporation: Origins, Evolution, and Attributes' (1981) 19 J. Econ. Lit. 1537. See also W. Bratton Jr 'The New Economic Theory of the Firm: Critical Perspectives from History', in S. Wheeler (ed.), *The Law of the Business Enterprise* (Oxford University Press, Oxford 1994) 153.

[21] See further on the concept of integration in chapter 5, section 5.3.2.

[22] It should be noted that legal factors also have a role to play in determining the location characteristics of the host state. The host state may use its political power to alter its location advantages through law and thereby influence the investment decisions of the enterprise (see Muchlinski, Multinational Enterprises (n 10) 38–40).

[23] See Kopits, 'Multinational conglomerate diversification' (1979) 32 Econ. Int. 99.

[24] See generally, A. Dewing, *Financial Policy of Corporations* (Ronald, New York 1953) 980–7. See also D. Milman, 'Groups of Companies: The Path towards Discrete Regulation', in D. Milman (ed), *Regulating Enterprise* (Hart Publishing, Oxford 1999) 221.

[25] See further on limited liability in the group context and more generally the legal problems associated with MEGs in chapter 2.

1.2.5 Flexibility in organizational structures of multinational enterprises

The combined model proposed by Dunning[26] has later been adapted to take account of the rise of multinational strategic alliances.[27] Such alliances may enhance each participating firm's ownership advantages and extend internalization advantages across the participants. Location advantages are considered in relation to their capacity to influence the extent and structure of localized centres of excellence into which strategic alliances may choose to locate and are also regarded as a parameter of the ownership advantages of the firm.[28] Accordingly, multinational enterprises' investment choices tend towards 'the creation of foreign direct investment "clusters" around locations offering the correct mix of location advantages for the enhancement of firm competitiveness'.[29] Such developments have led to changes, inter alia, in the business organization of multinational enterprises allowing for more flexible forms of organization.[30]

1.2.6 MEGs—a widespread phenomenon

Ultimately, multinational groups of various forms have come to be the modern reality.[31] These complex enterprises are based widely around the globe.[32] The impact of the MEG in world business is more significant considering operations taking place using various group structures, other than the conventional hierarchical structures and the full ownership of affiliates. The MEG may take

---

[26] N 18.

[27] See J.H. Dunning, *Alliance Capitalism and Global Business* (Routledge, New York 1997) ch. 3. See further on MEG structures in section 1.3.

[28] J.H. Dunning, 'Location and the Multinational Enterprise: A Neglected Factor?' (1998) 29 J. Int'l. Bus. Stud. 45.

[29] Muchlinski, *Multinational Enterprises* (n 10), 32.

[30] Ibid.

[31] P..I Blumberg et al, *Blumberg on Corporate Groups* (2005) [hereinafter, Blumberg et al, *Blumberg on Corporate Groups*] (5 Volumes) vol. 1, s. 1.04; Blumberg, *The Multinational Challenge* (n 3) 231. Professor Schmitthoff observed in 1989 that 'in modern business life, particularly on the transnational level, the single public limited company has virtually ceased to exist and one encounters only groups of companies' (C.M. Schmitthoff 'Introduction', in C. Schmitthoff and F. Wooldridge (eds.), *Groups of Companies* (Sweet & Maxwell, London 1991) xiv, ix). See also E. Ellis, 'Multinationals and the Antiquities of Company Law' (1984) 47 Mod. L. Rev 87, 92; K. Hofstetter, 'Multinational Enterprise Parent Liability: Efficient Legal Regimes in a World Market Environment' (1990) 15 N.C.J. Int'l L. & Com. Reg. 299, 301–02; D. Milman, 'Groups of Companies: The Path towards Discrete Regulation', in D. Milman (ed.), *Regulating Enterprise* (Hart Publishing, Oxford 1999) 235–6; P.L. Davies, *Gower and Davies' Principles of Modern Company Law* (Sweet & Maxwell, London 2008) [hereinafter: Davies, *Company Law*] 228–9.

[32] See Blumberg et al, *Blumberg on Corporate Groups* (n 31), vol. 1, s. 1.01. See, though, O. Sussman 'The economics of the EU's corporate-insolvency law and the quest for harmonization by market forces' [2005], *Oxford Financial Research Centre*, Working Paper 2005-FE-16, 18. Sussman found, in regard to five European countries (Germany, France, Spain, the UK, and Italy) in the period 2001–03 and in regard to 116,445 of Europe's top companies, that the phenomenon of foreign ownership (i.e. the degree of group operations across several jurisdicions) among sizable European companies is important though not overwhelming.

a multiplicity of forms including the more loosely connected networks of coordinated economic collaborations.[33] In particular, the phenomenon is intensified if those group enterprises linked by contract rather than equity are taken into account. Such undertakings include for example enterprises composed of franchisors and franchisees or licensors and licensees.[34]

All in all, the phenomenon is both significant in frequency and in complexity of its components. As observed by the authors of Blumberg on Corporate Groups:

> Multinational corporations of enormous size dominate the world's economy. These enterprises are corporate groups that typically conduct their operations throughout the world through numerous subsidiary corporations—domestic and foreign—incorporated under the laws of the country in which they conduct their business. The multinational groups are typically complex, multitiered corporate structures with first-tier, second-tier, third-tier, and even more junior-tier subsidiaries.[35]

In the context of insolvency, the intensity of the phenomenon is also reflected in the level of media coverage given to numerous large scale insolvency cases of multinational groups in recent decades, such as the collapse of the Maxwell Group, Worldcom, Global Crossing, Federal Mogul, MG Rover, Parmalat, to name just a few.[36]

1.3 What Constitutes a MEG

1.3.1 Introduction

A basic issue to establish before considering how the law should address insolvencies within MEGs is what may be regarded as a MEG in this respect. It was

---

[33] See Muchlinski, *Multinational Enterprises* (n 10) 33. See further section 1.3 (discussing MEG structures).

[34] It was observed that 'Franchising is the outstanding example of this development . . . In recent years, enterprises resting on franchise contracts have come to occupy an increasingly prominent position in certain industries, particularly hotels, fast-food and other restaurants, and motor vehicles sales and servicing.' (Blumberg et al, *Blumberg on Corporate Groups* (n 31) Vol. I, s. 6.04 [A]). Burns mentions in regard to UK based franchise systems that the phenomenon developed from a relatively small beginning to a big business which continues to grow in size and significance and to a large extent operates internationally (see T. Burns, 'Developing a Franchise: could securitization be a serious funding option for franchisors in the United Kingdom?' [2006] JBL 656).

[35] The authors note that the phenomenon has grown to surprisingly large dimensions and refers to UNCTAD 2005 World Investment Report, reporting of 69,727 multinational parent corporations conducting business through 690,391 foreign affiliates (UNCTAD, 2005 World Investment Report, 265 (Annex Table A.I.8). They also note that, in addition, there were many thousands of franchisees, licensees, dealers, and contractors for which statistics are unavailable (Blumberg et al, *Blumberg on Corporate Groups* (n 31) Vol 1, s. 1.01).

[36] These and other MEG insolvencies' cases will be discussed later on in this work. Indeed, an increase in number of collapses of enterprise groups is anticipated in the near future due to the current financial crises (with the collapse of the Lehman Brothers investment banking group as a major example). See further chapter 3 on the cross-border insolvency phenomenon.

already indicated (in the previous section) that foreign investment and operations via separate business units may take various forms. It is important now
to consider what those possible forms are in more detail, and to substantiate
whether these structures will be included under the term MEG for our purposes.
Essentially, both the linkage between the separate units and the foreign element
required for the 'group' and 'multinational' aspects of MEGs, respectively, should
be identified.

1.3.2   Equity-based hierarchical multinational corporate groups

The typical multinational group enterprises are those operating across borders via
subsidiary companies.[37] These are 'equity-based' forms of multinational enterprises and classically they are structured in the 'pyramid' hierarchical form of
ownership, where a parent company wholly owns (or holds the majority of shares)
and controls a subsidiary or a number of subsidiaries (domestic and foreign).[38] In
fact, these patterns may appear in more complex forms of multi-tier group structures, with subsidiaries and sub-subsidiaries either wholly or partly owned.[39]
Alternatively, a group may be created via the common ownership and control of
individual shareholders (or a family).[40] In all these structures, the group is equity
based, namely its components are linked by stock ownership, and the capacity to
control the management and operations of the various entities is what constitutes
the group. Control over a subsidiary (which includes membership in the subsidiary) cannot be easily defined. Yet, in general terms such a relationship exists
whenever the controller holds a strategic position within the corporate decision-
making facility of the subsidiary which gives it a power to directly or indirectly
influence its business affairs. It may therefore derive from a variety of situations

---

[37]   See Blumberg et al, *Blumberg on Corporate Groups* (n 31) Vol. 1, s. 1.01.

[38]   This is a widely used form of corporate groups, but it is especially typical of US and UK
enterprises of the 20th century (T. Hadden, 'Regulating Corporate Groups: An International
Perspective', in J. McCahery, S. Picciotto and C. Scott (eds.), *Corporate Control and Accountability*
(Oxford University Press, Oxford 1993) 343, 345–7; Muchlinski, *Multinational Enterprises* (n 10),
56–8 (Muchlinski mentions examples such as the Ford group (the US auto manufacturer) and
Cape Asbestos)).

[39]   Corporate groups may evolve into intricate networks of sub-holding companies (see
A. Muscat *The Liability of the Holding Company for the Debts of its Insolvent Subsidiaries* (Dartmouth
Publishing Group, Aldershot 1996) [hereinafter: Muscat, *The Liability*] 8. See also T. Hadden,
'Inside Corporate Groups' (1984) 12 Int. J. of Soc. of Law 271, 273; Blumberg et al, *Blumberg on
Corporate Groups* (n 31), vol. 1, s. 1.01.

[40]   See for example the relationship between Parmalat and Parmatour. The Italian Tanzi family held the Parmalat dairy group and also other family companies such as Parmatour (a tourism
business) (see *New York Times*, 'The Rise and Fall of Parma's First Family', 11 January 2004). All
those companies may be regarded as among themselves creating a group via the common control
of the family (see further on the Parmalat insolvency proceedings in chapter 6 mainly sections
6.2.1.4, 6.2.1.6, 6.2.2.1 and 6.2.2.2; chapter 7, section 7.5.4; chapter 8, section 8.2; and chapter 9,
section 9.2.4).

demonstrating ability to effectively control the subsidiary.[41] Control need not be actively exercised and a passive potential for control may suffice to form a group of linked entities.

When the entities comprising the group (be it the parent and a subsidiary, or different subsidiaries) are situated in more than one country the group is multinational.[42] The group components may all operate in the same line of business or there may be more diversity in the entities' operations.[43] A particular subsidiary may serve specific purposes, as with SPVs[44] used for example for securitization transactions.[45]

Equity-based linkages that may potentially form a multinational group could be a result of various forms of alliance between firms.[46] An example is the transnational merger in which two or more parent companies from different countries

---

[41] This may include situations where a person or a parent holds a small percentage of the shares yet with concentrated rights (in the general meeting or rights to nominate the members of the board of directors), either attached to the shares or as contemplated in the subsidiary's constitution, or as a result of agreements with other members. It can also happen where there is less than the majority of voting shares, but where ownership of the remaining shares is dispersed, or as a result of a control contract with the subsidairy (according to which the subsidairy renounces its autonomy and is subordinated to the directions of the parent) or where there are interlocking board directorates (See e.g. J.E. Antunes, *Liability of Corporate Groups—Autonomy and Control in Parent-Subsidiary Relationships in U.S., EU and German Law. An International and Compative Law* (Kluwer, Deventer 1994) 116–21; D.D. Prentice 'A survey of the law relating to corporate groups in the United Kingdom', in E. Wymeersch (ed.), *Groups of Companies in the EC* (De Gruyter, Berlin 1993). On control emerging in contractual networks see section 1.3.4 below.

[42] On the 'international aspect' see further section 1.3.6.2.

[43] See Blumberg, *The Multinational Challenge* (n 31), 142. See further chapter 5 on different levels of integration within MEGs.

[44] A special purpose vehicle (SPV; also referred to as special purpose entity (SPE) or special purpose company (SPC); this work uses the term SPV).

[45] Securitization has become one of the most important financing vehicles in the US, and its use is now rapidly expanding worldwide. It enables companies, inter alia, to obtain lower cost financing, increase liquidity and it better allocates risk and its distribution. The transaction involves transfer of revenue generating assets to a newly formed special purpose entity. The SPV then issues bonds or other securities (secured by assets sold). The funds that are raised by the bond issue will then be used to pay the originator company for the assets it transferred to the SPV. The main idea is to separate the receivables from risk associated with the originator company, and for this reason it is crucial that the SPV will remain insolvency remote. SPVs are usually corporate entities held by the originator company, but they may take other forms such as partnerships (on securitization transactions and the use of SPVs see S. Schwarcz, 'Structured Finance: The New Way to Securitize Assets' (1989) 11 Cardozo L. Rev. 607; S. Schwarcz, *Structured Finance: A Guide to the Principles of Asset Securitization,* 2nd edn (Practicing Law Institute, New York 1993); S. Schwarcz, 'The Alchemy of Asset Securitization' (1994) 1 Stan. J. L. Bus. & Fin. 133; S. Schwarcz, 'Securitization Post-Enron' (2004) 25 Cardozo L.Rev. 1539. See also C. Hill, 'Securitization: A Low Cost Sweetener for Lemons' (1996) 74 Wash U. L.Q. 1061; T. Burns, 'Developing a Franchise: could securitization be a serious funding option for franchisors in the United Kingdom?' [2006] JBL 656). On SPVs in the context of MEG insolvencies see chapter 6 section 6.2.1.1 and section 6.3.3.3 and chapter 9 section 9.5.1.

[46] See Michael Y. Yoshino and U. Srinivasa Rangan, *Strategic Alliances: An Entrepreneurial Approach to Globalization* (Harvard Business School Press, Cambridge MA 1995) 4–5 (an alliance can take a variety of forms, ranging from an arm's length contract to a joint venture). On contractual linkages between firms see section 1.3.4 below.

integrate their business operations and jointly hold a company.[47] A transnational merger may be achieved via the creation of a 'twin holding' company located in each home state, based on joint shareholding by the founding parent companies, and the transfer of operating activities to subsidiaries that may be jointly or separately owned and controlled by the holding companies.[48] As organizational structures may change over time, such enterprises may restructure the business to form a more unified operation for various commercial reasons, forming a new single parent company instead of two parents located in different countries.[49]

A transnational merger can also develop from an international joint venture. In fact, there is no precise legal meaning to the term 'international joint venture', but it is commonly associated with a scenario involving cooperation between two or more parent companies from different countries that share control over the venture, formed for the pursuit of a particular activity.[50] Initially, the joint venture is between independent parent undertakings, and is operating for a specific purpose, but this may develop into a more permanent undertaking and a more integrated form of business. Unlike parent–subsidiary relationship in which there is control by a single parent, the joint venture normally involves shared control, although one of the parent undertakings may exercise a dominant influence over the venture.[51]

---

[47] This is especially common in Europe (for a thorough review of this type of multinational organization see Muchlinski, *Multinational Enterprises* (n 10), 58–63).

[48] See the examples provided by Muchlinski (ibid), for instance the Eurotunnel group, which operated under two parent companies (jointly held French and English Holding companies)—Eurotunnel SA and Eurotunnel Plc, each owning respectively a French and English concessionary companies—France Manche SA and the Channel Tunnel Group Ltd. The group entered insolvency proceedings, and has been restructured (Eurotunnel SA and Eurotunnel Plc became subsidiaries of Groupe Eurotunnel SA and their names were changed to TNU SA and TNU Plc respectively; see further on the case in chapter 6, section 6.2.1.10). See also J. Keir, 'Legal Problems in the Management of a Group of Companies', in C.M. Schmitthoff and F. Wooldridge (eds.), *Groups of Companies* (Sweet & Maxwell, London 1991) (discussing the organization of the Unilever group, which took the dual holding company approach). See also T. Hadden, 'Regulating Corporate Groups: An International Perspective', in J. McCahery, S. Picciotto and C. Scott (eds.), *Corporate Control and Accountability* (Oxford University Press, Oxford 1993) 343, 347.

[49] See the unification of the Anglo-Dutch oil company Royal Dutch Shell. Until 20 July 2005 it took the twin holding form of enterprise, but then was unified by establishing a new parent company headquartered in the Netherlands and incorporated in the UK (Muchlinski, *Multinational Enterprises* (n 10), 59).

[50] This refers to joint ventures created by the formation of a separate undertaking (otherwise the joint venture may be created by contract). Muchlinski discusses, inter alia, the example of Renault-Nissan Alliance which is organized around a 50 per cent jointly owned strategic management company, Renault-Nissan BV, incorporated in the Netherlands. The structure has been adopted for the specific purpose of coordinating strategic cooperation while preserving the distinct corporate culture and brand identity of each partner (Muchlinski, *Multinational Enterprises* (n 10), 67). See also generally on the phenomenon of joint ventures in M. Lower, 'Joint Ventures', in D. Milman (ed.), *Regulating Enterprise* (Hart Publishing, Oxford 1999) 241.

[51] Muchlinski, *Multinational Enterprises* (n 10), 66–8.

1.3.3 Decentralized and heterarchical patterns

The elements of central control and strategic influence over the affairs of subordinated entities were emphasized above as 'glue' connecting bundles of entities (operating worldwide) to form a multinational group. This is mostly emphasized in vertically (rather closely) held enterprise groups. However, multinational enterprises (comprised of separate business units) may operate their business in more decentralized and even heterarchical patterns. In such decentralized or flatter structures of organizations the group may still achieve a degree of managerial control or otherwise may still coordinate the whole business.[52] Such forms of enterprise could also be regarded as multinational groups. The linkage then will not be limited to control or capacity to control, but will also include the capacity to coordinate the business.

In fact, it has been argued that with enterprise growth and maturity, more decentralized patterns may be chosen by firms, replacing the traditional hierarchical model as the primary leading form for multinational enterprises.[53] The group may thus spread certain functions geographically across the global enterprise and opt for more flexible and innovative driven structures. In such structures, the members of the group will tend to be more autonomous (less closely held or controlled). As a result, the group as a whole (or certain parts thereof) is decentralized.[54] This strategy in forming the enterprise group may also lead to the replacement of parent–subsidiary structures with free-standing companies linked to the 'parent' by contract. The next section will consider possible contractual forms of multinational groups.

[52] In Japan, special group structures have evolved as a result of statutory prohibition of monopolies. One form that emerged was the keiretsu, or families of firms. In this type of group of companies there is no principal holding company, but a complex network of small intra-group holdings operating in coordination by regular meetings of the managements and through interlocking directorships. It has been observed that there appears to be general acceptance in Japan of the value of informal cooperative structures (but the formal prohibition of holding companies is widely regarded as historical anachronism) (T. Hadden, 'Regulating Corporate Groups: An International Perspective', in J. McCahery S. Picciotto and C. Scott (eds.), *Corporate Control and Accountability* (Oxford University Press, Oxford 1993) 343, 352–3). The authors of *Blumberg on Corporate Groups* observe that while relatively minor amounts of securities in such cross-holdings are sufficiently significant to create some pressure for the corporate policies of the group entities to be conducted in some collaborative fashion it is normally a situation where there is a minor degree of common control (Blumberg, *Blumberg on Corporate Groups* (n 31), vol 5, s.180.03). Some systems limit to an extent such cross-holding structures by generally prohibiting extensive cross-ownership (e.g. in France and Germany cross-holding in excess of 10 per cent is prohibited (France: Law No. 66-537, July 24, 1966, Arts. 217, 217-1, 217-2; Ordinance No. 67-695, Aug. 17, 1967, Arts. 1, 6; Germany: Aktiengesetz, BGB III 4121-1, Sept. 6, 1965, s. 71(1)).

[53] See Muchlinski, *Multinational Enterprises* (n 10) 47–8.

[54] See J.H. Dunning, *Multinational Enterprises and the Global Economy* (Addison-Wesley Publishing Co, Wokingham 1993) [hereinafter: Dunning, *Multinational Enterprises*] 3; N. Hood and S. Young, *The Economics of Multinational Enterprise* (Longman, London 1979) 3; R. Caves, *Multinational Enterprises and Economic Analysis*, 2nd edn (Cambridge University Press, Cambridge 1996) 1; Muchlinski, *Multinational Enterprises* (n 10) 45–51.

1.3.4 Multinational businesses comprised of entities linked by contract

Multinational groups operating via parents and numerous subsidiaries are a major form of multinational organization.[55] But, such organizations will also typically vary their use of legal patterns for their operations and may conduct certain parts of the group's activities via affiliates other than subsidiaries by way of different types of agreement.[56] Alternatively, the entire group may be a bundle of contractually linked entities (termed by Teubner as 'network organizations' [57]).

In this type of structure, ownership does not feature (in those parts of the group not operating via conventional subsidiaries), and the entities are interconnected only via contractual relationship.[58] However, as with equity-based multinational groups, control may be the element constituting the group, or the ability to control or coordinate a unified business in the more heterarchical patterns.[59] In a way similar to a parent–subsidiary relationship, the contractually linked entity may be an integral part of the group and may be closely and commonly controlled.[60] Alternatively, the contractual based group may operate as a transnational network group with looser connections among the entities, yet still operating with a degree of coordination. Generally, it has been observed that there is a trend towards more open heterarchical organizations via contractual linkages, though this may depend on the particular industry and the degree of integrated control desired by the enterprise.[61]

As mentioned earlier the most common type of contractual group relationship is agreements between franchisors and franchisees.[62] Here, the franchisor and the franchisee are linked together by the franchise contract. The franchise

[55] Blumberg et al, *Blumberg on Corporate Groups* (n 31) vol. I, s. 6.04.

[56] Ibid, s. 1.01.

[57] See G. Teubner, 'The many-headed Hydra: networks as higher order collective actors', in J. McCahery, S. Picciotto and C. Scott (eds.), *Corporate Control and Accountability* (Clarendon Press, Oxford 1993) 41. See further G. Teubner, ' "Unitas multiplex: corporate governance in group enterprises', in D. Sugarman and G. Teubner (eds.), *Regulating Corporate Groups in Europe* (Nomos, Baden-Baden 1990) 87–92; G. Teubner, 'Beyond Contract and Organisation? The External Liability of Franchising Systems in German Law', in C Joerges (ed.), *Franchising and the Law: Theoretical and comparative Approaches in Europe and the United States* (Nomos, Baden-Baden 1992) 105; G. Teubner, *Law as an Autopoietic System* (Blackwell Publishers, Oxford 1993) ch. 7.

[58] See J.E. Antunes, *Liability of Corporate Groups—Autonomy and Control in Parent-Subsidiary Relationships in U.S., EU and German Law. An International and Compative Law* (Kluwer, Deventer 1994) 120.

[59] See section 1.3.3.

[60] Blumberg et al, *Blumberg on Corporate Groups* (n 31) vol. 1, s. 6.04.

[61] Muchlinski, *Multinational Enterprises* (n 10) 66.

[62] See n 34, and accompanying text. The group may also comprise both traditional subsidiaries and independently owned operational units of franchisees (the authors of *Blumberg on Corporate Groups* give the examples of Hilton, Holiday Inn and Hertz multinational enterprise and notes that the public eye cannot readily distinguish in regard to such enterprises whether the particular business conducted by the group is organized as a traditional subsidiary or a franchisee (Blumberg et al, *Blumberg on Corporate Groups* (n 31) vol. 1, s. 6.04[A]).

contract is typically of a standard form used throughout the chain, requiring operation by the franchisee in accordance with certain standards and procedures imposed by the franchisor and assuring the franchisor a dominant position over the franchisee in operational and related matters.[63] Hence, in such contractual forms of enterprises there may be a similar pattern of hierarchical close control as with the classic pyramid pattern of equity-based groups. A looser contractual network aimed at distribution (across borders) may take the form of simple distribution agreements with foreign distributors.[64] Other typical contractual linkages are those aimed at production, such as licensing networks.[65]

1.3.5 Supranational entities

As we are concerned with enterprises conducting business transnationally, it is worth mentioning particular forms of entity which are 'supranational' as such, in the sense that they are formed under laws adopted by regional organizations of states. Though, as this work is also concerned in particular with 'groups', it should be noted that any such supranational entity (although of a multinational nature) is in itself not a subject matter of this work (as it is a type of a single entity). Yet, obviously, such entities may be part of a multinational group. The 'European company' known as the 'Societas Europaea' (SE) is one example of such an entity. [66] It is a creation of the EC Statute for the European Company 2001,[67] and it applies to public companies. It is primarily aimed at facilitating cross-border mergers of companies on the basis of a single set of rules and a unified management and reporting system. The idea is to provide a community form of incorporation that will not be identified with any particular member state. Yet, the success of this concept is compromised mainly due to the absence of a Community registry and of comprehensive regulation for the SE.[68] The EU commission is currently proposing a new European Private Company Statute (*Societas*

---

[63] Blumberg et al, *Blumberg on Corporate Groups* (n 31) vol. 1, s. 6.04[A]. The degree of control exercised by franchisors tends to be significant as the purpose of the franchisor is to expand its products and brand image abroad in a uniform business format so as to develop its presence as an international business (Muchlisnki, *Multinational Enterprises* (n 10) 53.

[64] Here, the distributer, after purchasing the stock from the producer, is usually free to sell goods as it sees fit (Muchlinski, *Multinational Enterprises* (n 10) 53).

[65] For a description of license agreements in the contexts of groups and multinational enterprise see Muchlinksi, *Multinational Enterprises* (n 10) 45; Blumberg et al, *Blumberg on Corporate Groups* (n 31) vol. 1, s. 6.04[B].

[66] For a comprehensive account of supranational forms of international business see Muchlinski, *Multinational Enterprises* (n 10) 72–7.

[67] Council Regulation (EC) 2157/2001 of 8 October 2001 (European Company Statute) [2001] OJ L294/1.

[68] The SE is mainly governed by the law of member states where it is registered. See further Muchlinski, *Multinational Enterprises*, (n 10) 72–3 (noting the example of Allianz, the German insurer, as the largest European company to use the SE structure). Thus far there have been less than 200 SE registrations throughout the European community and only less than 70 have operations and employees (as opposed to being shelf companies) (see Company Law Newsletter, 'European

Privata Europaea (SPE)) designed for small and medium-sized enterprises. This will complement the statute for the European company as it will apply to private companies (and will require only a nominal minimum share capital). It will allow entrepreneurs to set up all subsidiaries in various member states in the same form, and thus (as the EU commission predicts) will save considerable costs.[69]

Another supranational form of business adopted by the European Community is the European Economic Interest Grouping (EEIG) established by EC Regulation.[70] The creation of such an entity is aimed at facilitation of cross-border cooperation between business entities operating within the EC. It is formed by the conclusion of a contract between the member companies (or individuals) and upon registration becomes a separate entity. However, according to the relevant regulation, the members shall have joint and unlimited liability, the effects of which are to be determined by national law.[71] The EEIG is of limited commercial scope, as it has to facilitate or develop the economic activities of its members and is therefore disqualified from certain commercial activities.[72]

1.3.6 In favour of a wide meaning of a multinational enterprise group

1.3.6.1 Considering the different types of groups and the range of different levels of connections among the entities

Evidently, enterprises conducting business on a worldwide basis via separate entities take different shapes. It can be a small business of parent and few subsidiaries, an intricate web of subsidiaries and sub-subsidiaries, a network of franchisor and franchisees, a joint venture, a parent operating its activities via subsidiaries as well as licensees' affiliates, and so forth (assuming that these enterprises operate on a worldwide basis). The question is whether all such types should be considered as possible subject matter in the treatment of insolvencies within MEGs.

In general, it seems that limiting a definition of a MEG to only certain patterns while excluding other possibilities used in practice will result in mismatch

Commission proposes European Private Company and Small Business Act', Sweet & Maxwell, August 7, 2008).

[69] The SPE statute will only provide a set of company law rules related to the company form and will not regulate other areas of law affecting companies (such as insolvency) (see Proposal for a Council Regulation on the Statute for a European Private Company (COM (2008) 396/3) (available at: http://ec.europa.eu/internal_market/company/docs/epc/proposal_en.pdf); see also *EU Focus* 2008, 237, 2–4, 'Small Business Act for Europe Unveiled'.

[70] Council Regulation (EC) 2137/85 of 25 July 1985 (Establishing the European Economic Interest Grouping) [1985] OJ L199/1.

[71] Ibid, Art 24(1).

[72] See further S. Israel, 'The EEIG—A Major Step Forward for Community Law' (1988) 9 Co. Law 14; M. Anderson, *European Economic Interest Groupings* (Butterworths, London 1990); Muchlinksi, *Multinational Enterprises* (n 10) 73–5; Davies, *Company Law* (n 31) 26–8.

between the law and the realities. More importantly, it seems that there is no real justification in 'discriminating' against certain patterns (excluding them from a potential definition) even though there is no real difference in substance between them and the patterns that are within a definition of an enterprise group. For example, as seen above, where an international business is carried out by means of contract, there may emerge a relationship of control and dominance by one party over the other in much the same way as in the traditional parent–subsidiary relationship. A counter argument is that limiting the definition to certain clearly defined patterns will enhance certainty, for instance if the definition only refers to majority holding of a subsidiary. Majority holding is a clear concept to apply and expanding the concept of a group to other types of linkages may result in vagueness, that is, lack of predictability and certainty.[73] But clearly, a definition that would not encompass what are in fact enterprise groups (operating in the same way as other types traditionally perceived as groups) would lose its significance. It may allow enterprises and their members to evade legal consequences or otherwise be deprived of benefits the law may provide to such commercial relationships (especially bearing in mind legal and economic creativeness and continuous changes in practice in terms of patterns used by enterprises for their global operations). The inevitable conclusion is that all potential forms of enterprises operating via separate entities which feature a relevant form of 'glue' connecting them should be within the term 'MEG', without discriminating against certain forms which are in fact no different in substance.

Another question is what should be the sufficient linkage between the entities. It is possible to apply a high or a low threshold in terms of the connections between the entities for the purpose of determining whether they result in an enterprise group relationship. This will not pose a problem in terms of emphasizing form over substance or distinguishing otherwise similar patterns from others, as, by limiting the degree of linkage, a particular legal pattern is not preferred over another. Rather, the same threshold can be applied for any legal pattern the enterprise may choose.

The question is thus whether to adopt a broad meaning of MEG in terms of the degree of linkage required, allowing for capacity to coordinate the entities comprising the group to suffice. Or, rather a narrower concept, that would require close control or at least capacity to control the affairs of the entities in the group. For our particular purposes, the question is whether this will imply a rigid application of remedies or procedures to be imposed or utilized by the group or its entities in the course of their insolvencies in all possible scenarios. If this were the case, then adopting a broad meaning of MEG could be problematic, especially when considering the possibility of making a parent liable for the debts of its

---

[73] In contrast, it is noted in Blumberg et al, *Blumberg on Corporate Groups* that in the public eye there is no way of differentiating between the majority holding and close contractual linkages (see n 62).

subsidiary. Even in a closely controlled traditional group, members of a group are normally not liable for the debts or omissions of the other members. Such an idea would contradict basic principles of legal responsibility.[74] Furthermore, this is especially inappropriate considering different areas of the law relating to groups. The group may be more readily recognized for certain purposes,[75] and less so in regard to other areas. But also within the confines of insolvency, there may be various rules and remedies that may be considered for a group (as will be discussed later on in this work), which are very different in nature, particularly in the extent to which they interfere with the concept of the separateness among the entities.

However, these problems subside if the approach taken to MEG insolvencies will adopt a flexible strategy. A broad term could capture all possible scenarios that may occur in practice, where legal rules (or a subset of legal rules) might be relevant. Thus, it will indicate the scope of relevant rules, albeit specific rules could be subject to additional conditions. Specific pre-requisites for imposing rules could be determined for the specific area in issue and in regard to specific devices. Critically here, consideration will need to be given to various degrees of control and unification of groups, which in turn may dictate the solutions (or rules) that may be applied.[76]

Considering insolvencies within multinational groups, it seems that narrowing the meaning of the term MEG *a priori* could be detrimental to a meaningful approach to this matter. In the various structures of multinational enterprises (comprised of separate entities) discussed above a degree of coordination or of mutual involvement may potentially occur. If insolvency within such enterprises occurs, the promotion of goals of insolvency may require having regard to the enterprise as the relevant body or giving effect to the inter-connections among its members. If a broad approach to what are the goals of insolvency is taken, exclusion of certain types of enterprises (comprised of separate entities) would be especially counter-productive.[77] Thus, for instance, a functioning bankruptcy system may, in the relevant circumstances, need to hold a group member which excessively dominated other group members in a way harmful to its creditors (be it as a result of equity holding or a contractual linkage) responsible for the insolvent members' debts. In other circumstances, such a system should allow for joint administrations of insolvency proceedings of multiple debtors that operated with a degree of coordination in their ordinary course of business as this would, for example, reduce costs in the handling of the proceedings. An insolvency

---

[74] See H. Collins, 'Ascription of Legal Responsibility to groups in Complex Patterns of Economic Integration' (1990) 53 Mod. L. Rev. 731, 734. See further on the issue of liability and corporate groups in chapter 2.

[75] See e.g recognition of groups for accounting purposes (chapter 2, section 2.4.2).

[76] For the purpose of this work, certain prototypes of organizational patterns combined with insolvency scenarios will be construed to assist in considering relevant solutions (see chapter 5).

[77] See chapter 4 (discussing insolvency goals in legal systems).

system may aim to promote business rescues and this may require, in the relevant circumstances, encompassing all the group entities in a plan, as the exlusion of an entity which was part of a coordinated business may impede the achievment of a rescue and be detrimental to a wide set of stakeholders.[78] In other words, a broad meaning assigned to the term MEG could better serve the objectives of insolvency systems.

I therefore suggest that it will be fit to follow the economists' perception of transnational businesses, viewing such enterprises as comprised of entities that may be tied by contract or by equity and may be organized with a high degree of decentralization. The vital link can thus be control, (actual, or capacity to control) or coordination between (or over) equity or contractually based entities, even when it is exerted over autonomous action centres.[79] A broad flexible approach should be taken as to what initially can be regarded as an enterprise group, including within the meaning the various possible patterns, appreciating that those may change over time, and that not every type can be anticipated by the law. This does not refer though to situations where there is mere 'collective dominance' of oligopolies (also termed tacit coordination),[80] among independent enterprises not otherwise linked by contract or equity. It also does not refer to networks or strategic alliances between firms that are focused on one-off or incidental transactions where there is no possibility to control or to coordinate the overall business. The term 'group' also does not refer to a relationship between entities and their creditors (in their capacity as creditors). Although a creditor (especially a secured creditor with substantial security over the undertaking) may exert significant control over a company, it is nevertheless an outsider to the enterprise business. Its relationship with a group may raise legal issues,[81] but it will not be part of the group.

1.3.6.2 The international element

In terms of the international element, it was generally referred above to the entities of the group (at least two of them) being 'situated' in different countries. The question is what precisely this means. Normally, it refers to entities being incorporated in different countries.[82] Indeed, incorporation has been the traditional standard for corporate nationality under international law.[83] Common

---

[78] See the discussions of insolvency solutions for insolvencies within MEGs in chapters 6–9.

[79] See e.g., Dunning, *Multinational Enterprises* (n 54), 3.

[80] See S. Baxter and F. Dethmers, 'Collective dominance under EC merger control—after Airtours and the introduction of unilateral effects is there still a future for collective dominance?' (2006) 27(3) ECLR 148.

[81] If the creditor was significantly involved in the management of the enteprise he may be exposed to 'lender liability' of some sort under certain jurisdictions (for example, creditors may be regarded as 'shadow directors' under the wrongful trading provision in the English Insolvency Act 1986 (s. 214)).

[82] See the OECD description of multinational enterpises in n 93.

[83] Blumberg et al, *Blumberg on Corporate Groups* (n 31) vol. 1, s. 48.02[A].

law national legal systems have also been utilizing the incorporation standard as the primary linkage of a company to a jurisdiction.[84] Civil law systems have traditionally referred to the location of the corporation seat, a notion that has been developed to refer to the 'real seat' of the company.[85] To an extent, incorporation generally loses its predominance as the sole manifestation of linkage to the country, and alternative standards based on notions of principal place of management and control are being used.[86] Indeed, incorporation may not represent a genuine connection of the corporation to the forum, in terms of economic realities, as a company may be incorporated in one place but conduct its business entirely elsewhere.[87] Especially considering insolvency issues, it may well be that the principal insolvency against a company will be held in its centre of main interests rather than its place of incorporation.[88] This may raise, for example, issues of how to handle the insolvency proceedings against related companies apparently centred in different jurisdictions.[89] Therefore, in considering whether a group is multinational, I suggest to have regard both to the test of incorporation and to other potential manifestations of company nationality.

1.3.7 Legal systems' approaches to the definition of groups and multinational enterprises

As will be further discussed in the next chapter, legal regimes normally lack a coherent law of corporate or enterprise groups. This is also reflected in an absence of consistent definitions of groups in legal systems. Normally, no general definition is offered, not even for domestic groups. Sometimes the key players in a group are defined, and typically this is done for specific purposes within the law. 'Control' is normally regarded as the key connection between the group's members in these cases, yet various factors are used to establish a relationship of control. Sometimes control is expressed only in terms of holding voting rights; other definitions are more elaborative and elements of 'effective' control are emphasized

---

[84] Ibid, s. 48.02[B].

[85] Ibid, s. 48.02[C].

[86] Ibid, ch. 48. But, see developments in Europe which to an extent undermines developments under national law towards standards based on economic realities. In the context of the freedom of establishment concept under the Rome Treaty, the European Court of Justice (ECJ) upheld the concept that the legal status of an existing entity incorporated in the EU must be respected by every Member State, even if the incorporation in a particular member state took place for the purpose of avoiding stricter incorporation laws in the other member state (*Centros Ltd v Erhvervs-og Selskabsstyrelsen* (C-212/97) [1999] ECR I-1459); *Überseering* [2002] ECR I-9919; *Inspire Art* [2003] ECR I-10155). See further on the incorporation factor in regard to jurisdiction in insolvency in chapter 6, section 6.2.1.9; chapter 7, section 7.3.2; and chapter 8, section 8.3.3.

[87] See E.T. Bicker, 'Creditor Protection in the Corporate Group' (University of Freiburg—Faculty of Law, Working Papers Series, July 2006).

[88] On the concept of 'centre of main interests' in regard to cross-border insolvency see chapter 3, section 3.4.2.2.

[89] See chapters 6–9 *passim*.

(the actual ability to exert dominant influence).[90] Definitions may refer only to parent–subsidiary relationship (i.e., not referring, for instance, to natural persons who may control several companies) or they may include different types of enterprise. Such differences in definition sometimes appear within the same legal system.[91]

On the international level, the OECD Guidelines[92] describe multinational enterprises in broad terms while observing that they usually consist of separate entities established in a number of countries. They focus on coordination rather than control as the possible manifestation of linkage between separate entities, and suggest that the amount of influence and control over affiliates may differ between enterprises with different degrees of autonomy enjoyed by affiliates.[93] The crucial characteristic of the multinational enterprise is the ability to coordinate activities between enterprises in more than one country. Other factors are not decisive. This description is broad enough to include both equity and non-equity-based groups, regardless of the legal form or ownership of the entities.[94] This is a broad conceptual guideline, and therefore involves some arbitrariness,[95]

---

[90] See e.g. American standard of 'control' in various legislation and court decisions which provide functional standards that turn on power over the management and operations of the company (Blumberg et al, *Blumberg on Corporate Groups* (n 31) vol. II, s. 90.04[A]; see also the Australian Corporation Act 2001, s. 50AA(1) (defining control as the capacity to determine the outcome of decisions about financial and operating policies). Cf. Canadian Business Corporations Act 1974–75–76, s. 2(3) (control is defined by formal requirements, i.e. reference to ownership of more than 50 per cent of the voting power for election of directors); New Zealand Companies Act 1993, s. 7 (defining control as the power to appoint or remove all the directors or 'such number of directors as together hold a majority of the voting rights at meeting of the board.').

[91] See e.g. English Companies Act which offers no formal definition of a group, though it seeks to define the key players within a group. For accounting purposes the definition refers to a group of undertakings embracing an elaborated list of optional connecting factors that can establish a parent undertaking, including concepts of major voting control (formal control concept), but also concepts of effective control. That is, a company is a parent to another company also if it has the right to exercise dominant influence over the subsidiary by virtue of its memorandum or articles or by virtue of a control contract, or if it has a participating interest in the undertaking and actually exercises a dominant influence over it or it and the other company are managed on a unified basis (s. 1162 and Sch 7 of the English Companies Act 2006). For other purposes the definition is narrower, refers only to body corporate and to formal control over a subsidiary (s. 1159 of the English Companies Act 2006). The latter definition is however a considerable improvement on the previous definition which did not focus on control, rather on holding a majority of the shares (voting or non-voting) (see Davies, *Company Law* (n 31) 234).

[92] OECD Guidelines for Multinational Enterprises 27 June 2000 (available at: http://www.oecd.org/dataoecd/56/36/1922428.pdf) [hereinafter: OECD Guidelines].

[93] See OECD Guidelines (ibid), 'Concepts and Principles' p. 3. The guidelines do not provide a precise definition of multinational enterprises, yet it states that such enterprises: '. . . usually comprise companies or other entities established in more than one country and so linked that they may co-ordinate their operations in various ways. While one or more of these entities may be able to exercise a significant influence over the activities of others, their degree of autonomy within the enterprise may vary from one multinational enterprise to another. Ownership may be private, state or mixed'.

[94] See also Muchlinski, *Multinational Enterprises* (n 10) 6–7.

[95] Ibid.

but it avoids exclusion of types of groups that may in substance encompass the same characteristics as others.

UNCITRAL Working Group V, which is at present considering the issue of treatment of enterprise groups in insolvency,[96] is currently proposing that the term 'enterprise group'[97] should be explained as 'two or more enterprises, that are interconnected by ownership or control'. It also explains that 'control' should mean 'the capacity to determine, directly or indirectly, the operating and financial policies of an enterprise', and that 'enterprise' includes any entity regardless of its legal form (yet one which is subject to insolvency laws).[98] It therefore currently adopts a wide meaning of the components of the group, as these are not confined to corporations. Additionally, it does not seem to be confined to groups linked by equity. It adopts a functional test of control, not resting solely on formal standards (such as specified percentages of ownership),[99] though it refrains from expanding the meaning to include groups operating in a coordinated manner.

---

[96] UN Comm'n on Int'l Trade Law (UNCITRAL), Working Group V (Insolvency Law) [hereinafter: UNCITRAL Working Group V or Working Group interchangeably]. The author is an adviser to the UK delegation in the deliberation of the Working Group. The views expressed in this study in regard to the work of Working Group V, however, are those of the author and do not necessarily reflect those of the UK delegation or of the Working Group. The book refers to various draft recommendations and other relevant notes or draft commentary from the working papers, mainly those which were the bases of the discussions in the fourth meeting of the Working Group (New York, 3–7 March 2008) on which a report has already been published, and to subsequent working papers which were provided as material for the fifth meeting of the Working Group (Vienna, 17–21 November 2008). It should be noted that at the time the book went to print the work is still in progress (another meeting of the Working Group for discussion of the topic of enterprise groups is scheduled for 18–22 May 2009, New York) and thus recommendations and commentary may be altered (including their numbering).

[97] The term is 'generic' and not limited to domestic groups (see Report of Working Group V (Insolvency Law) on the work of its thirty-third session, 16 November 2007, A/CN.9/643, para. 123; available at http://www.uncitral.org/uncitral/en/commission/working_groups/5Insolvency.html). [hereinafter: Report, thirty-third session].

[98] See Note by the Secretariat, Working Group V (Insolvency Law), 31 December 2007, A/CN.9/WG.V/WP.80; available at: http://www.uncitral.org/uncitral/en/commission/working_groups/5Insolvency.html [hereinafter: WP.80], para. II A (a); UN Comm'n on Int'l Trade Law (UNCITRAL), UNCITRAL Report of Working Group V (Insolvency Law) on the work of its thirty-fourth session, 14 March 2008, A/CN.9/647, paras. 14–23 [hereinafter: Report, thirty-fourth session], and UN Comm'n on Int'l Trade Law (UNCITRAL), UNCITRAL Note by the Secretariat, Working Group V (Insolvency Law), 1 September 2008, A/CN.9/WG.V/WP.82 [hereinafter: WP.82], paras. 2(a)–(d), 28–32 (all documents available at: http://www.uncitral.org/uncitral/en/commission/working_groups/5Insolvency.html). It was noted that the function of the glossary in the Working Group proposals should not be to provide statutory definitions of the relevant terms, but rather to provide readers with a general idea of how the concepts were used (Report, thirty-fourth session, ibid, para. 13).

[99] As it currently stands the definition can be interpreted as suggesting that ownership alone can be a sufficient linkage creating a group, as it refers to either control or ownership as the connecting factors. Yet, in its last meeting, the Working Group considered that the 'ownership' element should be qualified by adding the word 'significant' (so that it has to be substantial) (see UNCITRAL, UNCITRAL Draft report of Working Group V (Insolvency Law) on the work of its thirty-fifth session (Vienna, 17–21 November 2008) 18 November 2008, A/CN.9/WG.V/XXXV/CRP.1/Add.2 (on file with author) [hereinafter: Draft Report CRP.1/Add.2], para. 13. It is the author's

A committee of the International Insolvency Institute which is currently working on devising principles for coordination of multinational enterprise group insolvencies,[100] currently suggests that 'multinational enterprise group' or 'enterprise group' will mean 'a group of companies or enterprises established or centred in more than one country which are linked together by some form of control, whether direct or indirect, or ownership, by which linkage their businesses are controlled or coordinated.'[101] This definition is to an extent broader than the definition currently suggested by UNCITRAL Working Group V as it explicitly adopts the concept of coordination (resulting from a degree of control or ownership) as a possible manifestation of linkage creating an enterprise group.

1.3.8 Addressing the problem of definition in future reforms

To enhance consistency and clarity in legal systems on the one hand, and be compatible with economic realities and business innovations on the other, a broad all-encompassing meaning to the term MEG, centred on actual or capacity to control or coordinate the business (in functional terms) would be advantageous. This could be done primarily by explaining the term 'enterprise group', with further explanation as to international aspects.[102] Further conditions could then be added with regard to specific issues pertaining to the group; for our purposes, conditions relevant to issues pertaining to groups in distress.[103] A wide meaning given to MEGs would imply that the law matches with economic realities and will be general enough to serve the various problems that may be associated with groups. It also takes into account the dynamic nature of enterprises and the fact that a particular group form may become more dominant in the future, which again implies that some level of flexibility in the definition is suitable. Providing such guidance in legislation will enhance clarity and predictability, especially where 'players' from different regimes need to assess foreign laws (as we are dealing with a multinational setting). Adopting a broad flexible definition across legal regimes could further enhance consistency and harmonization, which would generally assist in dealing with multinational enterprises.[104]

---

view that a better definition will refer to ownership as only one factor in determining control (or coordination—see section 1.4).

[100] At the time the book went to print the work of the committee is still in progress. International Insolvency Institute (III), Committee on International Jurisdiction and Cooperation, Judicial Guidelines for Coordination of Multi-National Enterprise Group Insolvencies, Co-Chairs Hon. R.R. Mabey and J.L. Garrity, Reporter S.P. Johnston, Advisor I. Mevorach (Working Draft, on file with author) [hereinafter: III Draft Guidelines] (the author is an advisor to the committee; the views expressed in this work are those of the author and do not necessarily reflect those of the committee).

[101] See III Draft Guidelines (ibid), Definitions.

[102] As may be done by UNCITRAL Working Group V (see n 97).

[103] Relevant conditions for the purposes of international insolvency will be discussed in subsequent chapters.

[104] See further the problems associated with groups operating worldwide in chapter 2.

Alternatively, definitions of MEGs can be advanced in specific legislation in different areas of the law. In our area of interest, in a similar way, a broad meaning to MEGs would be suitable. As explained above, a variety of different issues may arise in connection to the MEG in distress, thus generality in the initial definition is beneficial. The meaning of an enterprise group currently suggested by UNCITRAL Working Group V[105] is a step in the right direction, suggesting a rather wide description (though as aforementioned it does not include coordination as a possible linkage). As aforementioned, the work is in progress[106] and it remains to be seen what would finally be included in the term (and in any accompanying explanatory notes or further explanations). In any case, for it to become practically significant it should be adopted within national legislation in as many countries as possible.[107]

In the absence of a universal definition for MEGs, and in places where there is room for manoeuvre in legal systems (in the absence of clear constraints imposed in the relevant legal system), courts could still consider enterprises as MEGs if this is the reality of the matter (emphasizing substance rather than form). This would only be a starting point prior to considering the specific purpose for which a business is to be recognized as a group. Therefore this should not drive parties to attempt considering new legal innovative patterns only to evade legal implications. Referring to a business as a MEG will not automatically imply rules, and where it does it can be for the benefit of companies, as will be discussed later on in this work in regard to certain procedures in insolvency that will be beneficial to the group as a whole.

1.4 Conclusion

The phenomenon of multinational enterprises conducting their business via separate entities is significant and widespread, both in quantity and in the scale of operations each enterprise may undertake. This may be driven by various economic advantages as well as legal incentives. MEGs do not appear in a single version, though. Rather, there is a range of different forms of international groups' structures. The strength and significance of the linkage between the entities comprising the group may also differ among different enterprises. A trend towards more open heterarchical organization of multinational enterprises which may use free-standing units linked to the parent by contract has been observed.[108] At the same time, there are clear advantages in the vertical parent–subsidiaries relationship, at least in certain industries, where a high level of integrated control

---

[105] See section 1.3.7.
[106] As of November 2008.
[107] See chapter 3, section 3.4 on instruments used by UNCITRAL and their adoption in national legislation.
[108] Muchlinski, *Multinational Enterprises* (n 10), 48–9, 65–6.

is desired as well as a less complex structure of the business.[109] It is therefore predicted that these patterns will continue to be used. Even when restructuring is desired by the group, networking may take time.[110] In any case, 'discriminating' between the different patterns even though a linkage emerges in much the same way, could be counter-productive. Similarly, limiting the degree of linkage only to capacity to control or even actual control is disadvantageous. This will exclude enterprises operating in more heterarchical patterns that may legitimately benefit from rules a legal system may provide for groups, or otherwise evade legal consequences. Certainly, the variety of groups may be relevant 'subject matters' in regard to issues of insolvency. For these reasons I suggest taking a more inclusive approach to what should initially be the meaning of a MEG. This work will therefore discuss MEGs (in insolvency) and generally refer to a bundle of entities (two or more) mutually connected either by common or interlocking shareholding,[111] or via contract, so that they can be controlled or may coordinate their businesses, and which are established or centred in different countries so that they may be subjected to different jurisdictions if they were to be considered separately.

The work uses the term 'enterprise' as the group may not necessarily consist only of corporations[112] (though this is normally the case), and it can be contractually based. If it is a corporation it can be either limited or unlimited. However, the focus of this work will be on limited corporations (that is, groups comprised of companies which are separate legal persons with their own rights and obligations distinct from those of their shareholders). This is the common scenario.[113] Generally, our focus is on corporate insolvency (rather than insolvency of individuals). Therefore, in particular scenarios where for example the group is comprised of an individual (or a number of individuals) and several entities (controlled by him), this study will focus on the 'sister' corporations and will not deal with the position of the individuals in terms of their bankruptcy or responsibilities. The primary focus of the work will also be on the parent and subsidiary relationship (i.e. multinational groups of companies linked by equity). However, indications of similar concerns arising in regard to contractual links will also be made.

---

[109] Ibid. See also T. Hadden, 'Regulating Corporate Groups: An International Perspective', in J. McCahery, S. Picciotto and C. Scott (eds.) *Corporate Control and Accountability* (Oxford University Press, Oxford 1993) 343, 346.

[110] Muchlinski, *Multinational Enterprises* (n 10) 48–9, 65–6.

[111] If this is allowed to occur under the relevant legal system (see n 52).

[112] It can be various types of business forms such as partnerships or trusts.

[113] Incorporation of most forms of business undertakings as limited liability companies is today the rule (D. Goddard, 'Corporate Personality—Limited Recourse and its Limits', in R. Grantham and C. Rickett (eds.), *Corporate Personality in the 20th Century* (Hart Publishing, Oxford 1998) 20, 63. See also T. Rapakko, *Unlimited Shareholder Liability in Multinationals* (Kluwer, The Hague, 1997) ch. 6 (discussing the universal adoption of the liability limitation in corporate law) [hereinafter: Rapakko, *Unlimited Shareholder Liability*].

2

'To Link or not to Link?' The Problem of the Multinational Enterprise Group Business Structure

2.1 Introduction

This chapter aims to set forth the first of two pillars supporting the issue of MEG insolvencies; that is, the problems associated with conducting businesses via a group of separate (multinational) entities.[1] Quite surprisingly, given the significance and considerable power of MEGs in the modern world,[2] this business form tends to be neglected by legal systems. This is mainly in the sense that the issues pertaining to enterprise groups (including those issues deriving from the international aspect) are not normally dealt with comprehensively or systematically. Certainly, approaches to the treatment of groups differ among legal systems. At its core any such approach needs to determine whether a group of entities should be treated as a single body or as a bundle of completely separate entities. This question is underlined by a tension between traditional 'entity principles' and modern 'enterprise principles'. The latter attempts to be more attentive to the commercial reality of the corporate group (which may in fact operate as a coherent entity) while the former adheres to the formal corporate structure of the enterprise—the separation between the group members and the limited liability granted to parent companies. This chapter presents the dichotomy between entity and enterprise principles, as well as their application in legal systems. The discussion identifies certain consistencies and prevailing concepts across legal regimes, which could also be justified on the policy level. This, in turn, will guide us when exploring (in subsequent chapters) the possibilities of linking among group components in insolvency in light of the specific underlying objectives and policies.

---

[1] The second would be the cross-border insolvency aspect and will be discussed in the next chapter.

[2] See chapter 1.

2.2　One Enterprise or Several Entities?

2.2.1　A gap between commercial realities and legal infrastructure

Despite the economic reality in which the enterprise group plays a major role,[3] laws relating to corporations and other business forms (on national or international levels) tend to deal with the single entity as if it was the norm. Legal systems normally deal with the 'group problem' from the point of view of company law, which is primarily designed to regulate the single company.[4] Yet, the enterprise group as such raises a variety of legal issues, which are either particular to groups, or intensified in a group context. Additionally, concerns regarding groups reach beyond core company law and penetrate areas such as taxation, insolvency, antitrust, and employment.[5] Essentially, the problem is that the treatment a group receives through traditional concepts of single entities, i.e. the corporate separate personality and the limited liability granted to its shareholders, might not match its economic reality.

'Separate personality' suggests that each company is a legal person distinct from its shareholders; hence it is capable of enjoying rights and of being subject to duties which are not the same as those enjoyed or borne by its members.[6] The concept of 'limited liability' suggests that the company's shareholders are not liable for the losses and debts of the company.[7] In a corporate group scenario this means that the assets of the entire enterprise are not available against liabilities incurred by one part of that enterprise.[8] Similarly in regard to contractual linkages creating a group enterprise,[9] contract law assumes an arm's length relationship between independent entities of equal bargaining. In addition, contracts between the controlling entity and other network members may include provisions to exclude the 'parent' liability.[10]

---

[3]　See chapter 1, section 1.2.

[4]　See C.M. Schmitthoff, 'Introduction', in C.M. Schmitthoff and F. Wooldridge (eds.), *Groups of Companies* (Sweet & Maxwell, London 1991) ix; M. Lutter, 'Enterprise Law Corp. v. Entity Law, Inc.- Phillip Blumberg's Book from the Point of View of an European Lawyer' (1990) 38 (4) American Journal of Comparative Law 949, 958. There are exceptions. See in particular the German *Konzernrecht*: para. 291 et seq of the *Aktiengesetz* (Stock Corporation Act) 1965 (reproduced in English in K.J. Hopt (ed.), *Groups of Companies in European Laws, Legal and Economic Analyses on Multinational Enterprises* vol. II (De Gruyter, Berlin 1982) 265–95) which explicitly and directly deals with the group problem, though it is still not comprehensive and has its own shortcomings (see further section 2.4.4 below).

[5]　See section 2.2.2.

[6]　See further section 2.3.2 (on the economic essence of the separate entity).

[7]　See further ibid.

[8]　R.B. Thompson, 'Piercing the veil: Is the Common Law the Problem?' (2005) Conn. L. Rev. 619, 621.

[9]　See chapter 1, section 1.3.4.

[10]　See generally on the gap between law and reality in regard to contractually linked groups in Blumberg et al, *Blumberg on Corporate Groups* (n 31 chapter 1) vol 1, s 6.05. See also on network organizations sources cited in n 57 chapter 1.

Yet, at least in certain scenarios of group operations, adhering to these concepts to the fullest extent may be commercially unjustified and may not serve the objectives of the particular area of the law. Group owners may seek to fragment a business into separate components, but still operate an integrated business with a 'group policy' (that is, with a view to making profits on an enterprise level). A particular group may operate with complete intermingling of assets and debts; stakeholders involved with groups may benefit from the strength of the group as a whole and so forth. In addition, there is a range of possible organizational structures of groups. Organizationally, MEGs may appear in different degrees of integration and centralization of management.[11] This does not necessarily correlate with the legal structure opted for by the enterprise (i.e. the corporate group form), which provides for full separation among the group companies. As a result, the application of concepts of separateness between entities and limited liability to the group case may collide with the actual way the group business operates, and therefore may achieve different outcomes compared with the single company case. This problem becomes clearer when considering the ability of enterprises to exploit the group structure to the detriment of certain stakeholders of the group, as well as the benefits the group may be deprived of if strict adherence to the legal separateness of its elements is always adopted.

2.2.2 The enterprise group problem arising in different areas of the law with further complexities in the international group case

Given the extended possibilities those in control of a group have, issues pertaining to the operation of the enterprise group may arise in a variety of areas of the law with further complexity resulting from the international setting of the group. These will be only briefly discussed here in order to illuminate the special condition and the challenges a MEG brings about across legal areas.[12] Hadden summarizes several major categories of potential issues associated with groups.[13] The first category he mentions is 'manipulation of control holding'. That is, the problems associated with the possibility of extensive cross-holdings between the companies comprising the group. A high level of cross-holdings between group members (where this is allowed by the legal system) might be used to entrench control over the group with a small commitment of personal or corporate capital. It can also

---

[11] See chapter 5, sections 5.3.2 and 5.3.3.

[12] This overview is by no means comprehensive. Its purpose is mainly to highlight a range of issues that may arise when dealing with MEGs, whereas the particular issues pertaining to MEG insolvencies will be explored in detail later on in this work.

[13] T, Hadden, 'Regulating Corporate Groups: An International Perspective', in J. McCahery, S. Picciotto and C. Scott (eds.), *Corporate Control and Accountability* (Oxford University Press, Oxford 1993) 343, 358–60.

be a means of supporting the share price in the relevant companies.[14] The second category, 'misleading accounts', relates to the disclosure of the financial state of companies. It had become apparent that annual reports, balance sheets, and profit and loss statements can be manipulated, for instance, by concealing losses using intra-group transactions designed to create profits.[15] 'Avoidance of taxation' may also be a particular problem in the group context, where profits and losses can be manipulated by transfer pricing and other intra-group transactions. These problems may increase the more the group structure is complex and transcends jurisdictional borders. For instance, groups might attempt to avoid taxation in high-tax jurisdictions by shifting profits to lower-tax jurisdictions or tax havens.[16] As explained by Hadden,[17] similar group gains may be produced in respect of other governmental incentives to locate plants in particular jurisdictions.

Another problem (termed by Hadden 'avoidance of antitrust, monopoly and other regulations') is that the group structure may be used to avoid the impact of certain forms of regulation. For instance, dominant enterprises could engage in anti-competitive practices among the group members, under the umbrella of a single concern (e.g., when operating in the form of a corporate group) if antitrust regulation is not specifically designed to cover such practices, whichever legal form is used by those concerns. Here combating such behaviour involves giving effect to the fact that the apparent single enterprise actually comprises independent undertakings.[18]

In other areas, the relationship among the group members and the fact that the group may operate as a coherent entity may need to be recognized to uphold the effect of various regulations. For instance, in regard to securing effective employee participation in corporate decision making (in those legal systems providing such protection),[19] or prohibiting financial assistance by companies for the acquisition of shares in the company, where the company may be a parent in a corporate group.

'Oppression of minority interests', a problem that also arises in the single company context (the conflicting interests between directors and minority and majority shareholders), may take on a particular shape in the context of groups. In this respect, the problem is that those running the group may favour the interests of the group as a whole (or certain parts of the group) over the interests of particular subsidiaries and shareholders.[20]

---

[14] Ibid, 359, 361.

[15] Ibid, 360, 362.

[16] Ibid, 360, 366. See also generally on taxation problems associated with multinational enterprises in Muchlinksi, *Multinational Enterprises* (n 10 chapter 1) ch. 7.

[17] T. Hadden, 'Regulating Corporate Groups: An International Perspective', in J. McCahery, S. Picciotto and C. Scott (eds.), *Corporate Control and Accountability* (Oxford University Press, Oxford 1993) 343, 360, 366.

[18] Ibid, 367.

[19] Ibid, 364–6.

[20] Ibid, 360, 362–3.

Furthermore, the group business form may be used to avoid liability. For instance where those running the group strategically form subsidiaries so that hazardous activities will be segregated and resulting liabilities will be avoided.[21] The danger increases in the international context where parent companies might carry out speculative and risky transactions through subsidiary companies (rather than via a branch for example) they control in another country. This might place the parent, which is the dominant entity responsible for the speculation, in a remote position, 'hiding' behind legal forms and jurisdictional boundaries.[22] A question then arises as to the liability of the controlling entity for the obligations or debts of the subsidiary.

When insolvency is anticipated the problem of excessive risk-taking increases. The shareholders have a greater incentive to engage in risky investments as they have nothing to lose, and the prospect of making a significant profit that may prevent insolvency is highly enticing.[23] Also, there may be attempts to conceal the financial situation of group components or shifting assets among group members (in the international setting this may involve moving assets to other jurisdictions).

Although consideration of the treatment of groups tends to focus on issues of liabilities and responsibilities of the group, relevant issues also arise in relation to the attribution of rights to the group as such, or to its components as a result of the inter-connections among the group members,[24] for instance with regard to tax exemptions.[25] In insolvency, questions may arise as to the possibility of coordinating or consolidating insolvency proceedings against group members in order to facilitate liquidation or reorganization on a group scale.[26] Where the group is transnational this brings forth further complexities in regard to the possibility of placing all proceedings in a single jurisdiction, and the law that should apply to these insolvencies.[27] Issues could also arise regarding the protection of the group from avoidance of responsibility by parties transacting with its members. For instance, an employee employed by a parent company as well as by its subsidiaries, although agreeing with the parent company to a restraint of trade provision (i.e., prohibiting the employee from working in a competitive business) may move on to work for a different company in direct competition with the parent's subsidiaries and invoke separate personality concepts to claim he did not breach the agreement with the parent company.[28]

---

[21] Ibid, 360, 364.

[22] See also C.M. Schmitthoff, 'The Wholly Owned and the Controlled Subsidiary' [1978] JBL 218, 222.

[23] See I.M. Ramsay, 'Models of Corporate Regulation: The Mandatory/Enabling Debate', in R. Grantham and C. Rickett (eds.), *Corporate Personality in the 20th Century* (Hart Publishing, Oxford 1998) 215, 259.

[24] See Blumberg, *The Multinational Challenge* (n 3 chapter 1) 237.

[25] See n 122 and accompanying text.

[26] An issue which will be discussed in detail in chapters 6–8.

[27] Ibid.

[28] See the English case, *Beckett Investment Management Group Ltd v Hall* [2007] EWCA Civ 613 (see also n 125–6, and accompanying texts).

Additional problems arise with respect to the international nature of the group. The MEG may present an economic reality that does not match piecemeal national regulation (since the enterprise as a global unit crossed borders) and thus regulating the risks of its operation becomes more complex. In fact, there are two basic aspects to the problem, as is comprehensively explained by Blumberg.[29] One is the question of 'home country extraterritoriality'. That is, the attempt to regulate foreign acts by foreign subsidiaries of domestic parent companies. The other is 'host country extraterritoriality' which involves imposing national law over foreign corporations not operating within the country by asserting jurisdiction over them and imposing liability upon them by reason of the activities of their local subsidiaries. This will normally present additional problems of recognition and enforcement of such judgements. Indeed, nation states may be under pressure to engage in extraterritoriality practices so as to avoid manipulation of the corporate group structure, yet this may produce conflicts among legal systems.[30] This is particularly problematic where the relevant jurisdictions adopt different policies. Surely if foreign components of the enterprise are not subject to the national controls, the enterprise may evade legal consequences by having the prescribed activity conducted by a foreign component.[31] From the point of view of parties involved with the group, conflict of law issues may pose an additional barrier (to that resulting from the fragmentation of the group to separate entities) on pursuing a claim against the relevant entity. From the firm's perspective, it may prevent it from benefiting from attribution of rights to the group as such, due to its fragmentation across borders.

2.2.3 Summary

It is apparent that the interface between different angles of the law and the enterprise group raises particular issues, and that the problems increase when the group is international. Nonetheless, as aforementioned, there is generally an absence of a coherent and comprehensive regulatory strategy of the group phenomenon. The question is whether traditional ways of allocating liabilities and regulating companies and other business forms should win through in the same way in a group context or whether legal obligations should be imposed (or rights attributed) upon the group as a whole (or obligations of one entity be imposed upon another group member) including its foreign elements. This is a critical question in attempting to address the case of MEGs in insolvency; that is, to what extent it should be allowed to link the group affiliates for the various purposes pertaining

---

[29] See Blumberg, *The Multinational Challenge* (n 3 chapter 1) ch. 8.
[30] See Blumberg et al, *Blumberg on Corporate Groups* (n 31 chapter 1) vol 1, s 1.01.
[31] See Blumberg, *The Multinational Challenge* (n 3 chapter 1) ch. 8. See also P.I. Blumberg, 'The Barriers Presented by Concepts of the Corporate Juridical Entity' (2001) 24 Hastings Int'l & Comp. L. Rev. 297, 299.

to their insolvencies. The debate here (which will now be overviewed) is between proponents of 'enterprise principles' and of 'entity law'.

2.3 The Theoretical Debate

2.3.1 Entity law versus enterprise principles

Entity law represents the traditional thinking, deeming the separate company as the main player, respecting the distinct corporate personality of the corporation and the limited liability of its shareholders.[32] The corporation is an artificial person which comes into life via the process of incorporation, and is then recognized as a legal person by a sovereign power.[33] This arguably corresponded fully with the economic realities of the nineteenth century where the single corporation was the norm. Namely, separate legal identity for the corporation and its shareholders matched the separation between single companies and their investors. The principle of limited liability provides protection to shareholders investing in companies.[34] Only in exceptional circumstances is the corporate veil to be ignored for various purposes when the enterprise has become objectionable.[35]

The concept of 'enterprise entity' suggests that in certain circumstances the enterprise may be regarded as the relevant entity or effect will be given to the relationship among group members. Here a 'new' entity is recognized, based on economic facts rather than on legal incorporation. That is, when the corporate

[32] Blumberg, *The Multinational Challenge* (n 3 chapter 1) 231; P.I. Blumberg, 'The Corporate Entity in an Era of Multinational Corporations' (1990) 15 Del. J. Corp. L. 283; C.M. Schmitthoff, 'The Wholly Owned and the Controlled Subsidiary' [1978] JBL 218, 219–22.

[33] There is extensive writing on the debate regarding the essence of the 'corporate person' concept. Some of the best-known writings are: F.W. Maitland, *Introduction to Gierke's Political Theories of the Middle Age* (Cambridge University Press, Cambridge 1900); Machen Jr. 'Corporate Personality' (1911) 24 Harv. L. Rev. 253; H.J. Laski, 'The personality of Associations' (1916) 19 Harv. L.R. 404; Vinogradoff, 'Juridical Persons' [1924] 24 Colum. L. Rev. 594; J. Dewey, 'The Historical Background of Corporate Legal Personality' (1926) 35 Yale L. J. 655; M. Radin, 'The Endless Problem of Corporate Personality' (1932) 32 Colum. L. Rev. 643; M. Wolff, 'On the Nature of Legal Persons' (1938) 54 LQR 494; HLA Hart, 'Definition and Theory in Jurisprudence' (1954) 70 LQR 37; D. Derham, 'Theories of Legal Personality', in L.C. Webb (ed.), *Legal Personality and Political Pluralism* (Melbourne University Press, Melbourne 1958); R. Hessen, *In Defence of the Corporation* (Hoover Institutional Press, Stanford 1979); Stein, 'Nineteenth Century English Company Law and Theories of Legal Personality' (1983) 1 Quaderni Fiorentini 503; M. Dan-Cohen, *Rights, Persons, and Organizations: A Legal Theory for Bureaucratic Society* (University of California Press, Chicago 1986); S.A. Schane, 'The Corporaion is a Person: the Language of a Legal Fiction' (1987) 61 Tul. L. Rev. 563; Teubner, 'Enterprise Corporatism: New Industrial Policy and the "Essence" of the Legal Person' (1988) 36 Am. J. Comp. L. 130; K. Iwai, 'Persons, Things and Corporations: The Corporate Personality Controversy and Comparative Corporate Governance' (1999) 47 Am. J. Comp. L. 583.

[34] Blumberg, *The Multinational Challenge* (n 3 chapter 1) 231. See further section 2.3.2 (for the rationales of limited liability).

[35] See A.A. Berle Jr, 'The theory of enterprise entity' (1947) 47 Colum. L. Rev. 343, 352. See further on lifting the corporate veil section 2.4.3.

personality does not correspond to the actual enterprise, but merely to a fragment of it.[36] Such an 'enterprise approach' has been referred to as 'a product of modern age', 'a pragmatic response of the legal and political system to changing political, social and economic realities'.[37] Enterprise principles will be thus concerned with matching rights and responsibilities to the collective economic activity (the business), i.e. to the enterprise comprised of separate but related companies.[38] Arguably this would better reflect current economic realities where enterprises operate as groups.[39] It has also been observed in this regard, that the application of limited liability in a group context may not be justified. Instead of protecting the investors (the owners of the company) it now protects the corporate layers of the enterprise. That is, it protects companies (rather than individuals) that are often part of the business of their subsidiaries.[40] Therefore, the newer enterprise conceptualization operates, as has been observed,[41] to address groups as such and to some extent redefine the legal boundaries of the business organization so that it fits with economic realities. With regard to MEGs operating as non-equity network organizations[42] a 'network liability' approach has been advocated according to which there may be a simultaneous assignment of responsibility for an act giving rise to a claim upon 'the network, the centre, and the individual unit'.[43] More generally, enterprise theory may apply 'relational law' to any type of group comprised of distinct entities where the group operated in terms of economic realities as a unified business.[44] This means that rights or duties may be attributed upon the controlling entity or upon 'sister' entities arising from the economic interrelationship among the entities, notwithstanding their legal formal separation and risk shifting (contractual or resulting from shareholding).[45] Relational law as the basis of enterprise principles thus rests on status and relationship rather than on the party's participation in the transaction or any contract, assumption, ratification, or other consensual act.[46]

[36] A.A. Berle Jr, 'The theory of enterprise entity' (1947) 47 Colum. L. Rev. 343, 348–50.

[37] Blumberg, *The Multinational Challenge* (n 3 chapter 1) 253.

[38] Ibid, 245.

[39] See chapter 1, section 1.2.

[40] Blumberg, *The Multinational Challenge* (n 3 chapter 1) 232. P.I. Blumberg, *Law of Corporate Groups: Enterprise Liability in Commercial Relationships, including Franchising, Licensing, Healthcare Enterprises, Successor Liability, Lender Liability and Inherent Agency* (Aspen Publishers Law & Business, Amsterdam 1998).

[41] Blumberg, *The Multinational Challenge* (n 3 chapter 1) 232–3.

[42] See chapter 1, section 1.3.4.

[43] See G. Teubner, 'The many-headed Hydra: networks as higher order collective actors', in J. McCahery, S. Picciotto and C. Scott (eds.), *Corporate Control and Accountability* (Clarendon Press, Oxford 1993) 59. See also other sources cited in n 57 chapter 1.

[44] See further on relevant factors to determine degree of unity and integration of the group in chapter 5, section 5.3.2.

[45] Blumberg et al, *Blumberg on Corporate Groups* (n 31 chapter 1) vol 1, s. 6.04.

[46] Ibid, s 6.02; P.I. Blumberg, 'The Transformation of Modern Corporation Law: The Law of Corporate Groups' (2005) 37 Conn. L. Rev. 605, 614 (citing, for example, R. Pound *The Spirit of the Common Law* (Marshall Jones Francestown NH 1921) 12–24; R. Pound *Jurisprudence* (Lawbook Exchange Ltd, 1959) 210–21). For a comprehensive survey of legal responses of American law to

Commentators in the US have identified a shift in US courts' approach, as well as in legal rules in other jurisdictions, from strict adherence to the entity doctrine to applying enterprise principles.[47] Elsewhere, it has also been argued that there are numerous indications in the law of western countries that there exist a set of legal rules dealing with the enterprise group (i.e. elements of an emerging 'enterprise law').[48] Yet, it seems that these new enterprise concepts do not suggest that entity law should be abolished and replaced by enterprise principles. Indeed, Blumberg in his seminal work on corporate groups stresses that enterprise law is not a transcendental doctrine reflecting the emergence of a new legal unit; mainly because the enterprise entity has none of the primary fundamental rights recognized for legal units, such as the right to sue or be sued, the right to contract or to own property. Therefore, it does not supersede entity law, except in discrete areas where it better serves the underlying policies and objectives of the law.[49] Berle emphasized that it is not always necessary to depart from legal incorporation; rather this should be done when the artificial person does not correspond to the fact.[50]

Yet, the degree of pervasiveness of enterprise law remains somewhat obscure. For instance, it is unclear to what extent the proponents of enterprise law invoke the abolishment of the application of limited liability upon groups as the ultimate aim,[51] and generally which of the two approaches should be adopted in any particular area. What seems to be clear is that in the eyes of enterprise law proponents, entity law 'no longer prevails as a transcendental concept dominating all corporation law',[52] but both entity law and enterprise law have a role to play in various areas of the law. Furthermore, which of the doctrines should be applied depends on the underlying objectives and policies of the law in the particular area.[53]

To further appreciate the implications of adhering to entity law or the extent to which it should give way to enterprise principles the economic significance of

the legal problems presented by enterprises linked by contract or other mutual arrangements see Blumberg et al, *Blumberg on Corporate Groups* (n 31 chapter 1) vol. 5, Part IX.

[47] For an extensive survey of the law of corporate groups and the pervasiveness of enterprise principles in legal systems, mainly in US law see Blumberg et al, *Blumberg on Corporate Groups* (n 31 chapter 1), and previously in P.I. Blumberg *The Law of Corporate Groups: Procedural Problems in the Law of Parent and Subsidiary Corporations* (Little Brown & Co, London 1983) (and 6 subsequent volumes); Blumberg *The Multinational Challenge* (n 3 chapter 1).

[48] M. Lutter, 'Enterprise Law Corp. v. Entity Law, Inc.- Phillip Blumberg's Book from the Point of View of an European Lawyer' (1990) 38(4) The American Journal of Comparative Law 949, 952. See further on legal regimes' approaches to the treatment of groups in section 2.4.

[49] See Blumberg, *The Multinational Challenge* (n 3 chapter 1), 237; Blumberg et al, *Blumberg on Corporate Groups* (n 31 chapter 1) vol. 1, s. 6.23; P.I. Blumberg, 'The Transformation of Modern Corporation Law: The Law of Corporate Groups' (2005) 37 Conn. L. Rev. 605, 611.

[50] A.A. Berle Jr, 'The theory of enterprise entity' (1947) 47 Colum. L. Rev. 343, 357.

[51] See further section 2.3.2.

[52] P.I. Blumberg, 'The Transformation of Modern Corporation Law: The Law of Corporate Groups' (2005) 37 Conn. L. Rev. 605, 606.

[53] Ibid, 611. See also R.B. Thompson, 'Piercing the veil within corporate groups: corporate shareholders as mere investors' (1999) 13 Conn. J. Int'l L. 379, 396.

allowing separateness among group members should be examined, in particular the role of fundamental principles of corporate law, the corporate separate personality, and limited liability.

2.3.2 The economic essence of the separate entity (and its limitations)

2.3.2.1 *The merits of corporate separateness in the single company scenario—reducing transaction costs*

In regard to corporations vis-à-vis shareholders, the doctrine of legal personality (i.e. the corporation being a juridical legal personality separate from the shareholders) is perceived to be economically efficient as it produces reductions in transaction costs by enabling the legal entity to own the business' assets. This means that the ownership interest in the company (the shares) can be transferred without the need to transfer the business itself, and capital can be raised from investors, over time, while avoiding costs of transfer of the assets when new shareholders join the company. In addition, it enables the business to operate on a limited liability basis.[54] Other advantages of incorporation as a legal entity include the ability of the company to borrow money and to grant charges to secure its indebtedness, including the floating charge.

In particular, the limited liability facility has long been recognized as a primary business benefit from operating as a legal entity, that is, the insulation of shareholders from liability for the debts of the company. It is a 'default rule' as shareholders may contract out of the rule by giving personal guarantees or forming an unlimited company. But it has significant economic advantages as it reduces various transaction costs.[55] It decreases the need for shareholders to monitor the managers of companies in which they invest because the financial consequences of company failure are limited; it provides incentives for managers to act efficiently and in the interests of shareholders, as well as enhancing market efficiency as it promotes free transfer of shares, due to the fact that under limited liability the price at which shares are traded does not depend upon an evaluation of the wealth of other shareholders; it permits efficient diversification by shareholders, which in turn allows shareholders to reduce their individual

---

[54] See D. Goddard, 'Corporate Personality—Limited Recourse and its Limits', in R. Grantham and C. Rickett (eds.), *Corporate Personality in the 20th Century* (Hart Publishing, Oxford 1998) 17–18 for a brief summary of the benefits in recognizing the legal personality of companies.

[55] That is: the costs of ensuring that each party's interests under the contract are protected. For the classic modern arguments see F. Easterbrook and D. Fischel, 'Limited Liability and the Corporation' [1985] 52 U. Chi. L. Rev. 89; L.E. Ribstein, 'Limited Liability and theories of the Corporation' (1991) 50 Mod. L. Rev. 80; F. Easterbrook and D. Fischel, *The Economic Structure of Corporate Law* (Harvard University Press, Cambridge MA 1991). For a convenient summary of the economic justifications for limited liability see I.M. Ramsay, 'Models of Corporate Regulation: The Mandatory/Enabling Debate', in R. Grantham and C Rickett (eds.), *Corporate Personality in the 20th Century* (Hart Publishing, Oxford 1998) 215, 251–2.

risk and it facilitates optimal investment decisions by managers who can invest in projects with positive net present values without exposing shareholders to the risk of losing their personal wealth. Goddard [56] observes that the rule is also of significant practical importance, since most business undertakings today are incorporated as limited companies, and the limited liability rule is present (and not contracted out) in the vast majority of contracts entered into in commerce today.

2.3.2.2 *The weaknesses of the economic rationales of corporate separateness in the group context*

In the context of groups, though, the strength of the economic rationales of limited liability has been questioned. Indeed, the discussion regarding the rationales for limited liability has been traditionally concerned with limited liability for shareholders. This ignores the different problems and policy issues relevant to corporate groups.[57] Certainly, many of the economic advantages claimed in support of limited liability may become less relevant when considering corporate groups.[58]

Thus, the rationale of encouraging investment by absentee investors is weaker in the context of a parent corporation which is normally not an absentee owner; rather it has a certain degree of control over the subsidiary.[59] Similarly the contention that limited liability promotes capital market efficiency as there is no need to monitor the wealth of fellow stockholders as well as the financial condition of the enterprise (and for the same reason provides incentives for managers to act efficiently) is weaker in the case of corporate groups, where the parent company may be the sole shareholder.[60] Furthermore, the arguments centred around avoiding alleged inefficiencies of unlimited liability (by reducing the need to supervise management decisions or to sue a large number of public shareholders) are also less relevant where liability is imposed on parent companies (rather than upon a large number of shareholders) who also tend to monitor the business of the subsidiary anyway. Encouragement of entrepreneurial risk-taking, which envisages shareholders investing in new businesses,

---

[56] D. Goddard, 'Corporate Personality—Limited Recourse and its Limits', in R Grantham and C Rickett (eds.), *Corporate Personality in the 20th Century* (Hart Publishing, Oxford 1998) 20, 63.

[57] See generally Blumberg et al, *Blumberg on Corporate Groups* (n 31 chapter 1) vol. I, ch. 5. See also P.I. Blumberg, 'Limited Liability and Corporate Groups' (1986) 11 J. Corp. L. 573, 575 (discussing the evolution of limited liability and its application to corporate groups); R.B. Thompson, 'Piercing the veil within corporate groups: corporate shareholders as mere investors' (1999) 13 Conn. J. Int'l L. 379 (discussing limited liability in the context of groups and the judicial response to the academic commentary on this issue).

[58] See e.g. Blumberg, *The Multinational Challenge* (note 4 above) ch. 6; K.A. Strasser, 'Piercing the Veil in Corporate Groups' (2005) 37 Conn. L. Rev. 637, 638–9.

[59] Blumberg, *The Multinational Challenge* (n 3 chapter 1) 125–6.

[60] Ibid, 126–7.

is less relevant when considering a group which conducts a common business, i.e. instead of conducting a business via a single company it fragments the business among separate entities.[61] There is no new investment here as the firm remains unchanged.[62]

It appears therefore that, especially when considering a typical group structure where a parent company is the sole or largely the sole shareholder engaged in the businesses of its subsidiaries, and where it is a unified business fragmented into separate entities, the rationales of limited liability which are centred around reduction in monitoring costs and promotion of risk diversification are weaker than in the traditional single company context.[63]

Indeed, it has been occasionally questioned whether limited liability is a justified concept in the group context. Farrar[64] notes that the strict application of the corporate separate personality notion to groups of companies, coupled with limited liability, has led to a system of limited liability within limited liability which was never countenanced by the early legislation, and has facilitated abuse. Griffin[65] argues that limited liability should be abolished in the context of subsidiary companies as it is prone to exploitation by dominant holding companies that might 'wash their hands' of all financial responsibility should the subsidiary fail, or prove too expensive in terms of attracting creditor or tort liability. Muscat[66] claims that the limited liability principle at least in the context of groups is due for a critical re-examination. Ramsay contended that as the rationales for limited liability are weaker in the group context it provides support for rethinking some aspects of the doctrine in the context of corporate groups.[67]

---

[61] Though it may be more relevant in those MEGs that operated as pure conglomerates and that normally seek to diversify their businesses (see Blumberg, *The Multinational Challenge* (n 3 chapter 1) 144–). See further chapter 5, section 5.3.2 on different organizational patterns of groups in particular in terms of the integration between the entities.

[62] Blumberg, *The Multinational Challenge* (n 3 chapter 1) 130–2.

[63] In this respect, Blumberg rejects Posner's arguments in favour of limited liability in the group context (see R. Posner, 'The Legal Rights of Creditors of Affiliated corporations: An Economic Approach' (1976) 43 U. Chi. L. Rev. 499), arguing that Posner has focused on parent companies which are pure investors, and failed to appreciate the type of groups that are themselves engaged in the operation of the subsidiary's business (see Blumberg, *The Multinational Challenge* (n 3 chapter 1), 41; see also J. Landers, 'A Unified Approach to Parent, Subsidiary and Affiliated Questions in Bankruptcy' (1975) 42 U. Chi. L. Rev. 589 and J. Landers, 'Another Word on Parents, Subsidiaries and Affiliates in Bankruptcy' (1976) 43 U. Chi. L. Rev. 572 (arguing that Posner built his model on conglomerates which do not represent the typical case where the enterprise involves interrelated businesses).

[64] J.H. Farrar, *Corporate Governance in Australia and New Zealand* (Oxford University Press, Oxford 2001), 229–33, 250.

[65] S. Griffin, 'Limited Liability: A necessary Revolution' (2004) 25 Co. Law 99.

[66] Muscat, *The Liability* (n 39 chapter 1) 154.

[67] I.M. Ramsay, 'Models of Corporate Regulation: The Mandatory/Enabling Debate', in R. Grantham and C. Rickett (eds.), *Corporate Personality in the 20th Century* (Hart Publishing, Oxford 1998) 215, 253.

2.3.2.3 *Segregation of groups of assets between the entities comprising the group*

Though these arguments about the weakness of limited liability in the group context are persuasive, it is certainly of merit at least in certain group scenarios, for example where the group was highly diversified.[68] Additionally, Hansmann and Kraakman[69] stressed that limited liability is part of a broader phenomenon of asset partitioning which serves important social interests. Limited liability, according to the argument, facilitates the segregation of groups of assets between investors and the company in the case of a single company, and between different entities in corporate groups. Therefore, limited liability of group constituents (or 'affirmative asset partitioning') works to the benefit of creditors, who are then protected from competing with creditors of other subsidiaries and can confine their monitoring efforts to the particular entity to which they advanced credit. This reduces the cost of credit for legal entities by reducing monitoring costs by creditors, protecting against premature liquidation of assets, and permitting efficient allocation of risk.[70] Therefore, in the context of corporate groups too, the most significant contribution of the law of organizations to commercial activity is its property law aspect, i.e. the shielding of the assets of the entity from claims of the creditors of the entity's owners or managers.[71]

2.3.2.4 *The risk associated with limited liability*

All in all, limited liability rests upon sound practical and economic justifications. Yet, permitting limited liability may create the possibility of externalization of some costs of the enterprise with risk falling on outsiders. Economic theoreticians' response to this problem is that creditors will compensate themselves for this risk via various methods, such as charging higher interest rates, taking securities over the companies' assets and demanding personal guarantees from the directors.[72] 'Private ordering' arguably resolves any risks of non-payment to creditors pertaining to limited liability and therefore there is no need to intervene (i.e. to provide any further protection to the company's creditors by statute or by the courts).

Yet, it is difficult to measure the potential harm that may be caused to different types of creditors by allowing limited liability, and at the same time the benefits to the enterprise, as well as to its creditors in adhering to this concept. Applying

---

[68] See n 61 above, and accompanying text.

[69] H. Hansmann and R. Kraakman, 'The Essential Role of Organizational Law' (2000) 110 Yale L.J. 387.

[70] Ibid, 398.

[71] Ibid, 387, 393.

[72] R. Posner, 'The Legal Rights of Creditors of Affiliated Corporations: An Economic Approach' (1976) 43 U. Chi. L. Rev. 499, 504.

Kaldor-Hicks analysis,[73] limited liability is arguably fair because it arranges resources so that the benefits to those who are better off exceeds the harm to those who are worse off (including where the losses in the transaction are hypothetically compensated by the winners), assuming that everyone had an equal chance beforehand of being on the winning side. Yet, this is not always a realistic assumption.[74] The argument rests on an efficient market hypothesis where 'all relevant information will be available to the market and that the market rapidly, if not instantaneously, digests all information as it becomes available'.[75] However, the market may not work efficiently where there is often incomplete information available to the parties. Additionally, such theoretical economic explanations generalize the creditors in terms of their need for recovery. The fact of the matter is that many creditors may have had little or no opportunity to calculate the risk, especially when the enterprise uses complex group structures.[76] Involuntary creditors such as tort claimants are not in a position to protect themselves from shareholders' opportunism.[77] Although voluntary creditors (who negotiated with the company) are supposed to be able to charge suitable interest rates (that will reflect the risk they are taking) or to include in the lending contract restrictions on activities of the company, an infallible adaptation to risks may be impossible. The costs of obtaining the information about the level of risk may be disproportionate

---

[73] The generally accepted measure of economic efficiency (named for N. Kaldor, 'Welfare Propositions of Economics and Interpersonal Comparisons of Utility' (1939) 49 Economic Journal 549, and J. Hicks 'The Foundations of Welfare Economics' (1939) 49 Economics Journal 696).

[74] See D. Farber, 'What (if Anything) Can Economics Say about Equity?' (2003) 101 Mich. L. Rev. 1791, 1795–6. The other often cited measure of efficiency—Pareto efficiency is virtually unattainable in the real world, as it demands that at least one person will be better off yet that no one else will be hurt. However, virtually any transaction inflicts uncompensated loss to parties which cannot be dealt with, or internalized by the terms of the contract (for an elaborated discussion of the limitations of Kaldor Hicks and Pareto efficiency measures in the context of limited liability see H. Anderson, 'Creditors' rights of recovery: economic theory, corporate jurisprudence and the role of fairness' (2006) 30 Melb. U. L. Rev. 1. See also R.J. Mokal, *Corporate Insolvency Law: Theory and Application* (Oxford University Press, Oxford 2005) [hereinafter: Mokal, *Corporate Insolvency*] 20–6; R. J. Mokal, 'Contractarianism, Contractualism, and the law of Corporate Insolvency' [2007] Singapore Journal of Legal Studies 51, 54–7, persuasively arguing that Kaldor Hicks and Pareto analyses are of limited use and are normatively odious).

[75] J.N. Gordon and L.A. Kornhauser, 'Efficenct Markets, Costly Information, and Securities Research' (1985) 60 New York University Law Review 760, 770–1.

[76] R.B. Thompson, 'Piercing the veil within corporate groups: corporate shareholders as mere investors' (1999) 13 Conn. J. Int'l L. 379.

[77] See H. Hansmann and R. Kraakman, 'Towards Unlimited Shareholder Liability for Corporate Torts' (1991) 100 Yale L.J. 1879. It is also acknowledged, though, that these risks may be better dealt with via other legal techniques such as imposing compulsory insurance as a condition for engaging in the risky activity (see e.g. in D. Goddard, 'Corporate Personality–Limited Recourse and its Limits', in R. Grantham and C. Rickett (eds.), *Corporate Personality in the 20th Century* (Hart Publishing, Oxford 1998) 11, 33). Additionally, the concept of direct liability in tort for the actual person who commits the tort may deter risky business activity of this sort. Yet, this is less likely to work in a corporate group setting where the responsibility will not be imposed on the individual shareholder (R.B. Thompson, 'Piercing the veil: Is the Common Law the Problem?' (2005) Conn. L. Rev. 619, 631–2).

to the amount of the transaction.[78] Dispersed creditors may lack incentives to undertake joint action to prevent opportunistic behaviour by the company.[79] Certain creditors, such as pre-paying customers, may not see themselves as extending credit and may be in a weak position to protect their interests.[80] Even sophisticated creditors may not be able to foresee all contingencies and contract for protection against them,[81] especially as risk may change over time and creditors may not be in a position to assess the implications of such changes.[82] The risk is more pronounced in the vicinity of insolvency.[83] As mentioned above,[84] when insolvency approaches, the problem of opportunism increases and the funds of the creditors are at greater risk.[85] Moreover, debtors may have misled creditors as to the creditworthiness of the company, or in a group context in regard to the entity with whom they have been dealing, or otherwise misused the corporate form to defraud creditors.[86]

Limited liability may need to be limited to achieve normatively desired results. Various stakeholders may need further protection and limited liability may need to be restricted, when taking into account the authentic business transaction

[78] J. Landers, 'Another Word on Parents, Subsidiaries and Affiliates in Bankruptcy' (1976) 43 U. Chi. L. Rev. 572, 529.

[79] V. Brudney, 'Corporate Bondholders and Debtor Opportunism: In Bad Times and Good' (1992) 105 Harv. L. Rev. 1821.

[80] See D. Prentice, 'Corporate Personality, Limited Liability and the Protection of Creditors', in R. Grantham and C. Rickett (eds.), *Corporate Personality in the 20th Century* (Hart Publishing, Oxford 1998) 99, 102, 109.

[81] I.M. Ramsay, 'Models of Corporate Regulation: The Mandatory/Enabling Debate', in R. Grantham and C. Rickett (eds.), *Corporate Personality in the 20th Century* (Hart Publishing, Oxford 1998) 215, 256.

[82] Especially creditors on long-term supply contracts that may lack up-to-date information (see D. Prentice 'Corporate Personality, Limited Liability and the Protection of Creditors', in R. Grantham and C. Rickett (eds.), *Corporate Personality in the 20th Century* (Hart Publishing, Oxford 1998) 99, 102, 109).

[83] See e.g. D. Goddard, 'Corporate Personality–Limited Recourse and its Limits', in R. Grantham and C. Rickett (eds.), *Corporate Personality in the 20th Century* (Hart Publishing, Oxford 1998) 11; P. Davies, Directors' Creditor–Regarding Duties in the Vicinity of Insolvency' (2006) 7 EBOR, 301.

[84] See section 2.2.2.

[85] See also D. Prentice, 'Corporate Personality, Limited Liability and the Protection of Creditors', in R. Grantham and C. Rickett (eds.), *Corporate Personality in the 20th Century* (Hart Publishing, Oxford 1998) 99, 105; I.M. Ramsay, 'Models of Corporate Regulation: The Mandatory/Enabling Debate', in R. Grantham and C. Rickett (eds.), *Corporate Personality in the 20th Century* (Hart Publishing, Oxford 1998) 215, 259; P. Davies, 'Directors' Creditor–Regarding Duties in the Vicinity of Insolvency' (2006) 7 EBOR, 301, 307–9 (Davies also explains that the problem of perverse incentives in the vicinity of insolvency arises even if in a particular legal system there are strong capital maintenance rules. High level of initial capital is no guarantee that assets will be maintained thereafter in the ordinary course. Additionally, capital maintenance rules regulate only losses of assets through distributions but not trade losses).

[86] See e.g. D. Goddard, 'Corporate Personality–Limited Recourse and its Limits' in R. Grantham and C. Rickett (eds.), *Corporate Personality in the 20th Century* (Hart Publishing, Oxford 1998) 11, 30.

that has taken place between the parties, and social aims beyond economic efficiency.[87]

Particularly in regards to groups, there may be a tension between granting limited liability to group members (as a corporate law default rule or as a matter of the contract between contractually-linked related companies) and the economic reality of the organization. Some have commented that group liability issues should therefore be dealt with by a different analysis and as a species of enterprise law.[88] Limited liability is a crucial facility even in regard to subsidiaries vis-à-vis parent companies in economic terms, yet a critical question is whether indeed the group operated as a bundle of separate companies or rather as a single entity. In addition, the question of cost externalizations, and opportunism by those running the enterprise is of particular weight in the context of groups, where issues such as dominance over subsidiaries and fragmentation of a single business into many components may arise.[89]

2.3.3 Distinguishing between 'levels of breaches' of the separateness between MEG entities and the role of enterprise law

It seems that it is commonly agreed that corporate personality (and generally legal separateness between economically linked businesses) coupled with limited liability are the primary rules also in a group context. Critically, the limited liability facility has been found crucial in encouraging commerce. In the group context, this is confronted with the need to fit with the economic realities of the way groups operate, and address the 'group problem' in an adequate way. Such considerations suggest that linking between the otherwise separate entities may be suitable in order to uphold the objective of a particular area of the law. Where such linkage involves imposing liability on the parent company (or other group siblings) this tension is in its highest degree. Ignoring the legal separateness in this way may defeat the strong economic merits of limited liability.[90] However,

---

[87] See H. Anderson, 'Creditors' rights of recovery: economic theory, corporate jurisprudence and the role of fairness' (2006) 30 Melb. U. L. Rev. 1, 9–13. Another version of economic efficiency theory claiming to be a sole viable notion of equitable outcomes is 'welfarism' theory according to which resources should be distributed so as to maximize overall social welfare. This theory too lacks a methodology that will select a normatively attractive social welfare function (for criticism of the theory in its claim to reduce equity to economics see e.g. D. Farber, 'What (if Anything) Can Economics Say about Equity?' (2003) 101 Mich. L. Rev. 1791).

[88] S.M. Bainbridge, 'Abolishing Veil Piercing' (2001) 26 J. Corp. L. 479; R.B. Thompson, 'Piercing the veil within corporate groups: corporate shareholders as mere investors' (1999) 13 Conn. J. Int'l L. 379; P.I. Blumberg, 'Limited Liability and Corporate Groups' (1986) 11 J. Corp. L. 573, 575. See also generally on this point in Blumberg et al, *Blumberg on Corporate Groups* (n 31 chapter 1) vol. 1, ch. 6.

[89] See section 2.2.2 above. Similar considerations arise in regard to groups linked by contract (see Blumberg et al, *Blumberg on Corporate Groups* (n 31 chapter 1) vol. 1, s. 6.05).

[90] See Blumberg et al, *Blumberg on Corporate Groups* (n 31 chapter 1) vol 1, s 3.02; P.I. Blumberg, 'The Transformation of Modern Corporation Law: The Law of Corporate Groups' (2005) 37 Conn. L. Rev. 605, 611.

the transaction costs benefits in adhering to this rule should only be sought if this will achieve just results, in particular considering the variety of stakeholders, the inefficiency of real markets and the possibility of opportunism and misconduct by enterprise controllers, with particular vigilance in the vicinity of insolvency.[91]

Thus, (and given the particular complexities of group structures and the problems arising in this regard in terms of possibilities of avoiding liabilities[92]) it is argued that enterprise law should play a role in shaping the circumstances where limited liability should be ignored, in order to achieve the objectives of the law (the area of law in the context of which the issue of liability arises) and correspond with commercial realities of group operations.

It should also be appreciated that in some circumstances interference with the group legal structure is not for the purpose of imposing liability upon the parent shareholder (or other group members) for another member's conduct, either in bankruptcy contexts or in the ordinary course of contractual or tortuous obligations of a group member. It was shown above that a variety of problems and issues may be at stake in the context of groups.[93] To address such problems the court or legislator may seek to give effect to the interrelations among group members. For instance, it might be necessary in order to prevent parties from evading certain regulations using a group structure. Alternatively, group relations will need to be taken into account in order to uphold actual intentions of parties to contracts (or interpret a statute) in regard to the actual relevant group member party to the contract (or the subject of the statute). It might also be necessary to enable effective procedures in the context of group operation and so forth. In such cases, the policy concerns underlying the doctrine of limited liability are absent[94] and therefore the tension is reduced when attempting to recognize the group as the relevant body. Here enterprise law should play a greater role where this meets economic realities and the objectives of the particular issues at stake.

Finally, certain attempts at interfering with group legal structures may not be strictly a matter of imposing liability, but may still involve the disregard of the division of debts and liabilities among entities (e.g., when attempting to substantively consolidate insolvency proceedings against group members[95]) and therefore may be less clear-cut.

In sum, recognizing the group as the relevant entity will not necessarily harm the key advantages of the law of organizations. On the other hand, it may serve to promote legal policy in particular areas where groups raise specific legal problems.

---

[91] See section 2.3.2.

[92] Section 2.2.2.

[93] Ibid.

[94] See P.I. Blumberg, 'The Transformation of Modern Corporation Law: The Law of Corporate Groups' (2005) 37 Conn. L. Rev. 605, 611. In general, cases apparently invading corporate separate personality are often not concerned with limited liability (see D. Goddard, 'Corporate Personality—Limited Recourse and its Limits' in R. Grantham and C. Rickett (eds.), *Corporate Personality in the 20th Century* (Hart Publishing, Oxford 1998) 17, 62).

[95] See n 155–6 below, and accompanying texts (and further in chapters 6–9, *passim*).

I therefore suggest to distinguish between different 'levels of breach' in terms of the extent to which ignoring the separateness between group members involves questions of liability (and interference with 'asset partitioning'). Where such questions are at stake (strong breach of separateness notion) more caution is required in making inroads into the separateness between the entities. Where recognition of the group and the inter-relations among its members does not interfere with limited liability, the scale may more easily shift towards enterprise law.

2.3.4 The entity–enterprise law dichotomy and state sovereignty

In cases where an enterprise approach is suitable it initially means that the relevant rule or judgement is to be applied on a group level, including the foreign affiliates. As indicated above,[96] if this is done unilaterally by nation states, imposing enterprise principles on the international group as a whole (by way of 'extraterritoriality' practices)[97] may be in conflict with laws regulating the foreign affiliates in their host countries. The particular problems this presents in the course of insolvency will be further discussed in the next chapter, when we consider the cross-border insolvency phenomenon. Yet, some general notes should be made here with regard to the problems of regulating multinationals in general.

What is at stake here is on the one hand the economic realities of the multinational group which may demand imposing enterprise principles over the entire enterprise, and on the other hand the fact that the world is divided into separate jurisdictions (different national states), and therefore there may be overlapping or conflicting interests of states and affected private interests. In this regard it has been observed that applying entity principles to international law contradicts the economic realities of the multinational group.[98] Assertion of extraterritorial jurisdiction by national laws may therefore be justified as it matches modern realities, especially if national regimes attempt to take into account in this process conflicts with foreign interests and balance them with national policies. It is certainly an inevitable result of legal systems' struggle to deal with the problems presented by world business.[99] However, it has also been argued that generally the effectiveness of such practices is open to question, as courts inherently find it difficult to balance competing foreign interests in an objective manner.[100] An alternative approach that has been suggested is that extraterritoriality conflicts

---

[96] Section 2.2.2.

[97] Ibid.

[98] Blumberg, *The Multinational Challenge* (n 3 chapter 1), 170. See also P.T. Muchlinski, 'Corporations in International Litigation: Problems of Jurisdiction and the United Kingdom Asbestos Cases' (2001) 50 ICLQ I; L.P. Kessel, 'Trends in the Approach to the Corporate Entity Problem in Civil Litigation' (1953) 41 Georgetown L.J. 525, 526–32; J.J. Fawcett, 'Jurisdiction and Subsidiaries' [1985] JBL 16; J.K. Rothpletz, 'Ownership of a subsidiary as a basis for jurisdiction' (1965) 20 New York University Intramural Law Review 127.

[99] See Blumberg, *The Multinational Challenge* (n 3 chapter 1), 192–3.

[100] See Muchlinski, *Multinational Enterprises* (n 10 chapter 1), 175.

could be avoided by adoption of a 'shared values' approach.[101] This approach provides that host countries should not resist foreign countries' extraterritorial rules as long as these rules express the shared values of both states (so that they do not impose a genuine threat to the national interests of the target state). The focus according to this approach is shifted from state sovereignty as a decisive factor to examination of the real threats to the nation state. This approach is compelling but limited given the lack of such 'shared values' among countries.[102]

It seems that the more effective way to deal with the problems associated with the operation of multinational businesses is to promote international mechanisms and frameworks applicable to such enterprises.[103] This could be achieved either via promotion of harmonization or convergence of substantive rules regarding multinationals,[104] or by devising international frameworks for conflict avoidance procedures.[105] Any such programmes may, however, be difficult to achieve due to states adhering to national interests.[106] There is also the risk of preventing local innovative solutions in various relevant areas, which should be taken into account.[107] In any event, it is clear that traditional legal concepts fail to deal adequately with the problems imposed by operations of multinationals, and this suggests that some changes in legal policy are required.[108] Various programmes have been taken on board, on regional and international levels, for the development of uniform substantive economic law by way of regulations, conventions, guidelines and other works attempting to mitigate conflicts. This exemplifies a tendency towards greater harmony in the treatment of multinational enterprises generally.[109] Finally, it should be born in mind that, in regard to multinational

---

[101] See B. Grossfeld and C.P. Rogers, 'A Shared Value Approach to Jurisdictional Conflicts in International Economic Law' (1983) 32 ICLQ 931.

[102] Muchlinski, *Multinational Enterrpises* (n 10 chapter 1), 175.

[103] Blumberg, *The Multinational Challenge* (n 3 chapter 1), 200–1.

[104] See K. Hofstetter, 'Multinational Enterprise Parent Liability: Efficient Legal Regimes in a World Market environment' (1990) 15 North Carolina J. of Int. Law and Comm. Reg. 299, 323–4. D. Milman, 'Groups of Companies: The Path towards Discrete Regulation', in D. Milman (ed.), *Regulating Enterprise* (Hart Publishing, Oxford 1999) 236, suggesting that the solution to national legislators' reluctance to regulate the peculiar legal problems posed by the group enterprise lie in regulation beyond the purely national level so as to eliminate potential economic disadvantage; Muchlinski, *Multinational Enterprises* (n 10 chapter 1) 41, arguing that the development of international law of foreign direct investment would serve to reduce the conflict caused by uncoordinated unilateral state policies. Harmonization of state policies will diminish misuse of internationalization advantages by multinational enterprises deriving from the diversity in national regulations.

[105] See Muchlinski, *Multinational Enterprises* (n 10 chapter 1), 175–6.

[106] See ibid, 41,

[107] On the debate reagrding harmonization in the context of cross-border insolvency see chapter 3, section 3.3.

[108] Muchlinski, *Multinational Enterprises* (n 10 chapter 1) 321.

[109] See e.g. the OECD Guidelines (n 92 chapter 1). These are recommendations addressed by governments to multinational enterprises operating in or from adhering countries. They provide voluntary principles and standards for responsible business conduct in a variety of areas including employment and industrial relations, human rights, environment, information disclosure, combating bribery, consumer interests, science and technology, competition, and taxation. See

groups, an enterprise approach will not always be suitable in the particular case. As we deal with multinationals that are operating via separate entities, in a case where entity law prevails, state sovereignty prevails (in regard to the group vis-á-vis its foreign members). Accordingly, universal tools may be unnecessary.

2.4 Legal Systems' Treatment of Enterprise Groups—Application of Entity or Enterprise Principles?

2.4.1 Introduction

It is often hard to detect what approach is adopted by legal regimes in relation to enterprise groups. That is, what is the system's stand on the entity–enterprise dilemma? This is due to a lack of a clear concept of groups, and in many cases a lack of explicit regulation, especially in common law systems.[110]

Additionally, the fact that the two traditional notions of company law—separate personality and limited liability—are often spoken of (in relation to companies) in unison, contributes to the difficulties in ascertaining the specific problems pertaining to corporate groups and the prevailing concept in a given legal system in dealing with those issues. The use of metaphors such as 'lifting the veil' certainly does not help as it further obscures the real issues at stake.[111] Piercing the veil doctrine has been the target of much criticism by commentators,[112] especially in the group context. Also, in construing rules regarding treatment of groups, there is often confusion between different areas of the law, preventing the development of consistent approaches appropriate to the specific objectives of the

---

also Council Regulation (EC) 44/2001 on Jurisdiction and the Recognition and Enforcement of Judgments in Civil and Commercial Matters [2001] OJ L12/1; Council Regulation (EC) 1346/2000 on Insolvency Proceedings (n 173 chapter 3) and the work of the Hague Conference on Private International Law (see D. McLean and K. Beevers, *Morris: The Conflict of Laws*, 6th edn (Sweet & Maxwell, London 2005) 15–16). See generally on international regulation of multinational enterprises in Muchlinski, *Multinational Enterprises* (n 10 chapter 1) chs. 15–18. The regional and international initiatives for addressing private international law issues particularly in regard to cross-border insolvency will be further discussed in chapter 3.

[110] M. Lutter, 'Enterprise Law Corp. v. Entity Law, Inc.- Phillip Blumberg's Book from the Point of View of an European Lawyer' (1990) 38(4) The American Journal of Comparative Law 949, 952.

[111] See *Berkley v Third Avenue Railway* 244 NY 84 (1926) at 94–5 (Cardozo C.J. remarked that: 'Metaphors in law are to be narrowly watched, for starting as devices to liberate thought, they end often by enslaving it').

[112] As it is applied 'freakishly' and it is 'unprincipled' (see F. Easterbrook and D. Fischel, 'Limited Liability and the Corporation' [1985] 52 U. Chi. L. Rev. 89, 89). Gower referred to lifting the corporate veil in the following terms: 'The results in individual cases may be commendable, but it smacks of palm-tree justice rather than the application of legal rules.' (L.C.B. Gower, *Gower's Principles of Modern Company Law,* 4th edn (London: Stevens, 1979), 138; I thank Professor Harry Rajak for drawing my attention to this quote).

particular field under consideration.[113] Nonetheless, it is attempted to highlight below some generalities in terms of trends in legal systems. This is not a comprehensive survey of national systems' regulation of groups;[114] and approaches and doctrines addressing group problems particularly in the context of international insolvency will be discussed in more detail in subsequent chapters.[115]

2.4.2 Inclination towards allowing recognition of the group where limited liability is not at stake

Generally speaking, legal systems tend to adhere to the concepts of corporate form and limited liability, and these concepts are generally applied in the same way to groups.[116] Yet, even in 'traditional' legal regimes, strictly wedded to the entity doctrine,[117] where limited liability is not at stake, there is often recognition of the group as the relevant entity (or imposition of rights or duties deriving from the interrelationship among group members) for various purposes. This is especially the case when it serves the policy of the particular area (both in legislation and in case law).[118]

For example, it is acknowledged that the group phenomenon cannot be ignored for financial disclosure purposes.[119] Indeed, in areas such as taxation and accounting, where the issues of limited liability do not arise, the economic unity of corporate groups is recognized, which is indicated by the adoption of enterprise concepts in these areas often in legislation.[120] Consequently, enterprise

---

[113] T.W. Cashel, 'Groups of Companies—Some US Aspects', in C.M. Schmitthoff and F. Wooldridge (eds.), *Groups of Companies* (Sweet & Maxwell, London 1991), 23, 27–8; K.A. Strasser, 'Piercing the Veil in Corporate Groups' (2005) 37 Conn. L. Rev. 637, 660–5.

[114] On which see sources cited in n 47.

[115] Chapters 6–9.

[116] See Muchlinski, *Multinational Enterprises* (n 10 chapter 1) 318 (indicating that even the most advanced corporate group law, the German Stock Corporations Act 1965 (*Aktiengesetz*) (on which see further below) seeks to preserve the subsidiary as a separate enterprise). See also Rapakko, *Unlimited Shareholder Liability* (n 113 chapter 1), ch. 6.

[117] Such as the strict application of *Salomon* in the UK (*Salomon v Salomon and Co. Ltd* [1897] AC 22). See C.M. Schmitthoff, 'The Wholly Owned and the Controlled Subsidiary' [1978] JBL, 218, 220 (Schmitthoff mentions that English law clearly favours the theory of legal separation, i.e. entity law).

[118] As aforementioned, enterprise law in general has been making inroads into entity law in different legal regimes. In particular, the authors of *Blumberg on Corporate Groups* have shown significant presence of enterprise law in US law, especially in areas not invovling limited liability. This includes also 'contractually linked enterprises' law' where especially franchise enterprises have come under substantial enterpise-wide regulation (see Blumberg et al, *Blumberg on Corporate Groups* (n 31 chapter 1) vol. 5, chs. 160–4).

[119] See Davies, *Company Law* (n 31 chapter 1) 233.

[120] Though such legislations are often complex and sometimes of uncertain application (see T. Hadden, 'Regulating Corporate Groups: An International Perspective', in J. McCahery, S. Picciotto and C. Scott (eds.), *Corporate Control and Accountability* (Oxford University Press, Oxford 1993) 343, 366; M. Lutter, 'Enterprise Law Corp. v. Entity Law, Inc.- Phillip Blumberg's Book from the Point of View of an European Lawyer' (1990) 38(4) The American Journal of Comparative Law 949, 951).

groups are usually obliged to prepare consolidated annual reports to be presented to the public. Similarly, taxation, although primarily applied to the single entity, will have regard to 'the enterprise' as the relevant player where particular objectives need to be fulfilled, such as protecting the revenue interests of governments (for instance, tax authorities may have the right to revisit transfer pricing structures),[121] or easing the tax burden that would otherwise result from the separate taxation of each member of the group. Thus, in most jurisdictions groups are permitted to offset profits and losses in affiliated entities.[122] In jurisdictions where financial assistance for purchasing shares in the company is prohibited, a subsidiary providing such assistance for purchasing shares in its parent may also be caught under the prohibition.[123] Current legislation in most jurisdictions is designed to cover violations of antitrust law, whatever the legal form used by those involved.[124] Examples in case law where groups were 'rather easily' regarded as one trading enterprise are where, for instance, a restraint of trade provision was interpreted widely to include the subsidiaries.[125] The court considered the reality of the case and the fact that the group was one concern with supreme control.[126] The court in the above case did not feel 'inhibited by a purist approach to corporate personality'. For various purposes related to employment law, the group may be regarded as an entity, for instance for questions of pensions and the protection of employees from layoff.[127]

[121] Transfer pricing refers to the pricing of goods and services within the corporate group. The choice of the transfer prices affects the allocation of the total profits among the group members, which in turn may affect taxing. A MEG may manipulate tax outcomes by for instance allocating most of the profit to a company operating in a country with low taxes (on taxation problems surrounding the activities of multinational enterprises see Muchlinski, *Multinational Enterprises* (n 10 chapter 1) ch. 7).

[122] It is the approach accepted by the OECD member states in the OECD Model Double Taxation Convention (see Muchlinski, *Multinational Enterprises* (n 10 chapter 1) ch. 7); T. Hadden, 'Regulating Corporate Groups: An International Perspective', in J. McCahery, S. Picciotto and C. Scott (eds.), *Corporate Control and Accountability* (Oxford University Press, Oxford 1993) 343, 366; M. Lutter, 'Enterprise Law Corp. v. Entity Law, Inc.- Phillip Blumberg's Book from the Point of View of an European Lawyer' (1990) 38(4) The American Journal of Comparative Law 949, 950–1. Attempts to consolidate enterprises for tax purposes are also done on regional level (see EC Seventh Company Law Directive (OJ 1983 L378/47) and EC Eleventh Company Law Directive (OJ 1989 L395/36).

[123] See, for example, s. 678 of the English Companies Act 2006.

[124] T. Hadden, 'Regulating Corporate Groups: An International Perspective', in J. McCahery, S. Picciotto and C. Scott (eds.), *Corporate Control and Accountability* (Oxford University Press, Oxford 1993) 343, 367 (Hadden shows that such regulatory legislation is applicable both to hierarchical and to network groups of all kinds).

[125] See in Canada *Manley Inc. v Fallis* (1977) 38 CPR (2d) 74. In the UK see *Beckett Investment Management Group Ltd v Hall* [2007] EWCA Civ 613 .

[126] *Beckett Investment Management Group Ltd v Hall* [2007] EWCA Civ 613 citing Lord Denning in *Littlewoods Organisation Ltd v Harris* [1977] 1 WLR 1472, 1482F.

[127] For instance, under French labour law, employees of a subsidiary may not receive lower pensions than the employees of the parent corporation. Additionally, the corporation may not lay off an employee of a subsidiary if a comparable position is vacant in another subsidiary or in the parent corporation (see M. Lutter, 'Enterprise Law Corp. v. Entity Law, Inc.- Phillip Blumberg's Book

2.4.3 The approach to limited liability in the group context

In contrast, a strict entity approach can be identified in cases which are clearly concerned with liability within groups (typically the liability of the parent company for the debts of its subsidiary). It seems that the concept of limited liability is strongly grounded in legal systems. Ignoring the corporate form in this context is rare and restricted.[128] But it is generally accepted that limited liability is not absolute, and liability will be imposed in exceptional scenarios.[129] Even in common law systems that strictly adhere to the entity doctrine, the corporate form is occasionally ignored,[130] for instance, where a company is a mere façade concealing the true facts.[131]

However, while recognizing that limited liability should be limited, legal systems tend to be obscure as to the instances where this concept might be overridden, especially in common law systems using vague concepts such as 'lifting the veil'.[132] Additionally, there is inconsistency to a large extent in this area (the instances where the veil of incorporation will be lifted) with certain strong arguments suggested in the commentary as discussed above. It was mentioned above that it is generally more justified to impose liability where involuntary creditors have been harmed, yet empirical data in relation to piercing the veil cases in certain common law jurisdictions show that courts pierce less often in tort than in contract contexts.[133]

from the Point of View of an European Lawyer' (1990) 38(4) The American Journal of Comparative Law 949, 950–1).

[128] See OECD, The Responsibility of Parent Company for Their Subsidiaries (1980), 'Summary of comparative findings', paras. 65–70 (this document is a comparative analysis of the legal situation concerning financial responsibility in OECD member countries) [hereinafter: OECD comparative findings]; R.D. Kauzlarich, 'The review of the 1976 OECD declaration on international investment and multinational enterprises' (1981) 30 Am. U.L. Rev. 1009, 1021 (explaining with regard to the OECD comparative findings that 'it was clear that the legal systems of all OECD countries upheld the principle of limited liability of companies in the absence of contractual liability, with certain fairly consistent but limited exceptions').

[129] By way of using the Anglo-American doctrine of 'lifting the corporate veil' or through concepts such as *actio Pauliana* (giving creditors powers over debtors who act in a manner prejudicial to the creditors' rights of execution) and *'abuse de droit'* (see J.M. Dobson ' "Lifting the veil" in four countries: the law of Argentina, England, France and the United States' (1986) 35 ICLQ 839). See also Muchlinski, *Multinational Enterprises* (n 10 chapter 1) 321 (explaining that the broad approach of existing laws is to provide ad hoc exceptions to the limited liability concept, which deal with individual abuses); OECD comparative findings (n 128).

[130] See C. Mitchell, 'Lifting the Corporate Veil in the English Courts: an Empirical Study' (1999) 3(1) Company Financial and Insolvency Law Review 15, for results of empirical research of 290 UK cases, in approximately half of which the court has lifted the veil, and comparisons to US and Australian results of similar studies, in which the courts have also occasionally lifted the corporate veil for various purposes.

[131] See, for instance, *Adams v Cape Industries plc* [1990] BCLC 479 (CA), the leading case in the UK in this area.

[132] See n 111–12, and accompanying texts.

[133] See R.B. Thompson, 'Piercing the Corporate Veil: An Empirical Study' (1991) 76 Cornell L.R. 1036, 1058 (a study of American cases); R.B. Thompson, 'Piercing the veil within corporate

Specifically, the degree to which any exceptions to limited liability can be grounded on group considerations (the interrelations among the group components) is largely uncertain and varies among legal systems.[134] In the UK for example, the 'single economic unit' argument, according to which the veil may be lifted if there were significant connections between the group members, as a basis for lifting the veil has been generally rejected.[135] Although English company law had recently undergone a significant reform, the issue of liability within corporate groups was not addressed, and it was thought that the matter is best dealt with by insolvency law.[136] Empirical studies of lifting the corporate veil cases in certain common law jurisdictions show that courts are more reluctant to lift the veil when a parent and a subsidiary are involved than in the case of single companies.[137]

In other common law jurisdictions, in particular in the US, a degree of shift from entity law to enterprise law has been identified in this respect, as courts sometimes apply enterprise principles in determining questions of liability, or put focus on factors relating to the interrelation among the group members.[138]

groups: corporate shareholders as mere investors' (1999) 13 Conn. J. Int'l L. 379, 385; I.M. Ramsay, 'Piercing the Corporate Veil in Australia' (2001) 19 Company and Securities Law Journal 250 (a study of Australian cases); C. Mitchell, 'Lifting the Corporate Veil in the English Courts: an Empirical Study' (1999) 3(1) CFILR 15 (a study of English cases).

[134] A classic example of such an approach is the *Deltec* case (*Compania Swift de la Plata, S.A. Frigorifica s/convocatoria de acreedores*, 19 J.A. 579, 151 La Ley 516 (1973)), in which the Argentine court extended the liabilities of an insolvent subsidiary to other group members relying on the unified structure of the group.

[135] The court in *DHN Food Distributions Ltd v Tower Hamlets London Borough Council* [1976] 1 WLR 852 was willing to treat group members as one entity, but this approach was largely rejected in other cases (see e.g. *Woolfson v Strathclyde Regional Council* 1978 SLT 159, 38 P& CR 521; *Adams v. Cape Industries plc* [1990] BCLC 479 (CA)).

[136] The issue was addressed by the UK Company Law Review Steering Group in a Consultation Document (*Modern Company Law for a Competitive Economy—Completing the Structure* (London, DTI November 2000) at chapter 10), where it was accepted that the arguments in favour of limited liability are weaker in relation to tort creditors. However, the Steering Group also noted that the British courts were unwilling to lift the corporate veil in such cases. It was thought that defining the circumstances in which the use of limited liability should be regarded as abusive would be difficult. The Final Report of the Steering Group contains nothing on corporate groups (see The Company Law Steering Group *Modern Company Law for a Competitive Economy Final Report* (London, DTI, 2001) (see P.T. Muchlinski, 'Holding multinationals to account: recent developments in English litigation and the Company Law Review' (2002) 23(6) Comp. Law. 1). See n 151 and accompanying text on remedies in insolvency.

[137] See empirical studies cited above (n 133). It was also indicated in regard to English cases, that cases in which the corporate veil has been disregarded are, by and large, cases where doing so has conferred some benefit on the group (see R.P. Austin, 'Corporate Groups', in R. Grantham and C. Rickett (eds.), *Corporate Personality in the 20th Century* (Hart Publishing, Oxford 1998) 71, 79–80, referring to the case of *DHN Food Distributions Ltd v Tower Hamlets London Borough Council* [1976] 1 WLR 852 where the parent was granted compensation, as opposed to cases such as *Adams v Cape Industries plc* [1990] BCLC 479 (CA) where the lifting of the veil would have exposed an entity to liability).

[138] Although the enterprise doctrine as such is minor compared to the 'main stream' veil piercing doctrine, it has been observed that even under the latter, certain aspects of group interrelations may be taken into account. Additionally, the court may not necessarily require all factors

2.4.4 Legal regimes with more explicit 'laws of groups'

There are certain legal regimes, such as the German system, that attempted to develop a particular law of groups (rather than view the single company as the norm).[139] In this sense they can be regarded exceptional. The German Stock Corporation Act 1965[140] deals with governance aspects of corporate groups and provides rules in regard to enterprise contracts and rules on de facto groups, in which cases liability may be imposed on the controlling entity. Thus, parent companies will be responsible for losses incurred by their subsidiaries if they adopted a 'control contract' (that is, they formalized their 'enterprise relationship'). This allows such groups to embrace 'group policy' (even if it is not in the best interests of particular subsidiaries).[141] In the absence of such a control contract a bundle of related companies may be regarded as a 'de facto group' when a company has been basically dominated by another company. This group regulation initially applied to public companies. However, German courts have extended it to private companies by analogy.[142] Although dealing with issues of abuse within groups in a direct manner, this system has been criticized for not being sufficiently effective, especially since in the course of applying the doctrines to private companies the court extended it dramatically. This has put shareholders at great risk and resulted in significant unpredictability. However, it has been indicated that there is now a shift in the German courts' approach toward a doctrine of liability based on wrongful behaviour rather than mere structural supremacy.[143] This brings

traditionally required for piercing the veil to be present (see Blumberg et al, *Blumberg on Corporate Groups* (n 31 chapter 1) chs. 12, 26–7, 59–60, 68–9; K.A. Strasser, 'Piercing the Veil in Corporate Groups' (2005) 37 Conn. L. Rev. 637, 650). See also A. Hargovan and J. Harris, 'Piercing the corporate veil in Canada: a comparative analysis' [2007] Comp. Law. 58 (on the Canadian approach and its similarities with the US one). In the case of franchise enterprises, in respect to imposition of liability of franchisors for the actions of their franchisees, the authors of *Blumberg on Corporate Groups* note that US courts, while in form rejecting the application of enterprise principles as such, have nonetheless often reached results consistent with the application of enterprise principles. In other contractually linked enterpises enterprise law plays a lesser role (Blumberg et al, *Blumberg on Corporate Groups* (n 31 chapter 1) vol 5, s 160.02).

[139] Such an approach was adopted in other systems, see the Brazilian Act No. 6404, 1976 about stock corporations, and the Portuguese Codigo das Sociedadas Commerciais (1986), Act No. 262/86 Articles 481–508 (Title VI: Sociedades cogligadas).

[140] See n 4.

[141] It is therefore not attempted to abolish limited liability within groups, as the parent owes duties of compensation to the creditors and minority shareholders of the subsidiary in return for the power of control (Muchlinski, *Multinational Enterprises* (n 10 chapter 1) 318).

[142] On the German *Konzernrecht* regime see K.J. Hopt, 'Legal Elements and Policy Decisions in Regulating Groups of Companies', in C.M. Schmitthoff and F. Wooldridge (eds.), *Groups of Companies* (Sweet & Maxwell, London 1991) 81; H. Weidemann, 'The German Experience with the Law of Affiliated Enterprise', in K.J. Hopt (ed.), *Groups of Companies in European Laws, Legal and Economic Analyses on Multinational Enterprises* vol. II ((De Gruyter, Berlin 1982) 21); V. Emmerich and J. Sonnenschein, *Konzernrecht* (München, 1997); A. Daehnert, 'Lifting the corporate veil: English and German perspectives on group liability' [2007] International Company and Commercial Law Review 393.

[143] A. Daehnert, 'Lifting the corporate veil: English and German perspectives on group liability' [2007] International Company and Commercial Law Review 393, 399.

the German approach closer to that of the common law systems, which impose liability on shareholders in more rare circumstances as aforementioned.

2.4.5 Developments on the EC level

Attempts to adopt an approach based on the German model on an international (regional) level, within the European Union, have failed. The EC draft 9th Directive on groups of companies [144] is based on the German model and provides for a legal structure for unified management of a public limited company and any other undertaking which has a controlling interest in it. The draft was never adopted by the full Commission being based on an approach very different than that taken by other member states. The current position of the European Commission is that there is no need to revive the directive, but that particular problems should be addressed through specific provisions. [145] Nonetheless, the High Level Group of Company Law Experts (on whose work the Commission's proposals are built) [146] proposed that member states should adopt the concept of a 'group policy' (pursuing the interests of the group as a whole even if it may be disadvantageous for a particular subsidiary), provided that, over time, there was a fair balance of burdens and advantages for the subsidiary. However, it also stressed that the principle of limited liability shall be retained in the corporate group except in rare occasions of abuse on the part of the group or the parent company leading to insolvency of a subsidiary. Therefore, it shares the general reluctance to interfere with limited liability, especially in the ordinary course of business. [147]

2.4.6 An entity approach in regard to directors' duties, and the possibility of dealing with group liability from the insolvency angle

The responsibility of parent companies for the losses or debts of subsidiaries and their stakeholders could be tackled via doctrines of directors' fiduciary duties. Here too, though, common law jurisdictions are generally wedded to an entity approach under which directors of a company owe their duties to the individual company of which they are directors, rather than to the group as a

---

[144] EC draft 9th Directive on groups of companies (Council Directive on the harmonization of company law) (9th Directive).

[145] See Final Report of the High Level Group of Company Law Experts on a Modern Regulatory Framework of Company Law in Europe, Brussels, 4 November 2002; Commission of the European Communities, 'Communication from the Commission to the Council and the European Parliament — Modernising Company Law and Enhancing Corporate Governance in the European Union — A Plan to Move Forward', 21 May 2003 (COM/2003/0284 final).

[146] Ibid.

[147] See further Davies, *Company Law* (n 31 chapter 1) 231–2; Teubner, 'Unitas multiplex: corporate governance in group enterprises', in D. Sugerman and G. Teubner (eds.), *Regulating Corporate Groups in Europe 67* (Nomos, Baden-Baden 1990) 92–393.

whole.[148] However, duty may be conferred upon parent companies for instance via doctrines of 'shadow director' and/or 'de facto director'.[149] Certain jurisdictions deal with the issue of group liability from the insolvency angle and explicitly in regulation. They can, therefore, be seen as adopting enterprise concepts in the context of insolvency.[150] In other regimes liability of parent companies in the context of insolvency may be tackled via doctrines primarily designed for the single company and its management, such as the fraudulent and wrongful trading type of provisions which are sometimes extended to parent companies.[151] It therefore seems that there is general adherence to entity law where issues of liability are at stake. However, various ways are offered in legal systems to tackle abuses by group controllers.

2.4.7 Further ambiguity as to legal regimes' approach to groups in the context of insolvency

In the area of insolvency, in addition to issues of group liability (that may arise in the context of insolvency), there are significant inconsistencies and obscurity in legal regimes' treatment of other issues arising in relation to groups in default.[152] For example,[153] it is not always clear whether a system allows for 'procedural consolidation' (or joint administration) of insolvency proceedings against group members. Some systems specifically allow this in legislation; other systems may permit it as a matter of practice.[154] In certain jurisdictions, insolvency proceedings against group members may be substantively consolidated with assets and debts pooled across the various entities, thus applying enterprise concepts.[155] However, even in jurisdictions where this is permissible it is often unclear to what extent and in which circumstances assets and debts should be mixed or

---

[148] T. Hadden, 'Regulating Corporate Groups: An International Perspective', in J. McCahery, S. Picciotto and C. Scott, (eds.), *Corporate Control and Accountability* (Oxford University Press, Oxford 1993) 343, 362–3.

[149] See e.g. the English Companies Act 2006, s. 170(5) providing that the general duties of directors apply to shadow directors where, and to the extent that, the corresponding common law rules or equitable principles apply.

[150] See New Zealand Companies Act 1993, ss. 271 and 272. See generally Blumberg et al, *Blumberg on Corporate Groups* (n 31 chapter 1) vol 2, ch. 90, and see further in chapter 9 on the issue of group liability in the insolvency context.

[151] See e.g. English Insolvency Act 1986, ss. 213 and 214. Such a type of provisions is to be found in various other jurisdictions (see further chapter 9, section 9.4.3).

[152] Though it has been observed that this is an area where entity law is in the process of erosion (Blumberg et al, *Blumberg on Corporate Groups* (n 31 chapter 1) vol 1, s. 3.02).

[153] These issues will be explored in more detail in subsequent chapters (chapters 6–9).

[154] See, for example, the US and the UK approaches, respectively (see further chapter 6, section 6.2.1.2).

[155] See e.g. US substantive consolidation doctrine (see further chapter 6, section 6.3.2; chapter 7, section 7.4; and chapter 9, section 9.3.4).

whether consolidation should only be procedural.[156] Certain regimes allow the subordination of debts of the parent company to those of external creditors in certain circumstances, taking into account the parent–subsidiary relationship, whereas in others subordination is generally not acceptable (other than of claims made by shareholders of the insolvent company in their capacity as shareholders).[157] On the international level, there are attempts at enhancing standardization in this area, by devising guidelines for legislators in regard to the treatment of groups in insolvency.[158]

2.4.8 Inroads into entity law with respect to jurisdiction

Problems of jurisdiction are generally dominated in practice by entity principles.[159] The usual approach is that each group member is a separate entity for purposes of jurisdiction, respecting legal form rather than commercial realities.[160] Yet, there are significant inroads into traditional entity law theory in this area. Here too, it is difficult to identify a clear trend. Various regimes have developed and applied extraterritorial enterprise principles in this context,[161] most prominently the US which is regarded as 'assertive' in the way it attempts to implement national policies over foreign elements of multinational groups.[162] It has also been using various doctrines including the use of enterprise principles to assert jurisdiction to adjudicate foreign components of the group.[163] In the area of international insolvency there have been developments driven in part by regional and international initiatives which shift legal regimes towards greater 'universality' in dealing with multinational debtors' insolvencies, as will be further explored in the next chapter.[164]

---

[156] Ibid.

[157] See the US and the UK approaches, respectively. Although subordination may be ordered under the English wrongful trading provisions (n 151). In the UK, the Cork Committee in 1982 (see Insolvency Law and Practice: Report of the Review Committee (Cmnd 8558) (London: HMSO, 1982) [hereinafter: The Cork Report]) struggled with the possibilities of reform of the law as it applies to groups in insolvency but drew back, due to the complexities involved and due to the wider implications this may have on other areas of the law (see further chapter 6, section 6.3.2; and chapter 9, section 9.4).

[158] See the work of UNCITRAL Working Group V on the matter (n 96 chapter 1). See further on the Working Group deliberations in chapters 6–9, *passim*.

[159] See Blumberg, *The Multinational Challenge* (n 3 chapter 1), 170–1.

[160] See the English case *of Adams v Cape* mentioned above (n 131). See also Blumberg et al, *Blumberg on Corporate Groups* (n 31 chapter 1) vol I, s 23.01.

[161] See e.g. the Argentine Draft Code of Private International Law: 24 ILM 269 (1985) Art. 10 (enabling extension of the law extraterritoriality on the basis of the economic unity of the enterprise); the EC Commission will extend jurisdiction over non-EC parent companies in competition cases, on the basis of presence of subsidiries in the EC (see *Imperial Chemical Industries Ltd v Commission* (Case 48/69) [1972] ECR 619).

[162] See Muchlinski, *Multinational Enterprises* (n 10 chapter 1) 174–5.

[163] Blumberg, *The Multinational Challenge* (n 3 chapter 1), 197–9.

[164] Chapter 3.

2.4.9 Summary

In sum, to a large extent, legal systems' approaches to group problems match the general conclusion in the previous section. That is, where there is minimum breach of the separateness between group entities (i.e. liability is not involved) there seems to be to an inclination towards allowing recognition of the group if this promotes the objective of the particular area of the law. Nevertheless, there is often lack of clarity as to a legal regime's stand on those matters and the degree of acceptance of enterprise principles. Where limited liability is at stake, there is general reluctance to ignore the separateness among group entities. But there is also significant ambiguity as to the circumstances when a legal regime will restrict limited liability. Generally, there is greater acceptance that liability may be imposed in the event of insolvency.

2.5 'To Link or not to Link' Between MEG Members in the Context of Insolvency—That is the Question!

Certainly, enterprise groups need to be 'taken seriously'. Globalization increases the use of this business form, so that it becomes the norm, while this also means that the rather chaotic platform currently supporting it is an even greater deficiency in terms of the ability to control and support the group operation and in terms of ascertaining the rules pertaining to the MEG. The present work aims to offer only a piece in the greater puzzle of the regulation of corporate groups, i.e. the insolvency aspect. It also focuses on the 'hard case' (but nevertheless nowadays a common case) in which problems associated with groups tend to arise— that of the MEG, with its added complexities deriving from the fact that the insolvency will be on an international scale.

The enterprise group (operating in more than one country) will therefore be placed at centre stage. Here the 'battle' is primarily along the lines of the entity– enterprise dichotomy as presented above. On the one side is the desire to find ways of connecting between the components of a global group for the purpose of benefiting the international insolvency process and promoting the reliability of the international insolvency system.[165] On the other side are the demands on behalf of traditional corporate theory that the integrity and distinctiveness of the corporate form be respected (or in MEGs linked by contract, respecting the contractual separation). An approach which attempts to unify what are legally separate entities, in their insolvencies, challenges these deep-seated notions. Hence, it entails the risk of diluting the business strategy of utilizing separate corporate formations as a method of ring-fencing financial risk.

---

[165] See chapter 4 for the discussion of goals of insolvency.

The discussion in this chapter revealed some of the main controversies between those advocating for entity law and those supporting the concept of enterprise law in the regulation of multi-element enterprises. It is apparent that entity law has strong merits, particularly with regard to the facility of limited liability. Indeed, there is also wide acceptance of entity law in legal regimes especially when a question of limited liability arises. Nevertheless, it is also apparent that entity law has its limits even more so in the case of the group form of business. The conclusion is therefore that both entity and enterprise law have a role to play when considering solutions to MEGs' operation or default.

A meaningful approach to insolvency within MEGs should thus encompass both entity and enterprise principles and attempt to find the right 'balance' in this respect. For that end, it will be important to appreciate the purpose of the linkage invoked and whether it involves defeating limited liability concepts. If limited liability is to an extent at stake enterprise law may have a more limited role to play (in clarifying the exceptions to the general rule), whereas where this is not the case use of enterprise law may be more pronounced in helping to close the gap between law and reality. In other words, we are constantly balancing on the scale 'entity' and 'enterprise' views. In addition, establishing the extent to which entity law should be adhered to (or rather that enterprise law should take centre stage) in the context of insolvency should ultimately depend on the degree to which it will achieve the objectives of this branch of the law, that is, the goals of insolvency. In other words, the approach should be 'goal-driven'. On top of that, the decision on appropriate solutions should take into account the type of MEG in default. As noted above there may be different types of MEGs with more or less close connections among the entities. Consequently, the approach taken should be 'adaptive' to the type of insolvency within MEGs in issue. I therefore suggest that a 'goal-driven adaptive balanced approach' to the entity–enterprise law dilemma in the context of insolvency within MEGs should be utilized.

Yet, as the subject matter is the transnational group, another fundamental question will be posed: the extent to which national borders will be ignored while linking between separate entities that operated in different countries in the course of their insolvencies. Clearly, an approach that may suggest unification between MEG members (in their insolvencies) entails a 'double interference' difficulty—a clash with the corporate entity and a clash with the country's (within which it operates) sovereignty and legal policy. This represents another axis of tension that will need to be resolved, in parallel to the entity–enterprise dichotomy, considering principles of cross-border insolvency. This issue will be discussed in the next chapter.

3

Global Frameworks or State-based Insolvencies—the Problem of Cross-border Insolvency

3.1 Introduction

The previous chapter considered the problems arising from businesses operating as groups, deriving from the gap between law and economic reality, and intensified in the case of the multinational groups. In essence the quandary was between two possible frameworks: 'entity law' and 'enterprise law'. The present chapter proceeds to examine the second 'pillar' supporting the discussion of the underlying problems of the MEG's insolvency—that of the cross-border insolvency element; namely, the questions pertaining to the handling and effects of insolvency proceedings against a debtor (or groups of debtors) with elements across borders.

The area of insolvency presents acute difficulties when it involves international dimensions. Here the crucial question is how to resolve clashes among legal systems when the case crosses national borders, including issues of jurisdiction, choice of law, recognition, and enforcement. Moreover, we ask to what extent the aim should be to unify the insolvency process across borders. The problems of home and host country extraterritoriality in regard to the regulation of multinationals in general were mentioned earlier.[1] The focus now is on the manifestation of the problem in the context of cross-border insolvency. The main theoretical approaches to this problem, of which the most prominent is the universalism–territorialism debate, will thus be presented and contrasted. Similarly to the previous chapter the approaches taken in the 'field' (as reflected in national systems and international models or initiatives in this area) will also be examined. Notwithstanding differences in approach, here too (as in the previous chapter) it is attempted to identify some prevailing concepts that can also be justified on the policy level, and which hence could guide us in tackling the problem of insolvencies within MEGs.

---

[1] See chapter 2, section 2.2.2.

3.2 The Essence and Significance of the Cross-border Insolvency Problem

Increasing globalization of trade and the rise of multinational enterprises[2] suggests that cases of default of companies may frequently occur in a cross-border context.[3] Cross-border insolvency may be a result of a collapsing company that has branches worldwide, or a MEG in insolvency.[4] Other factors and variables can render an insolvency case a cross-border one. This may include situations where the debtor company had dealings with one or more parties from other countries, the company had assets in different countries, its obligations were due to be performed abroad and so forth.[5] Several major cross-border insolvency cases that attracted much attention in the past decade were earlier mentioned.[6] Evidently, the number of corporate cross-border insolvency cases decided under the EC Regulation on Insolvency Proceedings is already substantial.[7] Similarly new cross-border insolvency cases are being considered under laws that recently implemented the UNCITRAL Model Law on Cross-Border Insolvency in various legal regimes.[8] These cases have been decided under cross-border frameworks.[9] There are of course other cross-border insolvency cases handled 'outside' any such regime,[10] including 'out of court' cross-border insolvency cases.[11]

The phenomenon of cross-border insolvency is thus significant and deserves attention. The current economic downturn makes things even more urgent. Indeed, recent years have introduced us to a number of noteworthy initiatives both on national and international levels for dealing with the problems associated

---

[2] See on the significance of the MEG phenomenon in chapter 1.

[3] This is not to say that it is a new phenomenon. Fletcher notes that even from the earliest recorded times insolvencies of debtors could have connections with different jurisdictions due to interaction between parties belonging to different countries and legal systems (See I.F. Fletcher, *Insolvency in Private International Law* (Oxford University Press, Oxford 2005) [hereinafter: Fletcher, *Insolvency*] 5).

[4] On the meaning of MEG see chapter 1, section 1.3.

[5] See Fletcher, *Insolvency* (n 3) 5–6.

[6] N 36, and accompanying text, chapter 1.

[7] There is no official collection of such decisions, yet <http://www.eir-database.com> accessed 1 November 2008, a website on case law and literature on the EC Regulation currently includes about 170 cases regarding business entities (including applications for opening main or secondary proceedings). The EC Regulation entered into force in May 2002 (see further on the EC Regulation in section 3.4.2.2).

[8] See e.g. <http://Chapter15.com> accessed 1 November 2008, a website dedicated to cases under Chapter 15 of the US Bankruptcy Code implementing the UNCITRAL Model Law on Cross-Border Insolvency in the US, entered into force in October 2005, which currently contains about 170 cases regarding business entities (this figure includes separate filings by companies or groups) (see further on UNCITRAL Model law in section 3.4.2.3).

[9] On which see further in sections 3.4.2.2–3.4.2.4.

[10] On national approaches to international insolvency see section 3.4.2.1.

[11] I.e. any sort of out of court arrangement or workout between the company and its stakeholders.

with cross-border insolvency.[12] By no means can these problems be easily solved. They arise due to the complexity of the fact that such cases contain international dimensions (so that the insolvency case is not neatly confined to a particular country and its legal system). The multi-location operations, stakeholders, or other elements concerned with the debtor mean that an insolvency case may be opened in more than one venue. In a world where national systems of insolvency differ in many ways,[13] the handling of such insolvencies may evoke significant difficulties and conflicts between systems. Although conflicts of laws issues are relevant in many areas of commercial law, they become more pronounced in the context of insolvency. Insolvency law is a sort of 'meta law' (overriding contract, property, and other legal rights that exist outside of insolvency).[14] The insolvency case will often involve different groups of stakeholders of different natures with potentially conflicting interests.[15] It will make sensitive decisions as to the future of the business and the distribution of the estate among the different stakeholders.[16] When this is encountered on a multinational level the result can certainly be a 'jurisdictional nightmare'.[17]

The question is how these problems should be addressed. Is harmonization of insolvency matters (i.e. aspects of the commencement, conduct, administration and conclusion of those insolvency proceedings and their effects) across national systems desirable, notwithstanding that such an attempt may 'strike at the heart of deep-seated cultural differences and legal codes founded on quite different principles'?[18] Alternatively, is it the goal to harmonize matters of private international law in the context of insolvency (establishing uniform rules in regard to jurisdiction, applicable law, recognition, and enforcement), or at least to encourage the resolution of clashes among jurisdictions and increase cooperation between separate insolvency proceedings opened against a debtor, or a group of debtors? Is it desirable to handle all aspects of insolvency proceedings against a debtor in a single court under a single set of rules even when it owns assets or has dealings

---

[12] See section 3.4.

[13] So 'as to oblige the realist to accept that the world essentially consists of separate, self-contained systems' (Fletcher, *Insolvency* (n 3) 11). The variations range from fundamental matters such as the underlying philosophy of the law, to the more specific questions concerning the manner in which such proceedings are conducted and the contents of the rules of substance or procedure as well as their systems of private international law (Fletcher observes that the differences in systems' private international laws in the area of insolvency are particularly pronounced (ibid, 7)).

[14] M. Balz, 'The European Union Convention on Insolvency Proceedings' (1996) 70 Am. Bankrp. L.J. 485, 486.

[15] Such as banks, tort victims, consumers, suppliers, employees and so forth.

[16] See E. Warren and J. Westbrook, 'Contracting out of bankruptcy: an empirical intervention' (2005) 118 Harv. L. Rev. 1197 (demonstrating empirically that business bankruptcy often involves numerous claimants of very different nature).

[17] R. Lechner, 'Note, Waking From the Jurisdictional Nightmare of Multinational Default: The European Council Regulation on Insolvency Proceedings' (2002) 19 Ariz. J. Int'l & Comp. L. 975.

[18] D.G. Boshkoff, 'Some Gloomy Thought Concerning Cross-Border Insolvencies' (1994) 72 Wash. U.L.Q. 931, 936.

or establishments (or even a subsidiary) abroad? These issues are at the core of this study insofar as they concern the specific case of the MEG. First, however, it is crucial to examine responses to these issues in the broader context of cross-border insolvency primarily in regard to single debtors. In subsequent chapters the focus will be narrowed to the particular case of the MEG insolvency.

3.3 The Theoretical Debate

3.3.1 Introduction

The main dispute regarding how international insolvencies should be dealt with is between two traditional approaches (positioned on the two ends of the 'theoretical spectrum' of this issue)—universalism and territorialism, with their supporting principles of unity and plurality, respectively.[19] These two polarities are very different in nature. One asserts separateness in the handling of the international insolvency; the other suggests a unified administration of the process. There are then various other approaches which offer pragmatic solutions, both within universalism and territorialism camps ('modified universalism' and 'cooperative territorialism') and outside (such as 'universal proceduralism'). Contractualism is another approach generally based on free choices by parties in regard to the international insolvency.

The perceived advantages or disadvantages of the different approaches to cross-border insolvency derive from certain basic concepts regarding insolvency theory and/or practical constraints in terms of current systems of insolvency. The discussion below will consider the merits as well as the downsides in regard to some of the main approaches in this context, ultimately highlighting what can be perceived as a set of main aspects of a desirable approach to the problem of cross-border insolvency.

3.3.2 The main schools of thought—pros and cons

3.3.2.1 Universalism

The universalists' camp takes its name from the theory of universalism which invokes (in its pure form) a universal effect to insolvency proceedings. It is also founded in the idea of 'unity of bankruptcy', according to which for every given debtor there should logically be a unified process of administration of the estate in the event of insolvency.[20] Thus, the ultimate aim of the universalists is the administration of multinational insolvencies by a single court applying a single insolvency law.[21] Although the case is international, it will not be split

---

[19] See Fletcher, *Insolvency* (n 3) 15.   [20] Ibid, 11–12.
[21] J.L. Westbrook, 'A Global Solution to Multinational Default' (2000) 98 Mich. L. Rev. 2276, 2292–7 (these two elements, single law and a single forum, are distinct and need not necessarily be

up among different jurisdictions but rather be assembled together (including the assets located in the different fora) to be administered in a unified manner. These ideas fully correspond with the assertion that as insolvency is a collective legal mechanism,[22] for an insolvency system to be effective it has to be symmetrical with the market, covering all or nearly all transactions and stakeholders in that market with respect to the legal rights and duties embraced by those systems.[23]

The reply of universalism to the questions raised in the beginning of this chapter—whether harmonization of rules of insolvency or of conflict of laws is desirable, and whether it is desirable to subject insolvencies to a single court and single law—would thus be generally 'yes', in the following order and ways.

Single law–single court system will be the ideal,[24] and this would supremely be achieved via unified international institutions that will establish a single international bankruptcy law and a single international bankruptcy court system.[25] Alternatively, this could be achieved by applying a unified set of private international law rules.[26] Such a method will be based on identifying the 'home country' of the multinational debtor, namely, the forum to which the debtor has the most substantial connections. Any assets located elsewhere in the world will be sent to this jurisdiction, in order for the property to be distributed to the creditors according to the local jurisdiction's distribution scheme. Preferably the forum administering the case will apply its own rules regarding matters of insolvency.[27] It is widely accepted that insolvency matters are to be governed by the law of the forum (*lex fori*) as insolvency is generally regarded as based on procedural norms. In addition, insolvency embodies fundamental values which should be protected by the forum.[28] The application of the law of the forum also avoids potentially costly and extensive litigation to determine issues of applicable law. As much as the insolvency law of the forum is applied in its entirety, the case is governed by a

conjoined, but ideally, the system will comprise both elements). See also K. Anderson, 'The Cross-Border Insolvency Paradigm: A Defense of The Modified Universal Approach Considering The Japanese Experience' (2000) 21 U. Pa. J. Int'l Econ.L. 679, 687–8; A.T. Guzman, 'International Bankruptcy: In Defence of Universalism' (2000) 98 Mich. L.Rev. 2177, 2179.

[22] This is a widely accepted notion in bankruptcy theory (Fletcher, *Insolvency* (n 4), 8–10) as will be further discussed in chapter 4.

[23] J.L. Westbrook, 'A Global Solution to Multinational Default' (2000) 98 Mich. L. Rev. 2276, 2283–8.

[24] Ideally, the system will comprise both elements (single law and single forum) (see J.L. Westbrook, 'A Global Solution to Multinational Default' (2000) 98 Mich. L. Rev. 2276, 2292–3. See also J.L. Westbrook, 'Theory and Pragmatism in Global Insolvencies: Choice of Law and Choice of Forum' (1991) 65 Am. Bankr. L.J. 457, 461).

[25] J.L. Westbrook, 'A Global Solution to Multinational Default' (2000) 98 Mich. L. Rev. 2276, 2292.

[26] The latter will likely generate less predictable outcomes due to difficulties in devising 'perfect' choice of law and choice of forum rules in terms of predictability of outcome, and generally the inconsistencies that may result from having multiple fora (J.L. Westbrook, 'A Global Solution to Multinational Default' (2000) 98 Mich. L. Rev. 2276, 2292).

[27] See J.L. Westbrook, 'Locating the Eye of the Financial Storm' (2007) 32 Brook. J. Int'l L. 1019, 1021–2.

[28] Fletcher, *Insolvency* (n 3) 89.

coherent system without applying different rules to creditors of the same nature. This also increases predictability (which in turn tends to reduce transaction costs and risk premiums), as under a unified approach to cross-border insolvency stakeholders would be able to refer to a single set of rules.[29] It also accords with the idea of equal treatment of all creditors on a global basis.[30]

Harmonization of laws will set the scene and make the conditions adequate for universalism to preside over cross-border insolvency. Universalism advocates that harmonization is inevitable in a field of law which operates on a global level. Thus, and because there are always pressures to make laws symmetrical with the market,[31] it is predicated that similarities among insolvency laws will increase resulting in high degrees of convergence and harmonization.

In a similar way to 'enterprise law' in regard to problems of multinational groups,[32] universalism is in line with the economic realities of the international insolvency. That is, universalism appreciates that businesses may have operated globally, rather than neatly within national borders. To match with this reality, adequate conceptual legal solutions should be available in the course of the insolvency of such businesses. As such, universalism has considerable appeal. Indeed it receives 'near unanimous support in the academic community'.[33]

What universalism does not currently fully correspond with, though, is 'legal realism'. Notwithstanding the increase in global insolvencies, legally there is much divergence in legal systems, and therefore attempts at 'internationalism' of insolvency still encounter problems of state sovereignty and expectations regarding the laws which are applicable. The legal reality is of a world of 'self contained legal systems',[34] which in turn makes it hard to achieve agreement on concepts such as a truly international court with direct effect on persons and corporations throughout the world (as is envisaged by universalism). Additionally, a particularly acute problem in developing a unified choice of law and choice of forum is the ability to devise clear and predictable rules for identifying the place where the globalized insolvency process will take place.[35] The 'indeterminacy' of the place where the 'single insolvency' will take place makes it also prone to manipulations.[36] Even if it would be achievable to identify such a venue, states may be

---

[29] J.L. Westbrook, 'A Global Solution to Multinational Default' (2000) 98 Mich. L. Rev. 2276, 2286; A.T. Guzman, 'International Bankruptcy: In Defence of Universalism' (2000) 98 Mich. L. Rev. 2177, 2179, 2181, 2270; R.K. Rasmussen, 'Resolving Transnational Insolvencies Through Private Ordering' (2000) 98 Mich. L. Rev. 2252, 2255.

[30] Fletcher, *Insolvency* (n 3) 11–12.

[31] J.L. Westbrook, 'A Global Solution to Multinational Default' (2000) 98 Mich. L. Rev. 2276, 2288–92.

[32] See chapter 2, section 2.2.1.

[33] A.T. Guzman, 'International Bankruptcy: In Defence of Universalism' (2000) 98 Mich. L. Rev. 2177, 2184. See also n 40.

[34] N 13.

[35] L.M. LoPucki, 'Cooperation in International Bankruptcy: A Post-Universalist Approach' (1999) 84 Cornell L. Rev. 696, 713–18.

[36] Ibid, 720–3.

reluctant to accept extraterritorial effects given to foreign laws in regard to insolvency issues.[37] There may also be practical difficulties in dealing with property located in a foreign jurisdiction from a distant base.[38] Furthermore, taking the local creditors' point of view, they may have dealt with the debtor on a local basis and expect the insolvency to be handled in that place and governed by the local laws.[39]

3.3.2.2 Modified universalism

Although the universalists' ideology is a widely held approach among scholars in the cross-border insolvency field,[40] those who generally take this approach realize the difficulty in putting such a regime into practice in the near future.[41] Hence, the current goal is to design an 'interim solution' until there is sufficient international consensus on the various legal matters pertaining to insolvency law so as to enable complete universalism. True (or pure) universalism is thus widely regarded as an appropriate or idealistic long-term solution.[42] An interim solution suggested by universalism is 'modified universalism'.

[37] Nations may be generally concerned about subordinating their own bankruptcy laws and policies to another jurisdiction which will control the case (see L.M. LoPucki, 'The Case for Cooperative Territoriality in International Bankruptcy' (2000), 98 Mich. L. Rev. 2216; R.S. Avi-Yonah, 'National Regulation of Multinational/enterprises: An Essay on Comity, Extraterritoriality, and Harmonization' (2003) 42 Colum. J. Transnat'l L. 5, 8–9, 12; F. Tung, 'Is International Bankruptcy Possible?' (2001) 23 Mich. J. Int'l L. 31; Fletcher, *Insolvency* (n 3) 12–13). See also on national approaches to international insolvency in section 3.4.2.1.

[38] Fletcher, *Insolvency* (n 3) 12.

[39] Ibid.

[40] See e.g. J.L. Westbrook, 'A Global Solution to Multinational Default' (2000) 98 Mich. L. Rev. 2276.; T. Kraft and A. Aranson, 'Transnational Bankruptcies: section 304 and Beyond' [1993] Colum. Bus. L. Rev. 329, 349–51; K. Anderson, 'The Cross-Border Insolvency Paradigm: A Defense of The Modified Universal Approach Considering The Japanese Experience' (2000) 21 U. Pa. J. Int'l Econ.L. 679; L. Arye Bebchuk and A.T. Guzman, 'An Economic Analysis of Transnational Bankruptcies' (1999) 42 J. L. & Econ. 775; R.J. Silverman, 'Advances in Cross-Border Insolvency Cooperation: The UNCITRAL Model Law on Cross-Border Insolvency' (2000) 6 Ilsa J. Int'l & Comp. L. 265; L. Perkins, 'Note, A Defense of Pure Universalism in Cross-Border Corporate Insolvencies' (2000) 32 N.Y.U. J. Int'l L. & Pol. 787; H.L. Buxbaum, 'Rethinking International Insolvency: The Neglected Role of Choice-of-Law Rules and Theory' (2000) 36 Stan. J. Int'l L. 23, 60; L. Unt, 'Note, International Relations and International Insolvency Cooperation: Liberalism, Institutionalism, and Transnational Legal Dialogue' (1997) 28 Law & Pol'y Int'l Bus. 1037; B.M. Devling, 'The Continuing Vitality of the Territorial Approach to Cross-Border Insolvency" (2002) 70 UMKC L. Rev. 435, 452; S.L. Bufford, 'Global Venue Controls Are Coming: A Reply to Professor LoPucki' (2005) 79 Am. Bankr. L.J. 105, 135.

[41] See J.L. Westbrook, 'A Global Solution to Multinational Default' (2000) 98 Mich. L. Rev. 2276, 2299-302. Though, Westbrook predicts that 'global economic integration is driving convergence of law at a surprisingly fast pace' and that 'this trend will make it possible to achieve a workable international bankruptcy system much sooner than might have been thought' (ibid, 2291). See also, Fletcher, *Insolvency* (n 3) 445 (explaining that an international treaty or an international court applying a single bankruptcy law is not within reach); H. Rajak, 'The Harmonisation of Insolvency Proceedings in the European Union' (2000) CFILR 180, 186 (stating that virtually no one considers creating a unified system attainable, at least in the short to medium term).

[42] See J.L. Westbrook, 'A Global Solution to Multinational Default' (2000) 98 Mich. L. Rev. 2276, 2299. See also Fletcher, *Insolvency* (n 3) 12.

Similarly to pure universalism, under 'modified universalism' international insolvency cases should be dealt with from an international perspective, embracing the view that assets should be collected and distributed on a worldwide basis. However, the approach takes into account the current situation in which insolvency laws differ among countries and where the cross-border insolvency case may demand that proceedings be opened in more than one state.[43] In this scenario of a multi-forum, multi-law world, courts applying the modified universalism approach will seek a solution as close as possible to the ideal of single court, single law resolution.[44] Furthermore, modified universalism aims at identifying a single place from where proceedings against the debtor could be handled. At the least such designated jurisdiction should be regarded as the 'main' venue for the proceedings, while using mechanisms such as 'ancillary' (in aid of a 'main' proceeding)[45] or 'secondary' proceedings handled in 'parallel' to the main process.[46] The idea is to either defer to another court which can be regarded as handling the main process of a debtor's insolvency, or to cooperate to the maximum extent with the principal insolvency process. Recognition of foreign proceedings and relief given to foreign representatives or foreign parties may not be automatic under such approaches. Rather, domestic courts may still have discretion to evaluate the fairness of the home-country procedures and to protect the interests of local creditors.[47] Modified universalism is thus regarded by universalist

[43] Until countries can agree on a specific single place to handle multinational insolvency. Even under the EC Regulation where the idea is that a single court will have international jurisdiction, in certain cases it is allowed to open a secondary process in another country or countries (see section 3.4.2.2).

[44] See J.L. Westbrook, 'A Global Solution to Multinational Default' (2000) 98 Mich. L. Rev. 2276, 2299332. This view was expressed by numerous universalists, e.g. R.A. Gitlin and E.D. Flaschen, 'The International Void in the Law of Multinational Bankruptcy' (1987) 42 Bus. Law. 307, 322; M. Sigal et al., 'The Law and Practice of International Insolvencies, Including a Draft Cross- Border Insolvency Concordat' 95 (1994) Ann. Surv. Bankr. L .1, 2; A. Nielsen et al., 'The Cross-Border Insolvency Concordat: Principles to Facilitate the Resolution of International Insolvencies' (1996) 70 Am. Bankr. L.J. 533, 534.

[45] Ancillary proceedings are not full domestic insolvencies, but rather are limited proceedings having a narrow purpose to assist the principal process (see J.L. Westbrook, 'Multinational Enterprises in General Default: Chapter 15, The ALI Principles, and The EU Insolvency Regulation' (2002) 76 Am. Bankr. L.J. 1, 8). See further on the ancillary mechanism included in the Model Law (section 3.4.2.3), and adopted in the ALI Principles (section 3.4.2.4).

[46] Parallel proceedings are full domestic insolvencies (as opposed to limited proceedings with a narrow purpose) in each country where the debtor has assets, and are generally regarded as favouring local law. Secondary proceedings can be viewed as a sub-category of the parallel-proceeding approach (see J.L. Westbrook, 'Multinational Enterprises in General Default: Chapter 15, The ALI Principles, and The EU Insolvency Regulation' (2002) 76 Am. Bankr. L.J. 1, 10–12). See further on the secondary proceeding approach adopted in the EC Regulation regime in section 3.4.2.2.

[47] See the system under the former s. 304 of the United States Bankruptcy Code (11 U.S.C. s. 304, repealed by Bankruptcy Abuse Prevention and Consumer Protection Act of 2005, Pub. L. No. 109–8, s. 802(d)(3), 119 Stat. 23, 146), and the recognition mechanism under the Model Law (section 3.4.2.3) and the ALI Principles (section 3.4.2.4). Cf. the system under the EC Regulation under which recognition is automatic (section 3.4.2.2).

supporters as the paramount solution for the short term and as such will foster the smoothest and fastest transition to complete universalism.[48]

Modified universalism's persuasiveness derives from its adherence to the goal of unification of insolvency proceedings on a global level while giving room to local policies and expectations (where differences among systems are the reality). The problem though is that in the attempt to modify pure universalism 'the exceptions may swallow the rule'. Thus, 'secondary proceeding' mechanisms could result in multiple local proceedings rather than a worldwide insolvency.[49] Modified universalism also currently does not sufficiently solve the problems of providing clear rules to identify the 'home country'. That is the tests and rules for identifying the venue for handling the 'main' process against the debtor company. In the absence of a clear venue standard the system remains uncertain and prone to strategic manipulations.[50] This can work to the detriment of creditors, especially those that are more vulnerable and have less means to protect themselves.[51] The vagueness of the venue is particularly acute, as under universalism (pure or modified) the main elements of the insolvency case are supposed to be governed by the law of that venue. This means that a lot is at stake in choosing the proper venue to administer the case.[52] In particular, commentators criticizing universalism have pointed to the indeterminacy of the 'home country' concept in the context of multiple entities operating worldwide (the case of MEGs).[53] Arguably, this is the 'Achilles' heel' of universalism—the difficulty in applying it to MEGs.[54] Especially, it is unclear 'whether the home country...is determined once for the entire corporate group, separately for each member of the group, or for the financially distressed entities of the group as a whole'.[55] Others suggest

[48] See J.L. Westbrook, 'A Global Solution to Multinational Default' (2000) 98 Mich. L. Rev. 2276, 2277, 2302; J.L. Westbrook, 'Locating the Eye of the Financial Storm' (2007) 32 Brook. J. Int'l L. 1019, 1020–1. See also E.J. Janger, 'Universal Proceduralism' (2007) 32 Brook. J. Int'l L. 819, 821 (stating that universalists hope the world will eventually be ready for true universalism).

[49] See L.M. LoPucki, 'Cooperation in International Bankruptcy: A Post-Universalist Approach' (1999) 84 Cornell L. Rev. 696, 734.

[50] See the problems with the concept of COMI under the EC Regulation (section 3.4.2.2). See also L.M. LoPucki, 'Cooperation in International Bankruptcy: A Post-Universalist Approach' (1999) 84 Cornell L. Rev. 696, 713–18, 720–3; S.M. Franken, 'Three Principles of Transnational Corporate Bankruptcy Law: A Review' (2005) 11(2) European Law Journal 232, 233–4, 248–54.

[51] See H. Eidenmuller, 'Free Choice in International Company Insolvency Law in Europe' (2005) 6 EBOR 423, 431.

[52] See J.L. Westbrook 'Locating the Eye of the Financial Storm' (2006–2007) 32 Brook. J. Int'l L. 1019, 1021–2.

[53] See L.M. LoPucki, 'Cooperation in International Bankruptcy: A Post-Universalist Approach' (1999) 84 Cornell L. Rev. 696, 716–25; L.M. LoPucki, 'Universalism Unravels' [2005] 79 Am. Bankr. L.J. 143, 152–58.

[54] LoPucki has claimed that 'the greatest uncertainty as to the meaning of "home country" results from the fact that most large firms are not single entities, but corporate groups' (L.M. LoPucki, 'Cooperation in International Bankruptcy: A Post-Universalist Approach' (1999) 84 Cornell L. Rev. 696, 716).

[55] L.M. LoPucki, 'Cooperation in International Bankruptcy: A Post-Universalist Approach' [1999] 84 Cornell L. Rev. 696, 716–17. See also L.M. LoPucki, 'Universalism Unravels' (2005) 79 Am. Bankr. L.J. 143, 143–4.

that universalism puts too much emphasis on solutions seeking coordinated proceedings. Possibly, as transnational enterprises normally operate as groups this may be undesirable from the perspective of the controllers of the group. After all, they may have structured the group in a way that certain subsidiaries will remain bankruptcy remote[56]—a choice bankruptcy law should respect.[57]

3.3.2.3 *Territorialism (and cooperative territorialism)*

Territorialism in international insolvency suggests that the effects of insolvency proceedings should be confined to such property as is located within the territorial jurisdiction of the country in which the proceedings are opened.[58] Similarly, the principle of 'plurality' of insolvency proceedings accepts that there may be two or more proceedings handled against the same debtor.[59] The idea is thus that national systems would each deal with any stake of the business located within their borders as a separate estate. Instead of managing the company's assets worldwide this approach opts for 'state by state' insolvency, irrespective of the fact that the enterprise operated globally. As a consequence, where the company had operations in several countries, then several independent bankruptcies might result. Accordingly, each court will decide, applying local laws and practices, in which manner to administer and distribute the debtor's assets.[60] This approach follows the ideas of 'vested rights' and national sovereignty that has also been at the core of traditional ideas of private international laws.[61] Essentially, these concepts stress that national sovereignty imposes the law of the sovereign on all that is within its territorial reach, and that law grants vested rights in assets so situated at the time an insolvency proceeding is instituted. Thus, the law of the *situs* controls the distribution of those assets, a system which is assumed to benefit local creditors.[62]

In stressing respect for state sovereignty, territorialism highlights the importance and unique distinctions between legal regimes, and strives to ensure minimum interference with domestic policies. This arguably corresponds with sovereignties' tendency to insist on applying their own insolvency laws to domestic

---

[56] Using SPVs for example (see n 44–5 chapter 1).

[57] See R.K. Rasmussen, 'The Problem of Corporate Groups, a Comment on Professor Ziegel' (2002) 7 Fordham J. Corp. & Fin. L. 395, 403 (see further on contractulaism section 3.3.2.5).

[58] Fletcher, *Insolvency* (n 3) 13–14.

[59] Ibid, 11.

[60] See L.M. LoPucki, 'Cooperation in International Bankruptcy: A Post-Universalist Approach' (1999) 84 Cornell L. Rev. 696, 701.

[61] See L.M. LoPucki, 'The Case for Cooperative Territoriality in International Bankruptcy' (2000) 98 Mich. L. Rev. 2216, 2218; F. Tung, 'Fear of Commitment in International Bankruptcy' (2001) 33 Geo. Wash. Int'l L. Rev. 555, 561; J.J. Chung 'The New Chapter 15 of the Bankruptcy Code: A Step Toward Erosion of National Sovereignty' (2007) 27 Nw. J. Int'l L. & Bus. 89, 93.

[62] See J.L. Westbrook, 'Multinational Enterprises in General Default: Chapter 15, The ALI Principles, and The EU Insolvency Regulation' (2002) 76 Am. Bankr. L.J. 1, footnote 19 at 5, explaining that these notions were firmly entrenched in the US.

assets and claimants.[63] It also avoids the problem of identifying a 'home country' for the multinational debtor, and the resulting concern that this venue will be prone to forum manipulation.[64] As aforesaid this is one of the main problems with the universalist approach.[65] Additionally, territorialists point to the fact that multinational enterprises may operate via subsidiaries neatly organized within national borders, therefore a territorial approach arguably fits properly with the way enterprises normally operate.[66]

Territorialism is highly criticized though in the commentary, as not providing ways to deal with the special problems of international insolvencies.[67] It is regarded as counter-productive to achieving financial reorganization or efficient liquidations for the entire company (as each jurisdiction handles the fraction of the case in a stand-alone manner).[68] In addition, it prevents a fair distribution of assets to creditors as it relies on arbitrary location of assets in the different jurisdictions; it does not attempt to resolve conflicts in priority rules and problems with debtors shifting assets to foreign jurisdictions. Foreign creditors are in an especially inferior position compared to local creditors. Territoriality precludes any universal control by foreign jurisdictions over local assets.[69] Rather, the local court may 'grab' any assets which are located in the jurisdiction for the purpose of distributing them among those creditors appearing in the local proceedings.[70] These will usually constitute local creditors as foreign creditors may be unaware of a local process handled against their debtor, with the lack of an international framework that aims to take into account the foreign elements of the case. With regard to corporate groups, territorialism's assumption that subsidiaries operate separately within each country of the local corporations fails to address the diversified scene of multinational groups, which may include occasions of mixed assets and debts among entities across borders, or significant interrelations among the group's members.[71]

---

[63] See n 37.

[64] L.M. LoPucki, 'Cooperation in International Bankruptcy: A Post-Universalist Approach' (1999) 84 Cornell L. Rev. 696, 751–3; L.M. LoPucki, *Courting Failure: How Competition for Big Cases Is Corrupting the Bankruptcy Courts* (The University of Michigan Press, Ann Arbor 2005) [hereinafter: LoPucki, *Courting Failure*] 183–205.

[65] See sections 3.3.2.1–3.3.2.2.

[66] L.M. LoPucki, 'Cooperation in International Bankruptcy: A Post-Universalist Approach' (1999) 84 Cornell L. Rev. 696, 750.

[67] See e.g. J.L. Westbrook, 'A Global Solution to Multinational Default' (2000) 98 Mich. L. Rev. 2276; R.K. Rasmussen, 'A New Approach to transnational Insolvencies" (1997) 19 Mich J. INT'L L. 1; Fletcher *Insolvency* (n 3) 13–14; See L.M. LoPucki, 'Cooperation in International Bankruptcy: A Post-Universalist Approach' (1999) 84 Cornell L. Rev. 696, 701 (making the point that 'the bankruptcy literature generally disparages territoriality').

[68] See e.g. J.L. Westbrook, 'A Global Solution to Multinational Default' (2000) 98 Mich. L. Rev. 2276, 2309–10.

[69] Fletcher, *Insolvency* (n 3), 13–14.

[70] See e.g. A.T. Guzman, 'International Bankruptcy: In Defence of Universalism' (2000) 98 Mich. L.Rev. 2177, 2179.

[71] As will be further discussed in chapter 5. See also chapter 1 for an overview of MEG structures.

Recognizing the increasing integration of the world economy, a moderate territorialist approach has emerged which invokes a system of territoriality that includes an element of 'cooperation'—a 'cooperative territorialism'. That is, a system for international cooperation in insolvency cases grounded in territoriality.[72] Under the proposed system each country would administer the assets located within its borders while cooperating with other countries in a variety of matters through treaty or convention. There are merits to this approach, as it follows 'legal realism' and thus requires minimal changes in current practices by allowing local jurisdictions to apply their own laws in regard to assets of the debtor located in the country. At the same time it ensures a degree of cooperation.

On the other hand, cooperative territorialism retains its main flaws as identified above.[73] It is still grounded on fragmentation of the law and forum that will govern the insolvency case and it is not symmetrical with the market in which the multinational debtor operated.[74] Although containing a 'cooperative' element, real cooperation in a territorial system is very limited.[75] Cooperation will come into force only where it will be apparently useful or 'mutually beneficial', while as a starting point each national court manages a separate process, according to national rules.[76] This may be particularly harmful in cases of reorganization attempts, which may require greater cooperation.[77] It might also defeat creditors' expectations and will fail to achieve justice, where, for example, national systems are free to deny priority treatment to foreign creditors, or where the location of the proceeding is to be grounded only on the whereabouts of assets rather than on more substantial predictable tests of jurisdiction.[78] This place may be elusive and easily manipulated, resulting in high unpredictability and susceptibility to fraud.[79] For the same reason, the 'vested rights' theory[80] is unpersuasive where the local availability of valuable assets will often be fortuitous and unpredictable

---

[72] See L.M. LoPucki, 'Cooperation in International Bankruptcy: A Post-Universalist Approach' (1999) 84 Cornell L. Rev. 696, 702; L.M. LoPucki, 'The Case for Cooperative Territoriality In International Bankruptcy' (2000) 98 Mich. L. Rev. 2216; LoPucki, *Courting Failure* (n 64) chs. 7 and 8; L.M. LoPucki, 'Universalism Unravels' (2005) 79 Am. Bankr. L.J. 143; L.M. LoPucki, 'Global and Out of Control?' (2005) 79 Am. Bankr. L.J. 79.

[73] See n 67–71, and accompanying texts.

[74] J.L. Westbrook, 'A Global Solution to Multinational Default' (2000) 98 Mich. L. Rev. 2276, 2308–09. See also Fletcher, *Insolvency* (n 3) 14.

[75] J.L. Westbrook, 'A Global Solution to Multinational Default' (2000) 98 Mich. L. Rev. 2276, 2302.

[76] L.M. LoPucki, 'Cooperation in International Bankruptcy: A Post-Universalist Approach' (1999) 84 Cornell L. Rev. 696, 750.

[77] J.L. Westbrook, 'A Global Solution to Multinational Default' (2000) 98 Mich. L. Rev. 2276, 2309.

[78] As advocated in L.M. LoPucki, 'Cooperation in International Bankruptcy: A Post-Universalist Approach' (1999) 84 Cornell L. Rev. 696, 744–8.

[79] J.L. Westbrook, 'A Global Solution to Multinational Default' (2000) 98 Mich. L. Rev. 2276, 2309; Fletcher, *Insolvency* (n 3) 14.

[80] See n 61–2, and accompanying texts.

and will grow even more so as assets become ever more quickly transferable from country to country.[81]

3.3.2.4 *Other universal-based approaches*

Another approach, which recognizes the need for a collaborative response to international insolvency while accepting the limitations of traditional universalism, is the 'internationalist principle' approach.[82] Mainly, it asserts that unless there is a treaty or agreement between countries, cross-border effects can take place only by use of private international law rules of the countries at hand. Nevertheless, countries should use private international law to achieve cooperation to its maximum extent. In addition, it suggests allowing both 'plurality' and 'unity' principles to apply (with none playing a dominant role). That is, it should be possible either to have the entire estate administered in a single jurisdiction or to have a number of proceedings being handled in several countries, depending on the circumstances of the case at hand, and on cost-efficiency considerations.[83] Hence, this approach appreciates the merits of universalism, yet at the same time the practical difficulties in achieving it.[84] It focuses particularly on the problems of attaining universal cooperation among countries which did not agree on some form of treaty providing for universal frameworks of some sort. Clearly in such situations the 'legal realism' of divergence in insolvency and conflicts regimes is at its most complicated form. Accordingly, a higher degree of modification to universalism ideas may be necessary.

Another approach advocates 'universal proceduralism'.[85] According to this approach, a system of international insolvency should consist of minimally harmonized rules of transnational insolvency procedure, a harmonized choice of law rules and non-uniform substantive law.[86] In other words, it should be possible to handle proceedings against a multinational business centrally on a worldwide basis and thus a uniform choice of forum rules will be beneficial. This should be accompanied by a uniform choice of law rules that will not necessarily provide that the forum's law will govern the case, rather the case may be fragmented in terms of the law that is applicable.[87] Arguably, 'one applicable law' should be avoided, as this will either create excessive incentives for forum shopping, or require excessive levels of harmonization.[88] The answer this approach gives to the questions raised in the beginning of this chapter is thus 'yes' to 'one court' but 'no' to 'one law', and generally 'no' to harmonization of insolvency rules. This approach has much in common with 'modified universalism', in that it advocates a constrained universalism that enables a universal process against the business to take place while

---

[81] See J.L. Westbrook, 'Multinational Enterprises in General Default: Chapter 15, The ALI Principles, and The EU Insolvency Regulation' (2002) 76 Am. Bankr. L.J. 1, 9.
[82] Fletcher, *Insolvency* (n 3), 15–17.
[83] Ibid.   [84] See section 3.3.2.1.
[85] E.J. Janger, 'Universal Proceduralism' (2007) 32 Brook. J. Int'l L. 819.
[86] Ibid, 821–2.   [87] Ibid, 846.   [88] Ibid.

still allowing for some diversity within the process.[89] It argues that limiting the efforts to such a regime is not only a matter of practicality (as advocated by modified universalism proponents[90]) but also normatively preferred.[91]

Universal proceduralism highlights certain important points as to the possibility and desirability of harmonization and uniformity of rules on the international level. First, it reminds us that competition among legal systems is a good thing when it generates a race to the top.[92] It is problematic though in the face of 'inter-jurisdictional' externality, that is where states attract firms through rules detrimental to stakeholders that may be located in other states, or where certain stakeholders can advantage themselves at the expense of other stakeholders in the firm.[93] Efforts to harmonize should therefore enable a certain degree of 'local variety' which is tolerable, while avoiding facilitation of harmful competition.[94]

Yet, the conclusion under this approach is apparently that uniformity of substantive rules on the international level is not desired. It is perhaps unattainable given the lack of a 'supranational authority that can command uniformity'.[95] It is therefore dependent on harmonization which in turn requires consensus. Here again the argument is that consensus is hard to reach, and even where this is achievable it may not be a real consensus, rather a result of dominant groups' pressures on account of other stakeholders.[96] Ultimately, it is not entirely clear to what extent this approach would support a degree of harmonization of substantive rules across jurisdictions.

The argument against harmonization even in the long run seems to underestimate current pressures (and future pressures as well, if globalization continues to increase) on legal systems to converge.[97] It is also the case that current efforts towards some degree of standardization in the field of insolvency are not necessarily driven by dominant groups. In fact, it seems that those efforts are considered by truly international bodies comprised of state representatives, and therefore can be considered as legitimate makers of global law in this area.[98] Universal

---

[89] See section 3.3.2.2.   [90] Ibid.

[91] E.J. Janger, 'Universal Proceduralism' (2007) 32 Brook. J. Int'l L. 819, 822.

[92] Ibid, 829. In particular, procedural innovations, well-run courts, economic infrastructure, well-trained work force, legal predictability or legal creativity should be encouraged (Ibid, 830, citing R. Romano, 'Law as a Product: Some Pieces of the Incorporation Puzzle' (1985) 1 J. L. Econ. & Org. 225).

[93] E.J. Janger, 'Universal Proceduralism' (2007) 32 Brook. J. Int'l L. 819, 829.

[94] Ibid, 830.

[95] Ibid, 831.

[96] Ibid, 834.

[97] Even gradually, and to start with more on regional levels within more coherent communities. See J.L. Westbrook, 'A Global Solution to Multinational Default' (2000) 98 Mich. L. Rev. 2276, 2288–92 and examples provided there of convergence of laws in various fields of law (which require market symmetry). See also section 3.4.1 on the major projects in the area of insolvency developing best practices, international standards, principles and recommendations to guide legal systems in reforming and renovating their insolvency laws.

[98] See mainly UNCITRAL Legislative Guide (n 137), and see S. Block-Lieb and T. Halliday, 'Incrementalisms in Global Lawmaking' (2007) 32 Brook. J. Int'l. L. 851, 899 (explaining that the

proceduralism certainly highlights the difficulties with harmonization but does not persuade that such efforts should be intentionally constrained to the minimum. In light of this, the argument is also less persuasive that the fact that 'one law' approach will demand harmonization is necessarily a flaw. Additionally, it is not clear that under a 'fragmented law' approach harmonization will not be desirable as well. It seems that the contrary is true. If the case is going to be referred to different legal regimes, considerable differences in those regimes may result in greater unfairness to similarly situated creditors, uncertainty as to the legal rules, and inefficiency in handling the insolvency of the business.[99] Nonetheless, and as is also stressed by the 'internationalist principle approach',[100] there may be scenarios where it will be more efficient and will meet expectations of local creditors to have such fragmentation of the case. It does not seem though that this is the rule desired in each and every scenario.

3.3.2.5 *Contractualism*

Contractualists' approaches to international insolvency are extensions to more general ideas of 'contract bankruptcy' or 'bargained bankruptcy'. The idea is that the debtor and its creditors should select the applicable bankruptcy regime by contract. This may be achieved in various ways, for instance, by providing a 'menu' system whereby the debtor chooses from a menu of several optional regimes and incorporates them into its constitution (articles of association). The choice is then unalterable unless the debtor obtains the agreement of all creditors.[101] Contractualists argue that a bankruptcy regime negotiated in the marketplace will be more efficient than any standardized 'contract' provided by a mandatory regime.

It has been proposed to take contractual bankruptcy concepts to the international level.[102] That is, to adopt a single insolvency law worldwide, but such that

---

legitimacy of the work undertaken by UNCITRAL is built on three foundations: representativeness, procedural fairness and effectiveness). Yet, it seems that universal proceduralism at least to some extent supports such initiatives currently underway by international organizations in the area of insolvency (and other areas) (see E.J. Janger, 'Universal Proceduralism' (2007) 32 Brook. J. Int'l L. 819, 821–2. Although Janger invokes a regime which will consist of ' "universal" but minimally harmonized rules of transnational bankruptcy procedure, harmonized choice of law, and non-uniform substantive law', he notes in a footnote: 'I do not oppose convergence or standardization of substantive bankruptcy law per se, though I do have reservation with regard to the proper scope of harmonization.').

[99] See section 3.3.2.1.

[100] Note 83, and accompanying text.

[101] See R.K. Rasmussen, 'Debtor's Choice: A Menu Approach to Corporate Bankruptcy' (1992) 71 Tex. L. Rev. 51, 100–11, 117. For other 'contractualist' academic ideas see e.g. B.E. Adler, 'Financial and Political Theories of American Corporate Bankruptcy' (1993) 45 Stan. L. Rev. 311, 319–24; L. Arye Bebchuck, 'A New Approach to Corporate Reorganizations' (1988) 101 Harv. L. Rev. 775, 776–7.

[102] See R.K. Rasmussen, 'A New Approach to transnational Insolvencies' (1997) 19 Mich J. Int'l L. 1; R.K. Rasmussen, 'Resolving Transnational Insolvencies Through Private Ordering' (2000) 98 Mich L. Rev. 2252; R.K. Rasmussen, 'Where are All the Transnational Bankruptcies?:

will be determined by the parties. The debtor would be free to select the country or countries that would administer the bankruptcy.[103] As with domestic bankruptcies the choice will be included in the articles of association, and could not be altered without the approval of the company's creditors. In the case of corporate groups, each entity in the group makes the *ex ante* choice (a choice which takes place prior to any insolvency event) in its charter. Here too, the argument is that this would generate the most efficient results. Arguably, it encourages the debtor to select and then file in the country with the most efficient bankruptcy law.[104]

The approach is attractive in its acceptance of economic integration and the need for an international approach to international insolvencies.[105] Yet, it does not invoke a single court system (the case could possibly be fragmented among different jurisdictions).[106] It further argues that a free choice of bankruptcy law to govern the case could lead to positive competition among jurisdictions in their attempt to attract companies to opt for their regime.[107] It can also resolve the problems of determining the proper venue (and associated problems of forum shopping) since the designated forum will be specified in advance (in incorporation) and then could be changed only with the consent of all creditors.[108]

However, contractualism fails to fully appreciate the multiparty nature of insolvency regimes and the divergence in the nature of claimants. In a bankruptcy case there will often be many claimants which means high negotiation and information costs in agreeing on a bankruptcy regime.[109] Additionally,

The Puzzling Case for Universalism' (2007) 32 Brook. J. Int'l L. 983. See also D.A. Skeel Jr., 'Rethinking the Line between Corporate Law and Corporate Bankruptcy' (1994) 72 Texas L. Rev. 471, 523; M. Franken, 'Three Principles of Transnational Corporate Bankruptcy Law: A Review' (2005) 11(2) European Law Journal 232, 242–7.

[103] Another suggestion is that the corporation will specify an arbitral institution in its articles of incorporation to perform the same function (see M.E. Diamantis, 'Arbitral Contractualism in Transnational Bankruptcy' (2007) 35 Sw. U. L. Rev. 327, 350).

[104] R.K. Rasmussen, 'A New Approach to transnational Insolvencies' (1997) 19 Mich J. Int'l L. 1, 20–1.

[105] See J.L. Westbrook, 'A Global Solution to Multinational Default' (2000) 98 Mich. L. Rev. 2276, 2303–07.

[106] R.K. Rasmussen, 'A New Approach to transnational Insolvencies' (1997) 19 Mich J. Int'l L. 1, 32. See also See J.L. Westbrook, 'A Global Solution to Multinational Default' (2000) 98 Mich. L. Rev. 2276, 2303 (explaining that Rasmussen does not propose a single court system); L.M. LoPucki, 'Cooperation in International Bankruptcy: A Post-Universalist Approach' (1999) 84 Cornell L. Rev. 696, 737 (explaining that Rasmussen is not entirely clear on this point, but that his approach may suggest a possible choice of territoriality).

[107] R.K. Rasmussen, 'Resolving Transnational Insolvencies Through Private Ordering' (2000) 98 Mich. L. Rev. 2252, 2273.

[108] R.K. Rasmussen, 'Debtor's Choice: A Menu Approach to Corporate Bankruptcy' [1992] 71 Tex. L. Rev. 51, 118. See also L.M. LoPucki, 'Cooperation in International Bankruptcy: A Post-Universalist Approach' (1999) 84 Cornell L. Rev. 696, 738 (noting that Rasmussen himself does not indicate combating forum shopping as one of the contractualist system's advantages, as he considers the problem of forum shopping insignificant).

[109] E. Warren and J. Westbrook, 'Contracting Out of Bankruptcy: An Empirical Intervention' (2005) 118 Harv. L. Rev. 1197, 1201 and 1248–54; L.M. LoPucki, 'Cooperation in International Bankruptcy: A Post-Universalist Approach' (1999) 84 Cornell L. Rev. 696, 737–42.

many of the claimants might be poorly adjusting creditors who would be unable to negotiate or adjust their prices.[110] The magnitude and diversity of claimants in insolvency is even more pronounced in the case of multinational firms.[111] Problems with transparency of information about the bankruptcy regime applicable are also more pronounced in international cases, which results in increased costs of obtaining information.[112] Another acute difficulty with a contractualist approach is the problem in enforcing the parties' bargain against debtor manipulation, where the system does not have control over the debtor's assets and thus cannot apply legal mechanisms against transactions contravening the bargain (e.g., a transaction preferring other creditors).[113]

Letting parties be in sole charge of choosing the insolvency regime may lead to undesirable manipulations of the forum ('forum shopping'). The firm and the most influential creditors will be those selecting the regime, and they may chose countries, not necessarily with the most efficient regimes, but with bankruptcy laws most favourable to their interests. This may also lead bankruptcies to 'insolvency havens' where the debtor may have little or no assets.[114] This is especially problematic considering once again the diversity in the nature of claimants that may not be able to participate in the control of the 'haven' proceedings.[115] Such jurisdictions may also lack adequate systems to deal with underlying objectives of insolvency,[116] especially as there are no significant links between the jurisdiction and the particular case, there is no real 'interest' in administering the case.

More constrained 'free-choice' international insolvency systems have also been suggested, whereby firms would be able to choose where to incorporate their business, and by doing that determine the forum that will administer their insolvency and the law applicable.[117] The law of the country of incorporation will

---

[110] The involuntary creditors (such as tort victims) will not have the opportunity to contract. Other mal-adjusting creditors with relatively little bargain power or creditors with too little at stake may also be excluded from meaningful participation (see L.M. LoPucki, 'Cooperation in International Bankruptcy: A Post-Universalist Approach' (1999) 84 Cornell L. Rev. 696, 739–42; E. Warren and J. Westbrook, 'Contracting Out of Bankruptcy: An Empirical Intervention' (2005) 118 Harv. L. Rev. 1197, 1224–48, 1253).

[111] L.M. LoPucki, 'Cooperation in International Bankruptcy: A Post-Universalist Approach' (1999) 84 Cornell L. Rev. 696, 739.

[112] L.M. LoPucki, 'Cooperation in International Bankruptcy: A Post-Universalist Approach' (1999) 84 Cornell L. Rev. 696, 739; J.L. Westbrook, 'A Global Solution to Multinational Default' (2000) 98 Mich. L. Rev. 2276, 2305–06.

[113] J.L. Westbrook, 'A Global Solution to Multinational Default' (2000) 98 Mich. L. Rev. 2276, 2305–06.

[114] D.C. Levenson, 'Proposal for Reform of Choice of Avoidance Law in the Context of International Bankruptcies from a U.S. Perspective' (2002) 10 Am. Bankr. Inst. L.Rev. 291, 296; J.L. Westbrook, 'Locating the Eye of the Financial Storm' (2007) 32 Brook. J. Int'l L. 1019, 1030–2.

[115] J.L. Westbrook, 'Locating the Eye of the Financial Storm' (2007) 32 Brook. J. Int'l L. 1019, 1030–2.

[116] See chapter 4.

[117] Following similar ideas within the realm of company law, whereby companies may be free to choose where to incorporate subjecting the company to favourable regulation while doing business elsewhere (see in Europe the cases of *Centros* (*Centros Ltd v Erhvervs- og Selskabsstyrelsen* (C-212/97)

not only govern issues of company law but will also be in charge of administering the insolvency proceedings according to the law of that forum.[118] Choice under this approach is not utterly open to the parties. It is a choice specifically given to the business and it has to be accompanied by registering the business in that place. It is mainly directed at solving the problems with uncertainty and sensitivity to manipulation of the home country standard in international insolvency under universalism.[119] To an extent it addresses the transnational character of the case, in accepting the need to conduct a global insolvency for multinational debtors (as the idea is to handle the international insolvency on a global basis in the place of incorporation under the laws of that country).[120] Yet, similarly to the criticism regarding other forms of contractualism, making the place of incorporation a decisive factor in determining the venue that will administer and govern the insolvency proceedings may lead to insolvencies being handled in places with no real connection to the insolvency case in issue. Bearing in mind the diversity of claimants and the fundamental issues involved in an insolvency case this is undesirable.[121]

Another way of letting parties chose the forum and law to administer the insolvency case is in agreements negotiated in the context of insolvency—either before insolvency proceedings are commenced or after their commencement, i.e. via what is called 'protocols'.[122] It can be used either for single multinational companies or corporate groups. Agreeing on protocols to resolve various problems in the context of the cross-border insolvency case can be highly beneficial in terms of achieving global solutions, in the absence of universal frameworks or in addition to them. The ad-hoc nature of this tool enables a degree of flexibility in tailoring solutions to the specific case, overcoming clashes between jurisdictions and achieving greater cooperation, in case such cooperation is desirable. Furthermore, if such protocols are often used in practice, it is then possible to build on previously used protocols to reduce costs of negotiating such protocols each time from scratch.[123] Still, however, in large global cross-border insolvencies involving a number of countries, agreeing on protocols may be a difficult and expensive task. Additionally, if it is open to the parties to decide on the forum to administer the case (with a strong recommendation that courts refrain from

[1999] ECR I-1459), *Überseering* (*Überseering* [2002] ECR I-9919) and *Inspire Art* (*Inspire Art* [2003] ECR I-10155), that strictly adhered to this concept).

[118] See H. Eidenmuller, 'Free Choice in International Company Insolvency Law in Europe' (2005) 6 EBOR 423, 432.

[119] See sections 3.3.2.1–3.3.2.2.

[120] But see the problems it raises in this respect when considering MEG insolvencies (in chapter 6, section 6.2.1.9).

[121] See n 115–16, and accompanying texts. See further on the issue of the venue standard and the place of incorporation factor (in the context of MEG insolvencies) in chapter 6, section 6.2.1.9; chapter 7, section 7.3.2; and chapter 8, section 8.3.3.

[122] See S.P. Johnston and J. Han, 'A Proposal for Party-Determined COMI in Cross-Border Insolvencies of Multinational Corporate Groups' (2007) 16 JBLP 811, 826–9.

[123] See below on the use of protocols in practice (section 3.4.2.1).

interfering with such choices) it may lead to the same problems identified above of directing the case to a venue with no real connection to the case.

3.3.3 Summary: universality–territoriality: a balanced scale

In sum, universalism is based on strong grounds and is widely accepted. It fits with general prevailing concepts in regard to the regulation of multinationals.[124] Essentially, effective and internationally harmonious legal control over multinationals requires the establishment of international legal controls co-extensive with the geographical scope of the activities being controlled.[125] To facilitate such global controls harmonization is desirable, especially if it emerges via compliance with what may be widely accepted as best practice standards, rather than agreements on what would be the lowest common denominators. Still, though, it has been forcefully highlighted that harmonization efforts should leave room for local innovations.[126]

Furthermore, universalism persuasively suggests conducting proceedings against multinational enterprises in a unified comprehensive manner, avoiding fragmentation of the case to achieve maximum market symmetry.[127] To an extent this has also been an aspiration of the contractualist approach. Nonetheless, there may be scenarios where it may be more expedient and just to conduct more than one proceeding for the enterprise at hand bearing in mind the divergence of legal systems.[128] It may also be beneficial in terms of allowing room for national laws, thus upholding the unique distinctions between national regimes.

Finally, universalism highlighted the need to subject the debtor to an insolvency regime to which it had a real connection. The cross-border insolvency should not be directed to 'haven' jurisdictions. Yet, the indeterminacy of the proper venue can undermine the efficacy of universalism. Contractualism strives to simplify identification of such location. To an extent it may assist in this task at least if it could direct the case to the place with a close connection to the debtor.

The discussion above highlights the appropriateness of both universalism and territorialism in different scenarios, and a possible role to be played by contractualism. In the context of MEGs a similar proclivity is needed. That is, handling the MEG case with all its diversity and complexity should draw upon flexibility in the approach and the mechanisms used. It was noted earlier when discussing the MEG phenomenon that these enterprises often exhibit diversified structures.[129] For instance, a given MEG could be closely controlled and centralized or otherwise more loosely linked. The consequent balance of universalism–territorialism may tip towards one side or another accordingly. Additionally, the problem of

[124] See chapter 2, section 2.3.4.
[125] Blumberg, *The Multinational Challenge* (n 3 chapter 1) 172.
[126] See section 3.3.2.4.   [127] See section 3.3.2.1.
[128] See sections 3.3.2.2–3.3.2.4.
[129] For an overview of different structures of MEGs see chapter 1, section 1.3.

identifying a 'home country' in international insolvencies (when a degree of universalism is sought) intensifies in the MEG scenario, where as a consequence of the legal separateness between the entities comprising the MEG, certain group members may have different home countries.

3.4 Universalism–Territorialism in Practice: Legal Systems' Treatment of Cross-border Insolvency

It is thus proposed that all of the approaches discussed above may have a role to play in cross-border insolvencies (and even more so in the MEG scenario). It will now be considered to what extent these approaches (and the conclusions reached here) already play a role in practice.

3.4.1 Harmonization of insolvency systems—the development of global insolvency norms with flexibility in the lawmaking process

In recent years, a considerable degree of effort has been put into the creation of global norms in the area of insolvency and the renovation of national laws in light of such global standards. These efforts are led by various leading global institutions, which have developed legislative guides, principles, or good practice standards in regard to various aspects of insolvency law.[130] Among these projects[131] are the International Monetary Fund Principles for Effective Insolvency Procedural Principles 1999,[132] the Asian Development Bank Good Practice Standards for Insolvency Law 2000,[133] the European Bank for Reconstruction and Development Core Principles for an Insolvency Law Regime 2004,[134]

---

[130] Some of the projects are indirectly related to insolvency. See e.g. U.N. Comm'n on Int'l Trade Law, UNCITRAL Legislative Guide on Secured Transactions (2008), available at: http://www.uncitral.org/uncitral/en/uncitral_texts/payments/Guide_securedtrans.html; EBRD (2003) *Core Principles for a Secured Transactions Law* (available at: http://www.ebrd.org/country/sector/law/st/core/model/core.htm).

[131] The initiatives mentioned here mainly focus on policies and matters at the core of insolvency law. Other initiatives which focus on private international law aspects of insolvency will be discussed below. The brief overview provided here of the magnitude of work on the international level in the area of insolvency has benefited from the *Taxonomy of Guidelines and Principles in International Insolvency* (not yet published, copy on file with the author) prepared with the assistance of Dr. Paul Omar in relation to the ALI/III Global Principles Project (see n 243). The author wishes to thank Dr. Paul Omar for providing a copy of the document.

[132] *Orderly and Effective Insolvency Procedures. Key Issues,* published by the legal department of the International Monetary fund (1999) (available at: http://www.imf.org/external/pubs/ft/orderly/index.htm). [hereinafter: the IMF Principles] (see generally, Fletcher, *Insolvency* (n 3) 500).

[133] 'Insolvency Law Reforms in the Asian and Pacific Region', published in *Law and Policy Reform at the Asian Development Bank* (2000), Volume 1 [hereinafter: the ADB standards] (see generally, Fletcher, *Insolvency* (n 3) 500).

[134] EBRD (2004) *Core Principles for an Insolvency Law Regime* (available at: http://www.ebrd.org/country/sector/law/insolve/core/index.htm) [hereinafter: EBRD Principles]. See also EBRD

Principles of European Insolvency Law 2003,[135] the World Bank Insolvency and Creditors Rights Systems Principles 2001,[136] the UNCITRAL Legislative Guide on Insolvency Law 2004,[137] and the World Bank-UNCITRAL Principles (draft, 2005).[138] Some initiatives are still in progress,[139] most importantly and relevant to this study is the work currently undertaken by UNCITRAL Working Group V in considering recommendations in regard to enterprise groups in insolvency.[140]

Insolvency Office Holder Principles (see J. Allen and N. Cooper, 'Law in Transition Online, EBRD Insolvency Office Holder Principles', 2007).

[135] W.W. McBryde, A. Flessner and S.C.J.J. Kortmann (eds.), *Principles of European Insolvency Law, Series Law of Business and Finance,* Volume 4 (Kluwer Legal Publishers, Deventer 2003) [hereinafter: *EU Principles*]. The EU Principles were developed by an international Working Group founded in 1999 and consisted of an academic group of fifteen professionals, originating from ten EU countries (See B. Wessels 'Principles of European Insolvency Law' *International Insolvency Institute* (available at: http://www.iiiglobal.org/downloads/European%20Union/Articles/21-_PEILABIjournal_appended.pdf).

[136] World Bank, 'Principles and Guidelines for Building Effective Insolvency Systmes and Debtor-Creditor Regimes' (2001) [hereinafter: World Bank Principles]. The text is under revision in conjunction with the UNCITRAL Legislative Guide (see n 137). The most recent revised draft published in 2005 (see Document, Principles and Guidelines for Creditor Rights and Insolvency Systems, based on The World Bank Principles and Guidelines for Effective Creditor Rights and Insolvency Systems and the UNCITRAL Legislative Guide on Insolvency Law (provisional text, January 2005, not yet published) (available at: http://web.worldbank.org/WBSITE/EXTERNAL/TOPICS/LAWANDJUSTICE/GILD/0,,contentMDK:20196839~menuPK:146205~pagePK:64065425~piPK:162156~theSitePK:215006,00.html). The original principles have emerged through a process of extensive international discussion and feedback. They were vetted by regional roundtables involving over 700 participants from 75 countries and have drawn upon feedback from regional forums (see R. Tomasic, 'Creditor Participation in Insolvency Proceedings' EBRD Meeting held on 27–28 April 2006 (available at http://www.oecd.org/dataoecd/41/44/38182698.pdf); see also Fletcher, *Insolvency* (n 3) 500–3).

[137] UNCITRAL (2004), *UNCITRAL Legislative Guide on Insolvency Law* (available at: http://www.uncitral.org/pdf/english/texts/insolven/05-80722_Ebook.pdf). [hereinafter: UNCITRAL Legislative Guide or the Legislative Guide, interchangeably]. 87 States, 14 inter-governmental organizations and 13 non-governmental organizations participated in developing the Guide. The legislative guide was adopted by consensus in 2004. Recognizing the importance to all countries of strong, effective and efficient insolvency regimes as a means of encouraging economic development and investment, the Legislative Guide was endorsed by the United Nations General Assembly on 2 December 2004 (see R. Tomasic, 'Creditor Participation in Insolvency Proceedings' EBRD Meeting held on 27–28 April 2006 (available at http://www.oecd.org/dataoecd/41/44/38182698.pdf).

[138] During 2005, a combined edition of the World Bank Principles and the UNCITRAL Legislative Guide was drafted with the aim of providing a comprehensive guidance avoiding overlaps and confusion resulting from having two main texts on matters of insolvency. The work is still in draft form (see n 136), yet it represents a most ambitious initiative towards greater harmonization (see Fletcher, *Insolvency* (n 3) 500–3).

[139] As of November 2008. See e.g. the revisions undertaken by the World Bank of the World Bank Principles (ibid).

[140] See n 96 chapter 1. This followed the exchange of views and information provided in a colloquium held by UNCITRAL (Vienna, 14–16 November 2005). The secretariat of UNCITRAL subsequently proposed that the topic of corporate groups would be referred to a working group for consideration (see United Nations (2006), A/CN.9/596, Insolvency law: possible future work, Note by the Secretariat http://daccessdds.un.org/doc/UNDOC/GEN/V06/517/90/PDF/V0651790.pdf?OpenElement). At the time the book went to print the Working Group had held five meetings (reports of the first four meetings are available at: http://www.uncitral.org/uncitral/en/

The multitude of initiatives demonstrates the worldwide appreciation of glo-balization and its consequences in the form of the need for legal tools to facilitate the operation and default of multinationals. Although not aimed at prescribing rules and creating identical insolvency regimes, there is nevertheless an attempt to achieve a degree of standardization among jurisdictions.[141] It therefore reinforces universalists' assertion of the need for legal change in a global context and the fact that a degree of harmonization is already underway in this field.[142]

Indeed, it seems that these initiatives operate under the presumptions that efforts towards harmonization should proceed with caution, should appreciate differences between legal regimes and should leave room for local innovations. Veritably, such initiatives provide guidelines which do not impose insolvency rules upon national systems. Rather, they are supposed to be of assistance in the assessment of legal regimes, and in considering and taking on board reforms in the area of insolvency.[143] In that, these endeavours are 'modest' in ambition while demonstrating considerable effort (enthusiasm) in designing core prin-ciples that can be generally followed across jurisdictions. Of particular signifi-cance in this respect is the UNCITRAL Legislative Guide, which is based on the earlier work done by the IMF, the ADB and the World Bank,[144] but goes well beyond them and provides detailed recommendations (mainly in regard to domestic insolvency laws), while still incorporating considerable flexibility to

---

commission/working_groups/5Insolvency.html; a report of the last meeting (17–21 November, Vienna) is expected to be published in 2009 prior to the forthcoming meeting of the Working Group in New York (18–22 May 2009)). It has been agreed by the Working Group that the cur-rent work was intended to complement UNCITRAL Legislative Guide (n 137) and UNCITRAL Model Law (n 212). It was also suggested that the possible outcome of that work will be in the form of legislative recommendations supported by a discussion of the underlying policy consid-erations (see UNCITRAL, UNCITRAL Report of Working Group V (Insolvency Law) on the work of its thirty-first session, 8 January 2007, A/CN.9/618; (available at: http://www.uncitral. org/uncitral/en/commission/working_groups/5Insolvency.html) [hereinafter: Report, thirty-first session], paras. 69 and 70. In particular, it will form Part III of UNCITRAL Legislative Guide. The Working Group's ongoing work is further considered in subsequent chapters (chapters 6–9, *passim*).

[141] See Fletcher, *Insolvency* (n 3) 499.
[142] See section 3.3.2.1.
[143] See e.g. the European Bank for Reconstruction and Development declaring that its princi-ples (n 134) '...are meant as guidelines only and speak more to the results to be achieved rather than the process by which to achieve them. Invariably, exceptions to these principles may have to be made in the context of a given country's legal system.' (see http://www.ebrd.org/country/sector/law/insolve/core/index.htm); UNCITRAL Legislative Guide states that its purpose is 'to assist the establishment of an efficient and effective legal framework to address the financial difficulty of debtors. It is intended to be used as a reference by national authorities and legislative bodies when preparing new laws and regulations or reviewing the adequacy of existing laws and regulations.' (see UNCITRAL Legislative Guide, n 137, Introduction, para. 1); Similarly the World Bank Principles (n 136) contain international best practice in the design of insolvency and creditor rights mechanisms and are used to benchmark strengths and weaknesses of existing systems. They allow flexibility in domestic policy choices and take comparative domestic laws and institutions into account (see further on the World Bank Principles: 'Towards international standards on insol-vency: the catalytic role of The World Bank', Law in Transition, spring 2000).
[144] See n 132, 133 and 136.

accommodate different policy choices and contexts. In a recent multi-faceted empirical study of UNCITRAL work it has been observed in regard to the Legislative Guide that new methods and strategies are used in the Guide to enable it to achieve the task of both modernization of insolvency laws and harmonization. It not only identifies common grounds but also aims to revise laws to meet new challenges.[145]

In other words, while the ultimate lawmaking is left to national regimes, and while it is recognized that national insolvency systems must be rooted in the country's broader cultural, economic, legal, and social context, global norms are devised to serve as a benchmark of what is internationally accepted to be a 'best practice'.[146] Such standards are by no means binding but rather serve as a source of authoritative gentle pressure to amend legislation accordingly. For instance, when the General Assembly endorsed the UNCITRAL Legislative Guide in 2004 it recommended in its formal resolution 'that all States give due consideration to the Legislative Guide when assessing the economic efficiency of their insolvency regimes and when revising or adopting legislation relevant to insolvency'.[147] It can therefore be perceived as an attempt to lay down the foundations for increased harmonization in the area of insolvency which in turn will facilitate the handling of cross-border insolvency. As has been observed elsewhere in regard to the Legislative Guide, ultimately the harmonization effect of such global initiatives will need to be measured 'over time' and 'on the ground'.[148]

Within these harmonization efforts, the topic of corporate groups has been given only preliminary thought so far. The UNCITRAL Legislative Guide addressed the topic by giving a brief commentary which essentially highlights the main difficulties pertaining to groups in insolvency.[149] However, it refrained from providing recommendations regarding this topic. The work currently

---

[145] See S. Block-Lieb and T. Halliday, 'Harmonization and Modernization in UNCITRAL Legislative Guide on Insolvency Law' (2007) 42 Tex. Int'l L. J. 475, 476–7 and 488–98. See further on the Guide in chapter 4 sections 4.2.–4.2.3 (considering insolvency objectives).

[146] See generally on the use of standards in legislation and law-making R. Tomasic, 'The Sociology of Legislation' in R. Tomasic (ed.), *Legislation and Society in Australia* (Allen & Unwin, Sydney 1980) 19–49. See also T.C. Halliday and B.G. Carruthers, 'The Recursivity of Law: Global Norm Making and National Lawmaking in the Globalization of Corporate Insolvency Regimes' (2007) 112 AJS 1135.

[147] United Nations General Assembly, Resolution 59/40. There is also initial evidence that recommendations are followed by legal regimes (see A.E. Pottow, 'Procedural Incrementalism: a model for international bankruptcy' (2005) 45(4) Virginia Journal of International Law 935, 1008, noting that the call by UNCITRAL to diminish special priorities by insolvency regimes 'has been heard').

[148] S. Block-Lieb and T. Halliday, 'Harmonization and Modernization in UNCITRAL Legislative Guide on Insolvency Law' (2007) 42 Tex. Int'l L.J. 475, 511 (noting that in order to assess the harmonization effect we will need to study the legislation the Guide has inspired and the implementation of that legislation by courts, insolvency representatives, and insolvency professionals).

[149] See UNCITRAL Legislative Guide (n 137) Part two, ch V, paras. 82–92.

undertaken by UNCITRAL Working Group V in regard to enterprise groups in insolvency is aimed at tackling this issue.[150]

3.4.2 Unifying private international law aspects of insolvency and cooperating in international insolvencies—approaches in practice

Clearly, if a considerable degree of harmonization of insolvency laws is achieved, private international rules in this area would become less significant in the absence of substantial conflicts.[151] However, as full convergence of insolvency laws is currently not within reach, improving problems related to jurisdiction, choice of law, recognition and access to foreign proceedings, and otherwise increasing assistance and cooperation in the context of cross-border insolvency is an outstanding task.[152] The main regional and international projects aimed at some uniformity of private international law issues in the context of insolvency will be considered below.[153] The section will start though with notes on approaches of domestic legal systems to transnational insolvencies and on courts and party-led ad hoc initiatives addressing problems of cross-border insolvencies, in the absence of standard rules. The discussion herewith is aimed at appreciating the conceptual approach taken by the various models, and certain key features demonstrating the approach. Furthermore, the degree to which these models address the problem of MEGs in insolvency will also be examined. In later chapters particular tools and concepts provided in any of the models, that will be relevant to the discussion of insolvencies within MEGs, will be referred to and cases applying the models will be discussed where relevant.[154]

3.4.2.1 *National approaches, courts, and party-led initiatives*

It is often claimed that although universalism (and modified universalism) is favourably embraced in legal literature, countries have generally applied a more territoriality-based method (a 'grab rule' approach).[155] This is only partially true.

---

[150] See n 140, and accompanying text. See also S. Block-Lieb and T. Halliday, 'Incrementalisms in Global Lawmaking' (2007) 32 Brook. J. Int'l. L. 851, 896–7 (explaining that the work of the Working Group on this topic aims to sharpen the focus on a particular topic, building 'vertically' on earlier work of UNCITRAL, i.e. UNCITRAL Legislative Guide (n 137) and the UNCITRAL Model Law (n 212; on which see in section 3.4.2.3)).

[151] Fletcher, *Insolvency* (n 3) 503.

[152] Ibid.

[153] Note that the projects mentioned in section 3.4.1 also normally contain principles or recommendations in regard to private international law in insolvency (on which aspects see further in Fletcher, *Insolvency* (n 3) 498–507).

[154] See chapters 6–9, *passim*.

[155] See J.L. Westbrook, 'Multinational Enterprises in General Default: Chapter 15, The ALI Principles, and The EU Insolvency Regulation' (2002) 76 Am. Bankr. L.J. 1, 8; D.C. Levenson, 'Proposal for Reform of Choice of Avoidance Law in the Context of International Bankruptcies from a U.S. Perspective' (2002) 10 Am. Bankr. Inst. L. Rev. 291, 293; E.J. Gerber, 'Not All Politics Is Local: The New Chapter 15 to Govern Cross-Border Insolvencies' (2003) 71 Fordham L.

Fletcher observes that it is not uncommon to find national laws expressed in terms which declare that the insolvency proceedings of that system shall enjoy universal effects. However, it is his experience that no state has yet adopted freely and unilaterally, a policy of according matching effect to insolvency proceedings conducted under the laws of foreign states, especially in regard to immovable property located within the state.[156] Similarly, in regard to corporate groups, countries may attempt to apply 'home country' extraterritoriality to extend control over the international subsidiaries in the course of insolvency, and vice versa—nations could also attempt to exercise 'host country' extraterritoriality by ascertaining jurisdiction over the foreign parent of a domestic subsidiary in the course of insolvency.[157] However, it may similarly be less likely that countries will recognize the extension of foreign proceedings of a parent over local subsidiaries or a judgment against a parent company given in the jurisdiction of the subsidiary.

Thus, to a certain extent, national approaches can be perceived as grounded in territoriality, yet at least in regard to the extraterritorial effect of proceedings opened inside the country, the approach tends to be that of universality. This may indicate acceptance by countries of the merits of universalism, i.e. the need to encompass all elements related to the insolvency case and consider them in a unified manner, yet in the lack of structured frameworks the result might be reluctance to subject local stakeholders to foreign proceedings. Indeed, it seems that where international frameworks are available there is a growing trend to use them.[158] As will be discussed below, there is a gradual embrace of UNCITRAL Model Law in countries' legislation.[159] The entry into force of the EC Regulation within the EU is another indication.[160]

But also in the absence of applicable international models, or as an additional route for overcoming private international law problems in the context of insolvency, parties and courts have utilized domestic private international laws

Rev. 2051, 2058; E.H. Biery et al, 'A Look at Transnational Insolvencies and Chapter 15 of the Bankruptcy Abuse Prevention and Consumer Protection Act of 2005' (2005) 1 Bost. Col. L. Rev. 23, 26–7. See, for example, the 'grab rule' approach which was taken by some jurisdictions in the case of the collapse of the BCCI banking group (n 436 chapter 6). A number of countries, including the US, in which the group had subsidiaries or branches 'ring fenced' assets insisting on giving priority to local claims against local assets with little regard to proceedings taking place elsewhere and despite the fact that the group's funds were extensively commingeled (see J.L. Westbrook and J.S. Ziegel, 'NAFTA Insolvency Project' (1998) 23 Brook. J. Int'l L. 8; see further on the BCCI collapse in chapter 6, sections 6.2.1.9, 6.2.2.3, 6.3.4; chapter 7, section 7.4.1; n 79, chapter 8; and n 81, chapter 9).

[156] Fletcher, *Insolvency* (n 3) 13. See also J.L. Westbrook, 'Multinational Enterprises in General Default: Chapter 15, The ALI Principles, and The EU Insolvency Regulation' (2002) 76 Am. Bankr. L.J. 1, 8.

[157] See also chapter 2, section 2.2.2.

[158] See J.L. Westbrook, 'Multinational Enterprises in General Default: Chapter 15, The ALI Principles, and The EU Insolvency Regulation' (2002) 76 Am. Bankr. L.J. 1, 8.

[159] See section 3.4.2.3.

[160] See section 3.4.2.2.

(or other more specific methods) in order to integrate universalistic ideas in the context of insolvency. A fundamental manifestation of this approach is the doctrine of 'comity'—the established tradition among judges within the common law legal camp to cooperate and assist foreign jurisdictions.[161] National regimes sometimes provide specific mechanisms for judicial assistance and cooperation in cross-border insolvency cases within their legislation.[162] Generally, ideas of universalism or internationalism seem to be infusing into practice, with courts showing increased flexibility in interpreting their inherent powers to promote universalism and comity.[163] However, as long as such assistance is largely based on discretion with no uniformity, such methods suffer from significant lack of certainty and predictability, which often results in foreign representatives being reluctant to commit resources to pursue such assistance.[164]

It is also common in practice to achieve global solutions using ad hoc mechanisms based on full reciprocity, mainly by way of agreed protocols.[165] These also

---

[161] Fletcher, *Insolvency* (n 3) 17.

[162] See e.g. s. 426 of the English Insolvency Act 1986 (restricted to cooperation with certain countries and territories); or the ancillary proceedings pursuant to former section 304 of the US Bankruptcy Code (on which see Fletcher, *Insolvency* (n 3), 225–62).

[163] See e.g. *Cambridge Gas Transp. Corp. v Official Comm. of Unsecured Creditors* [2006] UKPC 26, [2006] 3 WLR 689 (where the Privy Council recognized a Chapter 11 plan confirmed by a New York court against a group of companies, notwithstanding opposition of the principal shareholder of the parent company. The case was determined on general principles of English private international law, and the court stated, that at common law 'the domestic court must at least be able to provide assistance by doing whatever it could have done in the case of a domestic insolvency' so as to avoid the need for parallel proceedings); *McGrath and another v Riddell and others* [2008] UKHL 21 (where the House of Lords ruled, based on s. 426 of the English Insolvency Act 1986, that the English assets of the HIH group of companies were to be remitted to the Australian liquidators to be distributed in accordance with Australian law. It overturned the results of the decision at first instance, as well as the unanimous decision of the Court of Appeal, and gave a wide interpretation to s. 426 to enable a single universal scheme for insolvency distribution to be achieved); *In re Multicanal, SA*, 314 BR 486 (Bankr SD NY 2004) (where a US court recognized an Argentine pre-packaged plan, preventing parallel proceedings to take place in the US); *In re Bd. of Dirs. of Telecom Arg., S.A* (2d Cir NY May 29 2008) (where a US court recognized an Argentine restructuring plan despite differences between Argentine Insolvency Law and the US Bankruptcy Code); In *Maxwell Communication Corp. plc v Societe Generale* 93 F 3d 1036 (2nd Cir 1996) (where a US court deferred to English courts and laws based on the doctrine of international comity). Cf., for example, *Re Bank of Credit & Commerce International S.A. (No. 10)* [1997] 2 WLR 172 (where the English court applied its national concepts of *pari passu* (in regard to the doctrine of set-off) notwithstanding the ancillary nature of the English proceedings in this case. One point which is not clear is whether the common law route is still open to US bankruptcy courts to grant relief to a foreign representative on comity grounds in the absence of recognition under chapter 15 (implementing the UNCITRAL Model Law, on which see in section 3.4.2.3). The decision in *United States v JA Jones*, 333 BR 637, 639 (Bankr. EDNY 2005) suggests that chapter 15 is now the only source of relief (for criticism see G. Moss, 'The Mystery of the Sphinx–COMI in the U.S.' (2007) 20(1) Insolvency Intelligence 4–7).

[164] Fletcher, *Insolvency* (n 3) 225–7, 248.

[165] Mentioned above (section 3.3.2.5). UNCITRAL Secretariat has undertaken a project to enhance the use of protocols by conducting informal consultations with judges and insolvency practitioners to compile practical experience with respect to negotiating and using cross-border insolvency protocols (see the Report on the development of the work (Official Records of the General Assembly, Sixty-first session, Supplement No. 17 (A/61/17), para. 209 for the decision of the

include protocols in cross-border insolvency cases involving multinational corporate groups.[166] Protocols enable office holders to run concurrent insolvency proceedings taking place in different countries in a coordinated manner, and may even address deferral to any of the courts involved so as to avoid conflicts which may otherwise arise. Generally, protocols may cover a range of issues and will usually require the courts' approval.[167] The idea is to avoid potential clashes of jurisdiction and 'international chaos'.[168] This mechanism is sometimes used together with the appointment of 'examiners' or 'foreign representatives' by the courts involved. These office holders may act as mediators and facilitators of the parallel insolvency process and can also negotiate the protocols.[169]

Commission to undertake the work, and see UNCITRAL Notes on Cooperation, Communication and Coordination in Cross-Border Insolvency Proceedings, A/CN.9/WG.V/WP.83 (working text); available at: http://www.uncitral.org/uncitral/en/commission/working_groups/5Insolvency.html [hereinafter: Draft UNCITRAL Notes on Cooperation]). The International Insolvency Institute Committee on International Jurisdiction is currently working on devising principles for rescuing multinational enterprise groups (see III Draft Guidelines, n 100 chapter 1), where cooperation via the use of protocols is promoted. Within the European Community a non-binding set of guidelines aimed at enhancing communication and cooperation have been developed (see the European Communication and Cooperation Guidelines for Cross-border Insolvency, developed under the aegis of the Academic Wing of INSOL Europe by Professor Bob Wessels and Professor Miguel Virgos, July 2007; the guidelines are included in an article available at: http://bobwessels.nl/wordpress/wp-content/uploads/2007/09/icr-editorial-oct-07.pdf [hereinafter: The European Guidelines for Communication]). The European Guidelines for Communication strongly endorse the use of protocols as means to enhance coordination (see further on the above initiatives, in the context of MEG insolvencies, in chapter 6, *passim*). See also the ALI Principles and the ALI Guidelines for communication which encourage cooperation in cross-border insolvency including by way of agreed protocols (see section 3.4.2.4).

[166] The International Insolvency Institute has collected and published all of the cross-border protocols it could locate on its website at http://www.iiiglobal.org/international/protocols.html. Draft UNCITRAL Notes on Cooperation (n 165) contains many examples of the use of protocols in practice. These include use of protocols by enterprise groups in insolvency (see Annex to the Notes which includes summaries of the cases referred to in the text). See further examples mentioned in chapter 6, section 6.2.1.5.

[167] See S.P. Johnston and J. Han, 'A Proposal for Party-Determined COMI in Cross-Border Insolvencies of Multinational Corporate Groups' (2007) 16 JBLP 811, 822–6.

[168] See E.D. Flaschen, A.J. Smith, L. Plank, 'Case Study: Foreign Representatives in U.S. Chapter 11 Cases: Filling the Void in the Law of Multinational Insolvencies' (2001) 17 Conn. J. Int'l L. 7–13.

[169] See e.g. the Protocols used in the case of Maxwell (*Re Maxwell Communications Corp.* [1993] 1 WLR 1402 (Ch 1993); 170 BR 800 (Bankr. SDNY 1994)) and Nakash (*In re Nakash*, No. 94-13-44840 (BRL) (Bankr. SDNY May 23 1996); D.C. (Jm.) 1595/87, *In re Nakash* [1996]). In these cases the US court appointed examiners to coordinate and negotiate Protocols; and the Singer case in which the US court appointed a foreign representative to coordinate a consistent approach to the overall international conglomerate (*In re Singer Company N.V.*, 262 BR 257 (Bankr. SDNY 2001)). See also E.D. Flaschen, A.J. Smith, L. Plank, 'Case Study: Foreign Representatives in U.S. Chapter 11 Cases: Filling the Void in the Law of Multinational Insolvencies' (2001) 17 Conn. J. Int'l L. 7–18 (indicating the shortcomings of 'examiners' and protocols and proposing that the 'foreign representative' is an appropriate method for cross-border insolvencies to which the US is a party, as it enables to retain the 'debtor in possession' while appointing a facilitator and mediator sufficiently independent of the debtor).

Thus, although 'contractualism' in bankruptcy is not generally accepted in practice and remains mostly a theoretical idea,[170] there is scope in practice for party-determined choices in the event of insolvency. The use of protocols can also be perceived as reflecting cooperative territoriality, at least in those cases where it is used as a means to bridge over otherwise territorial parallel proceedings.[171] Bridging between parallel proceedings can also be achieved using direct communication between the courts involved. This can be done by various means such as telephone conversations, videoconferences, and exchanging emails.[172] As aforementioned, though, ad hoc mechanisms of this sort have limitations, especially where there are numerous parties involved which might be located in different time zones and use different languages. It was also mentioned above (when discussing the limitations of contractualism) that leaving it to the parties to agree on the forum to preside over the insolvency proceedings entails the risk of directing the case to a venue with no real connection to the case. Relying solely on courts or parties' initiatives as the way to resolve problems of cross-border insolvency may also be insufficient considering jurisdictions which require legislative direction before embarking on such initiatives.

3.4.2.2 The EC Regulation on Insolvency Proceedings[173]

Turning to a regional model for cross-border insolvency, the EC Regulation[174] recognizes the increasing number of companies operating on a worldwide basis,[175] and appreciates that in order to ensure the proper functioning of the internal market (within the EU) it is necessary to have a framework for cross-border insolvency at community level (rather than national level).[176] Accordingly,

---

[170] See E. Warren and J. Westbrook, 'Contracting out of bankruptcy: an empirical intervention' (2005) 118 Harv. L. Rev. 1197, 1201.

[171] See 'cooperative territoriality' above (section 3.3.2.3).

[172] Communication of this sort is also encouraged by international models for cross-border insolvency (see sections 3.4.2.3 and 3.4.2.4). See further on direct communication (in the context of MEG insolvency) in chapter 6, section 6.2.1.5.

[173] Council Regulation (EC) 1346/2000 on Insolvency Proceedings [2000] OJ L160/1 (available at: http://eur-lex.europa.eu/LexUriServ/LexUriServ.do?uri=OJ:L:2000:160:0001:0018:EN: PDF) [hereinafter: EC Regulation or Regulation, interchangeably]

[174] In force since 31 May 2002. For history and comprehensive commentaries on the EC Regulation see e.g. Fletcher, *Insolvency* (n 3) ch. 7; B. Wessels, 'The changing landscape of cross-border insolvency law in Europe' (2007) 12(1) *Juridica International* 116–124; H. Rajak, 'The Harmonisation of Insolvency Proceedings in the European Union' (2000) CFILR 180; G. Moss, I.F. Fletcher, S. Isaacs (eds.), *The EC Regulation on Insolvency Proceedings: A Commentary and Annotated Guide* (Oxford University Press, Oxford 2002) [hereinafter: Moss et al, *The EC Regulation*].

[175] See Recital (3) to the EC Regulation (n 173).

[176] See Recitals (1)–(8) to the EC Regulation (n 173). It should be noted that Article 1(2) of the EC Regulation excludes insurance undertakings, credit institutions, investment undertakings holding funds or securities for third parties and collective investment undertakings from its scope. Indeed due to the risks inherent in banking activities and the impact a bank failure can have on the economy of a country often financial institutions are treated differently than other businesses. Further legislation was introduced at EC level in this context, in the form of EC Directives

its aim is that every debtor will be subjected to a unitary insolvency process having universal effects. To achieve this purpose, the Regulation contains provisions regarding jurisdiction, recognition of judgments and the law applicable to the insolvency proceedings. These provisions are binding and directly applicable in member states. In other words, it creates internationally enforceable rules with multinational application (within the community). It is hence a rather drastic scheme, enabling close coordination of transnational insolvencies,[177] and as such is based on a universalist approach.[178]

A core feature of the Regulation is the concept of a 'centre of main interests' (COMI). That is, that the main proceedings against a debtor should take place in the jurisdiction where its centre of main interests is located.[179] The main proceeding has a universal scope and is intended to encompass the debtor's assets on a worldwide basis and to affect all creditors, wherever they may be located.[180] This enables the office holder to take speedy measures in other member states to assert his rights to control and administer the entire estate.[181] Only one set of main proceedings may be opened in the community against the debtor, thus reflecting the principle of unity. The Regulation clearly attempts to unify rules of jurisdiction.[182] This also encompasses the idea of single main proceedings

(see Directive 2001/17 on the reorganization and winding-up of insurance undertaking ([2001] OJ L110/28) and Directive 2001/24 on the reorganization and winding-up of credit institutions ([2001] OJ L125/15). The issue of banks' insolvencies (the specific problems arising in this context and the particular regulation applying to such institutions) is outside the scope of this book. See on this matter E. Hupkes, *The legal aspects of bank insolvency. A comparative analysis of Western Europe, the United states and Canada*, Studies in comparative Corporate and Finance Law, v.10 (Kluwer Law International, 2000) ch 7; B. Wessels, 'Banks in distress under rules of European Insolvency Law' (2006) 21 (6) JIBLR 301.

[177] See I.F. Fletcher, 'The European Union Regulation on Insolvency Proceedings' [2003] INSOL INTERNATIONAL, Cross-Border Insolvency 15. However, it is a regional instrument confined to the boundaries of the European community, and does not apply globally.

[178] It actually refers to the idea of 'market symmetry' when it states that its adoption is necessitated by the integration of the internal market.

[179] Hereinafter: COMI (Article 3(1) of the EC Regulation (n 173)). This is also the decisive criterion for the application of the Regulation. The Regulation applies only to proceedings where the debtor's COMI is located in the Community (Recital (14) to the EC Regulation (ibid). In the *Brac* case it was made clear by the English High Court that this includes companies incorporated in third states whose COMI was located in one of the member states (see *In re Brac Rent-A-Car Inc* [2003] EWHC 128 (Ch), [2003] BCC 248).

[180] M.Virgos and E. Schmit, 'Report on the Convention on Insolvency Proceedings' (1996) 6500/1/96, REV1, DRS 8 (CFC), para. 73. The Report has been issued to serve as an interpretive guide to the Insolvency Convention of 1995, which five years later was altered to become the Insolvency Regulation. The Report has been recognized as the unofficial guide for interpretation of the regulation [hereinafter: Report Virgos/Schmit]. The rules on jurisdiction are matched by mandatory rules for the recognition of such proceedings in other member states and of the effects deriving from such recognition. Member states can deny recognition only in the rare case where it will be contradictory to national public policy (see Articles 16–26 of the EC Regulation (n 173)).

[181] See I.F. Fletcher, 'The European Union Regulation on Insolvency Proceedings' [2003] INSOL INTERNATIONAL, Cross-Border Insolvency 15, 38–9.

[182] In this area, there has been generally a mismatch between two main national approaches, one which is based on the 'real seat' of the company, and another which focuses on the place of

being conducted in a place with close connection to the debtor.[183] However, the Regulation does not completely solve the problems associated with the identification of the debtor's 'home country'.[184] It does not offer a clear definition of COMI, except that Recital (13) (taken from the Report Virgos/Schmit)[185] explains that it is the place where the debtor conducts the administration of his interests on a regular basis and is therefore ascertainable by third parties.[186] Although it does not leave the question of proper venue completely open, the definition is prone to various interpretations and can be regarded as somewhat 'fuzzy'.[187] In any case, COMI apparently looks for the 'real seat' of the debtor,[188] and the place of the company's registered office is only the point of departure (a rebuttable presumption).[189] In addition, it does not provide any procedure or mechanism for determining the proper jurisdiction in cases where two or more countries can potentially compete as a proper forum, but merely grants primacy of effect to the first court to open proceedings.[190] The Regulation also provides a uniform choice of law concept, according to which the basic rule is that the law governing the insolvency matters is the law of the forum in which proceedings are opened.[191] Hence, to an extent it incorporates the idea of one law applying in the case, which should be the law of the court administering it.[192]

the registered office. The former approach which emphasizes economic realities and looks for the actual seat of the company is typically linked with the civil law countries.

[183] A concept invoked by universalism (see section 3.3.2.1).

[184] See section 3.3.2.1.

[185] Note 180, para. 75. See comments made in this regard in EC Regulation courts' decisions for instance *In re Brac Rent-A-Car Inc* [2003] EWHC 128 (Ch), [2003] BCC 248 and in *Geveran Trading Co Ltd v Skjevesland* [2003] BCC 209).

[186] The COMI is presumed to be in the place of the debtor's registered office. This presumption can be rebutted if a party can show that the company's main interests are centred in another member state in a manner which is ascertainable by third parties (Article 3(1) and Article 3(2) of the EC Regulation (n 173); see *Eurofood IFSC Ltd* (Case C-341/04) [2006] OJ 2006 C143/11. See also I. Verougstraete, *Manuel de la faillite et du concordat* (Kluwer Editions Jurdique Belgique, Waterloo 1998), 627; I.F. Fletcher, 'The European Union Regulation on Insolvency Proceedings' [2003] INSOL INTERNATIONAL CROSS-BORDER INSOLVENCY A Guide to Recognition and Enforcement, 15, 27–31).

[187] See H. Eidenmuller, 'Free Choice in International Company Insolvency Law in Europe' (2005) 6 EBOR 423, 447. See further on the interpretation of COMI (in the context of discussing MEG insolvencies) in chapter 6, section 6.2.1.9; chapter 7, section 7.3; and chapter 8, section 8.3.3.

[188] Thus, it is regarded as a victory for the civil law inspired 'real seat' theory of jurisdictional competence over the 'state of incorporation' theory traditionally espoused by the members of the Anglo-American common law 'family' (n 182, see also Fletcher, *Insolvency* (n 3) 367).

[189] See n 186.

[190] The possibility of requesting a preliminary ruling of the ECJ in such an event will be hardly effective, since only a 'supreme national court' (the court of the last resort) can seek such a ruling (see Article 68 of the Consolidated EC Treaty (formerly Article 73p ECT). This is due to the fact that the convention has been converted into a Regulation, adopted under Title IV of the EC Treaty. It means that this will be time consuming and costly (see I.F. Fletcher, 'The Challenge of Change: First Experiences of Life under the EC Regulation on Insolvency proceedings in the UK' Annual Review of Insolvency Law, 2003 (Carswell, Toronto 2004) 431, 436–7).

[191] Article 4 of the EC Regulation (n 173). This is subject to exceptions (Articles 5–15). See also on the choice of law rules under the EC Regulation in Fletcher, *Insolvency* (n 3) 396–420.

[192] A concept invoked by universalism (see section 3.3.2.1).

The EC Regulation attempts to balance the 'unity' principle with the need to have regard to legitimate expectations of creditors[193] with the result that it allows a local (rather than solely global) proceeding to take place, in the form of 'secondary' proceedings.[194] In addition, it provides a set of exceptions to the basic choice of law rule.[195] These modifications are the result of acknowledging the differences between member states' substantive laws.[196] Thus, the Regulation is, in fact, a form of 'modified universalism' with territorial elements incorporated within its scheme. Still, though, if territorial proceedings are opened in parallel to main proceedings (that is subsequent to the opening of main proceedings[197]) they do not take place in complete isolation. The Regulation provides that 'secondary' proceedings are subject to rules designed to ensure those proceedings are integrated into the overall process of administering the insolvent debtor's estate for the benefit of creditors generally.[198] In particular, the unity of the debtor's estate is maintained through rules based on the doctrine of hotchpot,[199] on the consolidation of any surplus left over at the conclusion of the secondary proceedings,[200] and on the right of all creditors to lodge claims in the main and in any secondary proceedings[201] and to participate in all proceedings, whether main or secondary.[202] In addition, once multiple proceedings emerge the insolvency representatives have to communicate information and cooperate with each other.[203] In sum, the Regulation can be perceived as grounded on universalism while accepting 'legal realism' and therefore containing territorialistic elements. The extent to which the balance is tilted to one of those approaches largely depends on whether in practice secondary proceedings are often opened against debtors.

[193] See Recitals (12) and (24) to the EC Regulation (n 173).

[194] Based on the debtor having an 'establishment' in the territory (Article 3(2) of the EC Regulation (n 173)). This essentially means ascertaining whether the debtor maintains a 'place of businesses' in the jurisdiction, based on external impressions of parties who had dealings with the debtor (see Fletcher, *Insolvency* (n 3) 376–7).

[195] Articles 5–15 of the EC Regulation (n 173). See also I.F. Fletcher, 'The European Union Regulation on Insolvency Proceedings' [2003] INSOL INTERNATIONAL, Cross-Border Insolvency 15, 31–8; Also see J.L. Westbrook, 'Multinational Enterprises in General Default: Chapter 15, The ALI Principles, and The EU Insolvency Regulation' (2002) 76 Am. Bankr. L.J. 1, footnote 122 at 34 (Westbrook expresses the opinion that some of the exceptions are large ones (e.g., for secured creditors) and seem regrettable).

[196] See Recital (11) to the EC Regulation (n 173).

[197] Territorial proceedings can also be opened in advance of any main proceedings. In this case they are 'free standing' (see Article 3(4) of the EC Regulation (n 173)).

[198] See Fletcher, *Insolvency* (n 3) 432–6.

[199] Article 20 of the EC Regulation (n 173) (the common law rule according to which a creditor that receives a distribution in a foreign insolvency proceeding must stand aside in a local distribution until creditors of the same class (under local law) have received as much from the local proceeding as the first creditor got from the foreign one).

[200] Article 35 of the EC Regulation (n 173).

[201] Article 32 of the EC Regulation (ibid)

[202] Article 32 of the EC Regulation (ibid).

[203] Article 31 of the EC Regulation (ibid).

The Regulation, however, does not contain provisions to deal with the issue of corporate groups. This was expressly indicated in the Report Virgos/Schmit.[204] Apparently, therefore, courts should identify the COMI of the debtor (as the basis for ascertaining jurisdiction) on a 'separate basis', notwithstanding its relationship with other affiliated companies.[205] Similarly, territorial (secondary) proceedings can be opened against a parent debtor, in another jurisdiction where it had an 'establishment' by way of local operations or a branch, but not a subsidiary company.[206] There are also no explicit provisions which provide for means of cooperation between proceedings taking place against related debtors.[207] Although several pan-European MEG restructurings have been successfully coordinated by placing all affiliated companies' proceedings under a single forum and single law, this was generally based on COMIs found in that jurisdiction for each company separately.[208] It seems thus that the Regulation (and its interpretation by the ECJ)[209] is currently largely based on an entity approach in the context of international insolvency.[210] Yet, the absence of rules regarding groups within the Regulation can also be a result of the complexity of these scenarios, and therefore it was left to be dealt with at a later stage.[211]

---

[204] Note 180. The report indicates in para. 76 that 'The Convention offers no rule for groups of affiliated companies (parent-subsidiary schemes). The general rule to open or to consolidate insolvency proceedings against any of the related companies as a principal or jointly liable debtor is that jurisdiction must exist according to the Convention for each of the concerned debtors with a separate legal entity. Naturally, the drawing of a European norm on associated companies may affect this answer'.

[205] See *Eurofood IFSC Ltd* (Case C-341/04) [2006] OJ 2006 C143/11, [26]–[37]. Though the court has not disqualified 'parental control' over a subsidiary as a relevant factor in determining the proper jurisdiction, the focus was on the whereabouts of the registered office and operations of the particular subsidiary (see further on the case in chapter 6, sections 6.2.1.6, 6.2.1.8 and 6.2.1.9; chapter 7, sections 7.3.2 and 7.5.2; and chapter 8, sections 8.1 and 8.2).

[206] See *Telia Soneria AB v Hilcourt 'Docklands' Ltd* [2003] BCC 856 (Ch). In the case, a creditor threatened to pursue winding-up proceedings against a Swedish company (a company whose registered office and centre of main interests was in Sweden) in the UK on the grounds that it had a subsidiary in the UK. The judge posited that, winding-up proceedings directed at Telia can only be brought in Sweden and that the courts of England and Wales have no jurisdiction. The reason for this judgment was apparently based on the notion that the separate personality of the subsidiary must be respected. See also B. Wessels, 'International Jurisdiction to Open Insolvency Proceedings in Europe, In Particular Against (Groups of) Companies' Working Papers Series, Institute for Law and Finance, Johann Wolfgang Goethe University, (available at: http://www.iii-global.org/country/european_union/InternJurisdictionCompanies.pdf.) 19; Fletcher *Insolvency* (n 3) 379–80.

[207] Moss et al, *The EC Regulation* (n 174) 173–4.

[208] See further discussion on the possibility of administering insolvencies of affiliated companies on a unified basis under the EC Regulation (and relevant examples) in chapter 6, section 6.2.1.6.

[209] Note 205, and accompanying text.

[210] See on the entity-enterprise law debate chapter 2, section 2.3.1.

[211] The Virgos-Schmit Report (n 180) refers to a possible new European law on associated companies (para. 76).

3.4.2.3　*The UNCITRAL Model Law on Cross-Border Insolvency*[212]

The Model Law is the most significant scheme for regulating cross-border insolvencies currently at hand in terms of the potential breadth of its application. It is an international initiative, targeted at every country that wishes to embrace it.[213] On the other hand, it is less 'pretentious' in the means and mechanisms it provides (compared to the EC Regulation[214]) and more modest in its goals.[215] It appreciates that it is currently unrealistic to have a wide global regime that includes substantive law rules and that attempts to be fully uniformly and consistently applied in nation states.[216] Thus, it deliberately refrains from including rules of direct jurisdiction or choice of law.[217] Designed as a set of model legislative provisions rather than an international treaty (or other sort of supranational legislation[218]), the Model Law is also not binding. The ultimate form of legislation which could result from the Model Law is left to each country. Thus, it has the merit of being acceptable to a wide circle of states.[219] Yet it is also prone to the danger of passivity, and lack of uniformity in application of the rules.[220] Currently, however, a significant adoption of the Model Law looks to be in reach, as a number of countries (some with substantial international commercial significance) have already

---

[212]　UNCITRAL, UNCITRAL Model Law on Cross-Border Insolvency with Guide to enactment, U.N. Sales No. E.99.V.3 (available at: http://www.uncitral.org/pdf/english/texts/insolven/insolvency-e.pdf) [hereinafter: Model Law, or UNCITRAL Model Law, interchangeably, and UNCITRAL Guide to Enactment].

[213]　It was adopted unilaterally by UNCITRAL in May 1997. For comprehensive reviews of the Model Law see Fletcher, *Insolvency* (n 3) ch. 8; R.W. Harmer, 'Documentation B, UNCITRAL Model Law on Cross-Border Insolvency' (1997) 6 Int. Insolv. Rev., 145; A.J. Berends, 'The UNCITRAL Model Law on Cross-Border Insolvency: A Comprehensive Overview' (1998) 6 Tul J Int'l & Comp L 309; J. Clift, 'The UNCITRAL Model Law on Cross-Border Insolvency—A Legislative Framework to Facilitate Coordination and Cooperation in Cross-Border Insolvency' (2004) 12 Tul. J. Int'l & Comp. Law 307.

[214]　See section 3.4.2.2.

[215]　See L.C. Ho, 'Overview', in L.C. Ho (ed.), *Cross-Border Insolvency, A commentary on the UNCITRAL Model Law* (Globe Law & Business, London 2006) 17; J.L. Westbrook, 'Chapter 15 At Last' (2005) 79 Am Bankr LJ 713.

[216]　See Fletcher, *Insolvency* (n 3) 443–6. See also J.A.E. Pottow, 'Procedural Incrementalism: a model for international bankruptcy' (2005) 45(4) Virginia Journal of International Law 935, 995 (pointing out that this narrow procedural focus of the model law is politically expedient as it refrains from being perceived as a threat to state sovereignty).

[217]　Cf. the provisions of the EC Regulation (in section 3.4.2.2.).

[218]　Such as the EC Regulation (ibid).

[219]　Its adoption can then provide an essential legislative direction especially important in case of civil law countries, as it will permit courts to cooperate with courts in other countries to manage cross-border insolvencies. In most adopting countries it is likely to make cooperation in reorganization cases much easier, while frustrating efforts to engage in manipulation of assets and other fraudulent activity (See J.L. Westbrook, 'A Global Solution to Multinational Default' (2000) 98 Mich. L. Rev. 2276, 2279–80).

[220]　See Fletcher, *Insolvency* (n 3) 486; R.W. Harmer, 'Documentation B, UNCITRAL Model Law on Cross-Border Insolvency' (1997) 6 Int. Insolv. Rev. 145, 152; H. Rajak, *Company Liquidations* (Sweet & Maxwell, London 2006) [hereinafter: Rajak, *Company Liquidations*] 360.

adopted the Model Law,[221] including the US[222] and the UK.[223] On the other hand, enactment is not always faithful to the terms provided in the Model Law, which might then diminish its practical value.[224] The Model Law will also have great effect if adopted within groupings of states (that may already be a party of regional cross-border insolvency models),[225] thus ensuring a high level of cooperation among those countries and the rest of the world.[226]

The Model Law aims to assist with three main issues: access to foreign courts; recognition of foreign insolvency proceedings; and relief primarily to protect assets in foreign jurisdictions. It thus facilitates access to a foreign insolvency proceeding, both for a foreign representative and foreign creditors.[227] It provides for a relatively simple, fast, and inexpensive procedure for the recognition of foreign insolvency proceedings, and the further assistance and relief provided to the foreign representative in the foreign jurisdiction.[228] Relief may include a stay of proceedings and executions and suspension of rights to transfer or to dispose

[221] Fifteen countries have so far enacted legislation based on the UNCITRAL Model Law, according to information contained in UNCITRAL Website (http://www.uncitral.org/uncitral/en/uncitral_texts/insolvency/1997Model_status.html). For accounts of the implementation of the Model Law in the various local jurisdictions see L.C. Ho (ed.), Cross-Border Insolvency, A commentary on the UNCITRAL Model Law (2006); B. Wessels, *International Insolvency Law* (Kluwer, Deventer 2006), Chapter III.

[222] See Chapter 15 of the US Bankruptcy Code [hereinafter: Chapter 15]. On Chapter 15 see e.g. J.L. Westbrook, 'Multinational Enterprises in General Default: Chapter 15, The ALI Principles, and The EU Insolvency Regulation' (2002) 76 Am. Bankr. L.J. 1, 18–24; R.G. Mason, 'United States', in L.C. Ho (ed.), *Cross-Border Insolvency, A commentary on the UNCITRAL Model Law* (Globe Law & Business, London 2006) 197–217.

[223] SI 2006/1030 (http://www.opsi.gov.uk/si/si2006/20061030.htm) [hereinafter: the British Model Law]. On the British Model Law see e.g. I.F. Fletcher, 'Better late than never: the UNCITRAL Model Law enters into force in Great Britain' (2006) 19(6) Insolv. Int. 86; Fletcher, *Insolvency* (n 3) supplement to second edition, 83–106); L.C. Ho, 'England', in L.C. Ho (ed.), Cross-Border Insolvency, A commentary on the UNCITRAL Model Law (2006), 65–95; S. Shivji, A. Smith and A. Walters, 'The Cross-Border Insolvency Regulation 2006: an Emerging Jurisprudence' [2008] Am. Bankr. Inst. J. 40.

[224] For instance, certain countries included a 'reciprocity condition', namely that reciprocity must be shown on the part of the foreign state in which the insolvency proceedings have opened. See the way the Model Law has been enacted in the laws of Mexico and South Africa as described in Fletcher, *Insolvency* (n 3) 489–90. In terms of uniformity, Japan's version of the Model law is regarded as the least uniform of those adopted so far (see ibid, 490; J.L. Westbrook, 'Multinational Enterprises in General Default: Chapter 15, The ALI Principles, and The EU Insolvency Regulation' (2002) 76 Am. Bankr. L.J. 1, 24).

[225] Such as the EU countries, or the NAFTA countries.

[226] See J.L. Westbrook, 'Multinational Enterprises in General Default: Chapter 15, The ALI Principles, and The EU Insolvency Regulation' (2002) 76 Am. Bankr. L.J. 1, 3–4 and 38–41. It should be noted that the Model Law may not cover all types of business undertakings. Thus, the Model Law does not specifically deal with the issue of bank insolvency. It leaves the exclusion or inclusion of financial institutions to the discretion of the enacting countries (see Article 1(2) of the Model Law (n 212)). As aforementioned the case of bank insolvency is outside the scope of this book (see n 176 and references provided there).

[227] Articles 9–14 of the Model Law (n 212).

[228] Articles 15–23 of the Model Law (n 212). See also R.W. Harmer, 'Documentation B, UNCITRAL Model Law on Cross-Border Insolvency' (1997) 6 Int. Insol. Rev. 145, 149–50.

of assets of the debtor,[229] and additional relief, most notably the possibility of entrusting the administration and the distribution of all or part of the debtor's local assets to the foreign representative (provided that the court is satisfied that the interests of local creditors are adequately protected).[230]

Recognition and relief involves the identification of the foreign proceedings either as 'main' or 'non-main' foreign proceedings, based on the EC Regulation concepts of COMI and 'establishment', as requirements differ depending on the degree of connection of the case to the opening state.[231] Hence, the Model Law too attempts to unify insolvency systems' concepts regarding forum choice. But it also envisages situations where proceedings related to the same debtor are taking place in foreign countries in any possible version (in parallel or as an ancillary process, ordinary lawsuits or combinations of the above) possibly causing problems of conflicts between the concurrent proceedings. It explicitly allows recognizing proceedings as non-main proceedings as mentioned above, and it additionally allows for concurrent proceedings to be opened in the recognizing jurisdiction if the debtor has assets in that jurisdiction.[232]

To deal with problems of conflict the Model Law explicitly directs the courts involved to cooperate 'to the maximum extent possible', including by way of direct communication,[233] and to ensure consistency in the relief they grant.[234] It further provides for the manner or methods by which cooperation may be most appropriately applied, including the use of protocols.[235] As such, the Model Law incorporates a modification of universalism. Territorial proceedings may be opened against the same debtor, but there is a strong emphasis on the requirement to cooperate to the maximum, which is a manifestation of universalist ideas.[236] Additionally, as aforesaid, the Model Law leaves choice of law issues open. Thus, the national law may apply its own laws or otherwise foreign laws in granting various sorts of relief.[237]

---

[229] Which is automatic upon recognition of proceedings as foreign main proceedings, and requires an application by the foreign representative in the case of foreign non-main proceedings (Article 20 of the Model Law (n 212); see n 231 and accompanying text on main and non-main proceedings). The problem is, though, that the stay of proceedings does not affect the right to commence individual actions or proceedings to the extent necessary to preserve a claim against the debtor (Article 20(3) of the Model Law (n 212)), and the stay may be modified or terminated for instance by opening concurrent proceedings in regard to the local assets (ibid, Article 28).

[230] Article 21 of the Model Law (n 212). See also on the relief available under the Model Law, Fletcher, *Insolvency* (n 3) 465–71.

[231] Article 2 of the Model Law (n 212) provides the definitions of main and non-main proceedings. See section 3.4.2.2 on the meaning of COMI and establishment under the EC Regulation, which the Model Law followed.

[232] Article 28 of the Model Law (n 212).

[233] Article 25 of the Model Law (n 212). See also J.L. Westbrook, 'Multinational Enterprises in General Default: Chapter 15, The ALI Principles, and The EU Insolvency Regulation' (2002) 76 Am. Bankr. L.J. 1, 17.

[234] Articles 28–32 of the Model Law (n 212).

[235] Article 27 of the Model Law (n 212).

[236] See section 3.3.2.1.

[237] See J. Clift, 'The UNCITRAL Model Law on Cross-Border Insolvency—A Legislative Framework to Facilitate Coordination and Cooperation in Cross-Border Insolvency' (2004) 12

It should also be appreciated, that such cooperation, international recognition, access, and relief as envisaged by the Model Law, may be restricted by local notions of public policy or requirement that local creditors will be protected.[238] In so much as such 'safety valves' are frequently invoked (especially if this implies a requirement that the foreign laws will provide similar protections to those offered locally), the tilt in the universality–territoriality balance will be towards territoriality.[239]

Similarly to the EC Regulations the Model Law does not deal explicitly with the issue of corporate groups. Rather, it deals with debtor companies whose insolvency involves international elements, or full insolvency proceedings taking place in more than one jurisdiction regarding the same debtor.[240] It seems that UNCITRAL took a pragmatic approach when refraining from dealing with the complex issue of corporate groups at the stage of construing the Model Law, and left it to a later stage. However, this task is now undertaken by an UNCITRAL Working Group [241] which currently considers possible solutions for international insolvencies of multinational enterprise groups.[242]

3.4.2.4 *The ALI Principles of Cooperation*[243]

Another major initiative essentially designed for use among the countries belonging to NAFTA [244] is the ALI Principles. Like the EC Regulation it is a regional solution,[245] yet it takes the form of unofficial best practice principles and recommendations,[246] developed by the private sector.[247] The Principles were designed in order to achieve closer integration and cooperation in the insolvencies of multinational companies within NAFTA, understanding that such

---

Tul. J. Int'l & Comp. Law 307, 324. See also generally J.L. Westbrook, 'Choice of Avoidance Law in Global Insolvencies' (1991) 17 Brook. J. Int'l L. 499; J.L. Westbrook, 'Universalism and Choice of Law' (2005) 23 Penn. St. Int'l L. Rev. 625.

[238] See Articles 6, 21(2) and 22 of the Model Law (n 212).

[239] See also n 163.

[240] See the scope of application and the definition of foreign proceeding (Articles 1 and 2 of the Model Law, n 212).

[241] Note 96 chapter 1.

[242] On which see chapters 6–9, *passim*.

[243] American Law Institute, 'Principles of Cooperation Among the NAFTA Countries Transnational Insolvency' (excerpt from *Transnational Insolvency: Cooperation among the NAFTA Countries* [2003] is available at: http://www.ali.org/doc/InsolvencyPrinciples.pdf) [hereinafter: ALI Principles].

[244] North American Free Trade Agreement. Namely, Canada, Mexico and the USA.

[245] However, another initiative of the ALI in collaboration with the International Insolvency Institute is aimed at evaluating the possibility of adapting the Principles so as to provide a standard statement of principles suitable for application on a global basis in international insolvency cases (Prof. Ian Fletcher and Prof. Bob Wessels were appointed by the International Insolvency Institute as Reporters of the project, approved by the Institute's Council in December 2005). For a report on this project see I.F. Fletcher, 'Maintaining the Momentum: The Continuing Quest for Global Standards and Principles to Govern Cross-Border Insolvency' (2007) 32 Brook. J. Int'l L. 767, 776–84.

[246] Whereas the EC Regulation is positive binding law (see section 3.4.2.2).

[247] The ALI (American Law Institute) is a private-sector law reform organization.

development is essential to the full realization of the free flow of investment contemplated by the NAFTA.[248] Here again we can see universalism concepts incorporated in practical solutions, resulting in some modification to pure universalism aspirations. The ALI Principles attempt to include proposals that reflect common grounds among the countries involved,[249] rather than recommending more ambitious broader mechanisms.[250] Thus, they expressly disclaim any attempt to adopt a choice of law rules,[251] the choice of ancillary versus parallel systems,[252] or any other substantive rules.[253]

Like the Model Law scheme, recognition is the central legal action. Recognition is not automatic but rather a procedure that should be sought in each relevant country.[254] Similarly, the effects of recognition (the relief available, granted by the local court) are not immediate. However, once a 'main' insolvency proceeding is recognized,[255] a broad moratorium can follow quickly.[256] In an attempt to maximize cooperation and achieve unity, the Principles urge that a recognized foreign representative will be granted control over local assets and that the transfer of assets out of a jurisdiction be permitted when that is appropriate.[257] The

[248] See J.L. Westbrook and J.S. Ziegel, 'NAFTA Insolvency Project' (1998) 23 Brook. J. Int'l L. 7; J.L. Westbrook, 'Managing Defaulting Multinationals Within NAFTA', in I.F. Fletcher, L. Mistelis and M. Cremona (eds.), *Foundations and perspectives of International Trade Law* (Sweet & Maxwell, London 2001) 465, 466; J.L. Westbrook, 'Multinational Enterprises in General Default: Chapter 15, The ALI Principles, and The EU Insolvency Regulation' (2002) 76 Am. Bankr. L.J. 1, 30.

[249] The Principles are also supported by intensive comparative studies of the three NAFTA countries' law and practice in insolvency matters, so that they promote predictability and facilitate cooperation among these countries (J.L. Westbrook, 'Multinational Enterprises in General Default: Chapter 15, The ALI Principles, and The EU Insolvency Regulation' (2002) 76 Am. Bankr. L.J. 1, 31).

[250] J.L. Westbrook, 'Multinational Enterprises in General Default: Chapter 15, The ALI Principles, and The EU Insolvency Regulation' (2002) 76 Am. Bankr. L.J. 1, 32.

[251] See ALI Principles (n 243), at section II, Topic D, Subtopic 2; Cf. the EC Regulation approach (section 3.4.2.2).

[252] Cf. the EC Regulation's 'secondary proceeding' approach (section 3.4.2.2). See also J.L. Westbrook, 'Managing Defaulting Multinationals Within NAFTA', in I.F. Fletcher, L. Mistelis, M. Cremona (eds.), *Foundations and perspectives of International Trade Law* (Sweet & Maxwell, London 2001) 465, 468, 470, 475 (the ALI Principles reflect some preference for an ancillary system).

[253] J.L.Westbrook, 'Managing Defaulting Multinationals Within NAFTA', in I.F. Fletcher, L. Mistelis and M. Cremona (eds.), *Foundations and Perspectives of International Trade Law* (Sweet & Maxwell, London 2001) 465, 468.

[254] ALI Principles (n 243), General Principle II, and Procedural Principles 1. Cf. the EC Regulation's approach (section 3.4.2.2).

[255] Following both the EC Regulation and the Model Law in the adoption of the 'main' insolvency proceedings concept and the 'COMI' test of the EC Regulation (see sections 3.4.2.2 and 3.4.2.3).

[256] ALI Principles (n 243), Procedural Principles 1, 2, 4. The same approach was adopted in the Model Law (see section 3.4.2.2); See also J.L. Westbrook, 'Managing Defaulting Multinationals Within NAFTA', in I.F. Fletcher, L. Mistelis and M. Cremona (eds.), *Foundations and Perspectives of International Trade Law* (Sweet & Maxwell, London 2001) 465, 471–2; Fletcher *Insolvency* (n 3) 307.

[257] ALI Principles (n 243), Procedural Principles 11 and 12.

Principles also adopt the concept of sharing of value.[258] That is, the notion of a worldwide perspective on the distribution of assets, urging the courts to determine distributions from a universalist perspective, and expressly contemplating the possibility of dismissing one or more full insolvency proceedings. This way a reorganization plan can be adopted in the main proceeding without the complications created by detailed differences in priority rules.[259] The Principles further facilitate the universal enforcement of an approved reorganization plan.[260]

The Principles comprehensively deal with the issue of communication among administrators and courts.[261] They strongly encourage such communication and contain a set of guidelines to facilitate this device.[262] They also contain exemplary protocols to facilitate cooperation in the form of agreements negotiated between the parties.[263] Various provisions aim at facilitating parallel insolvency proceedings, including the cross-border sales of assets.[264]

The Principles strive to achieve a solution as close as possible to what would have been achieved under a single transnational proceeding, by implementing a modified universalism approach. It is thus committed to full cooperation, under the current situation where the laws of the countries involved still differ.[265] Although the Principles accommodate both the ancillary and the parallel approaches they encourage deference to the 'main' proceeding.[266]

Unlike the previous models for cross-border insolvency discussed above,[267] the ALI Principles explicitly deal with the case of corporate groups to a certain

---

[258] Ibid, General Principle V.

[259] See J.L. Westbrook, 'Multinational Enterprises in General Default: Chapter 15, The ALI Principles, and The EU Insolvency Regulation' (2002) 76 Am. Bankr. L.J. 1, 35.

[260] ALI Principles (n 243), Procedural Principles 26 and 27.

[261] Conversely, the EC Regulation is silent on the subject of communication between courts (but see the European guidelines for communication (n 165)); The Model Law authorizes direct communication between courts and foreign representatives (see section 3.4.2.2).

[262] See ALI Principles (n 243), Procedural Principles 14 and 15; American Law Institute, Transnational Insolvency: Cooperation among the NAFTA Countries, Principles of Cooperation Among the NAFTA Countries, Guidelines Applicable to Court-to-Court Communication in Cross-Border Cases (2003) [hereinafter: ALI Guidelines for Communication]. The ALI in collaboration with the International Insolvency Institute are developing the ALI Guidelines for use in various regions of the world (see Institute's Guidelines for Court-to-Court Communication Gain International Approval, ALI Rep., Fall 2002, at 18; See also J.L. Westbrook, 'International Judicial Negotiations' (2003) 38 Tex. Int'l L.J. 567, 581).

[263] Appendix 3 of the ALI Principles (n 243); See also, J.L. Westbrook, 'Multinational Enterprises in General Default: Chapter 15, The ALI Principles, and The EU Insolvency Regulation' (2002) 76 Am. Bankr. L.J. 1, 37.

[264] ALI Principles (n 243), Procedural Principles 14–22.

[265] J.L. Westbrook, 'Managing Defaulting Multinationals Within NAFTA', in I.F. Fletcher, L. Mistelis and M. Cremona (eds.), *Foundations and Perspectives of International Trade Law* (Sweet & Maxwell, London 2001) 465, 468–9; Fletcher, *Insolvency* (n 3) 303–4; J.L. Westbrook, 'A Global Solution to Multinational Default' (2000) 98 Mich. L. Rev. 2276, 2299–2303.

[266] J.L. Westbrook, 'Managing Defaulting Multinationals Within NAFTA', in I.F. Fletcher, L. Mistelis and M. Cremona (eds.), *Foundations and Perspectives of International Trade Law* (Sweet & Maxwell, London 2001) 465, 470.

[267] The EC Regulation (section 3.4.3.3) and the Model Law (section 3.4.2.3).

extent.[268] However, recognizing the fact that international corporate group in insolvency is a complex issue which to some extent belongs to corporate law, the Principles restrict their scope to a limited number of legal issues, refraining from any attempt to deal with substantive issues, such as group liability, or the factors for applying substantive consolidation.[269] The Principles focus on facilitating the administration of affiliated companies' insolvency proceedings.[270] In particular they encourage allowing a global perspective over the group to enable effective reorganizations. At the same time they suggest caution and refrain from defeating the concept of corporate separateness.[271] These issues will be further discussed in Part III of this work.

3.5 Universality–Territoriality and the MEG

The previous chapter pointed out the need to 'take seriously' MEGs. In the context of cross-border insolvency there is a degree of neglect of this phenomenon, as it typically does not receive a full rounded consideration in national or international approaches (the current work in progress of UNCITRAL might prove to be an exception).[272] Nonetheless, existing approaches and solutions even if primarily designed for single companies could potentially be extended to apply to the group scenario. It is unclear though in which circumstances global solutions should and will apply to the case of group, and in which circumstances perhaps it is less desirable to even attempt cooperation between related companies' insolvency proceedings.

The question is thus whether, to what extent and, in which circumstances related companies should be linked in their insolvencies across borders, namely whether the balance should tip towards universalism or territorialism in this context. Indeed, it is evident that unity of cross-border insolvency has strong merits, but also that in the real world of separate legal regimes plurality of insolvency processes may be more just and efficient in certain circumstances (in the context of insolvency goals). Harmonization will support unity, but room for local inventiveness is also beneficial. Elements of contractualism may also assist in achieving

---

[268] See J.L. Westbrook, 'Multinational Enterprises in General Default: Chapter 15, The ALI Principles, and The EU Insolvency Regulation' (2002) 76 Am. Bankr. L.J. 1, 38 (explaining that the Principles 'put a toe in the water' on this difficult problem). See also Fletcher, *Insolvency* (n 3) 311 (the Principles offer 'somewhat tentative guidance on the approach to be followed').

[269] ALI Principles (n 243), 77. See also J.L. Westbrook, 'Managing Defaulting Multinationals Within NAFTA' in I.F. Fletcher, L. Mistelis and M. Cremona (eds.), *Foundations and Perspectives of International Trade Law* (Sweet & Maxwell, London 2001) 465, 474.

[270] In Procedural Principles 23 and 24. Note that the Principles do not provide what will constitute an affiliate (or a corporate group) for the purpose of this approach (see on the issue of the meaning of a multinational enterprise group in chapter 1, section 1.3).

[271] ALI Principles (n 243), 80.

[272] As of November 2008 the work of UNCITRAL Working Group V is still in progress.

suitable results especially in regard to difficulties in identifying the debtor's home country and in enhancing cooperation. Current approaches to the cross-border insolvency problem to a large extent reflect these contentions. The dilemma intensifies in the group context, especially due to the diversified scene of insolvencies within MEGs, and the difficulties in determining issues of jurisdiction in such cases. Fundamentally, establishing whether the case should be dealt with by (some variant of) universality or (some variant of) territoriality should depend on the degree to which it will achieve the goals of insolvency. On top of that, the decision on the approach should take into account the type of MEG in default as well as the degree of interference with state separateness which is invoked.

It is therefore suggested (similarly to the conclusion in chapter 2 with respect to the entity–enterprise dilemma) that a 'goal-driven adaptive balanced' approach should be utilized in regard to the universalism–territorialism dilemma[273] in the context of insolvency within MEGs.

---

[273] I refer to the territoriality–universality dilemma in abbreviate, though other approaches discussed above are not excluded from the consideration of the balanced approach.

PART II

GUIDING OBJECTIVES AND TYPICAL SCENARIOS

4

Insolvency Goals in Legal Systems

4.1 Introduction

In the chapters that will follow this part (chapters 6–9 in Part III) it is attempted to look at some of the key issues arising in regard to insolvencies within MEGs and possible ways to resolve them, according to the framework proposed in this book. As was repeatedly mentioned, essentially the question will be to what extent should the group constituents be linked in the context of insolvency. It was suggested in the preceding chapters (chapters 2 and 3) that the desirability of 'linking tools' in the context of the MEG insolvency and its implications for the two main relevant 'dilemmas'—entity versus enterprise approach, and the universality–territoriality question—should be considered in light of the objectives of insolvency, and the types of MEG that may be in issue. To an extent, various types of group and goals of insolvency were scarcely mentioned while discussing the problems of groups (in general) and the problem of cross-border insolvency (primarily in regard to single debtors). In order to systematically consider the particular case of the MEG in insolvency, these issues will be considered in this Part in more detail. The key objectives and tasks of insolvency law to which the work will be referring will be set out in this chapter. In the next chapter certain prototypes of MEG organizational structures (coupled with insolvency scenarios) will also be offered, that can be useful as a reference point in the subsequent investigation of linking tools.

4.2 Key Objectives and Tasks of Insolvency Law

4.2.1 Can shared objectives and tasks be identified?

In attempting to seek a meaningful approach to MEGs in insolvency it is important that such approach will have the potential to be accepted universally. It follows then, that part of the challenge here is to place 'the law of MEG insolvency' within a framework that could reflect some universal common grounds. As the approach is 'goal-driven', that is, it seeks to promote the insolvency goals, the goals pursued should be such that they represent a general acceptance among nation states. For the approach to be meaningful it should also encompass concepts which are consistent with normatively desired aims.[1] Thus, in case a universal statement of aims can be identified, the question will be whether these goals can be perceived as legitimate. Identifying shared insolvency objectives and their underlying legitimizing arguments can then assist us in assessing linking tools for MEG insolvencies, ensuring that the proposed system meets consistent purposes.

Bearing in mind the differences between various legal systems specifically in the context of insolvency law,[2] the possibility of identifying shared objectives among jurisdictions seems far fetched. However, as described in chapter 3, there are various multinational initiatives in the area of insolvency that can come to our aid. Those initiatives attempt at construing internationally accepted guidelines and principles to guide legal systems in renovating, assessing, or reforming their insolvency laws.[3] Most notably, it was mentioned that the UNCITRAL Legislative Guide,[4] which provides a set of elaborative recommendations, was devised by a truly international body and adopted by consensus.[5] The Legislative Guide in itself has been built on earlier work of other organizations (and thus there are great similarities in the objectives offered by the Legislative Guide to core principles offered in these other initiatives), however it is a much more elaborate effort at modernization and harmonization of insolvency laws.[6]

The Legislative Guide provides, in its Part One,[7] certain key objectives that should lead insolvency laws in formulating rules of insolvency. The Legislative Guide acknowledges differences between legal regimes while stressing that it is possible to identify uniform values, even if in some abstract broad form. It states before laying down the objectives that:

Although country approaches vary, there is broad agreement that effective and efficient insolvency regimes should aim to achieve the key objectives identified below in a balanced manner.[8]

The list of nine objectives delineated by the Legislative Guide includes provision of certainty in the market; maximization of value of assets; striking a balance between liquidation and reorganization; ensuring equitable treatment of similarly situated creditors; provision of timely, efficient, and impartial resolution of an insolvency; preservation of the insolvency estate; ensuring a transparent and predictable insolvency law; recognition of existing creditor rights and establishment

---

[1] See V. Finch, *Corporate Insolvency Law* (Cambridge University Press, Cambridge 2002) [hereinafter: Finch, *Corporate Insolvency*] ch. 2 (arguing that meaningful evaluations of proposals or existing insolvency regimes have to be made in light of clear expositions of the nature of aims and objectives of corporate insolvency). See also, Mokal, *Corporate Insolvency* (n 74 chapter 2) 10–16.

[2] As noted in chapter 3, section 3.2.

[3] Chapter 3, section 3.4.1.   [4] N 137 chapter 3   [5] Ibid.

[6] See chapter 3, section 3.4.1.

[7] The Legislative Guide (n 137 chapter 3) Part one, ch. 1.

[8] Ibid, para. 3.

of clear rules of priorities; and the establishment of a framework for cross-border insolvency.[9] These are the highest order principles that should lead insolvency systems when renovating or reforming insolvency laws.[10] They were devised by an international body with participation and agreement of representatives from large number of countries, and therefore it embodies a consensus on a wide scale. As such it can be argued that a universal statement of current goals of insolvency systems is at hand.

The key 'shared' objectives will be further elaborated below, primarily as stressed by the Legislative Guide, while also making references to manifestations of the proclaimed objectives in legal regimes to further demonstrate their wide acceptance. It will also be suggested that this set of 'objectives' (so named by the Legislative Guide) can reflect a normatively attractive set of insolvency ideals, which can be perceived as a framework for desirable insolvency systems. For this purpose, the next section will consider what could be perceived on the normative level as the key values of insolvency systems and their corresponding tasks. This will be based on existing theories of insolvency law. Following this discussion, the objectives in the Legislative Guide (and in legal regimes) will be examined in light of these key values.

4.2.2 Fair and efficient insolvency regimes—the key values and possible ways to achieve them

4.2.2.1 *Wealth maximization and costs reduction*

A prominent economic aspect of insolvency law is its attempt to maximize creditors' wealth.[11] In this regard, processes involved in insolvency should strive to be efficient and conducive to wealth maximization. Unnecessary transaction costs should be avoided.[12] Here, insolvency law should take into account costs involved with the prospect of default (*ex ante* costs) and costs which might occur after the enforcement of the debt (*ex post* costs), and aim to minimize them.

---

[9] Ibid, paras. 4–14.

[10] As mentioned in chapter 3, the Legislative Guide also offers detailed recommendations and commentary (in its other parts). In this respect it has been noted that the 'arrays of rule-types' used by the Legislative Guide (i.e. the different types of recommendation it provides which are not all of the kind stressing particular action to be taken) enable the Guide to adjust for the degree of diversity and dissent on the various issues (see S. Block-Lieb and T. Halliday, 'Harmonization and Modernization in UNCITRAL Legislative Guide on Insolvency Law' (2007) 42 Tex. Int'l L.J. 475, 502–6).

[11] This aim has been particularly stressed by commentators from the law and economics movement (see n 50–2, and accompanying texts).

[12] This draws on the literature on transaction cost economics (e.g. O. Williamson and S. Masten, *The Economics of Transaction Costs* (Edward Elgar Publishing, Aldershot 1999)). See also Mokal, *Corporate Insolvency* (n 74 chapter 2), 20–7. J. Armour, 'The law and economics of corporate insolvency: a review' [2001] ESRC Centre for Business Research University of Cambridge Working Paper No. 197, 15.

There are direct *ex post* costs relating to the handling of the insolvency process such as professional fees incurred; and more significantly such costs which result from inefficient deployment of the firm's assets.[13] First, there is the concern that when the debtor has more liabilities than assets, and many creditors, the creditors will engage in a wasteful race to collect assets. This is the famous 'common pool' problem created when diverse 'co-owners' assert rights against a common pool of assets. It has been long recognized that in order to preserve the estate and maximize returns to the creditors as a group, a mandatory collective procedure for enforcement of claims is beneficial. Consequently, creditors are prevented from pursuing their claims on an individual basis (for instance by imposing a moratorium on enforcement) and are required to cooperate.[14] An alternative solution to the common pool problem could theoretically be contracting for an insolvency procedure via negotiations in advance, before the company is in financial distress (and the creditors have individual enforcement rights and thus they are faced with the 'prisoner's dilemma').[15] However, this is highly problematic considering the magnitude and diversity of claimants and therefore the transaction costs that will be involved in agreeing on such contracts.[16] Other alternatives to mandatory insolvency procedures include non-legal solutions to the common pool problem. For instance, when some sort of 'workout' (a resolution of the debtor's financial distress without commencing formal proceedings) is arranged, or when 'pre-packaged' arrangements are agreed upon before entering into a formal insolvency.[17] The viability of these options largely depends on the transaction costs involved. These solutions are particularly problematic in cases where there is a significant number of creditors with diversity of interests.[18] In contrast, they can be highly efficient where claims are concentrated in a few relatively homogeneous lenders.[19]

In the absence of such alternatives, it is in the common interest of the debtors' stakeholders that the distribution of the debtor's assets will be carried out in an

[13] J. Armour, 'The law and economics of corporate insolvency: a review' [2001] ESRC Centre for Business Research, University of Cambridge, Working Paper No. 197, 15–17.

[14] See e.g. T.H. Jackson, 'Bankruptcy, nonbankruptcy and the creditors' bargain' (1982) 91 Yale L.J. 857.

[15] See R.K. Rasmussen, 'Debtor's Choice: A Menu Approach to Corporate Bankruptcy' (1992) 71 Tex. L. Rev. 51.

[16] See P. Aghion, O. Hart and J. Moore, 'The Economics of Bankruptcy Reform' (1992) 8 J. L. Econ. & Org. 523, 526. Additionally, many potential creditors will not be able to participate in such negotiations in a meaningful way (see also chapter 3, section 3.3.2.5 on the contractualist approach in the context of cross-border insolvency).

[17] See J. Armour, 'The law and economics of corporate insolvency: a review' [2001] ESRC Centre for Business Research, University of Cambridge, Working Paper No. 197, 35.

[18] See J. McConnell and H. Servaes, 'The Economics of Pre-Packaged Bankruptcy' (1991) 4 Journal of Applied corporate Finance 93; L. Qi, 'The rise of pre-packaged corporate rescues on both sides of the Atlantic' (2007) 20(9) Insolv. Int. 129, 131–2.

[19] T. Hoshi, A. Kashyap and D. Scharfstein, 'The Role of Banks in Reducing the Costs of Financial Distress in Japan' in Bhandari and L.A. Weiss (eds.), *Corporate Bankruptcy: Economic and Legal Perspectives* (Cambridge University Press, Cambridge 1996) 532, 535.

orderly manner, via a collective, centralized insolvency procedure.[20] Preventing creditors from 'grabbing' assets will also ensure that the estate is not dismantled, and thus it may be possible to profit from a sale of the whole estate, as in many cases the firm is worth more than the collection of its pieces.[21] Additionally, an inefficient deployment of assets may result in the loss of the going concern surplus of the firm (if indeed the whole is worth more than its parts) if the whole (in a going concern form) cannot be preserved.[22] An efficient resolution for the business may be bringing it back to full productivity, if it is a viable business. This option will be destroyed if creditors are able to collect the assets on an individual basis.[23] In this respect, some sort of a reorganization procedure may be conducive to achieving such results. Indeed, it may be possible to achieve going concern-based solutions without applying a reorganization process, as theoretically, buyers may offer to purchase the business as a going concern in a liquidation process.[24] However, there may be financing problems (raising cash for purchase of the whole business) and lack of competition which may impede such solutions.[25] It should be noted, that a going concern solution may not always be the best one in terms of value enhancing, as the piecemeal liquidation value of the business may sometimes exceed its going concern value.[26] Certainly, in many cases a full rescue will result in losses. In contrast, there may be cases where a sort of rescue of the business will generate a greater value. It is therefore desirable that an insolvency law will provide procedures that enable such solutions.[27]

[20] P. Aghion, O. Hart and J. Moore, 'The Economics of Bankruptcy Reform' (1992) 8 J. L. Econ. & Org. 523, 526.

[21] Ibid, 525.

[22] M.J. White, 'Corporate Bankruptcy as a Filtering Device: Chapter 11 Reorganizations and Out-of-Court Debt Restructurings' (1994) 10 J. L. Econ. & Org 268; M..J. White, 'The Costs of Corporate Bankruptcy: A US-European Comparison' in Bhandari, S. Jagdeep and A. Lawrence (eds.,) *Corporate Bankruptcy: Legal and Economic Perspectives* (Cambridge University Press, Cambridge 1996) 467; P. Aghion, O. Hart and J. Moore, 'The Economics of Bankruptcy Reform' (1992) 8 J. L. Econ. & Org. 523, 525.

[23] N.L. Georgakopoulos, 'Bankruptcy Law for Productivity' (2002) 37 Wake Forest L. Rev. 51, 53.

[24] Some law and economics scholars have argued that the most cost efficient solutions can be achieved via a liquidation procedure (such as the US Chapter 7 process (11 USC., Chapter 7)), as a going concern sale can be achieved without the costs involved with a reorganization (see e.g. D.G. Baird, 'The Uneasy Case for Corporate Reorganizations' (1986) 15 Journal of Legal Studies 127).

[25] P. Aghion, O. Hart and J. Moore, 'The Economics of Bankruptcy Reform' (1992) 8 J. L. Econ. & Org. 523, 527–8.

[26] P. Aghion, O. Hart and J. Moore, 'The Economics of Bankruptcy Reform' (1992) 8 J. L. Econ. & Org. 523, 527 (explaining that this could happen if the firm is inefficiently large but managers have been unwilling to split it up).

[27] See e.g. the UK administration regime, which although a 'rescue driven' procedure, it provides for a hierarchy of objectives that may be pursued by the administrator, including 'achieving a better result for the company's creditors as a whole than would be likely if the company were wound up' and 'realising property in order to make a distribution to one or more secured or preferential creditors' (Insolvency Act 1986, Schedule B1, para 3(1); see also S. Frisby, 'In Search of a Rescue Regime: The Enterprise Act 2002' [2004] MLR 247, 249). Ultimately the decision is a distributional one. For example, particular offers for the business may satisfy senior creditors who will

Crucially, in terms of the insolvency procedure, enhancing *ex post* cost efficiency demands collective decision-making that will be rapid, accurate, and will minimize strategic behaviour as a result of heterogeneous priorities (i.e. efficiently deal with the possible diversity of stakeholders' interests).[28] Costs involved with operating some sort of a reorganization procedure should be a particular concern. Such procedures may involve placing decisions in the hands of insolvency representatives, a supervising judge or the management,[29] which involves agency costs.[30] The judge or the office holder may have insufficient knowledge and incentives in order to make the right decisions in regard to the debtor. The managers' interests may not be aligned with interests of other groups of stakeholders. Creditors' involvement in the process may cause delays and result in considerable conflicts that may impede the reaching of fast decisions.[31] Thus, insolvency law should attempt to minimize these potential costs. Certain measures, such as majority voting, and the ability to reach certain decisions while avoiding prior consultation with creditors in cases where there is clear need of fast decisions, may be necessary.[32] There should also be a great deal of emphasis on a sufficient degree of expertise of agents to whom decision-making is delegated.[33] Crucially, in any given case, it is necessary to assess these potential costs against the potential benefits. Insolvency law should also aim to provide clear rules and to apply them in a consistent manner (so that it is difficult to manipulate the rules). This will minimize and resolve disputes with the least possible delay and expense. Vagueness in the rules may give the parties more cause for litigation and hence increase the costs of insolvency.[34]

4.2.2.2 *Respecting pre-insolvency entitlements and providing adequate incentives and measures to enhance* ex ante *efficiency*

The *ex ante* costs of financial distress are also of crucial importance, especially as they affect not only those firms (and parties concerned) that have entered into the insolvency process but also those firms and parties contracting with them that might potentially go into insolvency.[35] The rules of insolvency may influence

---

thus suffer from delaying such disposal of the assets, whereas delaying the decision may generate greater returns to the creditors as a whole (see n 56, and accompanying text).

[28] J. Armour, 'The law and economics of corporate insolvency: a review' [2001] ESRC Centre for Business Research, University of Cambridge, Working Paper No. 197, 20–5.

[29] Compare the US Chapter 11 regime under which typcially the debtor remains 'in possession' with the UK administration regime where control is transferred to the creditors represented by an insolvency office holder.

[30] P. Aghion, O. Hart and J. Moore, 'The Economics of Bankruptcy Reform' (1992) 8 J. L. Econ. & Org. 523, 529–30.

[31] Ibid, 528–30.

[32] See e.g. cases where courts took this approach in relation to the English administration regime (*Re T & D Industries plc* [2000] BCC 956; *Re Transbus International* [2004] EWCA Civ 932).

[33] Ibid, Finch, *Corporate Insolvency* (n 1) 49, 54.

[34] D.G. Baird, 'Bankruptcy's Uncontested Axioms' (1998) 108 Yale Law Journal 573, 595.

[35] See e.g. O. Hart, *Firms Contracts and Financial Structure* (Oxford University Press, Oxford 1995) Ch. 7.

the behaviour of the debtor or its stakeholders in the ordinary course of business. There are 'financial agency costs' to take into account in regard to management (and shareholders') behaviour near insolvency, i.e. managers maximizing their own utility (or the interests of the shareholders) at the expense of the creditors.[36] The prospect of default may give rise to managerial perverse incentives by significantly increasing risk thus shifting losses from shareholders to creditors. This is normally prevented by the need to maintain reputation, but it is less effective near insolvency at which time managers and shareholders may be less concerned with the potential need to return to the market for additional funding.[37] This may be particularly pronounced with regard to managers of closely held firms and 'shadow directors', who may be less affected by the discipline of the managerial labour market.[38] Insolvency law should be concerned with reducing these costs.

Creditors of the company may also have perverse incentives to place the debtor under insolvency (even where the business is viable) if they think they will gain benefit from the commencement of such proceedings, where insolvency law may offer them particular advantages which they did not possess under non-insolvency law.[39] In this respect rules of insolvency may affect the behaviour of creditors *ex ante*, which may result in the increase of *ex post* costs associated with the commencement of insolvency proceedings.

In this regard, it has been stressed that insolvency law should respect rights obtained by creditors prior to insolvency. Insolvency law should translate pre-bankruptcy assets and liabilities into the bankruptcy forum with minimal dislocation.[40] Security rights in loan covenants can work to constrain the firm's decision-making and thereby mitigate the problems generating from managers' perverse incentives to engage in high risks projects. Therefore, there should be the smallest possible interference with pre-existing priority contracts (i.e. insolvency should not be redistributive) so as not to reduce this advantage.[41] Additionally, respecting pre-existing entitlements may reduce incentives of creditors to commence insolvency where this is unnecessary, as they will not obtain any additional

---

[36] See Mokal, *Corporate Insolvency* (n 74 chapter 2) 274–7.

[37] See D. Prentice, 'Corporate Personality, Limited Liability and the Protection of Creditors', in R. Grantham and C. Rickett (eds.), *Corporate Personality in the 20th Century* (Hart Publishing, Oxford 1998) 99, 108–9; J. Armour, 'The law and economics of corporate insolvency: a review' [2001] ESRC Centre for Business Research, University of Cambridge, Working Paper No. 197, 17, 25. See also chapter 2, section 2.3.2.4 on the problems of risk shifted to creditors in the brink of insolvency (in the context of the group problem and limited liability).

[38] See Mokal, *Corporate Insolvency* (n 74 chapter 2) 284–92 (Mokal refers to a survey of English and Welsh cases applying the worngful trading provisions. Although the sample is small it shows that in most cases the issue of managers risk-shifting in the vicinity of insolvency in a way harmful to creditors arose in the context of such types of firms).

[39] D.G. Baird and T. Jackson, 'Corporate Reorganization and the Treatment of Diverse Ownership Intersts: A Comment on Adequate Protection of Secured Creditors in Bankruptcy' (1984) 51 U. Chi. L. Rev. 97; D.G. Baird, 'A World Without Bankruptcy' (1987) 50 Law and Contemporary Problems 173; D.G. Baird, 'Loss Distribution, Forum Shopping and Bankruptcy: A Reply to Warren' (1987) 54 U. Chi. L. Rev. 815.

[40] D.G. Baird, 'Bankruptcy's Uncontested Axioms' (1998) 108 Yale Law Journal 573, 580–2.

[41] A. Schwartz, 'A Theory of Loan Priorities' (1989) 18 Journal of Legal Studies 209.

gain from placing the debtor under insolvency (or prevent impeding the initiation of insolvency proceedings by those who lose out under the scheme).[42] In particular, security interests and other rights *in rem* which have been created prior to the onset of insolvency should be respected so that such creditors can rely on their rights and create appropriate arrangements to suit their particular needs. This is regarded as fundamental to the system of credit and a destructive impact upon such commercial confidence should be avoided.[43]

To an extent, certainty, clarity, and predictability of insolvency law rules (and consistent application of the rules) are also perceived as supporting minimization of transaction costs *ex ante*. They may facilitate the provision of credit and other forms of investment since parties can easily identify the rules pertaining to their transaction and rely with confidence on the rules provided by the insolvency regime in pricing the transaction and calculating their risk.[44] Clear and predictable rules may also enhance consensual dispute resolutions between the debtor and its creditors which may prevent entry into insolvency proceedings.

Returning to the problem of managers' (and controllers') perverse incentives (near insolvency), other methods to tackle this within the insolvency regime are by way of mandatory provisions imposing penalties on such behaviour *ex post* (if insolvency proceedings have eventually commenced). For instance, if managers continue trading in the firm without minimizing losses to creditors when insolvency is inevitable, they will be held accountable.[45] Such penalties can be seen as directed at minimizing pre-default incentives on managerial decision-making.[46] A different way of dealing with problems related to detrimental delays in entering into insolvency proceedings would be to offer benefits to managers and controllers in placing the debtor under insolvency, for instance by giving the debtor control over the process.[47]

Setting aside transactions entered into near default which are attempts at taking away assets from the debtor is another way of tackling opportunistic

---

[42] D.G. Baird and T. Jackson, 'Corporate Reorganization and the treatment of Diverse Ownership Interests: A Comment on Adequate Protection of Secured Creditors' (1984) 51 U. Chi. L. Rev. 97; D.G. Baird, 'A World Without Bankruptcy' (1987) 50 Law and Contemporary Problems 173; D.G. Baird, 'Loss Distribution, Forum Shopping and Bankruptcy: A Reply to Warren' (1987) 54 U. Chi. L. Rev. 815.

[43] Fletcher, *Insolvency* (n 3 chapter 3) 10.

[44] A.T. Guzman, 'International Bankruptcy: In Defence of Universalism' (2000) 98 Mich. L. Rev. 2177, 2179, 2181 (though Guzman raises doubts as to the degree to which certain creditors (the non-adjusting creditors (see also n 60, and accompanying text)) in fact rely on the bankruptcy regime in setting the terms of lending (ibid, 2193–4); R.K. Rasmussen, 'Resolving Transnational Insolvencies Through Private Ordering' (2000) 98 Mich. L. Rev. 2252, 2255.

[45] See e.g. the provisions on fraudulent and wrongful trading under the English Insolvency Act 1986 (ss. 213 and 214) (see further in chapter 9 the discussion of *ex post* penalties in insolvency, in the context of insolvency within MEGs).

[46] See R. Grantham, 'The Judicial Extension of Directors' Duties to Creditors' [1991] JBL 1.

[47] See e.g. the US approach to the management of reorganizations (see J. Armour, 'The law and economics of corporate insolvency: a review' [2001] ESRC Centre for Business Research, University of Cambridge, Working Paper No. 197, 29).

behaviour by managers.[48] If such measures (as imposing liability to losses of a company or cancelling transactions) are to be pursued collectively (rather than by creditors individually) this also fulfils the idea of collectivism, as aforementioned.[49]

4.2.2.3 *Widening the goals of insolvency (beyond wealth maximization and preserving relative entitlements)*

The classic 'contractarian' position though is that insolvency law's sole aim should be to preserve and maximize the insolvency estate and distribute it according to rights of creditors for which they have bargained prior to the insolvency event.[50] This position can be justified on the basis that it attempts to respect parties' autonomy. Creditors in a hypothetical bargain scenario would have agreed to such rule *ex ante* (before the event of insolvency) which can resolve the common pool problem as explained above. In the hypothetical bargain creditors will have different entitlements and so they will not consent to any changes which will make them worse off in the event of insolvency. They will also agree that all unsecured creditors (who did not bargain for any particular priority) will be paid the same proportion of their claims as all others similarly placed so that there will not be any transfer of value from secured to unsecured creditors. The role of insolvency law should be merely procedural—it should translate pre-insolvency law positions to insolvency. No other rights should be created and no other policies are relevant apart from those designed to ensure that return to creditors as a group is maximized and dividends are distributed according to pre-entitlements.[51] Rehabilitation of the firm, for example, is therefore not a legitimate objective of insolvency law except to the extent that pre-entitlement holders believe that such a path will generate greater recoveries.[52]

This approach has been strongly criticized as taking too narrow a view of the role of insolvency law, and as failing to appreciate other interests that should be considered by insolvency law apart from those of existing creditors.[53] The point

---

[48] See e.g. the undervalued transaction and preferences provisions under the English Insolvency law (English Insolvency Act 1986, ss. 238–241, 423–425) and 'fraudulent conveyances' under US bankruptcy law (US Bankruptcy Code, s. 548) (see further in chapter 9 the discussion of *ex post* penalties in insolvency, in the context of insolvency within MEGs).

[49] See J. Armour, 'The law and economics of corporate insolvency: a review' [2001] ESRC Centre for Business Research, University of Cambridge, Working Paper No. 197, 30.

[50] See e.g. T. Jackson, *The Logic and Limits of Bankruptcy Law* (Harvard University Press, Cambridge MA 1986); D.G. Baird and T. Jackson, 'Corporate Reorganization and the treatment of Diverse Ownership Interests: A Comment on Adequate Protection of Secured Creditors' (1984) 51 U. Chi. L. Rev. 97.

[51] See T. Jackson, *The Logic and Limits of Bankruptcy Law* (Harvard University Press, Cambridge MA 1986).

[52] Which may indeed be the case if the firm only suffers from financial distress (i.e. the firm's income is not enough to pay back its debts) and otherwise it is economically viable (See D.G. Baird, "Bankruptcy's Uncontested Axioms" (1998) 108 Yale Law Journal 573, 573–83).

[53] See e.g. E. Warren, 'Bankruptcy Policy' (1987) 54 U. Chi. L. Rev. 775, 800. See also E. Warren and J. Westbrook, 'Searching for Reorganization Realities' (1994) 72 Wash. Univ. L.Q.

has been made that insolvency law has a wider role to play and a wider range of interests to accommodate. Mainly, insolvency cannot avoid dealing with substantive issues of distribution. In fact, a central job of insolvency is allocating the losses of the debtor's default and this involves difficult policy decisions (as to where to let those losses fall).[54] Certain parties may need further protection in insolvency, taking into account their vulnerable position. This may result in an 'insolvency decision' to give a preferred position to certain parties who are perceived as vulnerable or deserving special protection. Alternatively, it could involve redistribution of wealth in the event of insolvency to achieve fair results, for example by making managers or shareholders contribute from their own personal assets to the insolvency estate in certain circumstances, or subordinate any debt owed to them to the debts of other ordinary creditors.[55] Certain paths may be taken in the insolvency process that may be beneficial to a wider set of stakeholders with little harm to existing creditors, which may be justifiable in fairness terms.[56] The *pari passu* rule, perceived as requiring equitable treatment to similarly situated creditors, in the sense that distribution is to be made according to the pre-insolvency claims (and creditors are repaid the same proportion of their claims as all others similarly placed) may be regarded as 'base-line rule on equality',[57] but could to an extent be rejected so as to achieve a fair result.[58]

Maximizing collective return as the sole objective also lacks normative justification. It is based upon a notional bargain (assuming what the parties to such a hypothetical scenario would have agreed upon) rather than on real-world negotiations and real-world parties (some of which may lack accurate information regarding

1257 (criticizing the way this approach uses theoretical constructs in regard to what happens in reality to reach policy conclusions without attempting to verify such contentions by empirical evidence); R. Goode, *Principles of Corporate Insolvency Law* (Sweet & Maxwell, London 2005) [hereinafter: Goode, *Insolvency*], 43–8; Finch, *Corporate Insolvency* (n 1), 28–33.

[54] E. Warren, 'Bankruptcy Policy' (1987) 54 U. Chi. L. Rev. 775, 810.

[55] See e.g. the wrongful trading provisions in the Englisn Insolvency Act (s. 214 of the English Insolvency Act 1986), which may be regarded as 'redistributive' in the sense that they create a new right against the directors operational only in insolvency (see Mokal, *Corporate Insolvency* (n 74 chapter 2) ch. 8). See further on wrongful trading (in the context of insolvency within MEGs) in chapter 9. See also Finch, *Corporate Insolvency* (n 1) 32–3.

[56] See Goode, *Insolvency* (n 53) 45.

[57] Finch, Corporate Insolvency (n 1) 32.

[58] Ibid. See also R.J. Mokal, 'Contractarianism, Contractualism, and the law of Corporate Insolvency' [2007] Singapore Journal of Legal Studies 51, 86–7. Mokal argues that *pari passu* should not be treated as a fundamental rule of insolvency, as in practice it plays little distributive role, since all available assets are distributed to secured and statutory preferential creditors. In England, for example, nothing goes *pari passu* in three-quarters of insolvency proceedings (see also Mokal, *Corporate Insolvency* (n 74 chapter 2) ch. 4; R.J. Mokal, ' "Priority as Pathology": The *Pari Passu* Myth' [2001] CLJ 581). Mokal also explains that often the *pari passu* rule is otherwise understood as referring to rateable distribution within classes created by insolvency law, yet the idea of creating preferred classes is to an extent contradictory with the idea of equal treatment to creditors. Another perception of the *pari passu* principle is that it deprives individualistic debt enforcements rights, yet this is in fact an aspect of collectivism aimed at the preservation of the estate, rather than its distribution (see Mokal, *Corporate Insolvency* (n 74 chapter 2) ch. 4).

the risks involved). It also considers only the voluntary creditors (who hypothetically bargained with the debtor).[59] Yet, in fact, the creditors of the company may be very different in nature and sophistication. Creditors often include involuntary creditors, like tort victims and taxing authorities, as well as mal-adjusting (or non-adjusting) creditors, like employees, small suppliers, and pre-paying customers (those who cannot adjust the terms of their lending to the risks they face).[60] This theory also excludes any other interests that may be affected by the insolvency law.

Indeed, various approaches to the question of the function of insolvency law stress that it has a wider role to play and that it should not focus only on wealth maximization. The 'communitarian vision' suggests that insolvency law should be concerned with weighing the interests of a broad range of different parties, giving centrality to distributional concerns. Insolvency law should be concerned with protecting community interests and thus should look to the survival of companies as well as to their orderly liquidation.[61] Others emphasized the importance of various procedural aspects in the context of insolvency law, seeing insolvency law as providing a forum within which all interests affected by the insolvency can be voiced. Insolvency laws should provide means of representation and participation.[62] The 'eclectic approach' proposed by Warren suggests a multiple value vision of insolvency law, which is not 'neat' but rather 'dirty, complex, elastic, inter-connected'.[63] This view encompasses 'economic and non-economic dimensions and the principle of fairness as a moral, political, personal and social value'.[64] Finch mentions the following goals as relevant to insolvency processes, under wider multiple-valued approaches:

distributing the consequences of financial failure amongst a wide range of actors; establishing priorities between creditors; protecting the interests of future claimants; offering opportunities for continuation, reorganization, rehabilitation; providing time for adjustments; serving the interests of those who are not technically creditors but who have an interest in continuation of the business (e.g. employees with scant prospect of re-employment, customers, neighbouring property owners, and state tax authorities); and protecting the investing public, jobs, the public and community interests.[65]

[59] See e.g. D.R. Korobkin, 'Contractarianism and the Normative Foundations of Bankruptcy Law' (1993) 71 Tex. L. Rev. 541; D.G. Carlson, 'Philosophy in Bankruptcy (Book Review)' (1987) 85 Mich. L. Rev. 1341, 1355; Mokal, *Corporate Insolvency* (n 74 chapter 2) ch. 2; Finch, *Corporate Insolvency* (n 1) 30–1; Goode, *Insolvency* (n 53) 46–7. See also chapter 2, section 2.3.2.4 on the problems with economic methods as sole measures of equality (in the context of the limited liability concept).

[60] See D. Prentice, 'Corporate Personality, Limited Liability and the Protection of Creditors' in R. Grantham and C. Rickett (eds.), *Corporate Personality in the 20th Century* (Hart Publishing, Oxford 1998) 99, 109–10; E. Warren and J. Westbrook, 'Contracting Out of Bankruptcy: An Empirical Intervention' (2005) 118 Harv. L. Rev. 1197, 1224–48, 1253.

[61] See a summary of this approach in Finch, *Corporate Insolvency* (n 1) 35–8.

[62] For a summary of the 'forum vision' see ibid, 38–9

[63] E. Warren, 'Bankruptcy Policy' (1987) 54 U. Chi. L. Rev. 775, 811.

[64] D.R. Korobkin, 'Rehabilitating Values: A Jurisprudence of Bankruptcy' (1991) 91 Colum. L. Rev. 717, 781.

[65] Finch, *Corporate Insolvency* (note 1) 40–1.

Finch also mentions other aims that can be added, such as seeking to ascertain the causes of failure and considering whether conduct merited punishment.[66] This provides a more fully reasoned answer as to what should be the values of insolvency.[67] The problem is that it offers a wide array of goals with little assistance to decision-makers in making the right balances between the different goals.[68] Finch attempts to formulate more explicit values while stressing their cumulative strength. Thus, she suggests that measures of insolvency law should refer to efficiency in producing outcomes, but also to questions of accountability, representativeness, expertise in decision-making, and fairness (in process and in substance—to achieve distributional justice).[69] She also emphasizes the need to make trade-offs between goals, yet without offering clear measures as to how to make such balances.[70]

Expanded 'contractarian' ideas get closer to such 'traditionalists' approaches (stressing wider goals to insolvency) in that they attempt to remedy the narrowness of the classic 'creditor bargain model'. They suggest that the 'hypothetical bargain' where creditors are placed behind a Rawlsian 'veil of ignorance'[71] negotiating the rules of insolvency law (initially suggested under the 'creditor bargain model' as explained above) should be more inclusive and take into account the interests of all affected parties. Under this model the parties will also not be permitted to know their particular positions (they will be placed behind a 'veil', ignorant of their legal status), and under such circumstances will negotiate principles of insolvency. These principles will arguably include the idea of taking into account all affected parties as well as mediating between conflicting interests, and where this is not possible protecting those parties who are the most vulnerable.[72] This implies that insolvency law should indeed be concerned with distributive issues and in this regard make evaluative judgments as to priorities among affected parties.[73] Thus, this approach too provides a more fully rounded account of the role of insolvency. However, problems of indeterminacy still remain, mainly as it fails to explain how agreements can be reached behind the veil regarding which parties are most vulnerable and deserve greater protection in the potential insolvency.[74] Generally, it is unclear to what extent

---

[66] Ibid, 41.   [67] Ibid, 42.   [68] Ibid.

[69] Ibid, 49–56.   [70] Ibid, 51.

[71] J. Rawls, *A Theory of Justice* (Harvard University Press, Cambridge MA 1971); J. Rawls, *Political Liberalism* (Columbia University Press, New York 1996).

[72] D.R. Korobkin, 'Contractarianism and the Normative Foundations of Bankruptcy Law' (1993) 71 Tex. L. Rev. 541. See also Mokal, *Corporate Insolvency* (n 74 chapter 2) ch 3. Mokal too suggests a Rawlsian approach to testing the fairness of insolvency rules (advocating an 'authentic consent model'), yet he admits to the bargain only those affected by insolvency law, which should not claim to be all-pervasive, rather it should deal with those 'unique difficulties that arise only in the context of an insolvency debtor's inability to satisfy [its] obligations as they come due.' (see ibid, 68 citing G.E. Brunstad, 'Bankruptcy and the Problems of Economic Futility: A theory on the Unique Role of Bankruptcy Law' (2000) 55 Bus. Law. 499, 505).

[73] J. Armour, 'The law and economics of corporate insolvency: a review' [2001] ESRC Centre for Business Research University of Cambridge Working Paper No. 197, 12.

[74] Finch, *Corporate Insolvency* (n 1) 35.

'*ex ante*' assumptions can be expected to match the complex realities of business life and to accommodate the many categories of decision makers and the variety of circumstances in which their decisions may have to be made'.[75]

4.2.2.4 Balancing between goals

The question of trade-offs is crucial when one asserts more than one goal to insolvency systems. Indeed, some cases can feature conflicting interests, and the question will be what the relative importance of the various values of the law is.[76] It has been convincingly argued that substantive fairness should be the ultimate (substantive) goal of insolvency systems, while efficiency should be perceived as a procedural goal.[77] Economic efficiency supports fairness considerations. It has a crucial role in ensuring the pursuit of normatively attractive goals more effectively, but in itself does not resolve distributional matters.[78] Determining what is fair in regard to loss bearing in the event of insolvency requires looking outside of economics.[79] Indeed, economics assists in assessing whether processes and rules of insolvency are conducive to wealth maximization and are beneficial in avoiding unnecessary transaction costs. However, it may well be that fairness will require the implementation of a redistributive rule when taking into account other values apart from wealth maximization.[80] This understanding of the roles of the fairness and efficiency goals (and the difference between substantive and procedural goals) helps in making relevant balances or trade-offs in pursing the goals.[81] It makes it clear that a procedural goal should not be traded-off with a substantive goal, since the former is not justified as a stand-alone.[82] However, there may be competition among different versions of a certain goal.[83]

4.2.2.5 Fairness in distribution

Vagueness remains in regard to the substantive issues, in particular what would justify a particular way of distribution of the estate, or taking a particular path

---

[75] Goode, *Corporate Insolvency* (n 53) 48.
[76] Finch, *Corporate Insolvency* (n 1) 50–1; J. Armour, 'The law and economics of corporate insolvency: a review' [2001] ESRC Centre for Business Research, University of Cambridge, Working Paper No. 197, 13.
[77] Mokal, *Corporate Insolvency* (n 74 chapter 2) 24–5.
[78] See D. Farber, 'What (if Anything) Can Economics Say about Equity?' (2003) 101 Mich. L. Rev. 1791, 1821; R. Mokal, 'Contractarianism, Contractualsim, and the Law of Corporate Insolvency' [2007] Singapore Journal of Legal Studies 51, 57.
[79] Finch, *Corporate Insolvency* (n 1) 53–54. See also chapter 2, section 2.3.2.4.
[80] Finch, *Corporate Insolvency* (n 1), 53–54.
[81] R.J. Mokal, 'On Fairness and Efficiency' [2003] MLR 452, 458–9.
[82] Ibid, 458. Mokal gives the extreme example of the Nazi administration providing an efficacious system of accountability and expertise yet by no means legitimate.
[83] Ibid, 459. Mokal gives the example of the *parri passu* rule which exemplifies a just compromise between the fairness benefits of making further enquiries about who should get what from the residual resources, and the fairness disadvantages of dissipating the estate so that the remaining claimants as a group get little or nothing.

that may be harmful to certain creditors. The idea of reaching a fair or just result is open ended and suffers from indeterminacy, precisely because it is not based only on norms of economic efficiency.[84] It can be stipulated, however, that fairness requires taking into account all relevant parties that are affected by the relevant law.[85] In our context, it means those affected by a particular insolvency issue once it is identified as a matter of insolvency. It should also treat them as equals.[86] This does not mean giving identical treatment to stakeholders in relation to the distribution of the resources ('flat equality'), but rather according equal respect and consideration to all relevant interested parties in the choice of insolvency law principles ('deep equality').[87] The latter requires examination of a wide array of factors impinging upon the stakeholders' interests, in particular, their bargaining power and vulnerability in regard to their ability to respond to insolvency risks *ex ante* (when extending credit or becoming a tort victim of the debtor) and their ability to bear insolvency loss *ex post* (after the debtor becomes insolvent).[88] It also means searching for efficient tools to minimize waste inherent to insolvency. As mentioned above, efficiency supports fairness and the pursuit of fair results should be done with minimum waste of resources.

It is also suggested that accepting the need to deal with complex distributive issues also requires that effort will be made to articulate guidance as to what is at stake when considering particular solutions in insolvency. Explicit instructions could then be given regarding the relevant parties that should be considered and the relevant evidence and circumstances (main considerations to take) that may influence decisions on the matter. This is not only beneficial in terms of clarity and predictability of rules,[89] but also it can better ensure that relevant parties and the factors affecting their interests are taken into account in similar scenarios of insolvency. In other words, it is not clarity per se which is suggested here, but rather clarity in support of fairness—a comprehensive and coherent account to be given in the law on what are the relevant factors to consider in particular situations pertaining to insolvency. This is not so much a matter of worrying about giving too much discretion to courts and thus the need to reduce vagueness in the rules.[90] Rather, it is worrying about significant relevant factors being 'lost' when making crucial distributive decisions and therefore, hindering fairness.

---

[84] J. Armour, 'The law and economics of corporate insolvency: a review' [2001] ESRC Centre for Business Research University of Cambridge Working Paper No. 197, 14.

[85] See H. Anderson, 'Creditors' rights of recovery: economic theory, corporate jurisprudence and the role of fairness' (2006) 30 Melb. U. L. Rev. 1, 3–6.

[86] See Mokal, *Corporate Insolvency* (n 74 chapter 2) 1–2.

[87] See R. Dworkin, *Sovereign Virtue: The Theory and Practice of Equality* (Harvard University Press, Cambridge MA 2000) 11.

[88] See e.g. E. Warren, 'Bankruptcy Policy' (1987) 54 U. Chi. L. Rev. 775, 778; Finch, *Corporate Insolvency* (note 2) 32–3; R.J. Mokal, 'On Fairness and Efficiency' [2003] MLR 452, 459.

[89] Which may have cost benefits for example in preventing litigation (see section 4.2.2.1).

[90] Such 'worries' regarding vagueness in the rules and granting discretion to bankruptcy courts (based merely on cost-efficiency concerns) are expressed by 'proceduralists' such as Baird (see D.G. Baird, 'Bankruptcy's Uncontested Axioms' (1998) 108 Yale Law Journal, 573, 595).

4.2.2.6 *Summary*

To summarize, in broad terms, insolvency regimes should be fair and efficient.[91] Arguments suggesting that insolvency is about pursuing a single goal of maximizing wealth to creditors and imitating the position of creditors prior to insolvency are weak. Insolvency law must be concerned with designing fair rules of distribution. This may demand a degree of redistribution of rights in order to achieve socially desirable results. In pursuing just substantive results insolvency law should treat parties as equals in the deep sense. It should also aim to use efficient mechanisms to reduce *ex ante* and *ex post* costs, as well as aim to ensure procedural fairness (namely accountability, transparency, creditor participation, and representativeness) in the insolvency process. Certain such mechanisms that may enhance efficiency and fairness were mentioned above. The question now is to what extent these norms and tasks are generally embraced in current regimes (even if with various degrees of differences in implementation). As aforesaid, this question is considered by primarily examining the UNCITRAL Legislative Guide,[92] as providing an exposition of aims on an international level.

4.2.3 A broad agreement on the key values and tasks for effective insolvency regimes

It is possible to read into the statement of objectives in the Legislative Guide[93] an attempt to further the values and the corresponding tasks discussed above, albeit to a large extent in a generalized form without prescribing the details of particular ways of pursuing the tasks and the ways to balance between goals.[94] This in turn reflects a degree of consensus on the main features and underlying goals of insolvency laws.

4.2.3.1 *An eclectic approach*

The Legislative Guide seems to avoid the idea of promoting one goal only (as suggested by classic contractarians).[95] Rather, it refers to both procedural and substantive matters, relating both to efficiency and fairness in the task it designated to insolvency laws, reflecting a more eclectic approach to the role of insolvency. Thus, it speaks of several key objectives that insolvency regimes should aim to

---

[91] See Finch, *Corporate Insolvency* (n 1) 54 (as aforementioned Finch identified several rationales for justifying insolvency processes: efficiency, expertise, accountability, and fairness. Yet, expertise and accountability can be conceptualized as procedural aspects of fairness and as aspects of efficiency (see also R.J. Mokal, 'On Fairness and Efficiency' [2003] MLR 452, 459–62 (persuasively suggesting that efficiency, expertise, and accountability are all procedural goals, while fairness is a substantvie goal)).

[92] Note 137 chapter 3.

[93] Ibid, Part One, ch. 1, paras. 3–9.

[94] Similar goals can be found in the second major initiative for providing key principles for insolvency regimes, that is the World Bank Principles (n 136 chapter 3).

[95] Section 4.2.2.

achieve 'in a balanced manner', rather than one all-encompassing procedural goal.[96]

4.2.3.2 Wealth maximization and respect for pre-insolvency entitlements as key goals

The Legislative Guide accepts the importance of maximizing wealth in the course of insolvency. The second objective in the Guide is stated to be 'maximization of value of assets',[97] and the sixth is preservation of the estate.[98] For this purpose it considers collectivism (by way of imposing a stay of creditor action) to be beneficial as it stops the race to collect.[99]

The Legislative Guide also accepts the primacy of existing creditors in that it stresses that insolvency laws should recognize existing creditor rights.[100] It also emphasizes the need to provide clear rules for the ranking of priorities and consistency in their application. These should 'be based upon commercial bargains'[101] (which is in accord with classic contractarians' views of the role of insolvency).[102] This, it is accepted in the Legislative Guide, will facilitate the provision of credit.[103] It correlates with the idea that respect of pre-entitlements reduces *ex ante* perverse incentives and upholds security interests and rights in rem.[104] In general, 'certainty and predictability' are perceived in the Guide as crucial in promoting economic stability and in fostering lending and investment, as well as preventing disputes 'by providing a backdrop against which relative rights and risks can be assessed and help define the limits of any discretion.'[105]

The Guide also points out that insolvency law should aim to provide timely and efficient resolution of insolvency,[106] as well as to promote dispensing information, so that it would be easier to assess the debtor's situation and consequently the most appropriate solution for the business.[107] Thus, there is clear emphasis on economic efficiency (both in *ex ante* and *ex post* terms) and respect of creditors' rights as obtained prior to the insolvency.

---

[96] The Legislative Guide (n 137 chapter 3), Part one, Ch. 1, para. 3.

[97] Ibid, para. 5 (Objective 2).

[98] Ibid, para. 10 (Objective 6).

[99] See also Fletcher, *Insolvency* (n 3 chapter 3) 9 (observing that the concept of collectivity is shared among legal systems).

[100] The Legislative Guide (n 137 chapter 3) Part one, Ch. 1, para. 13 (Objective 8).

[101] Ibid.

[102] Section 4.2.2.

[103] The Legislative Guide (n 137 chapter 3), Part one, Ch. 1, para. 13 (Objective 8).

[104] Section 4.2.2. See also Fletcher, *Insolvency* (n 3 chapter 3), 10 (observing that 'The principle of respect for such pre-bankruptcy rights is widely accepted by national laws, even if the nature of such rights and the conditions attaching to their creation are by no means uniform throughout the world').

[105] The Legislative Guide (n 137 chapter 3), Part one, Ch. 1, paras. 4, 11, 12, 13 (Objectives 1, 7, and 8).

[106] Ibid, paras. 8–9, (Objective 5).

[107] Ibid, para 12 (Objective 7).

4.2.3.3 Acknowledging the wider goals of insolvency law

However, the Legislative Guide does not stop here and proposes that insolvency systems will aim to pursue other goals, including enabling reorganizations, ensuring equitable distribution to creditors, and enhancing impartiality.[108] The Legislative Guide states that providing for reorganization procedures is compatible with wealth maximization, as it is 'predicated on the basic economic theory that greater value may be obtained from keeping the essential components of a business together, rather than breaking them up and disposing of them in fragments'.[109] However, it also suggests taking account of other aspects as well in deciding on the path for the business. It states that 'insolvency law should include the possibility of reorganization of the debtor as an alternative to liquidation, where creditors would not involuntarily receive less than in liquidation and the value of the debtor *to society and to creditors* may be maximized by allowing it to continue.'[110] It acknowledges the need to reach delicate decisions which 'may have implications for other social policy considerations, such as encouraging the development of an entrepreneurial class and protecting employment'.[111] This echoes the 'traditionalists' view that reorganization may be beneficial on the basis of wider values.[112] Possibly, the court may confirm a plan even when certain creditors will prefer to take the liquidation path, if it is convinced that they will receive as much as if allowed to seize the assets and sell them piecemeal, and that other goals may be fulfilled at the same time (such as job preservation, benefit to the community and/or to the managers and shareholders). The way to implement such plans and the particular reorganization procedure are not prescribed by the Legislative Guide.[113] It points out and suggests, though, that insolvency law will be flexible regarding different tasks a reorganization plan may serve, which may not necessarily be full rehabilitation (for example, a mechanism for selling the business as a going concern).[114]

---

[108] Ibid, paras. 6–9 (Objectives 3, 4 and 5).

[109] Ibid, para. 6 (Objective 3).   [110] Ibid (emphasis added).

[111] Ibid.   [112] See section 4.2.2.

[113] In Part Two, Ch. IV, though, the Legislative Guide (n 137 chapter 3) delineates such various methods, including their merits or disadvantages.

[114] Ibid, paras. 3–5. Fletcher observes that it is common in insolvency regimes to have an alternative procedure to outright liquidation (Fletcher, *Insolvency* (note 3 chapter 3) 10). See also G. McCormack, 'Control and Corporate Rescue—an Anglo-American Evaluation' (2007) 56 ICLQ 515 (explaining that in regard to UK and US insolvency regimes, that although generally regarded different (the former perceived as 'pro-creditor' especially in stressing the replacement of the debtor's management when insolvency commences, and the latter as 'pro-debtor' allowing inter alia for the debtor to remain in possession) the differences are not that profound. Both have legislatively declared reorganization alternatives to liquidation, and in both systems the reorganization procedure is not always geared towards full rehabilitation. Rather, in many cases it is more 'creditor oriented' (referring to D.A. Skeel Jr, 'Creditors' Ball: The "New" New Corporate Governance in Chapter 11' (2003) 152 U. Pa. L. Rev. 917, 918); H. Rajak, 'The Culture of Bankruptcy', in P.J. Omar (ed.), *International Insolvency Law Themes and Perspectives* (Ashgate, Aldershot 2008) 3, 24–5 (on the similarities between the UK and US regimes in regard to their approach to rescues). See also S. Block-Lieb and T. Halliday, 'Harmonization and Modernization in UNCITRAL Legislative

The Legislative Guide does not suggest a pure translation of the pre-insolvency rights to the insolvency law, but rather that redistributions are 'minimized'.[115] In pursuing equitable distribution,[116] and equitable treatment of similarly situated creditors,[117] the Legislative Guide states that 'creditors with similar legal rights should be treated fairly, receiving a distribution on their claim in accordance with their relative interests' and that 'all creditors do not need to be treated identically, but in a manner that reflects the different bargains they have struck with the debtor'.[118] It recognizes though that '[t]his is less relevant as a defining factor where there is no specific debt contract with the debtor, such as in the case of damage claimants (e.g. for environmental damage) and tax authorities.'[119] It also recognizes that 'the principle of equitable treatment may be modified by social policy on priorities and give way to the prerogatives pertaining to holders of claims or interests that arise, for example, by operation of the law'.[120] However, it stresses (within the same objective above) that still 'it retains its significance by ensuring that the priority accorded to the claims of a similar class affects all members of the class in the same manner'.

It seems, thus, that the Legislative Guide considers the principle of equitable treatment in a multilayered way. On the one hand, it recognizes its significance,[121] though it seems to refer to different notions of the principle, both prescribing equal treatment to creditors according to prior entitlements, and referring to equality among creditors of preferred classes as created by insolvency law.[122] On the other hand, it accepts that the concept is subject to social decisions on priorities. Here too, the Legislative Guide does not prescribe the way to design such priorities, and leaves it to national laws to determine on implementation of distributive issues. Yet, it explains that insolvency laws often attribute priority rights to certain claims, and that this is often based upon social, and sometimes political considerations.[123] It suggests that such priorities should be clearly stated,[124]

Guide on Insolvency Law' (2007) 42 Tex. Int'l L.J. 475, 508 explaining that: 'the Guide builds on international consensus on the desirability of enabling the reorganization of a viable commercial entity.[] The eight policy norms—those key objectives based on earlier work done by the IMF and World Bank and found in Part One of the Legislative Guide were instrumental in identifying reorganization as a central component in any "modern" insolvency statute and in providing policy-oriented touchstone to which the Guide could return, time and again, to justify both the tenor and content of reorganization-friendly recommendations.' (footnote omitted).

[115] Legislative Guide (n 137 chapter 3) Part one, Ch. 1, para. 13 (Objective 8).

[116] Ibid, para. 10 (Objective 6).   [117] Ibid, para. 7 (Objective 4).

[118] Ibid.   [119] Ibid.   [120] Ibid.

[121] It has been observed that the essential notion of equality of treatment of creditors and the *pari passu* rule of distribution are dominant principles in insolvency regimes (Fletcher, *Insolvency* (n 3 chapter 3) 9).

[122] For criticism of the latter interpretation of the notion of equality and *pari passu* see note 58.

[123] The Legislative Guide (n 137 chapter 3) 270. See also Fletcher, *Insolvency* (n 3 chapter 3) 9 (observing that 'most national insolvency laws have embraced a policy of according preferential treatment to certain species of liability ... Conversely, other types of claim may be relegated to the rank of postponed debts which are not eligible to participate in the distribution of the debtor's estate until all preferential and ordinary debts have been paid in full.').

[124] The Legislative Guide (n 137 chapter 3) Part two, Ch. V, para. 68.

and that certain social concerns can be addressed more readily by law other than insolvency law.[125] It identifies a tendency towards a lesser degree of priority classes,[126] while explaining that in the majority of states, certain workers' claims constitute a class of priority claims in insolvency.[127]

4.2.3.4 Additional tasks of insolvency law which support equitable distribution

The Legislative Guide continues to suggest that equitable treatment also 'permeates many aspects of insolvency law, including the application of the stay or suspension, provisions to set aside acts and transactions and recapture value for the insolvency estate, classification of claims, voting procedures in reorganization and distribution mechanisms.' [128] In this context it emphasizes that '[a]n insolvency law should address problems of fraud and favouritism that may arise in cases of financial distress by providing, for example, that acts and transactions detrimental to equitable treatment of creditors can be avoided.' [129] The idea is to tackle unfairness and promote commercial morality as well as to address the problem of such opportunism in an efficient way, while balancing this against problems of cost of the disruption to markets inherent in avoidance of transactions that are otherwise legitimate.[130] National regimes differ more widely, though, in regard to *ex post* penalties against managers and debtors.[131] However, it has been observed that even when comparing the UK and the US regime (which represent different approaches towards debtors and mangers),[132] there is still common ground to be found in this respect.[133]

[125] Ibid.

[126] See also J.A.E. Pottow, 'Procedural Incrementalism: a model for international bankruptcy" (2005) 45(4) Virginia Journal of International Law 935, 1008 (pointing to the reduction in number of priorities in legal regimes).

[127] The Legislative Guide (n 137 chapter 3), Part two, Ch. V, para. 72.

[128] Ibid, Part one, Ch. I, para. 7 (Objective 4).

[129] Ibid. See also the Legislative Guide (n 137 chapter 3) Part two, Ch. II, para. 150 (explaining that many insolvency laws include avoidance provisions). See also J.L. Westbrook, 'Locating the Eye of the Financial Storm' (2007) 32 Brook. J. Int'l L. 1019, 1021 (observing that avoiding powers are found in virtually every bankruptcy law). However, avoidance provisions are subject to crucial variations as between different jurisdictions (see Fletcher, *Insolvency* (n 3 chapter 3) 400; J.L. Westbrook, 'Avoidance of Pre-Bankruptcy Transactions in Multinational Bankruptcy Cases' (2007) 42 Tex. Int'l L.J. 899, 901–2).

[130] The Legislative Guide (n 137 chapter 3) Part one, Ch I, para. 5 (Objective 2).

[131] Indeed the guide does not provide recommendations on the question of liability of managers for trading the business when insolvency is inevitable. Yet, it provides in the commentary that 'if the consequence of the past conduct and behaviour of persons connected with an insolvent debtor is damage or loss to the creditors of the debtor (e.g. by fraud or irresponsible behaviour), it may be appropriate, depending upon the liability regimes applicable for fraud on the one hand and negligence on the other, for an insolvency law to provide for possible recovery of the damage or loss from the persons connected.' (The Legislative Guide (n 137 chapter 3) Part two, Ch. III, para. 34).

[132] See n 114.

[133] Although, under the US regime 'there is a general lack of sticks...if directors fail to put the interests of creditors first by filing early for reorganization' there are other methods to deal with unfairness and perverse incentives by directors such as the law on directors' duties 'and in a growing number of US cases the courts have held that managerial allegiance must shift from the

4.2.3.5 Creditors' participation, impartiality, and expertise of insolvency representatives

Other goals, which can be regarded as 'procedural', are also stressed by the Legislative Guide. For instance, impartiality [134] and voting by creditors [135] are also regarded as objectives, both as supporting equitable treatment of creditors. In regard to creditors' participation in insolvency proceedings,[136] the Legislative Guide further explains that this may take many forms in different legal systems. Generally, either indirect participation (via an insolvency representative) and/ or direct involvement of creditors is to be found in legal regimes as a result of acknowledging their significant interests in the debtor's business once insolvency proceedings are commenced.[137] The Legislative Guide stresses that a high level of creditor participation is desirable and should in fact be encouraged (which implies incorporating means to encourage participation as well as to provide adequate information and notice). It can also enhance efficiency as creditors may be in a good position to advise and assist in the decision-making process. However, this should be balanced against the need to ensure that the creditor representation mechanism remains efficient (avoiding creditors involving themselves in matters that will not have an impact on their interests).[138] It also explains the importance of the insolvency representative having sufficient expertise as to warrant an efficient and fair conduct of the proceedings and generally to ensure that there is confidence in the insolvency regime.[139]

4.2.3.6 Summary

It is apparent, that the Legislative Guide stresses a variety of goals. It also emphasizes the problems of trade-offs, and points out when contradictions may occur, however, without prescribing precise ways of balancing and implementing the desired goals. It also seems to link procedural goals to substantive ones. Hence, preservation of the estate is perceived as crucial to wealth maximization and is

---

shareholders to the creditors when a company approaches insolvency.' (see G. McCormack, 'Control and Corporate Rescue—an Anglo-American Evaluation' (2007) 56 ICLQ 515, 526–7). For the principle as expressed by English courts under which in the onset of insolvency, it is the creditors as opposed to the shareholders who become the residual claimants of the corporate assets see *West Mercia Safetywear Ltd (in liq) v Dodd* [1988] BCLC 250; see also the Australian case *Kinsela v Russel Kinsela Pty Ltd* (1986) 10 ACLR 395).

[134] The Legislative Guide (n 137 chapter 3) Part one, Ch. I, para. 8 (Objective 5).
[135] Ibid, para. 7 (Objective 4).
[136] Mentioned in ibid, para. 9 (Objective 5).
[137] The Legislative Guide (n 137 chapter 3) Part two, Ch. III, para. 75. See also R. Tomasic, 'Creditor Participation in Insolvency Proceedings' EBRD Meeting held on 27–28 April 2006 (available at: http://www.oecd.org/dataoecd/41/44/38182698.pdf.).
[138] The Legislative Guide (n 137 chapter 3), Part two, Ch. III, para. 75.
[139] Ibid, para. 74.

pursued so as 'to allow equitable distribution to creditors',[140] and 'impartiality supports the goal of equitable treatment'.[141]

In sum, there is wide agreement that insolvency regimes should be based on multiple values that encompass both substantive and procedural ends. The insolvency process should aim to maximize the value of the estate, encompassing both the possibility of liquidating or reorganizing the business. This should support equitable distribution of the estate to the stakeholders, according to established priority rules and equitable treatment of similarly ranked creditors. Although the primary focus here is on equitable treatment of creditors, there is regard to interests of other parties. The rules should be clear and predictable as much as possible and the process transparent. The balance to be made among (and within) goals may nevertheless differ among legal regimes as well as particular ways to implement the various goals and tasks. The Legislative Guide also identifies a shared objective to promote coordination and assistance in cross-border insolvencies.[142] This is clearly regarded by the Legislative Guide as essential in the 'modernization' of insolvency laws, and the need to meet the challenges of the future. This should be achieved, as explained in the Legislative Guide, by establishing a framework for cross-border insolvency, in particular by way of adopting the UNCITRAL Model Law on Cross-Border Insolvency.[143]

4.2.4 The consideration of the objectives in subsequent chapters

The chapters of Part III of the book examine various measures for addressing insolvency within MEGs which may assist in promoting insolvency goals, while putting them through the prism of the entity–enterprise law and universality–territoriality dilemmas. The issues which will be addressed will therefore be key aspects that are of particular relevance and interest to the MEG in insolvency problem. That is, those matters pertaining to insolvency which will be peculiar to the fact that the firm in hand is organized with separate entities (rather than a case of a single debtor), or the company in hand is part of a group and controlled by an entity rather than a shareholder. However, an attempt is not made to deal with all features of insolvency. Rather, the aim is to reveal the key traits of a meaningful approach to insolvency within MEGs.

The work will thus suggest ways to handle insolvency proceedings against the MEG (or parts thereof) fairly and efficiently. It will be considered what specific paths a MEG may take in its insolvency, in particular to what extent and in which circumstances it will be desirable to unify between the MEG units during this process. In this respect, relevant solutions will be examined in light of the goals

---

[140] Ibid, Part one, Ch. I, para. 10 (Objective 6).
[141] Ibid, para. 8 (Objective 5).
[142] Ibid, para. 14 (Objective 9).
[143] Ibid.

of wealth maximization, efficiency in decision-making, and promotion of rescues, as well as the *ex ante* effects of relevant rules for the administration of MEG insolvencies and questions of distribution, and matters of procedural justice (the issues will be discussed in chapters 6–8). It will also consider (in chapter 9) penalties or remedies that may be imposed in the course of insolvency within MEGs to combat opportunism in the group context. The goal of enhancing coordination and assistance in cross-border insolvency will also be relevant in all those matters as they all occur in an international insolvency context.

5

Prototypical Scenarios of Insolvency within Multinational Enterprise Groups

5.1 Introduction

It was mentioned earlier that there is considerable diversity in the ways MEGs are operating today.[1] MEGs conduct businesses in different sizes, legal patterns, and geographical spheres and operate in various degrees of integration and centralized control. In this respect, it was proposed earlier, that it is crucial for a meaningful approach to insolvencies within MEGs to be able to consider this variety of structures. A priori, any of those possible structures should not be excluded from being under the scope of a 'law of MEGs in insolvency'.[2] Yet, by definition, this poses a major difficulty in attempting to devise solutions to MEGs in insolvency, since there is no one pattern of MEG on which relevant rules could be applied. Moreover, the insolvency event itself is not of one nature and can occur in a variety of scenarios. Additionally, issues pertaining to insolvency are diverse so that certain solutions may be adequate for certain MEGs in insolvency while others may be only appropriate in other situations.

To be able to deal with this conundrum, the goal of this chapter is to delineate the main relevant features of the way MEGs are structured and operated that are significant to issues of insolvency within MEGs. Using these as dimensions we could then describe the entire spectrum of MEGs. That is, a given MEG could be classified according to these dimensions. While appreciating the diversity in the insolvency situations within a variety of MEG legal forms, the chapter will conclude with an attempt to classify certain prototypes of MEG (along the dimensions that will be suggested), hence, enabling some measure of generalization across cases and scenarios. As the dimensions selected are first and foremost relevant for the issue of international insolvency of the MEG, the result will be a suitable taxonomy that will facilitate discussion in the subsequent chapters on desirable linking measures for insolvency within MEGs, and guide the policy choices.

---

[1] See chapter 1.
[2] Ibid, section 1.3.6.

5.2 Key Factors Regarding the Structure, Operation, and Default of MEGs with Relevance to Insolvency within such Enterprises

The question at the core of this work is to what extent, in which cases, and for what purposes a linkage between the components of a MEG should be made in the course of their insolvency.[3] The factors pursued here should, therefore, relate to the issue of linking between foreign affiliates in their insolvencies. That is, the factors should bear relevance to issues pertaining to the creation of such linkage (on the global level).

In this respect, it is first suggested that the different types of insolvency in terms of the companies involved in the process are considered: it can be a case in which only one subsidiary of the MEG is under insolvency, or a case of a number of subsidiaries in distress (the entire group or part thereof). This will reflect on the appropriate global linking means to be applied. For instance, an insolvency of a subsidiary may put the focus on issues of liability,[4] while a total collapse may raise issues in regard to the handling of the insolvency process.[5] The particular insolvency scenario may also have effects on the issue of the proper venue.

Another important aspect is the level of integration and inter-dependence among the members constituting the MEG (or the degree of 'group unity' or otherwise 'affiliates' independence').[6] The legal structure of the firm may take various forms, based on equity linkages as well as contractual ones.[7] In any of these cases the interrelations among the entities may create an integrated group.[8] The question of integration and its degree will have profound implications on the appropriate global linking tools to be applied. For instance, a case could involve intermingling of assets and debts between entities and hosting states. Alternatively, it could feature a MEG that was operating in a more separate mode, neatly organized within national borders. Accordingly, certain solutions such as a pooling of assets and debts of entities located in different countries[9] may be effective in promoting insolvency goals in regard to the former scenario but may not be suitable for the latter.

---

[3] See chapter 2, section 2.5; and chapter 3, section 3.5.

[4] See chapter 9.

[5] See chapters 6–8.

[6] The degree of integration and interdependence among group consitutents has been stressed as playing an important role in court decisions regarding issues of corporate groups in general (see Blumberg et al, *Blumberg on Croporate Groups* (n 31 chapter 1) vol. 1, s. 6.02). Hadden stresses that a relevant factor for classification of groups for legal purposes may be defined in terms of the degree of autonomy of parts of the group (T. Hadden, 'Regulating Corporate Groups: An International Perspective' in J. McCahery, S. Picciotto and C. Scott (eds.), *Corporate Control and Accountability* (Oxford University Press, Oxford 1993) 343, 357–58).

[7] See chapter 1, section 1.3.

[8] Ibid.

[9] See chapter 6, section 6.3.

Finally, another important aspect of MEGs for our purposes is whether and to what extent the MEG was centrally managed and controlled. It is sensible to assume that the degree of centralization is also related to the degree of integration (that is, we expect a highly centralized MEG to be integrated as well[10]). However, an integrated MEG could also be decentralized. But, the degree of centralized control and the presence and function of a MEG 'centre' will be crucial in itself in determining issues of the proper venue in regard to the handling of MEG insolvency proceedings. It will also reflect on the kind of desired linkage on the cross-border front in the first place, i.e. to what extent it will be appropriate to have one or several insolvencies against the group in different countries,[11] and on questions of responsibility of controlling entities for the debts of their subsidiaries.[12] As these issues are at the core of finding solutions in international insolvency, this will be another important factor to consider.

These three factors will set the basic scene to assist the later discussion of a suitable approach to insolvencies within MEGs. Nevertheless, additional considerations will be added to these basic scenarios in later stages (as will be relevant to promoting particular objectives). For example, in terms of control, a crucial aspect will be the way control was exercised by those running the group (whether for instance control gave rise to disallowing a subsidiary to develop independent profit-making activities).[13] This may suggest linking tools aimed at combating mismanagement in the context of MEGs.[14] Or, in terms of insolvency scenarios, the viability of the business at hand will be an additional relevant factor in terms of rescue possibilities in the MEG context.[15] It is also worthwhile to note that other aspects may be relevant in determining some of the primary factors delineated above. For example, percentage of ownership may reflect on the degree of affiliates' autonomy.[16] Or, the size of the MEG may indicate the autonomy of companies and the complexity of the group and thus prove relevant to the degree of integration and centralization.[17] However, these aspects only indicate or reflect on the main factors mentioned above and therefore do not represent key factors in themselves.

5.3 Classifying each Factor into Main Representative Scenarios

Obviously, each of the key factors delineated above entails a range of possible scenarios or degrees along a continuum. Integration can be strong or weak (with all ranges of options in between), the MEG may be more or less centralized and so

---

[10] See section 5.3.2.
[11] See chapter 6, section 6.2.1.8.
[12] See chapter 9, sections 9.3 and 9.5.2.
[13] See chapter 9, section 9.3.
[14] Ibid.   [15] See chapter 6.
[16] See section 5.3.3.   [17] Ibid.

forth. Therefore, in order for the above mentioned factors to serve as the dimensions describing the spectrum of MEG scenarios we first need to classify each of the three factors mentioned above into a number of main representative classes. Here too, the representative categories reflect categorical differences in the need to link between affiliates of an MEG in the event of insolvency.

5.3.1 The insolvency scenarios

Most important for our purposes would be which parts of the group are in financial difficulties: whether it is a group of several affiliates that collapses (or that is undergoing financial distress so that it may enter an insolvency process), or is it a case of a specific member of a group in distress (for which some sort of insolvency proceeding may be considered)?[18] As aforementioned, a case of 'group collapse' will raise different issues than a case of a single member in distress. Typically, when there are several affiliates under insolvency, questions of ways to administer the process arise.[19] Conversely, in the single insolvency scenario (where an affiliate is under insolvency) the primary focus will be put on issues of group liability or the improper transfer of assets belonging to the affiliate.[20]

It is therefore suggested here, that the insolvency scenarios should be placed into two classes. The first class will feature the case of distress of more than one entity within a MEG (it can be a total collapse of a MEG or a collapse of a division thereof). This type of case will also include those instances where it appears that only one affiliate is in financial difficulties and in need of an insolvency procedure, but a closer examination will reveal that there is another affiliate (or affiliates) on the verge of collapse (which could also be the outcome of high dependence on the first distressed affiliate[21]). It will also include cases where a parent and a sub-subsidiary (second-tier subsidiary) are in financial distress,[22] or several sister companies are collapsing. The second class will focus on an insolvency of a particular affiliate within a MEG.

5.3.2 Degree of integration/interdependence

As mentioned above, the question of the degree of 'group unity' is crucial for our purposes. That is, to what extent the group actually operated as a single entity or rather its components were truly (not only legally, but economically) independent

---

[18] The relevant issue here is whether more than one entity may enter an insolvency process, and this may include solvent entities in financial difficulties, depending on whether this is allowed in the particular legal system. 'Insolvent' entity refers to where the entity's liabilities exceed the value of its assets, or where it is unable to pay its debts when they fall due (see UNCITRAL Legislative Guide on Insolvency Law (n 136 chapter 3), Preface, para. 12(s)).

[19] See chapter 6.   [20] See chapter 9.

[21] See chapter 6, section 6.2.1.1.

[22] Though typically issues of group administration in insolvency will be most relevant among subsidiaries and their immediate holding entity which may constitute an integrated business (see n 36).

entities. Economic integration is a major factor in ascertaining group unity,[23] which may be determined by examining the kind of operations performed by the members; that is, to what extent the companies comprising the group collectively carried out a common business.[24] There may even be commingling of accounts and difficulty in segregating individual assets and liabilities.[25] Generally, in ver- tically structured MEGs, the degree to which control over affiliates was actually exercised[26] is relevant in determining the degree of unity or otherwise business independence of affiliates. That is, to what extent the business of the affiliates was operated at an arm's length or in the other extreme closely dominated by a con- trolling entity.

Other factors are focused on the degree of interdependence. Thus, where group members significantly rely on other affiliates in the group for vital functions (such as legal, accounting, tax, insurance and so forth) the companies become consider- ably intertwined and their resemblance to independent corporations diminishes.[27] Similarly interdependence may result from 'group financing', such as loans rest- ing on cross guarantees of the group members.[28] In many groups, executive per- sonnel are rotated by the parent to successive assignments in different affiliated companies, and various programmes for employees are devised on a group basis resulting in the employees being identified with the group as a whole.[29] Another relevant factor in ascertaining the degree of group unity is how the group repre- sented itself to the public, and to what extent it was perceived as a single entity.[30]

Indeed, a central question important for the application of various insolvency techniques is whether the MEG was significantly unified in terms of its business or whether it was weakly (or non-) integrated. As will be discussed later on, in cases of integrated MEGs certain 'linking' methods may be desirable (irrespect- ive of whether the MEGs are also closely controlled or more loosely coordinated). What matters here is that there was 'business integration'. Such linking tools may be inadequate though in the case of non-integration (of whichever group structure).[31] Furthermore, it is also important to identify the special case in which there was actually a greater degree of integration/ inter-dependence in a way that resulted in a substantial mix between the entities comprising the group. This may suggest more interventionist tools to be applied in the course of insolvency, in terms of interfering with the corporate form and the location of the entities in different jurisdictions.[32] It is therefore suggested to classify the integration/ interdependence factors into three classes: the 'weak (or no) integration' cases, the 'business integration' cases, and the 'asset integration' scenarios of MEGs.

---

[23] See Blumbeg et al, *Blumberg on Corporate Groups* (n 31 chapter 1) vol 1, s. 6.02.
[24] Blumberg, *The Multinational Challenge* (n 3 chapter 1) 144–5.
[25] Blumberg et al, *Blumberg on Corporate Groups* (n 31 chapter 1) vol 5, s. 88.06.
[26] See ibid, vol 1, s. 6.02 (explaining that the way control was exercised is also relevant to the issue of attribution of responsibilities of the affiliate to the dominant entity, a matter which we will discuss in chapter 9).
[27] Ibid, vol 1, s. 6.02.   [28] Ibid.   [29] Ibid.
[30] Ibid.   [31] See chapter 6.   [32] Ibid, section 6.3.

'Asset integration' represents the integration situation where there is a significant degree of 'entity unity', in the sense that the financial affairs of the MEG entities were entangled. The term 'asset integration' is used for convenience purposes but it means to indicate intermingling of assets and/or debts. The focus is not so much on the integration of the *business*, but rather on the commingling of the contents of the *entities*.[33] This could be a result of negligence by those who ran the group (who might have commingled books and accounts of the various entities), a planned strategy,[34] or a way to deceive creditors and conceal assets from them, and it may also result in creditors relying on the group as a whole when dealing with it.

'Business integration' will refer to the scenarios where the business was operating with significant integration or inter-dependence, so that the group was unified in terms of its business.[35] This normally refers to MEGs which were operating a single worldwide business, namely, the subsidiaries or affiliates conduct only a part or fragment of the larger business of their parent, which is collectively conducted by the various affiliates under the control of the parent[36] (or jointly coordinated[37]). It is noteworthy that this category may also include conglomerate enterprises and other diversified groups. Although such businesses on their face may seem significantly independent (since the enterprises do not collectively carry out a common business[38]) they may, in fact, operate in an integrated way through financial and administrative interdependence.[39]

'Weak or non-integration' is where the MEG (or certain parts thereof) was not operating in an integrated manner. Here, the parent company may have had the capacity to control or coordinate the business, but in effect the subsidiaries were operating at arm's length, conducting truly separate businesses. Alternatively, the parent may control the subsidiaries without an overall coordination that results in an integrated business (for instance, when different subsets of subsidiaries

---

[33] See examples in ibid.

[34] This can be an economically efficient strategy (see J. Landers, 'A Unified Approach to Parent, Subsidiary and Affiliated Questions in Bankruptcy'"(1975) 42 U. Chi. L. Rev. 589, 592, arguing that free commingling of funds and properties may be highly desirable in order to maximize overall productive use of the capital and resources of the enterprise). See also W.H. Widen, 'Corporate Form and Substantive Consolidation' [2007] 75 Geo. Wash. L. Rev. 237, 255–62 (suggesting that economic theory predicts that high integration will occur in many enterprises seeking to become more cost efficient through growth). Commingling may be particularly frequent in smaller operations where the accounting and other records are prepared in an ad hoc manner on an enterprise level (see J. Dickfos, C. Anderson and D. Morrison, 'The Insolvency Implications for Corporate Groups in Australia—Recent Events and Initiatives' (2007) 16 Int. Insol. Rev. 103, 105–6).

[35] See examples in chapter 6, section 6.2.

[36] As will typically be the case in 'pyramid' hierarchical forms of MEGs, either linked by equity or contract (see chapter 1, section 1.3). It can be an integration between a subsidiary (or subsidiaries) and an immediate holding company, or a subsidiary and an ultimate holding company, yet it is assumed with regard to multinational structures, that more often subsidiaries and their immediate parent will constitute together a commercial division or enterprise in one sector. Other subsidiaries with their own immediate parent would constitute another enterprise in a different sector (see Musact, *The Liability* (n 39 chapter 1) 444).

[37] In the more decentralized or heterarchical structures of MEGs (see e.g. the Japanese 'model' of groups linked by cross shareholding with unity in management; chapter 1, sections 1.3.3 and 1.3.4).

[38] Blumberg, *The Multinational Challenge* (n 3 chapter 1) 144–5.

[39] Because of the opportunities for economies of scale and scope (ibid).

are coordinated separately). Low level of integration is more likely in pure conglomerates and other highly diversified groups.[40] The SPV mentioned earlier will
normally be designed to be remote from the group to achieve its purposes.[41] In
addition, typically, companies held for pure investment purposes will be truly
autonomous and removed from participation in the business operations. It is also
more likely that an autonomous company will be partly owned rather than fully
held by the holding company.[42]

5.3.3 Central control, location, and function

Whereas the previous factor focused on the degree of actual unity and intermingling of business/assets, here the focus is on the managerial pattern in terms of
the function and location within the geographical sphere of the decision-maker
in the MEG. The crucial aspect here is whether the MEG was centrally controlled
by a common head office or, although the MEG may have been integrated,[43] it
was operated with a significant degree of decentralization (and if so in what way).
In addition, we will ask whether there is geographical displacement between the
MEG's nerve centre and affiliates and whether the group had more than one head.

Various factors have been suggested in order to evaluate the degree of centralized control in multinational firms (and accordingly the level of autonomy granted
to local affiliates). The size of the group, the type of products it manufactures, the
degree of integration of activities with the other members of the group, the targeted market, and how the subsidiaries are owned are relevant factors to consider
when determining the degree of autonomy a group's constituent company has.
Less autonomy is expected if the company belongs to a large MEG established
in many foreign countries, if it manufactures fairly standardized products; if the
activities of the members are largely integrated; if it has been created to serve a
market larger than the country in which it is established; or if the parent company holds a large portion of the equity. Other factors to take into account are
the nationality and resulting business culture of the parent; the age of the subsidiary, in that centralisation may decrease over time; the method of entry into
the host state, in that a new establishment may be more closely controlled than
an acquired local company; the industrial sector in which the firm operates, in
that some industries will be more globally integrated and centralized than others;
the performance of the subsidiary, in that poor performance increases central

---

[40] An integrated business strategy does not include all groups of companies. In conglomerate
groups that operate diversified businesses the group structure may be used for various reasons other
than the imposition of a single business strategy (Davies, *Company Law* (n 31 chapter 1) 229). See
also R. Posner, 'The Legal Rights of Creditors of Affiliated corporations: An Economic Approach'
(1976) 43 U. Chi. L. Rev. 499, 510 (asserting that the group often may not constitute a single
enterprise, pointing not only to conglomerates but also to highly diversified enterprises conducting
distinct businesses sharing 'a few headquarters functions.'). Non-integration may also be present
among two MEGs joined together by common holdings (of a parent or indivuduals (see chapter 1,
section 1.3.2) but operating different businesses).

[41] See chapter 1, section 1.3.2.   [42] See n 47.

[43] Either in terms of 'business' or 'assets' (see also text preceding section 5.3.2).

control; and the tendency of geographically organized multinational enterprises to be less centralized than functional, product, or matrix-organized firms.[44]

As aforementioned, the degree of centralization/decentralization and generally the location and function of management will reflect on issues of venue and techniques of unification between foreign affiliates in their insolvency. Degree of centralization/decentralization will also reflect on issues of group responsibility.[45]

It is therefore suggested that this factor is classified into three prime categories with two additional variants. The first class is where the MEG is centrally controlled and managed via a single 'head' and where that head office is the policy-maker and directing 'brain'. This is typically (but not only) the case in the traditional equity-based vertically structured MEGs, with skills and senior decision-takers concentrated around the parent company[46] (this is most pronounced in smaller closely held (wholly or majority holding) ones).[47] It can similarly be the case in contractually linked MEGs where affiliates are subjected to common control.[48] (Hereinafter: 'centralized MEGs'.)

The second class is where the MEG was to a large extent decentralized (yet still integrated). That is, the MEG was subjected to a central head office, with the functions of the head more in the realm of coordination or supervision rather than close control. The group entities are significantly autonomous, with considerable presence of the subsidiaries in their jurisdiction, as they were locally managed (this may also include major contracts to which the subdsidiary is party governed by local laws, local employees are employed, creditors are dealing with the subsidiary locally and so forth). It was mentioned earlier, that when the group becomes multinational, mature and large in size, decentralized patterns tend to be most effective.[49] In these cases, the division of responsibilities and tasks between the headquarters, regional offices, and affiliates may change. In cases where the need to coordinate the global activities is important, the locus of decision-taking remains in the centre, though, the role of the head office may change. Instead of the ultimate policy-maker and directing 'brain' the headquarters will act as coordinator and identifier of new business opportunities and the creator of task force networks within the firm.[50] Where the managements of local units need a great deal of local information the locus of decision-taking may be largely decentralized to regional offices and/or local affiliates.[51] Additionally,

[44] OECD Structure and Organization of Multinational Enterprises (Paris, 1987), 35; Dunning, *Multinational Enterprises* (n 54 chapter 1) 225–6. See also P.T. Muchlinski, 'Corporations in International Litigation: Problems of Jurisdiction and the United Kingdom Asbestos Cases' (2001) 50 ICLQ I 1, 10; Muchlinski, *Multinational Enterprises* (n 10 chapter 1) 50–1.

[45] See section 5.2.

[46] See Muscat, *The Liability* (n 39 chapter 1) 56–7.

[47] See chapter 1, section 1.3.2.

[48] For instance a franchise contract may assure that the franchisor has a dominant position over the franchisee in operational and related matters (see chapter 1, section 1.3.4).

[49] See chapter 1, section 1.3.3.

[50] See Dunning, *Multinational Enterprises* (n 54 chapter 1) 223. See also Muchlinski, *Multinational Enterprises* (n 10 chapter 1) 48.

[51] Ibid.

MEGs may operate a diversified business or as a conglomerate in which the parent and subsidiaries are in different industries, however the parent supervises the operation to achieve integration in financial and administrative matters.[52] These patterns are also included in this class (hereinafter: 'decentralized MEGs').

The third class is where the MEG is decentralized but, moreover, it also lacks a common head office. Examples are in the form of heterarchical networks (or alliances) of contractually linked entities or networks of cross-shareholdings. Critically, for these structures to be considered as a group for the purposes of this work they need to show they operate in coordination which is achieved by interlocking directorship and/or management conferences and so forth.[53] (Hereinafter: 'heterarchical MEGs'.)

Within either the centralized or the decentralized class it is suggested that two particular categories are added. The first is where the integrated MEG was controlled or coordinated by more than one head. This could be achieved, for instance, via the creation of a 'twin holding' company (located in different states),[54] or a joint venture (which acquired a degree of permanence and achieved integration) where control is shared among the parent undertakings.[55] (Hereinafter: 'multiple head MEGs'.)

The second is where in terms of the geographical spread of the MEG its head was 'isolated', in the sense that the significant majority of the MEG's activities are concentrated in another country. In its extreme this would feature a large MEG with numerous subsidiaries, where the controlling parent is situated in a certain country while all the subsidiaries are located in another country. (Hereinafter: ' "isolated" head MEGs'.)

5.3.4 Portraying a concise picture of insolvency within multinational enterprise groups

Finally, it is important to bear in mind that the key factors identified above will sometimes have implications for more than one aspect pertaining to insolvencies within MEGs. For instance, the insolvency scenario may affect issues of group liability, as well as manner of administration and international jurisdiction.[56] In addition, there may be mutual influences among factors. Thus, as aforementioned the degree of centralized control may affect the degree of integration.[57] Hence, in order to properly evaluate the insolvency situation and determine the proper global means to apply to the case it will be necessary to portray the specific case along each of those dimensions together. Indeed, the identification of prototypes is geared exactly to this end and will be of assistance in this regard.

[52] See Blumberg, *The Multinational Challenge* (n 3 chapter 1) 144–5.
[53] See chapter 1, section 1.3.3.
[54] See n 48 and accompanying text, chapter 1.
[55] Notes 50–1, and accompanying text, chapter 1.
[56] As will be discussed in subsequent chapters (chapters 6–9).
[57] See section 5.3.2.

5.4　Defining 'Prototypes'

The above representative classes (distinctively classified along the three dimensions) can be combined together to provide 23 prototypes of potential insolvency events within possible organizational types of MEGs. As aforesaid, these prototypes do not attempt to cover all possible scenarios of MEGs in default, but rather concentrate on a number of possible cases which are most relevant to this work on issues of insolvencies within MEGs. Therefore, these prototypes derive from the combination of the concept of degree of integration in the variety of business forms[58] and the idea of degree of centralized control[59] coupled with the basic insolvency circumstances of whether several affiliates are collapsing or the focus is on a particular subsidiary.[60] The range of options which may occur along the three-dimensional classifications will be provided, yet later on in the work reference will be made only to those options bearing significance to the issues discussed (this will be accompanied by some concrete examples and actual cases to demonstrate these prototypes).

The table below depicts the various prototypes generated from the categories:

Table

| | Group insolvency | | | | | | | Insolvency of a single affiliate | | | | | | |
| | Centralized | | | Decentralized | | | Heterarchical | Centralized | | | Decentralized | | | Heterarchical |
	Single Head	Multiple Head	Isolated Head	Single Head	Multiple Head	Isolated Head		Single Head	Multiple Head	Isolated Head	Single Head	Multiple Head	Isolated Head	
Business Integration	A1	A2	A3	B1	B2	B3	C		I			J		K
Asset Integration	D1	D2	D3	E1	E2	E3	F							
No Integration				G1	G2	G3	H					L		M

Source: Author

The main Prototypes will be illustrated below. These will be accompanied by a brief explanation of what each illustration signifies. Some standardized visual symbols will be used throughout the various illustrations. First, a box will signify a legal entity. Second, the type of border used for these boxes will signify the insolvency status of the entity. That is, a solid box will represent a solvent company while a dotted box will represent an insolvent company. Third, arrows from one box to another will signify a linkage between affiliate entities (either equity or contractual

---

[58] Ibid.　　　[59] See section 5.3.3.　　　[60] See section 5.3.1.

relationships). Fourth, a star symbol will be used to indicate centralization or decentralization.[61] Finally, the weight of the ellipse surrounding the boxes will signify the degree of integration within the group. That is, a thin line will represent 'business integration' whereas a thick one will represent 'asset integration'.

Prototype A1: Business integrated centralized single head insolvent MEG

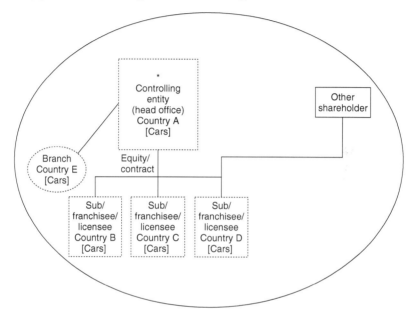

Source: Author

- In this case more than one entity is under insolvency (all companies surrounded by a dotted line).[62]
- This prototype includes a branch (taking the form of a small ellipse to distinguish it from a subsidiary) to illustrate the fact that the MEG may be comprised of affiliates as well as branches (subsequent prototypes will not include branches for simplicity reasons, however obviously branches can be present in any of the prototypes). Other forms of entity (such as partnerships) are not included as the focus is on companies.[63]
- It also includes a scenario where a subsidiary (the subsidiary in country D in the illustration) is also held by additional shareholders (only partly held by the controlling entity). This can also be the case in subsequent prototypes yet again for simplicity reasons it is illustrated only here.

---

[61] A star located only in the parent's (or controlling entity's) box signifies a centralized MEG, whereas a star appearing both in the parent and the subsidiary signifies a decentralized MEG.

[62] As in the first class of insolvency scenarios (see section 5.3.1).

[63] See chapter 1, section 1.4.

- The prototype uses a simple two-tiered structure of a parent and subsidiaries but it can be part of a larger group with multiple-tier subsidiaries (the prototype will always refer to the part of the group which is integrated).
- The ellipse around the enterprise group represents the integration between the components (here the companies are integrated (in business terms)).[64]
- In this case all companies operate in the same industry (the car industry in the above illustration) as is typically the case in integrated centralized MEGs.[65] The parent company in the example undertakes part of the business as well; however it could also be that it will operate merely as a holding company.
- The MEG is either equity based, or contractually linked (the illustration indicates the examples of franchisees or licensees).[66] Subsequent prototypes will just use the term 'affiliate' to indicate that it can be either a relationship with a traditional subsidiary or a contractual linkage with an affiliate.
- As explained above, the star [*] represents centralization. Here the enterprise is centralized with the head office controlling the entire business.[67] In the illustration the head office is located where the immediate parent or controlling entity is located (since this is typically the case[68]). However, it may be located elsewhere. The point is that the enterprise is commonly and centrally managed.
- In the illustration (and in the subsequent prototypes as well) each entity is situated in a different country (hence representing a multinational enterprise).[69] However, it can be that some of the entities are situated in the same place.[70]

Prototype A2: Business integrated centralized multiple head insolvent MEG

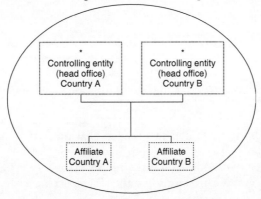

Source: Author

---

[64] As in the second class of the integration factor (see section 5.3.2).
[65] See sections 5.3.2 and 5.3.3.   [66] See chapter 1, section 1.3.4.
[67] As in the first class of the centralization factor (see section 5.3.3).
[68] N 46, and accompanying text.
[69] On the meaning of MEG and particularly the international element see chapter 1, section 1.3.6.2.
[70] For the particualr sitaution where the MEG is divided between two locations, resulting in an 'isolated' head see prototype A3.

- Here instead of one head office there are in fact two centres controlling the integrated business. This specific structure is based on joint shareholding. Thus, there are in fact two groups with two parents that together operate a single business as if they were one group (so that at the top of the integrated enterprise there is no single controller).[71]
- In the illustration there is a 'twin holding' structure. Another example is an integrated joint venture with control shared among the parent companies.[72]

Prototype A3: Business integrated centralized isolated head insolvent MEG

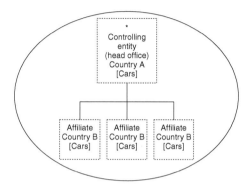

Source: Author

- Here the MEG's head is located in a different place than all the rest of its activities. To demonstrate this scenario, the parent in the illustration is located in a particular country, while all the subsidiaries are located in a different country.[73]

Prototype B1: Business integrated decentralized single head insolvent MEG

(1)

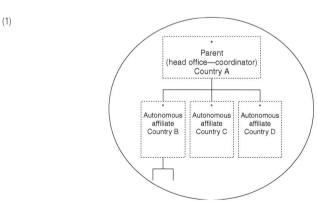

Source: Author

---

[71] As in the first variant within the centralization factor (section 5.3.3).
[72] See chapter 1, section 1.3.2.
[73] See the second variant within the centralization factor (section 5.3.3).

(2)

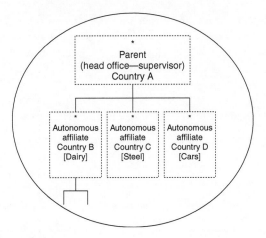

Source: Author

- The first figure (figure (1)) refers to decentralized MEGs.[74] The second figure (figure (2)) refers in particular to a conglomerate sort of enterprise (in which the companies operated different businesses), that may appear not to be integrated, however significant inter-links suggest it is an integrated MEG.[75] In both figures, although the MEG is relatively diversified or decentralized, it is integrated in the sense that there are considerable interrelations among the constituent companies or that the companies together comprise a single business jointly coordinated.[76]
- The enterprise is coordinated or supervised via the head office. The local affiliates are significantly autonomous and represent separate centres of control (this is represented by the star [*] that, as opposed to the previous Prototypes (A1–3), also appears within the local subsidiaries). However, the subsidiaries do not function completely independently.[77]

Prototype B2: Business integrated decentralized multiple head insolvent MEG

- This prototype is similar to the one depicted by prototype B1, only that here it is with multiple heads (similar to the way prototype A2 relates to A1).[78]

Prototype B3: Business integrated decentralized isolated head insolvent MEG

- This prototype is similar to the one depicted by prototype B1, only that here it is with an isolated head (similar to the way prototype A3 relates to A1).[79]

---

[74] As in the second category of the centralization factor combined with the scenario of business integration (sections 5.3.2 and 5.3.3). The affiliates are under insolvency (see the first category of the insolvency factor).

[75] See section 5.3.2 above.   [76] As in the second class of the integration factor (ibid).

[77] As in the second class of the centralization factor (see section 5.3.3).

[78] I.e., it is a combination of the first category of the insolvency factor, the second class of the integration factor, the second class of the centralization factor, and the first variant of the centralization factor (sections 5.3.1–5.3.3).

[79] I.e., it is a combination of the first category of the insolvency factor, the second class of the integration factor, the second class of the centralization factor, and the second variant of the centralization factor (sections 5.3.1–5.3.3).

Prototype C: Business integrated heterarchical insolvent MEG

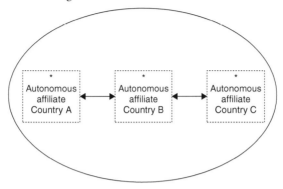

Source: Author

- This prototype represents a scenario where the MEG is integrated (and all affiliates are under insolvency),[80] yet it is organized as a network of affiliates with no principal head for the entire MEG.[81]
- Here too, it can be a contractually based network, or the affiliates may be linked by cross-shareholdings.[82]

Prototype D1: Asset integrated centralized single head insolvent MEG
Source: Author

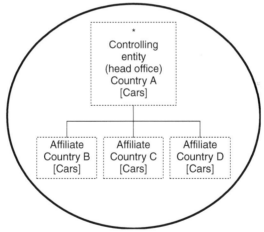

- The thick lined ellipse represents integration between the components, in terms of 'asset integration', rather than mere business unity.[83] Typically, there will be close centralized control,[84] and close business integration as well. However, a

---

[80] As in the first category of the insolvency factor (section 5.3.1).
[81] As in the third category class of the centralization factor (section 5.3.3).
[82] See chapter 1, sections 1.3.3 and 1.3.4.
[83] As in the first class of the integration factor (see section 5.3.2).
[84] As in the first class of the centralization factor (see section 5.3.3).

degree of asset integration (commingling of assets or liabilities) might appear in scenarios of lesser centralization.

- In this scenario all companies are under insolvency.[85]

Prototype D2: Asset integrated centralized multiple head insolvent MEG

- This prototype is similar to the one depicted by prototype D1, only that here it is with multiple heads (similar to the way prototype A2 relates to A1).[86]

Prototype D3: Asset integrated centralized isolated head insolvent MEG

- This prototype is similar to the one depicted by prototype D1, only that here it is with an isolated head (similar to the way prototype A3 relates to A1).[87]

Prototype E1: Asset integrated decentralized single head insolvent MEG

- This prototype is similar to the one depicted by prototype D1, only that here it is a decentralized scenario (as in prototype B1).[88]

Prototype E2: Asset integrated decentralized multiple head insolvent MEG

- This prototype is similar to the one depicted by prototype E1, only that here it is with multiple heads.[89]

Prototype E3: Asset integrated decentralized isolated head insolvent MEG

- This prototype is similar to the one depicted by prototype E1, only that here it is with an isolated head.[90]

Prototype F: Asset integrated heterachical insolvent MEG

- This prototype is equivalent to the one depicted by prototype D1, only that here it is a heterarchical scenario (as in prototype C).[91]

---

[85] As in the first insolvency scenario (see section 5.3.1).

[86] I.e, it is a combination of the first category of the insolvency factor, the first class of the integration factor, the first class of the centralization factor, and the first variant of the centralization factor (sections 5.3.1–5.3.3).

[87] I.e., it is a combination of the first category of the insolvency factor, the first class of the integration factor, the first class of the centralization factor, and the second variant of the centralization factor (sections 5.3.1–5.3.3).

[88] I.e., it is a combination of the first category of the insolvency factor, the first class of the integration factor, and the second class of the centralization factor (sections 5.3.1–5.3.3).

[89] I.e., it is a combination of the first category of the insolvency factor, the first class of the integration factor, the second class of the centralization factor, and the first variant of the centralization factor (sections 5.3.1–5.3.3).

[90] I.e., it is a combination of the first category of the insolvency factor, the first class of the integration factor, the second class of the centralization factor, and the second variant of the centralization factor (sections 5.3.1–5.3.3).

[91] I.e., it is a combination of the first category of the insolvency factor, the first class of the integration factor, and the third class of the centralization factor (sections 5.3.1–5.3.3).

Prototype G1: Non-integrated decentralized single head insolvent MEG

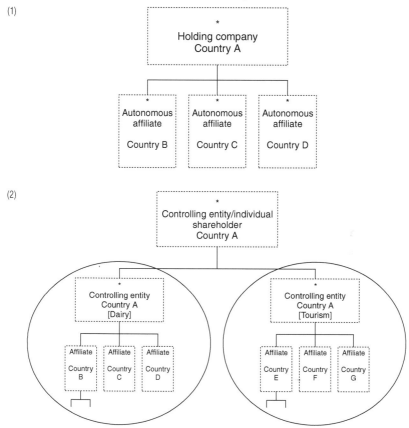

Source: Author

- This prototype represents a case of weak (or no) integration[92] within a collapsing enterprise.[93] The subsidiaries function independently, with no significant involvement of the parent in their business operations. Accordingly, the MEG is not centralized or considerably coordinated.
- Another example of no integration is given in figure (2), where two groups are controlled by a single holding company (or an individual shareholder). Although the groups are commonly controlled, they operate different businesses with no significant inter-relations among the two groups.[94]

---

[92] As in the third class of the integration factor (see section 5.3.2).
[93] As in the first insolvency scenario (see section 5.3.1).
[94] See chapter 1, section 1.3.2.

Prototype G2: Non-integrated decentralized multiple head insolvent MEG

- This prototype is similar to the one depicted by prototype G1, only that here it is with multiple heads.[95]

Prototype G3: Non-integrated decentralized isolated head insolvent MEG

- This prototype is similar to the one depicted by prototype G1, only that here it is with an isolated head.[96]

Prototype H: Non-integrated heterarchical insolvent MEG

- This prototype is similar to the one depicted by prototype G1, only that here it is a heterarchical scenario (as in prototype C).[97]

Prototype I: Insolvent affiliate in business integrated centralized MEG

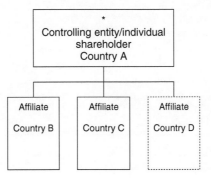

Source: Author

- This prototype represents a case of single company insolvency within a business integrated centralized MEG.[98] As aforementioned, there may be more than one affiliate collapsing in the particular case, so that different issues may arise in the course of this insolvency. Yet, the focus in this scenario is on issues pertaining to the relationship between the affiliate and its controller and the way control was exercised by the controller over the affiliate, and questions regarding transactions involving the assets of the particular affiliate.

---

[95] I.e., it is a combination of the first category of the insolvency factor, the third class of the integration factor, the second class of the centralization factor, and the first variant of the centralization factor (sections 5.3.1–5.3.3).

[96] I.e., it is a combination of the first class of the insolvency factor, the third class of the integration factor, the second class of the centralization factor, and the second variant of the centralization factor (sections 5.3.1–5.3.3).

[97] I.e., it is a combination of the first class of the insolvency factor, the third class of the integration factor, and the third class of the centralization factor (sections 5.3.1–5.3.3).

[98] A combination of the second class of the insolvency factor, the second class of the integration factor, and the first class of the centralization factor (sections 5.3.1–5.3.3).

- The insolvent affiliate in issue may also be the parent company.[99]
- The location of the MEG head may appear in the various versions (see prototypes A1–A3 above, and accompanying illustrations). Yet, in scenarios where the focus is on a particular subsidiary's insolvency, issues of handling joint insolvencies underlying the need for assessing the location of the head [100] are absent, and therefore these variants are not mentioned here.
- Note that 'asset integration' by definition refers to scenarios of collapse of all affiliates (which were 'asset integrated'),[101] and thus is not represented in the scenarios of a single affiliate insolvency.

Prototype J: Insolvent affiliate in business integrated decentralized MEG

- This prototype is similar to the one depicted by prototype I, only that here it is a decentralized scenario (as in prototype B).[102]

Prototype K: Insolvent affiliate in business integrated heterarchical MEG

- This prototype is similar to the one depicted by prototype I, only that here it is a heterarchical scenario (as in prototype C).[103]

Prototype L: Insolvent subsidiary in non-integrated decentralized MEG

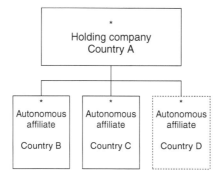

Source: Author

- This prototype is equivalent to the one depicted by prototype G (1–3) or H in which the MEG is non-integrated, only that here the focus is on the insolvency of a particular subsidiary.

---

[99] In regard to group liability the focus is on the insolvent subsidiary, however, when the insolvent affiliate is the parent company this may give rise to issues of avoidance (see chapter 9).

[100] See section 5.2.

[101] See section 5.3.2.

[102] I.e., it is a combination of the second category of the insolvency factor, the second class of the integration factor, and the second class of the centralization factor (sections 5.3.1–5.3.3).

[103] I.e., it is a combination of the second category of the insolvency factor, the second class of the integration factor, and the third class of the centralization factor (sections 5.3.1–5.3.3).

Prototype M: Insolvent subsidiary in non-integrated heterarchical MEG

- This prototype is similar to the one depicted by prototype L, only that here it is a heterarchical scenario (as in prototype C).[104]

Mixture of prototypes

The prototypes represent typical illustrative cases. However, it should be noted that a given MEG insolvency case may in reality contain a mixture of the prototypes that were described above. Thus, for instance, it could be the case of an integrated centralized single head insolvent MEG (as in prototype A1), with one (or more) subsidiary that was significantly autonomous (as in prototype B1)—demonstrated in the figure below:

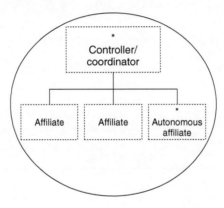

Source: Author

5.5 Summary

This chapter aimed at providing a taxonomy that will assist the following analysis of measures for insolvencies within MEGs by way of devising certain prototypical scenarios that primarily bear relevance to the issue of linking between members of a MEG in its insolvency (recognizing the group for various purposes). These prototypes were shaped along three key factors: the sort of insolvency scenario, the degree of integration, and the degree and manner of centralization. The use of the prototypes will become clearer when the issues pertaining to insolvencies within MEGs will be addressed. For example, when considering the merits of linking tools in the course of handling the insolvencies of several affiliates in light of wealth maximization and rescue attempts, the impact of any potential measures will be assessed in regard to 'asset integrated insolvent MEGs'

---

[104] I.e., it is a combination of the second category of the insolvency factor, the third class of the integration factor, and the third class of the centralization factor (sections 5.3.1–5.3.3).

(prototypes D–F) as well as the integrated scenarios (prototypes A–C), and possible nuances in this respect where the cases involves for example a single head centralized MEG (prototype A1) as opposed to a decentralized single head insolvent MEG (prototype B1) and so forth.[105] These discussions will be based on real cases of real MEGs, thus providing examples for the relevant scenarios.

---

[105] See chapter 6.

PART III

THE QUEST FOR APPROPRIATE SOLUTIONS FOR INSOLVENCY WITHIN MULTINATIONAL ENTERPRISE GROUPS

6

Preservation of the Estate, Maximization of Value, and Facilitation of Rescues

6.1 Introduction

The question this chapter deals with is whether and to what extent the MEG should be recognized as a unit (linking between its components) in the course of insolvency, for the purpose of preserving the insolvency estate, maximizing value, and enabling rescues in the handling of the insolvency process. Bearing in mind entity and territoriality concerns, the framework proposed in the previous parts of this work—the goal-driven adaptive balanced entity–enterprise, territoriality–universality approach—will be applied in answering this question. Essentially, the focus is on key *ex post* aspects of efficiency (i.e. after the event of default) in the handling of the insolvency process within MEGs. That is, reducing transaction costs in the course of insolvency and maximizing returns.[1] Another concern would be to facilitate reorganizations. In contrast this chapter will not deal with the effect of the rules on pre-entitlements of stakeholders, what would be a fair distribution of the estate among them, and the clarity and predictability of the rules.[2] Nor will it deal with issues of procedural justice that may pertain to such mechanisms.[3]

It was mentioned earlier that asset maximization requires a collective procedure, at least where other alternatives to mandatory insolvency procedures are impractical.[4] In an international insolvency case involving several entities, with many creditors with different interests located in different jurisdictions, the

---

[1] Though, several aspects also affecting the efficiency of the process will be discussed in later chapters. It was mentioned in chapter 4 that certainty enhances *ex ante* efficiency (before the event of default) but also *ex post* efficient resolution of disputes (within the insolvency process). This aspect (enhancing certainty and predictability) will be discussed in chapter 8. Expertise, accountability, creditors' participation may all affect *ex post* efficiency and will be discussed in chapter 7, section 7.5. Additionally, remedies in insolvency for combating group opportunism may swell the estate as well as reduce *ex ante* inefficiencies. This issue will be considered in chapter 9.

[2] These matters will be explored in chapters 7–9 (where they have particular relevance to the group case).

[3] On which see in chapter 7.

[4] See chapter 4, section 4.2.2.

likelihood of 'non-legal' solutions diminishes.[5] The main focus will thus be on formal collective procedures. Here, if the business as a whole is worth more than its parts or there is going concern surplus, the aim is to benefit from this prospect (in terms of increasing the insolvency estate). It is not in issue whether liquidation or rescue should be pursued, nor is it the purpose to suggest a particular type of reorganization procedure (including the type of representation—whether it is the debtor remaining in control over the process or professional appointees replacing the management[6]). It was mentioned earlier that the system should strive to provide a rescue procedure, yet this could take different shapes.[7] The issue here is whether both in rescue and liquidation, there are any particular concerns where a MEG is involved in terms of maximizing results. In this respect, the need for timely and efficient resolution of the insolvency was highlighted earlier, including easy use and access to information about the debtor to enable efficient assessment of its situation (which will assist in examining what is the most appropriate solution for the business).[8] These aspects should also be examined when considering the case of the MEG in distress.

In regard to single debtors operating worldwide, cross-border insolvency models, conscious of the risk that value will be lost due to fragmentation of the business among jurisdictions, postulate that insolvency proceedings should operate efficiently and effectively, maximizing value of the debtor's assets and increasing return to creditors.[9] In the case of a MEG matters are even more sensitive. Assets of the 'business' may be spread between different entities located within different states; solvent entities may be dependent on insolvent related companies; intergroup dealing may be difficult to ascertain; creditors may have claims against more than one entity and so on. Questions then arise as to whether to conduct separate proceedings against the group entities, or rather with a degree of unification (and to what degree). If the latter is taken on board, which of the entities will be included in such unification, and to what extent should it and can it be done across borders? Can a moratorium on enforcement apply in other countries? What will be the forum overseeing a unified process? What is the law that will apply to foreign entities? How can all relevant information be gathered? Can a 'unified plan' be binding in foreign jurisdictions? These, and additional related issues, are crucial to an efficient process of insolvency within MEGs.

---

[5] See L. Qi, 'The rise of pre-packaged corporate rescues on both sides of the Atlantic' (2007) 20(9) Insolv. Int. 129, 131–2.

[6] See chapter 4, sections 4.2.2.2 and 4.2.3.5. The work will use the term 'representative' to mean any type of person or body governing the insolvency process.

[7] Ibid, sections 4.2.2.1 and 4.2.3.3.

[8] Ibid.

[9] See e.g. Articles 13 and 17 of the Model Law (n 212 chapter 3) and the Recitals to the EC Regulation (n 173 chapter 3) especially Recitals (2) and (8). See also I.F. Fletcher, 'The European Union Regulation on Insolvency Proceedings', INSOL INTERNATIONAL CROSS-BORDER INSOLVENCY A Guide to Recognition and Enforcement (2003) 15, 20.

Appreciating the diversified scene of insolvencies within MEGs, the proto-types suggested in chapter 5 will assist in determining appropriate solutions. Ultimately, the purpose is to achieve the goals and tasks (in focus in this chapter) while making an appropriate balance in regard to the underlying conflicts inherent to MEG—that is, the entity–enterprise law, and territoriality–universality dilemmas.

6.2 A Global Unified Approach to 'Business Integrated' MEGs in Distress

6.2.1 Benefiting from package sales and going concern surpluses

6.2.1.1 Why and when 'linking' between the group entities across borders is beneficial

The first stage in maximizing value to the creditors as a whole is the preservation of the estate. The next is identifying what is most likely to maximize the firm's value. In many cases the answer to the latter question will be a sale of all or certain assets together, possibly as a going concern. In certain cases, it will be possible to rescue the business and bring it back to productivity. The question is what does that mean in the case of a MEG. A MEG is comprised of legally separate entities, located in different countries, and therefore such solutions (i.e., a sale of all assets, rescue of the business) may initially seem relevant for each entity in the group on a separate basis within states' boundaries. However, this may result in loss of value.

Consider prototypes A–C, (identified in chapter 5[10]), which depict business integration scenarios (in different variations, encompassing the degree of centralization as well[11]). In all these prototypes, there are several entities (a parent and a subsidiary or a number of subsidiaries, or several sister companies) in financial distress, so the focus is on insolvency solutions for a number of entities, which together constituted a business integrated enterprise.[12] In these types of MEG, the group operated either as a single business (on a worldwide basis), or as a conglomerate with more diversity of operations but with significant financial or administrative interdependence.[13] The entities comprising the MEG were linked either via equity or had contractual linkages (e.g. in franchisor–franchisees relationships).[14] Essentially, the more the business is inter-linked in any of these ways the more there is a potential for added value in considering the group as a

---

[10] See chapter 5, section 5.4.

[11] On this aspect see sections 6.2.1.8–6.2.1.10.

[12] See chapter 5, sections 5.3.1. Solvent member may also join a unified solution that may be designed for the business, yet this would be an ordinary business decision of the solvent entity (see further section 6.2.1.2).

[13] See chapter 5, section 5.3.2.

[14] See chapter 1, section 1.3 and chapter 5, section 5.2.

whole in its insolvency. This is simply because businesswise it was not really a case of several different firms. Hence, if the whole *is* worth more than its parts then the whole may well mean the whole of the business comprising the whole (or several) of the entities located in different countries. It may otherwise relate to a division of the business, which includes more than one entity in more than one jurisdiction. In terms of economic realities 'the whole' or the 'going concern' is not matched to an entity's assets or business within national borders.

A linkage (i.e. a unified solution, recognizing the group)[15] in 'business integrated' distressed MEGs thus may be needed, 'mimicking' the MEG's 'real' way of conducting the business in its 'golden days' and its operational links—in the course of insolvency. This is especially vital when considering rescues, either a pure rescue (saving the companies) or partial rescue (saving the business, selling it as a going concern). Here, a sort of collectivity on a group-global scale will be advantageous, first in order to preserve the estate (as a whole) and then to be able to make an intelligent use of the groups' assets, for the purpose of the continuation of the business. As this is crucial in a single multinational debtor scenario,[16] it should similarly be critical in the 'business integrated' MEG case. The stakeholders (viewed as a whole on a group-global-wide level) can then benefit from the strength of the group enterprise (which may have also gained a reputation as such in its 'golden days'),[17] and its variety of assets (although located and owned by different entities), which may be crucial for the MEG's business continuation.

In the absence of a global group-wide solution allowing for such unification, a sort of 'common pool' problem may arise.[18] Assuming that the usual common pool problem in regard to the creditors vis-à-vis their debtor is solved on the entity level, by subjecting each entity to an insolvency procedure; and that the international aspect of the problem (grabbing assets of the particular entity

---

[15] In the following sections below, a particular mechanism for achieving such a linkage will be considered.

[16] See chapter 3, sections 3.3.2.1 and 3.3.3. Indeed, in a reorganization of a single debtor, it is regarded as crucial that the debtor should be able to use all the assets which are important for the continuation of the business' operations, and that would be impossible if creditors in different jurisdictions can 'grab' them, or if assets are concealed in other jurisdictions (see e.g., Article 17 of the Model Law (n 212 chapter 3), explaining that '[t]o the extent there is a lack of communication...it is more likely that assets would be concealed or dissipated, and possibly liquidated without reference to other possible, more advantageous solutions'). See also K.S. Alwang, 'Notes, Steering the most appropriate course between admiralty and Insolvency: Why an International Insolvency Treaty should Recognize the Primacy of Admiralty Law over Maritime Assets' (1996) 64 Fordham L. Rev. 2613, 2625 (claiming that 'reorganization is unlikely if foreign creditors can attach, in multiple countries, the assets necessary for the debtor to continue operating').

[17] Landers notes that creditors may benefit from the multi-corporate nature of their debtor. He mentions the example of conglomerate mergers where the government may object to the acquisition of one concern by another on the basis that it makes the resulting concern too strong (see J. Landers, 'Another Word on Parents, Subsidiaries and Affiliates in Bankruptcy' (1976) 43 U. Chi. L. Rev. 527, 528, citing Turner, 'Conglomerate Mergers and Section 7 of the Clayton Act' (1965) 78 Harv. L. Rev. 1313, 1322–93).

[18] On the classic 'common pool' problem when the debtor is insolvent see chapter 4, section 4.2.2.1.

located in foreign jurisdictions) is resolved by subjecting the entity to a global collective process by applying some kind of cross-border insolvency model based on a degree of universalism;[19] still, we are left with a kind of group-wide international insolvency 'common pool' problem now occurring in a multiple-entity context within the insolvency process of the various entities vis-à-vis the MEG. Here, the whole group can be regarded as 'co-owned' by the stakeholders of the different entities, though in a limited way, in terms of entitlement to benefit from the surplus or premium deriving from the group strength rather than entitlement to the assets of other entities. Yet, in the absence of an orderly cooperation on a global group-wide scale, each entity's stakeholders may attempt to 'grab entities' (i.e. commence a local entity-based procedure), fearing that stakeholders or representatives of other entities will attempt to reach over them via other jurisdictions' extraterritorial rules (which may apply enterprise concepts and for example allow them to be placed under insolvency in the jurisdiction of the parent company). This can lead to a race to the courthouse placing subsidiaries under insolvency when this is perhaps unnecessary, and to loss of value from the possible cooperation that may enhance the estate of each entity. This may result in considerable damage to the whole group of stakeholders when viewed 'from the top' on a group-global scale, i.e. the prospect of maximizing value of the estate for the benefit of the stakeholders (of the MEG) as a whole.

What is needed is some sort of centralized control or coordination over the entire MEG. That is, the part of the MEG which is 'business integrated' as aforementioned.[20] The MEG may include solvent and insolvent entities. But, it may well be that all those parts which are integrated will eventually suffer from financial difficulty even if initially this is noticeable only in several entities of the business (as the financial state of a member of the group may jeopardize the financial survival of other affiliates).[21] A 'domino effect' may occur resulting from the interrelation between the group constituents, especially if there were significant cross-guarantees and mutual transactions, but also where there was otherwise interdependence in terms of the business. To be able to construe a global rescue it should be possible to consider the entire 'business integrated' MEG as much as possible at the same time. A single authority can then oversee the entire enterprise that will have all relevant information and accordingly direct it to a profitable way.[22] At the least, a degree of coordination between group members' proceedings is needed. This will also enable the devisal of various beneficial restructurings on

---

[19] See national and international solutions for cross-border insolvencies in chapter 3, section 3.4.2.

[20] See also I. Mevorach, 'The road to a suitable and comprehensive global approach to insolvencies within multinational corporate groups' [2006] JBLP 455 where an argument for a need for global solutions for integrated corporate groups is put forward.

[21] See also J.S. Ziegel, 'Corporate Groups and Crossborder Insolvencies: A Canada–United States Perspective' (2002) 7 Fordham J. Corp. & Fin. L. 367, 370.

[22] Creditors' participation in such decisions is another crucial aspect which will be considered later on (see chapter 7, section 7.5).

a group scale, ultimately reaching a global unified plan for all relevant entities. To succeed in such a mission, it may be necessary to close down particular divisions of the business (operating across entities), concentrating on specific more viable elements, or cutting down certain projects (that may take place across entities). Urgent measures may be necessary,[23] and unification may ensure this can be achieved on a group-wide level. Funding issues can then also be considered on a global group-wide level. If reorganization of some kind is sought, new finance for the operation of the business in the course of the insolvency process (normally termed 'post-commencement financing') is vital.[24] Considering the matter on a group level can broaden the opportunities in this respect too. For example, it may be possible to seek funding from group members, those that are under insolvency or solvent members (if the latter consent to give such funding[25]), or to provide securities or guarantees by certain members for financing received by other members. Basically, an overall control or coordination over the 'business integrated' MEG insolvency will allow the best utilization of the MEG's resources to be sought. Otherwise, it will be highly difficult to direct the way the business goes ahead. It would be extremely problematic to reorganize such a business if each part of it is managed separately and is left to pull in its own direction.

The 'destructive' effect one group member's financial state may have on another group member (both belonging to an integrated MEG) noted above, also implies that there are mutual interests among such entities and their stakeholders. The interest of any specific company within a group that anticipates better value if it is preserved, is that the entire business (or its viable part) will be preserved as well. Liquidation of another particular component may have a damaging effect upon the reputation of the rest of the group. It may also affect the viability of the other entities (and may possibly lead to their total shutdown). Conversely, when a certain subsidiary is a burden on the others then in order to stabilize the business it may be necessary to close it down.

The need for unification (for the sake of enhancing asset value) is somewhat less acute where rescue of sort is not pursued, where it is not the aim to benefit from the going concern surplus and the strength of the operating business of the entire MEG. However, it could still be the case that some sort of 'package sale' of assets (belonging to several entities) would generate greater value.[26] As explained earlier,[27] such deals are likely to increase cash receipts in selling groups of assets, compared with sales of assets on an isolated basis. The question then is which

[23] See chapter 4, section 4.2.2.1.

[24] See e.g. G. McCormack, 'Super-priority new financing and corporate rescue' [2007] JBL 701, 702.

[25] If the company is not under insolvency, it is a matter for that company to determine (under normal company law) whether it agrees to provide such finance.

[26] This will add to other possible cost benefits of unification in liquidation, for instance preventing multiplicity of claims resulting from the inter-connections among the group members (see section 6.2.2).

[27] See chapter 4, section 4.2.2.1.

entity of the group legally owns the relevant assets that together may create a beneficial 'group' in terms of returns. In 'business integration' scenarios it may well be the case that such assets are spread among the different foreign entities, especially in the first example of 'business integration' where the various entities altogether conduct a single business (so assets of same nature may be possessed by the entities). In such a case the same rationale of subjecting the whole MEG to some sort of unified global process that enables global deals of this sort to be conducted can enhance the estate's value.[28]

An obvious example will be when each company comprising the MEG owned a certain part of a complete product. In this case a combined sale may be both more practical and likely to result in higher consideration than separate sales. Consider for instance a railway network operating in a number of countries. The assets of this network are actually divided between subsidiaries incorporated in the different states in which the railway is operating. To sell the network in pieces may significantly reduce the price received. Similarly, if a number of related patents and licences are owned each by a different entity in a group then obviously selling the assets in parts is extremely disadvantageous. It may also be the case when assets of similar sort are scattered amongst various entities that are valuable as a mass of assets and less attractive if sold to different buyers. It is even likely that a buyer for an entire enterprise (although comprised of separate entities) may be willing to pay an added premium compared to the price of the assets alone or to the price of the separate activities of each component. Enabling global deals also broadens the opportunities available for the companies in distress. It gives the administrators 'a room for manoeuvre' in their attempt to reach the best deal and the best price. It may be, for example, financially wiser to reject certain offers that may be available to a specific component in a certain moment, since a larger and better deal is starting to form elsewhere.

It is not to say that in all scenarios of 'business integrated' MEGs the ultimate solution for the 'firm' is a group-wide rescue or package sale across the global group. A full global rescue may be unwise and unattainable (if for instance, the business is not viable) and similarly a package group-wide sale in liquidation may not be achievable (for example because of lack of funding or sufficient competition). Yet, because these prototypes depict 'business integration' it is beneficial to consider the option of such solutions for the MEG or parts thereof when determining 'what to do with the firm', as initially, in terms of commercial realities, the firm *is* the MEG. To be able to make such considerations the MEG entities' insolvencies should be 'linked'. Another thing to take into account is the degree of additional costs that may occur in conducting a separate process in a 'business integrated' MEG scenario.[29]

---

[28] Such package sales of corporate groups' assets are also envisaged in the ALI Principles as a potential benefit of global unified solutions in such cases (ALI Principles (n 243 chapter 3) Illustration to Procedural Principle 24).

[29] On which see section 6.2.2.

On the other hand in prototypes G–H,[30] i.e. when the MEG is weakly or non-integrated, or a particular entity is remote from the group (for instance was held for pure investment purposes, or is a special purpose vehicle (SPV) designed to stay remote),[31] there is a much smaller chance that the MEG's stakeholders will gain any benefit (added value to the MEG assets) from a unified global solution. Most often, the insolvency of one part of such a group will not affect the rest, so an entire collapse would be rare. Even if the insolvency will encompass the whole or several entities in the group, linking between the fragments of the group, typically, will not provide a significant advantage in terms of increasing revenues. The proceedings will involve a variety of unrelated businesses of different nature, assets of diverse sorts, and, generally, an assortment of components that do not represent one single business that would gain from reconstruction or from a joint sale. However, the dynamic nature of insolvency should be appreciated and the possibility that new information may be revealed (or new opportunities will come along) suggesting a linkage with such entities would benefit wealth maximization. Yet, the presumption in these cases is that linkage is not needed.

Returning to a situation when a global unified solution is predicted to be beneficial, a few points should be further clarified. First, a global unified solution is very likely to be beneficial to MEGs even if it is not a case where there was a 'mess' between the entities comprising the group, i.e. what was earlier termed 'asset integration' (prototypes D–F[32]), in which case the entities were commingled in the ordinary course of business.[33] This is a situation that may well demand linking tools, even 'stronger' ones.[34] But it does not have to be a case of 'asset integration' in order for unified global mechanisms to be beneficial in terms of adding value to the estate as explained in this section.

The existence of inter-group transactions or cross-guarantees is also not a prerequisite for a beneficial linkage (although, it adds a reinforcing justification for connecting between the insolvencies). It may be the case of a host of subsidiaries operating rather separately with independent administration, dealing mainly with outsiders. Still, the fact that all the fragments were connected in such a way that they all operated a single business and were ultimately managed or coordinated as a group suggests that it would benefit from global asset realizations in the event of insolvency. Similarly, if there were inter-group links this may result in a de facto integration even though the businesses may appear to be separate (the 'conglomerate' type of MEG that operates different businesses).[35] The fact that 'under the surface' linkages and interrelations (such as administrative support and financial interdependence) exist, may imply that the different companies are not truly commercially and financially independent. Rather, the 'concern' relates

---

[30] See chapter 5, sections 5.4.   [31] See ibid, section 5.3.2.
[32] See ibid, section 5.4.   [33] Ibid.   [34] See section 6.3.
[35] See chapter 5, section 5.3.2 and Figure 2 of prototype B1 (ibid, section 5.4).

to the MEG, and thus a linkage in the course of insolvency will be essential in order to consider unified solutions.

A global unified solution also does not necessarily stipulate a 'mess' across borders of each entity, i.e. a situation where the assets, debts, activities and so forth of each of the entities (of the business integrated MEG) are spread among different countries, so that they are not neatly organized within the borders of one country. In other words, each entity when viewed separately may be a domestic one with no 'international elements' apart from its connections with related entities. It suffices that the MEG business is one whole or that there were inter-links among its entities, that global unification of some sort should be considered.

It is only when the MEG is weakly or non-integrated (as explained above) that presumably there is no need for any sort of unification. Even then, though, each entity in its insolvency may require solutions based on a degree of universalism due to its own cross-border elements. This is, however, not the concern here, as this is a single entity (cross-border insolvency) situation.

In sum, in cases of 'business integrated' MEGs, unified global consideration of what to do with the firm (i.e. the MEG) is crucial in terms of enabling value enhancement for the stakeholders of the group as a whole. Thus, the decision-making process should take place with a view of the MEG in mind. Recognition of the MEG as such in terms of handling its various insolvencies is needed. A degree of enterprise–universalistic solutions is therefore envisaged. In that case, it should be considered to what extent such approach will result in excessive harm to concepts of entity law and territoriality. In order to appreciate what is at stake in this respect, 'enterprise law mechanisms' and global unifying methods should be considered.

6.2.1.2 Mechanisms for group-wide insolvencies

It was shown in chapter 2 that legal systems, although generally adhering to entity principles, do embrace various 'enterprise law' concepts, recognizing the group or the relationships among group members for various purposes.[36] In the context of insolvency certain legal regimes provide mechanisms for the 'consolidation' of insolvency proceedings of related companies. Essentially these are means to unify between the proceedings of different members of a group.

The mechanism of procedural consolidation[37] implies that only the procedural aspect of the insolvency is being consolidated (i.e. the proceedings can be administered jointly, instead of on a separate basis) but the actual entities remain intact. There is no consolidation of assets and debts. Each entity remains indebted to its own creditors and the owner of its assets. The idea is mainly to

---

[36] See chapter 2, section 2.4.

[37] The terms 'joint administration', 'administrative consolidation' and 'procedural coordination' are also being used for this sort of mechanism. This work will refer to these terms as well as to 'procedural consolidation', interchangeably.

facilitate reorganization of the affairs of the whole enterprise or to bring about a going concern sale.[38] This is to be distinguished from 'substantive consolidation'[39] where the entities are consolidated (a mechanism which will be discussed later on).

US bankruptcy law, for example, explicitly permits in legislation the procedural consolidation of insolvency proceedings of several affiliates (the components of a corporate group).[40] This is facilitated by the venue provisions allowing filing by affiliates in the same court (so long as the first petitioner has a sufficient connection with the jurisdiction).[41] The Bankruptcy Rules further allow for the election of a single trustee to preside over the joint process.[42] Thus, large Chapter 11 cases (the US reorganization procedure) of corporate groups will often result in a single reorganization plan for the entire group.[43] The common practice in such large bankruptcy cases is to open the proceedings in regard to all subsidiaries in the group (even if some of them are not insolvent at the time[44]), so as to avoid the inefficiency of having new proceedings being opened consecutively and disorderly and so that a plan for the group as a whole can be devised.[45] Under US law procedural consolidation does not have any substantive consequences and creditors are attached to the particular subsidiary.[46] It thus does not affect the substantive rights and liabilities of the stakeholders and the allocation of assets according to the priorities provided by the law, which will ascribe to each entity separately.[47] Procedural consolidation in the US is regarded as 'a matter of convenience and cost saving'.[48]

---

[38] See I. Mevorach, 'Appropriate treatment of corporate groups in insolvency—a universal view' (2006) 8 EBOR, 179, 189.

[39] Also sometimes termed 'pooling' of assets and debts. This work will refer to these terms interchangeably.

[40] See US Bankruptcy Rule 1015.

[41] See 28 USC, s. 1408. Separate filings are initially required, and thereafter a consolidation order is needed (see Blumberg et al, *Blumberg on Corporate Groups* (n 31 chapter 1) vol 2, s. 88.03).

[42] Fed. R. Bankr. P. 2009(a).

[43] See information provided by LoPucki in J.S. Ziegel, 'Corporate Groups and Crossborder Insolvencies: A Canada–United States Perspective' (2002) 7 Fordham J. Corp. & Fin. L. 367, 387).

[44] This is facilitated by the fact that under US bankruptcy law insolvency is not a prerequisite for commencing the process.

[45] I am indebted to Ron DeKoven of 3/4 South Square barrister chambers for sharing his views on common practices in the US with respect to procedural consolidations under Chapter 11.

[46] Blumberg et al, *Blumberg on Corporate Groups* (n 31 chapter 1) vol 2, s. 88.03.

[47] See D.G. Baird, 'Substantive Consolidation Today' [2006] 47 B.C.L. Rev. 5, 6; Blumberg et al, *Blumberg on Corporate Groups* (n 31 chapter 1) vol 2, s. 88.02. See also *In re Northeast Dairy Coop.* Fed'n, Inc., 88 Bankr. 21, 25 (Bankr. NDNY 1998) and *In re Chateauaugay Corp.*, 141 Bankr. 794 (SDNY 1992) in which the court emphasized the administrative nature (as opposed to substantive) of the procedural consolidation facility.

[48] See e.g. *In re Coles*, 14 BR 5, 5–6 (Bankr. ED Pa 1981).

Joint administration of this nature is also available in other jurisdictions.[49] In certain countries,[50] as a matter of practice, a single insolvency office holder can be appointed in respect of each group member enabling a de facto coordination of the process in regard to affiliates' insolvency proceedings.[51]

UNCITRAL Working Group V[52] (in considering the treatment of enterprise groups in insolvency) has discussed in its meetings certain draft recommendations concerning handling the insolvency proceedings against group members in a joint manner.[53] Thus, it is currently provided in the Working Group's working papers, that allowing a joint application for commencement of insolvency proceedings against group members would be beneficial in terms of facilitation of coordinated consideration of such applications, facilitation of efficiency, and reduction of costs.[54] It is further being considered, that it should then be possible to procedurally coordinate the proceedings; here too procedural efficiency concerns are emphasized.[55] It is also emphasized by the Working Group that under procedural coordination and joint applications, the separate legal entity

---

[49] See e.g. J.S. Ziegel, 'Corporate Groups and Crossborder Insolvencies: A Canada–United States Perspective' (2002) 7 Fordham J. Corp. & Fin. L. 367, 376; J.S. Ziegel, 'Canada-United States Cross-Border Insolvency Relations and the UNCITRAL Model Law (2007) 32 Brook. J. Int'l L. 1041, 1050 (noting that procedural consolidation is very common in Canada). UNCITRAL Note by the Secretariat, Working Group V (Insolvency Law), mentions (apart from procedural consolidation in the US) South Africa, Spain, France, Argentina and Mexico procedural consolidation regimes (see UNCITRAL Note by the Secretariat, Working Group V (Insolvency Law), 4 October 2006, A/CN.9/WG.V/WP.74/Add.1, p. 5 para. 12, available at: http://www.uncitral.org/uncitral/en/commission/working_groups/5Insolvency.html) [hereinafter: WP.74/Add.1].

[50] Including Australia, England, and Germany (see ibid, para. 14).

[51] Moss et al mention, in regard to English law based jurisdictions, that such cooperation is often ensured by having the same insolvency practitioners from the same major firm of accountants, appointed as liquidators to the various entities comprising a corporate group (see Moss et al, *The EC Regulation* (n 174 chapter 3) 173).

[52] See n 96 chapter 1.

[53] Note that at the time the book went to print the work is still in progress. As mentioned earlier, reference is made to relevant draft recommendations, notes or draft commentary, mainly from recent working papers which were the basis for discussions in the fourth Working Group meeting (New York, 3–7 March 2008) on which a report has already been published, and to subsequent working papers which were provided as material for the fifth meeting of the Working Group (Vienna, 17–21 November 2008) (see n 96 chapter 1 and n 140 chapter 3).

[54] See WP.80 (n 98 chapter 1), draft recommendation 1 (including the preceding purpose clause); Report, thirty-fourth session (n 98 chapter 1), para. 31; UNCITRAL Note by the Secretariat, Working Group V (Insolvency Law), 2 September 2008, A/CN.9/WG.V/WP.82/Add.1 available at: http://www.uncitral.org/uncitral/en/commission/working_groups/5Insolvency.html [hereinafter: WP.82/Add.1], draft recommendation 1 (including the preceding purpose clause) and paras. 5–17.

[55] See WP.80 (n 98 chapter 1), draft recommendations 2–8; Report, thirty-fourth session (n 98 chapter 1), paras. 36–44; WP.82/Add.1 (n 54), draft recommendations 3–9 and paras. 18–29. It is stressed though that a joint application against several group members would not necessarily lead to procedural coordination, though it might facilitate the court taking a decision on procedural coordination (ibid, para. 8).

of each group member should be respected.[56] In accordance with this notion, a proposal is further being considered, that creditors making an application for commencement of proceedings against group members in a joint manner will be able to do so only in respect of group members of whom they were creditors.[57] The Working Group is considering provisions that allow for flexibility in terms of the meaning of procedural coordination, which may include situations of a single court dealing with various insolvency proceedings of various members of a group as well as various courts coordinating with each other.[58]

It seems that the idea is to allow joint application by those who have standing to commence proceedings against the relevant entities. The possibility of procedural coordination can then be considered at the same time as the application of commencement or later on in the process. It could be an initiative of one of the parties or the insolvency representative.[59] The administration of the insolvency proceedings may then be coordinated for procedural purposes.[60] This can take place either under the supervision of a single court or via coordination among several proceedings opened in different courts.

Additional aspects of unified administration, pertaining to preservation of the estate and increasing asset value,[61] are also being considered. The Working Group currently stresses the importance of post-commencement financing in the group context.[62] The usual incentives that may be given to post-commencement lenders should be applied in the group context where a solvent member or an external lender provides finance to a group member under insolvency proceedings.[63] Additionally, the Working Group considers specific recommendations in regard to provision of post-commencement finance provided to one member subject to insolvency proceedings by another member also subject to insolvency proceedings. Apart from allowing the provision of incentives to such post-commencement finance, the provision of cross-entity support in these situations should be accompanied by considerations of possible harm that may be caused

---

[56] WP.80 (n 98 chapter 1), para B.1 (purpose clause); Report, thirty-fourth session (n 98 chapter 1), Para. 37; WP.82/Add.1 (n 54), purpose clause preceding draft recommendation 3.

[57] See WP.80 (n 98 chapter 1), draft recommendation 1(b); Report, thirty-fourth session (n 98 chapter 1), paras. 32–35; WP.82/Add.1 (n 54), draft recommendation 1(b) and para. 14.

[58] Report, thirty-fourth session (n 98 chapter 1), para. 24; WP.82 (n 98 chapter 1), para. 2(e); WP.82/Add.1 (n 54), paras. 18–21.

[59] See WP.80 (n 98 chapter 1), draft recommendation 4; Report, thirty-fourth session (n 98 chapter 1), para. 39. WP.82/Add.1 (n 54), draft recommendation 4.

[60] See WP.80 (n 98 chapter 1), draft recommendation 3; Report, thirty-fourth session (n 98 chapter 1), para. 38; WP.82/Add.1 (n 54), draft recommendation 3.

[61] See also the Working Group's discussions in regard to the issue of voting (chapter 7, section 7.2.2.1) and aspects of procedural fairness (chapter 7, section 7.5) pertaining to joint solutions for group insolvencies.

[62] See UNCITRAL, UNCITRAL Note by the Secretariat, Working Group V (Insolvency Law), 4 September 2008, A/CN.9/WG.V/WP.82/Add.2 [hereinafter: WP.82/Add.2], paras. 13–15. See also section 6.2.1.1.

[63] See recommendations 63–8 of the Legislative Guide (n 137 chapter 3); Report, thirty fourth session (n 98 chapter 1), para. 48; WP.82/Add.2 (n 62), paras. 16–19.

to creditors of the enterprise providing the support. This should be balanced by considering the overall gain in the long term which will generate from the provision of such financing.[64]

Furthermore, the Working Group currently considers enabling a single representative to be appointed for two or more group members under insolvency.[65] Otherwise, if more than one representative is appointed it suggests enabling cooperation among representatives (to the maximum extent possible).[66] It specifies a wide array of issues that may be the subject of such cooperation including the need to share information between the representatives,[67] division of power over the enterprise, responsibilities (and the possibility of any of the representatives taking a leading role), coordination of reorganization plans proposals, and coordination of administration of debtors' affairs including matters of funding, preservation, and selling of assets.[68]

It is also currently stressed by the Working Group, that insolvency law should permit a single reorganization plan for an enterprise group.[69] This may take place within a procedural coordination process or in the absence of a formal order of coordination. The Working Group envisages group-wide reorganization plans comprising several group members under insolvency, yet an enterprise group entity which is not subject to insolvency proceedings may participate in such a plan as well. This will be based on an ordinary business decision taken by that member, subject to applicable company law. It is further explained that the plan will need to be approved in regard to all members subject to the plan. Voting on and approving the plan is to be conducted by the creditors of each entity on a separate basis.[70]

---

[64] See WP.80 (n 98 chapter 1), draft recommendations 9–13; Report, thirty-fourth session (n 98 chapter 1), paras. 45–54; WP.82/Add.2 (n 62), draft recommendations 10–13, and paras. 20–9 (the commentary also notes that problems of conflict of interest may arise where for example a single representative is appointed and needs to determine on issues of intra-group post-commencement finance. On the issue of conflict of interests see chapter 7, section 7.5.4).

[65] See UNCITRAL, UNCITRAL Note by the Secretariat, Working Group V (Insolvency Law), 2 January 2008, A/CN.9/WG.V/WP.80/Add.1; available at http://www.uncitral.org/uncitral/en/commission/working_groups/5Insolvency.html [hereinafter: WP.80/Add 1], draft recommendation 24; Report, thirty-fourth session (n 98 chapter 1), para. 78; UNCITRAL, UNCITRAL Note by the Secretariat, Working Group V (Insolvency Law), 4 September 2008, A/CN.9/WG.V/WP.82/Add.3 [hereinafter: WP.82/Add.3], draft recommendation 26, and paras. 42–7.

[66] WP.80/Add 1 (n 65), draft recommendations 26 and 27; Report, thirty-fourth session (note 98 chapter 1), para. 80; WP.82/Add.3 (n 65), draft recommendations 28 and 29. Such cooperation may take place even in the absence of a formal procedural coordination order. It is also currently emphasized, that cooperation may be achieved directly between the courts (ibid, para. 44).

[67] This also has implications for cost reduction (see section 6.2).

[68] WP.80/ Add 1 (n 65), draft recommendation 28; Report, thirty-fourth session (n 98 chapter 1), paras. 76–80; WP.82/Add.3 (n 65), draft recommendation 30.

[69] UNCITRAL Working Group currently stresses a broad approach, so that joint administrations of insolvencies against group members may take different paths, not necessarily a reorganization (see WP.80 (n 98 chapter 1), para. 12).

[70] See WP.80/Add 1 (n 65), draft recommendations 29 and 30; Report, thirty-fourth session (n 98 chapter 1), para. 81; WP.82/Add.3 (n 65), draft recommendations 31 and 32, and paras.

These mechanisms described above are compatible with the notion of enabling asset preservation and maximization of value on a group level. It is possible under such regimes to place the various insolvencies under the authority of a single judge and appointee. In particular, as mentioned above, UNCITRAL Working Group V in its work in progress stresses flexibility in the way procedural coordination may take place (which may be a matter of coordination between concurrent proceedings, over which several representatives preside, acting in cooperation). Coordinated solutions for the business may also take place, as mentioned above, without a formal order of procedural coordination. This is of particular merit especially when planning for the international scenario which may demand more flexibility in terms of possible solutions.[71]

It is then possible under such regimes to consider the way ahead for the different entities on a joint basis, and if considered beneficial even devise a unified reorganization plan for all entities. Compatible with the idea of enhancing value for all otherwise separate entities (and stakeholders belonging to distinct entities) these mechanisms would normally not require the elimination of the distinction between the entities, but would encompass the idea of taking 'group considerations' for instance in meeting requirements for commencement of proceedings.[72]

It is not always clear which sort of groups could be the subject of procedural consolidation under such regimes (or other group-wide solutions such as a single reorganization plan achieved by way of cooperation with no procedural consolidation order). As mentioned in chapter 1 different jurisdictions provide different definitions for groups, some based on formalities (such as percentage of voting rights), and some provide broader definitions which encompass the scenario of integration.[73] A formal definition used in procedural consolidation in insolvency may preclude certain enterprises from enjoying the benefits of unification. On the other hand, determining whether to allow procedural consolidation based on the basic definition alone may result in applying procedural consolidation to enterprises which were not necessarily integrated. For example, if the definition regards capacity to control (by, for instance, holding the majority of the voting rights in the subsidiary) as sufficient to create parent–subsidiary relationship, control may not have been exercised and the subsidiary may have operated

---

48–55. See further chapter 7, section 7.2.2.1 on voting on group unified plans and fairness considerations, including reference to the Working Group discussions on the matter.

[71] As will be discussed below. See also I. Mevorach, 'Appropriate treatment of corporate groups in insolvency—a universal view' (2007) 8 EBOR, 179, 184–5 (proposing that in implementing rules regarding group insolvencies by domestic regimes, there should be planning ahead of the international scenario).

[72] Indeed, UNCITRAL Working Group considers that for the purposes of commencement of proceedings by insolvent entities, group considerations may be taken into account in determining whether a member is in imminent insolvency (see WP.80 (n 98 chapter 1), para. 13; WP.82/Add.1 (n 54), para.9).

[73] See chapter 1, section 1.3.7.

a completely separate business not integrated with the rest of the group. In such a case, procedural consolidation may not add benefits to the group as a whole. On the domestic level, however, the matter is less crucial, as it will most likely not cause additional harm in terms of costs.[74]

6.2.1.3 Procedural consolidation and entity law

I argued in chapter 2 that we should distinguish between different levels of breach of the corporate form in respect of measures for dealing with groups. Where the 'holy grail' of entity separateness (that is, the notion of limited liability) is not at stake, the scale can shift more easily towards enterprise law (i.e., recognition of the group and interrelations among the group, closing the gap between law and reality).[75] Procedural consolidation (and other variants of group-wide solutions based on cooperation for administrative purposes as delineated in the previous section) is in line with this contention. Although there is recognition of the group as such (and thus the tool can be regarded as based on enterprise concepts), it is not for the purpose of imposing liability on group members or mixing assets and debts in any way. The unification sought is only procedural, administrative, rather than 'substantive'. Therefore, it is not applied in strict circumstances.

This is only true, however, if the distinction between procedural and substantive effects of the consolidation is duly kept across the board (with respect to all issues that may arise in the course of the consolidation). Only then can it be proclaimed that entity law is kept intact. This includes issues such as commencing insolvency proceedings, voting on plans, distribution of proceeds, providing post-commencement finance and so forth. So long as this is done against the particular entity, and the benefit to the particular entity is safeguarded then entity law is not defeated. Each entity will receive proceeds from a sale according to its contribution to it. The different interests of each entity will be addressed in a unified plan, and the voting on it will be conducted on a separate basis. A question does arise, though, as to whether it should be possible to sacrifice particular entities for the sake of benefiting the group as a whole. For instance, will it be possible to subject a particular entity to the unified plan notwithstanding its dissent? Or, to reject a lucrative offer for sale of its assets for the sake of a package sale which will benefit the group as a whole? To answer these questions, issues of redistribution and fairness in insolvency (in light of the entity–enterprise law dilemma) should be further considered. These issues will be addressed in the next chapter.

For now, it is conceded that so long as preservation and maximization of the assets to the stakeholders of the group as a whole does not result in harm to particular entities (that would not have been otherwise caused, if the group as a whole was not being considered), procedural consolidation as an enterprise law

---

[74] On costs associated with consolidation see section 6.2.2.3.
[75] See chapter 2, section 2.3.3.

tool (and related mechanisms such as the appointment of a single representative and so forth) does not pose problems to entity law. Rather, the two live in peace. What it does is ensure greater gains to the elements of the group and their stakeholders, by taking into account the mutual influence and possible mutual destructiveness. That is, enterprise law steps in to ensure the law mimics commercial realities for the benefit of the group as a whole, where the gains for the whole do not contradict the gains for the parts.

But this is just half way in the quest for global unified measures that will assist in maximizing return in the MEG case. The group which is the subject matter of this work operates on a worldwide basis, and thus it should be considered whether procedural consolidation can be applied on a global basis; in particular, what mechanisms can be used for this purpose, and whether this raises further concerns in terms of entity law or territoriality.

6.2.1.4 *The need for global measures for 'business integrated' MEGs in distress*

In chapter 3 various national and international mechanisms addressing the problem of cross-border insolvency were reviewed. It was mentioned that although initially legal regimes are considered to be territorial in aspiration, in fact there is considerable movement towards greater universality.[76] There are substantial efforts towards harmonization in the realm of insolvency laws, as well as for achieving greater cooperation in international insolvencies and uniformity of private international laws.[77] The general scarceness of explicit consideration of the particular case of the MEG in distress to date was also mentioned.[78]

---

[76] See chapter 3, section 3.4.   [77] Ibid.

[78] The main exceptions are the ALI Principles which offer some solutions (see chapter 3, section 3.4.2.4; see also sections 6.2.1.5 and 6.2.1.6) and now UNCITRAL Working Group V's work in progress on the matter (n 96 chapter 1 and n 140 chapter 3). The latter has up until its last meeting (Vienna, 17–21 November 2008) mainly focused on domestic issues pertaining to enterprise groups. Yet, various materials have been produced by the Working Group's Secretariat on the international aspects pertaining to enterprise groups in insolvency, and the matter has been considered in the last meeting. Though, at the time the book went to print no recommendations (on the international issues) have yet been introduced and discussed by the Working Group (it is expected that such recommendations will be discussed in the next meeting of the Working Group (New York, 18–22 May 2009)). See Report, thirty-fourth session (n 98 chapter 1), paras. 85–91. See also Note by the Secretariat on the international issues in the material for the Working Group's thirty-fifth session (Vienna, 17–21 November 2008) (UNCITRAL, UNCITRAL Note by the Secretariat, Working Group V (Insolvency Law), 10 September 2008, A/CN.9/WG.V/WP.82/Add.4 [hereinafter: WP.82/Add.4]), and previous notes and reports regarding the international issues and the Working Group progress on these matters: UNCITRAL, UNCITRAL Note by the Secretariat, Working Group V (Insolvency Law), 4 October 2006, A/CN.9/WG.V/WP.74/Add.2; UNCITRAL, UNCITRAL Note by the Secretariat, Working Group V (Insolvency Law), 4 October 2006, A/CN.9/WG.V/WP.76/Add.2; Report thirty-first session (n 140 chapter 3), paras. 50–67; UNCITRAL, UNCITRAL Report of Working Group V (Insolvency Law) on the work of its thirty-second session, 25 May 2007, A/CN.9/622, paras. 85–92; Report, thirty-third session (n 97 chapter 1) (all documents available at: http://www.uncitral.org/uncitral/en/commission/working_groups/5Insolvency.html).

As the entities comprising the MEG in distress are located in different countries, a way to enable central control or coordination over their insolvency proceedings on a global level is needed so that procedural consolidation and related
procedures for joint considerations of group members' insolvency proceedings as
mentioned above are applied on a global level. In particular, it should be possible
to open proceedings against the affiliates in a single jurisdiction and handle the
proceedings centrally or otherwise to coordinate between concurrent proceedings taking place in different jurisdictions. The aim is to achieve a global unified
plan binding upon all affiliates and their stakeholders, or otherwise profitable
package sales on an international scale.[79]

A couple of international insolvency cases involving MEGs (one of a process
involving a sale of assets and one involving a restructuring) may exemplify the
loss of value and problems that may arise in uncoordinated proceedings against
'business integrated' MEGs in distress. In the case of KPNQwest N.V. data communication MEG,[80] the assets of the group's components were sold separately,
on an entity-by-entity basis. The result was a rock bottom sale.[81] The fact that
the sales were conducted disjointly was disadvantageous in terms of maximizing values. Since the companies' assets together comprised a data communication network (in this sense the group was 'business integrated', although different
components owned different parts of cable rings) it is very likely that it would
have been more beneficial to attempt to sell the European cyber centres network
as a global network of internet and data hosting facilities, rather than to sell it
in parts.[82] The commencement of the *Parmalat* multinational group's insolvency process, encompassing numerous entities that operated in different countries around the world[83] exemplified the difficulties that a global plan initiative
may face. In this case proceedings were opened in different countries with no

[79] This is also stressed by UNCITRAL Working Group's current discussions of international
issues pertaining to enterprise groups (n 78). It is explained in the Working Group's report that the
objective of the task in the cross-border context would be 'to consider how to maximize the value of
the group and the importance, in that regard, of reorganization' (see Report, thirty-fourth session
(n 98 chapter 1), paras. 90–91).

[80] KPNQwest group owned cables in Europe and across the Atlantic Ocean. The cables ran
through various countries and were owned by subsidiaries of the group situated in these countries.
On 31 May 2002 the Dutch parent company entered bankruptcy proceedings. As a result, many
of its subsidiaries were put under insolvency process as well (see R. Van Galen, 'The European
Insolvency Regulation and Groups of Companies', INSOL Europe Annual Congress, Cork,
Ireland, 16–18 October 2003 (http://www.insol-europe.org)).

[81] Estate Gazette, 'Leading data hosting site offered at a 55M GBP discount' 14 September
2002, NEWS, p. 43; *GLOBALTURNAROUND*, 'KPNQwest in sales drive', June 2002, issue 29,
p. 11.

[82] *GLOBALTURNAROUND*, 'Parmalat is not Europe's Enron It's Italy's Maxwell', January
2004, issue 48, p. 2.

[83] The Italian Dairy group of companies that was operated in Europe, but also in many other
parts of the world, including South America, South Africa, Canada, US and Australia, and that
was headquartered in Italy. The proceedings of Parmalat produced many different episodes of litigation (see in sections 6.2.1.4, 6.2.1.6, 6.2.2.1 and 6.2.2.2; chapter 7, sections 7.5.2 and 7.5.4;
chapter 8, section 8.2; and chapter 9, section 9.2.4).

sufficient cooperation and no one single direction for the entire group. The mandate of the Italian Extraordinary Administrator appointed by the Italian government for several companies in the group [84] was to try and design a reconstruction plan for the whole group, while continuing to operate the business as a going concern.[85] However, one of the greatest threats the administrator faced was disintegration, brought on by local creditors opening separate proceeding against Parmalat entities in different places around the world.[86] Such actions posed a major obstacle for the administrator as they reduced his hold on the units outside Italy and thus interfered with his efforts towards a global restructuring of the group. In general, the experience of the beginnings of the Parmalat insolvency process demonstrated a lack of sufficient cooperation and of central direction and single supervision.[87]

The question here too is what mechanism may assist in achieving greater cooperation for the purpose of promoting the goal of asset value maximization. There are various mechanisms which may potentially 'do the job'. All of which invoke a degree of cross-border linkage, and therefore the need to consider the extent to which such methods are harmful to territoriality concepts. Another matter to consider in this respect is whether any of the universal measures defeat entity law (i.e. considering the operation of entity law in the context of jurisdiction).

---

[84] The appointment took place at the end of the year 2003, in the wake of revelations of widespread fraud by executives.

[85] See Parmalat News Briefs, *DOW JONES Newsletters*, International Insolvency, 9 March 2004, p. 9.

[86] One example is the provisional liquidation process that was opened against three Cayman Islands subsidiaries by US insurance companies, and that were continued to be handled 'separately', after the Italian administrator's loss in gaining control over the process (see judgment of the grand court of the Cayman Islands in the administrator's application to replace the provisional liquidators appointed to a Cayman Islands subsidiary of Parmalat—Parmalat Capital Finance Ltd. (Grand Court of the Cayman Islands, March, 2004, on file with the author); see also 'Parmalat ask Kroll to find assets', *Financial Times*, 2 March 2004; D. Reilly, 'Judge Rejects Administrator's Push To Control Parmalat's Cayman Units', *DOW JONES Newsletters*, International Insolvency, 2 March 2004, p. 1, 3). Other examples are the Brazilian court's decision to appoint administrators to the Brazilian unit (see 'Brazil Unit Says Two Banks Will Provide Credit Lines', *DOW JONES Newsletters*, International Insolvency, 2 March 2004, p. 6); the administration order that has been given by a French court against Parmalat's milk supplier group Laitier des Pyrenees (see 'Parmalat is not Europe's Enron It's Italy's Maxwell', *GLOBALTURNAROUND*, January 2004, issue 48, p. 2); the Irish high court's decision to approve the appointment of Irish provisional liquidators to Parmalat's subsidiary Eurofood IFSC (see *Eurofood IFSC Limited* [2004] BCC 383 (see further on this case in sections 6.2.1.6, 6.2.1.8–6.2.1.9; chapter 7, sections 7.3.2 and 7.5.2; and chapter 8, section 8.2)).

[87] See 'Parmalat is not Europe's Enron it's Italy's Maxwell', *GLOBALTURNAROUND*, January 2004, issue 48, p. 2. See also the Cayman Islands' court decision (n 86) in relation to the agreement between the Italian administrator and the provisional liquidators appointed to the subsidiaries in the Cayman Islands. There, although the parties agreed upon a memorandum providing for cooperation and a mutual exchange and access to information and documentation, in reality 'there has been less than optimal cooperation extended by each party to the other under their memorandum of agreement' (ibid).

6.2.1.5   *Coordination and cooperation, access, recognition, and relief in regard to entities of the business integrated MEG in distress*

Coordination on a global scale may be achieved via means of cooperation between proceedings taking place against group members in different jurisdictions. This is a translation of the idea of (domestic) procedural coordination taking place between concurrent proceedings (against affiliate companies).[88] The notion of cooperation and coordination between concurrent foreign proceedings was mentioned earlier, in regard to the cross-border problem faced by single debtors.[89]

It was mentioned that national regimes may prevent local 'grabbing' of assets and recognize foreign proceedings by applying concepts of comity and judicial assistance especially where the foreign court seems competent and there is no infringement of local notions of public policy.[90] These notions can be applied in the group context in the sense that proceedings taking place against group members (belonging to the same integrated MEG) will be recognized in the jurisdiction where proceedings against other such MEG members are also being handled. Relevant assistance can then be given, providing relevant information to the foreign representative of the foreign affiliate and cooperating in regard to the various issues which may arise. It will be suggested below to be more ambitious in the attempt to harmonizing insolvency processes against group members and in the appropriate circumstances centralize the proceedings fully or partially, but at the least courts should use their discretion (where such is available) to promote cooperation between concurrent proceedings taking place against group members, and parties should be encouraged to resolve potential conflicts arising in this respect.

Further cooperation can be achieved via ad hoc attempts at devising agreements (protocols) or communicating between the foreign representatives or the courts.[91] It was noted in chapter 3 that protocols have been used in practice in cases of global groups to achieve such cooperation. This approach has, in most cases, resulted in efficient administration of the whole insolvency proceedings and, in some cases, enabled a worldwide settlement or an optimal combined plan of reorganization.[92] Communication and cooperation both through the use of

---

[88]   See section 6.2.1.2.
[89]   See chapter 3, sections 3.4.2.1, 3.4.2.3 and 3.4.2.4.
[90]   See chapter 3, section 3.4.2.1.
[91]   Ibid, section 3.4.2.1.
[92]   See, e.g., *In re ICO Global Communications Servs. Inc.*, Case No. 99-2933 (Bankr. D Del 1999); *Global Crossing Ltd* (Chapter 11 No. 02-40188-reg (REG) (Bankr. SDNY); *Re Maxwell Communications Corp.* [1993] 1 WLR 1402 (Ch 1993); 170 BR 800 (Bankr. SDNY 1994); *In re Inverworld* 267 BR 732, 740 n. 10 (Bankr. WD Tex 2001); *In re Smouha* 136 BR 921; *In re Loewen Group Int'l. Inc.*, No. 99-1244, 2002 U.S. Bankr. LEXIS 199 (Bankr. D Del 1999); *In re Enron*, No. 01-16034, 2001 Extra Lexis 304, at 2, (Bankr. SDNY Dec. 10, 2001); *In re Singer Company N.V.*, 262 BR 257 (Bankr. SDNY 2001). See also on cooperation between foreign courts and representatives, including in group cases: J.L. Westbrook, 'International Judicial Negotiations' (2003) 38 Tex. Int'l L.J. 567, 571–3; J.S. Ziegel, 'Corporate Groups and Crossborder

protocols and the use of direct judicial conversations is now a routine in cross-border insolvency cases involving Canada and the United States,[93] and to some extent it is also in use in other parts of the world.[94] To facilitate the use of this mechanism, parties and courts should be advised to consider 'precedents' of protocols, i.e. such agreements which were concluded between parties in previous cases of MEGs. In this respect, the work of UNCITRAL in construing a document which will contain the accumulative experience in devising such cross-border insolvency agreements is of significant merit.[95] The Draft UNCITRAL Notes on Cooperation[96] describes and analyses numerous such agreements as well as providing sample clauses from various such agreements which were concluded in practice. It thus provides judges and administrators with considerable information and explanations as to how such agreements may be used. It explains that such agreements may contain only general provisions emphasizing the need for cooperation, or more detailed specific provisions which establish a framework of principles to govern the multiple insolvency proceedings.[97] Such specific

Insolvencies: A Canada–United States Perspective' (2002) 7 Fordham J. Corp. & Fin. L. 367, 369; R.K. Rasmussen, 'The Problem of Corporate Groups, a Comment on Professor Ziegel' (2002) 7 Fordham J. Corp. & Fin. L. 395, 404; D.G. Baird and R.K. Rasmussen, 'The Four (or Five) Easy Lessons from Enron' (2002) 55 Vand. L. Rev. 1787; E.B. Leonard, 'Coordinating Cross-Border Insolvency Cases' International Insolvency Institute, June 2001 (http://www.iiiglobal.org/downloads/committees/Cross-Border%20Communications%20in%20Insolvency%20Cases/13-_Co-ordinating_Cross-Border_Insolvency_Cases.pdf); E.D. Flaschen, A. J. Smith, L. Plank, 'Case Study: Foreign Representatives in U.S. Chapter 11 Cases: Filling the Void in the Law of Multinational Insolvencies' (2001) 17 Conn. J. Int'l L. 7–13; L. Salafia, 'Cross-Border Insolvency Law in the United States and its Application to Multinational Corporate Groups' (2006) 21 Conn. J. Int'l L. 297, 301–16.

[93] See J.S. Ziegel, 'Corporate Groups and Crossborder Insolvencies: A Canada–United States Perspective' (2002) 7 Fordham J. Corp. & Fin. L. 367; R.K. Rasmussen, 'The Problem of Corporate Groups, a Comment on Professor Ziegel,' (2002) 7 Fordham J. Corp. & Fin. L. 395; S. Golick and M. Wasseman, 'Canada' in L.C. Ho (ed.), *Cross-Border Insolvency, A commentary on the UNCITRAL Model Law* (Globe Law & Business, London 2006), 46 (citing Justice J.M. Farley, 'The International Scene: A Judicial Perspective on International Cooperation in Insolvency Cases', March 1998 ABI Jnl 59, 59: The Ontario supreme court of justice has held that 'it has been estimated that there was a 40 percent enhancement or preservation of value as a result of the use of the protocol and the ensuing cooperation which it engendered amongst the parties').

[94] See court-to-court communication that took place in between US and English courts in *Cenargo* (*In re Cenargo International Plc* 294 BR 571 (Bankr. SDNY 2003); *Cenargo* (*Re Norse Irish Ferries & Cenargo Navigtion Limited* (unreported, 20 February 2003); see Insolv. Int. 2003, 16(6), 47–8 (NOTICEBOARD—Cooperation Between Courts); S. Moore, 'Cenargo: A Tale of two courts, comity and (alleged!) contempt!', January 2004 (available at: http://www.iiiglobal.org/downloads/country/USA/Articles/30-_cenargo.pdf). See also court-to-court communication between Dutch and German courts in the case of *BenQ* (*BenQ Mobile GmbH & Co. OHG [a trading partnership] and BenQ Mobile Holding B.V.*, Docket No. 1503 IE 4371/05 Munich, February 5, 2007); see C.G. Paulus, 'The aftermath of "Eurofood"—BenQ holding BV and the deficiencies of the ECJ decision' (2007) 20(6) Insolv. Int. 85). Cf. *Re T&N* [2004] EWHC 2878 (Ch), [26] where the English court refused to communicate directly with a US court on the basis that the proposed agenda involved 'matters of controversy between the parties'.

[95] See n 165 chapter 3.

[96] Ibid. As of November 2008 the document is still in draft form.

[97] See Draft UNCITRAL Notes on Cooperation (n 165 chapter 3), Part IIIA, paras. 4 and 24–6.

provisions may include court deferral, claims resolution procedures, procedures for communication between the courts and so forth, depending on the needs arising in each particular case, the interests of the parties and the relevant countries involved, in particular to what extent legal traditions are similar or different. In case of different legal traditions agreement may focus more on process and procedure.[98]

UNCITRAL Working Group V,[99] in addressing the international aspects pertaining to enterprise groups in insolvency[100] currently considers the Draft Notes of Cooperation as possible tool to be utilized in enterprise group insolvencies occurring in more than one country. As aforementioned, the work of the Working Group is in progress,[101] but possibly the Working Group may include in future recommendations on the international aspects of enterprise group insolvency reference to the Draft UNCITRAL Notes on Cooperation.[102] Such a recommendation will be of crucial importance. It will highlight to parties and courts that cooperation and particularly the use of protocols can and has been used in cases of MEG insolvencies, encourage them to utilize such means of cooperation and coordination in these cases, and in particular make use of provisions which were 'battle proven' in protocols in similar cases. This can be particularly useful for parties and courts in countries with limited experience with the use of protocols or other means of communication.

It is also critical to have clear reference to it and a suggestion for the utilization of this tool in cases of MEGs, as the current Draft UNCITRAL Notes on Cooperation does not explicitly refer to MEGs. Rather, it explains that cross-border agreements are agreements entered into for the purpose of cooperation and coordination of multiple insolvency proceedings in different states concerning the same debtor.[103] Particular reference to the case of MEGs is needed. Parties and courts should be encouraged to make use of protocols to achieve maximum cooperation in the handling of proceedings against members of integrated MEGs. This may include means to coordinate the proceedings (including language and frequency of such communications) as well as requirements to seek approval of the representatives or the courts presiding over the proceedings of the affiliate companies prior to taking particular actions (for example disposing of assets of the company). This may allow a global sale beneficial to the various members to be pursued (rather than separate sales with no consultation with the other insolvency representatives), or a global restructuring to be devised (accommodating differences in the types of reorganizations available in the jurisdiction).

---

[98] Ibid. See further section 6.2.1.6 on the possibility of achieving centralization via mechanisms for communication and cooperation .

[99] Note 96 chapter 1.

[100] See n 78.   [101] Ibid.

[102] See WP.82/Add.4 (n 78), para. 28.

[103] See Draft UNCITRAL Notes on Cooperation (n 165 chapter 3), Part IIIA, para. 4.

A protocol could also contain 'stronger' means of cooperation to achieve greater centralization of the process, as will be discussed below.[104]

It is suggested, though, that cooperation and assistance should also be enhanced via formal legislative provisions, which will guarantee that recognition, access, and assistance are provided in regard to the MEG insolvency and that cooperation is being achieved.[105] Relying on goodwill and ad hoc cooperation between parties or courts on a mere consensual basis with no pre-defined standard rules to this extent may not always succeed. As mentioned in chapter 3, in certain jurisdictions specific legislative direction may be necessary in order for the courts to be engaged in such cooperation and coordination. Generally, certain parties may be reluctant to initiate cooperation means and may prefer to pull in their own direction, failing to appreciate the merits of cooperation.[106] In the Draft UNCITRAL Notes on Cooperation, UNCITRAL too recognizes limitations to the use of protocols. It explains that such agreements may only be concluded if they fit with national laws.[107] In our context, if national laws lack recognition of tools for procedural consolidation [108] they may be reluctant to apply such concepts on a global level. I therefore argue that a legislative framework for pursuing cooperation with foreign courts or between insolvency representatives in cases of MEG insolvencies is necessary. Where no framework is available ad hoc cooperation would still significantly benefit from pre-defined principles and guidelines for cooperation and communication.

UNCITRAL Model Law[109] explicitly provides that courts and insolvency representatives of a state enacting the Model Law should cooperate and communicate with foreign courts and representatives.[110] The Model Law envisages inter alia situations where there are several proceedings taking place around the world against the same debtor and aims to achieve greater coordination of those proceedings.[111] The ALI Principles (being unofficial best practice principles and recommendations rather than binding rules) encourage cooperation and communication between foreign courts and administrators, and aim to facilitate parallel insolvency proceedings taking place against the same debtor (in case deference to a single court is not achievable).[112]

---

[104] See section 6.2.1.6.

[105] As noted earlier, especially civil law systems might lack the means to cooperate without specific authority and thus formal provisions of this kind can be of crucial importance (see n 219 chapter 3).

[106] See section 6.2.1.1 (the 'common pool' problem in the group context). Another problem could be that creditors may lack the incentive to cooperate if they consider that they will do worse under a unified solution, yet as will be suggested in Chapter 7, in certain circumstances global solutions should be pursued if they will benefit the stakeholders of the group as a whole even if it involves a degree of sacrifice by certain entities (see chapter 7, section 7.2.2).

[107] See Draft UNCITRAL Notes on Cooperaion (n 165 chapter 3), Part IIIA, para. 9.

[108] On which see section 6.2.1.2.

[109] N 212 chapter 3.

[110] See generally on the model law chapter 3, section 3.4.2.3 (n 221 chapter 3 delineates the countries which have so far enacted the Model Law).

[111] See chapter 3, section 3.4.2.3.

[112] Ibid, section 3.4.2.4 (in particular see the ALI Guidelines for Communication (n 262 chapter 3)). See also the European Guidelines for Communication (n 165 chapter 3).

Furthermore, UNCITRAL Model Law ensures that standing is given to foreign representatives and creditors (of proceedings taking place in the debtor's centre of main interests or where he has an establishment) in the local courts. It furthermore facilitates recognition of the foreign process, which may follow various types of relief including a stay of proceedings in regard to local assets and creditors, and delivery of relevant information.[113] Nonetheless, we are still missing explicit reference to the MEG scenario in this respect.

It is suggested that these ideas should be extrapolated to the MEG case. That is, instead of confining the tool to cooperation between different insolvency proceedings against the same debtor, here the cooperation (required in a formal standard rule) will involve different *affiliates'* insolvency proceedings. Jurisdiction for each company in the group will not be based on arbitrary location of assets, rather on a real connection of each affiliate to a jurisdiction, as required by universalism in regard to single debtors.[114] Yet, on the group scale coordination can be achieved between parallel territorial proceedings.

Thus, a foreign representative appointed over a foreign affiliate should be granted access to proceedings opened in another jurisdiction against another member of the same group, and the foreign proceedings against an affiliate should be recognized in the jurisdiction of the related company. This will allow making the necessary linkage between the two (or more) proceedings. Consequently, 'isolated' decisions taking place in regard to the local affiliates without having regard to proceedings taking place elsewhere in regard to the same group will be avoided, and a degree of global consolidation would be achievable so that enhancing values to the whole MEG would be possible.

An explicit recommendation to this extent is provided in the ALI Principles.[115] The Principles consider the possibility of two parallel proceedings (against related companies) taking place (although it suggests permitting a subsidiary to open insolvency proceedings in the home country of the parent company).[116] In case the subsidiary is in parallel proceedings in its home country the Principles urge that coordination will be sought between the two proceedings to achieve the benefits of consolidation where possible.[117]

An additional tool for promoting consolidation on a concurrent basis will be to recognize the effect of foreign affiliates' proceedings taking place elsewhere in regard to group members for the purpose of opening local proceedings against another member of the group. Here the scenario considered is where there are still no proceedings opened against a local member of the same group (against whose other members proceedings have been opened elsewhere). In this case, considering the foreign proceeding (that has been opened) in the country where an

---

[113] See chapter 3, section 3.4.2.3. See also on similar measures provided in the ALI Principles (chapter 3, section 3.4.2.4).
[114] Ibid, section 3.3.3.
[115] Ibid, section 3.4.2.4.
[116] ALI Principles (n 243 chapter 3), Procedural Principle 23.
[117] Ibid.

affiliate is operating can assist in establishing requirements for commencement of proceedings against that group member, if its financial stability is contingent upon the situation of the rest of the group.[118] For example, a creditor of the foreign subsidiary filing insolvency proceedings against it will be able to give as evidence for imminent insolvency of that subsidiary the fact that it is part of a MEG which has collapsed elsewhere. This will facilitate the placing of affiliates under insolvency, preserving their estates, sharing of information among these proceedings, and considering unified solutions for them in a coordinated manner. It can lead to and thus promote global (concurrent) consolidation.

I thus suggest an attempt to achieve maximum cooperation between multiple proceedings (in regard to the MEG), via various methods, including party-led (or court initiated) agreements but also more formalized ways of recognition, access, assistance, and cooperation. Here, what is to be recognized is the linkage between the affiliate companies and its effect in the course of insolvency, i.e. the need to consolidate the insolvency proceedings against the MEG affiliates. There is hence no added problem in terms of entity law under such an approach. It is the same idea of procedural consolidation taking place in domestic insolvency proceedings (here between concurrent proceedings), which generally does not interfere with the separateness between the entities.

In terms of the cross-border dilemma, though, a degree of universalism is sought in the sense that there will be an attempt at close linkage, cooperation, and other relief to be able to achieve asset preservation and maximization. However, interference with state sovereignty (in regard to the tools suggested for MEG insolvencies) is minimal if coordination is sought between parallel processes taking place locally against affiliates. Although it is based on the concept of proceedings against single debtors being handled in their home country, it does not reject modifications in this regard by way of 'secondary' or concurrent proceedings taking place for the same debtor as provided in existing models for single debtors.[119] Yet, in regard to the MEG, it avoids the additional problem of identifying a home country for the group, a concept perceived as problematic.[120] It also does not interfere with national laws, as (under coordination between a parallel proceedings regime) each jurisdiction handling the case against the local affiliate applies its own choice of law rules. There is also room for contractualism under such a 'cooperative global consolidation' approach, in the sense of giving parties freedom to determine various issues relating to the coordination of the process (by way of protocols for example).[121]

---

[118] See section 6.2.1.1. It may also be possible to persuade the local court to refrain from opening local proceedings against a local affiliate (see section 6.2.1.6).

[119] See chapter 3, sections 3.4.2.2–3.4.2.4.

[120] Ibid, section 3.3.3. But, see section 6.2.1.6 where stronger global measures are suggested requiring the identification of a 'group home country'.

[121] Though, the parties would not be free to choose the forum and law that will govern under this 'parallel' model of consolidation. Here, the protocols are subjected to the relevant courts' supervision and discretion. Jurisdiction is determined in regard to each entity according to the

To the extent that territoriality is defeated (to a degree) where coordination is applied between proceedings against affiliate companies (accompanied by other measures of access and relief), this is mitigated by the fact that such coordination will be required only for 'business integrated' MEGs and not for every type of MEG. The application of procedural consolidation should thus be narrowed down in the global arena where it is faced with territoriality concerns. Territorialism also highlights that there may be additional costs involved in global communications, and the seeking of such 'cross-entity recognition'.[122] But, in cases of 'business integrated' MEGs the goal of wealth maximization suggests that a degree of territorially can be sacrificed in order to achieve greater cooperation. For an integrated MEG, it will be crucial to provide such means for its insolvency (even more than for the national case). No doubt, it will be much more complicated to attempt a worldwide reorganization with no means of cooperation where different legal regimes are involved and entities are geographically dispersed across countries or continents.

However, a global group-wide procedure taking place via coordination among multiple local processes against the various affiliates may have its toll in terms of efficiency compared to more unified solutions. Ignoring for the moment costs that may be involved in having multiple proceedings,[123] it may just be unattainable to coordinate such a global operation, especially in cases of widespread groups operating in different time zones, and where numerous parties and entities are involved.[124] This is why both international models and national approaches often stress a greater degree of universalism in the sense of deferring to a foreign court and law, allowing closer coordination of cross-border insolvencies. The feasibility and justifications as well as the limitations of such an approach for the case of the MEG will now be considered.

6.2.1.6 *Stronger measures = greater prospects*

6.2.1.6.1 The concept of centralization of insolvency proceedings against MEG members

In cases where the MEG was integrated and thus joint administration of the insolvency proceedings against the different members is beneficial, then in the international case, if the proceedings against the affiliates can be centralized to a single jurisdiction and conducted under a single regime it will greatly facilitate

---

relevant rules applied (to the particular debtor) and the court determines the applicable law (which in regard to the insolvency matters will normally be the law of the forum (see chapter 3, section 3.3.2.1), unless a more 'centralized' approach is taken, on which see section 6.2.1.6).

[122] See section 6.2.2.3 on the costs involved in transnational attempts at cooperation.

[123] Ibid.

[124] In regard to the use of protocols, for example, these are normally used in proceedings involving two countries, normally counties of similar legal culture (most examples of protocols are of cross-border insolvency cases involving proceedings in the US and Canada (see S.P. Johnston and J. Han, 'A Proposal for Party-Determined COMI in Cross-Border Insolvencies of Multinational Corporate Groups' 16 JBLP 811, 817)).

their coordination and allow a more harmonious process.[125] This is a combination of enterprise law concepts—the idea of a single court and a single representative presiding over procedural consolidations of affiliates (sometimes provided domestically for groups [126]) with universalists' cross-border mechanisms envisaging a single court and a single law governing the case of a multinational debtor.[127]

It is suggested that such an approach could be especially beneficial in regard to global rescue attempts which involve more complex decision-making (compared to liquidations), including in many cases the need to take urgent measures.[128] Doing that within a system of 'equal' parties with no directing head can be problematic especially if the group is big and widespread. Additional problems may arise in conducting proceedings simultaneously in different jurisdictions due to differences in the insolvency laws. This may affect the ability to coordinate a global scheme, or at least pose considerable difficulties, where for example there are differences in the reorganization procedures.[129]

6.2.1.6.2 Current measures for centralization of proceedings against single debtors

It was mentioned earlier that the concept of COMI adopted in the EC Regulation,[130] and followed in the Model Law [131] and the ALI Principles [132] is an attempt to unify rules of jurisdiction in the context of insolvency, identifying the court that should preside over the principal proceedings against the debtor.[133] As much as this is recognized worldwide then duplication of proceedings is reduced (subject to the concept of secondary proceedings,[134] or the possibility to open concurrent proceedings [135]). Under the EC Regulation regime the recognition of the main proceedings is automatic; this jurisdiction will preside over the entire debtor's affairs and its rules will generally govern.[136] Under the Model law, a stay of proceedings will follow such recognition (if recognition has been given, as it is not automatic), and there is additional possible relief that may be granted, including allowing for the debtor's affairs to be administered by the foreign representative.[137] As explained earlier, the Model Law does not provide uniform choice of law rules, thus the court presiding over the case will apply its own choice of law system.[138]

---

[125] For advantages or concerns such an approach may raise in regard to other insolvency goals see chapter 7, section 7.3; and chapter 8, section 8.3.

[126] See section 6.2.1.1.

[127] See chapter 3, sections 3.3.2.1 and 3.3.3.

[128] See section 6.2.1.1.

[129] Most pronouncedly in a case involving affiliates located both in countries with developed insolvency laws and countries which lack basic tools for reorganizations. But it may create problems in less dramatic scenarios. See, for instance, the *Enron* case in which a complex plan needed to be designed in order to overcome the differences between the Chapter 11 and scheme of arrangement regimes (*In re Enron*, No. 01-16034, 2001 Extra Lexis 304, at 2, (Bankr. SDNY Dec. 10, 2001); *GLOBALTURNAROUND*, 'To scheme or not to scheme Lessons from Enron', October 2004, issue 57, p. 11).

[130] N 173 chapter 3.   [131] N 212 chapter 3.   [132] N 243 chapter 3.

[133] See chapter 3, section 3.4.2.   [134] Ibid, sections 3.4.2.2–3.4.2.4.

[135] Ibid, section 3.4.2.3.   [136] Ibid, section 3.4.2.2.

[137] Ibid, section 3.4.2.3.   [138] Ibid, section 3.4.2.3.

The ALI Principles urge the transfer of control over the debtor's affairs to the principle jurisdiction and representative so as to enable determination of distributions from a universal perspective to the maximum extent possible.[139] The ALI Principles too do not provide uniform choice of law rules.[140]

In the absence of pre-defined international concepts (that is, where international models do not apply), national measures of 'deference' to a foreign jurisdiction and its insolvency law may be applied by local courts (applying legal regimes' own concepts of a competent court) to achieve centralization of the process in terms of the court and law which will apply. This may also include recognition and enforcement of its decisions, including the binding effect of a reorganization plan upon all stakeholders of the debtor wherever located.[141] Party-led agreements (protocols) or other means of coordination and communication (such as direct communication between courts) may also be utilized to achieve such 'stronger' means of coordination. Thus, it may be agreed between the courts or the parties that a court will defer to another court in general or in regard to specific matters arising in regard to the insolvency of the debtor.[142]

6.2.1.6.3 Enabling centralization in the case of the MEG insolvency

Translating this notion to the MEG case, a home country of the MEG could be identified and be designated as the principal jurisdiction in which all proceedings (against the group affiliates) will take place.[143] In an EC Regulation type of regime (if it would have applied to groups[144]) this could then receive automatic recognition and almost 'total unity' as aforementioned. In a Model Law or ALI Principles types of system,[145] opening such proceedings could receive recognition as main proceedings and subsequent relief may be sought in the local jurisdiction, for instance preventing local creditors from opening proceedings locally, transferring all assets to the group home country, entrusting the administration and realization of the affiliate's assets located in the local states to the foreign representative (while satisfying the local court that local creditors' interests are adequately protected), and entrusting the distribution of those assets to the foreign representative, to achieve a centralized consolidation.

---

[139] Ibid, section 3.4.2.4.   [140] Ibid.

[141] Ibid, section 3.4.2.1. See in particular the examples of cases where courts took such an approach in ibid, n 162.

[142] See Draft UNCITRAL Notes on Cooperation (n 165 chapter 3), Part IIIB, paras. 71–4.

[143] 'Secondary' type of proceedings may still be opened in case any of the entities had establishments in other jurisdictions, according to the rules regarding single debtors (operating on a cross-border scale). See also section 6.2.1.8 for a discussion of the application of a secondary proceeding concept to the group scenario, and the proposal of further alternatives for MEG insolvencies apart from full centralization.

[144] Note that currently the EC Regulation does not provide rules dealing with corporate groups (see chapter 3, section 3.4.2.2). But see below in this section consideration of other ways in which the EC Regulation is being used to resolve MEG insolvency cases.

[145] As explained earlier, the Model Law currently does not provide explicit rules for groups in insolvency (chapter 3, section 3.4.2.3), but see below in this section discussion of the use of the Model Law in cases of MEG insolvencies. See also below (section 6.2.1.5) on the specific Principles in the ALI Principles dealing with groups.

This could be most effectively done by way of extrapolating the concept of COMI of a debtor (as provided in the international models mentioned above) to COMI of the group, and according this location recognition worldwide.[146] Alternatively, it can be done by stretching domestic laws' own concepts of a competent court as having an extraterritorial reach over all the debtor's affairs to include affiliates.

In terms of applicable law, in that case preferably there would be concentration of this aspect too, the law of the group forum mainly applying its insolvency law in the handling of the global consolidation (in respect to insolvency matters).[147] As aforementioned, this is the rule under the EC Regulation in regard to single debtors—the law of the forum generally governs the insolvency matters. Thus, the state where insolvency proceedings are opened determines the effects of insolvency proceedings, both procedural and substantive and also governs all conditions for the opening, conduct, and closure of the insolvency proceedings. However, under the EC Regulation, the exceptions to the rule are extensive and result in allocating some crucial jurisdiction elsewhere,[148] whereas the idea of uniformity and harmonization as well as certainty for parties involved in cross-border insolvency requires that such exceptions would be kept to the minimum.[149]

UNCITRAL Model Law[150] does not provide for international jurisdiction and uniform choice of law rules, yet it may allow the administration and distribution of the estate to be entrusted in the foreign representative.[151] Under many legal regimes

---

[146] See section 6.2.1.9 for consideration of the test for locating a MEG COMI.

[147] A different approach was taken in the case of *Midland* (*In re Midland Euro Exch.*, 347 BR 708, 710-11 (Bankr. CD Cal 2006). In this case, a corporate group was placed under insolvency proceedings in the US and was subject to substantive consolidation (on which see section 6.3). Notwithstanding the US court ascertaining jurisdiction over the corporate group, it refrained from applying its laws in regard to claims to avoid certain transactions to which one of the group affiliates was a party (see J.L. Westrbrook, 'Avoidance of Pre-Bankruptcy Transactions in Multinational Bankruptcy Cases' (2007) 42 Tex. Int'l L.J. 899, 910–11). See further on choice of law rules regarding avoidance transactions in chapter 9, section 9.6.

[148] See EC Regulation (n 173 chapter 3), Articles 5–15 (the special rules are concerned with third parties' rights in rem, set-off, reservation of title, contracts relating to immovable property, payment systems and financial markets, contract of employment, rights subject to registration, community patents and trademarks, avoidance of transactions (which are subject to the rules of the forum yet subject to exceptions, on which see further in Chapter 9 section 9.6), protection of third party purchasers and effects of insolvency proceedings on a lawsuit pending. Additionally, if secondary proceedings are opened, local assets will be subjected to distribution under local laws.

[149] In particular, those exceptions in regard to secured creditors are extensive (see J.L. Westbrook, 'Multinational Enterprises in General Default: Chapter 15, The ALI Principles, and The EU Insolvency Regulation' (2002) 76 Am. Bankr. L.J. 1, 34; D.T. Trautman et al., 'Four Models for International Bankruptcy' (1994) 41 Am. J. Comp. L. 573, 583–6; UNCITRAL Legislative Guide (n 137 chapter 3), Part two, Ch. I, para. 80)). See also section 6.2.2.2 on cost benefits in applying the forum's law, and see chapter 8 on the effect of the diversity in choice of law rules regarding matters of insolvency on the goals of certainty and predictability.

[150] N 212 chapter 3.

[151] Yet, another alternative is for the representative to seek various relief under the law of the recognizing state (see Fletcher, *Insolvency* (n 3 chapter 3) 471).

the bankruptcy forum will then mainly apply its laws in regard to insolvency matters.[152] Yet, the ability to achieve a harmonized solution in terms of applicable law under the Model Law regime should be acknowledged, as many countries adopt exceptions to the application of the law of the forum (to determine insolvency matters) which vary in number and scope.[153]

6.2.1.6.4 Centralization of MEG insolvency proceedings in practice

In the absence of explicit rules in regard to enterprise groups in international models, there are some solutions 'in practice' (for achieving centralization). Certain national regimes have been applying their own notions of universality and comity, to extend jurisdiction over related companies (and the corresponding jurisdiction—granting recognition to such insolvency proceedings). This has been especially significant between closely related jurisdictions.[154] On occasions, the courts even recognized and enforced a stay of proceedings granted by the foreign jurisdiction against local non-debtor solvent subsidiaries.[155] This does not accord, though, with the idea suggested above of recognizing the separateness among the entities, so that a moratorium against certain parts of the group cannot apply to other members, unless the latter are part of the insolvency process. Indeed, bringing the other entities into the proceedings should, as was suggested above, take into account the group interrelations and their effect on the financial state of the entities, but otherwise a stay should not automatically apply to stand-alone entities.

Ad hoc means of communication were also utilized to achieve centralization of proceedings in MEG insolvency cases. In the case of *Cenargo* (group of companies), proceedings were initially opened both in the UK and in the US. Each of the relevant courts restricted the other party from pursuing proceedings in the other jurisdiction. Eventually, the US court suspended the Chapter 11 proceedings finding that the 'centre of gravity' of the cases was in the UK. The 'battle' was solved by the respective judges holding a conference call in which they agreed on a number of key jurisdictional differences. Ultimately, a joint administration

---

[152] See UNCITRAL Legislative Guide (n 137 chapter 3), Part two, Ch. I, para. 80.

[153] Ibid.

[154] Such approach has been occasionally taken by US and Canadian courts (see L. Salafia, 'Cross-Border Insolvency Law in the United States and its Application to Multinational Corporate Groups' (2006) 21 Conn. J. Int'l L. 297, 329 (though it is noted that the approach is not followed in a consistent manner); J.S. Ziegel, 'Corporate Groups and Crossborder Insolvencies: A Canada–United States Perspective' (2002) 7 Fordham J. Corp. & Fin. L. 367, 386–7; J.S. Ziegel, 'Canada-United States Cross-Border Insolvency Relations and the UNCITRAL Model Law (2007) 32 Brook. J. Int'l L. 1041, 1050 (noting that procedural consolidation on a cross-border level involving Canadian and US affiliates has been occurring in practice).

[155] See *Re Babcock & Wilcox Canada (BW Canada)* (2000) 18 CBR (4th) 157, (2000) 5 BLR (3rd) 75 (Ont. S.C.J. [commercial]); Cf. *Bracon International Inc. v Everest & Jennings Canadian Ltd* [2001] 26 C.B.R. (4th) 154, 2001 Carswell Ont 396 (Ont SCJ). See also J.S. Ziegel, 'Canada-United States Cross-Border Insolvency Relations and the UNCITRAL Model Law' (2007) 32 Brook. J. Int'l L. 1041, 1050–2.

took place in the UK enabling successful rehabilitation of many companies in the group.[156]

Under the EC Regulation,[157] centralization of insolvency proceedings in MEG cases has been brought about in numerous multinational group cases. Though, the way in which this was possible is somewhat peculiar. Rather than identifying a single COMI for the group as a whole (as suggested above), in these cases the COMI identified for each affiliate separately pointed to a single location—resulting in all of them being placed under insolvency in the same place (administration orders were issued for each company, but all in the same court and same jurisdiction). The often-cited example is *Daisytek*,[158] the multinational computer peripherals group.[159] In this case an English appointee attempted to facilitate a pan-European restructuring by opening proceedings for all the affiliates comprising the European division of the group at the same place (the UK).[160] Thus, administration orders were requested for all the European subsidiaries that were part insolvent and part likely to become insolvent within a short time.[161] The aim was to administer the proceedings jointly, instead of having a 'patchwork of different cases in different countries' to achieve a cost efficient result.[162] This seemed especially advantageous as it was thought that the group would benefit from a reorganization type of procedure rather than liquidation.[163] The UK court managed to find that the COMI of each of the subsidiaries was in England.[164] There was, though, much controversy as to whether indeed the centre of the German and French subsidiaries was in the UK. In the absence of rules dealing with corporate groups in the EC Regulation the question of jurisdiction in regard to the foreign affiliates was not clear.[165] At a certain point in time main proceedings against the German and French subsidiaries were opened in their 'local' jurisdictions, based

---

[156] see S. Moore, 'Global Crossing versus Cenargo The right way and the wrong way' *GLOBALTURNAROUND*, January 2004, issue 48, p. 8; LoPucki, *Courting Failure* (n 64 chapter 3), 189, 191–3, 204–5; S. Moore, 'Cenargo: A Tale of two courts, comity and (aleged!) comtempt!', January 2004 (available at: http://www.iiiglobal.org/downloads/country/USA/Articles/30-_cenargo.pdf); S. Sandy and T. Richard, 'The Cenargo Case: A Tale of Conflict, Greed Contempt, comity and Costs' Insol World—Fourth Quarter 2003, 33–5).

[157] Note 173 chapter 3.

[158] For a comprehensive review of the proceedings in this case see Fletcher, *Insolvency* (n 3 chapter 3), 388–93.

[159] In re *Daisytek-ISA Ltd* [2003] BCC 562.

[160] In Daisytek 14 companies were at issue, amongst them a French trading company and two German trading companies as well as their German holding company. The question of jurisdiction arose in respect of the German companies and the French company. The court gave fourteen administration orders against the parent and thirteen subsidiaries.

[161] *In re Daisytek-ISA Ltd* [2003] BCC 562, 564.

[162] See S. Taylor, 'Daisytek chain reaction', *GLOBALTURNAROUND*, July 2003, issue 42, p. 10.

[163] *In re Daisytek-ISA Ltd* [2003] BCC 562, 564.

[164] Ibid.

[165] See further on certainty problems in chapter 8.

on the assertion that their centres as separate entities was in these jurisdictions.[166] Ultimately, the UK decision that the COMI of the group members was in the UK was recognized by the other foreign jurisdictions involved,[167] and the process was centrally handled (with the German local main proceedings which were opened for the German subsidiary—the parent of the two other German companies—converted to secondary proceedings).[168] This gave the group a chance of saving itself as a whole, rather than splitting up its various European assets.[169] If the COMI of some of the subsidiaries could not have been located in England, the process would have been 'broken up' between different jurisdictions, the EC Regulation not encompassing specific rules to ensure that a group process will be handled with coordination, even if a particular subsidiary has its own COMI locally.

There are numerous other examples of 'de facto' consolidations of European MEG insolvencies. That is, cases where the court of a member state extended jurisdiction over several affiliates finding that all of them had their COMI in that jurisdiction, opening separate proceedings against each affiliate but handling them under the authority of a single court through a single representative.[170] Yet, the decision of the ECJ in the case of *Eurofood*[171] may put obstacles in the way of achieving unified solutions based on the EC Regulation in its current shape.[172] Eurofood IFSC was a wholly owned subsidiary of Parmalat SpA (part of the Parmalat MEG in regard to which proceedings were opened

---

[166] See Tribunal de Commerce, Cergy-Pontoise, 1 July 2003; *PAR Beteiligungs GmbH*, AG Dusseldorf County Court, 6 June 2003 (502 IN 126/03), ZIP 30/2003. See further comments on this jurisdictional 'battle' in section 6.2.1.8; chapter 7, section 7.5.2; and chapter 8, section 8.2.

[167] See *Klempka v ISA Daisytek SA,* Cour D'Appel (Versailles) [2003] BCC 984; *Klempka v ISA Daisytek SA*, Cour de Cassation (France) [2006] BCC 841; *PAR Beteiligungs GmbH*, Dusseldorf Court of Appeal, 23 October 2003; 12 March 2004.

[168] *PAR Beteiligungs GmbH*, Dusseldorf Court of Appeal, 23 October 2003; 12 March 2004.

[169] See 'French breakthrough for Euro Regulation' *GLOBALTURNAROUND*, Oct 2003, issue 45, p. 9.

[170] See e.g. *Re Crisscross Telecommunications Group* (unreported, 20 May 2003), Ch D; *Cirio Del Monte,* Italian court of Rome, August, 2003 (unreported); '*Hettlage-Austria*', Munich District Court (Amtsgericht), 4 May 2004, AG Munchen Beschl.v.4.5.2004–1501 IE 1276/04; *Re Parmalat Hungary/Slovakia*, Municipality Court of Fejer, 14 June, 2004; *Collins & Aikman Corporation Group* [2005] EWHC 1754 (Ch); *Re TXU Europe German Finance BV* [2005] BCC 90 (Ch D); *Energotech SARL* (Tribunal de Grande Instance (France) [2007] BCC 123; *Re MG Rover Espana SA* [2005] BPIR 1162 (In Administration); *Eurotunnel Finance Ltd* (Tribunal de Commerce de Paris, 2 Aug 2006) (unreported); *MPOTEC GMBH* (Tribunal de Grande Instance, Nanterre [2006] BCC 681 (Fr); *Re Parkside Flexibles* [2006] BCC 589. See also *GLOBALTURNAROUND*, 'French revolution on COMI', March 2006, issue 74, p.1; M. Haravon, 'Recent Developments in France under EU Regulation 1346/2000' (2005) 18 Insolv. Int. 118; G. Moss and M. Haravon, ' "Building Europe"— the French Case Law on COMI' (2007) 20 Insolv. Int. 20; G. Moss, 'Group Insolvency—Choice of Forum and Law: the European Experience under the Influence of English Pragmatism' (2007) 32 Brook. J. Inl'l L. 1005 (demonstrating the wide adoption in Europe of 'English Pragmatism', i.e. placing proceedings of related companies in a single jurisdiction thus facilitating centralization of group insolvency proceedings).

[171] *Eurofood IFSC Ltd* (Case C-341/04) [2006] OJ 2006 C143/11.

[172] Although even after *Eurofood* courts have been able to identify mutual a COMI in group cases (see n 170).

in Italy for the purpose of devising solutions for the group in its insolvency [173]). The subsidiary was in essence a financing vehicle for the Parmalat group. Proceedings against this company were opened first in Ireland,[174] and then also in Italy.[175] There was a controversy as to the location of the centre of this company, the Italian administrator arguing it to be in Italy, mainly based on the connections between the subsidiary and the group.[176] The Irish creditors claimed it to be in Ireland based on (arguably) substantial presence of the subsidiary in that jurisdiction.[177] The issue was referred to the European Court of Justice (ECJ). In a preliminary opinion given by the Advocate General,[178] he asserted, inter alia, that the Regulation applies to individual companies and not to corporate groups. Accordingly, in terms of ascertaining jurisdiction nothing can necessarily be inferred from the fact that a debtor company is a subsidiary of another company. Each subsidiary within a group must be considered individually.[179] The ECJ upheld this opinion reinforcing the approach expressed by the Advocate General in respect to corporate groups.[180] It refrained from developing a 'group concept' and put little emphasis on the interrelations between the subsidiary and the parent. It stated that the COMI should be determined for the particular subsidiary. Though the fact that the subsidiary is controlled by a parent situated elsewhere may be a relevant factor, it seemed to receive little weight. At least it is not clear from the decision in which circumstances 'group consideration' will prevail. In the case of *Eurofood*, a separate process has been conducted in Ireland.[181]

The Model Law [182] is also currently 'in use' for such attempts at centralizing insolvency proceedings against MEG members (so that a unified coordination of the process can take place). Though, here too, in the absence of explicit rules, there is much obscurity as to the extent to which such solutions can be achieved. The same concept of COMI (and sometimes also that of 'establishment'—as a

---

[173] See n 83–5, and accompanying texts.

[174] An appointment of provisional liquidators was approved by the Irish High Court (see *Eurofood IFSC Limited* [2004] BCC 383).

[175] *Re Eurofood IFSC,* (Trib (I) 19 February 2004 [2004] I.L.Pr.14.

[176] The Italian court accepted the Italian administrator contentions (ibid*).*

[177] *Eurofood IFSC Limited* [2004] BCC 383.

[178] *Eurofood IFSC Ltd* (Case C-341/04) [2005] BCC 1021 (AGO).

[179] Ibid, paras. 106–26.

[180] *Eurofood IFSC Ltd* (Case C-341/04) [2006] OJ 2006 C143/11.

[181] See ibid, and the later decision of the Irish Supreme Court to dismiss the Italian administrator appeal. The Irish court decision was based on the ECJ ruling, mainly the fact that proceedings were first opened in Ireland (*Re Eurofood IFSC Ltd* (Unreported, 3 July 2006) (Sup Ct (Irl)); see further discussions of the case in sections 6.2.1.8 and 6.2.1.9; chapter 7, sections 7.3.2 and 7.5.2; and chapter 8, section 8.2 and 8.3.3. See generally on *Eurofood* in B. Wessels, 'Cross-Border Insolvency Law in Europe: Present Status and Future Prospects' (2008) 1 PER, 1, 14–17; S. L. Bufford, 'Centre of Main Interests, International Insolvency Case Venue, and Equality of Arms: the Eurofood Decision of the European Court of Justice' (2007) 27 Nw. J. Int'l L. & Bus. 351).

[182] N 212 chapter 3.

basis for opening non-main proceedings against a subsidiary) is being used to try and persuade the court that all proceedings against related companies should be handled in a unified manner in a single jurisdiction. An example is the case of the *Main Knitting* group.[183] In this case, a Canadian appointed representative has filed a petition in a US bankruptcy court (under the Model Law as adopted in the US bankruptcy code[184]) for recognition of Canadian proceedings opened against the MEG companies as foreign main proceedings.[185] In Canada, proceedings were opened in regard to a Canada incorporated parent company and two US subsidiaries (incorporated in Delaware). The parent company operated a garment manufacturing and distribution business in Montreal, and it had sales in Canada and the US. A US wholly owned subsidiary was engaged in the warehousing and distribution of the parent company's products in New York. Another US sub-subsidiary was engaged in the importation and wholesale of the parent's products in New York. Both subsidiaries' chief executive offices where located in Montreal.[186] The Canadian representative argued that recognition should be given to all proceedings as foreign main proceedings pursuant to the US Bankruptcy Code because the COMI of all debtors was in Canada as the debtors' chief executive offices were there. Accordingly, he asked for relief to be granted including a stay of proceedings.[187] A creditor of the American subsidiary objected, arguing that the American subsidiary had significant presence in the US and therefore recognition and relief should be denied.[188] Eventually the parties reached a settlement in regard to safeguarding certain rights of the creditor against property of the American subsidiary, and the court granted the recognition and relief sought subject to the stipulation.[189]

---

[183] *In Re Main Knitting Inc. Et al*, Nos. 08 (11272, 11273, 274) (Bankr NDNY, 2008).

[184] See chapter 3, section 3.4.2.3.

[185] *In Re Main Knitting Inc. Et al*, Nos. 08 (11272, 11273, 274), Petition for recognition of Canadian proceedings under 11 USC s.1515 ((Bankr NDNY, 24 April 2008).

[186] Ibid.

[187] Ibid.

[188] *In Re Main Knitting Inc. Et al,* Nos. 08 (11272, 11273, 274), Objection of HSBC Bank USA, National Association to the petition for recognition of Canadian proceedings under 11 USC s.1515 ((Bankr NDNY 1 May 2008).

[189] See *In Re Main Knitting Inc. Et al*, Nos. 08 (11272, 11273, 274), Order granting recognition of Canadian proceedings under 11 USC s. 1515 (Bankr NDNY 18 June 2008); Stipulation and order resolving objection of HSBC Bank USA, National Association to petition for recognition of Canadian proceedings under 11 USC s.1515 (US District Court. SDNY, 19 June 2008). See other recognition orders given under the US Chapter 15 in regard to MEGs (comprising foreign and local affiliates), e.g. *ROL Manufacturing (Canada), Inc. Et al,* No. 08-31022, Order granting recognition of foreign main proceedings (Bankr Southern district of Ohio, 17 April 2008); *Creative Building Maintenance Inc. Et al,* Nos. 06 (03586, 03587), Order recognizing foreign proceedings and granting further relief and additional assistance (Bankr WDNY, 29 December 2006) (in this case the proceedings opened in Canada in regard to the US subsidiary was recognized as non main proceedings); *Madill Equipment Canada Et al,* Nos. 08 (41426–41435) (Bankr. Western District of Washington, 2008).

6.2.1.6.5 Adopting universalist–enterprise law principles to enhance centralizations

It is thus possible to an extent to achieve a centralized coordination of insolvency proceedings against integrated MEGs under existing regimes. Yet, I suggest that relying only on the somewhat random attempt at locating the centre of each of the companies in the same place (as may be done under the models based on the concept of locating the debtor's COMI) may impede the achievement of centralization in the MEG context. Thus, in cases such as *Daisytek* discussed above, the UK court struggled to show how each of the subsidiary's COMI was in England (so as to enable coordinated proceedings of the entire group), without being able to rely in full transparency on the group scenario as a justification for unification in an explicit manner.[190] The use of protocols or other means of ad hoc communication may also fail to result in centralization especially in the absence of predefined guidelines or sufficient experience of the courts and the parties involved in using such strategies for centralizing MEG's insolvencies. Explicit rules based on enterprise principles (combined with universalism) are needed, so as to enhance centralization of integrated MEG members' insolvencies in the appropriate circumstances. Various initiatives along these lines have recently started to emerge.

Between the NAFTA countries, the ALI Principles specifically urge enabling a degree of centralization in the case of a parent and a subsidiary[191] each being incorporated and operating in a different NAFTA jurisdiction. It does not identify a home country for the group, and it does not provide in which cases centralization should be pursued as opposed to mere coordination,[192] but it suggests allowing a subsidiary to open insolvency proceedings in the jurisdiction where the parent has commenced insolvency proceedings, in the absence of a proceeding involving the subsidiary in the country of its main interests, and to have either procedural or substantive consolidation under applicable law.[193] It also stresses that corporate groups should be reorganized from a worldwide perspective.[194]

---

[190] *In re Daisytek-ISA Ltd* [2003] BCC 562 (Ch D), 5–8. But, see the case of TXU in which Mr Registrar Baister did expressly take into account (in his decision to place Irish and Dutch debtors' insolvency proceedings in the UK) the fact that a related company (of these debtors) was already the subject of an administration order in England. Placing all related companies 'under one roof', as was held, could 'achieve consequential savings in costs' and result in a better coordinated process (*Re TXU Europe German Finance BV* [2005] BCC 90 (Ch D)).

[191] The Principles mention that they could also apply to sister companies (ALI Principles (n 243 chapter 3) 79).

[192] See texts accompanying notes 115–17.

[193] ALI Principles (n 243 chapter 3) Procedural Principle 23. The Principles do not suggest though in which cases procedural consolidation should be sought and in which substantive consolidation is more adequate.

[194] Ibid, Procedural Principle 24. The principle continues to stress the need to consider issues of allocation of value having regard to the need to respect the corporate form (see further on this issue in chapter 7, section 7.2). See also on the ALI Principles and corporate groups J.L. Westbrook, 'Multinational Enterprises in General Default: Chapter 15, The ALI Principles, and The EU Insolvency Regulation' (2002) 76 Am. Bankr. L.J. 1, 38.

Non-binding judicial guidelines for coordination of MEG insolvencies are being devised by a committee of the International Insolvency Institute.[195] The Guidelines are specifically concerned with cases of MEGs, and they direct courts and parties involved in such cases to take a centralized approach. The courts, under these guidelines, should attempt to locate the single jurisdiction in which proceedings against group members would be handled (and defer to that court). This 'group jurisdiction' may then have jurisdiction over all assets of the enterprise. Protocols may also be used to further this objective. Yet, this depends on national laws which may limit the court's deference to the jurisdiction and the scope of a coordinating protocol.[196]

As aforementioned, UNCITRAL Working Group V[197] is currently considering how to address the international aspects of enterprise group insolvencies. In this respect, the Working Group may consider the use of protocols to achieve a degree of centralization in MEG insolvency cases, or even go further and reach an agreement on a concept and a definition of a proper centralized jurisdiction for MEG insolvencies.[198] The work is still in progress though,[199] and the feasibility of agreeing on such a concept is still not clear. It may be that the Working Group will address the notion of centralization, yet without limiting the jurisdiction of other proceedings which may be opened against group members (that is, the role of the centre jurisdiction may be limited and centralization will not be necessarily full).[200]

These initiatives are commendable. As aforesaid, in explicitly referring to the specific case of MEG there is a better chance that parties will indeed cooperate to the extent that centralization will be achieved or that courts will defer to other courts and so greater harmonization of the process will be achieved, and efficiency in the handling of the proceedings against MEG members will be enhanced. I suggest going further than that though (not only relying on ad hoc cooperation and non-binding guidelines) and devise principles for centralization within a legislative framework, providing where the proper jurisdiction for handling the MEG insolvency is located and the powers that will be allocated to this jurisdiction (and the insolvency representative). This can be done, for example, by encouraging legislators to renovate national laws to this extent, via recommendations in international guidelines, such as the Legislative Guide (and may indeed be achieved by recommendations on this topic if such will be provided by Working Group V). At the same time, notions of centralization of single debtors'

---

[195] See III Draft guidelines (n 100 chapter 1).
[196] III Draft Guidelines (ibid), Guideline 2. See further on the identification of the forum to handle the group proceedings in section 6.2.1.9.
[197] N 96 chapter 1.
[198] See WP.82/Add.4 (n 78), paras. 10–15, 26–8.
[199] As of November 2008.
[200] On the concepts of full and partial centralization see section 6.2.1.8. See further on the Working Group discussion of the concept of MEG COMI in section 6.2.1.9.

insolvency, as provided in international models for cross-border insolvency,[201] should be extended to explicitly refer to the case of MEGs.

In particular, ad hoc means for communication and cooperation as sole methods for achieving centralization are unsatisfactory, even where parties are well informed as to the possible use of protocols and communication for MEG cases. I have explained above that certain jurisdictions may require legislative direction before committing to such cooperation, and that cooperation may be hard to achieve in cases involving multiple jurisdictions.[202] Even when parties and courts do utilize such means (e.g. protocols) these in many cases are confined to general agreements in regard to coordination of the process (rather than 'stronger' means of centralization). This may be a result of differences in national laws and not because centralization is inadequate.[203] As I argued in chapter 3, it is also necessary to scrutinize parties' agreements in regard to jurisdiction as otherwise the case may be handled in a 'haven' jurisdiction.[204] Parties should cooperate 'in the shadow' of standard, widely accepted rules of proper jurisdiction and applicable law.[205]

The concept of global centralized consolidation [206] should thus be entrenched in national and international approaches to MEG insolvencies. An enterprise concept (i.e., the recognition of the group as such) would require courts to take into account 'group considerations' in determining the issue of jurisdiction of the sort expressed, for example, in the petition for recognition of foreign main proceedings in the *Main Knitting* case above,[207] or in the Italian representative's petition in regard to *Eurofood*.[208] The court should take into account in considering the issue of jurisdiction the benefits of locating a centre which is common to the entire group, thus, enabling a harmonized solution with maximum coordination. This will ensure that centralization in the appropriate circumstances can be achieved.

As will be suggested below, in certain scenarios full centralization may not be adequate, but the circumstances where it is or is not desirable to centralize such proceedings are currently unclear. Provisions in approaches to international insolvencies are needed which will clarify in which circumstances full centralization is adequate, and in which cases a lesser degree of centralization should be pursued (or no centralization at all). In case a degree of centralization is efficient and not particularly harmful, rather than grounding jurisdiction decisions

---

[201] See the Model Law and the EC Regulation regimes (section 6.2.1.6.2)

[202] See chapter 3, section 3.4.2.1.

[203] See section 6.2.1.5.

[204] See chapter 3, sections 3.3.2.5 and 3.4.2.1.

[205] Parties bargain against the backdrop of laws relevant to their transaction (see e.g. R. Cooter et al., 'Bargaining in the Shadow of the Law: A Testable Model of Strategic Behaviour' (1982) 11 J. Legal Stud. 225, 225).

[206] See section 6.2.1.6.1.

[207] N 183.

[208] N 175–6, and accompanying texts.

concerning group members on separate determination of venue, it is necessary to ascertain where the centre of the group is located, and allow this place to lead the proceedings.[209] Further provisions will also be needed clarifying the powers of the courts and the law which will apply where centralization of a sort is pursued. Before considering types of centralization and the question of identification of a group home country, the extent to which centralization may be harmful to entity law or territoriality should be appreciated.

6.2.1.7 *Centralization, entity law, and territoriality*

The question is whether a centralized approach for a MEG's insolvency proceedings poses a problem to either entity law or territoriality. In terms of entity law we have already moved past the potential barrier existing in regard to procedural consolidation. It was concluded that as long as the distinction between procedural and substantive consolidation is maintained there is no threat to the economic essence of entity law.[210] The change in jurisdiction if centralization is attempted (where an entity may be 'moved' to another venue due to 'group considerations') should not be regarded as a threat to entity law as such either, as the matter of jurisdiction is procedural.[211] Here too, there is no threat to limited liability, and thus enterprise principles (in this case, concentration of the proceedings based on the group interrelations) should be more easily applied where it promotes the goals of the relevant law. The concept of entity separateness does not encompass state separateness. It operates outside any territorial boundaries, and aims at encouraging commerce by enabling the segregation of assets and liabilities as between entities or an entity and its shareholders.[212] It does not envisage differences in legal regimes and local processes. It should not matter hence to entity law if the destiny of the entity is to be determined by another jurisdiction (the entity remains a legal person, only it is moved to a different location). Therefore, I suggest that in terms of entity law, it should be possible to recognize the group interrelations, i.e. the economic reality of the group operating in integration for the purpose of allocating jurisdiction, enabling the designation of a particular venue as encompassing an entire group. Jurisdiction in insolvency law is very much a concern of connection to the territory,[213] and if an entity has such a connection which is a result of a connection with another entity (as a matter of economic reality) jurisdiction should be ascertained.

What is clearly under threat here is territoriality and state sovereignty—the idea of states being able to control and impose their laws and procedures upon

---

[209] See on other harmful effects of absence of explicit rules on the goals of certainty and predictability in chapter 8, section 8.2.
[210] See section 6.2.1.3.
[211] See chapter 2, sections 2.3.3 and 2.3.4, and see section 2.4.8 where it was noted that there is a degree of acceptance in practice of enterprise law in the area of jurisdiction.
[212] See chapter 2, sections 2.3.2.
[213] See chapter 3, section 3.3.3.

local entities. It has been argued in this respect, that global segmentation provides each country with a discrete firm to focus on, and that firms may yield higher returns when administered on a territorial basis.[214] It has been further argued that, there is generally lesser need for universalism in regard to multinational corporations, as these tend to keep their operations in various countries separate, via the incorporation of separate entities in the countries of operation.[215] This argument however, is contested here as it fails to take into account the variations of MEG operations. As I stated at the beginning of this chapter, there is room for both universalism and territorialism in the context of MEGs. Importantly, though, in the appropriate circumstances (based on the prototypical scenarios) an enterprise–universalist approach should be allowed. Indeed, multinational corporations tend to operate via separate entities,[216] yet this does not mean that the enterprise will not benefit from a global solution. As explained above, in business integrated scenarios the goal of return maximization requires unification.[217]

It was explained earlier that the enterprise–universalist approach invoked here seeking to consolidate affiliates' insolvency proceedings globally should be confined to what we termed 'business integrated' MEGs. This is a way to balance universality and territoriality, led by the goal of return maximization. This way those entities operating as a stand-alone, not integrated with the rest of the group, will primarily conduct their insolvency on a separate basis. However, it should be appreciated that not all groups will operate in this way, and in that case, the group entities (and their stakeholders) should be able to enjoy the benefits of unification. Additionally, in these cases there are fewer significant implications for local policies anyhow, as the entities at stake are not entirely 'local' in essence—they are significantly economically connected to other entities in other jurisdictions. As has been observed elsewhere,[218] local policies are in any case difficult to apply to multinational companies.[219] Consequently, little surrender of local control will be needed by international governance of multinationals.

This alone, though, may result in an approach which is too dichotomized and somewhat missing the economic reality of MEGs where there are more nuanced

---

[214] R.K. Rasmussen, 'Resolving Transnational Insolvencies Through Private Ordering' (2000) 98 Mich. L. Rev. 2252, 2259).

[215] L.M. LoPucki, 'Cooperation in International Bankruptcy: A Post-Universalist Approach' (1999) 84 Cornell L. Rev. 696, 750.

[216] See chapter 1, section 1.2.

[217] Rasmussen indeed mentions that 'there may be firms that experience financial, but not economic, distress, and whose constituent parts are so well integrated that any successful reorganization will need the active cooperation of all countries in which the firm has an affiliate.' (R.K. Rasmussen, 'Resolving Transnational Insolvencies Through Private Ordering' (2000) 98 Mich. L. Rev. 2252, 2259). He also asserts the existence of a trend toward more integrated transnational operations (R.K. Rasmussen, 'A New Approach to Transnational Insolvencies' (1997) 19 Mich. J. Int'l L. 1, 31.

[218] See J.L. Westbrook, 'A Global Solution to Multinational Default' (2000) 98 Mich. L. Rev. 2276, 2298–9.

[219] Since, for example, the multinational company may have transferred assets out of nation states (ibid, 2298–9, 2310–11).

types of structure and operations. Bearing in mind territoriality concerns and with the goal of efficiency in mind certain additional variations of 'business integrated' insolvent MEGs should be considered.

6.2.1.8 Alternative methods of global consolidation—full or partial centralization

Territoriality suggests caution in applying global measures to the foreign related entities. It is therefore suggested here that the solutions should be derived from the type of MEG in distress. Mirroring the economic reality in this way will not only assist in ensuring that the goal of wealth maximization is indeed enhanced in the particular case, it will also provide a degree of flexibility allowing mitigating territoriality concerns. It will avoid the randomness of more rigid approaches that apply 'one size fits all' solutions to what is essentially a diversified form of business. Instead of suggesting that all groups should be handled on a separate, local basis in their insolvencies because of territoriality concerns, or otherwise always be handled in a unified manner, I argue that an attempt should be made to match the solution to the case.

I suggest that in the scenarios depicted by prototype A—the 'business integrated centralized insolvent MEGs'[220]—full centralization is appropriate, especially if reorganization is sought. By 'full centralization' I mean concentration of all insolvency proceedings against the members (belonging to the insolvent integrated centralized MEG) in a single jurisdiction as well as concentration of the law which will apply to the insolvency matters regarding those members. In this respect, I suggest that the forum which handles the group proceedings will apply its laws to all aspects of the commencement, conduct, administration, and conclusion of the insolvency proceedings against those group members and their effects.[221] This will correspond with the widely accepted choice of law rule according to which insolvency proceedings are governed by the forum state (the *lex fori concursus*).[222] I also suggest that exceptions to this rule will be kept to the minimum so as not to undermine the unity and harmonization of the process.[223]

---

[220] In the various variants A1-3 (single head, multiple head and isolated head; see chapter 5, section 5.4).

[221] As recommended in UNCITRAL Legislative Guide (n 137 chapter 3), Part two, Ch. I, Recommendation 31. See also the choice of law rules under the EC Regulation (chapter 3, section 3.4.2.2 and section 6.2.1.6.3)

[222] See section 6.2.1.6.3.

[223] Ibid. The approach recommended in the Legislative Guide (n 137 chapter 3) is adopted here. See UNCITRAL Legislative Guide (n 137 chapter 3) Part two, Ch. I, para. 80. The Guide refers to very limited exceptions in its recommendations regarding the issue of law applicable in insolvency proceedings (though it mentions more extensive possible exceptions in the commentary). One such exception refers to rights and obligations in a payment or settlement system or in a regulated financial market (the effects of insolvency proceedings on such rights should be governed solely by the law applicable to that system or market) (see Recommendation 32). The second refers to rejection, continuation and modification of labour contracts which may be governed by the law applicable to the contract (see Recommendation 33), so as to give workers, who may often have a relatively

It should be emphasized, that this concentrated choice of law concept applies only to insolvency matters and does not affect rules in regard to the creation of rights and claims. The latter continues to be governed by general conflict of law rules.[224] Thus, the insolvency forum will need to apply its conflict of law rules to determine which laws govern the creation of a right or claim outside insolvency.

Such centralization fits those cases where the relevant companies were integrated and defaulted (or will probably collapse in the near future), and where they were all closely controlled together via the head office of the group. This refers to cases where, for example, a subsidiary had its registered office locally, as well as assets, creditors, and dealings; however it was administered and managed in another jurisdiction. It did not have significant local autonomy and was very much associated with the 'managing jurisdiction'. Centralizing the insolvency process in such cases corresponds with the economic reality of how the group was managed in its ordinary course of business, and will enhance efficient proceedings, especially reorganization. Other 'insolvency concerns' may arise from the application of such a solution, mainly potential problems in regard to creditors' rights and predictability of insolvency outcomes, yet these issues will be addressed in subsequent chapters.[225]

In prototype B, depicting 'business integrated decentralized insolvent MEGs',[226] a 'decentralized' approach should be considered in the course of insolvency. Centralization should be pursued, but with a limited role allocated to the forum presiding over the case (thus, centralization will only be 'partial'). This is not a rigid formula and there may be 'hard cases', but the idea is that if in terms of economic realities the entities were only loosely controlled in the foreign jurisdiction, and had significant autonomy and 'locality' (all of them or particular entities) then it should be possible to treat them as locals also in their insolvency while still retaining the linkage to the principal proceedings (in the course of insolvency). That is, apart from recognizing a centre for the group, the local centres would also be recognized in the sense that local proceedings against the autonomous entities will take place under the local insolvency system. The forum of the centre of the group will lead the group process, be in charge of coordinating a global solution (if such a solution is beneficial), will collect the necessary information regarding the enterprise and generally direct the way forward. Yet, local processes will also take place and the local laws will apply to insolvency

---

weaker bargaining position, the specific protections they were given in their contract (and protect them from the rejection or modification of those contracts in insolvency). The guide also recommends that any additional exceptions should be limited in number and be clearly set forth or noted in the insolvency law (see Recommendation 34). On protection of creditors in applying universalism-based solutions (for MEG insolvencies) see chapter 7, section 7.3.1. On choice of law rules in regard to avoidance transactions and liability to debts of subsidiaries see chapter 9, section 9.6.

[224] Ibid, para. 82.

[225] See chapters 7 and 8.

[226] In the various variants B1–3 (single head, multiple head and isolated head; see chapter 5, section 5.4).

matters arising in regard to the local affiliates. It should be noted that the local proceedings may be themselves multinational, and could even preside over the insolvency process against various other group members if it represents a centre of a regional group. As described in chapter 5, MEGs may be multi-tiered and their organizational structure can be mixed. So, for example, the relationship between an ultimate parent and a subsidiary may be that of decentralization, whereas the subsidiary itself may serve a whole region and may centrally control an integrated centralized group.

What we do not want is an 'all or nothing' solution that may result in loss of value and considerable obstacles to rescue attempts. Especially when reorganization is sought (and the particular subsidiary is likely to be crucial for the global reorganization) the linkage with the local process could be most crucial—gathering of all information regarding the various affiliates to oversee the entire picture, and coordinating of the entire process by some ultimate authority will be critical in assessing and implementing the options that will be the most beneficial for the enterprise.

In other words, even if the situation suggests that local proceedings are necessary, it may still gain from a linkage and cooperation between the various proceedings. Thus, a significant improvement upon existing models, such as the EC Regulation,[227] is the possibility to recognize the group and the necessary linkage among its affiliates even where affiliates in the group had separate COMIs.[228] The amount of control exerted over the other affiliates' processes should be appropriate according to the circumstances, depending on the specific case and the amount of coordination required. Cases 'in between' should also be considered, where albeit there is significant presence in the local jurisdiction, many other elements of the group are located in the group centre, with additional factors suggesting centralization is efficient, in particular the need to reorganize the entire MEG. The future pattern of the organizational structure of the MEG (or any part thereof) should also be taken into account. For instance, it may have been the case that prior to the insolvency proceedings most of the MEG was decentralized. However, post-insolvency a reorganization plan is devised which requires a more centralized administration of the MEG.[229] This in turn will require greater centralization in the handling of the insolvency proceedings (at least in regard to some parts of the MEG). In such scenarios more 'universality' may be sought, driven by economic efficiency. Although efficiency concerns normally suggest that in a decentralization scenario it is more efficient to have a local process in terms of the costs involved,[230] in certain circumstances the overall costs and

---

[227] See sections 6.2.1.5 and 6.2.1.6.
[228] But see below in this section measures that may be taken under the EC regulation to achieve certain solutions for decentralized MEGs.
[229] I am indebted to Professor Jay Westbrook for this insight.
[230] See section 6.2.2.3.

benefits may suggest that full centralization (of all or certain parts of the MEG) is the most efficient solution even in such cases.

Scenarios like that of *Eurofood*,[231] or the German and French subsidiaries in the *Daisytek* case,[232] can typify decentralization. The subsidiaries in these cases were part of an integrated group. Eurofood had significant interrelations with the parent company in Italy, which guaranteed its debts and coordinated its affairs, and it operated as a financing vehicle for various affiliates in the group.[233] Daisytek's German and French subsidiaries were part of the pan-European reseller and whole-sale distributor (of electronic office supplies) that was managed as a group, ultimately coordinated via the head office in England. There were also cross-guarantees between the entities.[234] Evidently, both scenarios involve an integrated group, where the group managed a single business or the entities had significant interrelations.[235] Nonetheless, these subsidiaries had significant local autonomy. Eurofood had a local head office (in Dublin), its affairs were to an extent administered locally and governed by Irish law.[236] The German and French subsidiaries both had local employees and affairs managed locally, by local head offices, although a manager operating in the location of the English parent company was involved in the management of these subsidiaries.[237] This is to be distinguished from cases of non-integration, where although entities are part of the same group, operations took place on a separate basis, with very weak interdependence if at all.[238] In these cases, as aforementioned, the primary assumption is that no linkage is needed (with the non-integrated parts of the group) in the course of insolvency.[239]

---

[231] Discussed in section 6.2.1.6.

[232] Ibid.

[233] See *Re Eurofood IFSC* (Trib (I) 19 February 2004 [2004] I.L.Pr.14.

[234] See *Re Daisytek-ISA Ltd* [2003] BCC 562, 564–5. See also B. Wessels, 'International Jurisdiction to Open Insolvency Proceedings in Europe, In Particular Against (Groups of) Companies' Working Papers Series, Institute for Law and Finance, Johann Wolfgang Goethe University (available at: http://www.iiiglobal.org/downloads/European%20Union/Articles/11-_InternJurisdictionCompanies.pdf).

[235] See chapter 5, section 5.3.2.

[236] See *Eurofood IFSC Limited* [2004] BCC 383. Indeed, this was one of the arguments of this subsidiary's US bondholders (in their attempt to avoid transfer of the main proceedings to Italy). They argued that it was a standalone unit and irrelevant to the group restructuring (see 'Italian and Irish courts clash over Parmalat', *GLOBALTURNAROUND*, April 2004, issue 51, p. 3).

[237] See *Re Daisytek-ISA Ltd* [2003] BCC 562, 565; see also *In re Daisytek ISA Ltd* (Tribunal de Commerce, Cergy-Pontoise, 1 July 2003); AG Dusseldorf County Court, 6 June 2003 (502 IN 126/03); ZIP 30/2003; *Klempka v ISA Daisytek SA*, Cour de Cassation (France) [2006] BCC 841.

[238] See, for instance, the situation of Collins & Aickman vis-à-vis the US entity (*Collins & Aickman Corporation Group* [2005] EWHC 1754 (Ch D)) in which case, after the filing of Chapter 11 proceedings against the ultimate parent located in the US, the European operations were separately controlled via headquarters in the UK; the case of Brac (*Re Brac Rent-A-Car Inc.* [2003] EWHC (Ch) 128; [2003] BCC 248) where the European operations were in a virtually independent cluster; the case of *Daisytek* vis-à-vis the US operations (*Re Daisytek-ISA Ltd* [2003] BCC 562)—Daisytek operated an integrated group within Europe, though it was part of a wider group ultimately controlled by an American corporation, Daisytek Inc (see Fletcher, *Insolvency* (n 3 chapter 3) 388).

[239] Cf. S.L. Bufford, 'International Insolvency Case Venue in the European Union: The Parmalat and Daisytek Controversies' (2006) 12 Colum. J. Eur. L. 429, 469, arguing that cases

Subjecting the entire process to a single direction (in cases of 'decentralized business integrated insolvent MEGs') while conducting local proceedings against certain affiliates can be achieved by 'translating' the notion of 'secondary' proceedings provided in existing cross-border insolvency models (and the corresponding obligation to cooperate with the main proceedings),[240] to the MEG scenario. That is, the main proceedings will refer to the 'group proceedings' while the secondary proceedings to proceedings against related companies with local centres. This means that there is no need for multiple proceedings in the group centre against all the affiliates. One set of 'group supervisory' proceedings can be opened in the group centre, and additional local proceedings in the centres of particular subsidiaries. The court of the 'group centre' will have the authority to supervise and communicate with the entire process. Three main characteristics should be kept. The first is that local proceedings will be subjected to the supervision of the central process, (placed at the group's centre) and should coordinate with it to achieve global solutions, either within a liquidation process, or reorganization or a combination. Second, it should be possible to have either reorganization or a winding-up process locally.[241] Third, opening territorial proceedings against a subsidiary should be done only when it is indeed necessary (dependant on the scenario at hand), and not automatically in regard to any type of MEG. This will prevent the loss of potential benefits of complete centralization, and will ensure the 'correct portion' of universality to be applied in the case.

A proximate solution can otherwise be achieved under the existing models' concepts of COMI (for main proceedings) and establishment (for secondary/non-main proceedings). In case a COMI can be found in regard to all affiliates in the group at hand in a single jurisdiction, it is possible to then open secondary proceedings, in addition to the main proceedings, against particular subsidiaries, if they also had an establishment locally, i.e. an established place of business.[242] Indeed, in the decentralized MEG scenarios, the subsidiaries will have significant local presence. The disadvantage compared with the more explicit 'group solution' is that the proximate solution is dependent on the initial identification of the same place of COMI for each affiliate, which, if not taking into account the group interrelation as a major factor, may be impossible. For example, in

such as *Daisytek* (in regard to the German and French subsidiaries) demonstrate a case of non-integration and therefore proceedings should be administered on an individual separate basis. In my view, such an approach has the tint of a 'black or white' solution which may not benefit the stakeholders. A unified process for a business of the European-Daisytek type (which was operating a single business) could add value to the entire group, whilst still allowing local proceedings to take place. By identifying such a group as business integrated-decentralized (rather than non-integrated) the corresponding solution becomes clearer and more adequate.

[240] See chapter 3, section 3.4.2.2.

[241] To avoid destabilizing a 'rescue' process opened for the group as a whole (cf. EC Regulation (n 173 chapter 3) Article 3(3), under which secondary proceedings can only be winding-up proceedings).

[242] See e.g. proceedings opened against the German subsidiary in *Daisytek* (see section 6.2.1.6).

Eurofood, the Irish court determined (and the ECJ approved) that the COMI (of that subsidiary) was in the local jurisdiction (in Ireland),[243] and therefore centralization or a 'supervision' model (via the Italian proceedings) could not be applied.

6.2.1.9　A single jurisdiction to which the MEG as a whole has connection—identifying the MEG home country

Clearly a precondition for fulfilling the ideal of group centralization in the various levels suggested is the possibility of identifying a 'group centre' from which either all proceedings could be handled or (in the decentralized MEGs) supervised.[244] The feasibility of such an attempt will now be considered.

The main tests for jurisdiction in the context of insolvency (of single debtors) are those based on the debtor's place of incorporation (or formation, statutory seat, or registered office), the location of principal assets of the debtor (or its operations or activities or creditors), or central administration and control (aspects of management) of the debtor.[245] These tests may be combined to provide a standard venue, or the standard venue may utilize a presumption based on one test which may be rebutted by other tests. As aforementioned, a predominant standard test for jurisdiction for single debtors is that of 'centre of main interests' (COMI) (currently provided in all main international insolvency models). With the Model Law already adopted by a significant number of states, the test is becoming increasingly universal.[246] Under this concept, the principal proceedings should be handled or recognized as such if being opened in the centre of main interests of the debtor, which is presumed to be the place of the registered office (or incorporation).[247]

Therefore, incorporation plays a role in jurisdiction determination. Yet, when considering the MEG case, and as the goal of wealth maximization dictates that the standard venue will be such that could refer us to a single location—a 'group home country' (although we are dealing with separate entities)[248]—incorporation as a standard venue is unhelpful.[249] The incorporation test applied to groups will inevitably preclude any global consideration in cases of MEGs (where affiliates were incorporated in different jurisdictions). The MEG itself is not incorporated in a particular country (it is not as such a recognized legal entity[250]) so

---

[243] Ibid.
[244] See also on this issue I. Mevorach, 'The Home Country of a Multinational Enterprise Group Facing Insolvency' (2008) 57 ICLQ, 427.
[245] Ibid, 436.
[246] See chapter 3, section 3.4.2.3.
[247] See chapter 3, section 3.4.2.2.
[248] See section 6.2.2.2; chapter 7, section 7.3.2; chapter 8, section 8.3.3; and chapter 9, section 9.5 for additional considerations in respect to the chosen venue for a MEG in insolvency.
[249] It is also problematic considering fairness in distribution (see chapter 7, section 7.3.2). See also a consideration of the incorporation test in light of the predictability goal in chapter 8, section 8.3.3.
[250] See chapter 2, section 2.3.1.

there is no single country that can be identified as the place of incorporation of the group.[251]

The ECJ, though, dealing with a case of a subsidiary belonging to a MEG in the case of *Eurofood*,[252] did not attempt to mitigate the incorporation presumption in this context. As aforementioned it refrained from stressing a group concept, as such a notion is not available within the EC Regulation.[253] It has further put much focus on the whereabouts of the registered office of each subsidiary, explaining that rebutting the presumption requires factors both objective and ascertainable to third parties.[254] But, the example given to when rebutting the presumption will be successful is the rather extreme scenario of the subsidiary not having any operations at all in the (local) jurisdiction.[255] The judgment in *Eurofood* is somewhat mitigated by the subsequent decision of the ECJ in *Planzer Luxemburg Sarl*.[256] In interpreting the meaning of place of company's business (in the 13th EC Directive) the court explained that primary factors are the registered office but also the place of the company's central administration and other factors (and it refers by analogy to the decision in *Eurofood*).[257]

It has been rightly pointed out that the ECJ in *Eurofood,* in emphasizing the incorporation factor, was merely applying the EC Regulation which only deals with single debtors, and in this context the incorporation presumption

---

[251] An improvement could have been referring to the place of incorporation of the parent company of the MEG. However, this may lead to a place with no real connection to the group entities and thus raise other problems of costs and forum shopping (see section 6.2.2.2; chapter 7, section 7.3.2; and chapter 8, section 8.3.3).

[252] Discussed in section 6.2.1.6 above.

[253] Ibid.

[254] *Eurofood IFSC Ltd* (Case C-341/04) [2006] OJ 2006 C143/11, [26]–[37]. On ascertainability to third parties in this context see further in chapter 8, section 8.3.3.

[255] The court referred to a 'letterbox' company that is not carrying on any business in the country where its registered office is located (*Eurofood IFSC Ltd* (Case C-341/04) [2006] OJ 2006 C143/11, [26]–[37]). This approach was followed by the Dutch court in the case of *BenQ* (*BenQ Mobile GmbH & Co OHG [a trading partnership]* and *BenQ Mobile Holding BV*, Docket No 1503 IE 4371/05 Munich, 5 February 2007) where the court took jurisdiction over the parent company of that group based on the fact that the company had its registered office in the Netherlands and it performed some activities there, knowable to third parties, notwithstanding the fact that the group was managed from Munich. See also cases prior to *Eurofood* taking a similar approach to the presumption of incorporation, e.g. Tribunal de Commerce in Charleroi (Commercial Court Charleroi, Belgium), judgment of 16 July 2002, *Me Herstens v SARL Bati-France* [2004] Tijdschrift voor Belgisch Handelsrecht 81; *Rechtbank van Koophandel Tongeren* (Commercial Court Tongeren, Belgium), judgment of 20 February 2003; *Voorlopige bewindvoerders van de SPRL C v SPRL C* [2004] Tijdschrift voor Belgisch Handelsrecht 70 (where the courts seemed to be prepared to rebut the presumption only where the statutory seat was wholly fictitious).

[256] Case C-73/06) [2007] ECR I-5655.

[257] The case was not concerned, though, with the corporate group complications. See also other EC Regulation cases where courts have given lesser weight to the presumption of incorporation (e.g. Ci4net.com decided prior to the ECJ judgment in *Eurofood* (*Ci4Net.com. Inc.* [2005] BCC 277 (Ch D). See also R. Tett and N. Spenser, 'COMI: Presumption, what presumption' (2004) 17 Insolv. Int.); and other cases where the court found a mutual COMI to all companies comprising a group notwithstanding different registered offices (n 170).

has merits.[258] Yet, considering the significance of MEGs,[259] reference to the presumption in this context could have been more lenient. Even within the EC Regulation in its current form it could be possible to apply only a weak presumption that incorporation is the centre of main interests of the particular group affiliate, while giving factors relating to the group relationship greater emphasis.[260]

A test based on degree of operations is also problematic when assessed in light of the need to identify a single focus point for the entire group, as it lacks robustness. Assets and activities tend to be spread among the entities and the countries where the MEG operates, with none of them having a clear majority. In addition, some assets could be of a mobile nature and even be outside the boundaries of any country.[261]

What could be most useful for our purpose is a test based on elements of control in the MEG context, i.e. the central administration of the MEG, the place where the headquarters of the MEG is located.[262] In fact, this seems to be a key factor underlying the concept of COMI (for single debtors). As mentioned earlier,[263] the exact meaning of 'centre of main interests' is somewhat vague. Indeed, the EC Regulation does not define what the COMI of a company is (except for providing the presumption of incorporation). On its face, a COMI could be identified according to operations (or location of most assets) or otherwise it could be based on aspects of management. Nevertheless, both the Report Virgos/Schmit and the Recitals to the EC Regulation,[264] stress that the COMI should be at the place where the debtor conducts the administration of his business on a regular basis and that it should be ascertainable by third parties.[265] Interpretations of the

---

[258] See P. Torremans, 'Coming to terms with the COMI concept in the European Insolvency Regulation' in P. J. Omar (ed.), *International Insolvency Law Themes and Perspectives* (Ashgate, Aldershot 2008), 173, 181. See also H. Eidenmuller, 'Free Choice in International Company Insolvency Law in Europe" (2005) 6 EBOR 423, 447 (suggesting replacement of the COMI standard in the EC Regulation with registered office as the criterion for jurisdiction). But see additional deficiencies of the incorporation test discussed in chapter 7, section 7.3.2; and chapter 8, section 8.3.3 in regard to problems of forum shopping.

[259] See chapter 1, section 1.2.

[260] See though the discussion in section 6.2.1.8 suggesting that the *Eurofood* case itself demonstrates a scenario where local proceedings should have been opened, though with a linkage to the principal process.

[261] See L.M. LoPucki, 'Cooperation in International Bankruptcy: A Post-Universalist Approach' [1999] 84 Cornell L. Rev. 696, 716 (LoPucki gives the example of assets which were leases in satellites orbiting the earth). On other problems associated with this test see chapter 8, section 8.3.3.

[262] See also I. Mevorach, 'The road to a suitable and comprehensive global approach to insolvencies within multinational corporate groups' [2006] JBLP 455, 471–78; G. Moss, 'Group Insolvency—Choice of Forum and Law: the European Experience under the Influence of English Pragmatism' (2007) 32 Brook. J. Inl'l L. 1005; I. Mevorach, 'The Home Country of a Multinational Enterprise Group Facing Insolvency' [2008] 57 ICLQ, 427.

[263] See chapter 3, section 3.4.2.2.

[264] Ibid.

[265] Report Virgos/Schmit; Recital (13) of the EU Regulation. See also Virgos, 'The 1995 European Community Convention on Insolvency Proceedings: an Insider's View', in: *Forum International*, No 25, March 1998, 13, noting with regard to the need that the place will be ascertainable to third

COMI concept embedded in the UNCITRAL Model Law have also suggested that it directs courts to consider the country where the debtor's headquarters are located as the country of main insolvency proceedings.[266] At the least, the headquarters criterion is consistently listed as one of the key factors indicating a centre of main interests.[267] The rationale underlying the incorporation presumption discussed above is also derived from the assumption that normally the registered office of the company will accord with the actual head office.[268]

Applying the 'headquarters criterion' (or the main place of administration of the debtor's affairs) in the group case enables identification of the place of command and control of the 'business integrated' insolvent MEG. That is, the place from which the business as a whole was actually controlled, or coordinated (in the more decentralized patterns). Subsidiaries are generally directed and managed from headquarters of the group enterprise. The headquarters may be viewed as the brain and nerve centre, while the subsidiaries as the limbs.[269] Hence, the headquarters reflect the 'meeting point' for the various entities. The head office criterion can thus be the main 'connecting factor' for group venue, and should be identified considering the group as a whole looking at the group as an entity for the (limited) purpose of jurisdiction identification.[270] Having a decisive factor will then resolve situations where different connecting factors direct us to different countries. Thus, in a case such as *BCCI*,[271] where factors point in different directions (in *BCCI* the parent company was incorporated in Luxemburg with a 'brass plate' headquarters there, the group's assets were spread around the world and operational headquarters were based in London) the country of principal proceedings should be that in which the actual headquarters were located.[272]

---

parties that 'the place where the debtor conducts the administration of his business and centralizes the management of his affairs (e.g. contractual and economic activities with third parties) satisfies this requirement; not the place where the assets, whatever their value, are located, not the place where the goods are manufactured (e.g. the place of industrial establishment, etc)'. See also G. Moss and C.G. Paulus, 'The European insolvency regulation—the case for urgent reform' (2006) 19 Insolv. Int. 2 (suggesting optional definitions to COMI that focus on head office functions). On the aspect of ascertainability and predictability of COMI to third parties see chapter 8, section 8.3.3.

[266] See Memorandum from J.L. Westbrook to the National Bankruptcy Review Commission (29 July 1997, in National Bankruptcy Review Commission, Bankruptcy: The Next Twenty Years (1997), app E-1 at 7.

[267] See e.g. *Re Tri-Continental Exchange Ltd* 349 BR 627 (2006) (D (US)); *Re SPhinX, Ltd* 351 BR 103 (Bankr SDNY 2006), 117; *Re Bear Stearns High-Grade Structured Credit Strategies Master Fund, Ltd* 374 BR 122 (Bankr SDNY 2007), 128; *Re Bear Stearns High-Grade Structured Credit Strategies Master Fund, Ltd* (US District Court. SDNY 2008), 25–9; *In re Basis Yield Alpha Fund (Master)*, 381 BR 37 (Bankr. SDNY 2008).

[268] See Report Virgos/Schmit (n 180 chapter 3).

[269] See C. Tugendhat, *The Multinationals* (Eyre and Spottiswoode, London 1971) 22–3.

[270] See section 6.2.1.5.

[271] *Re Bank of Credit & Commerce International SA (No. 10)* [1997] 2 WLR 172 (Ch 1996) (see n 436 and further discussion of the BCCI collapse in sections 6.2.2.3 and 6.3.4; chapter 7, section 7.4.1; n 79 chapter 8 and; n 81 chapter 9).

[272] Indeed, commentators expressed the opinion that England was the actual centre of interests of the BCCI group although the main proceedings against the group took place in Luxembourg

Senior decision-takers may typically be concentrated around the parent company, though in fact they may have operated in a different location than that where the parent was incorporated or had business. The parent can be incorporated in one place or have activities in a particular country while the operational headquarters of the group are located elsewhere.[273] It should also be noted that the headquarters we are looking for are not necessarily those in relation to the entire group which has at its top the ultimate parent company, but only that of the 'business integrated' collapsing MEG.

Relevant circumstantial matters may assist in locating the operational headquarters of the group. This includes: the location where executive meetings were taking place, and where the financial affairs were directed; whether this management had the authority to direct or coordinate the global business (the various activities of the group companies throughout the world); whether the registered office or another head office is actually the address of principal executive offices or whether it is only a 'post box', and whether the majority of the administrative functions of the companies were conducted from this place; whether commercial policy was decided at this location; whether key contracts were subjected to that jurisdiction's laws. This is by no means an exhaustive list, but it presents several aspects that can usually assist in the identification of place of central control over an integrated group.

Bearing in mind possible errors in locating the COMI, and that there may be difficulties in collecting all necessary evidence (especially where considering groups with numerous entities) at the onset of the proceedings,[274] the standard venue should incorporate means of correcting error. Also, it should be possible to challenge in real time the decision regarding jurisdiction. Thus, when the proceedings are lawfully but inappropriately located it should be possible to ask for a transfer of the insolvency proceedings to be conducted from the proper jurisdiction.[275] Namely, it should be possible to transfer the jurisdiction of the principal

---

(see e.g. I.F. Fletcher, 'The European Union Regulation on Insolvency Proceedings' [2003] INSOL INTERNATIONAL, Cross-Border Insolvency, 15, 37). It would not be accurate to assert then that the *BCCI* case demonstrates the impossibility of identifying a single 'home country' for a distressed corporate group (an opinion expressed in L.M. LoPucki, 'Cooperation in International Bankruptcy: A Post-Universalist Approach' (1999) 84 Cornell L. Rev. 696,713–15) but rather it shows that there should be a clearer standard for an acceptable centre.

[273] In the case of *Crisscross* for instance, the actual headquarters of the group were in London at the place of incorporation of one of the group's subsidiaries but not of the parent company (*Re Crisscross Telecommunications Group* (unreported, 20 May 2003) (Ch D)). As aforementioned, in the case of *BCCI* the parent company was incorporated in Luxemburg whereas the actual headquarters were apparently in London (see *Re Bank of Credit & Commerce International SA (No. 10)* [1997] 2 WLR 172 (Ch 1996)).

[274] See further on problems associated with obtaining information in section 6.2.2.2. Distortions in allocating COMI may also be a result of forum shopping (see chapter 7, section 7.3.2).

[275] Similar to the power given to English courts in domestic bankruptcy cases. The courts have a general power of transfer that may be used to relocate proceedings in the court in which they can be most suitably and conveniently administered and a specific power to transfer proceedings in cases where it transpires that the proceedings have commenced in the wrong court (see

process to the appropriate forum, though this possibility should be carefully used, as it may have implications for the legal regime that will be applied and may involve significant additional costs. Particularly when proceedings are already underway such change should only involve subjecting local proceedings to the supervision of main jurisdiction rather than altering the locus of the proceedings altogether.[276] However, if the entity which exerted control over the various affiliates joins the process only after proceedings against the other affiliates have already started to a substantial level, then it should be permissible to move or alter the supervisory authority to the court where this entity is located.[277]

To some extent, this approach gains support in practice. It was shown above, that in numerous cases where proceedings were opened against MEGs under the EC Regulation[278] the courts took a pragmatic approach and placed all affiliates proceedings in a single jurisdiction.[279] In these cases, the COMI of each of the companies comprising the group was located in the venue of the group head office (although some of the subsidiaries were incorporated in countries other than that of the place of the group headquarters, and may even have had some operations locally). A similar tendency can be detected when considering cases applying the UNCITRAL Model Law in the context of groups. For example, in the cases of *Main Knitting* mentioned above,[280] the US court recognized and gave various relief to all Canadian proceedings opened against the group affiliates, including the US subsidiaries, based on the assertion that chief executive offices were located in Canada, notwithstanding incorporation of subsidiaries in the US and the presence of assets in that jurisdiction.[281] This inclination of courts to place insolvency proceedings of related companies at the place of the group headquarters correlates with the idea of looking for the centre of main administration of a

---

I.F. Fletcher, *Law of Insolvency*, 3rd edn (Sweet & Maxwell, London 2002) [hereinafter: Fletcher, *Law of Insolvency*], 131–2, 133–5, 582–3).

[276] Applying the model as suggested in section 6.2.1.8.

[277] See I. Mevorach, 'Centralizing insolvencies of pan-European corporate groups: a creditor's dream or nightmare?' [2006] JBL 468, 484.

[278] N 173 chapter 3.

[279] See section 6.2.1.6. See also I. Mevorach, 'The Home Country of a Multinational Enterprise Group Facing Insolvency' (2008) 57 ICLQ 427, 444–5.

[280] See section 6.2.1.6.

[281] As noted above, this was subject to debate, and indeed the opposing creditor based his argument on a combination of incorporation and main assets and activities tests (*In Re Main Knitting Inc. Et al,* Nos. 08 (11272, 11273, 274), Objection of HSBC Bank USA, National Association to the Petition for recognition of Canadian proceedings under 11 USC s. 1515 (Bankr NDNY May 1, 2008)). The recognition order was subjected to a settlement between the parties (see n 89, and accompanying text). See also the case of *Creative Building*, where recognition and relief was granted in regard to all proceedings opened in Canada against the group affiliates. In regard to the US subsidiary (CBM US) the basis for recognition was having an establishment in Canada (with the result that the relief was not automatic), anyhow the presence in Canada was based on the connection to the parent company—the fact that the subsidiary was owned and controlled via the head office in Canada (see *Creative Building Maintenance Inc. Et al,* Nos. 06 (03586, 03587), Memorandum of law in support of (1) verified petition under Chapter 15 for recognition of a foreign proceeding and (2) injunctive and other relief (Bankr WDNY November 15, 2006)).

debtor and it provides the opportunity to place all the proceedings of the group's members in one place which reflects a connection to the group as a whole.

It should be noted, that in cases of prototype B MEGs (the decentralized scenarios),[282] the headquarters criterion can apply in the same way, only now the proper venue may assume a somewhat different role—this time, looking at the head office's location as the centre of coordination (rather than centre of control) and designating the venue as holding the principal insolvency process. However, as divisions of the group were managed as autonomous units it may mean that the relevant entities will have strong mutual connections to the local management in terms of the way creditors dealt with the entities, the applicable law, the availability of information etc. Hence, though the role of the headquarters is operationally different it still reflects the meeting point of the various companies and the most significant connection the integrated group as a whole has to a particular place. Here as well, the headquarters test (in its specific characteristic as coordinator and supervisor) will accord with the way the business was actually operating. The same idea applies to those 'mixed' scenarios,[283] where the entire group is coordinated via a global headquarters, though there are centralized regional sub-groups. Each of these independent (to some degree) units can be handled centrally at the venue of their head office, while maintaining the linkage to the ultimate coordinator, if the latter was part of the integrated collapsing group. Of course, if there is only one such sub-group (and no global operation to coordinate) then the local centralized process will suffice.

It should also be noted that, if a consistent approach is taken for identifying the COMI of single companies, using the head office criterion as main factor, then it is most likely that identification of the COMI of each company in a group separately will fit with the identification of the group's COMI in those scenarios of centralized groups (prototype A[284]). Considering the group as a whole when determining the venue will in such circumstances only serve as reinforcement of the decision to locate the entities' COMIs in one place. It is submitted, that the incorporation presumption should be rebutted in cases where a member of a 'business integrated' MEG has its central administration in country Y albeit being incorporated in country X, which is the case in a centralized MEG scenario. The situation in those cases is similar to a debtor having its central administration in one country and a branch in another, only that here the branch is incorporated. This will normally be supported by other factors such as the law governing its affairs and the location of other affiliates. This should be the subsidiary's COMI even if the rest of the MEG is not collapsing, therefore generating consistent outcomes in cases where the MEG is insolvent. It is also important in situations where the insolvency starts off for a particular member only, but then progresses to include others. It will prevent the need to transfer the proceedings

---

[282] See chapter 5, section 5.4.   [283] Ibid.   [284] Ibid.

or otherwise conduct it in less than the most efficient way, as the subsidiary will be already placed in the MEG centre.

It is apparent that identifying a single or main home country for a MEG can (to some extent) be applied via existing models for cross-border insolvency, interpreting the concept of COMI in a way compatible with the MEG scenario. Though, I suggest that an improvement on the existing state of affairs would be directing parties and courts to ascertain jurisdiction for the group as a whole by investigating where the 'group COMI' is, using the operational headquarters criterion as key. This could be done by providing guidelines to courts in regard to handling MEG insolvencies or enhancing the use of protocols to achieve centralization via identification of a 'group COMI' based mainly on elements of actual control. More effectively (as explained above),[285] such a notion should be included within a legislative framework which will explicitly address insolvencies within MEGs.

As mentioned above, the International Insolvency Institute Committee on International Jurisdiction is currently working on devising (non-binding) judicial guidelines for coordination of MEG insolvencies.[286] As explained, the guidelines take a 'centralized approach' to MEG insolvencies and suggest concentrating proceedings in a single jurisdiction where possible (considering national laws). In this respect the guidelines attempt to define what a MEG COMI may be. They currently suggest that 'enterprise COMI' means 'the center of main interest of a multi-national enterprise group'. It is further explained that 'The Enterprise COMI should, however, be the place from which the enterprise is actually operated rather than merely a registered place of business with no relationship to the real management'.[287] It thus adopts the idea of locating the COMI of a group with notions of actual control (real management) as key factors in identifying such a centre.

UNCITRAL Working Group V's Secretariat, in introducing the international issues (as a basis for the current discussions by the Working Group of the international aspects pertaining to enterprise groups' insolvencies[288]), explains that it might be possible in some cases to commence in a single state insolvency proceedings against different group members located in different states. For this purpose, it suggests, a jurisdiction most central for the enterprise group may be identified.[289] The current working paper refers to various factors which may be utilized in order to determine whether insolvency proceedings against the subsidiary may be handled in a location other than its own place of incorporation. These are centred on determining the relationship between the subsidiary and its parent

---

[285] See section 6.2.1.6.5.
[286] N 100 chapter 1.
[287] III Draft Guidelines (ibid), Definitions.
[288] I refer to the material which was provided to the Working Group prior to its fifth meeting (Vienna, 17–21 November) (see n 78).
[289] WP.82/Add.4 (n 78), para. 11.

and the degree of interdependence of the former on the latter.[290] Additionally, it is provided that an enterprise COMI may be identified only for closely integrated groups, and in that case reference may again be made to various factors which may point to the degree of integration among the group members. These factors are focused on the degree of interdependence among the group members, and also include third party perceptions concerning the location of office functions including marketing, pricing, and delivery of products.[291] The working paper also observes that to be successful, a definition of group COMI would need to be internationally recognized, accepted and widely adopted.[292] The work is still in progress, yet, it was indicated in the report of the last meeting of the Working Group that although perhaps desirable, it would be difficult to reach a definition of an enterprise group COMI which is aimed at limiting, for example, the commencement of parallel proceedings.[293] Nonetheless, some suggestions were made as to how the COMI of the group might be identified. These included the place from which the financial affairs of the group are coordinated, the place where the group policy was set and management decisions made, the place where manufacturing occurred, and the place from which the group was controlled.[294] Reference was also made to the factors mentioned above regarding rebutting the presumption of incorporation in regard to the single companies and factors identifying integration.[295] It might be thus that a definition of COMI will eventually be agreed upon by the Working Group (by probably referring to a variety of factors which point to the real centre of gravity of the MEG), though this might eventually be used (in the context of the work of the Working Group) in order to achieve only partial centralizations, under which parallel proceedings may be opened while parties and courts are encouraged to acknowledge the centre forum as the ultimate coordinator of the group proceedings.[296]

6.2.1.10 Problems in identifying a home country

Territoriality concerns also instruct us to be cautious in proposing one court–one law regime, i.e. centralization in the group context (and this applies also to a supervisory concept), as this demands identification of a principal proceeding in the home country of the group, which might be a problematic task to perform.[297] Indeed, there may be 'hard cases' in this respect, where a single connection to

---

[290] Ibid, para. 6.

[291] Ibid, para. 13. On creditors' predictability of the insolvency forum see chapter 8, section 8.3.3.

[292] Ibid, para. 9.

[293] UNCITRAL, UNCITRAL Draft report of Working Group V (Insolvency Law) on the work of its thirty-fifth session (Vienna, 17–21 November 2008) 17 November 2008, A/CN.9/WG.V/XXXV/CRP.1/Add.1 (on file with author), para. 15.

[294] Ibid, para. 17.

[295] Ibid, para. 19; Draft Report CRP.1/Add.2 (n 99 chapter 1), paras. 1 and 2.

[296] Ibid, para. 1. See also section 6.2.1.8 on the concepts of partial and full centralization.

[297] See chapter 3, sections 3.3.2.3 and 3.3.3.

the MEG as a whole is difficult to ascertain, even when considering the rather straightforward head office criterion.[298]

One example is that represented by prototypes A3 and B3—the 'business integrated centralized (or decentralized) isolated head insolvent MEGs'.[299] That is, where although the head office of the MEG is in a certain country and it is real and operational, the majority of all other connecting factors are grouped in another country (i.e. the place of incorporation of the subsidiaries, their operations, creditors, and assets). In this situation the nexus to each of the two jurisdictions may actually be equal, even when looking at the group and its stakeholders as a whole. To illustrate, if all the subsidiaries of a group are incorporated in country X, the bulk of assets is there and all creditors are there, however the operational headquarters is in country Y, then there is a case to look at country X as an appropriate venue for the group's insolvency as well. Country X may be regarded as the centre of gravity of the entire group, as the headquarters in country Y are in fact 'isolated' (although not a façade) and as all other factors lead to country X, so that it is almost a case of a (country X) domestic group. This is a scenario very different to the cases where the constituent companies are spread over a number of countries; assets are located in various places and so on. Then, the headquarters test, as aforesaid, is certainly the best factor connecting the group to a single venue.[300]

Another set of 'hard cases' is that represented by prototypes A2 and B2—the 'business integrated centralized (or decentralized) multiple head insolvent MEGs', and prototype C—the 'business integrated heterarchical insolvent MEGs'.[301] The MEG may have had more than one head office managing the group operations. The business may have been split organizationally, and controlled via several sets

[298] These scenarios are also considered in I. Mevorach, 'The Home Country of a Multinational Enterprise Group Facing Insolvency' (2008) 57 ICLQ, 427, 445–8.

[299] See chapter 5, section 5.4.

[300] The case of *Maxwell* (*Maxwell Communication Corp.* 170 BR 800 (Bankruptcy SDNY 1994); *Maxwell Communication Corp.* [1993] 1 WLR 1402 (Ch 1993)) may demonstrate a scenario of such a 'balance of connecting factors'. The Maxwell group had most of its important subsidiaries located and managed in the US but on the other hand the parent company was incorporated in the UK and the UK was the financial and governance centre of the entire group. Indeed, from the point of view of the relevant courts, both the American and the UK courts believed they had an interest in handling the case (see also J.S. Ziegel, 'Corporate Groups and Crossborder Insolvencies: A Canada–United States Perspective' (2002) 7 Fordham J. Corporate & Financial L. 367, 379). Although it can be convincingly argued that the English court should have been the designated venue as the place of central administration, there is also a strong case in favour of the US jurisdiction where all the substance of the group business was located (see J.L. Westbrook, 'The Lessons of Maxwell Communication' (1996) 64 Fordham L. Rev. 2531, 2538). In this case a protocol (which was approved by the courts in the US and the UK) was devised and a coordinated reorganization plan has been achieved via cooperation among the two concurrent insolvency proceedings (see E.D. Flaschen and R.J. Silverman, 'The role of the examiner as facilitator and harmonizer in the Maxwell Communication Corporation international insolvency', in J.S. Ziegel (ed.), *Current Developments in International and Comparative Insolvency Law* (Clarendon Press, Oxford 1994) Chapter 25).

[301] See chapter 5, section 5.4.

of management. Or, the group may have been structured in a way that there was no single head exercising control over subsidiaries. Thus, instead of having one 'head' and 'brain' controlling or coordinating the entire group (in its ordinary course of business), there may be in fact two (or more) heads of the enterprise. It could also be a case where decision-making takes place as between managements of equally positioned entities (in the heterarchichal scenarios). These scenarios may actually represent a non-integrated group, however to the extent that the different headquarters coordinated the management of the group to create a single group business (or the managements of entities in the heterarchichal scenarios) then we are faced with a 'business integrated' MEG that requires coordinated solutions, however the head office test is hard to use.[302]

Yet, even in a case where a centre may be an elusive notion, a global unified solution should not be abandoned. Contractualism of a sort could assist in such situations of difficulty in locating a home country,[303] encouraging the parties to agree on the venue between the options representing equal connections between the MEG and the jurisdiction (neither may be the one having the clear connection to the group as a whole, but will be the 'next best thing').[304] Thus, courts should be equipped with further discretion to defer to the proximate jurisdiction to which the group has many connections, considering the other tests mentioned (incorporation, assets, and operations) and taking into account any agreements the parties may have reached regarding the jurisdiction to assist in the decision.

It may well be, though, that a single centre cannot be found in these kind of cases, but once again, refraining from a 'one size fits all' solution, and driven by the insolvency goal (here maximizing returns to creditors and promoting rescues) alternative solutions should be sought. That is, global consolidation should be attempted by applying other means. If centralization or supervision is not achievable, cooperation and coordination between parallel proceedings could still be a possible way ahead, and should be pursued.[305] For instance, consolidation could be achieved by conducting two or more main proceedings which coordinate the group insolvency together (in the various head offices controlling or coordinating the group, or the head office and the place of the majority of activities). Flexibility in ways of implementing procedural consolidation (or cooperation

---

[302] An example is the case of *Eurotunnel* (*Eurotunnel Finance Ltd* (Tribunal de Commerce de Paris, 2 Aug 2006) (unreported), mentioned in n 170) where there were two parent companies (French and English) owning the global integrated operation (see n 48 chapter 1). Indeed the decision of COMI in this case was not 'clear cut'. Eventually the global restructuring took place under the French 'Procedure de Sauvegarde'. The French court concluded inter alia that the various group entities' management was largely concentrated in France, as was also described in the annual reports of the parent companies (see C. Mallon, 'Eurotunnel', presentation delivered in Eighth Annual INTL Insolvency (III) Conference, Berlin, 9 June 2008 (on file with author)).

[303] See chapter 3, sections 3.3.2.5 and 3.3.3.

[304] See also chapter 7, section 7.3.2 for concerns regarding parties' choice of COMI.

[305] See section 6.2.1.5.

and coordination among courts and representatives) on a global level is thus particularly beneficial.[306]

6.2.2 Promoting timely and efficient resolution of the insolvency process

6.2.2.1 Reducing excessive and complex litigation

The event of insolvency of 'business integrated' MEGs might elicit multiple cross-border claims. Parent companies may have claims against their subsidiaries and vice versa (as a result of inter-group loans for instance). A creditor may have claims against several companies regarding the same debt (as a consequence of cross-guarantees for instance). Several creditors of different components may have claims regarding the same asset (resulting for instance from intra-group transactions and cross-credits). In a global context this may result in a flood of contested proceedings, jurisdictional conflicts, a need to shuttle claims to different entities in different countries etc. All such claims and disputes evidently could result in high costs and lengthy processes. It is enough that the companies had a significant amount of mutual transactions to cause complexities and substantial magnitude of litigation.

Extensive litigation may also be a result of the way the group was managed and controlled and the behaviour practised by the corporate group. Various affiliates may have causes of action against the controlling entity or other affiliates in regard to liability for their losses or voidable transactions.[307] If all such litigation is taking place trans-nationally with duplications with regard to the causes of action or parties involved then inevitably costs increase. Here as well, jurisdictional and choice of law conflicts will generate growing expenditure. Furthermore, the 'territorial' scenario of concurrent jurisdictions may result in the refusal of a certain court to enforce judgments given by other foreign courts. This is costly also because it might require repetitive procedures over the same issues in the courts of the various entities of the group relevant to the dispute.[308]

Another aspect of further litigation may revolve around questions of control over assets and over subsidiaries. That is, administrators appointed to reconstruct or to liquidate a company, which in fact was related to a wider business with operations (through subsidiaries) across the globe may attempt to expand control over

---

[306] As suggested above, the current proposal of UNCITRAL Working Group (n 96 chapter 1) to give procedural coordination a broad meaning encompassing a variety of solutions, as well as the wide array of means of cooperation among courts and representatives currently suggested by the Working Group is especially important when considering the international scenario (see section 6.2.1.2).

[307] See chapter 9.

[308] See K. Hofstetter, 'Multinational Enterprise Parent Liability: Efficient Legal Regimes in a world Market Environment' (1990) 15 North Carolina J. of Int'l Law and Comm. Reg. 299, 330, further stating that there is a potential for mutual opportunism and conflicting assertions among host country courts (in which a certain subsidiary is located) and home country courts (in which a parent is located) in applying checks on regulatory and adjudicatory powers.

cross-border assets and subsidiaries in order to be able to design a workable plan for the business or to maximize value for creditors in any possible way. However, since different administrators might be appointed to supervise the group's companies rather than one of them presiding over the entire group, such intentions are bound to end up in clashes. Disputes with other administrators appointed to supervise affiliates' proceedings or otherwise with local creditors might emerge, in addition to extensive jurisdictional battles, all of which are obviously expensive and time-consuming.

In the case of *Parmalat*,[309] for example, the attempts of the Italian Extraordinary Administrator to gain control over foreign units of the group resulted in significant costs. Since the enterprise was sprawled all over the world, the administrator needed to get a grip on the non-Italian units as well. For this purpose he tried either to place non-Italian subsidiaries under Italian jurisdiction, or to place its own people as supervisors of foreign subsidiaries.[310] However, this effort was not all successful, as separate administration proceedings were opened against Parmalat's subsidiaries in different countries.[311] The administrator 'fought back' trying to regain control over the subsidiaries and keep his control on the outspread assets,[312] thus incurring additional costs on Parmalat's estate.[313]

Further to increasing the burden of expenses on the insolvency proceedings, such amount of litigation may also slow down the whole process. It may seriously interfere with the effort to have a rapid and efficient sale of assets in liquidation. The commencement of the Lehman Brothers US investment banking group insolvency proceedings, encompassing numerous entities around the world, demonstrates these potential problems. Different types of insolvency proceedings have already been initiated against the group's entities in the US, Europe, and Asia. It is anticipated that the divergence of laws and regimes governing the group collapse will complicate the insolvency process, especially as there are indications of extensive intra-group transfers which took place prior to the collapse of the group. These alleged transfers have already led some internal creditors

---

[309] See n 83.

[310] For instance, the Italian administrator succeeded to get five Dutch subsidiaries (Parmalat Finance Corporation B.V., Parmalat Netherlands B.V., Parmalat Capital Netherlands B.V., Parma Food Corporation B.V. and Dairies Holding International B.V.) and two Luxemburg Parmalat entities (Olex S.A. and Parmalat Soparfi S.A) to be placed under Italian jurisdiction (see 'Parmalat unit account unfrozen', *Financial Times*, 26 February 2004, p. 29; P.J.M. Declercq, 'Restructuring European Distressed Debt: Netherlands Suspension of Payment Proceeding…The Netherlands Chapter 11?' (2003) 77 Am. Bankr. L.J. 377, 383).

[311] See n 86.

[312] For instance, the administrator was seeking to replace the provisional liquidators appointed for the Cayman Islands' subsidiary. The Cayman Islands' court rejected the request and confirmed the appointment of the provisional liquidators (see n 86). An extensive litigation has been taking place with regard to the Irish unit (ibid).

[313] One observer commented with regard to Parmalat when the case was ongoing that 'there is only about US$1 Billion of value left in Parmalat. At the rate things are going, half that could go in legal fees. And, if all this litigation continues, the restructuring could be held up for years' ('Parmalat at legal crossroads' News, *GLOBALTURNAROUND*, May 2004, issue 51, p. 4).

(group members) to press claims against other divisions of the group. It has been noted that the insolvency process is unlikely to be completed for several years, given (among other reasons) the high chances of litigation and the jurisdictional complexities.[314]

Extensive litigation may also impede the possibility of quickly stabilizing a distressed business and presenting a restructuring plan for it (in cases where it is perceived beneficial). In order to prevent a total collapse of the estate, and to be able to use assets wisely in addition to securing refinance for going forward, claims must be resolved speedily with real time responses to conflicts arising in the course of the insolvency.

Having 'global consolidation' concepts in place can reduce these costs. The more such cases will be directed at centralization, the easier it will be to deal with extensive litigation, especially if a single coherent law is applied. A single representative could make informed decisions as to which claims to pursue, having regard to the costs and benefits that may be involved, and the possibility of combining efforts across affiliates in pursuing particular claims.[315] A single court can consider claims of similar origin, applying the forum's laws (to insolvency matters) with which it is most familiar. But settling legal problems to an extent can also be achieved with other means of consolidation such as a coordinated global consolidation via a supervisory lead or on a parallel basis as suggested above.[316] At the least, the insolvency representative and courts can engage in communication and cooperation which can enhance faster resolution of claims.[317] It will also reduce the disputes regarding the control of assets and subsidiaries' proceedings within the MEG as administrators involved in the group's insolvency process will share a common cause and interest. Additionally, direct communication between courts can be used in order to quickly and efficiently resolve jurisdictional battles once they have started.[318] It should be explicitly provided that in cases of connected

---

[314] See 'KPMG discloses Lehman's Asia Risk', *Financial Times*, 27 November 2008; V. Heany, 'Winding Up Lehman', Accountancy (2008) 142 (1383) 94. Lehman Brothers operated globally with its main headquarters in New York, with regional headquarters in London and Tokyo and with many offices in other parts of the world. In September 2008, the ultimate parent company, Lehman Brothers Holdings Inc., a US company, filed for bankruptcy protection under Chapter 11 of the US Bankruptcy Code; the principal trading company of the Lehman group in Europe, Lehman Brothers International (Europe) (incorporated and headquartered in the UK) as well as other members of the group have entered administration proceedings in the UK, and the Japanese companies, Lehman Brothers Japan Inc. and Lehman Brothers Holdings Japan Inc. filed for bankruptcy protection in Tokyo. Note, that at the time the book went to print, the Lehman Brothers' insolvency proceedings were in their beginning phase. Note also that bank insolvency may present special problems outside the scope of this study (see n 176 and n 226 chapter 3 and references provided there).

[315] The issue of claims against group entities in the course of insolvency will be discussed in chapter 9.

[316] See sections 6.2.1.5 and 6.2.1.8.

[317] See section 6.2.1.5.

[318] See e.g. the use of this tool to resolve the jurisdictional battle in the case of *Cenargo* (n 94 and 156).

affiliates, each having proceedings commenced or heard in a different court, communication should be used as a fast track to prevent forum shopping and prolonged battles.[319] Devising clear and predictable rules will further decrease causes for litigation. This matter will be discussed separately later on.[320]

6.2.2.2 *Reducing expenses and time waste on obtaining information*

A major mission of office holders appointed to supervise insolvency proceeding of a distressed company is to gather all relevant information and data regarding its affairs. Such information usually includes the company's financial situation, its activities and customers, its assets and liabilities, the market within which it operates etc. In turn, this information (as well as the current situation on all fronts) will also be disseminated to parties involved. Especially where reorganization is being considered, such information, and its speedy collection are crucial.

In the case of 'business integrated' insolvent MEGs, such information is needed in regard to the entire business, including the financial state of each entity, the cross-entity transactions, the available assets and possible claims against outsiders. From the point of view of the particular entities, they may need information relevant to their own business that may be in the possession of other related entities (for instance, if assets were transferred from one company to another). In case the MEG is split up in the course of insolvency, obtaining such information will inevitably induce more efforts and costs. On the other hand, a global centralized procedural consolidation can result in 'centralized information'. The representative in the principal proceedings (opened against all the entities of the 'business integrated' MEG in distress) should thus be able to easily gather information from any other place in the world where such information may be located (where group entities may have operated), following recognition given to the principal process. Indeed, such relief is generally available upon recognition of foreign proceedings, for example under the Model Law.[321] Critically under the approach proposed here, all proceedings against the related entities are jointly handled, and the representative can seek the information in regard to all those entities. Further enhancing convenience in obtaining relevant information will be achieved if a standard venue is embraced which represents a real connection to the MEG as a whole.[322] It is most probable that such a venue (especially the group operational headquarters[323]) will hold the relevant documentation and information regarding the group affairs.

---

[319] See further on problems of forum shopping in chapter 7, section 7.3.2; and chapter 8, section 8.3.3.

[320] See chapter 8.

[321] See chapter 3, section 3.4.2.3.

[322] See section 6.2.1.9.

[323] As opposed to a criterion solely based, for example, on the place of incorporation of the parent company. The parent can be just a holding company with no significant operations, workforce, or management (see chapter 7, section 7.3.2 for further concerns in directing the case to a jurisdiction with no real connection to the MEG).

On a separate insolvencies system, actions being made in the course of the insolvency process regarding any of the group's members, such as motions filed to court, or attempts to sell assets or to negotiate with potential investors (which are, for example, in the same industry of that of other entities under insolvency) may also be relevant to the ongoing process of other related members, and seeking this information will further increase costs. Administrators might eventually do the same 'job' twice since any particular activity being done for a certain company may be relevant for another and vice versa. The case of *Parmalat*[324] exemplifies this kind of redundancy in actions and costs. On one occasion for instance, the Italian administrator needed to examine the records of one of the subsidiaries,[325] which was located in Malta.[326] However, both he and the provisional liquidators (appointed to supervise this subsidiary's liquidation) went to Malta for the same task of reviewing these documents, ending up with double expenses when costs are viewed on a group-wide level.[327]

In case a centralized approach is impractical or inadequate,[328] then a globally coordinated procedural consolidation, either in the supervisory model or on an 'equal' parallel basis can still reduce the complexities and costs of obtaining information. It can minimize the need to seek data that has already been gathered by a related company. It can enable easy and quick access to information regarding other affiliates or information that is held by such. This again demands application of the ideas of cooperation, communication, and sharing of information among courts and representatives in different jurisdictions where proceedings against those entities have been opened.[329]

6.2.2.3 Reducing costs related to conducting multiple insolvency proceedings, transnational communication, and relocation of proceedings

A clear merit of global consolidation which is concentrated in a single jurisdiction is that it reduces costs of multiple proceedings and hearings. In the MEG scenario it is not only a question of one versus a number of processes dealing with the group, it is also a matter of multiple processes held in different countries. This inevitably raises the costs of transferring information as mentioned above, and of any sort of communication that will usually involve travelling between countries and overcoming language and sometimes time zone differences. It is

---

[324] See n 83.
[325] Parmalat Capital Finance Ltd, which is a member of the Parmalat group of companies.
[326] The direct parent of this subsidiary was a company incorporated in Malta.
[327] See the Cayman Islands' court decision in the case of *Parlamat Capital Finance Ltd* mentioned above (n 86) at 15, 16. The court eventually decided that the costs issue is not a major factor compared with the views of third party creditors willing to have the separate provisional liquidators remain in place (on the issue of creditors rights and centralization see chapter 7, section 7.3).
[328] See sections 6.2.1.8–6.2.1.10.
[329] See section 6.2.1.5.

widely accepted that when a single debtor with branches abroad is placed under insolvency proceedings and consequently proceedings are being conducted in all those places where it had activities, there are wasteful costs involved.[330] Likewise, multiple proceedings being held in different places regarding the same 'business integrated' collapsing MEG are to some extent duplicate processes and therefore wasteful. Having several insolvency proceedings instead of one joint together, will entail having hearings for each company separately, as well as notices for creditors and meetings. On many occasions parties involved would need to be represented in more than one proceeding due to dealings they may have had with various entities of the group.

Such problems were quite prominent in the case of *BCCI* banking group's insolvency proceedings.[331] In this case a globally coordinated effort was conducted in order to close all the group's operations.[332] However, since the group had operations (part through subsidiaries and part through branches) in many countries liquidators were appointed in more than 50 different jurisdictions (with the three main proceedings taking place in London, Luxemburg, and the Cayman Islands from where *BCCI* was ultimately regulated). The liquidators ended up commuting between jurisdictions in an expensive and time-consuming operation.[333] Dealing with multiple insolvency proceedings under different time zones was also a difficulty the administrators of *Barings Bank* had to face subsequent to the bank's collapse in 1995.[334] The restructuring of the *Global Crossing*

---

[330] See Articles 3(1), 3(2) and Recital (12) to the EC Regulation (n 173 chapter 3). See also I.F. Fletcher, 'The European Union Regulation on Insolvency Proceedings' [2003] INSOL INTERNATIONAL, Cross-Border Insolvency, 15, 27–31; R.K. Rasmussen, 'A New Approach to transnational Insolvencies' (1997) 19 Mich J. Int'l L. 1, 18; J.L. Westbrook, 'Theory and Pragmatism in Global Insolvencies: Choice of Law and Choice of Forum' (1991) 65 Am. Bankr. L.J. 457, 461.

[331] Note 436 (and see further discussions of the BCCI collapse in section 6.3.4; chapter 7, section 7.4.1; n 79 chapter 8; and n 81 chapter 9).

[332] Ibid.

[333] See *GLOBALTURNAROUND*, February 2004, issue 49, p. 11; J. Willcock, Letter from the Editor, *GLOBALTURNAROUND*, June 2003, issue 41, p. 2.

[334] Barings collapsed in February 1995 as the result of trading activities carried on in the Far East. The holding company of the group was Barings Bank PLC. On 26 February 1995 Knox J made administration orders in respect of both the holding company and certain subsidiaries and appointed joint administrators to manage the affairs of these companies in London (see in *Barings plc and Anor v Internationale Nederlanden Group NV* [1995] CLY 777 1995 WL 1082385 background on the Barings administration). On 27 February 1995 judicial managers were appointed in Singapore to manage the affairs of Barings Singapore (see generally C. Brown, 'Report of the Board of Banking Supervision Inquiry into the Circumstances of the Collapse of Barings' JIBL 1995, 10(10), 446-52; S.C. Bair, 'Remarks, Lessons from the Barings collapse' (1996) 64 Fordham L. Rev. 1). The creditors were eventually rescued from a $1.4 billion debt as a result of a buyout by a Dutch bank and insurance firm in March 1995. However, the lack of an orderly process for administration of the insolvent multinational enterprises aggravated the debt (see J.K. Londot, 'Handling priority rules conflicts in international bankruptcy: assessing the international bar association's Concordat' (1997) 13 Bankr. Dev. J. 163, 167). Note that the issue of bank insolvency raises particular problems outside the scope of this study (see n 176 and n 226 chapter 3).

MEG[335] involved parallel proceedings taking place in the US and Bermuda.[336] Although successful, the process was highly expensive, as a result of the need to oversee and coordinate parallel proceedings for 16 different subsidiary companies. The multi-jurisdictional element added a further layer of intricacy to an already large-scale assignment.[337]

Global and centralized procedural consolidation is thus beneficial in this respect as well. Yet, as aforementioned, reallocation of proceedings to a single centre in the global case should be done more cautiously, while considering the particular scenario. Generally, it was suggested that such solutions be applied in cases of integrated groups. Indeed, in terms of costs, if the companies comprising the MEG were not integrated then usually what is being done in one of the affiliates' proceedings will not hold significant relevance to the rest of the group. If a joint administration will not be required and therefore will not be conducted then substantial communication, shuttle of information and so forth will not be needed in the first place. Consequently no added costs will occur as a result of the fact that there are multiple proceedings taking place with regard to that sort of group. Even in the integrated MEG cases, changing forum and applicable laws for a business that prior to the event of insolvency had substantial activities and operated under a rather different regime may turn out to be inefficient. It may add complexities rather than facilitate the process, since the business was well established in a specific country working under certain rules.[338] Conducting local process in cases of 'decentralized integrated' MEGs whose entities had significant local autonomy (though possibly supervised by a lead court), as suggested above,[339] hence also corresponds with the goal of costs reduction.

6.2.2.4 *Reducing the inefficiency resulting from successive filings*

The fact that the MEG business is divided into several entities might mean that in the event of financial distress not all companies will become insolvent simultaneously or file for insolvency at the same instance.[340] However, as aforementioned

---

[335] *Global Crossing Ltd* (Chapter 11 No. 02-40188-reg (REG) (Bankr SDNY)).

[336] The group comprised over 200 companies registered in 27 jurisdictions. The top holding companies were Bermudian registered (for tax reasons). However, the group's business was conducted primarily from the US. As a result, when the group sought protection from its creditors it simultaneously filed for Chapter 11 in the US. and sought the protection of the Bermudian court through provisional liquidation proceedings (see S. Moore, 'Global Crossing versus Cenargo The right way and the wrong way, *GLOBALTURNAROUND*, January 2004, issue 48, p. 8.; 'How Global Crossing made it to safety', *GLOBALTURNAROUND*, January 2004, issue 48, p. 6).

[337] 'How Global Crossing made it to safety', *GLOBALTURNAROUND*, January 2004, issue 48, p. 6.

[338] With regard to a single debtor, this is indeed one of the reasons why under the EC Regulation it is permitted to open secondary proceedings against the same debtor (Recital (19) to the EC Regulation (n 173 chapter 3)).

[339] See section 6.2.1.8.

[340] See L.M. LoPucki, 'Cooperation in International Bankruptcy: A Post-Universalist Approach' (1999) 84 Cornell L. Rev. 696, 723 (arguing that filings by one or more members of the group followed later by filings of other members are common).

it is most probable that the collapse of one member within a group will affect other members as well, if they were both integrated; especially if there were significant inter-company links, such as mutual transactions and cross-guarantees.[341]

In terms of administrative costs this may suggest increased complexities. If parts of the group continue to operate regularly, then it might be more difficult to get information relating to their financial state, existing assets, and managers' actions. Administrators would need to update and modify their approaches, predictions, and plans constantly, obviously resulting in inefficient administration. A global procedural consolidation system which allows considering the group interrelations when determining on the opening of proceedings against related companies[342] will enable the entire group to be considered as much as possible in the same instance, and thus eliminate some of these costs.[343]

6.2.3 Global procedural consolidation for 'business integrated' insolvent MEGs—a summary

Preserving and increasing the value of assets, enabling rescues and reducing costs involved with the process suggest that global consolidations for 'business integrated' insolvent MEGs are desirable. The idea is to be able to control or coordinate in a unified manner the insolvency proceedings against the related companies, to consider all relevant entities' situations, to determine the best way ahead for the business, and to conduct the process with reduced efforts and complexities. Especially where reorganization is sought, such linking tools are beneficial.

Yet, as the MEG is comprised of separate entities one caveat is the need to maintain this separateness in the course of insolvency. Thus, the MEG is not to be regarded as a single entity. In order to maintain the proper balance between entity and enterprise principles in this context, each entity in the course of insolvency should have its own debts, assets, and claims and thus separate interests which mean separate voting in the case of reorganization, separate distributions and so forth. It therefore should also be maintained that decisions or orders given in regard to any such group entities in the course of their insolvency would not be enforced against other group members that are not part of the process, unless there is particular cause of action against the outsider entity.[344] The effect of the consolidation in regard to the various issues pertaining, including the powers of

---

[341] See section 6.2.1.1.

[342] See sections 6.2.1.5 and 6.2.1.6.

[343] See, for example, the approach taken in the case of *Daisytek*, where the English court considered the opening of proceedings against all the integrated group entities, some of which were insolvent and some likely to become insolvent (n 160–1, and accompanying texts).

[344] Chapter 9 will address the issue of penalties against group members. Another 'positive' linkage may be sought in the course of insolvency on a voluntary basis in regard to funding of the insolvency processes of the insolvent members. Solvent entities outside the process may be willing to extend financing to the insolvent part of the group which may be crucial for purposes of the group rescue (see section 6.2.1.1).

the representative (or representatives), the assets available, the optional solutions, the restraints upon creditors, the binding effect of a reorganization plan, should all depend on the inclusion of the various entities in the consolidation, i.e. placing them under the insolvency process and linking between them in the course of the event.

Recognizing the group in this context (applying 'enterprise law') means considering the interrelations among the entities in determining whether to place an affiliate under insolvency. It also means linking between the insolvencies (against the related companies) in terms of coordination of efforts and decision-making. Furthermore, it means taking up group considerations when ascertaining jurisdiction, enabling the entire process to be placed under a single regime in appropriate circumstances. As aforementioned, a further question (which will be addressed in the next chapter) is whether entity law should be interfered with, even if in a minor way, in scenarios of 'business integrated' insolvent MEGs. In particular, the mere consideration of solutions beneficial to the MEG as a whole might involve sacrifice on part of creditors vis-à-vis the specific entity.

In balancing territoriality with universality further constraints should be put on the global means for consolidation. Procedural consolidation on a global level will apply to 'business integrated' MEGs as opposed to non-integrated MEGs (or particular entities with significant autonomy within the MEG).[345] In the latter case it is also less likely that major benefits will generate from linkage in the course of insolvency. Complete centralization should be typically imposed in cases of MEGs which were centralized. In decentralized types of cases, on the other hand, a supervisory model can be applied, where the lead proceedings coordinate the entire process. Some flexibility is needed here, in terms of the degree of linkage that may be needed. The purpose of the process should also be taken into account in determining whether complete or 'partial centralization' (where the central proceedings only coordinate the entire process) should be applied, since in a case where reorganization is sought closer linkage is needed. In cases where the home country problem prevents centralization of any sort, coordination between related companies' insolvency proceedings should still be exercised.

To some extent, these courses of action could be taken under existing national or international models (in regard to the groups of countries bound by such models). Mechanisms provided for single debtors' cross-border insolvency could be 'stretched' to apply to the case of groups, in so much as courts will be willing to apply enterprise law—universal solutions (under the suggested limitations) and take group considerations in reaching the relevant decisions. Using the proposed prototypes in the way suggested can assist in applying global group-wide

---

[345] Keeping in mind though the dynamics of the case and the possibility that a linkage may need to be made in case new information is revealed suggesting this will be beneficial (see section 6.2.1.1).

solutions matching economic realities in a way that is not excessively harmful to entity or territoriality.

An improvement on the existing situation would be to provide explicit rules for the case of groups. Then, applying consolidation when required, based on the prototypes and using the various methods, would form the required nuanced approach. This will ensure that group considerations and enterprise universal solutions are not missed and that ultimately maximization of returns is enhanced as much as possible.

At the same time, it would be desirable to promote the adoption of the concept of global procedural consolidation within domestic regimes. A particular national regime may not be subjected to a global framework for cross-border insolvency which may enable de facto consolidation. Even where the case is dealt with under a framework for cross-border insolvency which may allow concentration of the process, the legal regime presiding over the affiliates' proceedings may lack the means or relevant rules to allow procedural consolidation of sort within its jurisdiction. Therefore, having the concept of procedural consolidation and its application to MEG as proposed here in place in the jurisdiction will facilitate the conduct of such proceedings. Additionally, a wide adoption of the concept of COMI in its application to MEGs will assist in enabling centralization of proceedings against group members. In other words, a degree of harmonization should be sought, in the sense of recognizing the concept of procedural consolidation and the possibility of centralization when the case is global, across jurisdictions.[346]

A degree of flexibility in the way such concepts can be implemented should be provided, appreciating the need for room for manoeuvre by local regimes,[347] as well as the need to accommodate the various sorts of procedural coordination that may be applied in various circumstances on the international level. This also refers to group-wide unified solutions which may be achieved in the absence of a formal procedural consolidation order. Differences may be, for instance, in regard to the sort of representatives that may preside over such proceedings and the forms of cooperation among courts and representatives in achieving unified solutions.[348] Essentially, however, entity separateness should be kept while allowing for sufficient coordination to enable asset maximization. Stronger harmonization is required in regard to the COMI concept which is specifically directed

---

[346] This can be done by adoption of concepts that may be proposed 'from the top' by international initiatives (such as recommendations in this area that may be provided by UNCITRAL Working Group V) within national laws (see I. Mevorach, 'Appropriate treatment of corporate groups in insolvency—a universal view' (2006) 8 EBOR, 179, 182).

[347] See chapter 3, section 3.3.3.

[348] See section 6.2.1.1 for various aspects of procedural consolidation (and related unified solutions for group entities in insolvency), and see further on issues of representation in this context in chapter 7, section 7.5.

at the international level and will thus lack usefulness when interpreted and implemented differently by different legal regimes.[349]

6.3 Additional Linking Tools for 'Asset Integrated' MEGs

6.3.1 Maximizing returns and facilitating rescues in 'asset integrated' MEGs

In cases of those MEGs featuring 'asset integration'—prototypes D–F (either in MEGs linked by equity or by contract),[350] additional more interventionist tools may be needed for the purpose of reducing transaction costs and enabling reorganizations. These situations once again refer to scenarios of several entities in financial distress (either a parent and a subsidiary or several sister companies, or any other combination), and the focus is on the administration of their insolvencies. However, here there was integration in terms of the 'contents' of the entities to a significant degree. In other words, the separateness between the entities was ignored with the result of making it either impossible or very costly to treat the entities as separate in terms of the allocation of assets or debts to the particular affiliate in the course of their insolvency. This may occur in different variations, for example, assets being transferred around the enterprise with no proper book keeping, intra-group claims being unascertainable, external debts mixed and various combinations therof.

When such intermingling of affairs is significant it may make it very complicated to turn the wheel back and reconstruct the situation so that assets or debts are related to the particular affiliate. As mentioned earlier in describing the 'asset integrated' type of MEGs, the entanglement in the affairs of the MEG entities may not necessarily be a matter of fraud on creditors.[351] If it is a matter of misuse of the corporate form, then it may explain the intermingling, and support a conclusion to this extent. Yet, misuse per se (not necessarily attached to intermingling) is a matter that will be discussed later on, where particular remedies to deal with misbehaviour will be considered.[352] Similarly, reliance of creditors on the group as a single entity can support the conclusion that it was 'asset integrated', yet 'asset integration' is ultimately a conclusion based on the facts post-insolvency petition.[353]

---

[349] See I. Mevorach, 'Appropriate treatment of corporate groups in insolvency—a universal view' (2006) 8 EBOR, 179, 191. See also the merits of harmonization in terms of certainty and predictability in chapter 8, sections 8.4 and 8.5.

[350] In the various permutations of degree of centralization (see chapter 5, section 5.4).

[351] See ibid, section 5.3.2.

[352] See chapter 9.

[353] See further on the 'reliance' factor in the context of substantive consolidation in chapter 7, section 7.4.2.

In regard to prototypes A–C depicting 'business integrated' MEGS,[354] it was emphasized that the linkage sought in the course of insolvency was procedural, administrative; such that will not generally defeat the separateness between legal entities. Although the idea was to jointly coordinate and (where adequate) centralize the insolvency of such MEGs, entity law concerns required keeping the entities intact in the course of liquidation or reorganization, and assets (and value generated from them) and debts were to remain attached to the particular entity (in the same way as was the situation pre-insolvency). Yet, in the scenarios considered here, the corporate separateness may need to be ignored to an extent if considering the goal of asset maximization and enabling rescues.[355] Regarding the contents of the entities of the 'asset integrated' MEG as completely separate in the course of insolvency will mean alteration of their operational structure pre-insolvency. This alteration, the 'work' of disentangling the web of connections, separating what de facto is one pool of assets and/or debts, ascertaining which creditor belongs to which entity, who owes what and who owns which assets (notwithstanding, for example, the latter being moved around the group while ignoring the corporate form)—all this will be a burden on the insolvency estate, consuming the assets available for distribution. It may also be an impossible task, if the necessary information and evidence is missing. This may also include difficulties relating to the veracity and magnitude of inter-company claims. If the group was integrated to the extent depicted here then inter-company trading or inter-company loans (that in the event of insolvency may become a basis for disputes within the group) may have been conducted with no sufficient records and documentation, as a consequence of the entanglement of the entities. In such circumstances, trying to determine who within the group owes what to any of the other members will again entail very expensive and prolonged proceedings with no guarantee of a successful ending.[356]

Especially if some sort of reorganization may be sought, wasting such time and money on ascertaining claims and the real ownership of assets can be highly detrimental to the ability to have sufficient resources for the continuation of the business and the need for urgent measures as discussed above.[357] But, also in the case of liquidation, the burden on the estate resulting from a need to separate the entities' estates can significantly reduce returns to the stakeholders as a whole.

In terms of coordinating the insolvency, the more the web of inter-connection is complex and the entities operated while ignoring the legal separation, the more

---

[354] See chapter 5, section 5.4.

[355] Other goals will be considered in subsequent chapters.

[356] This problem is also highlighted in I. Mevorach, 'The road to a suitable and comprehensive global approach to insolvencies within multinational corporate groups' [2006] JBLP 455, 488–9. See also H. Peter, 'Insolvency in a Group of Companies, Substantive and Procedural Consolidation: When and How?' in H. Peter, N. Jeandin and J. Kilborn (eds.), *The Challenges of Insolvency Law Reform in the 21st Century* (Verlag Schulthess, Zurich 2006), 199, 201–2. See also the impact of fraud on the reliability of intra-group claims n 33 chapter 7, and accompanying text).

[357] Section 6.2.1.1.

it is likely that unified strategies in terms of the business were also implemented and the enterprise was one whole with high interdependence among the entities. In this case normally there will be an even stronger need for global unification, not only in terms of pooling certain content of the entities but also in terms of considering solutions for the business in the course of insolvency.[358] This is also true in regard to joining efforts when it comes to pursuing claims against controllers and other outsiders regarding various transactions and other misbehaviour in respect to the way the MEG business has been run prior to the insolvency.[359] These matters may be more pronounced in the 'asset integrated' MEG insolvencies where the corporate form was not kept.[360]

The 'domino effect' which was expected to occur in the 'business integrated' scenarios[361] is likely to be even more prominent here, where the separateness among the entities was not kept. Thus (and even to a larger extent than in the 'business integrated' MEG) it would be beneficial in these cases to be able to consider the entire 'asset integrated' MEG in the course of the insolvency process. It will also be a matter of further costs and efforts—to ascertain which parts of such MEGs are insolvent or truly solvent (in case insolvency is a requirement for entering into the relevant insolvency procedure). What may appear in an entity's balance sheet as solvency may be fallacious taking into account the inter-company debts, transfers of assets as between the entities, and so forth.

If the MEG was operating to a large extent as a single entity in the ordinary course of business, either as a result of a planned strategy or as a result of negligence in the way it has been running, reducing costs and enabling effective reorganizations demand mimicking this economic reality in the course of insolvency.[362] In the context of 'asset integrated' MEGs this would imply treating the MEG as a single entity, in the sense that the 'contents' of the entities are mixed (rather than merely the procedures involved in their insolvency).[363] If a 'merger of contents' is perceived desirable, then it should also be possible to achieve such a solution in the smoothest way, using measures such as delegation of powers to office holders and other mechanisms avoiding the need for consensus on the

---

[358] See in regard to 'business integrated' MEGs section 6.2.1.

[359] See section 6.2.2.1.

[360] The issue of remedies to combat group opportunism will be discussed in chapter 9. See also H. Peter, 'Insolvency in a Group of Companies, Substantive and Procedural Consolidation: When and How?' in H. Peter, N. Jeandin and J. Kilborn (eds.), *The Challenges of Insolvency Law Reform in the 21st Century* (Verlag Schulthess, Zurich 2006), 199, 202 (stressing that such claims may be abandoned in cases the entities are acting individually, as they are likely to lack the necessary knowledge or resources to do so successfully).

[361] See section 6.2.1.1.

[362] Other rationales or problems which may arise in respect to imposing such 'strong' linking mechanims will be discussed in chapters 7, section 7.4; and chapter 8, sections 8.3.2 and 8.4.

[363] It is not necessary though to establish a new entity for this purpose. The separate legal entities may remain intact; what is crucial here is the mixture among the assets or liabilities imitating the way these were handled in the ordinary course of business.

part of stakeholders (if this cannot be sought) and overcoming potential strategic behaviour.[364]

On the other hand, the need for 'strong' linking tools is less prominent in regard to those entities within the MEG which were not 'asset integrated' with the rest of the group, as in regard to those entities there is no problem in ascertaining their assets and debts. They may also stay solvent, if not affected by the financial state of the other affiliates, especially if they are not dependant on those affiliates.[365] It is also not necessary to mingle encumbered assets, where it is clear that they are allocated to a particular secured creditor. The same rules in regard to secured creditors in the course of insolvency proceedings may apply here in such circumstances. That is, secured creditors may surrender their security and participate in the collective distribution, or enforce their rights against the asset. In case reorganization is sought, it may be possible under the particular legal regime to subject secured creditors to a moratorium and allow disposition of such assets subject to adequate protection given to the secured creditor.[366]

It may be argued, though, that attempting to merge the contents of the estates of the MEG entities may in itself generate costs of litigation, as a result of parties objecting to this line of action.[367] However, if in terms of the factual circumstances it is reasonable to expect that the costs of disentangling the assets and debts will outweigh the costs of such litigation, in a way that will be detrimental to the group stakeholders as a whole, then return maximization still suggests that such linkage is beneficial. Additionally, as the linkage envisaged here is based on 'asset integration' scenarios, the advantages or disadvantages to different stakeholders are very much uncertain (as it is not clear to which entity they may have belonged and what is the real financial situation of that entity). In a commingling scenario it might be impossible to argue that some creditors will gain advantages and some will not, as the situation suggest that all creditors will be better off. In these circumstances there are no real incentives to litigate a different approach for the business. Yet, an important feature of such linking mechanism would be placing conditions upon them to allow for exclusion of aspects of the group which are not 'asset integrated'.

It will be considered herewith whether methods which enable such 'strong' linkage in the course of insolvency are already in place in legal regimes, whether

---

[364] See chapter 4, section 4.2.2.1. The question of redistribution of rights of certain creditors will need to be addressed though (see chapter 7, section 7.4).

[365] But other remedies may be sought in regard to such entities (see issues of group liability in chapter 9).

[366] See on treatment of secured creditors in insolvency proceedings UNCITRAL Legisaltive Guide (note 137 chapter 3), Annex I (setting forth the sections of the Guide addressing this issue). Security interests might be subject, though, to avoidance provisions (on voidable transactions in the context of MEGs see chapter 9).

[367] See D. Staehelin, 'No substantive consolidation in the insolvency of groups of companies' in H. Peter, N. Jeandin and J. Kilborn (eds.), *The Challenges of Insolvency Law Reform in the 21st Century: Facilitating Investment and Recovery to Enhance Economic Growth* (Verlag Schulthess, Zurich 2006), 213, 218.

and how they ought to be adopted universally, and how they should be applied in the international scenarios. Examining the linking solutions will be based, once again, on an approach which pursues a goal of insolvency, being adaptive and striking a balance in terms of the entity–enterprise, and universality–territoriality dilemmas.

6.3.2 Pooling 'the substance' of entities in the course of insolvency—available mechanisms

Essentially, we need means to merge assets and debts in cases where these aspects of the entities where intermingled in the normal course of business. Assets will be merged so that the aggregate of the assets would be available to meet all the creditors' obligations. Debts will be merged so that distribution of the assets to creditors can be done on a group level, ignoring allocation of creditors to particular entities. This, in turn, would enable costs to be saved and returns to be maximized, as well as achieving effective rescues where this is a viable solution. We also seek some flexibility in terms of available solutions, bearing in mind the different possible circumstances of 'asset integration'. Furthermore, we seek to be able to achieve such solutions within the various insolvency procedures, either in cases of liquidation or reorganization processes.

The doctrine of 'substantive consolidation',[368] in use in certain legal regimes, allows for such 'mergers' of entities in the course of insolvency. Here, not only the insolvency proceedings are being consolidated but also the entities themselves (or otherwise the assets or the debts, while the entities themselves remain intact). In any event it allows for a merger of the contents of the entities.[369] This can be regarded as another example of a degree of acceptance of enterprise concepts within legal regimes (which are normally wedded to the entity doctrine), though as was earlier noted there is much obscurity in this area and it is not explicitly provided in all or even in most legal regimes.[370]

Few regimes allow for substantive consolidation in legislation.[371] Section 271(1)(b) of New Zealand's Companies Act 1993 is such an example. Under this provision, courts are given wide discretion to order that liquidation proceedings of two or more related companies[372] will proceed together as if they were one company, i.e. that assets and debts will be pooled. A set of factors should

---

[368] Also termed 'pooling of assets and debts' (the terms will be used interchangably in this work).

[369] See I. Mevorach, 'Appropriate treatment of corporate groups in insolvency—a universal view' (2006) 8 EBOR, 179, 187. In some cases and in certain regimes substantive consolidation may be extended to include individuals (typically the controlling shareholder), yet the situation of individuals is outside the scope of this work, as explained in chapter 1, section 1.4.

[370] See chapter 2, section 2.4.7.

[371] UNCITRAL mentions that the doctrine is not widespread (see WP.74/Add.1 (n 49), 11).

[372] See chapter 1, section 1.3.7 on approaches to definitions of groups.

be considered prior to taking such course of action.[373] Such pooling orders apply to unsecured creditors only. Finally, the fact that creditors of a company in liquidation relied on the fact that another company is, or was, related to it is not a ground for making an order under the provision.[374] Essentially, courts have ordered pooling in cases where management has failed to operate the constituent companies as independent units, with the result that inter-company transactions were poorly documented, not documented at all, or used to prejudice creditors of the insolvent company.[375] Thus, pooling of assets and debts is possible in what was termed here as 'asset integration' scenarios, i.e. where there was intermingling of the contents of the estate while ignoring the corporate form. The fact of integration is also considered in relation to the question of solvency of the particular member.[376] Pooling may also be allowed in other circumstances as is implied from the wide-ranging authority given to the court,[377] and the guidelines provided under section 272 of the Act, directing courts to consider inter alia the behaviour of the related company in regard to the insolvent subsidiary.[378] These circumstances are not so much concerned with reducing administrative costs; rather they are directed at remedying unfairness in the context of groups (ameliorating harm caused to certain entities).[379] There is flexibility in terms of possible variations of pooling orders under the New Zealand regime, as orders may be subject to conditions.[380]

---

[373] The four guidelines that the court is directed to take into account are the extent to which the related company took part in the management of the company in liquidation; the conduct of the related company towards the creditors of the company in liquidation; the extent to which the circumstances that gave rise to the liquidation of the company are attributable to the actions of the related company, and the extent to which the businesses of the companies have been intermingled. Finally the court can consider any other matters as it thinks fit (New Zealand Companies Act 1993, s. 272(2)). See also chapter 9, section 9.4.4 on contribution orders under the New Zealand's Companies Act 1993. The provisions are regarded as unique in providing enterprise treatment of group members in the course of insolvency (see Blumberg et al, *Blumberg on Corporate Groups* (n 31 chapter 1), vol 2, s. 90.05[B]; Watson, 'Liability of a Company for the Debts of an Insolvent "Related Company"' [1983] J. Bus. L. 295, 295–6; Weiss, 'The New Zealand Companies Amendment Act, 1980' (1981) 9 Austl. Bus. L. Rev. 290, 293).

[374] New Zealand Companies Act 1993, s. 272(3).

[375] See *Re Pacific Syndicates* (NZ) Ltd (1989) 4 NZCLC 64, 757; *Re Dalhoff and King Holdings Ltd* (1991) 2 NZLR 296. See also M. Ross, 'Tangled Webs: Unravelling the Strands after a Corporate Group Collapses' ICCLR 1992, 3(11), 385–7.

[376] See e.g. *Re Dalhoff and King Holdings Ltd* (1991) 5 NZCLC 66, 959, where the court took into account the fact that the financial situation of each group company affected that of others, due to the high integration among the entities, and that to ascertain whether each entity was truly solvent required very costly proceedings to take place.

[377] Ibid.

[378] See n 373.

[379] Misconduct of the related company may also be the subject of a contribution order under New Zealand Companies Act 1993 (as noted in n 373). This issue will be discussed in chapter 9. See also chapter 7, section 7.4.2 discussing the viability of the factor of 'creditors' reliance' in this context.

[380] See also the Australian company law regime which has undergone reform, and now provides a scheme for statutory pooling for corporate groups. This includes pooling determination by a liquidator subsequent to creditors' approval, and court ordered pooling which is based on

Otherwise, substantive consolidation may rest on judicial authority. American bankruptcy courts, for example, have been using their general 'equity powers' provided in the Bankruptcy Code to give such orders for the pooling of assets and debts of affiliate companies including the elimination of intra-group claims.[381] To an extent the US doctrine of substantive consolidation is still 'vulnerable' due to its questionable statutory basis and the fact that it has not been 'formally embraced' by the US Supreme Court.[382] It is also routinely stressed by the US courts that this method is to be applied in rare circumstances, yet in practice it is commonly used.[383]

Anyhow, the underlying justification for the doctrine is the need to achieve 'just and equitable' results. In this context, the US courts have applied a variety of factors and tests for the application of the doctrine, to a degree that it has been commented that the doctrine is in a 'mess'.[384] Nonetheless, US courts are increasingly focusing on two main factors: whether creditors dealt with the entities as a single economic unit and did not rely on their separate identity in extending credit, and whether the affairs of the entities are so entangled that consolidation will benefit all creditors.[385] Thus, hopeless intermingling of assets and debts of affiliates is normally regarded a proper basis for consolidation under US substantive consolidation too. It is perceived as just and equitable as it reduces costs in a scenario of 'asset integration' where untangling the affairs of the entities will be detrimental to all creditors.[386] The other factor rests on fairness to particular creditors based on their expectations and reliance on the creditworthiness of the

determining whether it is just and equitable to make such an order. Pooling schemes in Australia are also being achieved via voluntary administrations (see n 392, and accompanying text). On pooling arrangements under the Australian regime see e.g. J. Dickfos, C. Anderson and D. Morrison, 'The Insolvency Implications for Corporate Groups in Australia—Recent Events and Initiatives' (2007) 16 Int. Insol. Rev. 103; J. Harris, 'Corporate group insolvencies: Charting the past, present and future of pooling arrangements' (2007) 15(2) Insolvency Law Journal 78; J. Harris, 'Pooling' (2007) 19(1) AIJ 16.

[381] See 11 USC, s. 105 (2000). See Blumberg et al, *Blumberg on Corporate Groups* (n 31 chapter 1), vol 2, ss. 88.01–88.11[c]. Another example is the Canadian regime, where courts may use their inherent power to consolidate the administration of bankrupt estates (see ibid, s. 90.05).

[382] See D.G. Baird, 'Substantive Consolidation Today' (2006) 47 Bost. Col. L. Rev. 5, 15.

[383] Empirical research shows that the doctrine is used in the majority of US large bankruptcy cases (see W.H. Widen, 'Corporate Form and Substantive Consolidation' (2007) 75 Geo. Wash. L. Rev. 237, 239; W.H. Widen, 'Report to the American Bankruptcy Institute: prevalence of substantive consolidation in large public company bankruptcies from 2000 to 2005' [2008] 16(1) ABI L. Rev. 1).

[384] See ibid; M.E. Kors, 'Altered Egos: Deciphering Substantive Consolidation' (1997) 59 U. Pitt. L. Rev. 381, 384; T.E. Graulich, 'Substantive consolidation—a post-modern trend' (2006) 14 Am. Bankr. Ins. L. Rev. 527, 530.

[385] See *Union Saving Bank v Augie/Restivo Baking Company, Ltd (In re Augie/Restivo Baking Co.)*, 860 F.2d 515 (2d Cir 1988); *In re Owens Corning*, 419 F.3d 195 (3d Cir 2005). On the development of the US case law on substantive consolidation see T.E. Graulich, 'Substantive consolidation—a post-modern trend' (2006) 14 Am. Bankr. Ins. L. Rev. 527.

[386] *Union Saving Bank v Augie/Restivo Baking Company, Ltd (In re Augie/Restivo Baking Co.)*, 860 F.2d 515, 519 (2d Cir 1988).

group, a matter which will be considered in the next chapter.[387] US courts have also emphasized the feasibility of reorganization as an important justification for substantive consolidation. In case the business can be rehabilitated there is stronger merit in allowing a more unified operation of the insolvency.[388]

The US substantive consolidation doctrine can be partial, as well as complete, with particular claims or priorities against an affiliate preserved with respect to assets of that affiliate.[389] Though, such partiality of the consolidation is not frequently applied due to difficulties in ascertaining the need for protection for particular creditors in the face of inadequate or missing records that either defy reconstruction or make it very expensive.[390] Partial consolidation may also be achieved via reaching settlements with particular creditors who may be able to show they have dealt with a particular entity.[391]

Substantive consolidation may also be achieved via procedures for voluntary arrangements for distressed companies.[392] Even in legal regimes generally strictly adhering to entity law,[393] such pooling arrangements may be applied in cases of intermingling of assets and debts, even in the absence of legislative guidance or a wide discretion for authorizing substantive consolidation.[394]

UNCITRAL Working Group V,[395] which currently addresses issues pertaining to enterprise groups in insolvency, is considering a recommendation that substantive consolidation (pooling assets and debts of several affiliates together) will

---

[387] See chapter 7, section 7.4.2.

[388] See e.g. *Chem. Bank. N.Y. Trust Co. v Kheel*, 369 F.2d 845, 847 (2d Cir 1966); *Re Commercial Envelope Manufacturing Co.*, 3 Bankr. Ct. Dec. (LRP) 647, 650 (Bankr SDNY Aug. 22, 1977); *Re Worldcom*, Chapter 11 No. 02–13533 (AJG), 2003 WL 23861928 (Bankr SDNY 2003). See also Blumberg et al, *Blumberg on Corporate Groups* (n 31 chapter 1), vol. 2, s. 88.06[B].

[389] See e.g. *In re Parkway Calabasas Ltd*, 89 Bankr. 832, 837 (Bankr CD Cal. 1988).

[390] Blumberg et al, *Blumberg on Corporate Groups* (n 31 chapter 1), vol. 2, s. 88.04.

[391] See *Re Worldcom*, Chapter 11 No. 02-13533 (AJG), 2003 WL 23861928 (Bankr SDNY 2003). See also D.G. Baird, 'Substantive Consolidation Today' (2006) 47 Bost. Col. L. Rev. 5, 10–11; D.A. Skeel, 'Groups of Companies: Substantive Consolidation in the U.S.' in H. Peter, N. Jeandin, J. Kilborn (eds.), *The Challenges of Insolvency Law Reform in the 21st Century* (Verlag Schulthess, Zurich 2006), 229, 232.

[392] See, for example, pooling measures in voluntary administrations in Australia in J. Harris, 'Corporate group insolvencies: Charting the past, present and future of pooling arrangements' (2007) 15(2) Insolvency Law Journal 78; J. Harris, 'Pooling' (2007) 19(1) AIJ 16.

[393] See for example the strict adherence to the 'Salomon doctrine' under the English legal regime (chapter 2, section 2.4.3).

[394] See e.g. *Re Bank of Credit & Commerce International SA (No. 3)* [1993] BCLC 1490 (see n 436) (in this case the English court approved a compromise under which the assets and liabilities of several companies in liquidation would be pooled because the affairs of the entities were intermingled (see further on the case in section 6.3.4); *Re Exchange Securities & Commodities Ltd (In Liquidation)* [1987] BCLC 425; *Taylor* 1993 SLT 375. See also S. Bowmer, 'To pierce or not to pierce the corporate veil—why substantive consolidation is not an issue under English Law' (2000) 15 JIBL 193 (expressing the view that English courts generally do not follow the US doctrine of substantive consolidation); Cork Report (n 157 chapter 2), which favoured a more comprehensive review of groups within English law, and referred, inter alia, to the pooling order mechanism available in New Zealand, but eventually refrained from reaching conclusions due to its possible implication for company law, though it expressed the need for a reform to be considered (ibid, 438–9).

[395] N 96 chapter 1.

be allowed in certain limited scenarios, among which is the situation where there was such an extensive intermingling of assets of the enterprise group members that it will be impossible to identify the individual assets of each company without a disproportionate expense or delay.[396] Persons permitted to make an application for substantive consolidation may include an enterprise group member, the insolvency representative of any group member or a creditor of any such group member.[397] Applying for substantive consolidation may be done at the time of the application for commencement of insolvency proceedings with respect to several group members or at a subsequent time.[398] The option of having a partial order for substantive consolidation, excluding certain assets or claims (in case ownership is undoubtedly clear) from such an order is also provided.[399] It is also provided that security rights are respected under a substantive consolidation order,[400] as well as priorities established in the individual insolvency proceedings.[401] The effects of the order are the termination of intra-group debts and claims, the pooling of claims, and the consolidation of creditors' meetings.[402] Much emphasis is put on the need to respect the corporate form, substantive consolidation being the exception to be applied in limited scenarios.[403]

In sum, merging assets and debts in the course of insolvency is possible under the doctrine of substantive consolidation. Concerns about extensive administrative costs are generally dominant, and sometimes the need to enable efficient reorganizations is also regarded as a relevant factor. Some flexibility is possible under substantive consolidation, which means in the scenarios of intermingling

---

[396] See WP 80/Add.1 (n 65), draft recommendation 17(a); Report, thirty-fourth session (n 96 chapter 1), para. 60; WP 82/Add.3 (n 65), draft recommendation 17(a). Consolidation would generally involve the group members subject to insolvency proceedings, but it may extend to apparently solvent group members whose affairs were closely intermingled with those of the other members so that further investigation shows them to be actually insolvent. In such a case the consolidation may extend only to the net equity of the solvent member (ibid, para. 20). Draft commentary also explains that consolidation may also be possible on the basis of consensus or via a reorganization plan (ibid, para 16). Other possible bases for substantive consolidation will be discussed in chapters 7 and 9.

[397] WP 80/Add.1 (n 65), draft recommendation 19; Report, thirty-fourth session (n 96), para.68; WP 82/Add.3 (n 65), draft recommendation 18(a).

[398] WP 82/Add.3 (n 65), draft recommendation 18(b).

[399] WP 80/Add.1 (n 65), draft recommendation 18; Report, thirty-fourth session (n 96), para. 67; WP 82/Add.3 (n 65), draft recommendation 21.

[400] Unless it is owed between group members and is terminated by the order, or the court determines that the security was obtained by fraud in which the creditor participated or the transaction granting the security is subject to avoidance provisions (see WP 80/Add.1 (n 65), draft recommendation 23; Report, thirty-fourth session (n 96), para. 73; WP 82/Add.3 (n 65), draft recommendation 20; on avoidance provisions see chapter 9).

[401] See WP 82/Add.3 (n 65), draft recommendation 19(c). See further on the effects of substantive consolidation on securities and priorities in section 6.3.3.1.

[402] See WP 82/Add.3 (n 65), draft recommendation 19(a), (b) and (d).

[403] See WP 80/Add.1 (n 65), draft recommendation 16, and the preceding purpose clause; Report, thirty-fourth session (n 96), paras. 57 and 59; WP 82/Add.3 (n 65), draft recommendation 16, and the preceding purpose clause. See also WP 82/Add.3 (n 65), para. 14. It should be recalled that at the time the book went to print the work of the Working Group is still in progress.

that, notwithstanding general 'asset integration', if certain claims can be ascertained against certain entities or assets they may be excluded from the pool. The need to respect the corporate form is very pronounced in the rhetoric of legislation or court decisions, though substantive consolidations are not that rare at least in some jurisdictions.

6.3.3 Substantive consolidation and entity law

6.3.3.1 *Allowing substantive consolidation in cases of a façade of 'asset partitioning'*

In chapter 2, the economic benefits of the doctrine of legal separateness were emphasized. This was particularly pronounced in regard to the concept of limited liability which encourages investment and risk taking, enhances capital market efficiency, and reduces costs of monitoring the management of the company.[404] It was shown that legal systems normally respect the corporate form and generally refrain from 'lifting the veil'.[405] It was therefore concluded that caution is needed in applying 'linking tools' in the course of insolvency where these may interfere with this concept. I suggested that in terms of balancing between entity and enterprise principles, where limited liability is at stake the balance should be tilted in favour of entity law.[406] In contrast, it was also shown that some of the cost benefits of limited liability are less pronounced in the context of groups, that the MEG structure is more prone to opportunism and that generally in the group context there is a tension between the legal separateness and economic realities.[407] Thus, enterprise law should play a role even in the case where limited liability may be defeated so as to close the gap between law and reality, and outline circumstances where opportunism should be remedied. I suggested taking the same approach in regard to entities linked by contract, where enterprise theory may apply 'relational law' and ignore contractual risk shifting in order to fit with economic realities or defeat opportunistic behaviour.

In this regard substantive consolidation was mentioned (in chapter 2) as a doctrine which interferes with the group legal structure to a significant extent. However, it is not, strictly speaking, a matter of imposing liability. Thus, the conclusion (regarding the entity–enterprise balance) may be less clear cut in this context.[408] Substantive consolidation suggests mixing of liabilities and ignoring the corporate form.[409] However, whereas determining whether to ignore limited

---

[404] See chapter 2, section 2.3.2.
[405] Ibid, section 2.4.   [406] Ibid, section 2.5.
[407] Ibid, section 2.3.2.   [408] Ibid, section 2.3.3.
[409] See e.g. I. Mevorach, 'Appropriate treatment of corporate groups in insolvency—a universal view' (2006) 8 EBOR, 179, 188–9; D.A. Skeel, 'Groups of Companies: substantive consolidation in the U.S.', in H.Peter, N. Jeandin and J. Kilborn (eds.), *The Challenges of Insolvency Law Reform in the 21st Century: Facilitating Investment and Recovery to Enhance Economic Growth* (Verlag Schulthess, Zurich 2006), 229; D. Staehelin, 'No substantive consolidation in the insolvency of

liability is primarily a competition between the creditors of the company and the shareholders (the latter being protected by limited liability), substantive consolidation involves a competition between the creditors.[410] It is not a scenario of the creditors of a company versus its shareholders, rather the creditors of each and every affiliate (subject to the consolidation) versus all the creditors of the other affiliates, and vice versa. It can hence be argued that substantive consolidation is not a direct interference with limited liability and thus should be more easily allowed.

Nevertheless, substantive consolidation certainly interferes with 'asset partitioning'.[411] That is, the segregation of assets and debts among the affiliates, which allows the creditors of each affiliate to confine their monitoring efforts to that subsidiary only, because they are assured they will not need to compete with creditors of other entities.[412] Substantive consolidation suggests ignoring this segregation. And therefore, the transaction costs related to monitoring in financing of entities in groups will increase if parties act 'in the shadow' of a rule suggesting substantive consolidation for groups in insolvency.[413] The case for caution in the application of substantive consolidation is hence well grounded. In times when credit is hard to obtain further restrains on devising rules which may increase the cost of credit are needed. At the same time it is of crucial importance to allow effective insolvency proceedings to take place, especially when reorganization is pursued.

I therefore suggest that substantive consolidation, as a tool for reduction of administrative costs and facilitation of rescues, should be applied in clearly defined scenarios depicting situations where asset partitioning was merely a 'façade'. It should be applied only in 'asset integrated' insolvent MEGs—a prototype representing a situation where it appears in the event of insolvency that there was no partitioning de facto, as a matter of economic reality. Where the assets and debts cannot be reasonably ascertained, it should be possible to pool them together.[414] Accordingly, the proceeds from assets sales should be distributed to the creditors

---

groups of companies" in H. Peter, N. Jeandin and J. Kilborn (eds.), *The Challenges of Insolvency Law Reform in the 21st Century* (Verlag Schulthess, Zurich 2006), 213, 214.

[410] J. Landers, 'A Unified Approach to Parent, subsidiary and Affiliated Questions in Bankruptcy' (1975) 42 U. Chi. L. Rev. 589, 634 (arguing that the doctrine of limited liability is not involved in the issue of consolidation).

[411] H. Hansmann and R. Kraakman, 'Towards Unlimited Shareholder Liability for Corporate Torts' (1991) 100 Yale L.J. 1879 (see further chapter 2, section 2.3.3).

[412] Ibid.

[413] See n 205.

[414] For a different approach see D. Staehelin, 'No substantive consolidation in the insolvency of groups of companies' in H. Peter, N. Jeandin and J. Kilborn (eds.), *The Challenges of Insolvency Law Reform in the 21st Century* (Verlag Schulthess, Zurich 2006), 213, 217 (ruling out substantive consolidation including in the scenario of intermingling of assets, claiming that the intermingling is always partial and therefore substantive consolidation would be unjustified in relation to certain creditors. It is argued below that the complementary measure of partial consolidation resolves this problem (see section 6.3.3.4)).

as a whole, or otherwise a reorganization plan should be implemented on the entire estate while dividends are distributed to all the creditors as if there was one single estate (according to a set priority under the applicable law). The intra-group claims as between the members subject to the substantive consolidation should then be terminated.[415] Intra-group claims in regard to members not party to the substantive consolidation should normally be treated as claims of other creditors (so in an 'asset integration' scenario they will be part of the pool).[416] Pre-insolvency entitlements of creditors should be respected though their respective rank may be different than that which they had when they were attached to a separate entity. When all creditors are pooled together the ranking depends on which other classes of creditors are now within the pool.[417] Security interests of external creditors should also be respected. In case securities are not over specific identifiable assets (for example the security relates to the entire undertaking of one of the entities), and it is impossible to ascertain what those assets are due to the intermingling situation, such securities should extend to the pool of assets. The relevant creditors' priority should be respected but as aforementioned the relative ranking may change as a result of joining the new pool of assets and claims.[418]

An obvious problem in these scenarios would be identifying the situation as 'asset integration' without first going through the 'job' of disentanglement of the financial affairs of the MEG entities to realize that it is impossible or dis-proportionate (a work we want to avoid).[419] However, this is not an unfamiliar problem in the area of insolvency. Critical decisions need to be taken at an early stage regarding the way ahead for the business, based on examination and valu-ation of the financial situation. Indeed, these decisions are more complex in an

---

[415] It should be noted that in this regard deferring the intra-group claims in priority ('subor-dination', on which see chapter 9) may not suffice, as here the mere existence and the amount of the claims are uncertain or would demand disproportionate effort to resolve. See on the difference between the elimination of inter-company claims in substantive consolidation and the equitable subordination doctrine in Blumberg et al, *Blumberg on Corporate Groups* (n 31 chapter 1), vol. 2, s. 88.10 (The authors of *Blumberg on Corporate Groups* note, that the differences may be theoretical, not practical, since in most cases when relegated to a junior rank, the subordinated claim in fact will never be paid).

[416] But intra-group claims may be subject to subordination in specific circumstances (see chapter 9).

[417] To give an example, prior to the substantive consolidation, entity X may have had only one class of creditors, thus this class was ranked first. After the substantive consolidation another class of creditors (initially belonging to entity Y) ranking higher compared with the class of creditors of entity X joined the pool and thus the creditors of entity X will now rank second.

[418] As currently specified in UNCITRAL Working Group V's draft recommendations on the matter of substantive consolidation, respect of securities is subject to scenarios of fraud in which the creditors participated and to avoidance provisions (see n 400, and see chapter 9 on avoidance provisions in the context of MEG insolvencies).

[419] See W.H. Widen, 'Corporate Form and Substantive Consolidation' (2007) 75 Geo. Wash. L. Rev. 237, 292–3.

intertwined MEG scenario. In this respect the importance of the expertise of those in charge of the process is more pronounced.[420]

Consistent with this analysis and still in regard to insolvency concerns with wealth maximization and costs (as this chapter ignores other insolvency concerns), substantive consolidation (which uses harsh enterprise concepts) should not be imposed on the parties on the grounds of mere convenience in the handling of closely related entities. It may be that administrative costs could be reduced in situations where the enterprise is integrated even if not intermingled. It may be easier to pool assets and debts together instead of ascertaining separate ownerships which may involve some effort, even where undoubtedly it is not impossible or disproportionate. Yet, doing so will interfere with 'asset partitioning' in an unbalanced way.

6.3.3.2 *The merits of entity law are less pronounced in closely linked MEGs*

'Merging' the substance of the entities therefore is very much a matter of matching the solution to the particular scenario (taking the 'adaptive' approach). Confining substantive consolidation to 'asset integration' scenarios also fits with concerns regarding limited liability in general, as in closely linked groups the merits of limited liability are less pronounced. In these scenarios there is less relevance in encouraging new investment and reducing levels of monitoring, where in any case the group has been operating with great unification, monitoring the subsidiaries' managements and largely running the same business.[421] Indeed, the prominent debate between Posner and Landers in regard to the justifications for enterprise solutions in the course of insolvency (including substantive consolidation) was largely drawn from focusing on different types of groups.[422]

The possibility of 'asset integration' occurring in more decentralized structures should also be acknowledged, though more caution is needed in these scenarios in applying substantive consolidation, where typically there will be less monitoring of management in the ordinary course of business and more divergence of business, which results in a greater need to keep limited liability intact.[423] In any type of integrated MEG, though, a further enquiry should be made as to the actual existence of commingling of the substance of the entities. Integration alone is not sufficient to justify substantive consolidation.[424] The group may operate with significant interdependence or conduct an overall single business, but still keep the

---

[420] See chapter 7, section 7.5.5.
[421] See chapter 2, section 2.3.3.
[422] See n 63 chapter 2, and accompanying text.
[423] See chapter 2, section 2.3.3.
[424] Cf. C.W. Frost, 'Organizational Form, Misappropriation Risk, and the Substantive Consolidation of Corporate Groups' (1993) 44 Hastings L.J. 449, 493–4 (arguing that the typical rule for vertical integrated groups should be substantive consolidation in insolvency).

separateness among the entities for reasons of fundraising, ring fencing of risks and so forth.[425]

6.3.3.3 Substantive consolidation and SPVs

The benefits of 'asset partitioning' could then be adequately maintained in the cases where asset segregation has been kept. There would be no real threat, for example, to the use of SPV entities, a practice with important benefits.[426] SPVs are specifically designed as entities holding assets separate from the assets of the rest of the group. As long as the originator company (which initiated the scheme, and transferred the rights to the SPV)[427] truly sold the assets to the SPV [428] and thereafter the corporate form has been kept between the companies, then (under the model proposed here) the SPV would not be joining in a consolidation if that will be applied in the course of insolvency.

It is important though that the corporate form is kept in terms of the substance i.e. the assets and liabilities are segregated, rather than merely in terms of 'corporate personality formalities' (such as identity of managers, joint strategies, joint administrative functions, and so forth). Indeed, as mentioned at the beginning of this chapter,[429] the SPV will typically be truly solvent (as it will be independent and separate from the originator) and thus outside the consolidation (procedural or substantive).

6.3.3.4 Different levels of substantive consolidation (partial substantive consolidation)

In addition, allowing different 'levels' of pooling arrangements can further ensure that the solution is applied in regard to those aspects of the MEG which were merged in the ordinary course of business. This is not only important in terms of reducing causes for litigation as mentioned above,[430] but also in terms of upholding the merits of entity law. First, as derived from the prototypes, those parts of the group, not being 'asset integrated' with the rest should be excluded (subject to the possibility of agreeing to join the consolidation [431]).

Second, as provided under available doctrines of substantive consolidation, certain creditors' claims [432] against certain assets may be excluded from the consolidation, either by court order or as a matter of settlement, based on the fact

---

[425] Yet, in certain circumstances this may be regarded as abusive which may require the application of certain remedies to cure the harm caused (see chapter 9).

[426] See n 44 and 45 chapter 1.

[427] Ibid.

[428] See S. Schwarcz, 'Securitization Post-Enron' (2004) 25 Cardozo L.Rev. 1539, 1543. If there is no 'true sale' the transaction may be attacked and avoided (see chapter 9, section 9.5.1).

[429] Section 6.2.1.1.

[430] Section 6.3.1.

[431] See section 6.3.3.5.

[432] This may include intra-group claims of members not party to the 'asset integrated' insolvent MEG.

that their debt can be reasonably ascertained. This, of course, does not mean that the assets or creditors excluded from the substantive consolidation are not subject to a moratorium where this is applicable, or to a unified plan. In addition, entities excluded from the substantive consolidation may be joined to the group by procedural consolidation. It is only that their creditors' claims will be eventually ascertained against these entities' assets.

6.3.3.5 Substantive consolidation by consent

Even if there was no actual intermingling of assets or debts, the MEG stakeholders may consider it beneficial that substantive consolidation will be applied, especially as it may save costs and facilitate a reorganization of the group. In such situations substantive consolidation may be achieved by consensus, and it may include solvent entities. A creditor should be able to waive his 'asset partitioning' benefit, but creditors in general should be assured that 'asset partitioning' will not be interfered with unless they will agree to such a waiver.

It could also be achieved by way of a reorganization plan implemented with creditor approval. However, courts should be particularly conscious in such situations of examining whether there may be creditors that will be prejudiced by such course of action, even if they have not actively objected to the substantive consolidation or were party to an international agreement on substantive consolidation. Especially, in an international context, it may be that certain creditors could not properly participate in the global process; their interests must nevertheless be taken into account.[433] It may be possible to compensate a party which would otherwise be prejudiced by the substantive consolidation and thus enable substantive consolidation to be applied.[434]

6.3.3.6 Summary

Substantive consolidation, applied in the way and under the conditions as suggested above, strikes a suitable balance between entity and enterprise principles, while promoting asset maximization in insolvency. It is adaptive to the relevant scenario and in that it is cautiously invoked, not as a matter of rarity, but as a matter of matching economic realities. It should still be considered though whether any harm might be caused by this solution to specific creditors, or whether this solution should be applied in other circumstances to meet other insolvency concerns. This will be addressed in subsequent chapters of this Part.

---

[433] See E.A. Webber, 'Consensual Substantive Consolidation: Comments on the Working Papers of Professor Skeel and Dr. Staehelin', in H. Peter, N. Jeandin and J. Kilborn (eds.), *The Challenges of Insolvency Law Reform in the 21st Century* (Verlag Schulthess, Zurich 2006), 235, 242–6, raising concerns about substantive consolidation reached through negotiations. Webber notes that it is possible that negotiations were not properly conducted with all parties heard and being adequately considered. On the matter of creditors' participation in the international insolvency process see chapter 7, section 7.5.

[434] See n 391, and accompanying text.

6.3.4 Global measures and the universality–territoriality dilemma

6.3.4.1 Greater need for international coordination in cases of 'asset integrated MEGs'

It will be recalled that on the international level further costs may be incurred by attempts at cooperation on a global level suggesting a further measure of caution in applying universalism-based tools. This also derived from territoriality concerns demanding greater prudence when procedural consolidation is applied internationally. On the other hand, where the group was integrated, and also international, coordination is even more important in terms of costs.[435] It becomes more acute in 'asset integration' cases where there was intermingling of the affairs. In such cases the disposition of assets and claims are difficult to resolve with greater complexities in the MEG scenario since assets are located within different countries and proceedings are being handled in competing jurisdictions. Hence, I suggest that in terms of asset maximization, in case of global 'asset integration', global substantive consolidation is desirable.

This was evident, for example, in the case of *BCCI*, involving a collapse of a group on a very large international scale.[436] Here, the representatives appointed[437] concluded that the main entities comprising the group were inextricably intermingled. The representatives realized that it would be extremely difficult to ascertain which asset belonged to which BCCI component and which BCCI creditors and which BCCI debtors were the creditors or debtors of which BCCI company. The manner in which many of the BCCI books had been kept prevented clear answers to these questions and suggested prospects of lengthy and expensive litigation on the path to reaching sustainable resolutions

---

[435] See section 6.2.1.5.

[436] The BCCI group collapsed in July 1991 and was closed down by banking regulators. It was a multinational banking organization with operations in approximately seventy countries. The group was comprised of three different corporations: BCCI Holdings, BCCI SA, and BCCI Overseas. BCCI Holdings operated as a holding company in Luxemburg, and owned the two other subsidiary banks, BCCI SA and BCCI Overseas, incorporated in Luxemburg and the Cayman Islands respectively. Each of these subsidiaries operated worldwide through branches and subsidiaries, one of the main branches was in the United Kingdom with the preponderant volume of BCCI SA located there (see *Re Bank of Credit & Commerce International S.A. (No. 10)* [1997] 2 WLR 172 (Ch 1996)). Note that bank insolvencies present special problems outside the scope of this study (see n 176 and n 226 chapter 3 and references provided there). In any case, the administration of BCCI which operated internationally may teach lessons equally relevant for the handling of other business insolvencies (see J.L. Westbrook and J.S. Ziegel, 'NAFTA Insolvency Project' (1998) 23 Brook. J. Int'l L. 8). On the BCCI collapse see H.S. Scott, 'Supervision of International Banking Post-BCCI' (1992) 8 Ga. St. U. L. Rev. 487; H.S. Scott, 'Multinational Bank Insolvencies: The United States and BCCI' in J. S. Ziegel (ed.), *Current Developments in International and Comparative Insolvency Law* (Clarendon Press, Oxford 1994) 733; E. Hupkes, *Legal aspects of bank insolvency. A Comparative analysis of Western Europe, the United States and Canada*, Studies in Comparative Corporate and Finance Law, v.10 (Kluwer Law International, 2000), 139–51.

[437] Insolvency representatives were appointed by the courts in Luxemburg, the UK and the Cayman Islands.

of these difficulties.[438] It was therefore expected that a pooling concept applied to the case would maximize returns to creditors, as the MEG at hand was 'asset integrated'. Notwithstanding a lack of pre-defined international legislative models applied to the case, a way to resolve the expected inefficiencies (and other insolvency problems that arose in this context)[439] was achieved via national courts' judicial assistance concepts, and the use of international agreements (protocols) approved by the relevant courts.[440] Thus, the provisional liquidators devised an improvised 'pooling' solution to avoid the winding up of the group from being lost in a morass of legal argument.[441] Although, the majority of the BCCI's components were formally solvent,[442] they were all lumped together and were subjected to the insolvency process (taking into account the intermingled scenario). The idea was to create a structure under which all BCCI assets would be pooled, hence the tracing and recovery of assets would be a joint enterprise, and creditors in each of the liquidations would receive the same level of dividend from a central pool.[443] Additionally, a degree of deference to one of the foreign courts in terms of the handling of the process was applied. One of the liquidations was granted a 'supervisory' role in the sense that it was regarded as the principal proceedings.[444] The determination of the claims of BCCI's creditors were to be carried out in accordance with this supervisory liquidation and most of the proceeds of the realization of BCCI property was to be transmitted to this place.

---

[438] See *Re Bank of Credit & Commerce International S.A. (No. 10)* [1997] 2 WLR 172 (Ch 1996).

[439] See questions of distribution in general, and issues of remedies in insolvency to combat group opportunism discussed in chapter 7, section 7.4; and chapter 9, respectively. In particular see the references to the *BCCI* case in chapter 7, section 7.4.1; n 79 chapter 8; and n 81 chapter 9.

[440] See section 6.2.1.5.

[441] See the Luxemburg winding up order (concluding that 'it results from the submissions of the supervisory commissioner of BCCI S.A. that the affairs of BCCI S.A. were inextricably linked with those of other entities of the BCCI group'), and *Re Bank of Credit & Commerce International S.A. (No. 10)* [1997] 2 WLR 172 (Ch 1996) (referring to the English court hearing of the winding-up petition on 2 December 1991 indicating 'the truly gargantuan task of preserving and realising assets of BCCI worldwide').

[442] BCCI Overseas was the only insolvent company.

[443] See the Luxemburg winding-up order (*Bank of Credit and Commerce International S.A.* (District Court of Luxemburg, 3 January, 1992)) in which the Luxemburg court explained that according to the supervisory commissioner's opinion it is essential to coordinate the liquidation operations by means of cooperation agreements to be concluded with the liquidators of the different foreign entities, subsidiaries and branches, with a view to creating a common pot and a common administration.

[444] Luxemburg was the country of principal liquidation (clause 3.1 and 3.11 of the pooling agreement (see *Re Bank of Credit & Commerce International S.A. (No. 10)* [1997] 2 WLR 172 (Ch 1996)). See also *In re BCCI S.A. (No. 2)* [1992] BCLC 715 (where the English courts determined that the insolvent estate of BCCI S.A. was to be administered in Luxemburg in accordance with Luxemburg law (though see n 163 chapter 3 referring to the English court decision to apply its own laws in regard to the set-off issue and n 155 chapter 3 referring to the approach taken by some of the jurisdictions involved which 'ring fenced' assets favouring local creditors).

6.3.4.2 Global substantive consolidation and centralization

Indeed, global substantive consolidation may be achieved via such ad hoc mechanisms (as discussed above in regard to procedural consolidation) implementing cooperation among concurrent proceedings taking place in different parts in the world even with a degree of deference to one of the courts involved.[445] But the toll in terms of efficiency is clear. It was mentioned above how in cases such as *BCCI* where the group was comprised of numerous entities, transnational communication is costly and time consuming.[446] This includes devising the pooling arrangement between many jurisdictions, which is prone to further complexities, bearing in mind potential disagreements. A supervisory mechanism as was applied in the case of *BCCI*—subjecting the process to a single principal jurisdiction that will supervise the operation and will apply mainly its laws—improves the inherent inefficiency. Otherwise, it may become extremely complicated to treat the companies as one unitary entity and to distribute dividends to all creditors as if they were all related to a single entity.

In terms of territoriality, applying pooling arrangements does not raise further concerns. In itself it only increases the enterprise concepts applied. However, the scenario of 'asset integration' which typically invokes substantive consolidation also suggests that the stronger global linking tools (i.e. centralization) will be desirable, in terms of wealth maximization and enabling reorganizations. For such a mechanism as substantive consolidation (which involves a tight linkage among the foreign affiliates) to work well, centralization is key. Even where the MEG involves more autonomous parts, as long as they were nevertheless intermingled with the rest of the group in terms of their substance, this should be a further justification for centralization. Otherwise, in a supervisory model the cooperation among the proceedings should be tighter with more deference to the main proceedings.

6.3.4.3 Various means for achieving global substantive consolidation

Centralization can be achieved by applying the same concepts which were proposed above—identification of a home country for the MEG as a whole and placing the affiliates under insolvency in that jurisdiction which will mainly apply its laws in regard to insolvency matters arising. Otherwise, existing concepts of the home country of single debtors can be applied which may lead to a single jurisdiction.[447] It should also be recalled that the ALI Principles, while urging to permit filing of proceedings by a subsidiary in the jurisdiction where proceedings against the parent company has been commenced, suggest that the court will then apply either procedural or substantive consolidation under applicable law.[448] In terms of cost efficiency, these various mechanisms in place in cross-border

---

[445] See section 6.2.1.5.   [446] See section 6.2.2.3.
[447] See sections 6.2.1.6 and 6.2.1.9.   [448] See n 193, and accompanying text.

insolvency models (enabling the concentration of the proceedings against MEG affiliates) may provide the necessary infrastructure for the application of substantive consolidation. Then, the jurisdiction handling the case should be able to apply substantive consolidation doctrines. In certain regimes such a doctrine is already in place (in various versions). An improvement will be to allow for this mechanism universally, based on the factors suggested here. This can be done by way of an international framework. Additionally, as proposed above in regard to procedural consolidation, a degree of harmonization (adopting the concept of substantive consolidation within domestic regimes) should be promoted. This will ensure the availability of this tool even when the particular jurisdiction is not subjected to an international framework that may allow for substantive consolidation, or to such that may provide global linking tools without explicit rules regarding substantive consolidation.[449] Such harmonization may be achieved if the work of UNCITRAL Working Group V reaches a successful ending, providing legislative recommendations in regard to substantive consolidation, and if such recommendations are widely adopted within national laws.[450] Substantive consolidation can be provided in various versions within national regimes.[451] What is crucial is that it will enable cost savings in scenarios of 'asset integrated' insolvent MEGs (allowing pooling in the intermingling of assets and debts situations).

In the scenarios where it will be impossible to locate a single centre in which to centralize the process or to supervise it (with greater powers to the main proceedings and deference to its laws),[452] I suggest that cooperation and coordination between parallel proceedings should be applied. This will need to encompass a mechanism for facilitating the joint realization of assets and distribution of proceeds (including agreeing on the law that will apply to the joint distribution).

The case of *Bramalea*[453] exemplifies a centralized approach combined with substantive consolidation taken by courts (applying national solutions for cross-border insolvency). The Bramalea group was a real estate enterprise with direct and indirect subsidiaries and joint ventures in Canada and the US. When it collapsed it was placed under insolvency proceedings in Canada, the Canadian court extending jurisdiction over the entire group, on the basis of its integration and the practical need to restructure the business on a consolidated basis.[454] Both

[449] See also I. Mevorach, 'Appropriate treatment of corporate groups in insolvency—a universal view' (2006) 8 EBOR, 179, 182.

[450] As mentioned earlier, the work of the Working Group is still in progress (see n 140 chapter 3). See section 6.3.2 on the draft recommendations (on substantive consolidation) currently proposed by the Working Group.

[451] For examples of how this doctrine is applied in different legal regimes see section 6.3.2.

[452] See section 6.2.1.10.

[453] A US–Canadian group (an unreported case in the Ontario Court of Justice); for a description and discussion of the case see R.G. Marantz, 'The Reorganization of a Complex Corporate Entity: The Bramalea Story' in J. S. Ziegel (ed.), *Case Studies in Recent Canadian Insolvency Reorganizations* (Carswell Legal Publications, Toronto 1997) 1. The case took place before the formulation of the UNCITRAL Model Law and its adoption within the US bankruptcy regime.

[454] Ibid, 6, 15–17.

solvent and insolvent subsidiaries were included in the proceedings, notwithstanding that insolvency was a requirement for receiving protection under the
Canadian regime for bankruptcy creditors' arrangements. The court accepted
the claim that the so-called solvent companies (based on a balance sheet analysis)
could not remain viable without Bramalea's support.[455] The Canadian court also
accepted the claim that Canada was the centre of the entire group. The US subsidiaries (incorporated in the US) apparently had assets and carried on business in
Canada, as various officers of the US affiliates were physically located in Canada
at Bramalea's head office. Additionally, many of the creditors which had loaned
to the US subsidiaries had in fact negotiated their loans with officers of the parent
in Canada, and had received guarantees from the parent company. Although the
US subsidiaries were operated and managed locally, large strategic decisions were
dealt with in Canada.[456]

The Canadian court decision was not contested, as Bramalea managed to reach
various settlements with specific creditors (including exclusion of some creditors and assets from the scope of the plan), thus avoiding possible objections.[457]
Although a coordinated insolvency was apparently efficient in this case (for the
group as a whole),[458] it is doubtful whether according to the model suggested
here substantive consolidation was justifiable, when confronted with entity law
concerns. Indeed, the Canadian court based its decision to substantively consolidate on the fact of 'integration' alone, and at least in regard to some of the
subsidiaries it was clear that they were not 'asset integrated' with the group. Thus,
in the case of US subsidiaries which had US property financed by US lenders
it was clear who the creditors of those subsidiaries were (US lenders) and what
assets they owned (the US property).[459] Applying substantive consolidation to
such subsidiaries was therefore detrimental to entity law, as explained above.[460]
Thus, if objections would have been raised in this case, or if sufficient settlements
could not have been reached, there was certainly room for rejecting substantive
consolidation at least in regard to certain creditors. Procedural consolidation, on
the other hand, is a different matter,[461] and could have been a justifiable solution
in this case, in order to promote efficiency, enable the restructuring, and at the
same time strike the right balance between entity and enterprise principle.

On the global front, it seems that the designation of the Canadian court as representing the group centre is compatible with the model proposed here (normally
referring the group central proceedings to the group operational head office).[462]
However, it seems that in regard to the US subsidiaries which were significantly

---

[455] Ibid, 6.   [456] Ibid, 17–18.
[457] Ibid, 19.   [458] Ibid, *passim*.
[459] Ibid, 17. See also L.M. LoPucki, 'Cooperation in International Bankruptcy: A Post-
Universalist Approach' (1999) 84 Cornell L. Rev. 696, 719–20.
[460] Section 6.3.3. This is also problematic in terms of promoting other insolvency goals on
which see chapter 7 section 7.4.
[461] See sections 6.2.1.2–6.2.1.3.
[462] See section 6.2.1.9.

autonomous (operated and managed locally with only ultimate strategic decisions made in Canada), if procedural consolidation had been applied, local proceedings supervised by the process in Canada should have been considered.[463] Agreeing to substantive consolidation though, there was indeed merit in full centralization. The alternative could have been conducting local proceedings with tight cooperation and supervision by the main process.

6.3.5 Global substantive consolidation for 'asset integrated' insolvent MEGs—summary

It is suggested that reducing costs and enabling rescues requires the application of 'strong' enterprise concepts combined with universal mechanisms in MEGs featuring 'asset integration'. If, however, the MEG was only integrated in terms of the business (or even non-integrated), or in case a particular subsidiary is of this nature, or is truly solvent, it is suggested that it should not be included within the global consolidation unless by way of consensus carefully scrutinized by the courts. In the 'asset integrated' MEGs substantive consolidation is desirable. It should be possible to apply it on a global level, preferably by referring the affiliates' proceedings to a single jurisdiction. This could be achieved either by using existing concepts of locating a centre for each debtor, or by employing the more robust concept of a 'group home country' as proposed earlier in this chapter.

6.4 Conclusion

Applying the 'goal-driven adaptive balanced entity–enterprise, territoriality–universality approach' and focusing on certain goals of insolvency—asset maximization and rescues for viable businesses—suggests that certain linking tools are justifiable in the course of a MEG insolvency. In scenarios of 'business integration', a distressed MEG and its stakeholders as a whole will benefit, in terms of the goals in question, from joint administration (procedural consolidation) on a global level. There is not a lot at stake in terms of entity law when applying such a doctrine, as long as the unification is applied in terms of procedures and coordination only. On the other hand, this has considerable benefits in terms of promoting the insolvency goal. On the global level it requires cross-border cooperation, and even centralization of the process, which to an extent conflicts with territoriality concerns. The balance is restored though when applying the 'adaptive' approach; that is, making use of the different levels of global linkages in the appropriate circumstances, based on the typical scenarios proposed. To ensure the application of centralization in the proper circumstances it was proposed to

---

[463] See sections 6.2.1.8–6.2.1.9.

adopt standard tests for the identification of a single jurisdiction that will be able to control (or supervise) the entire process and whose laws will mainly govern the insolvency issues. In scenarios of 'asset integration', a distressed MEG and its stakeholders as a whole will benefit, in terms of the goal in issue, from a more robust linking tool—pooling the substance of the affiliates together in the course of insolvency. Here much more is at stake in terms of the economic benefits of entity law, and thus strictness was suggested in depicting the situations where such a tool will be applied. On the global level, applying pooling arrangements suggested inclination towards the stronger global linking tools.

Both in regard to procedural and substantive consolidation, it was suggested that harmonization in terms of adoption of such tools universally will ensure that these mechanisms will be available when the case arises in any given juris-diction or jurisdictions. Standardization in the form suggested here can ensure asset maximization, but also suggest that harmonization should be feasible, as the boundaries of enterprise law are clearly put in place. Cross-border insolvency systems will also be improved if providing clear rules to allow coordinated solu-tions to MEGs in insolvency and ensuring that the best solution for the MEG as a whole will be pursued. Pending possible reform, courts and representatives should aim to achieve such solutions by applying existing models and tools where these are available, to achieve unification in appropriate circumstances. Additional concerns should be taken into account, though, in pursuing such tools, as will be discussed in subsequent chapters.

7

Equitable Distribution and Accountability

7.1 Introduction

The previous chapter suggested a number of 'linking tools' that should be applied in the course of MEG insolvency (depending on the circumstances). Essentially, global consolidation (in a variety of degrees and ways of implementations) was proposed as a tool which will enhance wealth maximization and costs reduction in the handling of the insolvency process and facilitate rescues. Nevertheless, I have concluded earlier, that the goal of asset maximization and efficiency of the process should not be treated as a sole stand-alone aim of insolvency. Other goals should be pursued as well.[1] In particular, insolvency laws should be concerned with fairness in distribution.[2] It should also be the aim to provide a fair insolvency process allowing for participation of creditors and adequate representation.[3] These matters are the focus of this chapter. A particular aspect of fairness in distribution is addressing wrongful acts, fraud, or favouritism in the context of financial distress. This issue will be discussed (in the context of MEG insolvency) separately in chapter 9.

In terms of distribution, it was concluded earlier that insolvency law should translate pre-bankruptcy entitlements into the bankruptcy forum with minimal dislocation.[4] However, pursuing an overall fair result may require redistribution in certain circumstances to accommodate the range of interests. The importance of respecting pre-petition rights of stakeholders as well as the justification for derogation from this rule to achieve socially desirable results is also stressed in universal statements of insolvency goals.[5] It was also desired to promote procedural fairness and ensure transparency and accountability of the insolvency process.[6] That is, ensuring a collective process not only in the negative sense of precluding the 'race to collect',[7] but also in assuring inclusiveness, enabling all creditors to participate and look to the presiding insolvency representative to both represent their interests and to bring them to account if they fail to

---

[1] See chapter 4, section 4.2.2.3.
[2] Ibid.
[3] Ibid, especially section 4.2.2.3.
[4] Ibid, section 4.2.2.2.
[5] Ibid, section 4.2.3.
[6] Ibid, sections 4.2.2.3 and 4.2.3.5.
[7] Ibid, section 4.2.2.1.

do so.[8] Another closely linked aim is the effective supervision of those handling the process, who should have sufficient expertise.[9] It can thus warrant a fair conduct of the proceedings.[10]

The case of a MEG in distress presents once again further difficulties in the context of distribution. Here, on top of the usual problems (in regard to single debtors) of addressing the differences between the stakeholders, the multiplicity of debtors and the international nature of the enterprise increase the challenges. The entities of the MEG may be in very different financial positions, and thus creditors of the different debtors may not have coherent interests—even if they hold the same type of security or other rights, or are in the same 'degree of vulnerability'. Some may have dealt with a stronger entity than the other group members, perhaps even one which is still solvent. Certain creditors may have thought they were dealing with the group as a 'group' while others only with a local component. Solutions for the MEG as a whole in the course of insolvency may improve the position and be beneficial to certain stakeholders, while others may prefer to stay detached from the group in the course of insolvency.

On the cross-border level, in regard to single entities there is the fear that foreign similarly situated creditors will not be treated equally.[11] In the case of a MEG, the fragmentation of the business into separate entities presents further difficulties as although creditors belong to separate entities, with separate estates, creditors of foreign related entities may be affected by solutions applied in regard to other related entities. The cross-border dimension also implies difficulties resulting from differences between legal regimes. For instance, creditors may have certain rights in insolvency if subjected to the laws of the country where the debtor is incorporated, which are not necessarily similar to the rights provided in another system to which the proceedings may need to 'move' in order to enable global solutions for the MEG (e.g., the ranking of a particular debt may

---

[8] See S. Frisby, 'In Search of a Rescue Regime: The Enterprise Act 2002' [2004] MLR 247, 250.

[9] See Chapter 4, sections 4.2.2.2, 4.2.2.3 and 4.2.3.5. There is an overlap to an extent between expertise and accountability. Expertise of the agent ensures competence and accuracy of judgment which in turn may reduce the need for accountability. Indeed, we have seen that legal regimes in practice may trade off between the two goals. Courts may express trust in specialists allowing them to reach decisions in the course of insolvency even without prior involvement of the creditors, especially in matters of urgency (Chapter 4, section 4.2.2.2).

[10] Both accountability and expertise can be perceived as components of efficiency as well (see R.J. Mokal, 'On Fairness and Efficiency' [2003] MLR 452, 459–62). Sufficient degree of expertise of the agents to whom decision-making is delegated will promote *ex post* efficiency—the handling of the process with minimum delays and accuracy of decisions. It also promotes confidence in the insolvency regime and consistency of outcomes. Accountability and creditor participation also enhance confidence in the process—ensuring that the agent's decision-making is aligned with creditors' interests. Participation may also assist in advice on decisions so long as this involvement does not turn to be counterproductive to cost-effectiveness (chapter 4, sections 4.2.2.1 and 4.2.3.5).

[11] Indeed, cross-border insolvency models stress that equality should be maintained, and creditors of similar ranking, whether local or foreign should share equally from the estate (see e.g. Recitals (12) and (24) of the EC Regulation, n 173 chapter 3). See also H. Rajak, *Company Liquidations* (n 220 chapter 3), 133–4, 347 (Rajak stresses that in the international context the principle of equitable treatment of creditors faces strong dangers of ring fencing assets and applying a 'grab rule').

be different under different insolvency regimes). Thus, a particular creditor may gain a lower (or higher) recovery from the estate of the company according to the location in which the proceedings are held.

Another concern involves forum manipulation.[12] As a change in the forum may change the legal system applicable, manipulation of the forum may deprive creditors of their rights. Indeed, the lack of uniformity in insolvency laws (and differences in attitudes of different forums) may motivate parties to shop for a 'better' forum in which to handle proceedings.[13] It may particularly affect non-adjusting creditors.[14] Indeed, cross-border insolvency regimes (for single debtors) stress the need to combat forum shopping.[15] In addition, manipulations (even from the outset, by debtors or strong creditors) may direct the proceedings to 'haven courts'.[16] As indicated earlier, allowing 'havens' to preside over cross-border insolvency is generally undesirable in regard to single debtors.[17] It is even more detrimental in the case of MEGs where parties' interests are likely to be more diverse, where 'haven' courts may lack the means to take into account all relevant interests and achieve just results. Generally, in the case of MEGs the risk of forum shopping increases as the MEG may have more room for manoeuvre comprised as it is of various separate entities located in different jurisdictions.[18]

The cross-border dimension and the multiple debtor scenarios both also raise further complexities when considering the procedural goals of accountability and expertise. The judgments to make in the course of MEG insolvency are

[12] Forum shopping is also detrimental to certainty and predictability in the context of MEG insolvency (see chapter 8).

[13] See A. Bell, *Forum Shopping and Venue in Transnational Litigation* (Oxford University Press, Oxford 2003), ch. 2. See also L.M. LoPucki, 'Cooperation in International Bankruptcy: A Post-Universalist Approach' (1999) 84 Cornell L. Rev. 696, 721. LoPucki claims that a successful international shop could offer great rewards. The shop might change the priority among creditors, render security interests invalid, or change the law governing avoiding powers. Shops might take cases to countries with corruptible judges, different languages, different treaty relationships, or locations inconvenient to creditors.

[14] See chapter 3, section 3.3.2.5. See also D.A. Skeel, 'European Implication of Bankruptcy Venue Shopping in the U.S.' (2007) 54 Buff. L. Rev. 439, 463, suggesting that if managers are permitted to make a venue choice at the last minute (anticipating insolvency) they may not face the same market discipline as they would if the filing location is determined in advance. The manipulating of the venue may be done for the benefit of the group insiders (and perhaps influential creditors) but not other mal-adjusting creditors.

[15] See Recitals (4), (12) and (23) to the EC Regulation (n 173 chapter 3).

[16] There are in fact countries that already compete as 'havens' for international bankruptcies such as Bermuda, Luxembourg and the Cayman Islands (L.M. LoPucki, 'Cooperation in International Bankruptcy: A Post-Universalist Approach' (1999) 84 Cornell L. Rev. 696, 721; see also LoPucki, *Courting Failure* (n 64 chapter 3), 193–200). It has also been observed that the Netherlands and the UK have become 'successful' in attracting debtors, wishing to place the insolvency process where they have the best chance of surviving a bankruptcy (see P.J.M. Declercq, 'Restructuring European Distressed Debt: Netherlands Suspension of Payment Proceeding...The Netherlands Chapter 11?' (2003) 77 Am. Bankr. L.J. 377, 378; *GLOBALTURNAROUND*, 'French breakthrough for Euro Regulation', October 2003, issue 45, p. 9; *GLOBALTURNAROUND*, 'Europe leads world in Forum Shopping', June 2003, issue 41, p. 1).

[17] See chapter 3, sections 3.3.2.5 and 3.3.3.

[18] See section 7.3.3.

inherently complex. The court and representative overseeing the case will need to deal with greater diversity of interests (as creditors will also belong to different entities), entities operating in different legal regimes, and creditors residing in foreign jurisdictions. Ensuring a democratic process can be a challenging task in cross-border cases. Accountability may further be in jeopardy where a process encompasses multiple separate entities. Particular questions arise as to the nature and responsibilities of the agents in charge of decision-making in the MEG context, and the possibility of a global group-wide process of MEG insolvencies to be sufficiently transparent and accountable.

Various issues should therefore be addressed when considering aspects of distribution and procedural fairness. Should a system allow 'sacrifices' to be made by certain entities and their stakeholders for the sake of the greater (group) good? Do global means such as 'centralization' ensure that rights of creditors are protected? Can a global system combat forum manipulation and ensure that cases are not directed to 'haven' forums and laws? Is mixing assets and debts in the course of insolvency redistributive? In case it is, is it nonetheless justified? Can the 'linking tools' suggested ensure adequate representation and creditors' participation?

It will be recalled that the framework applied in this work is goal-driven and adaptive. It aims to achieve the insolvency goals, and to take into account the type of MEG in default. It also aims to strike a proper balance between entity and enterprise law regarding the problems of enterprise groups, and universality and territoriality in regard to the cross-border insolvency aspects of the MEG in insolvency.[19] The question here is, therefore, whether global consolidation applied as suggested in the previous chapter, will also prove to be fair overall when considering issues of distribution and procedural fairness. Otherwise, what other characteristics may it require in order to fulfil these goals? In other words, will the balance between entity and enterprise law, and territoriality and universality change now that we consider the goal of fairness in distribution so that the linking tools proposed in the previous chapter will need to be modified?

7.2 Joint Solutions (for MEG Insolvencies) and Redistribution

7.2.1 The basic rule: maintaining the separateness among the MEG entities under procedural consolidation

The goal of asset maximization suggested that in cases of 'business integrated' insolvent MEGs (prototypes A–C)[20] the entire MEG should be considered in deciding on solutions for the enterprise in the course of insolvency. For this purpose 'global procedural consolidation' (in various possible forms) was suggested.[21]

---

[19] See chapter 2, section 2.5; and chapter 3, section 3.5.

[20] See chapter 5, section 5.4.

[21] The term procedural consolidation is used here to refer generally to the coordination of the proceedings among group members and the application of group-wide solutions in the course

Preserving the economic essence of entity law has suggested putting constraints on the application of procedural consolidation. It required that procedural consolidation would maintain the distinction between the entities and recognize the group (to benefit from global sales or global reorganization plans) without sacrificing certain entities. This also ensures that pre-insolvency entitlements are not affected by the procedural consolidation. Therefore, it fits with another insolvency goal—the respect for rights of creditors. This has efficiency advantages, as mentioned earlier,[22] in particular preventing perverse incentives for creditors to file for insolvency (against an entity which will gain from the consolidation at the expense of other entities) when this is unnecessary.

7.2.2 Maintaining equitable distribution: a case for stronger enterprise law-based solutions

Nonetheless, the question is whether, considering fairness in distribution, a degree of inroad into entity law (and thus affecting rights of creditors against the separate entity) is justified in the above prototypes A–C,[23] so that in certain circumstances the good for the whole can prevail even if it involves a degree of sacrifice by certain entities. Indeed, in chapter 2 it was concluded that although the economic benefits of entity law should be maintained, this is subject to fairness considerations, in particular tackling opportunistic behaviour in the MEG context and considering the particular traits of MEGs in terms of the tension they depict between law and reality.[24] As mentioned above, it was also conceded in discussing insolvency goals that notwithstanding the merits of insolvency law translating pre- insolvency law positions to insolvency, in certain circumstances derogation from this concept will be necessary in order to achieve a just solution.[25] All relevant parties affected by the insolvency matter —the procedural consolidation in this context—should be considered and accorded equal respect to their interests. This may suggest establishment of various rules in insolvency which may give priority to certain creditors, or demand contribution to the insolvency estate from certain parties, or enable taking certain paths in the course of insolvency which are beneficial even if they involve a degree of redistribution.[26]

7.2.2.1 *Voting on reorganization plans*

Consider, for instance, the issue of voting on a reorganization plan. In cases where it is conceded that the MEG at hand is viable, a single reorganization plan for the entire enterprise may prove the best way ahead for the business.[27] It was suggested

of insolvency. Such solutions may actually take place with or without a formal procedural consolidation order, via various means of cooperation among the group members' insolvencies (see chapter 6, section 6.2).

[22] See chapter 4, section 4.2.2.2.   [23] N 20, and accompanying text.
[24] See chapter 2, section 2.3.2.   [25] See chapter 4, section 4.2.2.3.
[26] Ibid.   [27] See chapter 6, section 6.2.

in chapter 6 that the plan will be voted on by each entity separately.[28] However, in case a particular entity dissents should it still be possible to approve such a reorganization plan? This is to an extent contrary to the entity being entirely separate and thus entitled to reject a plan. It also conflicts with rights of creditors vis-à-vis the particular entity. However, letting a minority entity or entities undermine a plan which could prove beneficial to the majority of the entities seems an unbalanced solution when considering all parties involved in the procedural consolidation, and the economic reality of the scenarios at hand. The subject matter here is a plan for an entire MEG which is 'business integrated'. It is different from a scenario where the creditors of a company address a plan on an entirely separate basis. Ignoring this difference might yield unjust outcomes. A more balanced solution would take into account the economic reality of the MEG at hand and the parties involved with it, which includes other secured and unsecured creditors, the possibility and scale of job preservation and the benefit to the shareholders.

For this purpose, the present model should draw on tools which are often recognized in regard to voting on single debtors' reorganization plans, and translate them to the 'business integrated' insolvent MEGs scenarios in order to become more flexible and adaptive to various situations and to accommodate the variety of interests involved. Confirmation of a plan (for single debtors) or addressing creditors' objections to a plan may demand demonstrating that a required majority has agreed to the plan, that creditors will receive under the plan at least as much as they would have received in liquidation (unless they agreed to receive less) and that a dissenting class shall receive under the plan full recognition of its ranking under the insolvency law.[29] In the MEG insolvency, in case the plan was not approved by all entities, further consideration could be given to the majority agreeing to the plan on a group level according to a pre-defined formula (such as majority of entities weighted by their debt, or majority of creditors in each class across the group), and then making it binding on the dissenting entity while providing adequate safeguards to its creditors. This will be especially advantageous in case the entity's participation in the unified plan is crucial to its success. In approving a plan in this way the court may enquire whether the objecting creditors have received full recognition of their ranking under the applicable law and the distribution to that class under the plan fits with that ranking. Further consideration can be made to any concrete indication regarding specific opportunities that the entity would have had if it was administered on a separate basis and consequently any harm caused to the dissenting creditors as a result of the unified plan.

It should be noted that UNCITRAL Working Group V (whose current draft recommendations in regard to procedural coordination and unified reorganization

---

[28] Ibid, section 6.2.1.3.
[29] Such measures are recommended as best practice standards in the UNCITRAL Legislative Guide (see UNCITRAL Legislative Guide (n 137 chapter 3), Part two, Ch. IV, Recommendation 152).

plans have been discussed earlier in this work)[30] has considered whether or not to recommend such an approach. The Working Group had expressed a view that it should not be allowed to consider approval of a plan on a group basis and allow the majority of creditors of the majority of members to compel approval of a plan for all members,[31] taking a strict view in regard to respect of the corporate form. Though, it seems that current draft commentary on the matter leaves some leeway to consider the consequences of rejection of a plan by particular group members.[32]

I suggest that though respect to entity law is crucial in these types of cases, a degree of flexibility in reaching solutions in the course of insolvency will better reflect the interests of all parties involved deriving from the interrelations among the entities, and the fact that the exclusion of a particular entity from the plan may have a damaging effect on the entire MEG.

Another concern in regard to voting rights in the MEG context is whether the same voting rights should be given to 'insiders' (i.e. to the MEG members which may also be creditors) and 'outsiders' (external creditors). Consistent with the approach of respecting pre-insolvency entitlements and the corporate form it is submitted that normally voting rights should not be altered on the grounds of being a related company, unless there was some opportunistic behaviour involved which requires further scrutiny in regard to the claim of the group member.[33]

7.2.2.2 Global group-wide sales

Another example of conflict between the interests of the MEG as a whole and those of the particular entity may arise in the course of a sale of the MEG assets as a going concern where all the group's creditors may be subjected to a moratorium under the applicable law (in case global procedural consolidation of sort has been applied to the 'business integrated' MEG).[34] Take for instance, the secured creditors of a particular subsidiary who may consider that the encumbered assets of that subsidiary can generate greater returns if they sell it on a separate basis (detached from the group). They thus require to be excluded from the moratorium. In the

---

[30] See n 96 chapter 1; n 140 chapter 3; and chapter 6, section 6.2.1.2.

[31] In WP.74/Add.1 (n 49 chapter 6), para. 22, the secretariat of Working Group V proposed for consideration enabling the approval of a plan on a group basis (the safeguards to the dissenting creditors would then possibly include ensuring that the unified plan is fair to the rejecting creditors in relation to their position relative to creditors of other group members). The approach was generally rejected (see Report, thirty-third session (n 97 chapter 1), paras. 114–15).

[32] See WP.82/Add.3 (n 65 chapter 6), para. 52. Note that at the time the book went to print the work of the Working Group is still in progress (see n 140 chapter 3).

[33] See chapter 9 in which problems of opportunism in the MEG context are discussed. See e.g. the Cayman Islands' court approach in the case of subsidiaries of the *Parmalat* group. In considering Parmalat's members' wishes presented to the court with regard to the appointment of provisional liquidators to the subsidiaries in the Cayman Islands, the court considered the intra-group claims as unreliable as a result of the alledged fraud and gave them lesser weight in considering the views of creditors (the Cayman Islands' court's decision mentioned in n 86 chapter 6, pp. 9–10). See also UNCITRAL Legislative Guide (n 137 chapter 3) Part two, Ch. V, Recommendation 184(a) (suggesting that insolvency laws should specify that claims by related persons should be subject to scrutiny, and where justified the voting rights of the related person may be restricted).

[34] See chapter 6, section 6.2.1.

circumstances, the subsidiary has no unsecured creditors and if considered on a separate basis the secured creditors may be granted relief.[35] Yet, this may conflict with the interests of the group as a whole if the latter is likely to gain from including these assets in the going concern sale of the entire business. The question is whether the secured creditors' request can be rejected on the basis of the harm that will be caused to the rest of the group if a separate sale takes place.

Another variant of such a question may involve a global package sale, while independently a concrete offer has been made to a particular subsidiary offering high consideration for its assets. The ALI Principles[36] consider such a situation (in regard to its recommendation to allow global consolidations to NAFTA corporate groups).[37] The example given there is of a subsidiary holding domestic intellectual property for which it is offered a good price by a local competitor seeking to suppress competition.[38] The question is, whether the local offer can be rejected in favour of a package sale. The ALI Principles suggest that such a lucrative offer given to a local subsidiary can be rejected but that the rights of the creditors vis-à-vis the subsidiary should be safeguarded by making an adequate allocation of value to that subsidiary from the proceeds of the global sale, so that the subsidiary will receive from the package sale at least the same amount as was offered to it separately.[39]

Indeed, considering the question of distribution in this context, and the entity–enterprise law dilemma, it seems that with regard to the above issues ('group level sales') it should be possible to reject separate offers or possibilities which may be beneficial to creditors of specific entities in order to enable the group as a whole to enjoy the accumulative value of the MEG assets. At the same time, rights of creditors against the separate entities should be safeguarded. I would argue that if it is a 'business integrated' MEG and it was placed under procedural consolidation then all parties involved in this process should be taken into account when considering the alternatives for the business or its assets. In certain scenarios, it may mean taking alternative courses of action that will benefit the entire group, although a particular subsidiary could have sold its assets in a way that would benefit its own creditors but incur harm to the entire group. If the damage to the particular subsidiary is not significant it would be fair to allow a course of action that will be beneficial to stakeholders of other related entities. In safeguarding rights of the subsidiary's creditors regard should be had to the value of the subsidiary's assets, especially if there is clear indication that greater proceeds would have been received in an independent separate sale.

---

[35] See for example UNCITRAL Legislative Guide (note 137 chapter 3), Part two, Ch. II, Recommendations 52–62, suggesting as a standard, that insolvency laws should permit the use and disposal of assets of the estate including encumbered assets, subject to preserving rights of the secured creditors and unless relief from the stay has been granted.

[36] N 243 chapter 3.

[37] See sections 3.4.2.4, 6.2.1.5 and 6.2.1.6.

[38] ALI Principles (n 243 chapter 3), p. 81.

[39] Ibid.

7.2.3 Summary

In sum, fair systems for MEGs' insolvencies should allow consideration of profitable solutions for the group as a whole where it is a 'business integrated' insolvent group and where it will not significantly harm particular entities. This implies only a slight change of the balance between entity and enterprise concepts towards enterprise law in the sense that the benefits from various solutions are considered on a group level. Yet, the balance is restored by ensuring adequate protection to creditors in regard to their rights vis-à-vis the separate entities. Ultimately, it also means minimal interference with pre-insolvency entitlements. Procedural consolidation can accommodate such an approach and at the same time ensure *ex post* efficiency in the handling of the process. The availability of a procedural consolidation mechanism of this sort should be promoted via efforts at harmonization insolvency systems as suggested earlier.[40] In 'de facto' procedural consolidation applied in MEG cases via existing cross-border insolvency frameworks (in the absence of an explicit model for MEG insolvencies)[41] courts should (within the constraints of applicable law) adopt such flexible solutions to achieve fair results.

7.3 The Global Measures (Supporting Consolidation) and Issues of Distribution

7.3.1 Protecting creditors in applying universalism-based solutions in MEG cases

Turning to the global linking tools which were suggested in support of procedural (or substantive[42]) consolidation,[43] the question now is whether the balance suggested in chapter 6 between universality and territoriality in this respect should be maintained in the same way when considering issues of distribution. In particular, the concern is with possible changes in the law applicable (following a change in the forum as a result of the quest for efficient solutions),[44] and the ability of the relevant courts to take all relevant parties' interests into account.

It was concluded in chapter 3, that a system of 'one forum and one law' has the merit of ensuring equitable treatment of all creditors of the debtor, wherever situated, preventing 'grabbing of assets'; and that this system should be the one to which the debtor has most connections.[45] Nonetheless, it was appreciated that

---

[40] See chapter 6, section 6.2.3.
[41] See ibid, sections 6.2.1.5–6.2.1.6.
[42] On substantive consolidation and issues of distribution see section 7.4.
[43] See chapter 6, sections 6.2.1.5–6.2.1.10, 6.3.4.
[44] The rules regarding the forum may be cause for other concerns related to the ability of creditors to participate in the process (see section 7.5).
[45] See chapter 3, section 3.3.

in certain circumstances upholding rights of creditors will mean that a degree of 'locality' is required, in terms of exceptions to the usual choice of law rule referring to the law of the forum, and/or conducting local proceedings in regard to certain aspects of the debtor.[46] It was also noted that this approach ('modified universalism') is generally predominant in practice;[47] and that the common test for allocating the jurisdiction to which the debtor has the most connection is that of COMI (the debtor's centre of main interests).[48]

Creditors' rights in insolvency are thus normally determined by the law of the debtor COMI. Does the model for MEG insolvency alter this notion? It is suggested that normally it does not, i.e. it does not interfere with right of creditors vis-à-vis the local debtor as determined by the local legal system. It will be recalled that in prototype A, where the MEG is integrated and centralized,[49] the model (invoked in chapter 6) suggests subjecting all the relevant entities to the laws of the jurisdiction representing the centre of the group.[50] Yet, as explained there, placing all subsidiaries in a single centre in those scenarios will match what should be perceived as their COMI anyhow, if there is consistent application of the COMI concept based on central administration as key.[51] Therefore, there is no alteration in the applicable insolvency system and rights of creditors vis-à-vis the subsidiary. In prototypes B and C, where the MEG was decentralized or heterarchical,[52] the subsidiaries have a local COMI, a centre of their own, in a different country where they operated with a significant degree of autonomy and were managed by a local management.[53] For these scenarios it was suggested that 'partial centralization' be applied, i.e. to enable local insolvency proceedings to take place under the local insolvency system (while subjecting them where possible to the COMI of the group which will serve as the supervisory jurisdiction).[54] Again, this means that the forum which may mainly apply its laws is that of the COMI of each particular entity.

On the group level the model for 'global procedural consolidation' ensures that all creditors of those entities which, in terms of economic realities, had the same centre, will receive the same treatment, in the sense that they will be subjected to

---

[46] Ibid.

[47] Ibid, section 3.4. Though modified universalism is applied in cross-border models in different ways. For example, some regimes offer a unified choice of law rule (see the EC Regulation model, ibid, section 3.4.2.2) while others do not (see UNCITRAL Model Law and the ALI Principles models, ibid, sections 3.4.2.3 and 3.4.2.4 respectively).

[48] See chapter 3, section 3.4.

[49] And the equivalent prototype D in the 'asset integrated' insolvent MEGs scenarios (see chapter 5, section 5.4).

[50] See chapter 6, section 6.2.1.8.

[51] Ibid, section 6.2.1.9.

[52] And the equivalent prototypes E and F in the 'asset integrated' insolvent MEGs scenarios (chapter 5, section 5.4). Though, see n 58, and accompanying text, in regard to flexible solutions in cases of 'asset integration' with degrees of decentralization.

[53] Chapter 5, section 5.3.3.

[54] See chapter 6, section 6.2.1.8.

the same system. Apart from the *ex post* costs benefits (in the course of insolvency) of such a scheme,[55] it guarantees that there are no distortions in terms of distribution. Creditors are placed in the same position vis-à-vis their entity as creditors in other entities in the 'integrated centralized insolvent MEG' (prototype A). On the other hand, in the decentralized/heterarchical scenarios, creditors may receive a different treatment, as they are in a different position, having dealt with an autonomous local entity. The model ensures nevertheless that such fragmentation is operated with minimum waste, providing for linkage to be made between the central group process and the proceedings against the autonomous subsidiaries.[56]

Additionally and most importantly, the idea of centralization (full or partial) enables a global perspective over the group as a whole, considering the position of connected affiliates and their stakeholders and not focusing on interests of local creditors.[57] As aforementioned, decisions regarding affiliates may affect other members in an integrated group, and thus a narrow view by a local court may neglect the interests of relevant parties.

Earlier, allowing for a degree of flexibility in applying the solutions, thus allowing centralization, albeit various degrees of decentralization or problems in allocating COMI, was suggested. It was proposed that a centralization concept should be considered also where the purpose of the proceedings (reorganization, substantive consolidation) reinforces a need for tighter global linkages, and/or there are various factors relating a subsidiary to the group centre (even though it was significantly present in its local jurisdiction).[58] Similarly, systems for single debtors' cross-border insolvency may allow avoiding opening secondary proceedings (where this is normally permitted) for the purpose of enhancing *ex post* efficiency and allowing a unified reorganization plan.[59] It was also suggested attempting to identify a 'group COMI' in 'hard cases' which may be the 'proximate' proper jurisdiction, which consequently means that rights of creditors may be altered.[60] In all such scenarios, though, there should be awareness of the effects of such solutions on rights of creditors. As the system allows for some flexibility in terms of the forum, it should be accompanied by flexibility in terms of the law applicable, in particular in order to uphold specific protections given to vulnerable creditors in the local insolvency law of their debtor.[61] If the local law offers greater protection to such parties,[62] the law of the forum handling the

---

[55] Ibid, section 6.2.
[56] See chapter 6, section 6.2.1.8.
[57] See I. Mevorach, 'The road to a suitable and comprehensive global approach to insolvencies within multinational corporate groups' [2006] JBLP 455, 502.
[58] Chapter 6, sections 6.2.1.8 and 6.3.4.
[59] See e.g. Article 3(2) of the EC Regulation (n 173 chapter 3).
[60] See chapter 6, section 6.2.1.10.
[61] Either in terms of their ability to adjust to risks associated with their debtor *ex ante* or to bear losses *ex post* (see chapter 4, section 4.2.2.5).
[62] Although as was mentioned earlier there is a general tendency towards a lesser degree of priority classes (chapter 4, section 4.2.3.3), the majority of countries afford priority to workers,

consolidation should take this into account and enable compensation accordingly in order to achieve just results. Such creditors may have conducted themselves under the assumption that they are protected in case of insolvency. Failing to take the effects of alterations in the forum on creditors' rights into account may (justifiably) invoke notions of national public policy usually incorporated in regimes for cross-border insolvency.[63] Such flexible approach has been taken in practice by courts on certain occasions. In the *MG Rover* group case (in which the EC Regulation was applied), for example, the English court overseeing the main proceedings against eight group members (the national sales companies through which cars were sold in Europe), allowed payment to employees equivalent to what they would have received in secondary proceedings in the local jurisdiction.[64] This way, opening secondary proceedings in the local jurisdictions of the particular entities (based on presence of an establishment), a step which was considered to be costly and such that would undermine the coordination of the insolvency process by the joint administrators within the main proceedings, was avoided. In policy terms, the courts ensured that efficiency (in having a unified process) was not traded off with fairness. It should also be noted that in that case, initially there was an attempt to prevent recognition of the main proceedings opened in England based on Article 26 of the EC Regulation[65] (i.e. on public policy grounds[66]). However, the French court ruled against the application of the public policy provision in this case mainly because the local creditors' rights were protected in the English proceedings.[67]

I thus propose that an international system for MEG insolvencies will be fair if it retains the same balance between the global/local distribution systems for single debtors (with worldwide operations). Additionally, it should ensure that creditors dealing with entities operating in the same geographical sphere are subjected to similar insolvency systems. This is achieved where centralization is pursued in scenarios of 'centralized' MEGs, and in more decentralized scenarios where different proceedings against subsidiaries are taking place (as suggested in chapter 6). This also enables the process to be handled with minimum costs. In cases where centralization is pursued, yet this may have resulted in a change in the forum (compared to that which applied to the debtor), then fairness requires ensuring that protections provided in the local systems are upheld in the group

and there are differences among states in regard to the degree of priority given and their specific ranking (see UNCITRAL Legislative Guide (n 137 chapter 3), Part two, Ch. V, paras. 72–3).

[63] See chapter 3, section 3.4.2.

[64] See *Re MG Rover Beluxl SA/NV (In administration)* [2006] EWHC 1296 (Ch); *Re MG Rover Espana SA (In Administration)* [2005] BPIR 1162; *Re Rover France SA*, CA Versailles, 15 December 2005. See also a similar approach taken in the *Collins & Aikman* case (*Collins & Aikman Corp* [2005] EWHC 1754 (Ch D)).

[65] N 173 chapter 3.

[66] See chapter 3, section 3.4.2.2.

[67] See M. Haravon, 'Recent Developments in France under EU Regulation 1346/2000' (2005) 18 Insolv. Int. 118, 120–1.

insolvency as well. Hence, compared to the model as was suggested in chapter 6, fairness considerations would require that the balance be restored by applying entity law and territoriality to the enterprise–universalism mechanism of centralization in these circumstances.

7.3.2 The standard test for the group central proceedings and fairness considerations

It is submitted that the 'group operational headquarters' (aspects of management and actual control on the group level) suggested in chapter 6 as a key standard for ascertaining jurisdiction in case of integrated MEGs,[68] apart from being beneficial in terms of locating a single centre for a whole group,[69] will also protect creditors' rights and promote just results. It ensures that the system presiding over the case is the one with the closest connection to the MEG as a whole thus preventing leading the case to 'haven' laws, and it is less prone to manipulation (compared with other potential standards). Therefore it is more likely to ensure safeguarding of creditors' rights and the handling of the case by a court with most interest in the case, which is more likely to take into account all relevant interests.

This test suggests that the central proceedings in regard to the MEG will be in the place of the real central administration of the MEG, not an artificial headquarters. This is the common meeting point of the group as a whole, the place where the business was actually managed, according to functional realities.[70] It requires that the MEG as a whole will have real economic presence in the jurisdiction. It is not based on formalities, but rather acknowledges the economic reality of the group. In theoretical terms, it takes an enterprise–universal approach to COMI allocation in the case of MEGs (mitigated by alternative solutions depending on the type of the case[71]), in that, it prevents MEGs from exploiting the group legal structure—i.e. the separateness between entities—to subject the group to a particular jurisdiction to which the group has no real connection, or otherwise subject a particular entity to a jurisdiction to which it has thin connection, by artificially separating it from the rest of the group. The venue choice has 'group sense'.

In contrast, I argue that place of incorporation (or registered office)[72] is not only detrimental to the task of finding a single 'group COMI' as incorporation is not done on a group level,[73] it may also direct cases of related companies to places

---

[68] For the purpose of full centralization or coordination of the process from this venue (see chapter 6, section 6.2.1.9).

[69] Ibid.

[70] See I. Mevorach, 'The Home Country of a Multinational Enterprise Group Facing Insolvency' (2008) 57 ICLQ, 427, 442.

[71] See chapter 6, sections 6.2.1.9 and 6.2.1.10.

[72] Another common venue standard (see chapter 6, section 6.2.1.9).

[73] Ibid.

to which they had little connection and may be prone to manipulations which may be harmful to creditors.[74] The only way to achieve centralization using this test is if one of the member's, for instance the parent's, place of incorporation will be designated as the group COMI. Yet, again, this may well mean that the central case might be handled in the place to which the group had no real connection (for instance where the parent is a holding company with no significant operations, workforce, or management). An insolvency process against a whole group would then be handled or supervised from a place where the group had no presence whatsoever apart from a 'letter box'. Incorporation as a key standard or even a strong presumption for ascertaining jurisdiction is therefore problematic in this respect to.

Indeed, as aforementioned, international models for cross-border insolvency adopting the concept of COMI as the test for opening main proceedings provide that the incorporation factor is only a rebuttable presumption.[75] That is, it is accepted under these regimes that such formalities as the place of incorporation are not determinative in ascertaining the venue for the insolvency process, but rather functional realities are key factors. The concept of COMI is thus based on the idea that the proposed place for opening proceedings should be the one to which the debtor is substantially linked, and in this regard it was shown that central administration is a key factor.[76] Under these regimes, incorporation is also not a decisive link for the purpose of opening secondary or 'non-main' proceedings. Rather, there should be real economic presence by way of an 'establishment' for such proceedings to be opened or recognized.[77]

Still, the question is how much weight is given to this factor. Courts applying the EC Regulation,[78] have sometimes stressed that incorporation was only one of many factors that were considered.[79] However, it was shown earlier how in the case of *Eurofood*, the ECJ has given the presumption much emphasis.[80] Nonetheless, the court did provide that the presumption can be rebutted by objective factors ascertainable to third parties, and especially where the place of incorporation was only a 'letter box'.[81] Cases decided under laws applying UNCITRAL Model Law,[82] also stressed the need to give evidence for real presence of the debtor in the

---

[74] See chapter 3, section 3.3.2.5.
[75] Ibid, sections 3.4.2.2–3.4.2.4 (especially n 186).
[76] See chapter 6, section 6.2.1.9.
[77] See chapter 3, section 3.4.2.2 (especially n 194).
[78] N 173 chapter 3.
[79] See e.g. *Ci4Net.com. Inc* [2005] BCC 277 (Ch D). See also R. Tett and N. Spence, 'COMI: presumption, what presumption' (2004) 17(9) Insolv. Int. 139. See also cases mentioned in n 170 chapter 6, where courts opened main proceedings against group members in the jurisdiction where the group head office was located, notwithstanding that some of the affiliates were incorporated in different jurisdictions.
[80] See chapter 6, section 6.2.1.9.
[81] Ibid.
[82] N 212 chapter 3.

foreign jurisdiction in order to establish main proceedings. The fact of incorp-oration is no more than a presumption, and the court will not recognize the for-eign proceedings in circumstances where it is not the COMI, even if there is no objection to such recognition. Similarly, in order to recognize foreign proceed-ings as non-main proceedings, evidence of economic presence in that jurisdiction should be provided.[83] On the normative level, as aforesaid, not only wealth maxi-mization but also fairness in distribution requires that incorporation will be no more than a presumption, the role of which is not more than to promote predict-ability.[84] The incorporation test focuses on form rather than substance, therefore may only be fiction, 'surreal'.[85] It was persuasively argued in this context that incorporation as a strong factor for ascertaining jurisdiction may have the effect of permitting 'bankruptcy havens' to serve as the chosen jurisdiction, which may lack acceptable outcomes.[86]

I suggest that the alternative types of test mentioned earlier, based on amount of activities, assets, or creditors[87] are also useful in terms of directing a case to a place with real economic presence, yet in terms of promoting other goals it is less efficient than the headquarters test.[88] It will thus be more helpful as a supportive, second best test, rather than the robust decisive standard. We thus end up with the operational group head office as a key standard test for the central proceed-ings against a MEG, and with additional factors as supportive of the general rule, or as assisting in cases where there was no single head office presiding over the group.[89] In the latter scenarios, I also suggested that parties will be able to pre-sent their choice to assist in identifying a 'proximate' COMI. In such a case, their choice is limited to alternative COMIs, not to places with no connection to the group, and thus there is no fear that the case will be directed to a place with no real connection to the MEG.

As the test requires real presence it is also rather stable, less manipulable com-pared with jurisdictional rules which may require a thinner connection to the jur-isdiction. The more the connection required is 'fragile' (for instance, some assets in the jurisdiction as a sufficient connection) the more it will be easy to meet the requirement and cherry pick a desirable forum prior to insolvency. Debtors

---

[83] *Re Bear Stearns High-Grade Structured Credit Strategies Master Fund, Ltd*, 374 BR 122 (Bankr SDNY 2007); *Re Bear Stearns High-Grade Structured Credit Strategies Master Fund, Ltd* (US District Court. SDNY 2008). A different approach was taken in the case of *SphinX* (*Re SPhinX, Ltd*, 351 BR 103 (Bankr SDNY 2006); *Re SPhinX, Ltd*, 371, B.R. 10 (SDNY 2007)).

[84] On which aspect see chapter 8, section 8.3.3.

[85] See I. Mevorach, 'The Home Country of a Multinational Enterprise Group Facing Insolvency' (2008) 57 ICLQ, 427, 438.

[86] See J.L. Westbrook, 'Locating the Eye of the Financial Storm' (2007) 32 Brook. J. Int'l L. 1019, 1030–2. See also chapter 3, section 3.3.2.5.

[87] See chapter 6, section 6.2.1.9.

[88] See ibid (in regard to wealth maximization), and chapter 8, section 8.3.3 regarding predict-ability aspects.

[89] See chapter 6, section 6.2.1.9.

(and perhaps influential creditors) may seek to substitute the otherwise applicable system with another in order to alter creditor priorities.[90]

Arguably, though, notwithstanding the headquarters factor being a realistic one, it can be manipulated.[91] In fact, any of the optional standards may be altered prior to the insolvency if debtors wish to pick a more favourable venue. Lopucki claims that multinational companies can change both their places of incorporation and the location of their headquarters rather easily.[92] To an extent the location of assets and operations are more difficult to change, but even this can be changed.[93] MEGs have even greater opportunities and tools for changing their centres, as they can achieve that through acquisitions and divestitures.[94] Additionally, MEGs may change their operational structure prior to insolvency, to become for example a centralized MEG rather than decentralized which at the time of insolvency arguably suggests (if taking a centralized approach) that only a single process should take place at that centre.[95]

---

[90] An example of this kind of forum shopping can be seen in the case of Cenargo (*Re Norse Irish Ferries & Cenargo Navigation Limited* (unreported, 20 February 2003); *In re Cenargo International Plc*, 294 BR 571 (Bankr SDNY 2003)). Cenargo, foreseeing its collapse, attempted to pick the US regime as its bankruptcy jurisdiction as it enabled the directors to remain in control through the 'debtor in possession' notion. For this purpose, the English parent (Cenargo International Plc) and various subsidiaries presented a Chapter 11 petition in the US, even though the only connection the group had to this country were bank accounts opened shortly prior to the opening of proceedings and the fact that certain creditors (a group of bondholders) were based in the US. However, the group was essentially European. Eventually, the US court suspended the Chapter 11 proceedings finding that the 'centre of gravity' of the cases was in the UK (see S. Moore, 'Global Crossing versus Cenargo The right way and the wrong way' *GLOBALTURNAROUND*, January 2004, issue 48, p. 8; LoPucki, *Courting Failure* (n 64 chapter 3), 189, 191–3, 204–5; S. Moore, 'Cenargo: A Tale of two courts, comity and (alleged!) comtempt!', January 2004 (available at: http://www.iiiglobal. org/downloads/country/USA/Articles/30-_cenargo.pdf); S. Sandy and T. Richard, 'The Cenargo Case: A Tale of Conflict, Greed Contempt, Comity and Costs' Insol. World, Fourth Quarter 2003, 33–35). Another example is the attempt of Yukos, the Russian oil company to seek Chapter 11 protection in the US. Yukos had no business interests in the US apart from bank accounts established on the eve of filing the bankruptcy petition. Eventually, the US court dismissed the case on the grounds that the company did not have enough of a presence there (*Re Yucos Oil Co* (Unreported, 24 February 2005) (SD Tex (US)). See also *GLOBALTURNAROUND*, 'Yukos court battle over chapter 11', February 2005, issue 61, p. 1,3; *GLOBALTURNAROUND*, 'Yukos abandons Chapter 11', April 2005, issue 68, p. 7); G. Moss, 'Dismissal of Yucos Chapter 11 Proceedings' (2005) 18(5) Insolv. Int. 77–8.

[91] See e.g. the case of *BCCI* (n 436 chapter 6) where the group's headquarters were moved to Abu Dhabi shortly before filing bankruptcy (see R. Donkin, 'Troubled BCCI Shifts Base to Abi Dhabi', *Financial Times* (London), 20 September 1990, p. 34).

[92] LoPucki, *Courting Failure* (n 64 chapter 3), 229. But see D.A. Skeel, 'European Implication of Bankruptcy Venue Shopping in the U.S.' (2007) 54 Buff. L. Rev. 439, 463, arguing that a rule that will require companies to file for bankruptcy in their place of incorporation will make the venue more certain and less manipulable (on certainty and predictability concerns see further chapter 8, section 8.3.3).

[93] LoPucki, *Courting Failure* (n 64 chapter 3) 229.

[94] Ibid.

[95] See actions taken by the PIN Group prior to its insolvency. All the group activities and head office functions were moved from Luxemburg to Germany prior to opening insolvency proceedings. The group apparently was 'transformed' from a decentralized group, with self-dependent entities operating in Luxemburg, to a centralized group (with the centre in Germany). Insolvency

A meaningful system for insolvency within MEGs should aim to overcome cynical attempts at moving the centre when anticipating insolvency. At the moment, under current regimes for cross-border insolvency in regard to single debtors (adopting the concept of COMI),[96] jurisdiction should be determined by examining the debtor's characteristics at the time of the opening of insolvency proceedings. There is no explicit prohibition in regard to a change of the centre of main interest at the eve of insolvency.[97] A better approach would be to guide courts to draw a distinction between a cynical attempt to move the centre (in our context, the centre of control in regard to the MEG as a whole) shortly before insolvency proceedings are commenced and a restructuring of the enterprise for sound commercial reasons before insolvency proceedings.[98] As was stated in the case of Ci4net.com[99] (an EC Regulation[100] case) with regard to alteration of a debtor's COMI, an 'artificial' change of the company's centre should not be regarded as altering the COMI for the purpose of the Regulation, whereas a real move of the centre could.[101] Hence, the place identified as the proper jurisdiction to handle the MEG insolvency process should be the centre of the group for a set amount of time prior to the insolvency.[102] In this regard, in order to resolve situations where there was more than one such place within this period of time, a model should presume that the venue in which the centre was residing the longest is the COMI.[103] However, the reasons for the change should be closely examined

proceedings were then opened in Germany (see A.J. Weissbrodt, 'Disproving the COMI presumption' (2008) *Eurofenix*, issue 32, 14).

[96] See chapter 3, section 3.4.2.2–3.4.2.4.

[97] See Fletcher, *Insolvency* (n 3 chapter 3) 367–8.

[98] See I. Mevorach, 'Centralizing insolvencies of pan-European corporate groups: a creditor's dream or nightmare?' [2006] JBL, 468, 483–4.

[99] *Ci4net.com Inc & Anor* [2005] BCC 277.

[100] Note 173 chapter 3.

[101] See also R. Tett and N. Spence, 'COMI: Presumption, what presumption' Insolv. Int. 2004, 17(9), 139–41.

[102] In *Ci4net.com* mentioned above (n 99) the judge stressed that the COMI must have some degree of permanence (it should not move around with the location of the directors). Certainly, moving the centre of main interests after lodging a request to open insolvency proceedings (but before the proceedings are opened) should not affect the decision regarding the appropriate jurisdiction. As was explained by the ECJ in the case of *Staubitz-Schreiber*, a transfer of jurisdiction from the court originally seized to a court of another member state on the basis of the debtor moving its centre after submitting the request would be contrary to the objectives pursued by the Regulation, mainly the intention to avoid incentives for the parties to transfer assets or judicial proceedings from one member state to another, seeking to obtain a more favourable legal position (*Staubitz-Schreiber* (Case C-1/04) [2006] OJ 2006 C60/3). See also the case of *Interdil* (Corte de Cassazione Civile, Sezioni Unite 28.01.2005 no 10606) where the Italian court ruled that a transfer of seat carried out by an insolvent company shortly before the opening of insolvency proceedings does not affect the jurisdiction of the insolvency court (see C. Carrara, 'Forum shopping and why timing is crucial' *Eurofenix* (2008) 20–1).

[103] Resembling the English rule that resolves a jurisdictional dilemma which arises when the debtor's residential address or business address (or for a company, the 'registered office') has changed from one insolvency district to another within a six-month period prior to the presentation of insolvency petition. The insolvency rules provide that the court within whose jurisdiction the debtor has been resident for the longest time prevails even if it is not the current address at the

and if it is apparent that the centre was genuinely placed at the new jurisdiction (though this was for a shorter period, as the company entered insolvency) this place should be designated as the proper venue.

Another sort of manipulation MEGs (or their creditors) may be engaged in is manipulating the order of filing of insolvency proceedings in regard to MEG members, to pick a preferable jurisdiction for the MEG in anticipated distress. For instance, MEGs may file proceedings initially by one or more members of the group followed later by filings of other members, postponing for instance the filing of the controlling entity to a later stage, making it difficult to then transfer the process to the centre of the group.[104] In this regard, I suggest that the concept suggested in chapter 6,[105] according to which a global consolidation system would allow considering the entire group as much as possible at the same time, will assist in overcoming such manipulation that may be the reason for the successive filings.[106] Additionally, the mechanism for 'correcting error' suggested earlier,[107] would provide the necessary flexibility in the jurisdictional rule to overcome manipulations, as certain entities may join the process at a later stage despite efforts to place the entire group under insolvency at once.

7.4 Global Substantive Consolidation and Redistribution

For 'asset integrated' insolvent MEGs (prototypes D–F),[108] it was suggested that substantive consolidation would typically be adequate in terms of maximizing returns. Notwithstanding the conflict with entity law, it was concluded that in the circumstances depicted by these prototypes there was actually a 'façade of asset partitioning' and thus such a tool wouldl achieve the goal of wealth maximization without unduly defeating entity law. The question now, when considering respect of rights and distribution in insolvency, is twofold. First, whether substantive consolidation for 'asset integrated' insolvent MEGs also fits with these goals, and second, whether these goals suggest that substantive consolidation should be sought in other scenarios as well (so that the balance will further shift towards enterprise concepts), in particular in case creditors have relied on the MEG as a whole.

---

time of filing (Insolvency Rules 1986, rr. 6.9(4), 6.40(2)(c); see also Fletcher, *Law of Insolvency* (n 275 chapter 6) 131–2.

[104] L.M. LoPucki, 'Cooperation in International Bankruptcy: A Post-Universalist Approach' (1999) 84 Cornell L. Rev. 696, 722–3.

[105] See section 6.2.3.4.

[106] See also I. Mevorach, 'Centralizing insolvencies of pan-European corporate groups: a creditor's dream or nightmare?' [2006] JBL, 468, 484.

[107] Chapter 6, section 6.2.1.9.

[108] In the various degrees of centralization (see chapter 5, section 5.4).

7.4.1 Asset integration

The problem with substantive consolidation is said to be that 'unless the asset to liability ratio is equal, substantive consolidation will necessarily reduce the bankruptcy distribution to some group of creditors or equity owners.'[109] This may be particularly problematic when considering entities in the 'pool' which are solvent or apparently richer than the others. Arguably, substantive consolidation is thus redistributive. However, in case of 'asset integration', where assets and debts are intermingled and inter-corporate liabilities are untraceable, it would be impossible to claim to what extent there is redistribution and even if there is any at all (without first going through the costs of untangling the web of connections). A creditor would not know what option will gain more for him (recovering from the separate entity or from the MEG as a whole). In these scenarios, ascertaining the actual assets and debts of each subsidiary is either impossible or would involve disproportionate efforts. In addition, if a particular company is allegedly solvent but in fact its assets and debts are commingled with those of other entities then the apparent worth of its assets may be unrealistic and the whole picture is actually unstable or incorrect. The intermingling between the entities in these scenarios results in a situation where all creditors in fact belong to the MEG as a whole, and therefore a fair distribution means that all assets of the MEG should be available for distribution to all creditors. A substantive consolidation mechanism allows for that, and also eliminates costs of attempting to untangle the web of connections.

Indeed, in the case of *BCCI*, which was earlier mentioned as an example of 'asset integrated' insolvent MEG,[110] the pooling solution which was applied was regarded as the only way to enable a fair distribution of the group assets. The businesses were so intermingled that a creditor could not possibly have shown that a certain company was by all means solvent or that he would gain more in a separate distribution. A prerequisite for such a claim would have been to conduct a long and expensive process of untangling the assets and debts to ascertain which assets and liabilities belonged to which group component. Therefore, the representatives in this case concluded that a pooling mechanism was essential also in order to ensure an equal treatment to the creditors as a whole.[111]

---

[109] C.W. Frost, 'Organizational Form, Misappropriation Risk, and the Substantive Consolidation of Corporate Groups' (1993) 44 Hastings L.J. 449, 451. See also D.G. Baird, 'Substantive Consolidation Today' (2006) 47 Bost. Col. L. Rev. 5, 6 (claiming that under substantive consolidation scheme 'some general creditors fare better and others worse').

[110] See n 436 chapter 6 and see further discussions of the BCCI collapse in chapter 6, sections 6.2.1.9, 6.2.2.3 and 6.3.4; n 79 chapter 8; and n 81 chapter 9).

[111] See *In re Bank of Credit and Commerce International S.A.* (District Court of Luxemburg, 3 January 1992). The court indicated that the supervisory commissioner 'is of the opinion that it is essential in order to ensure an equal treatment to all creditors of the group to coordinate the liquidation operations by means of cooperation agreements to be concluded with the liquidators of the different foreign entities, subsidiaries and branches, with a view to create a common pot and a

The possibility of excluding certain entities or certain claims from the substantive consolidation (applying partial substantive consolidation)[112] further ensures that there is no redistribution.

7.4.2 Reliance

It was shown earlier that certain legal regimes providing for substantive consolidation allow its application not only in circumstances of intermingling, but also based on other factors, related to the behaviour of those controlling the group (in regard to the way they ran it), and fairness to creditors who relied on the strength of the group as a whole when extending credit.[113] Under the New Zealand pooling regime, one of the factors to be considered in deciding whether to make a pooling order is 'the conduct of any of the companies towards the creditors of any of the other companies'.[114] This was interpreted as essentially meaning the degree of confusion of the creditors of the companies as to which company they had been dealing with,[115] although mere reliance by creditors of a company on the fact that another company is, or was, related to that company is not a ground for making such an order.[116]

Under the US bankruptcy regime, substantive consolidation apparently may be allowed in cases where creditors of affiliate companies have dealt with these entities as a single economic unit, and have not relied on their separate identities when extending credit.[117] Substantive consolidation is regarded as an equitable tool and may also be used as a remedy against improper and misleading corporate behaviour.[118]

The issue of fraud or misleading of creditors or other wrongful behaviour in regard to the way the group was operated and control was exercised (in the context of insolvency) will be discussed later on.[119] It will be argued that in such

---

common administration (Pooling Agreement) of all assets realised or to be realised by the different entities, in order to guarantee an equal distribution to creditors of those entities'.

[112] See chapter 6, section 6.3.3.4.

[113] See also I. Mevorach, 'The road to a suitable and comprehensive global approach to insolvencies within multinational corporate groups' [2006] JBLP 455, 512–13.

[114] Section 272(2)(b) of New Zealand Companies Act 1993.

[115] See *In Re Dalhoff & King Ltd* (1991) 5 NZCLC 66, 959.

[116] New Zealand companies Act 1993, s. 272(3).

[117] See e.g. *Soviero v Franklin National Bank* 328 F. 2d. 446 (2nd Cir 1964); *Union Sav. Bank v Augie/Restivo Baking Company (In re Augie/Restivo Baking Co)* 860 F 2d 515 (2d Cir 1988); *In re Owens Corning*, 419 F.3d (3d Cir 2005)). See generally, Blumberg et al, *Blumberg on Corporate Groups* (n 31 chapter 1) vol 2, s. 88.06[A].

[118] *In re Snider Bros., Inc.* 18 BR 230, 234 (Bankr. D. Mass. 1982); *Chemical Bank N.Y. Trust Co. v Kheel* 369 F.2d 845, 847 (2d Cir 1966)); *Union Sav. Bank v Augie/Restivo Baking Company (In re Augie/Restivo Baking Co)* 860 F 2d 515 (2d Cir 1988). See also E.A. Webber, 'Consensual Substantive Consolidation: Comments on the Working Papers of Professor Skeel and Dr. Staehelin', in H. Peter, N. Jeandin and J. Kilborn (eds.), *The Challenges of Insolvency Law Reform in the 21st Century* (Verlag Schulthess, Zurich 2006), 235, 237.

[119] See chapter 9.

circumstances other remedies which primarily aim to tackle group opportunism including fraudulent transactions will be more adequate (rather than substantive consolidation).[120] Creditors' belief that they have dealt with one single enterprise rather than with an individual member of the group may itself be a result of encouragement to this extent by those in control of the group, so that the creditors were misled to believe they were dealing with a greater entity, but as mentioned, this will be a matter to consider separately. It may also be the case that the entities of the MEG in hand were 'asset integrated' operating veritably as a single entity. In these cases, the fact the creditors relied on the MEG as a whole can serve as supportive argument in concluding that substantive consolidation should be applied to save costs *ex post* (in reconstructing the separate businesses during the insolvency proceedings).

The question is what should be the rule where creditors relied on the MEG (thus on the availability of assets owned by other entities), but there was no de facto confusion as to the ownership of assets and debts (it is not a case of 'asset integrated' MEG), and no actual misleading of creditors or identifiable 'vulnerable' transactions.[121] In other words, the question is whether reliance on the part of creditors can be a sufficient ground for substantive consolidation. A relevant scenario is where the MEG entities or several of them had an identifiable separate business. The business may have been functionally interdependent (a 'business integrated' MEG) but the assets and debts were not extensively intermingled, and at least can be ascertained with reasonable effort. However, creditors were not aware of that and their impression was that the assets of those entities were part of the entire estate. In this case conducting the insolvency for the group as a whole as if it was one entity will not necessarily save costs, but indeed it may increase returns to certain creditors (which may belong to a relatively 'weak' entity). Here though there is clearly redistribution. Unless there is an equal asset to liability ratio,[122] there will be diversity of creditors' interests with regard to the distribution of the group's estate, not only in terms of the different priority position within each entity, but also (particular to our context) in terms of the different prospects of payments from the particular entity.[123] It means that it may well be, for example, that creditors will have an incentive to place any of the MEG entities in insolvency to gain an advantage they would not have gained outside insolv-

---

[120] Ibid, section 9.5.   [121] On which see chapter 9, section 9.2.

[122] See n 109, and accompanying text.

[123] Rasmussen provides an example where creditors of one group member have claims that in total roughly equal that member's assets, while creditors of another member in the same group have claims that vastly exceed the assets of that member. The latter group of creditors will have an interest to pool assets and debts together while the former would insist on respecting the corporate form (see R.K. Rasmussen, 'The Problem of Corporate Groups, a Comment on Professor Ziegel' (2002) 7 Fordham J. Corp. & Fin. L. 395, 396). See also H. Peter, 'Insolvency in a Group of Companies, Substantive and Procedural Consolidation: When and How?' in H. Peter, N. Jeandin and J. Kilborn (eds.), *The Challenges of Insolvency Law Reform in the 21st Century* (Verlag Schulthess, Zurich 2006), 199, 206 (referring to US case law, such as *In re Augie/Restivo Baking Co.*, 860 F.2d 506 (2d Cir 1988)) that has shown that consolidation may not be necessarily in all creditors' interests).

ency.[124] Outside insolvency a claim to recover debt from other entities would have had proceeded on some sort of legal doctrine allowing to 'lift the veil',[125] which most likely would not have succeeded bearing in mind the strict adherence to entity law in legal regimes.[126] As we are not dealing here with a case of fraud or any other misbehaviour, or a façade of entities,[127] but rather the entities had their own businesses, a case for ignoring limited liability is weak. It is also not the case of giving a particular privilege in insolvency to a certain group of creditors which is of need of specific protection, so that it can be argued that redistribution is justified on that basis.[128] Rather, it will be a mixture of assets and debts of all entities, where certain creditors will recover at the expense of the others. It is also not taking assets from the controllers because they were perhaps responsible for the debts of their subsidiaries,[129] but rather making certain creditors pay for the reliance of others on a particular state of affairs.

It will also be based on rather subjective viewpoints of creditors, which may not be coherent across the group. It may be that some creditors thought they were dealing with the debtors as one economic unit, while others did not. Indeed, under the regimes allowing for consolidation on this basis, normally creditors who relied on the single entity can attempt to defeat substantive consolidation. Under the US regime, it may be possible to oppose substantive consolidation by showing that a creditor has 'relied on the separate credit of one of the entities and that it will be prejudiced by the consolidation.'[130] However, such creditors may not be able to show that the harm to them outweighs the benefits to other creditors from the consolidation.[131]

Substantive consolidation applied on this basis is also in direct conflict with entity law, particularly 'asset partitioning' and its advantages in reducing monitoring costs.[132] Creditors knowing that the substance of an entity to whom they were extending credit may be mixed with other entities in insolvency because the majority of creditors of a group to whom this entity is related (or may be related in the future, if it will be acquired by an enterprise at some point) will manage to prove they relied on the group as whole, are likely to invest in monitoring the financial state of the other related entities (or even not extend credit at all).[133] The costs may be even more substantial in a MEG where the enterprise has components in different parts of the world.

---

[124] See chapter 4, section 4.2.2.2.   [125] See chapter 2, section 2.4.3.

[126] Ibid.   [127] Ibid.   [128] See chapter 4, section 4.2.2.3.

[129] Ibid (and see the discussion of remedies in insolvency for combating group opportunism in chapter 9).

[130] *In re Auto-Train Corp.*, 810 F.2d 270, 276 (DC Cir 1987). See also *In re Owens Corning*, 419 F.3d at 212 (3d Cir 2005). See also, Blumberg et al, *Blumberg on Corporate Groups* (n 31 chapter 1) vol 2, s. 88.06[A].

[131] See D.G. Baird, 'Substantive Consolidation Today' (2006) 47 Bost. Col. L. Rev. 5, 9.

[132] See chapter 2, section 2.3.2.3. See also T. E. Graulich, 'Substantive consolidation–a postmodern trend' (2006) 14 Am. Bankr. Ins. L. Rev. 527, 529 (arguing that the liberal trend of bankruptcy courts in the US to make substantive consolidation the rule is in direct conflict with corporate separateness).

[133] See chapter 2, section 2.3.2.3.

The inevitable conclusion is that, at least when considering what should be the factors for such a strong linking tool to be adopted universally, reliance and creditors' subjective beliefs should not be decisive factors which will lead to substantive consolidation.[134] A fair system would allow mixing assets and debts where these are in fact scrambled so that separating them will harm all creditors, but otherwise it will refrain from enriching certain creditors at the expense of others, unless the latter agree to the scheme and the court is satisfied that creditors are not harmed as a result of the substantive consolidation.[135] Nevertheless, the consideration of creditors' beliefs may still serve two different functions. First, it can reinforce the argument in favour of pooling when the intermingling test suggests the same. By the same token, it will support the exclusion of certain creditors and assets from the consolidation (applying partial consolidation [136]) where the particular creditor relied on the separate existence of an entity. Second, it can assist in revealing situations where the group actually misled creditors to think that they would be able to recover from a financially stronger entity or other circumstances of fraud, which may suggest the application of remedies aimed at tackling 'group opportunism'.[137]

Therefore, in regard to substantive consolidation I suggest adhering to the model as was suggested in chapter 6, i.e. allowing substantive consolidation in 'asset integrated' insolvent MEG scenarios. This can be a standard for a universally accepted 'enterprise law' mechanism to be available in cases of MEG insolvencies of this nature. It will enhance fairness and efficiency, goals which are perceived attractive on a global level, without unduly harming entity law. The global mechanisms in support of substantive consolidation for MEGs apply, and their justifications in terms of efficiency and distribution have been discussed above.

7.5 Creditors' Participation and Adequate Representation in the Proceedings

7.5.1 Accountability on a global group-wide basis

The goal of fairness of the process and adequate representation (including expertise of the representatives) seems to raise doubts as to the desirability of any application of universalism and enterprise concepts for the MEG in insolvency.

---

[134] UNCITRAL Working Group V (n 96 chapter 1) has been discussing the doctrine of substantive consolidation (see chapter 6, section 6.3.2), and is currently rejecting the inclusion of the factors of appearance and reliance as bases for substantive consolidation, as they do not meet the standard of objectivity (see WP.80/Add.1 (n 65 chapter 6), draft recommendation 17(c); Report, thirty-fourth session (n 98 chapter 1), para. 64; WP.82/Add.3 (n 65 chapter 6), draft recommendation 17).

[135] See chapter 6, section 6.3.3.2.

[136] Ibid.

[137] I. Mevorach, 'Appropriate treatment of corporate groups in insolvency—a universal view' (2006) 8 EBOR, 179, 188. On the issues of group liability and voidable transactions see chapter 9.

Arguably, this only complicates the state of affairs. It requires sensitive decision-making, and it adds problems of conflict of interests, where it suggests allowing (in certain circumstances) single representation over what are separate entities. Additionally, full centralization will require creditors belonging to a local subsidiary to be subjected to a foreign process (where the 'group COMI' is located),[138] where otherwise they could just be involved in the process against the subsidiary locally, in the easiest and most accessible manner.

Arguably due process and objective representation is best achieved by a territorial–entity approach. However, here too, this approach would miss the economic reality of the MEG insolvency scenario. I have suggested earlier, that in integrated insolvent MEG scenarios (either in 'business' or 'asset' terms) there are mutual interests among the entities and their stakeholders.[139] A complete entity–territorial approach would ignore these mutual interests and would not allow adequate input or consideration of interests of creditors of other related entities.[140] In addition, substantive fairness requires consideration of the entire MEG stakeholders by those in charge of the process, taking a global group-wide perspective.[141]

The enterprise–universalism-based concepts of procedural and substantive consolidation accompanied by centralization and supervision thus ensure a more inclusive process where creditors of related companies can be given a stage on which they may present their views and can be taken into account. In other words, I argue that accountability should be considered on a global group-wide perspective in the relevant type of cases (i.e. prototypes A–F—the (business/asset) integrated MEGs[142]). Accordingly, all participants in a type of global procedural coordination of MEG proceedings[143] should have access to proceedings of the related companies involved. This does not mean an equal level of participation of creditors of the particular entity and those belonging to related companies (in the case of global procedural consolidation, i.e. for prototypes A–C scenarios—'business integrated' insolvent MEGs[144]). This will conflict with entity law in these circumstances as suggested earlier, as well as have a toll in terms of efficiency, since in procedural consolidation each entity remains separate and solutions are considered primarily on a separate basis.[145] Participation of creditors should not reach an extent where it becomes counter-productive; especially, creditors should not participate in matters that will not have an impact on their

---

[138] See chapter 6, section 6.2.1.9.

[139] Ibid, section 6.2.1.1.

[140] See I. Mevorach, 'Centralizing insolvencies of pan-European corporate groups: a creditor's dream or nightmare?' (2006) JBL, 468, 474.

[141] See section 7.3.1.

[142] See chapter 5, section 5.4.

[143] As suggested earlier, global consolidation may take various forms. It can be pursued via concurrent proceedings or by centralization or supervision, depending on the type of MEG in hand (see chapter 6, sections 6.2.1.5–6.2.1.8).

[144] See chapter 5, section 5.4.   [145] See chapter 6, section 6.2.1.3.

interests.[146] Bearing these limitations in mind, creditors of MEG members sub-ject to global consolidation of a sort should have standing in the proceedings of related entities and should be able to challenge decisions that may affect their rights vis-à-vis their entity. It is also important to note that creditors of entities belonging to the MEG but that are not integrated with it, and are outside the joint process should not have such rights.

Most importantly, it is suggested that representatives overseeing a unified process (which may be either centralized or decentralized) should be account-able to all the stakeholders (of the relevant entities subject to the joint process). They should be required to consider the best interests of the stakeholders of the various entities included in the process. This does not mean, however, that the entities are blurred. The primary duty is to each entity separately. There should be consideration, though, of the effect of decisions regarding certain entities on the stakeholders of other entities. And, vice versa, if a unified solution of sorts is taken (such as a global package sale) for the benefit of the group as a whole, then the harm that might be caused as a result to any particular entity should be taken into account and be addressed.[147] This will support and ensure substantive just-ice is actually followed—the representative pursuing the purpose of the process and taking all relevant parties' interests into account. If several representatives are appointed in a decentralized process (though subject to joint administration), they too should be primarily accountable to the particular entity they are admin-istering, but they should have a duty to cooperate with the supervisory process so that they will not act in a way unnecessarily harmful to creditors of other entities. In case substantive consolidation is applied,[148] the separate entities to an extent become one,[149] and thus normal rules for single debtors regarding accountability and participation should apply.

On the face of it, this approach imposes greater responsibility on those pre-siding over MEG insolvencies, thus complicating their task. However, in fact, it matches what insolvency representatives would have in many cases perceived as the right way ahead for the business in the relevant circumstances; only in the absence of relevant rules to this extent they may have found themselves in a diffi-cult position to justify their approach. On the one hand, they will normally have owed a duty to the particular entity for which they were appointed under the applicable company law. On the other hand, the economic reality of the enter-prise in hand demands taking a unified solution. The duty of the representative will not be fulfilled if they ignore this economic reality. For example, if the MEG is 'asset integrated', i.e. the assets and debts of the constituent companies are extensively intermingled, the insolvency representative (or the various representa-tives appointed for each constituent company) will not fulfil their duty to the

---

[146] See chapter 4, section 4.2.3.5.   [147] See section 7.2.2.
[148] In case of 'asset integrated' insolvent MEGs (see chapter 6, section 6.3; and section 7.4.1).
[149] See ibid.

particular company if they insist on keeping the separateness between the companies. An enterprise–universalist approach (within the limitations suggested) only ensures the law follows this reality. It gives justification (accompanied by responsibility) to the insolvency representative to take on board unified solutions. If they pursue a unified solution in the relevant circumstances, then they have not breached their duty to the creditors of the particular entity. Providing 'linking tools' and allowing unification ensures that insolvency representatives can fulfil their duties properly.[150]

7.5.2 Adequate notifications and consideration of relevant information as measures to enhance global group-wide creditors' participation

To allow participation on a global group-wide level (within the limitations suggested), a system for MEGs' insolvencies should ensure that adequate notices are given to relevant parties, and relevant information is properly disseminated. Thus, stakeholders of MEG members, party to a joint process, should be notified about the opening of such joint proceedings. This should contain information about the sort of global linking tools sought,[151]—and should be accompanied by adequate information in regard to the basis for the decision (in particular, the type of MEG in hand). Subsequently, creditors should be notified of the specific path sought for the enterprise. Especially, if substantive consolidation is applied, a clear explanation should be given on the justifications for taking this approach (i.e. the rationale for the decision, in particular whether it rests on an 'asset integration' scenario, and whether certain entities or claims are excluded from the process).[152] Creditors (of any of the entities included in the proposed substantive consolidation) should be able to challenge the decision or participate in the decision-making. It may be by way of voting on a plan if the substantive consolidation is proposed as part of a reorganization plan, or by way of seeking court approval (by the representative) subject to a right to object. In cases outside the limitations proposed in this work for substantive consolidation,[153] more scrutiny will be required ensuring that no creditor is harmed.[154] Clearly, notice on any order given by the court in this context for procedural or substantive consolidation (or partial substantive consolidation) including the terms of the order should be given to the relevant parties.

---

[150] This seems to be a key reasoning for the provisions of pooling arrangements in Australia (see J. Dickfos, C. Anderson and D. Morrison, 'The Insolvency Implications for Corporate Groups in Australia—Recent Events and Initiatives' (2007) 16 Int. Insol. Rev. 103, 120).

[151] Whether it is full centralization, supervision (including the location of the central process), or other means of cooperation.

[152] On partial consolidation see chapter 6, section 6.3.3.4.

[153] See chapter 6, section 6.3; and section 7.4.

[154] Ibid.

UNCITRAL Working Group V [155] in addressing the topic of enterprise groups' insolvencies (in regard to the domestic issues arising in this respect) is currently considering recommending that laws will establish requirements regarding the giving of notice and relevant information on the procedural coordination application and order, especially where the law makes provision for cases commenced in different jurisdictions to be transferred to, or administered by, a single jurisdiction and that transfer may affect procedural aspects of the proceedings.[156] The Working Group also considers providing similar recommendations in regard to substantive consolidation.[157] Such recommendations are highly commendable and should similarly (and even more meticulously) apply in the international context.

The International Insolvency Institute Committee on International Jurisdiction in its working draft judicial guidelines for coordination of MEG insolvencies [158] currently suggests that notice should be given to all members of the MEG when proceedings are commenced against any of the MEG members as well as the opportunity to be heard before determining the member's jurisdiction (COMI).[159]

As the case is international there is nevertheless a risk of neglecting 'remote' creditors if a subsidiary's insolvency is handled in some externally identified centre.[160] Certain creditors who might not have the sufficient means to embark on a multinational legal expedition may not be consulted even when a decision that pertains to them is taken. Furthermore, as was indicated with regard to single debtor cross-border insolvencies, there are practical disadvantages for foreign creditors due to language, distance and the differences between procedural requirements imposed by states' insolvency laws.[161] I suggest that a system for MEG insolvencies should strive to overcome this inherent inferiority of foreign creditors (in terms of ability to participate) by being extra cautious about issues of notice and information.[162] Courts should be reassured they are provided with the entire picture when considering the path a MEG insolvency process should take

---

[155] N 96 chapter 1.

[156] See WP.80 (n 98 chapter 1), draft recommendations 6 and 7; Report, thirty-fourth session (n 98 chapter 1), paras. 41 and 42; WP.82/Add.1 (n 54 chapter 6) draft recommendation 9 and paras. 25–8.

[157] See WP.80/ Add 1 (n 65 chapter 6), paras. 23 and 24; WP.82/Add.1 (n 54 chapter 6), draft recommendation 9 and paras. 34–6.

[158] III Draft Guidelines (n 100 chapter 1).

[159] Ibid, Guideline 1.

[160] See I. Mevorach, 'Centralizing insolvencies of pan-European corporate groups: a creditor's dream or nightmare?' [2006] JBL, 468, 475.

[161] See I.F. Fletcher, 'The European Union Regulation on Insolvency Proceedings' [2003] INSOL International, Cross-Border Insolvency, A Guide to Recognition and Enforcement 15, 41.

[162] The EC Regulation in offering a framework for cross-border insolvency for single debtors takes into account the disadvantageous situation of foreign creditors, and thus requires taking immediate steps to inform them about the opening of insolvency proceedings including notification of related issues such as time limits and information regarding the lodgment of claims (Article 40 of the EC Regulation (n 173 chapter 3)).

or with regard to other matters pertaining to the insolvency (this may include the decision on the location of proceedings, the administration and supervision of the process or the decision on any sort of consolidation to be imposed, and so on). The court should be able to take into account interests of all creditors relevant to the process, appreciating the consequences of particular decisions on creditors' rights.[163] This also means that creditors' interests should be considered even if they are not physically present in court.[164]

A tool (of 'last resort') that local courts (of local affiliates) will be able to use is the public policy notion. Thus, in cases of clear infringement of due process in a disproportionate manner and no adequate justification, local courts can refuse to recognize the central proceedings.[165] However, local courts should not give creditors a 'second chance' to participate and to be heard in an ancillary process of recognition, in scenarios where they had their opportunity to participate in the central process (and where there are no local proceedings taken place against the subsidiary in the local jurisdiction, i.e. in case of full centralization).[166]

---

[163] In the case of *Daisytek*, for example, there was a strong debate regarding the reasoning given by the English court when it opened the proceedings against each member of the group, and with respect to the representation of the subsidiaries in this process (see C.G. Paulus, 'Zustandigkeitsfragen nach der Europaischen Insolvenzverodnung', International Insolvency Institute (available at: http://www.iiiglobal.org/downloads/country/Germany/Articles/12-_ insolvenzverordnung.pdf); see also B. Wessels, 'International Jurisdiction to Open Insolvency Proceedings in Europe, In Particular Against (Groups of) Companies', Working Papers Series, Institute for Law and Finance, Johann Wolfgang Goethe University (available at: http://www.iii-global.org/downloads/European%20Union/Articles/11-_InternJurisdictionCompanies.pd); the case was discussed earlier (see chapter 6, section 6.2.1.6). In the case of *TXU* the court considered the possibility that there would be cases where the court would require evidence detailing extensively the circumstances in which the jurisdiction (in that case—the United Kingdom) has come to be or is said to be the centre of main interests of a foreign company in order to avoid prejudice of creditors' rights (*Re TXU Europe German Finance BV* [2005] BCC 90 (Ch D); see also G. Moss, 'Creditors voluntary liquidation for foreign registered companies' (2005) 18 Insolv. Int. 12–13).

[164] I. Mevorach, 'Centralizing insolvencies of pan-European corporate groups: a creditor's dream or nightmare?' [2006] JBL, 468, 485.

[165] Similar to the provisions in cross-border insolvency models with regard to foreign creditors of a single debtor (see Articles 40–2 of the EC Regulation (n 173 chapter 3); Article 6 of the Model Law (n 212 chapter 3)). See the ECJ decision in *Eurofood* which stated that the right to receive procedural documents and more generally the right to be heard (however—regarding proceedings held against the particular subsidiary) are considered as fundamental rights, thus member states may refuse to recognize proceedings that were opened in breach of this rights on the grounds of the public policy exception provided in the EC Regulation (*Eurofood IFSC Ltd* (Case C-341/04) [2006] OJ 2006 C143/11, [60]-[68]). Previously the Irish Supreme Court in considering the question of COMI in regard to *Eurofood*, found that there were major due process violations by the Parma court which required denial (on public policy grounds) of recognition of the Italian decision to open main proceedings against Eurofood in Italy (*Re Eurofood IFSC Ltd* [2004] BCC 383). But see also n 167. See also I. Mevorach, 'Centralizing insolvencies of pan-European corporate groups: a creditor's dream or nightmare?' [2006] JBL, 468, 485; I. Mevorach, 'The road to a suitable and comprehensive global approach to insolvencies within multinational corporate groups' [2006] JBLP 455, 504.

[166] See chapter 6, section 6.2.1.6. Such approach has been recently taken (in regard to recognition of a restructuring plan of a single debtor) by the US Second Circuit Court of Appeals. Upholding a US Bankruptcy Court's decision to grant recognition of an Argentine court-approved restructuring plan, it deferred to the Argentine court's findings, and enforced the restructuring

Additionally, regard should be made to possible trade-offs between the procedural rights to be heard and the urgency for a ruling to be given.[167] Generally, remedies for infringement of procedural justice should be sought within the jurisdiction in charge of the MEG insolvency process, as if the case was local. This will reduce clashes between jurisdictions and allow better coordination of the global process, while ensuring due process within the central process.

7.5.3 Handling the case in the proper venue

Finally, as mentioned above, the unified approach suggested in this work also ensures that the central proceedings are handled in a place to which the MEG as a whole has a real substantial connection, and prevent it from being handled in 'haven' jurisdictions.[168] This is important from the accountability perspective too as such jurisdiction may lack sufficient mechanisms to ensure a transparent process.[169]

7.5.4 Dealing with conflicts of interest

Adequate representation of the stakeholders' interests also requires expertise and objectiveness of those handling the global process. Objectiveness in the case of MEGs is particularly acute, as a single representative (or a bundle of representatives working together) may preside over the centralized or the coordinated process.[170] However, unless the case is going to be handled while applying full

---

plan despite differences between Argentine Insolvency Law and the US Bankruptcy Code. The Court of Appeals rejected a dissident note holder for failing to object to the foreign restructuring plan. *Argo Fund Ltd v Bd. of Dirs. of Telecom Arg., S.A. (In re Bd. of Dirs. of Telecom Arg., S.A.)*, 2008 U.S. App. LEXIS 11397 (2d Cir. NY May 29, 2008). L. P. Harrison, 'New York Circuit Court Upholds Recognition of an Argentine Plan Finding Creditor Should Have Objected In Foreign Proceedings' INSOL INTERNATIONAL NEWS UPDATE, Issue No. 7, July 2008 (noting that the decision seems to suggest that if a creditor fails to participate in a foreign proceeding in which it was provided with due process, then that creditor should not expect 'a second bite at the apple' in an ancillary proceeding in the US).

[167] In *Eurofood*, the ECJ explained that any restrictions on the exercise of the right to be heard should be duly justified and surrounded by procedural guarantees that it would be possible to challenge the urgent decisions (n 165). Generally, it stressed that invoking public policy should be a measure of last resort and can be used only in extraordinary circumstances (ibid). The ECJ did not rule whether on the facts in *Eurofood* public policy could have been invoked as this was outside the scope of the decision. See further on *Eurofood* in section 7.3.2; chapter 6, sections 6.2.1.6, 6.2.1.8 and 6.2.1.9; and chapter 8, sections 8.2 and 8.3.3. See also on the issue of public policy and the case of *Eurofood* in S.L. Bufford, 'Centre of Main Interests, International Insolvency Case Venue, and Equality of Arms: the Eurofood Decision of the European Court of Justice' (2007) 27 Nw. J. Int'l L. & Bus. 351, 394–402, 404–5, 411–18.

[168] See section 7.3.2.

[169] J.L. Westbrook, 'Locating the Eye of the Financial Storm' (2007) 32 Brook. J. Int'l L. 1019, 1031.

[170] Depending on the particular linking tool that will be applied (see chapter 6, sections 6.2.1.5–6.2.1.8).

substantive consolidation, each entity is supposed to remain intact, and its stake-holders' interests considered primarily on a separate basis. The representatives, if handling the whole proceedings together, may be representing different interests. The representatives are, on the one hand, operating for the benefit of the group as a whole (and the creditors in general), but on the other hand are dealing with separate entities that might have contradicting interests. Surely, this problem is more pronounced when the same representatives handle all the proceedings (against all members), but it is also quite prominent even if separate representatives handle the various entities, as operating as a closely tied group of representatives can result in an all too 'cosy' situation, with the potential to neglect certain creditors' interests.[171]

Legal regimes allowing procedural consolidation to take place, and permitting the same insolvency representative to preside over all group members sometimes provide means to deal with such conflicts. For example, the insolvency representative may be required to give an undertaking or be subject to a practice rule or statutory obligation to seek direction from the court in the event a conflict arises. In addition, additional representatives may be appointed if necessary.[172]

It will be advisable to embrace such mechanisms within national regimes (as part of promoting harmonization of the procedural consolidation tool),[173] as well as in international regimes for cross-border insolvency, so as to ensure adequate representation and resolution of potential conflicts. Flexibility and discretion in applying such mechanisms should be given to courts dealing with MEG insolvencies in order to allow them to trade off between possible problems of representation, and *ex post* efficiency in the handling of the process. The merits of single representation have been stressed earlier,[174] and where possible these advantages should not be defeated. An example of striking such a balance by a court presiding over proceedings against related companies (although in this particular case all operating in the same jurisdiction) is the decision of the Cayman Islands court to approve the appointment of liquidators over a Parmalat subsidiary,[175] notwithstanding their position as liquidators of other related

---

[171] See I. Mevorach, 'Centralizing insolvencies of pan-European corporate groups: a creditor's dream or nightmare?' [2006] JBL, 468, 475.

[172] See the background on treatment of corporate groups (domestic issues) provided by the Secretariat of UNCITRAL Working Group V (WP.74/Add.1 (n 49 chapter 6), para. 14). UNCITRAL Working Group V also considers a draft recommendation in regard to appointment of insolvency representatives for the purpose of facilitating coordination of related companies' proceedings (operating domestically), suggesting that insolvency laws will specify measures to address a conflict of interest, for example the appointment of additional insolvency representatives for group members in regard to which a conflict exists. Reference to the Legislative Guide (n 137 chapter 3) requirements for disclosure in relation to conflicts of interests may also be included (see WP.80/Add 1 (n 65 chapter 6), draft recommendation 25; Report, thirty-fourth session (n 98 chapter 1), para. 79; WP.82/Add.3 (n 65 chapter 6), draft recommendation 27).

[173] See chapter 6, section 6.2.3.

[174] Chapter 6, sections 6.2.1.1, 6.2.1.6, 6.2.2 and 6.3.4.

[175] On the *Parmalat* case see n 83–7, and accompanying texts, chapter 6.

companies. The decision was approved by the Court of Appeal of the Cayman Islands. Subsequently, the Privy Council has heard an appeal from the decision of the Cayman Islands Court of Appeal. Dismissing the appeal, the Privy Council held that the local court had taken proper matters into account. There was consideration of the advantages in having the same liquidators in place; in particular the efficiency in avoiding duplications of efforts[176] while stressing that possible conflict of interest could be dealt with by the court on the application of the liquidators.[177]

7.5.5 Expertise of insolvency representatives handling MEG insolvency cases

Regarding expertise, the particular concern in the MEG insolvency context is the magnitude of the case, being a worldwide insolvency of possibly a complex enterprise. The risk here is that centralized control or supervisory powers will be given to a single representative who will take a 'national view' over the case, and will be mainly concerned with local interests. Evidently, in the course of the insolvency proceedings (especially due to the legal separateness among the entities comprising the MEG) sensitive decisions may need to be taken. For example, judgments as to whether substantive consolidation is justified may be made in scenarios appearing to be of 'asset integrated' insolvent MEGs,[178] without engaging in the timely and costly operation of actually untangling the assets and debts.[179] It is therefore a concern to ensure that the administration supervising a group's process is capable of representing a variety of interests relevant in the case of a MEG and of supervising such complex operations.

In this respect, an international firm oriented to the taking of an international perspective over cross-border insolvencies and having the specialism in international insolvencies may be more adequate to deal with MEG cases (relative to a nationally oriented administrator), especially those involving large groups operating across the globe.[180] The insolvency representative may also need to facilitate the development of a protocol in case concurrent proceedings are taking

---

[176] See on this aspect chapter 6, section 6.2.2.
[177] See *Parmalat Capital Finance Ltd v Food Holdings Ltd (in liq.)* [2008] BCC 371.
[178] Prototypes D–F (chapter 5 section 5.4).
[179] See chapter 6, section 6.3.3.
[180] See, for example, concerns of local creditors of Cayman Islands subsidiaries of the Parmalat group about the administrator's (appointed over the Italian group) ability to act in their interest. Indeed, the way the Parmalat's administration was handled has been criticized as being too nationalized, focusing on seeking 'an Italian solution' and lacking a sufficient international perspective (see *GLOBALTURNAROUND*, January 2004, Issue 48, p. 3 and February 2004, Issue 49, p. 4). Creditor groups involved in the Parmalat process 'raised eyebrows' with regard to the sort of representation provided for such a large-scale, international case (ibid) (see further on *Parmalat* and the Cayman Islands' subsidiaries in n 86 chapter 6, and accompanying text and chapter 8, section 8.2); see also I. Mevorach, 'Centralizing insolvencies of pan-European corporate groups: a creditor's dream or nightmare?' [2006] JBL, 468, 485–6.

place and the need arises to agree on means of cooperation or more particular conflicts which need to be resolved. Here too, the task of the representative may be considerable and may require relevant expertise and experience in handling such cases. In this respect, the III Draft guidelines[181] currently emphasize the need for such officer to be acceptable to the parties in the different jurisdictions. They also suggest that preferably such a person will have experience in performing those tasks. They thus currently recommend generating a central listing of persons with such recognized stature in the international insolvency community to be maintained by one or more of the organizations concerned with international insolvencies.[182]

A system for MEG insolvency should thus require special qualifications for administrators of that scale. If the system allows for the debtor to remain in possession in case of insolvency, consideration should be given to the particular circumstances and scope of the case. In the absence of issues of corruption or other misbehaviour of the management and where the scope of the case allows, the latter may be well equipped for continuing managing the entire operation. Alternatively, especially in the decentralized scenarios, combined solutions could be established, for example local managements may remain in possession while the ultimate governing of the central proceedings is given to outsider appointees.

7.6 Conclusion

Fairness in distribution in the context of MEGs in distress suggests that in 'business integrated' insolvent MEG cases coordinated solutions (via procedural consolidation mechanisms) should be pursued if this will benefit the group as a whole while not significantly harming certain entities. Where there is a conflict between the good for the whole (the various entities) and the good for particular debtors and their stakeholders, the system should be able to proceed with the profitable solution while ensuring adequate protection to the otherwise harmed entities.

Other than that, the system should respect rights of creditors vis-à-vis the particular entity to whom they belong, and not mix assets and debts across the MEG as if it was a single entity, except in cases of 'asset integration'. In these cases redistribution is irrelevant as the financial position of each of the entities is uncertain to a significant extent. This is also why in cases of 'asset integration' substantive consolidation is not perceived as unjustifiably harmful to entity law. Substantive consolidation will be redistributive where it is grounded merely on 'reliance' (and will then also be in direct conflict with entity law's advantages of 'asset partitioning'). Expectations of creditors to recover from the MEG as a whole might

---

[181] N 100 chapter 1.
[182] Ibid, commentary to guideline 2.

be based in these circumstances not on actual rights, but rather on impressions. Meeting these expectations might result in transfer of wealth.

On the global level, pursuing procedural or substantive consolidation, using the alternative tools as suggested in chapter 6 (based on the prototypes suggested in chapter 5) will ensure that creditors' rights, provided in the legal system governing the debtor, are protected and that the court supervising the case takes a global perspective and considers all relevant parties' interests. To the extent that there is some mismatch between the enterprise–universalist measure applied (i.e. centralization) and the relevant type of MEG in hand, the system should be conscientious to ensure that protection provided to certain creditors in the legal system are not forsaken—'falling back' to territoriality and entity law. It is also critical in this respect that the forum presiding over the case is the one to which the MEG has a real connection, and manipulations of the forum will be as much as possible avoided. In this respect the 'operational head office' of the MEG was found to be a desirable key standard test for the proper venue.

Such an enterprise–universalism-based solution is also critical for ensuring accountability, that is hearing and giving participation rights to all those parties affected by the insolvency process (in the relevant prototypical scenarios). Being aware of the risks unification and especially centralization entails in this context, the insolvency system should provide mechanisms to encourage participation and ensure that all interests are taken into account. It should also ensure sufficient expertise of those in charge of a global process and be able to resolve possible problems of conflicts in representation.

Existing models for global insolvencies do not currently offer explicit guidelines regarding the way to coordinate proceedings against MEGs. International insolvency systems will be improved by providing relevant tools which can ensure that fairness to the stakeholders is achieved. On the domestic level, it was suggested that a degree of harmonization will be beneficial in terms of ensuring that substantive and procedural consolidations will become recognized and available tools. Considering the concerns that were raised in this chapter, standardization of procedural and substantive consolidation in the way proposed can ensure that fairness is achieved. As discussed in chapter 6, exiting models for cross-border insolvency as well as various national law concepts are utilized to enable 'de facto' consolidations on a global level. Pending possible reform which may provide a detailed framework in this respect, courts and representatives should be aware of what is at stake when employing such tools in terms of creditors' rights, as explained in this chapter. They can then use inherent powers they may have or tools provided in applicable laws in a way that will be beneficial to the creditors as a whole while not causing undue harm to others, and while ensuring adequate participation and representation.

8

Certainty and Predictability

8.1 Introduction

Thus far, it has been shown that the model proposed in this work for handling MEG insolvency proceedings is conducive to wealth maximization and can ensure a fair distribution of the insolvency estate. The question we turn to now is whether it could also be certain and predictable. It was important to establish first that the choice of the rules is legitimate (according to the analyses in the previous chapters), and only now we assess whether it could also be predictable. Otherwise we could have ended up with suggestions which will meet expectations of creditors, be clear and could be applied consistently but wrong nonetheless.

It is clearly beneficial for an insolvency system to ensure that any rules proposed under its framework are not vague and incomprehensible. Therefore, the 'goal driven' approach discussed in this book should attempt to achieve these goals as well. As mentioned in chapter 4, clarity and predictability of rules can reduce various costs. Clear rules can reduce causes for litigation as well as enhance expeditious dispute resolution.[1] Additionally, parties recognizing and predicting outcomes in insolvency can calculate risk and price the transaction with the debtor accordingly.[2] This is confined though to voluntary creditors (involuntary creditors did not extend credit to the debtor in the first place). It is also debatable whether or not the non-adjusting voluntary creditors do in fact rely on the bankruptcy regime in setting their terms of lending.[3]

Furthermore, certainty and predictability of desirable rules can also support fairness in ensuring that the circumstances which should be taken into account and the parties to be considered in the relevant insolvency decisions are clear.[4] These goals are also stressed to be of crucial importance in international statements of insolvency objectives.[5]

In regard to single debtors operating worldwide, cross-border insolvency models stress that predictability and creditors' expectations are fundamental to

---

[1] See chapter 4, section 4.2.2.1.
[2] Ibid, section 4.2.2.2.   [3] See Guzman's views in n 44 chapter 4.
[4] Ibid, section 4.2.2.5.   [5] Ibid, section 4.2.3.2.

issues of jurisdiction and cooperation.[6] As explained earlier, the change in the forum may change legal rights.[7] Therefore, preferably creditors should be able to foresee where the insolvency of a company is going to take place and calculate their risk accordingly. The unpredictability of the 'home country' standard even in regard to single debtors was identified as one of the key problems of a universalist system.[8] Yet, these problems should be put in perspective acknowledging the lack of clear data as to how much creditors actually assess in advance the foreign law that will govern the insolvency.[9] *Ex post* (after the debtor's default), creditors and representatives should be able to ascertain and rely on what foreign systems provide in the context of cross-border insolvency and be able to seek relief accordingly.[10] In the multiple debtor scenario different types of MEG may call upon different solutions. Parties and courts need to ascertain in these cases what sort of cooperation should be sought and whether unification is desirable at all. Where relevant, they need to ascertain what will be the venue of insolvency, as well as the applicable law, and whether these will be determined in regard to each MEG entity separately or for the MEG as a whole (or part of the MEG).

Problems of forum shopping are also of concern here, as it may defeat predictions regarding the venue and applicable law and the certainty and consistency of outcomes. As mentioned earlier, there is greater risk of venue competition and manipulation in cases of MEGs.[11] In addition, there is also the possibility that claims of creditors will be pooled together with those of the other related entities. That is, on top of the usual problems of assessing the financial situation of the debtor and the position of the creditor in this respect, the option of substantive consolidation provides another crucial issue for *ex ante* assessment or *ex post*

---

[6] Thus, the EC Regulation applying the idea of having one centre for single debtor EU-wide insolvency, provides that a major factor in determining where the main proceedings of the debtor should be taking place is third-party expectations (Recital (13) of the EC Regulation, (n 173 chapter 3) provides that the fact that a particular place is the centre of the debtor's main interests must be 'ascertainable by third parties'). See also Report Virgos/Schmit (n 180 chapter 3), and various EC Regulation cases in which 'ascertainability to third parties' factor was much emphasized: *Geveran Trading Co. Ltd v Skjevesland* [2003] BCC 209; *In re Daisytek-ISA Ltd* [2003] BCC 562 (Ch D); *Eurofood IFSC Ltd* [2004] BCC 383; *Re Parmalat Hungary/Slovakia* (Municipality Court of Fejer, June 14, 2004); *Ci4net.com Inc* [2005] BCC 277 (Ch D); *Eurofood IFSC Ltd* (Case C- 341/04) [2006] OJ 2006 C143/11, [33]–[37]. See also B. Wessels, 'International Jurisdiction to Open Insolvency Proceedings in Europe, In Particular Against (Groups of) Companies', Working Papers Series, Institute for Law and Finance, Johann Wolfgang Goethe University (available at: http://www.iiiglobal.org/downloads/European%20Union/Articles/11-_InternJurisdictionCompanies.pdf).

[7] See chapter 3, sections 3.3.2.1 and 3.3.3; chapter 7, section 7.1.

[8] See chapter 3 , section 3.3.2.1.

[9] See J.L. Westbrook, 'Locating the Eye of the Financial Storm' (2007) 32 Brook. J. Int'l L. 1019, 1023.

[10] UNCITRAL Guide to Enactment (n 212 chapter 3), stresses that insolvency systems provide rules for judicial cooperation, recognition of foreign insolvency proceedings and access for foreign representatives to courts by specific legislation rather than based purely on discretionary means, to enhance predictability and reliability.

[11] See chapter 7, section 7.1.

litigation and courts' and representatives' decision-making. In regard to all these matters, different creditors may have different predictions, especially as they were dealing with different entities.

The aim is thus to enhance the clear understanding of the legal consequences of a failure occurring within a worldwide group of companies and the predictability of outcomes in this context. It will be submitted, that the 'adaptive' framework suggested throughout this work is helpful here too, and that the balance which was maintained thus far between 'entity' and 'enterprise law', and 'territoriality' and 'universality' will also fit the bill in relation to the predictability goal. Consequently, the solutions invoked by the model proposed here could normally be predictable, and their adoption can enhance certainty and clarity. The chapter will also suggest additional means which a system for MEG insolvency could embrace in order to further improve predictability.

8.2 Problems of Predictability in Regard to MEG Insolvencies under Current Regimes

Cases of MEG insolvencies under existing regimes for cross-border insolvency[12] highlight problems generating from the uncertainty and unpredictability of rules in this context. In particular, the unpredictable nature of the rules that will apply to these cases, as well as the choice of venue or generally the lack of any clear doctrines to MEG insolvency might result in parties attempting to 'grab control' over the process, resulting in greater disputes in the course of insolvency. The lack of explicit guidelines as to the considerations to be made in devising solutions for MEGs also poses a threat to the protection of creditors' rights. For example, the proceedings may progress from a parallel administration to a sort of substantive consolidation,[13] without taking into account all relevant parties' interests. Parties themselves may be unwilling to support a unified process for the group (even where such approach would have been for the benefit of the group as a whole).[14] In cases of 'business' or 'asset' integrated MEGs,[15] perhaps some of the parties, courts and representatives involved may be driven to try and devise practical solutions for efficient liquidations or restructurings of MEGs. However, lacking sufficient structured guidelines, courts may be inclined towards the direction in which local creditors pull: either to protect creditors in the 'territory' (or those dealing with the local subsidiary) thereby sacrificing the global economic consequences it may have, or to enforce control over foreign members without

---

[12] On the various cross-border insolvency models see chapter 3, section 3.4.2.

[13] On substantive consolidation see chapter 6, section 6.3 and chapter 7, section 7.4. See also section 8.3.2.

[14] See also I. Mevorach, 'Centralizing insolvencies of pan-European corporate groups: a creditor's dream or nightmare?' [2006] JBL, 468, 476–80.

[15] Prototypes A–F (chapter 5, section 5.4).

sufficient consideration of their interests. Both of these options may be applied in a way which may defy the goals of cost reduction and fair distribution as well as contradict parties' expectations. The following paragraphs discuss several cases demonstrating these problems, some already mentioned in other contexts in this work, yet here the focus is on the particular concerns of certainty and predictability.

Recall that, in the *Eurofood* case,[16] the Italian administrator wished to subject the Irish company to Italian jurisdiction in order to facilitate a global group-wide restructuring for the Parmalat group.[17] However, creditors of the Irish subsidiary were reluctant to accept that. They feared the consequences of such an act and could not be confident that their rights would be adequately safeguarded. They were concerned, for example, that the assets of the Irish subsidiary would be lumped together with those of the rest of the group.[18] They preferred to have control of the subsidiary's future and thus strove to place its proceedings in Ireland. They were also concerned that an attempt would be made to move the centre of main interests of the company from Ireland to Italy. Consequently, two main parallel proceedings were opened. Indeed, the Irish court in its decision to approve the appointment of Irish provisional liquidators to the subsidiary emphasized the Irish company's creditors' predictions regarding jurisdiction and how they viewed the company's location.[19] The court held that it was clearly Ireland in which the creditors expected a default to be handled as creditors were dealing with investments issued in Ireland and subject to Irish fiscal and regulatory provisions.[20] The Italian court, on the other hand, in its decision to open main proceedings in Italy (in relation to the same company) seemed to have focused more on the entire group's operational structure and the Irish company's position within it.[21] Clearly, there was a lack of structured guidelines for the courts to follow in determining on the proper jurisdiction in a case of a group of companies. Consequently, each pulled to the other direction to meet the interests of the local creditors or the administrator in the other jurisdiction presiding over proceedings against other affiliates of the group. The decision of the ECJ in the case (upholding the Irish court claim to be the proper jurisdiction)[22] arguably reduced uncertainties as it strengthened the incorporation presumption. It entrenched

---

[16] On which see chapter 6, sections 6.2.1.4, 6.2.1.6, 6.2.1.8 and 6.2.1.9; and chapter 7, section 7.3.2.

[17] See chapter 6, section 6.2.1.4.

[18] See 'Italian and Irish courts clash over Parmalat', *GLOBALTURNAROUND*, April 2004, Issue 51, p.3.

[19] *Eurofood IFSC Ltd* [2004] BCC 383.

[20] Ibid.

[21] It pointed out the fact that the Irish company carried out activities instrumental to the Italian parent's group, that it was ancillary to the parent, that the parent guaranteed all transactions and that all operating and policy decisions were made from Italy (*Re Eurofood IFSC* (Trib (I), 19 February 2004 [2004] I.L.Pr. 14).

[22] *Eurofood IFSC Ltd* (Case C-341/04) [2006] OJ 2006 C143/11 (see also n 180–1 chapter 6, and accompanying texts).

the idea of ascertaining jurisdiction for each subsidiary separately, focusing on the ascertainability to third parties of the particular company.[23] However, this did not resolve the real conflicts inherent in these cases; it only highlighted the lack of rules that would clarify how to address the particular needs in cases of MEGs in insolvency.

In another matter related to the Parmalat group, in regard to a Cayman Islands' subsidiary of the group, the Cayman Islands' court's decision also reflected an inclination to avoid 'surrender of control' over the insolvencies of local subsidiaries in the absence of clear rules as to how proceedings against affiliates of a global group should be addressed, and how the interests of local creditors will be safeguarded.[24] Thus, the court refused to subject the company to the Italian administrator's control, approving the appointment of separate representatives. The court acknowledged the effect it might have on the cost-efficient operation of the whole process but nevertheless justified its decision by the fact that this was the wish of third-party creditors—to have separate representatives and to conduct a local process.[25] However, such a solution (segregation in handling the group's process) posed a threat at the time on the chances to engineer a global rescue plan and undoubtedly increased costs and complicated the proceedings.

It was also mentioned earlier,[26] how in the case of *Daisytek* although a practical solution was imposed (the entire European part of the group was placed under administration in a single jurisdiction facilitating a pan-European restructuring), it involved much confusion and discontent on the part of foreign members of the group. The question of jurisdiction in the case of groups was not clear and resulted in litigation on the issue in all jurisdictions involved.[27] Also recall the controversy that was involved in the case of *Main Knitting* (decided under the US chapter 15 implementing the UNCITRAL Model Law[28]), where a creditor of a local (US) subsidiary attempted to prevent recognition of the proceedings against the affiliate in Canada.[29] Other EC Regulation MEG cases, subsequent to *Daisytek*, exemplify a rather consistent approach to enable 'group solutions' and place all affiliates of MEGs in a single jurisdiction.[30] Yet, the extent to which and circumstances where this can be done, at least within the European Community in light of the ECJ decision in *Eurofood,* is unclear.[31]

---

[23] *Eurofood IFSC Ltd* (Case C-341/04) [2006] OJ 2006 C143/11, [26]–[37].

[24] See the judgment of the Grand Court of the Cayman Islands in the administrator application to replace the provisional liquidators appointed to a Cayman Islands' subsidiary of Parmalat— Parmalat Capital Finance Ltd (Grand Court of the Cayman Islands, March, 2004) (n 86 chapter 6). See also D. Reilly, 'Judge Rejects Administrator's Push To Control Parmalat's Cayman Units' in *DOWJONES Newsletters*, International Insolvency, 2 March 2004, p. 1.

[25] See also the concerns regarding adequate representation (n 180 chapter 7).

[26] See chapter 6, section 6.2.1.6.   [27] Ibid.

[28] N 212 chapter 3.   [29] Ibid.

[30] See examples provided in n 170 chapter 6.

[31] See Fletcher, *Insolvency* (Supplement to 2nd Edition, 2007), 121–2.

The case of *Bramalea* (discussed earlier[32]) demonstrates how in the absence of clear rules for administering MEGs in insolvency attempts at construing beneficial solutions for the MEG may result in prejudicing creditors' rights. Recall that the Canadian court took a 'flexible' pragmatic approach in this case facilitating a global group-wide reorganization. Although specific rules regarding administration of MEG insolvencies were lacking the court allowed the opening of proceedings against all the group members, including those incorporated and operating in the US, in Canada. It also pooled all assets and debts in relation to the group entities together and allowed a unified reorganization plan to take place, with voting to be done by creditors as if belonging to a single entity. All these actions were justified by the court based on Bramalea's claim that it was an integrated group. It seems that this course of action did not take all parties' interests involved into account. In particular, the assumption of US lenders with regard to US subsidiaries was that they had insulated themselves from the risk of financial distress in other parts of the group.[33] Lack of clarity could thus result in either unfairness or extensive litigation contesting the decision. In this case, to avoid litigation, extensive negotiations took place to achieve settlements with creditors.[34]

8.3 Global Linking Tools Compatible with Typical Expectations of Voluntary Creditors

The experience of MEG insolvencies under current regimes indicates that in terms of certainty and predictability there is room for improvement. I suggest that the model proposed in this work for coordination and unification (and sometimes substantive consolidation) of insolvency proceedings against MEG affiliates can improve the situation considerably.

8.3.1 Universal or territorial process for the MEG and problems of predictability

The crucial issue in the case of a worldwide group in insolvency is determining whether the insolvency proceedings should be handled jointly in a single forum, or completely separately, or whether some other measures for linking between the group components should be applied in the course of the insolvency. Can the particular approach to be taken—somewhere along the range between universality and territoriality—be clear and predictable?

---

[32] See chapter 6, section 6.3.4.
[33] R.G. Marantz, 'The Reorganization of a Complex Corporate Entity: The Bramalea Story', in J.S. Ziegel (ed.), *Case Studies in Recent Canadian Insolvency Reorganizations* (Carswell Legal Publications, Toronto 1997) 1, 17.
[34] Ibid, 19.

Arguably for the sake of predictability (ignoring other goals of insolvency) it is better to have a rule of thumb suggesting that the location of proceedings of any member of a group (and the corresponding law and forum that should supervise the process) should always be determined for each company separately. That is, without any considerations of the connections a particular member may have had with another related company or with a 'group'. Supposedly, creditors expect to enforce their rights upon the entity with whom they have dealt, not with a greater group, and thus to be able to open insolvency proceedings in the place of its main operations regardless of any possible links to some 'group centre'. If this is the case, then in the name of unification, a centralized approach may collide with creditors' expectations and may not fit with their views regarding the forum that should supervise the process. One may argue that a 'one size fits all' approach suggesting that each company in a group is to be treated separately in insolvency is simple and clear.

However, I suggest that as this 'separateness' rule does not always match with economic reality, it turns out to be misleading rather than straightforward (as it might seem to be). As was noted earlier,[35] a MEG may not operate purely as a bundle of separate entities (in business terms). Indeed, MEGs may exhibit diversified ways of operation.[36] Thus, a 'one size fits all' solution may not only be detrimental to achieving asset maximization and fair distribution,[37] but might also not fit with parties' predictions in regard to the way the business is to be treated in case it collapses.[38] In fact, in many insolvency cases of groups at least certain parties sought to have a unified centralized process for the MEG.[39]

It is submitted that parties' predictions regarding the location of the business' centre very much derive from the way the business was actually operating. Therefore, an 'adaptive' approach (which is an aspect of the framework suggested in this work[40]) is useful for ensuring that jurisdictional measures for MEG insolvencies are generally predictable. The prototype of the MEG operation[41] can be usually regarded as the basis for the expectations (unless there was an attempt at misleading creditors, a matter which will be discussed later on[42]). The model suggested earlier would typically direct parties and courts to seek a centralized solution (i.e. a strong 'universalist' approach) in cases of 'centralized' 'business' (or 'asset') integrated insolvent MEGs.[43] In these cases, the real centre of each

---

[35] See chapter 5, section 5.3.2.
[36] See chapter 1, section 1.3; and chapter 5, sections 5.3.2 and 5.3.3.
[37] See chapters 6 and 7.
[38] See I. Mevorach, 'Centralizing insolvencies of pan-European corporate groups: a creditor's dream or nightmare?' [2006] JBL, 468, 470–4.
[39] See, for example, the cases mentioned in section 8.2.
[40] See chapter 2, section 2.5; and chapter 3, section 3.5.
[41] See chapter 5 for the suggestion of prototypical scenarios.
[42] See chapter 9.
[43] Prototype A in the 'business integration' scenario, and prototype D in the 'asset integration' scenarios (see chapter 5, section 5.4).

of the entities comprising the group (the part which is centralized and integrated) is that of the group centre.[44] The various entities were centrally controlled altogether in the ordinary course of business. This would normally be reflected in the way the MEG has dealt with its creditors. Consequently, it will normally be the case that in these scenarios creditors had dealings with group members via the group central management, negotiated terms of contract with the group management, or their contracts may have been subjected to the laws under which the parent company controlling the group was operating, they may have received a guarantee from the parent company, and so on. As stressed earlier,[45] a centralization solution should be a matter of mimicking what was the situation prior to the insolvency process, in terms of commercial realities. The idea that the forum handling the case will mainly apply its laws (in regard to insolvency matters) further enhances predictability.[46] As has been argued in regard to single multinational debtors, predictability is enhanced if stakeholders are referred to a single set of rules rather than a fragmentation of laws of different systems.[47]

It has been argued elsewhere, that a 'universalist' solution based on an 'integration' test completely defeats predictability.[48] Arguably, integration is a matter of complex factual circumstances which lenders cannot predict when extending credit. Yet, as I suggested above, in 'centralized' MEGs ascertaining the integrated nature of the business and its concentration in the place of central administration does not require extensive investigation by creditors. It is rather the way lenders have dealt with the business. Nevertheless, there are certainly situations of integration where the inter-connections among the companies are more subtle. A relevant example is the case of conglomerates operating a diversified business though the members are significantly interdependent by various connections 'under the surface'.[49] Other scenarios of less straightforward interrelations are the types of decentralized MEGs or heterarchical operation, where although local entities had significant autonomy the MEG as a whole was altogether coordinated resulting in an integrated business.[50] In these scenarios there is more likelihood that parties transacting with the business had normally dealt with a particular local entity—negotiations took place with local management, laws of the system where the entity operates mainly governed potential disputes between the parties and so forth. There will typically also be some dealing with the ultimate head of the group in these cases, for instance by way of receiving guarantees from the holding company. However, for these types of MEG, the model provided in

---

[44] See chapter 6, section 6.2.1.9; and chapter 7, section 7.3.

[45] See chapter 6, section 6.2.1.8.

[46] See also the benefit of such an approach in the context of MEGs in terms of *ex post* efficiency in ibid, sections 6.2.1.6 and 6.2.2.1.

[47] See chapter 3, sections 3.3.2.1 and 3.3.3.

[48] See L.M. LoPucki, 'Cooperation in International Bankruptcy: A Post-Universalist Approach' (1999) 84 Cornell L. Rev. 696, 720.

[49] Prototype B (figure (2)) (see chapter 5, section 5.4).

[50] Prototypes B and C (ibid).

chapter 6 suggests 'lesser universalism' in the sense that local proceedings will be opened in regard to the autonomous subsidiary, and the insolvency matters will normally be subjected to local laws. On top of that, the various proceedings will be linked and supervised by the group centre.[51] Thus, the potential prediction of parties that their debtor is local but also connected to a coordinating entity will once again fit with the model suggestion. This is not surprising, as both the parties' expectations and the model derive from the way the MEG and its components conducted their business.

Predictions regarding law and forum can therefore largely be met under the 'adaptive balanced' approach suggested in this book. It also gives clear rules as to the circumstances where any type of global linking tool should be sought, subject to a degree of flexibility. This includes the scenarios where a group centre cannot be identified.[52] The use of prototypes enhances clarity, as it enables some measure of generalization. It offers on the one hand a reasonable range of alternative combinations, and on the other hand it narrows this to a small number of typical cases, which reduces vagueness. There is still a degree of flexibility without a significant sacrifice of predictability.[53]

Nevertheless, it is suggested that a too simplified approach in considering predictions on the part of parties dealing with the MEG should be avoided. At the end of the day, expectations cannot be a stand-alone goal. To an extent expectations will always be based on subjective impressions. Thus, different creditors involved with the group may have different impressions regarding the way the MEG was operating. Moreover, elements of different types of dealing could be found among creditors of the same company within a group. Creditors may also present their expectations to the court in a particular way which they believe will support their interests, rather than be an objective account of events.[54] There is also the problem of diversity among the stakeholders. As mentioned above, creditors like tort victims in any case could not predict (before suffering the injury) the law and forum that will apply. Certain creditors may not rely on the insolvency system when extending credit anyhow.[55] If predictions are taken into account, it may be that large sophisticated creditors find it easier to ascertain whether they have dealt with a separate entity or a group whereas small unsecured creditors may show greater difficulty in identifying the corporate actor with whom one was contracting.[56]

---

[51] See chapter 6, section 6.2.1.8.

[52] Ibid, section 6.2.1.10.

[53] See L.J. Westbrook, 'Locating the Eye of the Financial Storm' (2007) 32 Brook. J. Int'l L. 1019, 1023 (explaining that predictability is always in tension with correctness of result, and thus a balance between predictability and flexibility must be drawn).

[54] See section 8.3.3 below (on the problem of forum shopping).

[55] See section 8.1.

[56] See J.L. Westbrook, 'A Global Solution to Multinational Default' (2000) 98 Mich. L. Rev. 2276, 2314.

Focusing on the business reality of the MEG could assist the court in verifying creditors' expectations. I also suggest that the court in MEG cases should 'step back' and examine the way creditors dealt with the group from an objective perspective (using the notion of what a 'reasonable creditor' would have expected in the specific scenario) rather than basing its decision on the expressed subjective beliefs of creditors. It should also be dedicated to a global group-wide perspective when faced with a MEG case, so that predictions of all parties concerned with an interrelated MEG will be considered.[57] Ultimately, expectations and the way creditors dealt with the group (or entities within the group) should be perceived as a factor (or accumulation of factors) related to the identification of the type of group at hand.

8.3.2 Procedural or substantive consolidation for MEGs and certainty–predictability demands

The model suggested in this book puts clear boundaries between procedural and substantive consolidation in terms of the circumstances where each of these doctrines should apply, and in terms of the characteristics of each scheme.[58] Essentially, it is a matter of ascertaining whether the MEG is integrated, 'non-integrated' or 'asset integrated'.[59] In case there was no extensive intermingling, the coordination of the process on a unified basis should keep the separateness between the entities.[60] Parties can then have a clearer notion as to what is at stake when a case is directed to a single jurisdiction. Courts and representatives would also then have clear guidelines as to how to handle the case, what are the limitations of any option that may apply, and what should be taken into account in taking any of the paths. The availability of partial substantive consolidation can also assist in better matching the solutions to expectations, as where certain creditors have dealt with a separate entity, and so long as their debt can be ascertainable, it will be possible to exclude it from the pool.[61] Alternatively, a whole entity can stay outside the substantive consolidation.[62]

The 'adaptive balanced' approach applied in this context is of particular merit considering the goals in focus here, as it is based on clear and objective tests.[63] If the remedy is largely based on discretion and applied whenever the court perceived it to be 'just and equitable' (in a rather ad hoc manner) certainty and

---

[57] See also on creditors' participation chapter 7, section 7.5.
[58] See chapter 6, mainly sections 6.2.1.3, 6.2.1.5 and 6.3.3; chapter 7, sections 7.2 and 7.4.
[59] See chapter 5, section 5.3.2; chapter 6, mainly sections 6.2.1.1, 6.2.1.5 and 6.3.3; and chapter 7, sections 7.2 and 7.4.
[60] Ibid.
[61] See chapter 6, section 6.3.3.4; chapter 7, section 7.4.1.
[62] Ibid.
[63] See I. Mevorach, 'Appropriate treatment of corporate groups in insolvency—a universal view' (2006) 8 EBOR, 179, 183–4, 188–9.

predictability are greatly undermined.[64] These goals therefore reinforce moving away from equivocal factors towards a stricter notion of when substantive consolidation should apply. As explained earlier, this does not mean that it should be rarely applied.[65] Rather, the circumstances where it ought to be applied should be clearly stated. In this respect, it is also desirable to have a clear notion as to the circumstances where other somewhat resembling remedies for dealing with issues pertaining to MEG insolvencies in the sense that such remedies may also involve interfering with the separateness between the entities (for example the giving of contribution orders against related companies[66]) may be more adequate. These circumstances will be discussed in the next chapter.[67]

8.3.3 Unequivocal and stable home country standard

It is submitted that the group operational head office suggested as the key standard for allocating the proper jurisdictions for MEG insolvencies[68] also makes the right balance between certainty and predictability and other goals. It will be recalled, that an 'enterprise–universalist' approach was suggested (mitigated with entity law and territoriality, depending on the type of MEG at stake) to allocating the venue in case of MEGs. That is, identifying a single venue for the whole group from which the proceedings can be centralized or coordinated.[69] It was concluded that this will promote asset maximization as well as ensure that the proceedings are handled in a place with real connection, avoiding manipulations or the placing of the proceedings in 'haven' jurisdictions.[70]

Still, it may be argued that in terms of certainty and predictability the most straightforward predictable test is the place of incorporation of a company.[71] The extent to which this contention is correct is open to doubts. The information

---

[64] See for instance the broad discretion given to New Zealand courts under the pooling provisions (see chapter 6, section 6.3.2), or the doctrine applied under the US system, where the courts use their 'equity powers' to give such orders if it is 'just and equitable' to do so (ibid). Indeed, many US commentators argue that the US system of substantive consolidation is unsettled, unpredictable, unclear and inconsistent (see e.g. S. Schwarcz, 'Collapsing Corporate Structures: Resolving the Tension between Form and Substance' (2004) 60 The Business 142; T.E. Graulich, 'Substantive consolidation- a post-modern trend' (2006) 14 Am. Bankr. Ins. L. Rev. 527, 530; M.E. Kors, 'Altered Egos: Deciphering Substantive Consolidation' (1997) 59 U. Pitt. L. Rev. 381, 384).

[65] See chapter 6, section 6.3.3.

[66] See chapter 9, sections 9.4.3 and 9.4.4.

[67] Chapter 9.

[68] See chapter 6, section 6.2.1.9.

[69] Ibid.

[70] See chapter 7, section 7.3.3.

[71] See, for instance, L. Perkins, 'A Defence of Pure Universalism in Cross-Border Corporate Insolvencies' (2000) 32 N.Y.U. J. Intl L. & Policy 787, 815. See also the contractualist approach suggesting that debtors should be able to choose the bankruptcy venue by designating the place of incorporation as the standard venue in insolvency (chapter 3, section 3.3.2.5). See also the ruling of the ECJ in the case of *Eurofood*, where the incorporation presumption was given considerable weight (see chapter 6, section 6.2.1.9).

regarding the place of incorporation may not be always apparent to all creditors.[72] Anyhow, place of incorporation is highly problematic in case of MEGs in terms of allocating a single and meaningful (real) jurisdiction for the MEG as a whole.[73] It is also prone to manipulation and in that it may also defeat predictability (to an extent).[74] Therefore, a different standard test, as the leading factor for allocating jurisdiction, should be sought. As aforementioned, certainty and predictability, even if they play a role in practice, should not be perceived as stand-alone goals, and may be traded off with other goals.

Bearing this in mind, we seek to meet predictability and certainty without forsaking other goals. It is the objective that the designated venue will normally accord with creditors' legitimate expectations regarding jurisdiction for insolvency proceedings (a place which can be generally foreseeable to voluntary creditors) and that can be relatively easily identified and predicted by relevant parties.[75]

An option that was considered earlier for a test for jurisdiction was based on amounts of assets, creditors, or operations.[76] These types of factors are problematic in terms of certainty and predictability as key tests for jurisdictions. The need to measure and weigh between quantities entails a high level of complexity which makes the venue unpredictable and prone to manipulations. In particular, applying such a test in a group context may have a highly unpredictable outcome. Individual group members may each have their own principal asset or operation location with no clear mutual locus for the entire group. Furthermore, trying to identify a single place as the centre of gravity by summing up the entire group's assets or operations and the proportionate part located within the various entities (measuring quantities on a group scale) would require a costly operation which will result in debatable outcomes. It will be difficult to identify the place in which most of the assets of a single debtor reside, and to predict in advance what will be the evaluation of a future court in this regard. On a group scale where, for instance, the entities comprising the group were handling a variety of different operations and accordingly owned different sorts of assets or had different kinds of activities predicting the group's centre of gravity in advance would be equivalent to guesswork.[77] Therefore, in principle, these sorts of test at least as standalone standards are problematic when confronted with the goals of certainty and predictability in the group context.

---

[72] See J.L. Westbrook, 'Locating the Eye of the Financial Storm' (2007) 32 Brook J. Int'l L. 1019, 1029 (explaining that we generally have weak laws regarding disclosure of jurisdiction of incorporation).

[73] See chapter 6, section 6.2.1.9.

[74] See chapter 7, section 7.3.3.

[75] See I. Mevorach, 'The Home Country of a Multinational Enterprise Group Facing Insolvency' (2008) 57 ICLQ, 427, 435–6.

[76] See chapter 6, section 6.2.1.9.

[77] See I. Mevorach, 'The Home Country of a Multinational Enterprise Group Facing Insolvency' (2008) 57 ICLQ, 427, 438–9.

In contrast, the headquarters criteria could generally meet the goals of certainty and predictability. It targets the main proceedings at the actual meeting point of the enterprise in accordance with the way it was handled in the normal course of business including the way it had dealings with creditors, and it does not involve the need to weigh between amounts of operations or assets in different states, thus it is relatively clear. The emphasis is on objective criteria, rather than subjective beliefs of creditors. An additional merit of this approach is that it gives a particular factor—the group's actual headquarters—the lead while other factors (such as amount of assets) are supportive.[78]

It ends up with a test which is rather straightforward.[79] This will be a considerable improvement on the current situation under cross-border insolvency models, where COMI is an open textured notion incorporating a variety of factors. Especially in MEG cases, it may result in different jurisdictions legitimately claiming jurisdictions, as was demonstrated in various examples mentioned in this work.[80] It will also improve certainty and predictability if the insolvency regime applied to MEGs in insolvency will refrain from leaving too much room for discretion in the application of the jurisdictional rule. This seems to be the approach taken in cross-border insolvency models for single debtors embracing the notion of the COMI of the single debtor as determining the jurisdiction issue.[81] Courts are expected to determine COMI (or establishment, for non-main proceedings) based on the presence of a centre or establishment and that is it. They are not supposed to open insolvency proceedings or recognize foreign proceedings on other grounds (such as inherent powers to grant recognition based on comity for example).[82] This idea should be embraced for the case of MEGs as well.

On the other hand, 'ascertainability to third parties' which is another component of COMI under the current interpretation[83] should be examined with caution. Indeed, it is argued here that predictability of the venue is one of the goals the system should strive to achieve. However, this should not be a separate

---

[78] See chapter 6, section 6.2.1.9.

[79] See how it could resolve a 'conflict of factors' such as exemplified in the case of *BCCI* (see n 271–2 and accompanying texts, chapter 6). In the 'hard' cases, where the head office test does not lead to a clear-cut solution courts can be assisted by parties' agreements as suggested earlier (see chapter 6, section 6.2.1.10).

[80] See for instance, the examples mentioned in section 8.2. Indeed, results of an empirical research of companies operating in the EU have raised concerns as to the effect of the COMI notion under the EC Regulation on the cost of borrowing. It was found that since the entry into force of the Regulation companies decreased their level of gearing which may be explained by an increase in the level of legal uncertainty (see O. Sussman, 'The economics of the EU's corporate-insolvency law and the quest for harmonization by market forces' [2005], Oxford Financial Research Centre, Working Paper 2005-FE-16).

[81] On which see chapter 3, sections 3.4.2.2–3.4.2.4.

[82] See *Re Bear Stearns High-Grade Structured Credit Strategies Master Fund, Ltd* (US District Court. SDNY 2008). See also J.L. Westbrook, 'Locating the Eye of the Financial Storm' (2007) 32 Brook. J. Int'l L. 1019, 1022–8. Cf. *Re SPhinX, Ltd*, 351 BR 103 (Bankr SDNY 2006).

[83] See chapter 3, section 3.4.2.2.

stand-alone key aspect of the test. As suggested above, expectations of creditors in regard to solutions for the MEG should be examined while taking an objective point of view over the entire MEG and the stakeholders' interests.[84] The same approach should be taken in regard to the jurisdiction identification. Courts should be cautious of creditors' forum shopping—they may present to the court a biased account of their expectations in regard to the group (or a particular subsidiary) COMI. As aforementioned, the so-called 'expectations' might actually be a manifestation of particular interests of particular creditors.[85]

Additional mechanisms should be taken on board to further improve the potential predictability of the designated forum for the MEG insolvency, and the possibility that most expectations will be focused on a single location. The functional test suggested could be combined with a disclosure mechanism, i.e. an obligatory publication of the group COMI by the relevant companies.[86] This information could then become available to creditors dealing with the MEG or any parts thereof, and so enable a clear prospect of the location of proceedings (in case insolvency should occur). It may also be backed by an externally certified, systematic confirmation of the correspondence between claimed COMI and the ongoing realities, dependent upon some annually occurring process such as the audit.[87] This will help in avoiding the potential gap between 'impression' and 'reality' of the companies' operations and their effects on jurisdiction matters. Courts determining the proper venue will be able to initially rely on the COMI published by the group, unless there was convincing proof that the debtor was 'living a lie' (for instance for the purpose of enjoying the advantages of the bankruptcy haven in which the COMI had been stated to be). In such a case the court will make use of other evidence related to the organizational structure of the group to identify the place of command and control over the group.

8.4 Statutory Basis for the Linking Tools Invoked

It was mentioned earlier, that providing for the various linking tools suggested for MEGs in insolvency in legislation will ensure the availability of the tools in different jurisdictions, especially in cases where a system requires specific authority

---

[84] See section 8.3.1.

[85] See also I. Mevorach, 'Centralizing insolvencies of pan-European corporate groups: a creditor's dream or nightmare?' [2006] JBL, 468, 473–4.

[86] See I. Mevorach, 'The Home Country of a Multinational Enterprise Group Facing Insolvency' (2008) 57 ICLQ, 427, 442; I. Mevorach, 'Centralizing insolvencies of pan-European corporate groups: a creditor's dream or nightmare?' [2006] JBL, 468, 482.

[87] And accompanied by suitable sanctions (aimed at compensating the creditors) in case of false representation of the COMI against those responsible for enabling the company to perpetrate such a deception.

for the courts to apply certain concepts.[88] It is almost obvious, that this also improves certainty and predictability.[89]

This is even more crucial on the international level, where parties may need to ascertain what foreign systems provide in this context. Clearly, if the various 'enterprise measures' (the linking tools such as pooling orders or procedural consolidation, or centralization based on some notion of centre of the debtor) are only applied in practice, or by using inherent powers of the courts, stakeholders from other systems are likely to find it too difficult to calculate their risk when extending credit. Similarly, the lack of statutory basis for the linking tools available is likely to put obstacles in the way of parties utilizing any of the mechanisms a particular system provides *ex post* (after the default of the MEG or any parts thereof), for example seeking various sorts of assistance from the court of an affiliate company.

Having the relevant doctrines provided in legislation can further ensure consistency in their application, and thus a more rapid development of a body of precedents eventually building up to a reliable and steady system. This in turn will promote predictability.

8.5 Conclusion

It was noted earlier that the legal platform supporting MEGs' operations is generally chaotic.[90] This is certainly the case in the area of insolvency. It is unclear under the current state of affairs, what will actually happen with a collapsing MEG. It is almost a matter of a guess where the insolvency case will take place: in a group centre, or separately for each subsidiary (and what is the key standard test to apply in order to identify a single jurisdiction in case this is desirable). In case the proceedings are concentrated in some way, it is not clear what optional solutions are available for the MEG—to what extent the MEG components can be linked in the course of insolvency, whether linking tools will be available at all in the jurisdiction presiding over the case and what factors will determine the linking tool to be applied. This renders the system of MEG insolvencies considerably unpredictable and prone to manipulation.

The approach proposed in this work can improve predictability. It suggests a variety of linking mechanisms, which attempt to match to typical cases of MEG insolvency, and by that balance between 'entity law' requirements and 'enterprise law', 'universality' and 'territoriality'. The approach is flexible yet generalized

---

[88] See chapter 6, sections 6.2.1.5, 6.2.3 and 6.3.4.

[89] Indeed, UNCITRAL Working Group V (n 96 chapter 1), in its last published report (on the work on the issue of enterprise groups in insolvency) emphasizes that the purpose of including provisions in legislation regarding substantive consolidation (based on objective standards) is inter alia to ensure predictability (see Report, thirty-fourth session (n 98 chapter 1), para. 58).

[90] See chapter 2.

enough to provide clarity of the rules. In that, it could be generally foreseeable by voluntary creditors. It also provides clear distinctions between the different linking mechanisms, mainly the procedural and substantive consolidation, and centralization versus other 'lighter' global linking tools. This is accompanied by a relatively clear standard for ascertaining a single jurisdiction for the entire MEG, where proceedings can be centralized or supervised.

Nonetheless, it is suggested that giving predictability a lead role in construing the rules for MEG insolvency or in determining the measures that will apply to the case after insolvency has occurred should be avoided. The question of which linking tool should apply (if at all) needs to be considered in light of the various goals of insolvency, and the result should be fair overall.

Pending possible reform in the area which could clarify rules for MEGs in insolvency, predictability would be improved if decisions regarding MEGs in insolvency were based on functional realities rather than subjective accounts of creditors presented to courts in the various local jurisdictions (or in the one which may be perceived as the 'global'). Additionally, predictability will be enhanced if courts apply objective and clear factors in determining on various linking tools, refraining from open-ended justifications which may only have an ad hoc merit.

9

Responsibility for Debts of MEG Members and Vulnerability of Intra-group Transactions

9.1 Introduction

This chapter focuses on a particular aspect of fairness in distribution, addressing such problems as wrongful acts, fraud, or favouritism ('opportunistic behaviour') in the context of financial distress within MEGs.

It was concluded in chapter 4 that policy decisions in regard to loss allocation may justify redistribution of wealth in certain circumstances.[1] This may include making managers or shareholders who were involved in some mismanagement of the debtor contribute wealth to the insolvency estate of the debtor or subordinate any debt owed to them to the debts of other ordinary creditors to achieve fair results.[2] It may also include the reversal of transactions entered into by the debtor prior to insolvency which may have unjustly enriched certain stakeholders at the expense of the general body of creditors or undeservedly depleted the assets of the debtor.[3] Such measures are also conducive to minimizing pre-default incentives on managerial decision-making.[4]

In the context of insolvency within MEGs, questions regarding the vulnerability of transactions and responsibility for losses of the debtor are particularly complex. It was mentioned earlier that the group structure enables more legroom for such opportunistic behaviour.[5] Intra-group transactions may be numerous and hard to track back, shuttling of assets or favouritism towards group members may be part of the group strategy, creditors may be misled to believe they deal with a group rather than a particular entity and so forth. The international nature of the MEG complicates matters. Assets may be shuttled outside the jurisdiction to a foreign subsidiary; a particular foreign subsidiary may be abandoned (although it may have been previously presented as supported by the international group) in order to evade liability as the jurisdiction of the subsidiary may lack remedies for such situations. Generally, the international context raises conflict of laws issues which set up additional obstacles for any attempt to control group behaviour.

---

[1] Chapter 4, section 4.2.2.3.
[2] Ibid, sections 4.2.2.3 and 4.2.3.4.
[3] Ibid, section 4.2.2.2 and 4.2.3.4.
[4] Ibid, section 4.2.2.2.
[5] See chapter 2, section 2.2.2.

Questions then arise as to whether 'group consideration' should be taken when assessing intra-group transactions and behaviour of related companies vis-à-vis members which became insolvent. For instance, are there circumstances where a solvent parent company should be liable for the debts of its insolvent subsidiary (a similar question may also arise in a scenario where the parent company is also insolvent). Furthermore, what measures may be adequate to tackle those cases of group opportunism, so that they are fair and efficient, as well as sufficiently clear and predictable. It is also a concern how these issues can be resolved on the international level. In order to answer these questions, once again the 'goal-driven adaptive balanced entity–enterprise, territoriality–universality approach'[6] is applied. The attempt is to pursue the insolvency goals while maintaining an adequate balance between entity and enterprise law, territoriality and universality, appreciating the diversified scene of insolvency within MEGs.

9.2 'Group Considerations' in Avoiding (or Upholding) Intra-group Transactions

9.2.1 The typical avoidance provisions and their key elements

As mentioned earlier insolvency laws usually contain 'avoidance provisions'.[7] These are generally designed to uphold fair distribution of the insolvency estate by preventing fraud, favouritism and opportunistic behaviour.[8] There are different variations of avoidance provisions in different legal regimes.[9] Nevertheless, UNCITRAL Legislative Guide[10] mentions three types of avoidance transactions that are found in most legal systems.[11] These are the transactions intended to defeat, hinder or delay creditors from collecting their claims; transactions at undervalue; and transactions with certain creditors that could be regarded as preferential. As it is not the concern here to deal with the details of avoidance provisions in different jurisdictions (but rather to highlight particular considerations in the group context) it is sufficient to mention the usual common conditions for avoiding such transactions. For avoidance under the fraudulent transactions provision, it is required to prove the intent of the debtor, normally

---

[6] See chapter 2, section 2.5; and chapter 3, section 3.5.

[7] See chapter 4, section 4.2.3.4.

[8] UNCITRAL Legislative Guide (n 137 chapter 3), Part two, Ch. II, para. 151. Avoiding transactions will also result in swelling the insolvency estate which may be conducive to return maximization. Yet, consideration should also be given to the potential cost of litigation and likelihood of success. This demands expertise especially in the more complex situation of default within a MEG (see chapter 7, section 7.5.5).

[9] See n 129 chapter 4.

[10] N 137 chapter 3.

[11] Ibid, Part two, para. 170.

by identifying circumstances that are common to this type of transactions.[12] Undervalue transactions would generally be avoidable where the value received by the debtor as the result of the transaction was either nominal or non-existent, such as a gift, or much lower than the true value or market price, provided the transaction occurred within a suspect period, i.e. some (pre-defined) time prior to the commencement or application for insolvency proceedings. Some laws also require that the transaction has had a critical effect on the financial situation of the debtor. The law may provide defences so that the transaction is not avoided if certain conditions are satisfied, such as that the beneficiary acted in good faith, the transaction was entered into for the purpose of carrying on the debtor business and that there were reasonable grounds for believing that the transaction would benefit the debtor's business.[13] Preferential transactions are normally subject to avoidance if they took place within a suspect period, they involved a transfer to a creditor on account of an antecedent debt and as a result of the transaction the creditor received a larger percentage of its claim than other creditors. Another typical requirement is that the debtor was insolvent or close to insolvency when the transaction took place and some laws further require an intention to prefer. There are normally defences available, for example when it can be shown that the transaction was consistent with normal commercial practice between the parties or that new value was given.[14]

9.2.2 Applying avoidance provisions to intra-group transactions

Are there any particular 'group considerations' to take into account where the transaction in hand involves members of the same group? In other words—is there need to apply 'linking tools' in this context, in the sense of recognizing the MEG as such or the interrelations among the group members? This question could, in fact, be divided into two steps. Initially we can consider whether transactions among group members should be at all attacked under any available avoidance provisions. Alternatively, the MEG could be regarded as a single entity, and thus any transfer within the group should be conceived as if it was made within 'departments' of the same debtor. In such a case there is no issue of setting aside transactions as there is no actual transaction between two parties— possessions of one entity in the group are in fact, also possessions of another and vice versa (the property transferred has remained the property of the debtor).[15] In case there is relevance in attacking intra-group transactions then the (second) step would be to consider whether these should be judged with additional scrutiny (when recognizing the connection between the parties to the transaction), or rather the other way round—transactions should be upheld taking into account

---

[12] Ibid, para. 172.   [13] Ibid, paras. 174–6.   [14] Ibid, paras. 177–9.
[15] See Blumberg et al, *Blumberg on Corporate Groups* (n 31 chapter 1) vol 2, s. 85.19.

the interrelation among group members even if in other circumstances (not involving related companies) the transaction would have been avoided.

As suggested above, an adaptive approach is taken. A 'one size fits all' solution ignores the diversified scene of MEG insolvencies.[16] In contrast, considering various prototypes of MEG insolvencies[17] can assist in highlighting what solutions may be needed in order to promote just results. The focus here is on the particular affiliate and intra-group transactions involving its assets (rather than the handling together of several insolvencies). Prototypes I–K and L–M are therefore relevant as they all focus on the particular affiliate's insolvency. The insolvent affiliate is a member of either a 'business integrated' MEG or a 'non-integrated' MEG (which may be linked either by equity or contract, and may operate in various degrees of centralization).[18] Yet, it should be noted that similar issues may arise in the case of a total collapse of a MEG (insolvency of several MEG members); that is in the equivalent prototypes: A–C and G–H scenarios ('business integrated' insolvent MEGs or 'non-integrated' insolvent MEGs).[19] In these cases, the issue of avoiding transactions will occur during the insolvency of several group members—both issues of administration of group proceedings and issues of avoidance will need to be determined.[20] In the 'asset integration' scenarios (depicted by prototypes D–F)[21] there will be by definition a situation of total collapse (as a result of the intermingling and inability to ascertain solvency/insolvency among the intermingled entities). This particular scenario will be considered shortly.

It was already concluded that in cases of non-integration or even ('business') integration the insolvency of group entities should take place while respecting the corporate form, and thus creditors should recover their assets from the particular entity with whom they were dealing.[22] So, in considering fairness in distributing the estate of the particular entity, rights of creditors vis-à-vis the entity with whom they were dealing should be upheld unless there is justification for redistribution.[23] In this regard if the debtor's assets were depleted or certain creditors were preferred at the expense of other creditors of the same debtor, the corporate form should be respected and the transaction should be attacked on the basis of equitable treatment among the creditors of the particular entity. That is, even if the party to the transaction is a related entity creditor, or an undervalued transaction was favourable to another group member, these transactions should be attacked and reversed. As the creditors will not normally be able to recover their

---

[16] On which see chapter 1, section 1.3.

[17] See chapter 5 which delineated a set of relevant prototypes of insolvency within MEGs (see section 5.4).

[18] Ibid.

[19] Ibid.

[20] Ibid. See chapters 6–9 on the issues pertaining to the administration of group proceedings.

[21] The scenario of intermingling of assets/debts among the MEG entities, in the various degrees of centralization (see chapter 5, section 5.4).

[22] See chapter 6, section 6.2.1.3.

[23] See chapter 7, section 7.2.

debts from other group members,[24] it is crucial to ascertain which assets legally belong to which legal entity and to be able to reverse transactions favouring certain entities at the expense of others. Otherwise, to take the extreme example, one entity may remain with no assets at all, if the assets were all transferred to another entity. The creditors of the particular entity will end up with nothing if it is impossible to reverse the transaction. It is suggested therefore that in general it should be possible to apply avoidance provisions to group members.

9.2.3 Eliminating intra-group transactions in cases of 'asset integration'

On the other hand, in cases where the MEG was operating as a single entity in terms of the substance of the entities, transferring assets among the entities might have taken place excessively and even without record keeping (as if this is not a transaction between separate entities, but rather the moving of assets within what is economically the same entity). If this occurred, then it might be impossible or extremely difficult to detect the actual transactions that took place among the group members and eventually ascertain which entity owns which assets or which entity's assets were depleted as a result of intra-group transactions. Untangling the intra-group transactions will be either impossible or disproportionately costly. Indeed, in cases of prototypes D–F depicting 'asset integration'[25] it was suggested that substantive consolidation will typically apply (i.e. the pooling of assets and debts of the various entities together), in which case the intra-group transactions (among the members subject to the pooling order) are eliminated.[26] Otherwise, it should be possible to examine and, if necessary, to avoid (in the course of insolvency) vulnerable intra-group transactions.

9.2.4 Greater scrutiny in applying avoidance provisions to intra-group transactions

As was mentioned earlier, in the group context and more so in MEGs (groups operating worldwide), there are generally greater possibilities for opportunistic behaviour, especially on the brink of insolvency.[27] The MEG members are in a position to be knowledgeable of the financial position of the various group members, normally before this is clear to outsiders. They may attempt in such circumstances to shift assets from a distressed entity to other entities in the group and thus make sure that the assets are not to be distributed to the creditors of the distressed entity, but rather they will be utilized by other members of the group.

---

[24] Subject to particular circumstances as will be considered below (section 9.3), and the circumstances of 'asset integration' as discussed herewith (see also chapter 6, section 6.3; and chapter 7, section 7.4.1).

[25] See chapter 5, section 5.4.

[26] See chapter 6, section 6.3.

[27] See chapter 2, section 2.2.2.

As aforementioned, in the international setting this may involve moving assets to other jurisdictions.[28]

The risk of fraud and favouritism is considerable in the context of groups even if the parties to the transaction are non-integrated (i.e. in the circumstances depicted by prototypes L–M—the insolvency of a single affiliate member of a non-integrated MEG, and the equivalent prototypes for the cases of 'group collapse'—G-H[29]). Assets may be shifted, for example among non-integrated sister companies (i.e. companies which did not operate together a single business or did not have considerable mutual inter-connections[30])—a move that may be perpetrated by the group shareholders.[31] The fact that the same shareholder (or shareholders) controls both entities makes pre-insolvency transactions among the entities more vulnerable (compared to transactions between non-related parties). The related company party to the transaction although not integrated with the insolvent entity, is a member of the same group according to a definition of group adopted in this work, due to the controlling position of the shareholders over both companies.[32]

In such circumstances, of either prototypes I–K (insolvency of an affiliate member of an integrated MEG) or L–M (insolvency of an affiliate member of a non-integrated MEG), or the equivalent prototypes in a group collapse scenario[33] there is a need for tools to link between the entity in insolvency and the entity into which assets were diverted or which was otherwise favoured[34] so as to ensure that such transactions will be reversed in case they were detrimental to the insolvent affiliate.

9.2.5 Upholding intra-group transactions based on 'group considerations'

On the other hand, transactions between group members even (and in many cases especially) on the brink of insolvency may have commercial sense particularly

---

[28] Ibid.

[29] See chapter 5, section 5.4. Recall that 'non-integration' does not necessarily refer to the entire MEG, but may refer to relationship between certain members of the MEG.

[30] Ibid, section 5.3.2.

[31] See e.g. allegations regarding diversions of funds between the two different businesses controlled by the Tanzi family who controlled the Parmalat group (n 40 chapter 1). According to statements of Parmalat's officers during interrogations funds were diverted from Parmalat Finanziaria SpA to Parmatour, the controlling family's tourism business (see The Associated Press, 'Ex-Parmalat CFO Reportedly Blames Tanzi', *New York Times*, 3 October 2004). See further on the Parmalat insolvency proceedings in chapter 6, mainly sections 6.2.1.4, 6.2.1.6, 6.2.2.1 and 6.2.2.2; chapter 7, sections 7.5.2 and 7.5.4; and chapter 8, section 8.2).

[32] See chapter 1, sections 1.3.6–1.3.8.

[33] See chapter 5, section 5.4.

[34] The linking tool referred to here is somewhat different from those linking tools (such as consolidation) that were proposed in previous chapters. That is, it is not aimed at conducting insolvency proceedings under the same roof, but rather it is aimed at acknowledging the special relations between different affiliates in that they are not entirely independent of each other.

because they took place within a group of entities. Such transactions, if taking place among 'strangers' could be attacked as preferential or as depleting an affiliate's assets (this refers to transactions which are not fraudulent). Prototypes I–K should be particularly relevant for these considerations, namely the cases of the 'insolvent affiliate in business integrated MEG' (in the various degrees of centralization).[35] Where the affiliate in issue is part of an integrated MEG (in particular, the affiliate and the party to the transactions are integrated affiliates) certain transactions which are otherwise 'vulnerable' may not be regarded as such if considering the economic reality of integration. Here, the linkage needed is such that recognizes the group for the purpose of considering the actual detriments and benefits flowing to and from the insolvent entity, and in appropriate circumstances upholding intra-group transactions.

In regard to undervalued transactions, determining the value (i.e. the fair consideration) to the insolvent affiliate in issue may need to take into account the fact of integration. For instance, one affiliate may give a guarantee or security to the lender of another group member for the purpose of allowing the latter to raise further funds crucial for the continuance of its business. Indeed, between unrelated parties the transaction may seem unfavourable to the guarantor, in certain circumstances it may seem as a pure gift for no consideration if the guarantor does not receive any fees or anything tangible in return. However, considering the integration between these two entities may typically mean that the company guaranteeing the debt was to an extent dependent on the other affiliate (e.g., in terms of supply of products or services). The guarantor in an integrated MEG may have a true commercial interest in strengthening the financial position and the business of other group members. Therefore, it could be assumed that the guarantor entity may be receiving a proper benefit in consideration for the guarantee when recognizing the group and the integration of its components.[36]

In case it appears that the guarantor truly benefited from giving the guarantee, it seems unfair to reverse it to the detriment of the entity in favour of which the guarantee was given to the lender. Indeed, the lenders of the receiving entity will be the main beneficiaries of upholding the guarantee. This is contrasted with the guarantor entity and its stakeholders which may be non-adjusting creditors and tort victims, i.e. more vulnerable creditors.[37] However, regard should also be had to the benefit to the receiving entity and its other stakeholders from the strengthening of its financial position. The latter entity may be in financial difficulties as well. This may well be the situation in a case of integration between the

---

[35] Or the equivalent prototypes in the group collapse scenario. See chapter 5, section 5.4.

[36] See Blumberg et al, *Blumberg on Corporate Groups* (n 31 chapter 1) vol 2, s. 85.05[A]; Muscat, *The Liability* (n 39 chapter 1) 232.

[37] See Blumberg et al, *Blumberg on Corporate Groups* (n 31 chapter 1) vol 2, s. 85.20. See also chapter 4, sections 4.2.2.3 and 4.2.2.5 on different types of creditors in the context of insolvency goals.

entities.[38] The positions of the entities—the guarantor and the other affiliate—within the MEG should also be borne in mind. The guarantor may have been the parent company which may have exercised control over the affiliate in hand, in the ordinary course of business, in a way detrimental to the subsidiary and its stakeholders.[39] This adds an additional force to the finding that sufficient value was allocated to the guarantor in the giving of the guarantee. Upholding guarantees in such circumstances will also encourage the giving of credit to distressed affiliates. A routine attack on guarantees in such circumstances may deter lenders from providing funding in circumstances where the only security can be given by an affiliate knowing that the guarantee is likely to be attacked in the case of the guarantor liquidation. Especially in times where financing may be scarce it is crucial to provide adequate assurances to lenders that securities for lending will be respected.

Similar considerations may take place in regard to transactions which may seem preferential.[40] The insolvent affiliate may have paid an antecedent debt to a related company shortly before entering into insolvency, i.e. within the suspect period.[41] As between the debtor and an external creditor this may be regarded as preferring the latter. Conversely, in a group context, if the parties to the transaction belong to an integrated MEG there may be pure commercial reasons for the 'preference'. It may have been crucial for the continuance of the business of the (now) insolvent affiliate to pay the amount to its related company because of the interdependence among the group members.[42]

9.2.6 Summary

In sum, it should be possible to reverse intra-group transactions where these were detrimental to the affiliate in hand; yet such reversal of transactions should be avoided where in terms of economic realities the affiliate was not injured by the transaction. In any of these situations the 'group' should be recognized in order to close the gap between law and reality and reach fair and efficient solutions. Avoidance tools applied to the MEG case may assist in enhancing fairness in certain circumstances where the particular affiliate and its creditors were injured by the transaction. However, there may be other scenarios where creditors of the insolvent affiliate may need protection and where the use of avoiding transactions methods may not suffice. We turn to consider such circumstances.

---

[38] See chapter 6, section 6.2.1.1 (considering the likelihood of a 'domino effect' in such circumstances).
[39] See section 9.3.3.
[40] See n 14, and accompanying text.
[41] Certain laws will also require a desire to prefer the creditor (see e.g. English Insolvency Act 1986, s. 239). See n 14, and accompanying text.
[42] See also Muscat, *The Liability* (n 39 chapter 1) 237.

9.3 Protecting Creditors of 'Vulnerable Entities'—Fraud, Wrongful Trading, and False Impression of Creditworthiness by Group Members

9.3.1 Introduction

It was mentioned earlier that when insolvency is anticipated the problem of excessive risk-taking by the business managers augments.[43] Perverse incentives of this sort may be particularly significant in cases of 'shadow directors', for example a firm controlling a subsidiary.[44] Penalties imposed on managers in the event of the debtor's insolvency may reduce such incentives.[45] Crucially, fairness in distribution may require that in circumstances where managers took excessive risk at the expense of the creditors (knowing that most likely the company will not be able to meet its debts) they should bear some responsibility for the failure of the debtor, although they are normally shielded from such liability. This may mean requiring the managers to contribute from their personal funds to the estate of the debtor, or deferring any claim they may have against the company (if they are also its creditors) to claims of other external creditors.[46]

In this regard, it was mentioned that although national laws defer in the ways they deal with mismanagement in the course of insolvency there is broad acceptance of the notion that (to an extent) managerial allegiance shifts from the shareholders to the creditors when a company approaches insolvency.[47] In this respect, the particular issue to consider when addressing insolvencies within MEGs is the protection of creditors from mismanagement in the group context, and thus the possibility of 'linking' an insolvent affiliate to other group entities for the purpose of compensating the creditors of the insolvent affiliate for loss caused to them as a result of such mismanagement.

9.3.2 Extending the notion of 'management' to the controlling entity

Consider first such a case as just depicted where excessive risk was taken by a subsidiary in the vicinity of its insolvency without due consideration to the creditors. In the group context the 'management' responsible may well be the parent company controlling the entity (notwithstanding any responsibility of

---

[43] See chapter 4, section 4.2.2.2.
[44] Ibid.
[45] Ibid.
[46] Ibid, sections 4.2.2.3 and 4.3.2. Other measures may be imposed on directors, e.g. criminal sanctions and disqualification measures (see P.J. Omar, 'The European Initiative on Wrongful Trading' (2003) 6 Insolv. Law 239, 239).
[47] See chapter 4, sections 4.2.2.3 and 4.3.2. (a more controversial issue is the degree to which directors owe duties to creditors in the ordinary course of business, but this is outside our scope).

the directors of the subsidiary). This is because in the group context the notion of 'management' may be blurred in terms of the economic realities. Especially in 'integrated centralized' MEGs,[48] the management of the particular entity may be very much intertwined with a central management of the group, normally via the parent company.[49] The parent in this type of MEG may have had significant influence on the decision-making of the subsidiary and the policy taken by the group as a whole by way of the centralized control over the entire group, even if local entity management has been handling the daily affairs of the particular subsidiary.[50] Therefore, in case the applicable law considers particular circumstances as amounting to mismanagement (in the context of insolvency anticipation) and would order contribution of funds by managers in such circumstances then, although the parent is a separate entity, in case it has actually controlled the subsidiary in terms of policy and decision-making, we need measures for demanding contributions from its own funds to the insolvency estate of the subsidiary. In other words, we need to be able to create a 'link' between the entity in insolvency and the entity responsible for the excessive trading in the circumstances mentioned above. This could be particularly desirable from the point of view of the subsidiary's creditors in situations where the parent entity is solvent and its pockets are deep. Thus, such a contribution may enlarge the assets of the subsidiary available for distribution. This will then also contribute to return maximization in the course of insolvency.[51]

Prototypes I–K are therefore the typical relevant scenarios, i.e. the insolvent affiliate in 'business integrated' MEG in various degrees of centralization, where the MEG may be linked by equity or contract[52] (especially prototype I where the group was also centrally controlled).[53] In particular, the focus is on scenarios where the insolvent affiliate in issue is a subsidiary and the relationship in focus is with the solvent parent.[54] That is the situation of 'one-sided' integration in the

[48] Prototype I (in the scenarios focusing on the single subsidiary's insolvency) or A (in the scenarios of group collapse) (see chapter 5, section 5.4).

[49] See chapter 5, section 5.3.3.

[50] See D. Prentice, 'Corporate Personality, Limited Liability and the Protection of Creditors', in R. Grantham and C. Rickett (eds.), *Corporate Personality in the 20th Century* (Hart Publishing, Oxford 1998) 99, 117 (making this point in regard to the application of the concept of wrongful trading to parent companies, on which see further section 9.4.3).

[51] See chapter 4, section 4.2.2.1 and chapter 6 (in the context of a group collapse). Though, as mentioned above, the costs of litigation and the likelihood of success of allegations against the parent company should be borne in mind.

[52] See chapter 5, section 5.4. Recall, that the meaning of group applied in this work is not limited to equity-based 'hierarchical' groups involving parent-subsidiary relationships (see chapter 1, section 1.3.6). It was explained that enterprises comprised of entities linked by contract may display similar systems of managerial control, and that duties may be attributed to the controller based on its economic relations with the linked entity rather than on the formal legal separation and contractual risk shifting (see chapter 2, section 2.3.1).

[53] See chapter 5, section 5.4.

[54] Usually the immediate holding company, depending on the way the group was operated and which was the entity controlling the subsidiary (see n 36 chapter 5). Though, responsibility may also extend to other group members and may be relevant in other scenarios of integration

sense that the subsidiary was controlled or dependent on the controlling entity (typically the parent company), yet in terms of the parent it was not itself necessarily dependent on the subsidiary.

However, the factual circumstances of integration and control are only indicative of scenarios of involvement in the management of the subsidiary, and ultimately what matters is that there was evidence of actual mismanagement and actual involvement in the decision-making of the subsidiary. It should also be noted that other persons may be responsible for the debts of the insolvent member, such as lenders, individual shareholders, and as aforementioned the directors of the debtor or of the parent company. Yet, the position of these persons is outside the scope of this work which only focuses on the relationship among the group legal entities.[55]

9.3.3 Considering circumstances of 'mismanagement' in the group context

The notion of 'mismanagement' may also have specific meanings in the context of groups that should be appreciated by an approach to insolvencies within MEGs. It was noted earlier, that there are generally additional complexities in terms of fraudulent or wrongful behaviour towards creditors in anticipation of insolvency in the group context, as the group structure presents special opportunities in this respect.[56] Thus, there may be attempts to conceal the financial situation of group components, or to shift assets among group members as mentioned above.[57] This may reach the degree of fraud on creditors if actual dishonesty was involved. There may be various remedies outside insolvency addressing such problems. However, to the extent that the problem was not addressed prior to the insolvency, then in the course of the proceedings there is need for proper solutions that will be fair and cost-efficient.

---

notwithstanding a degree of decentralization, where other entities may have been involved in the fraudulent or wrongful act towards the creditors (see chapter 2, section 2.3.1 on the notion of 'network liability').

[55] Regarding lenders' liability in the group context see e.g. Blumenrg et al, *Blumberg on Corporate Groups* (n 31 chapter 1) vol 5, ch. 174; K.T. Lundgren, 'Liability of a creditor in a control relationship with its debtor' (1984) 67 Marq. L. Rev. 523; K. Hofstetter, 'Multinational Enterprise Parent Liability: Efficient Legal Regimes in a World Market Environment' (1990) 15 North Carolina J. of Int. Law and Comm. Reg. 299; R.K. Rasmussen, 'The Problem of Corporate Groups, A Comment on Professor Ziegel' (2002) 7 Fordham J. Corp. & Fin. L. 395, 397 (asserting that sophisticated creditors are well aware of managerial decisions concerning the structuring of the group and the allocation of assets when they extend credit). Generally, in the case of the individual shareholders a strict adherence to the limited liability concept should be kept since it is the essential advantage and purpose of the principle of limited liability: to safeguard 'natural' persons (see Muscat, *The Liability* (n 39 chapter 1) 194–5). On the liability of directors in this context see e.g. Muchlinski, *Multinational Enterpises* (n 10 chapter 1) 326–31.

[56] See chapter 2, sections 2.2.2 and 2.3.2.

[57] See ibid, and section 9.2.4.

In particular, the parent company may engage in commingling of funds, shifting assets outside the insolvent affiliate without sufficient record keeping (which will enable the transactions to be traced back to determine which assets actually belong to the subsidiary in hand).[58] This could happen either in order to hide assets from creditors (which will clearly amount to fraud), or as a general strategy for the maximization of the overall productive use of capital by the group. If such a strategy took place in a situation where the controllers realized that this is likely to result in the insolvency of the subsidiary it can be regarded as 'mismanagement' harming creditors in the sense explained above. Generally, the subsidiary may be in a position where it is not operating as a profit centre and only 'serves' the parent or the group as a whole.[59] The result may be to deprive the subsidiary of assets and sufficient funds, so that it may be trading while its controllers reasonably expect it to fail. In this respect, there is also greater danger of operating with no sufficient funds, due to availability of funds from other companies in the group which reduces the practical importance of adequate capitalization.[60] The holding company may fail to provide the subsidiary with the reasonably required financing to enable it to undertake the business activity for which it was incorporated.[61] Thus, from the moment the subsidiary started trading, it might have been insolvent.[62] This is a situation that may occur in a single company context, yet as aforementioned the risk for its occurrence augments in the group context.

It was also mentioned earlier how in the group context there is greater risk of avoidance of liability, as those running the group may have attempted to form

---

[58] See J. Landers, 'A Unified Approach to Parent, Subsidiary and Affiliated Questions in Bankruptcy' (1975) 42 U. Chi. L. Rev. 589, 597; Muscat, *The Liability* (n 39 chapter 1) 290–2. See also section 9.3.4 for the distinction between these scenarios and the voidable transactions scenarios or 'asset integration' scenarios.

[59] Landers mentions that creditors dealing with groups are in greater danger (compared with those dealing with single companies) inter alia due to inability of the subsidiary to develop independent profit making activities (see J. Landers, 'A Unified Approach to Parent, Subsidiary and Affiliated Questions in Bankruptcy' (1975) 42 U. Chi. L. Rev. 589, 597). Muscat classifies such situations under the term the 'subservient subsidiary situation' in which case a parent corporation dominates the subsidiary. Accordingly, its business is not conducted with the sole view of its own interests (rather possible interests of the parent, other affiliates, or of the group as a whole guide its operation). This may lead to group profit maximization, transfer pricing, diversion of corporate opportunities, manipulation of assets, allocation of financial support for the group and operation of the subsidiary without a profit motive (see Muscat, *The Liability* (n 39 chapter 1) 200–1).

[60] See J. Landers, 'A Unified Approach to Parent, Subsidiary and Affiliated Questions in Bankruptcy' (1975) 42 U. Chi. L. Rev. 589, 597.

[61] Muscat, *The Liability* (n 39 chapter 1) 312–16.

[62] See the English case *In Re Purpoint Ltd* [1991] BCC 121 where in considering allegations under the English wrongful trading provision (see section 9.4.3) the court expressed the view that arguably the company being dealt with in the case was, at the outset, so undercapitalized in relation to its business undertaking that it might have been insolvent from the moment of commencement of business and a prudent manager should not have let it trade. Though, ultimately the court decided that this was not the case on the facts, and thought that to imply knowledge upon the director that the company was doomed to fail would impose too high a test. See also B. Pettet, *Company Law*, 2nd edn (Pearson Longman, 2005), 36.

subsidiaries so that hazardous activities will be segregated.[63] In this respect it has been observed[64] that a particular form of such segregation might result in abusive behaviour in regard to the particular insolvent subsidiary. This is where the enterprise was artificially fragmented into legal units for no functional reason, but rather for the sole purpose of insulating the enterprise from potential claims. In these circumstances too, the entity controllers could have concluded that the specific unit is likely to collapse, which (in the case where no measures have been taken to safeguard its creditors) would amount to mismanagement harmful to creditors in anticipation of insolvency.

Finally, another aspect of mismanagement in the context of MEG insolvencies is where the subsidiary was represented to its creditors as part of a group or as supported by the parent or other entities, giving an impression of the subsidiary's financial viability based on its connection to the group.[65] In the vicinity of insolvency this allows the subsidiary to trade beyond its actual capability. If the rest of the group or the parent company 'abandon' the subsidiary where the latter enters insolvency, then it means that in the period leading to insolvency the parent let the subsidiary trade and take risks while it actually had insufficient funds to meet the debts incurred. In case creditors are misled in regard to the creditworthiness of the subsidiary with which they are dealing then both adjusting and non-adjusting creditors are injured by this strategy.[66] Tort victims are normally not affected by representations, but they will suffer as part of the general body of creditors from the depletion in the subsidiary's assets as a result of trading in the vulnerable circumstances. The creditors of the subsidiary as a whole are in a vulnerable situation.[67] Although the actual misrepresentation may well be performed by the

[63] See chapter 2, section 2.2.2.

[64] Muscat, *The Liability* (n 39 chapter 1), 399–401.

[65] Ibid, 421–3 (Muscat makes the distinction between mere 'group persona' strategy which normally benefits the subsidiary and does not cause harm to creditors (unless there was abusively dominating behaviour or undercapitalization as discussed above), and scenarios where this involved misrepresentation. Such impressions were given for example in the English case of *Augustus Barnett* (in *Re Augustus Barnett & Son Ltd* [1986] BCLC 170) where a parent company of a subsidiary in financial difficulties provided letters of comfort and general assurance that it was willing to provide the subsidiary with financial support as was necessary to enable it to continue trading (the subsidiary eventually collapsed and the court did not find the parent company responsible (see further n 119 and accompanying text)). The issue of misrepresentation as to the financial situation of a company has recently arisen in the English case of *Contex Drouzhba v Wiseman* ([2007] EWCA Civ 1201) in the context of liability of directors to creditors of their company. The court has found a director liable in the tort of deceit as he indicated to the company's suppliers that the company would in future be able to pay in full for supplies delivered. It was in effect an assurance as to future solvency of the company. By this representation the director had impliedly promised that the company would be able to meet its future obligations, although it was insolvent at the relevant time. The issue did not arise in the context of formal insolvency proceedings, and the court mentioned that the finding of implied representation of the type found in the case may also make directors guilty of fraudulent trading on the application of a liquidator (English Insolvency Act 1986, s. 213) (see D. Milman, 'Case Comment, Two cases of interest for company directors operating in the twilight zone' (2008) Insol. Int. 25).

[66] See chapter 2, section 2.3.2.4.

[67] In a similar way, the fundamental policy underlying the English old 'reputed ownership' clause (see s. 38(c) of the UK Bankruptcy Act 1914), which provided that property belonging to

subsidiary's own management (its directors),[68] as aforementioned (especially in prototype I scenarios—the insolvent affiliate of a 'business integrated' 'centralized' MEG),[69] the management is much intertwined with that of the parent. Also in other scenarios of MEGs (typically the integrated MEGs), the harm to creditors may have been caused as a matter of a group policy and strategies taken by the group controllers, and thus we need to be able to extend liability to other entities in the group (typically the parent company) in such cases.

In all these scenarios, the subsidiary is trading in situations where it is either doomed to fail or while misleading creditors. Unless measures are taken to safeguard the position of the subsidiary's creditors then this can be regarded as mismanagement harmful to creditors, and in the group context it should be possible to reach the responsible entity for adequate compensation. All affected parties should be taken into account (as well as their comparable positions and ability to adjust to loss *ex ante* and *ex post*),[70] and in this context the parent company and its stakeholders' interests should also be considered. Comparing the position of the subsidiary's creditors to the situation of the harming entity's creditors, the former are normally in a more vulnerable position. The harming entity is typically solvent so the creditors can recover their debts.[71] If the 'harming' entity may become insolvent as a result of imposing liability or deferring its debts still it is likely that this entity (and its stakeholders) is in a better position being the entity influencing the group policy and manipulating the affiliate in hand. In the contest between the two sets of creditors it seems that the subsidiary's creditors should normally prevail.

9.3.4 Scenarios of mismanagement distinguished from circumstances of voidable transactions or 'asset integration'

To an extent, there may be an overlap between the scenarios depicted here and scenarios of harm caused to the insolvent affiliate as a result of specific (voidable)

---

another person (than the debtor) may be taken by the creditors, was to prevent the gaining of false credit by persons who conveyed the impression of wealth by means of property which they do not in fact own. This clause is no longer part of English insolvency law and was criticized as 'verging upon the capricious', while its effectiveness was open to question. The outcome could have been quite devastating to the true owner who would have needed to prove in the bankruptcy for the value of his lost property, along with the other ordinary creditors (see I.F. Fletcher, *Law of Bankruptcy* (Macdonald & Evans, London 1978), 168–75). In the case of a corporate group, however, the relationship between the debtor and its affiliate makes them 'closer' parties (compared with a debtor and a 'remote' true owner of the property) which reinforces the problem of reliance on the portrayed image of the debtor and justifies more strongly putting the risk on the affiliate and not on third party creditors.

[68] See Muscat, *The Liability* (n 39 chapter 1) 424.

[69] See chapter 5, section 5.4.

[70] See on the notion of fairness in distribution chapter 4, sections 4.2.2.3–4.2.2.5.

[71] This is the typical scenario referred to above, i.e. prototypes I–K (see n 52 and accompanying text).

transactions.[72] A transaction involving the shifting of assets from a group entity can be regarded as voidable.[73] It can also be part of a pattern of abusive behaviour towards a subsidiary in the sense that its assets are transferred to other members or used for the purpose of the group but not to its own 'separate' benefit, in a way making the subsidiary's insolvency unavoidable and causing harm to the subsidiary's creditors.

However, the scenarios discussed in this section envisage behaviour which will not necessarily fall under particular avoidance provisions (even if those are properly applied to MEGs).[74] Thus, shifting of assets may have occurred on a routine basis, and may have involved a considerable amount of transactions, to the extent that it is impractical to examine each in light of the particular conditions of any avoidance provisions.[75] The misbehaviour may also fall outside the particular types of avoidance transactions available in the legal system.[76] For example, misrepresentation of creditworthiness of the subsidiary with no intent to defraud or letting it operate with insufficient funds might not fit within avoidance provisions.

There may also be an overlap with the scenarios for which other 'linking tools' were suggested, i.e. substantive consolidation.[77] As aforementioned (while discussing the avoidance of intra-group transactions), in cases where such transactions are untraceable with reasonable effort,[78] they may be eliminated under a pooling order.[79] Generally, the way the group entities were managed may have resulted in confusion between the assets and debts of the various group members suggesting that substantive consolidation is desirable.[80] It may well be that this scenario (of 'asset integration') involved excessive control and opportunistic behaviour of the sort depicted here.[81] In such circumstances, though, issues of

---

[72] See section 9.2.

[73] Ibid.

[74] Ibid.

[75] See Muscat, *The Liability* (n 39 chapter 1), 237–8. See also H. Peter, 'Insolvency in a Group of Companies, Substantive and Procedural Consolidation: When and How?' in H. Peter, N. Jeandin and J. Kilborn (eds.), *The Challenges of Insolvency Law Reform in the 21st Century Century* (Verlag Schulthess, Zurich 2006), 199, 203.

[76] See Muscat, *The Liability* (n 39 chapter 1), 234–5.

[77] See chapter 6, section 6.3; and chapter 7, section 7.4.1.

[78] That is, it is a case of 'asset integration' depicted by prototypes D–F (see chapter 5, section 5.3.4). Recall that 'asset integration' may occur in various variations (intermingling of assets or debts and/or the intra-group claims).

[79] See chapter 6, section 6.3.3.

[80] Ibid, section 6.3.

[81] See e.g. fraud and commingling of assets in an 'asset integrated' MEG scenario in the case of *BCCI* (n 436 chapter 6). There, the 'asset integration' was part of severely fraudulent behaviour by those who controlled the group, in this case the individual shareholders controlling the group. Of the serious illegalities in which BCCI participated, the most significant was the formation of a 'network' which involved an intricate money laundering arrangement (BCCI laundered drug money by transferring funds to its affiliates in the United States, and transferring funds to Luxemburg, and eventually London, where it was dispatched to one of its affiliates in another country in the form of a certificate of deposit; see T. McInerney, 'Towards the next stage in international banking

liability (of the entity which is part of the pooling order) become irrelevant as all assets and debts are mixed and intra-group claims eliminated.[82] Yet, in cases where there was no such intermingling (or otherwise an agreement on consolidation or the consolidation is only partial[83]) there may be room for applying other linking tools aimed at compensating the harmed entity or preventing the 'misbehaving' entity from competing for the assets of the harmed entity, in the event that it is also its creditor.

9.4 Available 'Enterprise Law' Remedies for Adequate Assessment of Intra-group Transactions and Creditor Protection in Insolvency

Our quest is thus for relevant 'linking tools', i.e. enterprise law mechanisms that will enable recognition of the group for various purposes and in appropriate circumstances reach the group controllers for contribution of funds or alteration of their ranking as creditors of the subsidiary, or reverse (or otherwise uphold) intra-group transactions. The subsequent section will assess whether such linking tools maintain an adequate balance with entity law, but first this section considers possible approaches, penalties, or relevant remedies available in legal regimes.

9.4.1 'Group considerations' in avoidance provisions

Avoidance provisions where these are in place[84] typically acknowledge the inter-relationship among group members for the purpose of facilitating the reversal of such transactions. They normally provide certain specific rules directed particularly at transactions between 'connected persons'.[85] Transactions between members of groups are usually covered by a definition of connected persons.[86] In regard to connected persons, avoidance provisions normally contain stricter conditions, in particular in regard to the length of suspect periods as well as the provisions of

regulation' (1995) 7 DePaul Bus. L.J. 143, 144; D.M. Laifer, 'Putting the Super Bank in the Supervision of International Banking—Post BCCI' (1992) 60 Fordham L. Rev. 467, 484). When the group eventually collapsed, it was essential to find a way to fairly distribute the assets (that were available for distribution) amongst the creditors, taking into account the fact that assets were diverted and money was circulated prior to the insolvency amongst the different entities within the group (see chapter 6, section 6.3.4.1).

[82] See chapter 6, section 6.3.3.1.
[83] On partial substantive consolidation see ibid, section 6.3.3.4.
[84] See section 9.2.
[85] Also termed 'related persons' or 'insiders' (see UNCITRAL Legislative Guide (n 137 chapter 3), Part two, Ch. II, para. 182).
[86] UNCITRAL Legislative Guide, for example, provides a definition of 'related person' which includes members of a corporate group (UNCITRAL Legislative Guide (n 137 chapter 3), Introduction, para. 12(jj)).

presumptions and shifted burden of proof (to the related person) regarding the requirements that the debtor was insolvent at the time of the transaction or was rendered insolvent as a result of the transaction.[87] UNCITRAL Working Group V[88] further considers explicitly suggesting that laws will encompass specification of the manner in which the various elements to be proved in regard to avoidance provisions (the burden of proof, specific defences and the application of special presumptions) would apply to avoidance of intra-group transactions.[89]

It is less clear to what extent legal regimes allowing avoiding transactions in the course of insolvency permit taking into account 'group considerations' (enterprise law concepts) for *upholding* transactions between group members. It has been argued that normally in this regard an entity approach is taken. That is, a transfer among connected persons will normally be avoided under the various avoidance provisions if it fulfils the normal pre-conditions, without giving special effect to the value or indirect benefit arising from the benefit to the other affiliate by virtue of the interrelations among the members.[90] However, courts may on occasion apply enterprise principles, either via 'piercing the corporate veil' doctrine[91] or on 'independent' enterprise concepts to uphold intra-group transactions. For instance, courts may determine that there was 'fair consideration' in a transfer by one affiliate that benefited another affiliate within the corporate group, acknowledging indirect benefit to affiliates from the support they provide to other group members.[92]

---

[87] See e.g. English Insolvency Act 1986, s. 240(2)(b) (in regard to a transaction at an undervalue—if the transaction is entered into with a person connected with the company, it is presumed that the company was insolvent at that time, or became insolvent by virtue of entry into the transaction); s. 240(1)(a) (in regard to voidable preferences—in the case of a preference which is given to a person connected with the company the suspect period is two years instead of six months for other persons); s. 239(6) (in regard to voidable preferences—in case of a preference which is given to a person connected with the company there is a presumption that the giving of the preference was influenced by a desire to prefer the connected person). See also UNCITRAL Legislative Guide (n 137 chapter 3) Part two, Ch. II, para. 182. The Legislative Guide contains recommendations in regard to voidable transactions with related persons suggesting that insolvency laws may specify that the suspect period for avoidable transactions involving related persons is longer than with transactions with unrelated persons (see ibid, recommendations 90 and 91).

[88] N 96 chapter 1.

[89] See WP.80/Add.1 (n 65 chapter 6), draft recommendation 15; Report, Thirty-fourth session (n 98 chapter 1), para. 55; WP.82/Add.2 (n 62 chapter 6), draft recommendation 15 and paras. 33–4. Note that at the time the book went to print the work of the Working Group is still in progress (n 140 chapter 3).

[90] See Blumberg et al, *Blumberg on Corporate Groups* (n 31 chapter 1) vol 2, s. 85.19[A] (explaining that US courts tend to treat subsidiaries and other entities of the group as separate in this context, referring to cases such as *In re Computer Universe, Inc.*, 58 Bankr. 28 (Bankr MD Fla 1986 and *In re Chase & Sanborn Corp.*, 68 Bankr. 530, 533 (Bankr SD Fla. 1986), aff'd, 813 F.2d 1177 (11th Cir 1987)). See also Muscat, *The Liability* (n 39 chapter 1) 228 (explaining that an entity analysis in regard to intra-group transactions would be expected from the English courts and appears to be the prevailing approach adopted by American courts).

[91] See generally chapter 2, section 2.4.3.

[92] See Muscat, *The Liability* (n 39 chapter 1) 228; Blumberg et al, *Blumberg on Corporate Groups* (n 31 chapter 1) vol. 2, s. 85.05[A], s. 85.18 and s. 85.19[B]. Under the English avoidance transactions regime, for example, the issue of 'group considerations' have not been explicitly considered,

UNCITRAL Working Group V[93] in addressing the issue of enterprise groups is currently considering proposing that in examining voidable intra-group transactions courts may have regard to the circumstances of the enterprise group (among whose members the transaction took place). This may include the degree of integration between the members (parties to the transaction), the purpose of the transaction, and whether the transaction granted an advantage to the group members that would not normally be granted between unrelated parties.[94] Thus, the recommendation proposes including explicit mention in legislation of group considerations beyond the mere reference to 'connected persons' (and the accompanied stricter conditions applied to such persons as explained above).

9.4.2 Group liability via lifting the corporate veil or directors' duties doctrines

Beyond circumstances of voidable transactions among group members, there is generally more reluctance to impose any kind of group liability (making shareholders, including legal entity shareholders contribute their own funds to cover debts of another entity). It will be recalled that legal regimes tend to strictly adhere to entity law when the issue of liability is at stake.[95] This may also suggest that shareholders, who are distinct from the entity they hold, can lend it funds and thus will be regarded as normal creditors.

It was also noted, though, that various doctrines are used (albeit normally in strict circumstances) which may allow the corporate form to be ignored to impose liability on the shareholder.[96] The concept of 'lifting the veil' in common law systems was mentioned.[97] It was noted that usually 'group considerations'

---

however it seems that there is room for such consideration under the provisions as formulated in the Insolvency Act. For example, in the case of an intra-group guarantee the affiliate may use the defence provided under the Act (see English Insolvency Act, s. 238(5)) to argue that at the time of the guarantee 'there were reasonable grounds for believing that the transaction would benefit' the affiliate (guarantor)—due to the commercial reality of integration among the group entities, and that the affiliate granted the guarantee in good faith (ibid) (see also Muscat, *The Liability* (n 39 chapter 1) 232–3).

[93] N 96 chapter 1.

[94] See WP.80/Add.1 (n 65 chapter 6), draft recommendation 14; Report, Thirty-fourth session (n 98 chapter 1), para. 55; WP.82/Add.2 (n 62 chapter 6), draft recommendation 14 and paras. 30–2. The Working Group also considered how the 'suspect period' (where the law enables avoidance of a transaction only if it took place within a specified period) in regard to voidable transactions in general to which any of the group members may have been party will be calculated in cases where substantive consolidation has been applied. It currently suggests that the specified date may be either different for each group member included in the order (being either the date of application for or commencement of insolvency proceedings) or common for all members included in the order, being the earliest of the dates of application for or commencement of proceedings with respect to those group members (see WP.80/Add.1 (n 65 chapter 6), draft recommendation 21; Report, thirty-fourth session (n 98 chapter 1), para.71; WP.82/Add.3 (n 65 chapter 6), draft recommendation 22).

[95] See chapter 2, section 2.4.3.

[96] Ibid.

[97] Ibid.

(or circumstances particular to groups) may not provide sufficient grounds for imposing liability under the lifting the veil jurisprudence. Yet, in certain legal regimes (e.g. the US regime) 'enterprise law' does play some role in this respect, with courts occasionally applying enterprise principles in determining questions of liability (both in regard to equity based and contractually linked entities), and focusing on factors relating to the interrelation among the group members.[98] The doctrine is not specific to insolvency, though, and thus does not guide courts in considering the particular concerns inherent to this area. Generally, it has been observed that the present rules underlying the lifting the veil doctrine 'neither guide good decision-making nor produce consistent or defensible results.'[99]

Liability of parent companies for debts owed to creditors may be imposed via doctrines of fiduciary duties of directors and concepts of 'shadow director' and/or 'de facto director'.[100] As aforementioned, there is much controversy as to the extent to which directors owe duties to creditors in the ordinary course of business. However, in insolvency and seemingly also when companies approach insolvency there is wider acceptance that managers should have regard to the interests of creditors in particular.[101] Such duties may be provided in specific legislation. The fraudulent and/or wrongful trading types of provisions discussed below postulate exactly that.

9.4.3 Group liability via fraudulent or wrongful trading regimes

Fraudulent and wrongful trading types of provisions are not uncommon and are to be found in different legal regimes albeit in different variations.[102]

Fraudulent trading may require participation in the conduct of the business with intent to defraud or for other fraudulent purposes.[103] Wrongful trading,

[98] Ibid.

[99] See K.A. Strasser, 'Piercing the Veil in Corporate Groups' (2005) 37 Conn. L. Rev. 637 (mentioning that there is near unanimity on the matter).

[100] See chapter 2, section 2.4.6.

[101] See section 9.3.1.

[102] Provisions of this type can be found, for example, in insolvency or company laws in the UK, Australia, New Zealand, South Africa, Canada, France, Belgium, Netherlands, Spain and Germany (on such types of provisions in commonwealth jurisdictions see Blumberg et al, *Blumberg on Corporate Groups* (n 31 chapter 1) vol 2, s. 90.02[C], s. 90.03[B], s. 90.05[B], s. 90.06); see also D. Prentice, 'Corporate Personality, Limited Liability and the Protection of Creditors', in R. Grantham and C. Rickett (eds.), *Corporate Personality in the 20th Century* (Hart Publishing, Oxford 1998) 99, 110–23. For a comparative analysis of such provisions in European jurisdictions see P.J. Omar, 'The European Initiative on Wrongful Trading' (2003) 6 Insolv. Law. 239. The High Level Group of Company Law Experts set up by the European Commission (see n 145 chapter 2) has also reached the conclusion in its final report (High Level Group of Company Law Experts on a Modern Regulatory Framework of Company Law in Europe, Final Report, Brussels, November 4, 2002) that wrongful trading rules should be introduced within the EU jurisdictions to cover situations where directors foresee or ought to foresee that the company cannot continue to pay its debts (see P.J. Omar, 'The European Initiative on Wrongful Trading' (2003) 6 Insolv. Law. 239, 243).

[103] See e.g. English Insolvency Act 1986, s. 213; New Zealand Companies Act 1993, section 380. See also Blumberg et al, *Blumberg on Corporate Groups* (n 31 chapter 1) vol 2, s. 90.02[C] and

on the other hand, is designed to be wider in scope and to reach non-fraudulent misconduct.[104] It is generally directed at mismanagement normally at some time leading to insolvency, specifically the trading of the business when the company is insolvent and where the trading only deepens this financial situation and reduces the availability of assets for recovery of debts to creditors.[105] The law may require that the director concluded or ought to have concluded that there was no reasonable prospect that the company could avoid going into insolvent liquidation.[106] Under certain legal regimes directors may escape liability based on various types of 'defences' that may be provided in the legislation. For instance, in the event of proof that after the directors first acquired deemed knowledge that insolvency is inevitable they took every step with a view to minimize the potential loss to creditors as they ought to have taken.[107] Other types of defences in this context exempt directors from liability if they had reasonable grounds to expect, and did expect, that the company was solvent at the time and would remain solvent even if it incurred that debt and other debts incurred at that time, or in the event of proof of receiving adequate professional advice regarding the solvency of the company.[108] The remedies for such behaviour are diverse as well, but at least in certain jurisdictions it is provided that the managers will contribute funds to the insolvency estate to compensate for the harm caused.[109] Recovery normally goes to the insolvent company (not to a particular creditor that may have been injured) and thus becomes part of the pool of assets available for distribution.[110] The amount of contribution is normally subject to the court discretion. In some regimes the courts demand that the sum contributed will reflect the loss caused, as it is of a compensatory nature.[111]

s. 90.05[B]; P.J. Omar, 'The European Initiative on Wrongful Trading' (2003) 6 Insolv. Law. 239, 243–9.

[104] Blumberg et al, *Blumberg on Corporate Groups* (n 31 chapter 1) vol 2, s. 90.02[C].

[105] See e.g. English Insolvency Act 1986, s. 214; French Commercial Code, Art. L624–2.-6; Australian Corporation Act 2001, ss. 558, 588. See also Blumberg et al, *Blumberg on Corporate Groups* (n 31 chapter 1) vol 2, s. 90.02[C] and s. 90.03[B]; P.J. Omar, 'The European Initiative on Wrongful Trading' (2003) 6 Insolv. Law. 239, 243–9.

[106] See English Insolvency Act 1986, s. 214(2)(b). See also D. Prentice, 'Corporate Personality, Limited Liability and the Protection of Creditors', in R. Grantham and C. Rickett (eds.), *Corporate Personality in the 20th Century* (Hart Publishing, Oxford 1998) 99, 118.

[107] See English Insolvency Act 1986, s. 214(3). See also D. Prentice, 'Corporate Personality, Limited Liability and the Protection of Creditors', in R. Grantham and C. Rickett (eds.), *Corporate Personality in the 20th Century* (Hart Publishing, Oxford 1998) 99, 118–20.

[108] See Australian Corporation Act 2001, s. 588X. See also Blumberg et al, *Blumberg on Corporate Groups* (n 31 chapter 1) vol 2, s. 90.03[B].

[109] See e.g. English Insolvency Act, s. 214(1); Australian Corporation Act 2001, s. 558V; See also P.J. Omar, 'The European Initiative on Wrongful Trading' (2003) 6 Insolv. Law. 239, 239; Blumberg et al, *Blumberg on Corporate Groups* (n 31 chapter 1) vol 2, s. 90.02[C], s. 90.03[B], s. 90.05[B], s. 90.06.

[110] See e.g. English Insolvency Act 1986, s. 214(1); Australian Corporation Act 2001, s. 588X. Blumberg et al, *Blumberg on Corporate Groups* (n 31 chapter 1) vol 2, s. 90.03[B].

[111] See the English case *Re Produce Marketing Consortium Ltd* [1989] BCLC 513. See also D. Prentice, 'Corporate Personality, Limited Liability and the Protection of Creditors', in R Grantham

The liability of a parent corporation under such regimes is less straightforward. Some regimes do not deal with the matter at all.[112] In others, a parent company may be similarly liable for mismanagement under various constructions, applying the general provisions of wrongful trading on parent companies. Under the English wrongful trading regime, for example, a parent company may be liable for mismanagement under the circumstances as explained above, if it fulfils the definition of a 'shadow director'.[113] A 'shadow director' is a person in accordance with whose instructions or directions the directors are accustomed to act.[114] This may require demonstrating that the parent company[115] significantly and consistently interfered with the management of the subsidiary.[116] Yet, the extent to which a parent may be made liable under this provision is unclear. Some commentators have argued that it gives a fairly wide discretion to bring a parent company within the definition of a shadow director in various circumstances.[117] However, the need to demonstrate pervasive interference in the management of the subsidiary may render the application of the provision to parent companies limited.[118] It seems, for example, that a parent company which abandons its subsidiary and allows it to enter insolvency, even though it supported it previously and created the impression that it stands behind the subsidiary, will not be subject to liability.[119] On the practical level, the application of the provisions on parent

and C. Rickett (eds.), *Corporate Personality in the 20th Century* (Hart Publishing, Oxford 1998) 99, 122.

[112] The South African wrongful trading provision (South African Companies Act 1973, s. 424), for example, does not impose liability on the parent company. Though, some commentators suggest that a parent company may be liable under the section at least where the director's knowledge of the unfair acts might be imputed to it (see D. Botha, 'Groups in South African Company Law' (doctoral dissertation, University of Pretoria 1981; see also Blumberg et al, *Blumberg on Corporate Groups* (n 31 chapter 1) vol 2, s. 90.06).

[113] The wrongful trading provision being applicable to a 'director' including a 'shadow director' (see English Insolvency Act 1986, s. 214(7)).

[114] English Insolvency Act 1986, s. 251.

[115] Note that the definition may extend to other persons, including the lenders (whose position in this context is outside the scope of this work).

[116] See *Re Hydrodan (Corby) Ltd* [1994] 2 BCLC 180. See also D. Prentice, 'Corporate Personality, Limited Liability and the Protection of Creditors', in R. Grantham and C. Rickett (eds.), *Corporate Personality in the 20th Century* (Hart Publishing, Oxford 1998) 99, 115–17.

[117] See A. Wilkinson, 'Piercing the Corporate Veil and the Insolvency Act 1986' (1987) 8 Co. Law. 124, 125. See also Blumberg et al, *Blumberg on Corporate Groups* (n 31 chapter 1) vol 2, s. 90.02[C].

[118] Cf. the interpertation of 'shadow director' under the French wrongful trading provisions. A parent company may be considered a shadow director of its subsidiary if it plays an important role in management decisions, or where both companies give the appearance of being interdependent and under the same management (see P.J. Omar, 'The European Initiative on Wrongful Trading' (2003) 6 Insolv. Law. 239, 246).

[119] See *In re Augustus Barnett & Son Ltd* [1986] BCLC 170. The case was decided under s. 213 of the English Insolvency Act 1986 (the fraudulent trading provision). The court found that the directors had not been fraudulent and that the parent did not participate in the management of the subsidiary. As indicated by Prentice, seemingly the case would be decided no differently under the wrongful trading provision (English Insolvency Act 1986, s. 214), as the parent would not be a shadow directo (see D. Prentice, 'Corporate Personality, Limited Liability and the Protection of

companies seems to have had little effect on the law. Generally, there are only a few instances of use of the provisions to pursue claims against directors.[120]

Under Australian law the wrongful trading provisions impose a liability for mismanagement on the holding company of a subsidiary. The Australian regime specifically provides in this regard that in examining the knowledge of the parent company regarding the insolvency of the subsidiary and the effect of incurring further debts, regard is to be had to the nature and extent of the parent's control over the subsidiary's affairs and any other relevant circumstances.[121]

9.4.4 Explicit consideration of group liability in insolvency

The New Zealand regime provides a specific tailor-made provision in regard to group liability in insolvency.[122] Similar to some of the fraudulent and wrongful trading regimes mentioned above, the purpose of the legislation is specifically to enable contribution of funds to the insolvency estate, though here the target of a contribution order is a related company and the circumstances where such contribution should be ordered are provided with the scenarios of relationships between group members in mind. Generally, liability is imposed in circumstances of involvement or misconduct of the related company towards the debtor in question. It is at the court's discretion to order that the related company pay the debtor's liquidator the whole or part of its debts.[123] The court is required to consider whether making a related company liable for the debts of the insolvent subsidiary

Creditors', in R. Grantham and C. Rickett (eds.), *Corporate Personality in the 20th Century* (Hart Publishing, Oxford 1998) 99, 116–17). Indeed, the Cork Committee has recognized the potential for the abuse of the corporate group and observed that, even with the introduction of wrongful trading, the law would remain in an unsatisfactory state (Cork Report (n 157 chapter 2) ch. 51).

[120] This may be a result of liquidators being cautious not to waste funds of an insolvent subsidiary in bringing claims where the likelihood of success may be unclear (see P.J. Omar, 'The European Initiative on Wrongful Trading' (2003) 6 Insolv. Law. 239, 245). This may be especially so in regard to liability of a parent company, in regard to which the scope of the wrongful trading provision is not entirely clear. But see the survey of English and Welsh cases applying the wrongful trading provision which showed that in most cases, the issue of managers risk-shifting in the vicinity of insolvency arose in the context of either closely held firms or in regard to shadow director (see n 38 chapter 4).

[121] A defence will arise if the parent corporation proves that it took all reasonable steps to prevent the subsidiary from incurring the debt. See Australian Corporation Act 2001, ss. 588V–588X. See also Blumberg et al, *Blumberg on Corporate Groups* (n 31 chapter 1) vol 2, s. 90.03[B].

[122] See New Zealand Companies Act 1993, ss. 271–272. Reform along these lines was also recommended in Australia, in the Harmer Report (see the Australian Law Reform Commission Report No. 45 General Insolvency Inquiry, AGPS, Canberra, 1988) though Australian legislation in regard to group liability was eventually limited to the wrongful trading provisions (see n 121, and accompanying text). The Cork Committee in the UK (n 157 chapter 2) has referred to the New Zealand legislation as providing possible solutions to the problems of abuse within corporate groups (see also n 119).

[123] As mentioned earlier, it is also possible, in the appropriate circumstances, that the assets and debts of a related company will be pooled together with the debtor, winding up both companies as if they were one (see chapter 6, section 6.3.2).

is 'just and equitable'.[124] In this regard, the court should take into account the set of factors delineated in the Act. That is, the extent to which the related company took part in the management of the company being wound up, its conduct towards the creditors, and the extent to which the winding up is attributable to the actions of the related company. The court is also authorized to consider such other matters as it thinks fit.[125] The provisions are thus wide in scope and give much discretion and flexibility to courts in determining group liability in the context of insolvency.[126] Potentially, parent companies may be held liable for the debts of their insolvent subsidiary in any possible circumstances if the courts find it just and equitable. Nevertheless, examination of the case law indicates that the court will scrutinize the factors closely prior to making an order under the provisions.[127] It has been observed that this legislation is 'revolutionary' in terms of its utilization of enterprise principles, yet that it has not been significantly utilized in practice to date.[128]

Another measure in insolvency which is sometimes used to tackle unfair behaviour in the group context is the substantive consolidation or pooling orders which were discussed earlier.[129] In certain jurisdictions allowing for such measures, these may be used to combat abuse within groups. For example, pooling orders under the New Zealand regime may be ordered in a variety of circumstances if the court considers the giving of such an order 'just and equitable' and the related companies are both in liquidation. The factors that should be considered include the conduct of the related company towards the other company in liquidation.[130] Recall, in addition, that under the US regime substantive consolidation is regarded as an equitable tool and may also be used as a remedy against improper and misleading corporate behaviour.[131] Substantive consolidation under the US regime is also available between a debtor and a non-debtor.[132]

UNCITRAL Working Group V[133] in addressing the issue of enterprise groups in insolvency and in considering recommending the substantive consolidation doctrine,[134] currently suggests applying it not only in scenarios of intermingling

---

[124] New Zealand Companies Act 1993, s. 271(1).

[125] Ibid, s. 272.

[126] See R.P. Austin, 'Corporate Groups', in R. Grantham and C Rickett (eds.), *Corporate Personality in the 20th Century* (Hart Publishing, Oxford 1998) 71, 84–5; Blumberg et al, *Blumberg on Corporate Groups* (n 31 chapter 1) vol. 2, s. 90.05[B].

[127] See J. Dickfos, C. Anderson and D. Morrison, 'The Insolvency Implications for Corporate Groups in Australia—Recent Events and Initiatives' (2007) 16 Int. Insol. Rev. 103, 119 (examining reforms in Australia with comparisons to the US and New Zealand regimes).

[128] Blumberg et al, *Blumberg on Corporate Groups* (n 31 chapter 1) vol 2, s. 90.02.

[129] See chapter 6, section 6.3; and chapter 7, section 7.4.

[130] See New Zealand Companies Act 1993, s. 272(1)(b).

[131] See chapter 7, section 7.4.2.

[132] See *In re 1438 Meridian Place, N.W., Inc.,* 15 Bankr. 89 (Bankr DDC 1981); *In re Crabtree* 39 Bankr. 718 (Bankr ED Tenn 1984).

[133] See n 96 chapter 1.

[134] See chapter 6, section 6.3.2.

of assets and debts,[135] but also in cases where two or more enterprise group members were engaged in fraudulent schemes or activity with no legitimate business purpose.[136] Otherwise the Working Group is currently not suggesting in draft recommendations additional measures to tackle misconduct (in particular in the case of a solvent company in regard to the insolvent subsidiary) apart from the elaboration on avoidance provisions.[137] It explains in a report and in draft commentary that legal regimes may apply measures available in their laws to remedy such situations (such as 'lifting the veil' doctrines and wrongful trading).[138]

9.4.5 Deference of group members' claims in insolvency

Another measure that is sometimes used to remedy misconduct relates specifically to scenarios where the parent company has a claim against the insolvent entity as a creditor. If considerations of fairness support it, the parent's claim could be deferred to the claims of the external unsecured creditors of the subsidiary or even debts of other shareholders.[139] Similarly to the wrongful trading provisions, in some jurisdictions this measure is primarily designed to address directors' mismanagement, while in others it could be directly applicable to group members.

Thus, subordination of claims is sometimes a remedy provided alongside the remedy of a contribution order in cases of wrongful trading by managers.[140] For example, under the English fraudulent and wrongful trading provisions the court may order the subordination of a debt owed to a director, wholly or in part, to all other debts of the company.[141] Thus, in circumstances of fraudulent trading or

---

[135] Ibid.

[136] See WP.80/Add.1 (n 65 chapter 6), draft recommendation 17(b); Report thirty-fourth session (n 98 chapter 1), para. 63; WP.82/Add.3 (n 65 chapter 6), draft recommendation 17(b) and para. 22). The Working Group considers, though, that misleading creditors to believe that the group operated as a single business should not be a basis for substantive consolidation, rather may give rise to other remedies (see ibid, para.64). Additionally, in regard to fraudulent schemes or activities with no legitimate business purpose as bases for substantive consolidation, the draft recommendation requires that the court is satisfied that substantive consolidation is essential to rectify the scheme or activity. If another remedy is available to achieve that result, it should generally be adopted (see WP.80/Add.1 (n 65 chapter 6), draft recommendation 17(b) and Part E, para. 11; WP.82/Add.3 (n 65 chapter 6), draft recommendation 17(b)).

[137] See section 9.4.1. See also n 150 in regard to the Working Group discussions of the subordination doctrine.

[138] See Report thirty-third session (n 97 chapter 1), para. 94; WP.82/Add.3 (n 65 chapter 6), paras. 4–13.

[139] The parent company may be a secured creditor so that without subordination it will rank ahead of the unsecured creditors, or if it is an unsecured creditor it will compete with them on the remainder of the assets. Otherwise if the related company is only an equity holder then under most insolvency laws its claim will be in any case deferred to all debts of the debtor (see UNCITRAL Legislative Guide (n 137 chapter 3), Part two, Ch. V, para. 76).

[140] See section 9.4.4. Note, that subordination agreements (where a creditor which may be a parent company agrees to subordinate its debts to debts of external creditors or minority shareholders) are a different matter, and maybe more widely recognized.

[141] See English Insolvency Act 1986, s. 215(4). See also Goode, *Principles of Corporate Insolvency* (n 53 chapter 4), 543.

mismanagement in the vicinity of insolvency, and in case the parent company can be shown to be sufficiently involved in the management of the subsidiary (to be regarded as a shadow director) its debt as a creditor may be deferred to debts of other external creditors.

In the US, the courts developed a doctrine of equitable subordination, which is primarily directed at loans by a parent company to its subsidiary.[142] The doctrine is bankruptcy-specific and thus designed to implement bankruptcy policy.[143] It thus aimed inter alia to remedy unfairness and abuse of control by controlling entities harming creditors and investors.[144] Thus, courts are allowed to inquire into the conduct of the parties and the nature of the financial arrangement which gave rise to the debt and defer the debt to the claims of the external creditors. Subordination is discretionary and may be ordered in a wide variety of circumstances where equitable principles so require. That is, where the conduct of the parent has been in some way unscrupulous. In particular, the court may inquire whether the subordinated creditor has engaged in some type of inequitable conduct; that this conduct has resulted in injury to other creditors or conferred an unfair advantage on the subordinated creditor; and that equitable subordination is not inconsistent with the provisions of the Bankruptcy Act.[145] It may order subordination in case the subsidiary was greatly undercapitalized, or in case of manipulations of intra-group transactions to its own advantage at the expense of external creditors, or generally if the parent acted unfairly.[146]

Equitable subordination is not supposed to be punitive, rather the aim is to compensate for the harm caused by the subordinated entity, and therefore it is accepted that it should be imposed only to the extent necessary to remedy the injury to creditors or shareholders.[147] Yet, if the conduct is pervasive and complex (so that it is not possible for example to identify a particular transaction as abusive) then complete subordination to the claims of the injured creditors or members will be ordered.[148] In appropriate cases, *pari passu* subordination may be ordered (ordering that the parent and the creditors of the subsidiary will share *pari passu*). It has been observed that this is especially appropriate in cases where the parent company is also insolvent and the competition is between two sets of innocent creditors. However, there is no general bar on full subordination in cases

[142] The doctrine is now incorporated by reference in s. 510(c) of the federal Bankruptcy Code.

[143] Cf. the 'lifting of the corporate veil' doctrine mentioned above (section 9.4.2).

[144] Blumberg et al, *Blumberg on Corporate Groups* (n 31 chapter 1) vol. 2, s. 87.19.

[145] *Re Mobil Steel Co*, 563 F.2d 692 (5th Cir 1977); *Wooley v Faulkner* (*In re SI Restructuring, Inc.*), No. 07–50872, 2008 WL 2469406 (5th Cir June 20, 2008).

[146] Indeed, American courts have often subordinated claims of dominant shareholders to those of unsecured creditors on the basis that the shareholder breached the rules of 'fair play and good conscience' and the 'fiduciary standards of conduct which he owes the corporation, its stakeholders and creditors.' (see *Pepper v Litton* 308 U.S. 295 (1939), 310–11. See also Muscat, *The Liability* (n 39 chapter 1), 250).

[147] Blumberg et al, *Blumberg on Corporate Groups* (n 31 chapter 1) vol. 2, s. 87.01.

[148] Ibid. See *Taylor v Standard Gas & Elec. Co.*, 306 U.S. (1939).

of insolvent parent companies.[149] This seems to give wide discretion to courts to defer debts owed to parent companies in various types of 'inequitable conduct'.

UNCITRAL Legislative Guide considered the issue of subordination and explains the scenarios where it might be applicable under different legal regimes. It also recommends that insolvency law should specify that claims by related persons should be subject to scrutiny and where justified, the claim may be subordinated. Otherwise, the Guide does not recommend the subordination of any particular types of claim under the insolvency law.[150]

9.5 Conflicts with Entity Law—Balanced Solutions

9.5.1 Avoidance of intra-group transactions and the entity–enterprise law dilemma

It is suggested that recognizing the group and interrelations among the group members in regard to voidable transaction involves only minimal interference with entity law. It will be recalled that the conclusion reached in chapter 2 was that when limited liability is not involved, there is lesser conflict with entity law and therefore the tension decreases when attempting to recognize the group as the relevant body. In such cases, it was submitted that enterprise law should play a greater role where this meets economic realities and the objectives of the particular issues at stake.[151] In the context of voidable transactions, giving effect to the interrelations among group members may prevent group members from bypassing avoidance transactions regulations. In other scenarios, group considerations will be relevant for upholding the actual intentions of the parties and the commercial sense of the transaction in hand.[152] The prototypical classification of MEGs in insolvency can assist in making the decisions. As aforementioned, in considering the detrimental effect of an intra-group transaction on the insolvent affiliate greater scrutiny is needed both in respect of integrated and non-integrated MEGs. On the other hand, benefit generating in particular from group inter-connections is typically relevant in integration scenarios.[153]

---

[149] See Blumberg et al, *Blumberg on Corporate Groups* (n 31 chapter 1) vol 2, s. 87.06.

[150] See UNCITRAL Legislative Guide (n 137 chapter 3) Part two, Ch. V, paras. 48, 60 and 61, and Recommendation 184(c). See also Recommendation 189(d) where the Guide notes that subordinated claims would rank after claims of ordinary unsecured creditors. UNCITRAL Working Group V (n 96 chapter 1) has considered whether to provide additional recommendations regarding subordination in the context of enterprise groups, yet is currently not suggesting such recommendations (see Report, thirty-third session (n 97 chapter 1), para. 60; WP.82/Add.2 (n 62 chapter 6), paras. 36–44).

[151] See chapter 2, section 2.3.3.

[152] See section 9.2.

[153] Ibid.

Otherwise, the group entities should be regarded as separate in examining the transactions. In fact, the examination of intra-group transactions must recognize the separateness among the group members, or else, as mentioned above, there is no transaction at all. The only scenario where the entities are mixed to become one (at least partially) is where substantive consolidation is applied. This, as suggested, should be done in 'asset integrated' insolvent MEGs (i.e. in regard to those group members whose assets and debts were mixed in the ordinary course of business, so that it is either impossible or involves considerable costs to disentangle the different businesses and trace back transactions) or with the consent of the creditors.[154]

Recall, that it was concluded that substantive consolidation, apart from the circumstances of 'asset integration', will contravene 'asset partitioning' (the economic essence of entity law), thus collapse the bargain and in turn be redistributive without justification.[155] On the other hand, reversing particular transactions is less interventionist—only the particular transaction is reversed, and it only deprives the creditors of the relevant entity (involved in the transaction) to the extent that they have benefited from a transaction outside the terms of the original bargain, because the transaction was preferential, fraudulent, or undervalued as explained above. Avoidance of transactions in such circumstances is also widely accepted outside the context of enterprise groups. And, in any case the conditions of the particular avoidance provisions have to be met also in regard to related companies. Thus, for example, in regard to undervalued transactions provisions, if it appears that there was fair consideration provided to the insolvent affiliate there should be no problem in upholding the transactions. In case fraudulent transactions involved the forming of separate entities (into which, for example, assets were shifted so as to hide them from creditors), corporate separate personality should be ignored as part of the decision to avoid the transactions, as in such circumstances the corporate form has been used for improper purposes.[156]

In this respect, transactions involving SPVs are often mentioned.[157] The fear is that the transaction will be avoided in insolvency as it is between related companies. However, as has been noted elsewhere, the risk is small as normally there is a 'true sale' between the company originator and the SPV and thus the transaction is not vulnerable.[158]

---

[154] See chapter 6, section 6.3.

[155] Ibid.

[156] It will be recalled that UNCITRAL Working Group (n 96 chapter 1) is currently suggesting allowing substantive consolidation in the scenario where group members were engaged in fraudulent schemes (see n 136). A better solution would be to attack the fraudulent transactions under relevant avoidance provisions (see Legislative Guide (n 137 chapter 3), Part two, Recommendation 87(a)), for the reasons explained above. Indeed, the Working Group currently stresses in the relevant recommendation that the court should be satisfied that substantive consolidation is essential to rectify the scheme or activity, and if another remedy is available to achieve that result it should generally be adopted (n 136).

[157] On the SPV transaction see n 45 chapter 1. On SPV and substantive consolidation see chapter 6, section 6.3.3.3.

[158] See S. Schwarcz, 'Securitization Post-Enron' (2004) 25 Cardozo L. Rev. 1539, 1543–4, 1551–3 (Schwarcz explains that the usual securitization transactions are fundamentally different

Therefore, applying regulations regarding avoidance of transactions to intra-group transactions in the way described above will enable restoration for the harm caused to the creditors of the insolvent affiliate. As a result, it will also swell the affiliate's insolvency estate. Or, where transactions are legitimate it will prevent their rejection. Ultimately it will enable fair results to be achieved when considering all relevant parties—the affiliate and its stakeholders, primarily the creditors, and the related company (typically the parent company) and its stakeholders—without causing considerable harm to entity law.

Measures provided in legal regimes to ensure greater scrutiny in regard to avoidance of intra-group transaction are thus useful for the purposes invoked here. However, clear rules in regard to giving effect to group considerations in assessing benefits to the insolvent affiliate are usually missing. As stressed earlier, certainty and predictability are important (as supportive goals for substantive fairness) especially in the international context.[159] Thus, a system for insolvency within MEGs should further promote clarification of this aspect. The current proposals of UNCITRAL Working Group V discussed above[160] provide for such additional clarity and are therefore highly commendable.

9.5.2 Balanced 'linking tools' for group liability

9.5.2.1 Caution in imposing liability or subordinating claims

As aforementioned, there may be cases of opportunistic behaviour and undue harm to creditors which do not fall within conditions of avoidance transactions.[161] Fairness may suggest the need for compensation (typically from the parent company) to restore harm caused to the insolvent affiliate. In case the parent was also a creditor, the deference of its claim against the insolvent entity might also be suggested.[162] The problem is that imposing liability on the parent shareholder (or any other related company) is harmful to entity law. As concluded in chapter 2, ignoring limited liability (where the parties themselves have not contracted out of the rule) defeats crucial economic benefits accompanying the doctrine.[163]

Subordinating claims to those of external creditors may be argued to be less intrusive (compared with imposing liability), as like consolidation it only involves competition among creditors[164] (the creditors of the insolvent affiliate and the

---

from the use of SPVs for mere financial-statement manipulation as was done in the case of *Enron*); P.V. Pantaleo et al, 'Rethinking the Role of Recourse in the Sale of Financial Assets' (1996) 52 Bus. Law. 159, 185.

[159] See chapter 8, section 8.4.
[160] See section 9.4.1.
[161] See section 9.3.4.
[162] Ibid.
[163] See chapter 2, sections 2.3.2.
[164] As has been claimed by Landers (see J. Landers, 'A Unified Approach to Parent, Subsidiary and Affiliated Questions in Bankruptcy' (1975) 42 U. Chi. L. Rev. 589, 634).

parent company as a creditor, or in the case where the parent is insolvent, between two sets of creditors). Yet, the benefits of 'asset partitioning' are clearly at stake.[165] The prospect of equitable subordination of intra-group debts increases the risk of non-payment to the subordinated party and therefore induces the creditors of that company to investigate the other affiliates' creditworthiness.[166] Subordination may also deter intra-group lending. Ultimately, subordination serves a similar function as veil piercing as if the claims of a parent company are subordinated, the creditors of the insolvent affiliate will be satisfied from assets that would otherwise serve to partially satisfy the claims of the parent company.[167] It is therefore also redistributive and in the absence of clear justifications should be avoided.

9.5.2.2 The role of enterprise law

Nonetheless, it was also concluded that economic theories stop short in resolving opportunistic behaviour and misleading of creditors, and that especially in the group context greater scrutiny in regard to limited liability is required.[168] It was suggested that the role of enterprise law in this context should be confined to identifying the interests and the relevant circumstances pertaining to group operations that should be taken into account when considering exceptions to the basic limited liability rule.[169] In this respect, the need for clear rules is crucial, not only in terms of any benefits in efficiency,[170] but also to support fairness in terms of ensuring that all relevant parties and circumstances are considered.[171]

It was appreciated that certain creditors may be particularly vulnerable to opportunistic behaviour. Involuntary creditors may not be able to calculate the risk involved with the debtor's default, and other mal-adjusting creditors may be in a weak position to protect their interests.[172] However, in the context of insolvency when considering liability upon the parent company it is not the specific creditor or a group of creditors which is considered, but rather swelling the assets for the benefit of the unsecured creditors as a whole (to be distributed according to the priorities under the applicable law), as the widely accepted notion of collectivity requires.[173] Therefore, imposing liability on the parent company in the

---

[165] See chapter 2, section 2.3.2.3.

[166] Though the potential liability under the subordination regime of the parent is limited to the amount of the loan, whereas imposing general liability may amount to the entire subsidiary's debts (see R. Posner, 'The Legal Rights of Creditors of Affiliated Corporations: An Economic Approach' (1976) 43 U. Chi. L. Rev. 499, 517–19).

[167] Blumberg et al, *Blumberg on Corporate Groups* (n 31 chapter 1) s.87.01.

[168] See chapter 2, section 2.3.2.4.

[169] Ibid, section 2.3.3.

[170] See chapter 4, sections 4.2.2.1 and 4.2.2.2.

[171] Ibid, section 4.2.2.5.

[172] See chapter 2, section 2.3.2.4.

[173] See chapter 4, section 4.2.2.1. See also D. Prentice, 'Corporate Personality, Limited Liability and the Protection of Creditors', in R. Grantham and C. Rickett (eds.), *Corporate Personality in the 20th Century* (Hart Publishing, Oxford 1998) 99, 122.

course of insolvency should be confined to circumstances of harm caused to the creditors as a whole and the compensation to them as a group.

It was indicated earlier,[174] that the creditors as a whole are at risk at times near insolvency when controllers of the debtor might engage in excessive risks not accompanied with sufficient disclosure and safeguards taken to ensure harm is not caused to creditors as a result of such risks. Making group controllers liable for the harm caused as a result (or subordinating their debts to those of external creditors) will align their interests to those of creditors of the subsidiary in the vicinity of insolvency.[175] If the contribution sought is also only compensatory and proportionate to the harm caused then creditors will not have perverse incentives to enter insolvency, as insolvency will not offer them an advantage.[176] It is therefore desirable to have measures for compensating the insolvent entity's creditors for injury caused as a result of mismanagement by group controllers prior to insolvency.

The various doctrines available in certain legal regimes mentioned above[177] could potentially provide such measures. The problem is that the measures delineated above normally suffer from one of two deficiencies (and sometimes from both of them) in the context of enterprise groups. Either they are too vague and therefore may unduly defeat entity law. Or, the measure is clear and strict for the case of directors but fails to explicitly consider the case of enterprise groups and their specific circumstances (or it does not consider it at all), in other words it does not give sufficient room for enterprise principles.

A desirable approach to insolvencies within MEGs should encompass such measures but clarify the scenarios where liability (or deference of claims) may be imposed in the group context. In this respect it was suggested above, that the group reality should be taken into account both for the purpose of identifying the 'management' in charge of the harm caused, and in order to consider circumstances of mismanagement.[178] These notions can be incorporated within available methods for group liability and/or subordination. In other words, enterprise law should assist in clarifying the scenarios which require the application of such measures in the group context. Indeed, this was the role designated (by the principles underlying the proposed framework[179]) to enterprise law where limited liability is involved. Entity law should remain the main rule and thus, outside the pre-defined scenarios, the separateness among the entities should be maintained.

Consequently, in measures focusing on liability of directors,[180] the liability of a parent company which influenced the management should be considered as

---

[174] See chapter 2, section 2.3.2.4.

[175] See chapter 4, section 4.2.2.2.

[176] See R.J. Mokal, 'Contractarianism, Contractualism, and the Law of Corporate Insolvency' [2007] Singapore Journal of Legal Studies 51, 91.

[177] Sections 9.4.2–9.4.5.

[178] Sections 9.3.2 and 9.3.3.

[179] See chapter 2, section 2.5.

[180] Doctrines of directors' duties or the fraudulent and wrongful trading type of provisions and the corresponding remedies—contribution and/or subordination (see sections 9.4.2–9.4.3).

well.[181] Typically, if the group is 'integrated centralized' via the parent company, the parent company may be liable for the harmful mismanagement. It suffices that as a matter of general pattern the affiliates (or the particular subsidiary) did not have significant autonomy but rather were in fact centrally controlled by the parent company which directed its affairs.[182] There should not be a need to demonstrate intrusive day-to-day running of the subsidiary. Rather, an overall strategic control is what matters, as in terms of economic realities such control is sufficient to invoke the necessary influence that makes the parent responsible. To some extent this could also facilitate arguments on the facts. The decision could be based on objective criteria regarding the degree of control exercised over the subsidiary instead of fulfilling more stringent conditions showing sustained and pervasive interference in the management.[183]

The same sort of tools should also explicitly acknowledge various circumstances particular to the group context that can be regarded as mismanagement by the group controllers. As mentioned above, in particular, it should be assessed whether these circumstances transpired in the vicinity of insolvency at the expense of the insolvent subsidiary's creditors.[184] That is, such managerial actions, specific to group structures, as excessive undercapitalization, asset shifting, diversion of opportunities from the insolvent affiliate, artificial integration and misrepresentation of the insolvent affiliate as being supported by the group, where these actions meant that the insolvency of the subsidiary was inevitable and where no sufficient safeguards were taken to prevent harm caused to creditors of the now insolvent subsidiary as a result,[185] should be acknowledged as mismanagement by the groups controllers. These kinds of misconduct may typically occur in the various types of integrated MEGs[186] (yet not necessarily the 'integrated centralized' types[187]). An 'abused' entity may operate with much autonomy most of its lifetime (with separate management, local dealings with creditors, contracts governed by local laws and so forth), yet for example the whole role of this entity was to provide support to the group.

As aforementioned, in 'asset integration' scenarios, substantive consolidation should typically be the solution.[188] Yet, in case of opportunistic behaviour within the MEG, if there was no intermingling of assets and debts as a matter of fact, substantive consolidation would typically not be the adequate remedy for the

---

[181] Indeed, this is provided in certain legal regimes (see ibid).

[182] See section 9.3.2.

[183] As seems to be required, for example, under the 'shadow director' concept embodied in the English wrongful trading provision (see section 9.4.3 above).

[184] See section 9.3.3.

[185] Ibid.

[186] Prototypes I–K (insolvency of an affiliate within an integrated MEG), or prototypes A–F depicting collapsing integrated MEGs (see chapter 5, section 5.4).

[187] Prototype I (insolvency of an affiliate within a centralized integrated MEG), or the equivalent prototype A in a group collapse scenario (see ibid).

[188] See sections 9.2.3 and 9.3.4.

injured creditors.[189] Opportunistic behaviour should be the subject of liability, avoidance, or subordination. First, if the 'misbehaving' entity is solvent, substantive consolidation will drag it into the insolvency process, whereas this will not necessarily be the case if the other means are used. Furthermore, even if it is also insolvent, substantive consolidation will involve a total mix of assets and debts (i.e. a complete redistribution where certain creditors win and others lose on a rather arbitrary basis). The other remedies discussed above will be less 'dramatic' in this respect.

9.5.2.3 The available provisions for group liability considered in light of entity/enterprise law concerns

To some extent, the sorts of mechanisms discussed above for dealing with group liability are already included within the 'director oriented' type of measures (at least in those tools that impose the measures on groups as well, for example via the concept of 'shadow director').[190] Apparently, gross undercapitalization is a relevant circumstance within the English wrongful trading provision.[191] In contrast, where such circumstances arose the court was reluctant to impose liability.[192] Clearly, the relevant scenarios that would be subject to wrongful trading in the group context need to be further clarified. For example, misleading of the creditors to believe that the parent supports the subsidiary (and eventually abandoning it) should be a circumstance subject to the provision, as it defeats expectations of the creditors of the subsidiary as a whole.[193]

A similar approach may be taken in applying the other type of measures more directly aimed at tackling the corporate group cases (contribution order against related companies and equitable subordination).[194] The circumstances suggested here may be fairly easily incorporated within such measures as they are flexible and involve much discretion.[195] However, this is exactly why these solutions may be problematic. They may go too far in the remedies they offer, and thus improperly risk entity law. Such tools can accommodate the necessary linkage invoked here while maintaining a proper balance between entity and enterprise law if

---

[189] Cf. the approaches taken by legal regimes allowing for substantive consolidation also as a remedy for misconduct (section 9.4.4).

[190] See section 9.4.3.

[191] See the Cork Report (n 157 chapter 2), para. 1785, p. 400 which considered that '[t]rading when a business is heavily under-capitalised will often come within the concept of "wrongful trading".' See also D. Prentice, 'Corporate Personality, Limited Liability and the Protection of Creditors', in R. Grantham and C. Rickett (eds.), *Corporate Personality in the 20th Century* (Hart Publishing, Oxford 1998) 99, 117.

[192] See *Re Purpoint Ltd* [1991] BCC 121 (see also n 62).

[193] Cf. in *Re Augustus Barnett & Son Ltd* [1986] BCLC 170; but see *Contex Drouzhba v Wiseman* in the context of liability of directors (see n 65 and 119).

[194] See sections 9.4.4 and 9.4.5.

[195] Ibid.

the circumstances for their applicability are further clarified.[196] A contribution order, for example, may be grounded on general fairness considerations, as the court may impose liability if it is 'just and equitable' in the circumstances. It may take into account the conduct of the related company towards the creditors of the company in liquidation (or any other matters as the court thinks fit).[197] Potentially, such factors may attract liability in circumstances beyond misleading of creditors and excessive risk at the expense of creditors.

Equitable subordination is also discretionary and may be ordered in a wide variety of circumstances where equitable principles so require.[198] Crucially, allowing wide discretion and factors such as 'just and equitable' to be determinative may be particularly undesirable in terms of certainty and predictability as well as fairness (which should ensure that all parties are involved and their positions are taken into account).

Finally, the lifting the veil doctrine seems to suffer from both deficiencies— being too wide and too unclear as to its applicability to corporate groups. On the one hand, in most jurisdictions the doctrine is rarely used, and courts are reluctant to lift the corporate veil. There is normally no group consideration taken in this respect.[199] Entity law is thus strictly adhered too, and there is little room for enterprise law, even where this may be perceived necessary. On the other hand, where it can be used, the circumstances relevant for invoking the doctrine are unclear and unpredictable so potentially it may go too far in lifting the veil where this is unjustified.[200]

9.5.2.4 Summary

Linking tools for group liability confined to the circumstances suggested above can maintain a proper balance between entity and enterprise law. They may be applied in various variations. However, entity law takes the lead as limited liability is involved, and thus the separateness should be normally maintained. The prototypes suggested in this work assist in matching solutions to types of cases appreciating the diversified scene of insolvency within MEGs, yet the enterprise structure itself is not the cause for liability. Integration and control per se are insufficient grounds for liability; rather, it is the mismanagement that we aspire to defeat. Clear mechanisms will also clarify the likelihood of success of litigation ensuring the pursuance of compensation when the case suggests it is justifiable, and increasing the assets of the insolvent affiliate in the right cases.

---

[196] See I. Mevorach, 'Appropriate treatment of corporate groups in insolvency—a universal view' (2006) 8 EBOR, 179, 191–3.
[197] See section 9.4.4.
[198] See section 9.4.5.
[199] See chapter 2, section 2.4.3. But, see section 9.4.2 as to its utility under the US regime.
[200] See section 9.4.2.

9.6 Global Measures and the Universality–Territoriality Dilemma

As explained in chapter 2, the international nature of the MEG complicates its regulation.[201] Generally, litigation involving issues of liability in the context of MEGs brings forth conflict of laws problems and thus further difficulties in combating group opportunism. The home country court of a parent company, for example, may dismiss a claim brought within the jurisdiction for imposing liability on the parent for debts of a subsidiary, applying doctrines such as *forum non convenience*.[202] Or, it may refuse recognition of liability imposed by a foreign court (under the laws of the subsidiary's jurisdiction) upon the parent company, based on doctrines such as national public policy.[203] Issues of jurisdiction and recognition of foreign judgments may add a real barrier to promotion of insolvency goals on the global level especially as the concept of limited liability is at stake.[204] As explained in chapter 2, in many legal regimes there is strict adherence to entity law. The circumstances where it is possible to impose liability upon a parent company tend to be obscure. Courts in the home country of parent companies in deciding, for example, whether to recognize a decision of a foreign court imposing liability upon the parent company, may feel it necessary to carefully examine the basis of the decision and the extent to which it was grounded on a similar approach to that of the court's own jurisdiction to entity law. Attempts to lift the veil based on wider notions of enterprise law may encounter jurisdictional obstacles.[205]

As submitted earlier, a degree of harmonization in the area of international insolvency is desirable. It will facilitate control over multinationals in terms of issues pertaining to their default.[206] It was also concluded though that harmonization and modernization should allow flexibility to leave room for local innovations. Applying these concepts to the context here, the adoption of relevant linking tools to combat group opportunism should be encouraged, ensuring the promotion of insolvency goals on a global level. The specific legal methods may

---

[201] See chapter 2, section 2.2.2.

[202] See e.g. *In re Union Carbide Corporation* Gas Plant disaster at Bhopal India in December 1984 634 F. Supp 842 (SDNY 1986). See also K. Hofstetter, 'Multinational Enterprise Parent Liability: Efficient Legal Regimes in a world Market Environment' (1990) 15 North Carolina J. of Int'l Law and Comm. Reg. 299; P.T. Muchlinski, 'Corporations in International Litigation: Problems of Jurisdiction and the United Kingdom Asbestos Cases' (2001) 50 ICLQ I).

[203] See e.g. The *Deltec* litigation (Gordon, M.W., 'Argentine jurisprudence: The Parke Davis and Deltec cases' (1974) 6 Law. Am. 320; *Deltec Banking Corporatin v Compania Italo-Aregentina de Electricidad SA* 171 NYLJ 18 Col 1 3 Aril 1974). See also Blumberg et al, *Blumberg on Corporate Groups* (n 31 chapter 1) vol. 2, s. 76.04[A].

[204] For a comprehensive discussion of problems of foreign imposition of liability see Blumberg, *The Multinational Challenge* (n 3 chapter 1) ch. 8; Blumberg et al, *Blumberg on Corporate Groups* (n 31 chapter 1), ch. 154.

[205] See Blumberg et al, *Blumberg on Corporate Groups* (n 31 chapter 1) vol 5, s. 154.08.

[206] See chapter 3, section 3.3.3.

vary between jurisdictions. Importantly, this should be done with as much clarity as possible, preferably in legislation,[207] and should maintain a proper balance between entity and enterprise law, as suggested above.[208] Harmonization and modernization may be promoted in various ways, for instance by proposing relevant measures as best practices or guidelines to states in renovating or reforming their laws (i.e. by proposals 'from the top' by international initiatives).[209]

A degree of harmonization of insolvency will also diminish problems of private international law.[210] Regardless of where the case will take place similar solutions may be applied, and recognition and enforcement of judgments could be given more easily without invoking notions such as 'public policy'. Generally, full harmonization of substantive laws of insolvency is not within reach in the near future,[211] and the probability of achieving this in regard to issues of liability may be particularly doubtful.[212] As mentioned earlier, developments in the area of private international law in the context of insolvency are thus of considerable importance.[213]

In the area of bankruptcy jurisdiction, an increasingly prevailing concept is that of the debtor's COMI for determining the venue to handle the main insolvency proceedings.[214] The EC Regulation also provides a uniform choice of law rule according to which most matters of insolvency will be resolved under the laws of the forum in which proceedings are commenced.[215] UNCITRAL Model Law in providing a global framework for cross-border insolvency does not include harmonized conflict of laws rules for adoption by enacting states, thus leaving these matters to established rules and practices in national laws.[216] However, rules of private international law in legal systems typically designate the law of the bankruptcy forum as governing insolvency matters.[217] This would normally be subject to various exceptions.[218] Additionally, even where an international model provides that there should be automatic recognition of judgments of the bankruptcy forum, this is usually subject to the public policy exception.[219]

---

[207] See chapter 8, section 8.4.
[208] Section 9.5.2.
[209] See also chapter 3, section 3.4.1; and chapter 6, section 6.2.3.
[210] See chapter 3, section 3.4.2.
[211] Ibid.
[212] See e.g. the approach taken by UNCITRAL Working Group V (n 96 chapter 1) to this issue (currently refraining from adopting recommendations on group liability, apart from suggesting that substantive consolidation may be used to remedy group opportunism in certain circumstances (see section 9.4.4)).
[213] See chapter 3, section 3.4.2.
[214] Ibid.
[215] Ibid, section 3.4.2.2. See also chapter 6, section 6.2.1.6.3.
[216] See chapter 3, section 3.4.2.3; and chapter 6, section 6.2.1.6.3. See also UNCITRAL Legislative Guide (n 137 chapter 3), Part Two, Ch. I, para. 80.
[217] Ibid.
[218] Ibid.
[219] See chapter 3, section 3.4.2.

Issues of MEG opportunism in the context of insolvency may be resolved under the above frameworks, in the cases where the insolvency is of a single debtor. That is, in prototypes I–M (the insolvency of a single affiliate within an integrated or a non-integrated MEG)[220] —where the parent company (or another related company in issue) is solvent and not consolidated in any way with the insolvent affiliate in issue. The COMI forum of the insolvent affiliate may handle the proceedings and apply its laws to resolve issues of group opportunism in the context of insolvency.

The EC Regulation specifically includes avoidance rules as matters to be determined under the laws of the forum.[221] However, it also subjects this to an exception. Thus, the law of the forum will not apply where the person who benefited from a legal act detrimental to all the creditors provides proof that: (i) the act in question is subject to the law of a member state other than that of the state of the opening of proceedings; and (ii) that law does not allow any means of challenging that act in the relevant case.[222] Under the UNCITRAL Model Law[223] the insolvency representative may seek remedies under the laws of the recognizing state, which will then apply its own private international law rules to determine the applicable law.[224]

Yet, the issue of applicable law in regard to voidable transactions is subject to much uncertainty and incoherence in legal regimes. There are various alternative rules. These are summarized in the ALI Transnational Insolvency Project—International Statement of United States Bankruptcy law.[225] Five alternatives are delineated as possible choice of law rules for avoidance transactions. The first suggests that a transaction will be avoided only if it is avoidable under home country law. The second suggests that it will be avoided only if it is avoidable under the law of the territory where the key event or events took place (the *situs* law). The third provides that a transaction can be avoided only if it is avoidable under both home country and the law of the territory (the *situs* law). The fourth provides that the transaction can be avoided if it is avoidable under either home country or the law of the territory (*situs* law), and the fifth option is that it can be avoided if it is avoidable under the law chosen by applying case specific choice of law rules based on the contacts and state interests presented in each case.[226]

---

[220] See chapter 5, section 5.4.

[221] See Article 4(2)(m) of the EC Regulation (n 173 chapter 3).

[222] See Article 13 of the EC Regulation (ibid). See also Fletcher, *Insolvency* (n 3 chapter 3), 401–2.

[223] Note 212 chapter 3.

[224] See Fletcher, *Insolvency* (n 3 chapter 3), 471.

[225] On the ALI project see chapter 3, section 3.4.2.4.

[226] See e.g. adoption of the fifth option in the case of *Maxwell* (*Maxwell Communication Corp.*, 170 BR 800 (Bankr SDNY 1994), aff'd, 186 Bankr. 807 (SDNY 1995) (see also Blumberg et al, *Blumberg on Corporate Groups* (n 31 chapter 1), s. 86.10); *In re Midland Euro Exch.*, 347 BR 708, 710–711 (Bankr CD Cal 2006).

The EC rule (and exception to the rule) explained above resolves (to an extent) the potential application of a choice of law rule which requires the cumulative application of the rules of more than one system in order to decide whether the ransaction is valid. As has been observed elsewhere, this may result in much difficulty in bringing about the avoidance of prior transactions.[227] The effect of the EC Regulation rule is that under most circumstances only a single avoidance rule—that of the law of the forum—will apply. Only in the specific situation covered by the exception,[228] the other party to the transaction with the debtor can defend the transaction showing that it is valid and unimpeachable according to the law by which it is properly governed (provided that it is a law of a member state).[229] Nonetheless, this exception provided in the EC Regulation to the basic choice of law rule may still put obstacles in the way of achieving fairness and combating voidable transactions, as the effect may be that at least in some scenarios the transaction will escape avoidance unless it would be avoidable under the laws of both the home country and the country whose laws otherwise govern the transaction.[230]

It was mentioned earlier that generally, in terms of promoting the idea of uniformity and harmonization for parties involved in cross-border insolvency, exceptions to the concept of single forum–single law should be kept to the minimum.[231] It was also concluded in chapter 3 that the universalist concept of single law and forum is commendable in terms of predictability.[232] In regard to avoidance transactions, it has been persuasively argued elsewhere, that the best choice of law rule is a universalist one, according to which the home country of the debtor's bankruptcy would apply its laws.[233] Territorialism does not offer a coherent choice of law rule for avoidance provisions, as it generally seeks to control only the local assets. It thus admits that the problem of strategic removal of assets from the debtor and its home country is more severe under territorialism (compared with universalism).[234] Applying the home country law to control voidable transactions is a choice of law rule that can be predictable and transparent.[235] The other

---

[227] See Fletcher, *Insolvency* (n 3 chapter 3), 401–2.

[228] Article 13 of the EC Regulation (n 173 chapter 3).

[229] See Fletcher, *Insolvency* (n 3 chapter 3) 402.

[230] See J.L. Westbrook, 'Choice of Avoidance Law in Global Insolvencies" (1991) 17 Brook. J. Int'l L. 499, 519 (FN 82); L.J. Westbrook, 'Avoidance of Pre-Bankruptcy Transactions in Multinational Bankruptcy Cases' (2007) 42 Tex. Int'l L.J. 899, 903 (FN 25).

[231] See chapter 6, section 6.2.1.8.

[232] See chapter 3, sections 3.3.2.1 and 3.3.3.

[233] See J.L. Westbrook, 'Choice of Avoidance Law in Global Insolvencies' (1991) 17 Brook. J. Int'l L. 499, 500; L.J. Westbrook, 'Avoidance of Pre-Bankruptcy Transactions in Multinational Bankruptcy Cases' (2007) 42 Tex. Int'l L.J. 899.

[234] Although it suggests that return of fleeing assets could be ensured by way of treaties among countries (see L.M. LoPucki, 'Cooperation in International Bankruptcy: A Post-Universalist Approach' (1999) 84 Cornell L. Rev. 696, 758). See also J.L. Westbrook, 'Avoidance of Pre-Bankruptcy Transactions in Multinational Bankruptcy Cases' (2007) 42 Tex. Int'l L.J. 899, 901.

[235] J.L. Westbrook, 'Choice of Avoidance Law in Global Insolvencies' (1991) 17 Brook. J. Int'l L. 499, 530; J.L. Westbrook, 'Avoidance of Pre-Bankruptcy Transactions in Multinational

option relying on the territory in which the transaction occurred is manipulable and unpredictable.[236] Otherwise applying case specific choice of law rules based on the contacts and state interests presented in each case also raises problems of predictability.[237] In addition, a home country rule accords with the fact that the purpose of avoiding powers in the course of insolvency is to redistribute the debtor's assets according to a set of priority rules which are also to be determined by the home country court and laws.[238]

Contribution orders imposing liability on related companies or subordination of debts owed to related companies should also be a matter to be determined by the courts and under the laws of the home country which will distribute the contribution funds among the creditors under its system of priorities. These issues too are matters of insolvency and thus should be handled by the insolvency forum under its laws. In the case of the subsidiary's single insolvency this will be the home country of the subsidiary.

Issues of group opportunism may alternatively arise within MEG insolvency, e.g. where the relevant parties to an avoidable transaction are under insolvency. If they are also integrated it was suggested earlier to apply a sort of consolidation, either procedural or substantive depending on the degree and type of integration.[239] In these scenarios, in case the MEG was integrated and centralized it was suggested that a 'group home country' (the operational head office representing a mutual COMI for all affiliates) will adjudicate the case.[240] Consequently, in these cases, issues of group opportunism would be determined by the 'group jurisdiction' under its laws. This will greatly facilitate combating abuse and manipulation, and achieving fairness in distribution, as it will overcome potential problems of recognition of the judgment of the insolvency court. This advantage of consolidation in a particular jurisdiction is also envisaged by the ALI Principles.[241] The consolidation encouraged by the ALI Principles is supposed to enable inter alia a reconciliation of past manipulation by the parent company of its subsidiary's affairs.[242]

Yet, in cases where there was decentralization (i.e. significant local autonomy of the subsidiaries) it was suggested earlier that the identified 'group home country' (the head office of the group from where the group was coordinated) will

Bankruptcy Cases' (2007) 42 Tex. Int'l L.J. 899, 902. See also UNCITRAL Legislative Guide (n 137 chapter 3), Part two, Ch. I, Recommendation 31(g) (proposing that the insolvency law of the state in which insolvency proceedings are commencened may apply to avoidance of certain transactions that could be prejudicial to certain parties).

[236] J.L. Westbrook, 'Avoidance of Pre-Bankruptcy Transactions in Multinational Bankruptcy Cases' (2007) 42 Tex. Int'l L.J. 899, 902.

[237] Ibid, 902–3.

[238] Ibid, 903–4.

[239] See chapter 6.

[240] Ibid, section 6.2.1.6–6.2.1.10.

[241] See n 243 chapter 3. On the ALI Principles see chapter 3, section 3.4.2.4. On the Principles regarding corporate groups see in chapter 6, sections 6.2.1.5–6.2.1.6.

[242] See Flecther, *Insolvency* (n 3 chapter 3), 311–12.

supervise the operation while local proceedings will be opened for the autonomous subsidiary, and local laws will apply.[243] In addition, where a mutual home
country cannot be identified parallel proceedings may take place with maximum
cooperation among the various jurisdictions.[244] Such an approach (as suggested)
maintains a proper balance between universalism and territorialism concerns in
the context of MEGs.[245] The same approach is followed in regard to the issues
considered here. Thus, in the scenarios where full centralization is not applied,
the subsidiary's home country will determine issues of group opportunism (in
regard to harm caused to the subsidiary's stakeholders). Thus, we end up with
balanced linking tools (in terms of universality and territoriality) in the group
context. And still, the supervision of the main group proceedings or the cooperation between the courts (as suggested earlier) can enhance the resolutions of any
potential conflicts between subsidiaries and parent's jurisdictions.

9.7 Conclusion

Applying the 'goal-driven adaptive balanced entity–enterprise, territoriality–
universality approach' supports the notion that certain 'linking tools' are justifiable in the course of insolvency within MEGs for combating group opportunism
and dealing with intra-group transactions.

The MEG and the interrelations among its members should be recognized
for the purpose of ensuring effective insolvency regulation against vulnerable
transactions. In certain cases giving effect to the interrelations among group
members will have the effect of upholding an intra-group transaction, in others
it will ensure that a transaction is reversed for the benefit of the general body of
creditors. Promoting clarity in the treatment of vulnerable intra-group transactions in legal regimes is crucial for ensuring efficiency and fairness of insolvency
processes no matter where proceedings are going to take place and under which
laws. The threat to entity law on the other hand is minimal.

Where opportunism in the group context cannot be attached to a particular
transaction, which can be attacked with reasonable effort, other measures are
required in order to achieve fairness in distribution. Here, linking between the
entities involved is needed in order to impose liability, and thus interference with
entity law is at its peak. Therefore, such linking mechanisms should be applied in
strict conditions, essentially directed at tackling excessive risk taking in the vicinity of insolvency and misleading of creditors. Specifically, the circumstances in
which the measures are applicable should encompass the group scenario. Drawing
upon enterprise law to assist in identifying such relevant scenarios, reference was

---

[243] See chapter 6, sections 6.2.1.8–6.2.1.9.
[244] Ibid, section 6.2.1.10.
[245] Ibid, sections 6.2.1.7–6.2.1.10.

made to circumstances of excessive undercapitalization, asset shifting, diversion of opportunities from the insolvent affiliate, artificial integration and misrepresentation of the insolvent affiliate (as being supported by the group) as sufficient grounds for imposing liability in the group context, where these actions meant that the insolvency of the subsidiary was inevitable and where there were no sufficient safeguards taken to prevent harm caused to creditors.

Promoting the adoption of such tools with a degree of standardization will ensure availability of relevant mechanisms and certainty for parties involved with cross-border insolvencies. In this regard, further recommendations by international bodies in regard to measures for imposing liability in the context of insolvency (in particular in regard to groups) could promote the relevant insolvency goals on a universal basis.[246]

Additionally, frameworks providing uniformity of jurisdiction and choice of law rules regarding issues of group opportunism in the context of insolvency enhance predictability as well as avoid evasion of the rules. As a result, any problems of group opportunism can be better controlled on a global level and fairness to the general body of creditors of the relevant debtor ensured. In the context of insolvency of a number of MEG members a framework for handling such processes was suggested earlier, essentially invoking joint administration of integrated MEG insolvencies and providing various measures accommodating concerns of territorialism. The concentration or coordination of such processes also facilitates resolution of potential problems of group opportunism. Ultimately, the measures suggested here can promote insolvency goals while retaining an adequate balance between universalism and territorialism, entity and enterprise law.

---

[246] UNCITRAL Working Group V (n 96 chapter 1), though, is currently not suggesting additional measures to tackle misconduct (apart from specific circumstances where substantive consolidation may be applied, the elaboration on avoidance provisions and a general reference to the Legislative Guide in regard to subordination without specifying circumstances where subordination may be applied in the enterprise group case). Currently, it generally directs parties in such circumstances to utilize available measures in legal regimes such as 'lifting the veil' doctrines and wrongful trading. Yet, it does not provide further recommendations encouraging legal systems to adopt such mechanisms nor the circumstances and conditions where such remedies should be invoked in the context of groups (see sections 9.4.1, 9.4.4. and 9.4.5).

Summary and Conclusion

Evidently, a collapse of a multinational enterprise group is often an event of great difficulty and complexity. Numerous stakeholders are involved in multiple locations in the world, loss of money is at stake as well as potential loss of jobs and other destructive effects. Complex issues arise even where one affiliate of the multinational group is facing insolvency. Legal systems are then called forth to facilitate and expedite handling of the insolvency event to the benefit of those concerned and deal with the intricate issues arising. However, thus far legal regimes have refrained from explicitly tackling the problem. Nevertheless, it seems that the 'winds of change' are blowing these days and the phenomenon and its implications are being considered by various international bodies. It is therefore of clear import to provide a comprehensive account of the problem, the legal theories that support it and the practical suggestions that would apply to it.

It was the purpose of this work to provide such an account so that an appropriate approach for handling insolvencies within MEGs (both in building on tools and mechanisms already available and in setting the ground for future reform) will be defined. To that end, the work invoked the 'goal-driven adaptive balanced entity–enterprise, territoriality–universality' framework. In essence, this framework attempts to cover all relevant aspects of the law and theory which impinge on the complex case of MEG insolvency. Thus, it is argued in the work that when assessing insolvency within MEGs a special consideration should be given to its group aspect balancing entity–enterprise conflicts. Similarly, a special consideration should be given to its multinational aspect balancing universality–territoriality conflicts. Furthermore, it is evident that many variations of MEGs in insolvency exist. Consequently, the suggested framework must adapt to the specific case at hand. This is done here by providing a nomenclature for classifying MEGs in insolvency. Thus, the framework can adapt to the specific case by identifying which prototypical scenario best describes the current case. Ultimately, the framework is conjured for handling insolvencies and thus it is put to the test in the context of what insolvency law strives to achieve, i.e. wealth maximization, promotion of rescues in proper circumstances, fairness in distribution, procedural fairness and generally certainty and predictability of the system.

In the course of the application of this framework to the questions at hand it was revealed that certain insolvency measures (primarily targeted at linking between the entities comprising the MEG) can be beneficial (and sometimes critical) for the treatment of MEG insolvencies. 'Beneficial' in this respect not only implies positive outcomes in terms of the goals of insolvency law but also with regard to the balance between entity–enterprise concepts and universality–territoriality concepts. Indeed, these balances were used in shaping the appropriate linking tools.

Generally, it was argued that global group-wide solutions in the course of MEG insolvencies should first and foremost be applied to integrated MEGs (i.e. those groups that operated in the ordinary course of business with a significant degree of interdependence or as single global business) but not to non-integrated MEGs or particular entities non-integrated with the rest of the MEG (namely entities which conducted a truly separate businesses). Accordingly, unification in the course of insolvency (if several affiliates of such an enterprise, collapse) will most likely result in considerable gains in terms of wealth maximization, cost reduction and promotion of reorganizations. If integration was only in 'business terms' then procedural consolidation suffices (i.e. the merger of the process but not of the entities). This in turn ensures 'entity law' is only minimally interfered with, and pre-insolvency entitlements are respected. Nevertheless, a degree of 'group perspective' was suggested when considering solutions for the enterprise (in the course of devising reorganizations in relation to MEG members or negotiating sale of MEG members' assets) so that courses of action beneficial to the majority of stakeholders across the group can be pursued while ensuring safeguards to opposing entities.

For MEGs that were integrated in terms of their substance (which were termed in the book 'asset integrated') more intrusive solutions are required (and justified). In cases where intermingling of assets and debts of the entities comprising the MEG occurred in the normal course of business, fairness in distribution as well as wealth maximization suggests that the entities should (to some extent) be merged in their insolvencies by pooling assets and debts together. This is, however, in direct interference with entity law (as the 'partitioning of assets' is not respected) and should therefore be applied only where there was in fact a façade of partitioning in the ordinary course of business in terms of economic reality (or otherwise when the relevant creditors consent). Reliance of creditors on the group as a whole (rather than the particular entity) or mere convenience in handling the proceedings should therefore not suffice as sole bases for a pooling order. Indeed, if pooling is ordered in such circumstances it will also result in unjustified redistribution of creditors' rights, were some creditors may gain advantage at the expense of others. This will contravene fairness in distribution and will also be counter-productive to efficiency.

On the global level, procedural and even more so substantive consolidation rely on close cooperation among the jurisdictions in which the various affiliates were operating and potentially will work most effectively if all proceedings are concentrated in a single venue. Yet, the more the process would be centralized, the more territoriality may be interfered with. Here too, the adaptive element of the approach is called upon in order to maintain a proper balance between universalism and territorialism. Usually, for the centralized MEGs (which were centrally controlled by the group head office in the normal course of business) a concentrated solution in the course of the global insolvency is suggested. In contrast, for the more decentralized patterns (where affiliates had significant local autonomy) an analogous solution would suggest local proceedings for the affiliates supervised by the principle group process. Other solutions are required for situations where concentration or coordination/supervision is not feasible. It was also found that determining on the global measure should also take account of the purpose of the process (whether reorganization or piecemeal liquidation is sought) and the degree of consolidation required. To the extent that a solution may distort the economic reality and transfer a case to a foreign jurisdiction (due to 'group considerations') even though the affiliate had separate autonomous territorial presence as an entity, measures should be taken to ensure rights of creditors vis-à-vis the local entity are protected (e.g., applying local protections of vulnerable creditors although the case is handled in a foreign forum).

It was apparent that global consolidation of the group process also enables a global perspective over the entire business (the integrated group as a whole), considering all relevant affected parties. It also ensures a more inclusive process where creditors of related companies can be given a stage on which they may present their views and can be taken into account. In other words, using global consolidation can help a wide array of insolvency goals to be achieved. However, this requires greater responsibility and expertise on the part of those handling the process (e.g., the court or the insolvency representative) who need to be able to consider the benefit for a global group while maintaining objectiveness as to the interests of its parts (in case only procedural consolidation is applied). Thus, it became apparent that measures for ensuring due process and avoidance of conflict of interests and adequate representation are required.

It was also suggested in the book that 'the law of MEG insolvencies' should attempt maximum certainty and predictability so to enhance efficiency and support fairness. To the extent parties can predict insolvency outcomes and do rely on them, it was argued that the enterprise/universalist concepts suggested (mitigated by entity/territoriality concerns) enhance predictability and consistency of outcomes. This is mainly because they rely on economic realities (much like all relevant stakeholders).

In this respect, this work also attempted to tackle what has been argued to be the 'Achilles' heel' of universalism. That is, the arguable indeterminacy of the home country rule, in particular in its application to corporate groups.[1] It was suggested, here, that a predictable rule that will enable concentration or

---

[1] See L.M. LoPucki, 'Cooperation in International Bankruptcy: A Post-Universalist Approach' (1999) 84 Cornell L. Rev. 696, 716–25; L.M. LoPucki, 'Universalism Unravels' (2005) 79 Am. Bankr. L.J. 143, 152–8 (as mentioned in chapter 3, sections 3.3.2.1–3.3.2.2).

coordination of a group process and refrain from diverting group cases to insolvency 'havens' can be devised. Essentially, it is suggested that an integrated MEG insolvency can be centralized or coordinated from a single location—predominantly in the operational head office of the group (the integrated part thereof). It was concluded that such a 'standard venue' test has a range of benefits. Yet, its limitations were also revealed. To an extent these could be overcome by applying contractualism concepts. That is, in cases of competition between various possible proper venues (in those cases where it is difficult to point to a single home country) parties' contracts can assist in indentifying the forum to govern the case. Alternatively, parties' agreements can assist in promoting cooperation in case where concurrent proceedings are inevitable and a global coordination is pursued among several full territorial proceedings.

Issues of group liability were particularly problematic when examined in light of the framework suggested. Although essential as part of a system which strives to achieve fairness in distribution, some of the insolvency measures for protecting creditors from group opportunism are in direct interference with limited liability. Here too, enterprise law was applied carefully—only in order to delineate exceptions to the basic rule of limited liability so that opportunism in the context of insolvency can be combated while the balance between entity law and enterprise law is still maintained. It became clear that in terms of entity law it is preferable to apply less intrusive measures such as avoiding particular vulnerable intra-group transactions. It was also acknowledged, though, that such measures may not provide complete solutions to problems of opportunism, and thus other remedies to tackle group responsibility in the context of insolvency were suggested. Here too, global measures were required so as to harmonize conflict of law in order to minimize obstacles put on the ability to control such behaviour.

To an extent it was shown that the various linking methods could be applied in cases of MEGs based on various available frameworks on national and international levels. Nevertheless, there is quite a lot of room for further reform, renovation and modernization of laws in this area. Measures such as procedural consolidation, substantive consolidation or contribution orders are not always available in legal regimes, and to the extent that they are, there is often a significant degree of obscurity as to their application, with the result that predictability as well as fairness are considerably undermined. For example, it is not entirely clear in which circumstances substantive consolidation (where it is available in the legal regime) can be applied, in particular to what extent reliance by creditors will be a sufficient factor (which will be detrimental to fairness and efficiency according to the analysis in this work). On the cross-border insolvency front, although current frameworks may be utilized to accommodate the MEG case, they would be considerably improved if made to explicitly deal with these scenarios. This could be achieved, for example, by explicitly providing that insolvency proceedings against members of 'centralized integrated' MEGs would be concentrated in a single jurisdiction, using the 'operational headquarters' as the key factor in identifying this forum. Such clarification of the jurisdictional rule can reduce jurisdictional quarrels, forum shopping and ensure concentration of the process in the proper circumstances which will in turn enhance fairness and be conducive to wealth maximization.

Some opposition for such an approach which aims to 'link' between MEG entities in the course of insolvency (and possible reform along its lines) is nonetheless anticipated, first and foremost as it confronts the long-established company law fundamental—the respect of the corporate form. Any attempt at disturbing this notion may be unwelcome, especially where it is proposed from the insolvency angle. However, a recurring theme of this work (which is incorporated in the suggested framework) was that 'linking tools' in the course of insolvency must bear in mind entity law. Crucially, this book proposes various measures, not all of which pose a critical threat to entity law (e.g., procedural consolidation and centralization).

To the extent that limited liability is at stake, the measures aim to tackle only those clear occasions were limited liability is 'annulled', either it was abused at the expense of creditors, or it was not kept at all so there was no segregation of assets and liabilities. In addition, the proposed linking tools are also such that are crucial for pursuing insolvency goals, and do not unnecessarily extend beyond this area. In regard to group liability (perhaps the most contentious aspect of group insolvency law), the measures proposed are confined to orders given in the course of insolvency to compensate for harm caused to creditors at times were the interests of creditors should be taken into account. Liability is extended to other entities in this respect only to the extent that in terms of economic reality they were the perpetrators of the mismanagement. In terms of company law, introducing group liability in insolvency will mean that in the vicinity of a subsidiary's insolvency (at times where it is clear that insolvency of the subsidiary is inevitable) its controllers should consider the interests of the subsidiary's creditors. In some jurisdictions a general concept to this extent is already in place (though as elaborated in chapter 9, they often require further clarification).

Considering the attempt to combat group opportunism, the argument may take another form, and provide that the measures proposed are superfluous as MEGs will normally come to the rescue of a distressed subsidiary in any case.[2] Veritably, in cases where subsidiaries were not abandoned and otherwise there was no issue of opportunism, issues of group liability will not arise in the course of insolvency. The international insolvency system, however, should have means to ensure fairness in distribution is kept in circumstances where such problems do occur. Previous cases, both of national and international groups, where subsidiaries entered insolvency and were no longer supported by the group were mentioned in chapter 9 of the book. It was also mentioned that issues of wrongful trading tend to arise inter alia in regard to shadow directors. Additionally, even where the

---

[2] See Muchlinksi, *Multinational Enterprises* (n 10 chapter 1) 334 (referring to empirical evidence suggesting that multinational enterprises are unlikely to allow their subsidiaries to go bankrupt).

group controllers supported their subsidiaries the group as a whole might eventually collapse, and it might then be revealed, for example, that the group strategy in the course of business prior to insolvency resulted in extensive shift of assets from a particular subsidiary in a way that its insolvency was inevitable and the interests of its creditors were not kept. Consequently, measures for compensation of the subsidiaries' creditors may be justified even though the controlling entity is also under insolvency.

On the global measures front some argue that a home country rule for international bankruptcies would drive cases away from less developing countries to industrial countries, as the latter normally host multinational debtors' head offices.[3] Similarly, it could be argued that promoting a jurisdictional rule which directs cases of MEG insolvencies to a 'group home country' is also biased against developing countries (as the group headquarters tend to be in industrial countries). There is an element of truth in this argument. This can be perceived as an integral part of territorialism concerns which seek to ensure state sovereignty over local assets. Yet, another theme of this work was to bear in mind territorialism concerns when devising tools for MEG insolvencies. In cases of significant autonomy of subsidiaries in the local jurisdictions it was proposed to allow the opening of territorial proceedings against the subsidiary while maintaining a linkage with the proceedings of other related companies and where possible supervise the entire process from the group home country. In cases of non-integrated groups it was suggested that the typical rule should be that no unification is sought. It is not the case then that all MEG affiliates' proceedings are shifted to the group head office jurisdiction. The dynamics and changes in world commerce and market forces should also be kept in mind when presenting arguments based on differences between developing and industrial countries in terms of hosting multinational's centres. The traditional division between developing and developed countries may be in any case blurred at some point in terms of nationality of leading enterprises. A trend towards 'real globalization' has been identified, under which there will be real competition on Western domestic markets and new global players will arise from emerging countries. There is already considerable growth of worldwide exports and worldwide foreign direct investment which marks the beginning of such 'real globalization'.[4]

A real concern can be raised in regard to the competency of courts to supervise complex insolvency proceedings involving a host of affiliates from different jurisdictions. The book has presented arguments in favour of global group-wide responsibility to be taken by courts and representatives and the need to refrain from a narrow national perspective. It was mentioned that the issues that may arise in this context will require considerable expertise. This is perhaps one of the

---

[3] See e.g. F. Tung, 'Skepticism about Universalism: International Bankruptcy and International Relations' (2 April 2002), Berkeley Program in Law & Economics, Working Paper Series, Paper 43. (Available at: http://repositories.cdlib.org/blewp/43/), 29, FN 93.

[4] See R. Berger, 'Future through proactive change', presentation delivered at Eighth Annual INTL Insolvency Institute (III) conference, Berlin, 9 June 2008 (on file with author).

main challenges for the future—promoting the international cooperative spirit among courts and insolvency representatives handling international insolvencies in general. Schemes taken by global organizations such as UNCITRAL for enhancing cooperative concepts among the judiciary[5] no doubt go in this direction and promote expertise and global 'responsibility' in cases of cross-border insolvency.

In conclusion, appreciating the international nature of many enterprises (which will commonly take the form of a host of affiliates operating in the various jurisdictions), insolvency laws should strive to pursue their inherent goals on a global level. This means that in reforming or renovating national laws the international case should be borne in mind and addressed, as well as the possibility that it will occur in regard to enterprises that were comprised of separate legal entities. It is also critical to consider 'international standards' in this respect so that measures taken locally may be compatible (at least to an extent) with approaches elsewhere. Consequently, the establishment of a coherent and consistent system of law for insolvency of multinationals will be promoted. This merits the importance of devising best practices and standards on the international level as well as more binding measures for harmonization (on regional or international level) such as a European directive. Once again the call is for comprehensive consideration of MEG insolvencies on those levels. Additionally, in reforming or construing cross-border insolvency frameworks, the enterprise group insolvency should be given adequate treatment

The current efforts of UNCITRAL Working Group V,[6] addressing the problems of enterprise groups are therefore much welcomed. It remains to be unveiled what will be the ultimate product of the group. Once this is achieved, it will then be a crucial matter to promote the adoption of consensual standards in this area within legal systems in as much as possible a coherent way. On the European front, the European Commission is required to report on the EC Regulation[7] by 1 June 2012 and, if necessary, to produce proposals for its adaptation. Within this process it is hoped that the matter of corporate groups will be addressed.

It is hoped that this book will contribute both to future efforts in reforming or renovating laws in this area and to the general debate and practice of the 'law of corporate groups' and its intersection with the law of international insolvency.

---

[5] See n 165 chapter 3.　　　[6] N 96 chapter 1.　　　[7] N 173 chapter 3.

Bibliography

Adler, B.E., 'Financial and Political Theories of American Corporate Bankruptcy' (1993) 45 Stan. L. Rev. 311

Aghion, P., Hart O., and Moore, J., 'The Economics of Bankruptcy Reform' (1992) 8 L. Econ. & Org. 523

Allen J., and Cooper, N., 'Law in Transition Online, EBRD Insolvency Office Holder Principles' 2007

Alwang, K.S., 'Note, Steering the most appropriate course between admiralty and Insolvency: Why an International Insolvency Treaty should recognize the Primacy of Admiralty Law over Maritime Assets' (1996) 64 Fordham L. Rev. 2613

American Law Institute, 'Principles of Cooperation Among the NAFTA Countries Transnational Insolvency' (excerpt from *Transnational Insolvency: Cooperation among the NAFTA Countries* [2003] is available at: http://www.ali.org/doc/InsolvencyPrinciples.pdf)

American Law Institute, Transnational Insolvency: Cooperation Among the NAFTA Countries, Principles of Cooperation Among the NAFTA Countries, Guidelines Applicable to Court-to-Court Communication in Cross-Border Cases (2003)

American National Bankruptcy Review Commission, Bankruptcy: The Next Twenty Years [1997]

Anderson, H., 'Creditors' Rights of Recovery: Economic Theory, Corporate Jurisprudence and the Role of Fairness' (2006) 30 Melb. U. L. Rev. 1

Anderson, K., 'The Cross-Border Insolvency Paradigm: A Defense of the Modified Universal Approach Considering the Japanese Experience' (2000) 21 U. Pa. J. Int'l Econ. L. 679

Anderson, M., *European Economic Interest Groupings* (Butterworths, London 1990)

Antunes, J. E., *Liability of Corporate Groups—Autonomy and Control in Parent-Subsidiary Relationships in U.S., EU and German Law. An International and Comparative Law* (Kluwer, Deventer 1994)

Armour, J., 'The Law and Economics of Corporate Insolvency: A Review' [2001] ESRC Centre for Business Research, University of Cambridge, Working Paper No. 197

Asian Development Bank, 'Good Practice Standards for an Insolvency Regime', in Law and Policy Development at the Asian Development Bank, April 2000

Austin, R.P., 'Corporate Groups', in R. Grantham and C. Rickett (eds.), *Corporate Personality in the 20th Century* (Hart Publishing, Oxford 1998) 71

Australian Law Reform Commission Report No. 45 General Insolvency Inquiry, AGPS, Canberra, 1988

Avi-Yonah, R.S., 'National Regulation of Multinational/enterprises: An Essay on Comity, Extraterritoriality, and Harmonization' (2003) 42 Colum. J. Transnat'l L. 5

Baird D.G., 'The Uneasy Case for Corporate Reorganizations' (1986) 15 Journal of Legal Studies 127

Baird, D.G., 'A World Without Bankruptcy' (1987) 50 Law and Contemporary Problems, 173

Baird, D.G., 'Loss Distribution, Forum Shopping and Bankruptcy: A Reply to Warren' (1987) 54 U. Chi. L. Rev. 815

Baird, D.G., 'Bankruptcy's Uncontested Axioms' (1998) 108 Yale Law Journal, 573

Baird, D.G., 'Substantive Consolidation Today' (2006) 47 Bost. Col. L. Rev. 5

Baird D.G., and Jackson, T., 'Corporate Reorganization and the Treatment of Diverse Ownership Interests: A Comment on Adequate Protection of Secured Creditors' (1984) 51 U. Chi. L. Rev. 97

Baird, D.G., and Rasmussen, R. K., 'The Four (or Five) Easy Lessons from Enron' (2002) 55 Vand. L. Rev. 1787

Balz, M., 'The European Union Convention on Insolvency Proceedings' (1996) 70 Am. Bankrp. L.J. 485

Baxter, S., and Dethmers, F., 'Collective Dominance Under EC Merger Control—After Airtours and the Introduction of Unilateral Effects is there still a Future for Collective Dominance?' (2006) 27(3) ECLR 148

Bebchuck, L.A., 'A New Approach to Corporate Reorganizations' (1988) 101 Harv. L. Rev. 775

Bebchuk, L.A., and Guzman, A.T., 'An Economic Analysis of Transnational Bankruptcies' (1999) 42 J. L. & Econ. 775

Bell, A., *Forum Shopping and Venue in Transnational Litigation* (Oxford University Press, Oxford 2003)

Berends, A.J., 'The UNCITRAL Model Law on Cross-Border Insolvency: A Comprehensive Overview' (1998) 6 Tul. J. Int'l & Comp. L. 309

Berger, R., 'Future Through Proactive Change', presentation delivered at Eighth Annual INTL Insolvency Institute (III) conference, Berlin, 9 June 2008

Berle Jr, A.A., 'The Theory of Enterprise Entity' (1947) 47 Colum. L. Rev. 343

Bicker, Eike, T., 'Creditor Protection in the Corporate Group' (University of Freiburg—Faculty of Law, Working Papers Series, July 2006)

Biery, E.H., et al., 'A Look at Transnational Insolvencies and Chapter 15 of the Bankruptcy Abuse Prevention and Consumer Protection Act of 2005' (2005) 1 Bost. Col. L. Rev. 23

Bjork, J.E., 'Notes & Comments, Seeking Predictability in Bankruptcy: an Alternative to Judicial Recharacterization in Structured Financing' (1998) 14 Bankr. Dev. J. 119

Black J., and Dunning J.H. (eds.), *International Capital Movements* (Macmillan, London 1982)

Block-Lieb, S., and Halliday, T., 'Harmonization and Modernization in UNCITRAL Legislative Guide on Insolvency Law' (2007) 42 Tex. Int'l L.J. 475

Block-Lieb, S., and Halliday, T., 'Incrementalisms in Global Lawmaking' (2007) 32 Brook. J. Int'l L. 851

Blumberg News, 'Report Says Banks Helped Parmalat Hide Fraud', 22 July 2004

Blumberg, P.I., *The Law of Corporate Groups: Procedural Problems in the Law of Parent and Subsidiary Corporations* (Little Brown & Co, London 1983) (and 6 subsequent volumes)

Blumberg, P.I., 'Limited Liability and Corporate Groups' (1986) 11 J. Corp. L. 573

Blumberg, P.I., *The Multinational Challenge to Corporation Law: the Search for a New Corporate personality* (Oxford University Press, Oxford 1993)

Blumberg, P.I., *Law of Corporate Groups: Enterprise Liability in Commercial Relationships, including Franchising, Licensing, Healthcare Enterprises, Successor Liability, Lender Liability and Inherent Agency* (Aspen Publishers Law and Business, Amsterdam 1998)

Blumberg, P.I., 'The Barriers Presented by Concepts of the Corporate Juridical Entity' (2001) 24 Hastings Int'l & Comp. L. Rev. 297

Blumberg, P.I., 'The Transformation of Modern Corporation Law: The Law of Corporate Groups' (2005) 37 Conn. L. Rev. 605

Blumberg, P.I., Strasser, K.A., Georgakopoulos, N.L., and Gouvin, E.J., *Blumberg on Corporate Groups* (Aspen Publishers, 2005) (5 vols)

Bornschier V., and Stamm, H., 'Transnational Corporations', in S. Wheeler (ed.), *The Law of the Business Enterprise* (Oxford University Press, Oxford 1994)

Boshkoff, D.G., 'Some Gloomy Thought Concerning Cross-Border Insolvencies' (1994) 72 Wash. U.L.Q. 931

Botha, D. 'Groups in South African Company Law (doctoral dissertation, University of Pretoria 1981)

Bratton Jr, W.W., 'The New Economic Theory of the Firm: Critical Perspectives from History', in S. Wheeler (ed.), *The Law of the Business Enterprise* (Oxford University Press, Oxford 1994) 333

Brown, C., 'Report of the Board of Banking Supervision Inquiry into the Circumstances of the Collapse of Barings' (1995) JIBL 10(10) 446

Brudney, V. 'Corporate Bondholders and Debtor Opportunism: In Bad Times and Good' (1992) 105 Harv. L. Rev. 1821

Brunstad, G. Eric, Jr., 'Bankruptcy and the Problems of Economic Futility: A Theory on the Unique Role of Bankruptcy Law' (2000) 55 Bus. Law, 499

Buckley P. I., and Casson, M., *The Future of Multinational Enterprise* (rev. edn Holmes & Meier, New York 1991)

Bufford S.L., 'Global Venue Controls Are Coming: A Reply to Professor LoPucki' (2005) 79 Am. Bankr. L.J. 105

Bufford, S.L., 'International Insolvency Case Venue in the European Union: The Parmalat and Daisytek Controversies' (2006) 12 Colum. J. Eur. L. 429

Bufford, S.L., 'Centre of Main Interests, International Insolvency Case Venue, and Equality of Arms: the Eurofood Decision of the European Court of Justice' (2007) 27 Nw. J. Int'l L. & Bus. 351

Burns, T., 'Developing a Franchise: Could Securitization be a Serious Funding Option for Franchisors in the United Kingdom?' [2006] JBL 656

Buxbaum, H.L., 'Rethinking International Insolvency: The Neglected Role of Choice-of-Law Rules and Theory' (2000) 36 Stan. J. Int'l L. 23

Carlson, D.G., 'Philosophy in Bankruptcy (Book Review)' (1987) 85 Mich. L. Rev. 1341

Carrara, C., 'Forum Shopping and Why Timing is Crucial' *Eurofenix* (2008) 20–1

Cashel, T.W., 'Groups of Companies—Some US Aspects', in Schmitthoff C.M. and Wooldridge F. (eds.), *Groups of Companies* (Sweet & Maxwell, London 1991) 23

Caves, R., *Multinational Enterprises and Economic Analysis* (Cambridge University Press, New York 2007)

Clift, J., 'The UNCITRAL Model Law on Cross-Border Insolvency—A Legislative Framework to Facilitate Coordination and Cooperation in Cross-Border Insolvency' (2004) 12 Tul. J. Int'l & Comp. Law 307

Collins, H., 'Ascription of Legal Responsibility to Groups in Complex Patterns of Economic Integration' (1990) 53 MLR 731

Company Law Newsletter, 'European Court of Justice Resolves Parmalat Jurisdictional Battle under EC Insolvency Proceedings Regulation', 9 May 2006

Company Law Newsletter, 'European Commission Proposes European Private Company and Small Business Act', Sweet & Maxwell, 7 August 2008

Company Law Review (CLR), Completing the Structure, URN 00/1335, November 2000

Company Law Review (CLR), Final Report, Volume I, URN 01/943, July 2001

Cooter, R., et al., 'Bargaining in the Shadow of the Law: A Testable Model of Strategic Behaviour' (1982) 11 J. Legal Stud. 225

Cork Report, Report of the Review Committee, Insolvency Law and Practice, Cmnd. 8558 (1982)

Daehnert, A., 'Lifting the Corporate Veil: English and German Perspectives on Group Liability' [2007] ICCLR 393

Dan-Cohen, M., *Rights, Persons, and Organizations: A Legal Theory for Bureaucratic Society* (University of California Press, Chicago 1986)

Davies, P., Directors' Creditor—Regarding Duties in the Vicinity of Insolvency' (2006) 7 EBOR 301

Davies, P.L, *Gower and Davies' Principles of Modern Company Law*, 8th edn (Sweet & Maxwell, London 2008)

Declercq, P.J.M., 'Restructuring European Distressed Debt: Netherlands Suspension of Payment Proceeding... The Netherlands Chapter 11?' (2003) 77 Am. Bankr. L.J. 377

Derham, D. 'Theories of Legal Personality', in L.C. Webb (ed.) *Legal Personality and Political Pluralism* (Melbourne University Press, Melbourne 1958) 1

Dewey, J. 'The Historical Background of Corporate Legal Personality' (1926) 35 Yale L. J. 655

Dewing, A., *Financial Policy of Corporations* (Ronald, New York 1953)

Diamantis, M.E., 'Arbitral Contractualism in Transnational Bankruptcy' (2007) 35 Sw. U. L. Rev. 32

Dickfos, J., Anderson, C., and Morrison, D., 'The Insolvency Implications for Corporate Groups in Australia—Recent Events and Initiatives' (2007) 16 Int. Insol. Rev. 103

Dobson, J.M. '"Lifting the Veil" in Four Countries: the Law of Argentina, England, France and the United States' (1986) 35 ICLQ 839

Donkin, R., 'Troubled BCCI Shifts Base to Abi Dhabi', *Financial Times* (London), 20 September 1990, p. 34

DOWJONES Newsletters, International Insolvency, 'Judge Rejects Administrator's Push To Control Parmalat's Cayman Units', 2 March 2004, p. 1, 3.

DOWJONES Newsletters, International Insolvency, 'Brazil Unit Says Two Banks Will Provide Credit Lines', 2 March 2004, p. 6

DOWJONES Newsletters, International Insolvency, Parmalat News Briefs, 9 March 2004, p. 9

DTI Consultative Document, Modern Company Law For a Competitive Economy (March 1998)

DTI Consultative Document, Modern Company Law For a Competitive Economy—Completing the Structure (London, DTI November 2000)

DTI The Company Law Steering Group, Modern Company Law For a Competitive Economy Final Report (London, DTI, 2001)

Dunning, J.H., *International Production and the Multinational Enterprise* (Allen & Unwin, London 1981)

Dunning, J.H., *Explaining International Production* (Allen & Unwin, London 1988)

Dunning, J.H., *Multinational Enterprises and the Global Economy* (Edward Elgar Publishing, Cheltenham 1993)

Dunning, J.H., *Alliance Capitalism and Global Business* (Routledge, New York 1997)

Dunning, J.H., 'Location and the Multinational Enterprise: A Neglected Factor?' (1998) 29 J. Int'l Bus. Stud. 45

Dworkin, R., *Sovereign Virtue: The Theory and Practice of Equality* (Harvard University Press, Cambridge MA 2000)

Easterbrook, F., and Fischel, D., 'Limited Liability and the Corporation' (1985) 52 U. Chi. L. Rev. 89

Easterbrook, F., and Fischel, D., *The Economic Structure of Corporate Law* (Harvard University Press, Cambridge MA 1991)

EBRD (2003) *Core Principles for a Secured Transactions Law* (available at: http://www. ebrd.com/country/sector/law/st/core/model/core.htm)

EBRD (2004) *Core Principles for an Insolvency Law Regime* (available at: http://www. ebrd.org/country/sector/law/insolve/core/index.htm)

Eidenmuller, H., 'Free Choice in International Company Insolvency Law in Europe' (2005) 6 EBOR 423

Ellis, E., 'Multinationals and the Antiquities of Company Law' (1984) 47 Mod. L. Rev.

Emmerich V., and Sonnenschein, J., *Konzernrecht* (München, 1997)

Estate Gazette, 'Leading Data Hosting Site Offered at a 55M GBP Discount' 14 September 2002, NEWS, p. 43

EU Focus 2008, 237, 2–4, 'Small Business Act for Europe Unveiled'

European Communication and Cooperation Guidelines for Cross-border Insolvency, Developed under the aegis of the Academic Wing of INSOL Europe by Professor Bob Wessels and Professor Miguel Virgos, July 2007; available in an article at http:// bobwessels.nl/wordpress/wp-content/uploads/2007/09/icr-editorial-oct-07.pdf)

Farber, D., 'What (if Anything) Can Economics Say about Equity?' (2003) 101 Mich. L. Rev. 1791

Farley, J.M., 'The International Scene: A Judicial Perspective on International Cooperation in Insolvency Cases', March 1998 ABI Jnl 59

Farrar, J. H., *Corporate Governance in Australia and New Zealand* (Oxford University Press, Oxford 2001)

Fawcett, J. J., 'Jurisdiction and Subsidiaries' [1985] JBL 16

Financial Times, 'Parmalat Unit Account Unfrozen', 26 February 2004, p. 29

Financial Times, 'Parmalat Ask Kroll to Find Assets', 2 March 2004

Financial Times, 'Judge Seizes Assets of Ex-Parmalat Chiefs', 30 September 2004

Financial Times, 'KPMG Discloses Lehman's Asia Risk', 27 November 2008

Finch, V., *Corporate Insolvency Law* (Cambridge University Press, Cambridge 2002)

Flaschen, E.D., and Silverman, R.J., 'The Role of the Examiner as Facilitator and Harmonizer in the Maxwell Communication Corporation International Insolvency', in J.S. Ziegel (ed.), *Current Developments in International and Comparative Insolvency Law* (Clarendon Press, Oxford 1994) Chapter 25

Flaschen, E.D., Smith, A.J., and Plank, L., 'Case Study: Foreign Representatives in U.S. Chapter 11 Cases: Filling the Void in the Law of Multinational Insolvencies' (2001) 17 Conn. J. Int'l L. 3

Fletcher, I.F., *Law of Bankruptcy* (Macdonald & Evans, London 1978)

Fletcher, I.F., *Law of Insolvency*, 3rd edn (Sweet & Maxwell, London 2002)

Fletcher, I.F., 'The European Union Regulation on Insolvency Proceedings' [2003] INSOL INTERNATIONAL CROSS-BORDER INSOLVENCY A Guide to Recognition and Enforcement, 15

Fletcher, I.F., 'The Challenge of Change: First Experiences of Life Under the EC Regulation on Insolvency Proceedings in the UK', Annual Review of Insolvency Law, 2003 (Toronto, Carswell, 2004) 431—55

Fletcher, I.F., 'Better Late Than Never: the UNCITRAL Model Law Enters into Force in Great Britain' (2006) 19(6) Insolv. Int. 86

Fletcher, I.F., 'Maintaining the Momentum: The Continuing Quest for Global Standards and Principles to Govern Cross-Border Insolvency' (2007) 32 Brook. J. Int'l L. 767

Fletcher, I.F., *Insolvency in Private International Law* (Oxford University Press, Oxford 2005, supplement 2007)

Franken, S.M., 'Three Principles of Transnational Corporate Bankruptcy Law: A Review' (2005) 11(2) European Law Journal 232

Frisby, S., 'In Search of a Rescue Regime: The Enterprise Act 2002' [2004] MLR 247

Frost, C.W., 'Organizational Form, Misappropriation Risk, and the Substantive Consolidation of Corporate Groups' (1993) 44 Hastings L.J. 449

Galloni, A. and Mollenkamp, C., 'Ex-Parmalat Banker Says He Misappropriated $27 Million, International Insolvency', *DOW JONES Newsletters*, 2 March 2004, p. 5

Georgakopoulos, N.L., 'Bankruptcy Law for Productivity' (2002) 37 Wake Forest L. Rev. 51

Gerber, E.J., 'Not All Politics Is Local: The New Chapter 15 to Govern Cross-Border Insolvencies' (2003) 71 Fordham L. Rev. 2051

Gilbert, J.S., 'Substantive Consolidation in Bankruptcy: A Primer' (1990) 43 Val L.R. 205

Gitlin, R.A. and Flaschen, E.D., 'The International Void in the Law of Multinational Bankruptcy' (1987) 42 Bus. Law. 307

GLOBAL TURNAROUND, 'KPNQwest in Sales Drive', June 2002, issue 29, p. 11

GLOBAL TURNAROUND, 'Europe Leads World in Forum Shopping', June 2003, issue 41, p. 1

GLOBAL TURNAROUND, Letter from the Editor, June 2003, issue 41, p. 2

GLOBAL TURNAROUND, 'Crisscross is First Group Admin', June 2003, issue 41, p. 3

GLOBAL TURNAROUND, 'French Breakthrough for Euro Regulation', October 2003, issue 45, p. 9

GLOBAL TURNAROUND, 'Parmalat is not Europe's Enron It's Italy's Maxwell', January 2004, issue 48, p. 2

GLOBAL TURNAROUND, 'How Global Crossing Made it to Safety', January 2004, issue 48, p. 6

GLOBAL TURNAROUND, 'Cenargo: The Shape of Things to Come' January 2004, issue 48, p.10

GLOBAL TURNAROUND, 'The New European Pastime', March 2004, issue 50, p. 6

GLOBAL TURNAROUND, 'Italian and Irish Courts Clash over Parmalat', April 2004, issue 51, p. 3

GLOBALTURNAROUND, 'Parmalat at Legal Crossroads' News, May 2004, issue 51, p. 4

GLOBALTURNAROUND, 'US Company Fails to Escape Euro Regulation', July 2004, issue 54, p. 1

GLOBALTURNAROUND, 'To Scheme or Not to Scheme Lessons from Enron', October 2004, issue 57, p. 11

GLOBALTURNAROUND, 'Yukos Court Battle over Chapter 11', February 2005, issue 61, p. 1,3

GLOBALTURNAROUND, 'Yukos Abandons Chapter 11', April 2005, issue 68, p. 7

GLOBALTURNAROUND, 'MG Rover, Europe's Biggest COMI', May 2005, issue 64, p. 3

GLOBALTURNAROUND, 'Collins & Aikman, Europe's Biggest COMI Filing', August 2005, issue 67, p. 1

GLOBALTURNAROUND, 'Canada Follows US with Insolvency Reform', December 2005, issue 71, p. 1

GLOBALTURNAROUND, 'French Revolution on COMI', March 2006, issue 74, p. 1

Goddard, D., 'Corporate Personality—Limited Recourse and its Limits' in R. Grantham and C. Rickett (eds.), *Corporate Personality in the 20th Century* (Hart Publishing Oxford, 1998) 11

Golick, S., and Wasseman, M., 'Canada', in L.C. Ho (ed.), *Cross-Border Insolvency, A commentary on the UNCITRAL Model Law* (Globe Law & Business, London 2006) 46

Goode, R., *Principles of Corporate Insolvency Law* (Sweet & Maxwell, London 2005)

Gordon, J.N. and Kornhauser, L.A., 'Efficient Markets, Costly Information, and Securities Research' (1985) 60 New York University Law Review 760

Gordon, M.W., 'Argentine Jurisprudence: The Parke Davis and Deltec Cases' (1974) 6 Law. Am. 320

Gower, L.C.B., *Gower's Principles of Modern Company Law*, 4th edn (London: Stevens, 1979)

Grantham, R., 'The Judicial Extension of Directors' Duties to Creditors' [1991] JBL 1

Graulich, T.E., 'Substantive Consolidation—A Post-modern Trend' (2006) 14 Am. Bankr. Ins. L. Rev. 527

Griffin, S., 'Limited Liability: A Necessary Revolution' (2004) 25 Co. Law 99

Grossfeld, B. and Roggers, C.P., 'A Shared Value Approach to Jurisdictional Conflicts in International Economic Law' (1983) 32 ICLQ 931

Guzman, A.T., 'International Bankruptcy: In Defence of Universalism' (2000) 98 Mich. L. Rev. 2177

Hadden, T., 'Inside Corporate Groups' (1984) 12 Int. J. of Soc. of Law 271

Hadden, T., 'Regulating Corporate Groups: An International Perspective', in J. McCahery, S. Picciotto and C. Scott (eds.), *Corporate Control and Accountability* (Oxford University Press, Oxford 1993) 343

Halliday T.C. and Carruthers, B.G., 'The Recursivity of Law: Global Norm Making and National Lawmaking in the Globalization of Corporate Insolvency Regimes' (2007) 112 AJS 1135

Hansmann, H. and Kraakman, R., 'Towards Unlimited Shareholder Liability for Corporate Torts' (1991) 100 Yale L.J. 1879

Hansmann, H. and Kraakman, R., 'The Essential Role of Organizational Law' (2000) 110 Yale L.J. 387

Haravon, M., 'Recent Developments in France Under EU Regulation 1346/2000' (2005) 18 Insol. Int. 118

Hargovan A. and Harris, J., 'Piercing the Corporate Veil in Canada: A Comparative Analysis' [2007] Comp. Law. 58

Harmer R.W., 'Documentation B, UNCITRAL Model Law on Cross-Border Insolvency' (1997) 6 Int. Insolv. Rev. 145

Harris J., 'Corporate Group Insolvencies: Charting the Past, Present and Future of Pooling Arrangements' (2007) 15(2) Insolvency Law Journal 78

Harris J., 'Pooling' (2007) 19(1) AIJ 16

Harrison, L. P., 'New York Circuit Court Upholds Recognition of an Argentine Plan Finding Creditor Should Have Objected In Foreign Proceedings' INSOL INTERNATIONAL NEWS UPDATE, Issue No. 7, July 2008

Hart, O., *Firms Contracts and Financial Structure* (Oxford University Press, Oxford 1995)

Heany, V., 'Winding Up Lehman' Accountancy (2008) 142 (1383) 94

Hessen, R., *In Defence of the Corporation* (Hoover Institutional Press, Stanford 1979)

Hicks, J., 'The Foundations of Welfare Economics' (1939) 49 Economics Journal 696

High Level Group of Company Law Experts on a Modern Regulatory Framework of Company Law in Europe, Final Report, Brussels, 4 November 2002

Hill, C., 'Securitization: A Low Cost Sweetener for Lemons' (1996) 74 Wash. U. L.Q. 1061

Ho, L.C. (ed.), *Cross-Border Insolvency, A Commentary on the UNCITRAL Model Law* (Globe Law & Business, London 2006)

Ho L.C., 'England' in L.C. Ho (ed.), *Cross-Border Insolvency, A Commentary on the UNCITRAL Model Law* (2006), 65–95

Ho L.C., 'Overview', in L.C. Ho (ed.), *Cross-Border Insolvency, A Commentary on the UNCITRAL Model Law* (Globe Law & Business, London 2006) 17

Hofstetter, K., 'Multinational Enterprise Parent Liability: Efficient Legal Regimes in a World Market Environment' (1990) 15 North Carolina J. of Int. Law and Comm. Reg. 299

Hood, N. and Young, S., *The Economics of Multinational Enterprise* (Longman, London 1979)

Hopt, K.J. (ed.), Groups of Companies in European Laws, Legal and Economic Analyses on Multinational Enterprises, vol. II (De Gruyter, Berlin 1982)

Hopt, K.J., 'Legal Elements and Policy Decisions in Regulating Groups of Companies', in C.M. Schmitthoff and F. Wooldridge (eds.), *Groups of Companies* (Sweet & Maxwell, London 1991) 81

Hoshi, T., Kashyap A., and Scharfstein, D., 'The Role of Banks in Reducing the Costs of Financial Distress in Japan', in Bhandari and L.A. Weiss (eds.), *Corporate Bankruptcy: Economic and Legal Perspectives* (Cambridge University Press, Cambridge 1996) 532

Hupkes, E., *Legal Aspects of Bank Insolvency. A Comparative Analysis of Western Europe, the United States and Canada*, Studies in Comparative Corporate and Finance Law, v. 10 (Kluwer Law International, 2000)

Hymer, S. and Rawthorn, R. 'Multinational Corporations and International Oligopoly: The Non-American Challenge', in Kindleberger (ed.), *The International Corporation* (MIT Press, Cambridge MA 1970) 57

Hymer, S. *The International Operations of National Firms: Study of Foreign Direct Investment* (MIT Press, Cambridge MA 1976)

'Insolvency Law Reforms in the Asian and Pacific Region', published in *Law and Policy Reform at the Asian Development Bank* (2000), Volume 1

Insolv. Int. 2003, 16 (6), 47–8 (NOTICEBOARD—Co-operation Between Courts)

Int'l Monetary Fund, *Orderly & Effective Insolvency Procedural Principles: Key Issues* (1999) (available at: http://www.imf.org/external/pubs/ft/orderly/index.htm)

International Insolvency Institute (III), Committee on International Jurisdiction and Cooperation, Judicial Guidelines for Coordination of Multi-National Enterprise Group Insolvencies, Co-Chairs Hon. R.R. Mabey and J.L. Garrity, Reporter SP. Johnston, Advisor I. Mevorach (Working Draft)

Israel, S., 'The EEIG—A Major Step Forward for Community Law' (1988) 9 Co. Law 14

Iwai, K., 'Persons, Things and Corporations: The Corporate Personality Controversy and Comparative Corporate Governance' (1999) 47 Am. J. Comp. L. 583

Jackson, T.H., 'Bankruptcy, Nonbankruptcy and the Creditors' Bargain' (1982) 91 Yale L.J. 857

Jackson, T.H., and Scott, R., 'On the Nature of Bankruptcy: An Essay on Bankruptcy Sharing and the Creditors' Bargain' (1989) 75 Virginia Law Rev. 155

Jackson, T., *The Logic and Limits of Bankruptcy Law* (Harvard University Press, Cambridge MA 1986)

Janger, E.J., 'Universal Proceduralism' (2007) 32 Brook. J. Int'l L. 819

Johnston, S.P., and Han, J., 'A Proposal for Party-Determined COMI in Cross-Border Insolvencies of Multinational Corporate Groups' (2007) 16 JBLP 811

Kaldor, N., 'Welfare Propositions of Economics and Interpersonal Comparisons of Utility' (1939) 49 Economic Journal 549

Kauzlarich, R.D., 'The Review of the 1976 OECD Declaration on International Investment and Multinational Enterprises' (1981) 30 Am. U.L. Rev. 1009

Keir, J., 'Legal Problems in the Management of a Group of Companies', in C.M. Schmitthoff and F. Wooldridge (eds.), *Groups of Companies* (Sweet & Maxwell, London 1991) 53

Kessel, L.P., 'Trends in the Approach to the Corporate Entity Problem in Civil Litigation' (1953) 41 Georgetown L.J. 525

Kopits, G., 'Multinational Conglomerate Diversification' (1979) 32 Econ. Int. 99

Korobkin, D.R., 'Rehabilitating Values: A Jurisprudence of Bankruptcy' (1991) 91 Colum. L. Rev. 717

Korobkin, D.R., 'Contractarianism and the Normative Foundations of Bankruptcy Law' (1993) 71 Tex. L. Rev. 541

Kors, M.E., 'Altered Egos: Deciphering Substantive Consolidation' (1997) 59 U. Pitt. L. Rev. 381

Kraft T. and Aranson, A., 'Transnational Bankruptcies: Section 304 and Beyond' [1993] Colum. Bus. L. Rev. 329

Laifer, D.M., 'Putting the Super Bank in the Supervision of International Banking Post BCCI' (1992) 60 Fordham L. Rev. 467

Landers, J., 'A Unified Approach to Parent, Subsidiary and Affiliated Questions in Bankruptcy' (1975) 42 U. Chi. L. Rev. 589

Landers, J., 'Another Word on Parents, Subsidiaries and Affiliates in Bankruptcy' (1976) 43 U. Chi. L. Rev. 527

Laski, H.J., 'The Personality of Associations' (1916) 19 Harv. L.Rev. 404

Lechner, R., 'Note, Waking From the Jurisdictional Nightmare of Multinational Default: The European Council Regulation on Insolvency Proceedings' (2002) 19 Ariz. J. Int'l & Comp. L. 975

Legal Framework for the Treatment of Foreign Investment (Volume II, Guidelines) (World Bank, 1992), reproduced 31 ILM 1363 (1992)

Leonard, B.E., 'Coordinating Cross-Border Insolvency Cases' International Insolvency Institute, June 2001 (available at: http://www.iiiglobal.org/downloads/committees/Cross-Border%20Communications%20in%20Insolvency%20Cases/13-_Co-ordinating_Cross-Border_Insolvency_Cases.pdf)

Levenson, D.C., 'Proposal for Reform of Choice of Avoidance Law in the Context of International Bankruptcies from a U.S. Perspective' (2002) 10 Am. Bankr. Inst. L. Rev. 291

Londot, J.K., 'Handling Priority Rules Conflicts in International Bankruptcy: Assessing the International Bar Association's Concordat' (1997) 13 Bankr. Dev. J. 163

LoPucki, L.M., 'Cooperation in International Bankruptcy: A Post-Universalist Approach' (1999) 84 Cornell L. Rev. 696

LoPucki, L.M., 'The Case for Cooperative Territoriality In International Bankruptcy' (2000) 98 Mich. L. Rev. 2216

LoPucki, L.M., 'Global and Out of Control?' (2005) 79 Am. Bankr. L.J. 79

LoPucki, L.M., 'Universalism Unravels' (2005) 79 Am. Bankr. L.J. 143

LoPucki, L.M., *Courting Failure: How Competition for Big Cases Is Corrupting the Bankruptcy Courts* (The University of Michigan Press, Ann Arbor 2005)

Lower, M., 'Joint Ventures', in Milman D. (ed.), *Regulating Enterprise* (Hart Publishing, Oxford 1999) 241

Lundgren, K.T., 'Liability of a Creditor in a Control Relationship with its Debtor' (1984) 67 Marq. L. Rev. 523

Lutter, M., 'Enterprise Law Corp. v. Entity Law, Inc.—Phillip Blumberg's Book from the Point of View of an European Lawyer' (1990) 38(4) American Journal of Comparative Law 949

Machen, Jr., 'Corporate Personality' (1911) 24 Harv. L. Rev. 253

Maitland, F.W., *Introduction to Gierke's Political Theories of the Middle Age* (Cambridge University Press, Cambridge 1900)

Mallon, C., 'Eurotunnel', presentation delivered at Eighth Annual INTL Insolvency (III) Conference, Berlin, 9 June 2008

Marantz, G.R., 'The Reorganization of a Complex Corporate Entity: The Bramalea Story', in J.S. Ziegel (ed.), *Case Studies in Recent Canadian Insolvency Reorganizations* (Carswell Legal Publications, Toronto 1997) 1

Martinez, J.L. and Jarillo, J.C., 'The Evolution of Research on Co-ordination Mechanisms in Multinational Corporations' (1989) 20 Journal of International Business Studies, 489

Mason, R.G., 'United States' in L.C. Ho (ed.), *Cross-Border Insolvency, A Commentary on the UNCITRAL Model Law* (Globe Law & Business, London 2006) 197–217

McBryde, W.W., Flessner, A., and Kortmann, S.C.J.J., (eds.), *Principles of European Insolvency Law, Series Law of Business and Finance* (Volume 4, Kluwer Legal Publishers, Deventer 2003)

McConnell, J. and Servaes, H., 'The Economics of Pre-Packaged Bankruptcy' (1991) 4 Journal of Applied Corporate Finance 93

McCormack, G., 'Control and Corporate Rescue—an Anglo-American Evaluation' (2007) 56 ICLQ 515

McCormack, G., 'Super-priority New Financing and Corporate Rescue' [2007] JBL 701

McInerney, T., 'Towards the Next Stage in International Banking Regulation' (1995) 7 DePaul Bus. L.J. 143

McLean D. and Beevers, K., *Morris: The Conflict of Laws*, 6th edn (Sweet & Maxwell, London 2005)

Memorandum from Jay L Westbrook to the National Bankruptcy Review Commission (29 July 1997, in National Bankruptcy Review Commission, Bankruptcy: The Next Twenty Years (1997), app E-1

Mevorach, I., 'Appropriate Treatment of Corporate Groups in Insolvency—A Universal View' (2006) 8 EBOR 179

Mevorach, I., 'Centralizing Insolvencies of pan-European Corporate Groups: A Creditor's Dream or Nightmare?' [2006] JBL 468

Mevorach, I., 'The Road to a Suitable and Comprehensive Global Approach to Insolvencies Within Multinational Corporate Groups' [2006] JBLP 455

Mevorach, I., 'The Home Country of a Multinational Enterprise Group Facing Insolvency' (2008) 57 ICLQ 427

Milman, D., 'Groups of Companies: The Path Towards Discrete Regulation', in D. Milman (ed.), *Regulating Enterprise* (Hart Publishing, Oxford 1999) 218

Milman, D., 'Case Comment, Two Cases of Interest for Company Directors Operating in the Twilight Zone' (2008) Insol. Int. 25

Mitchell, C. 'Lifting the Corporate Veil in the English Courts: an Empirical Study' (1999) 3(1) CFILR 15

Mokal, R.J., '"Priority as Pathology": The *Pari Passu* Myth' [2001] CLJ 581

Mokal, R.J., 'On Fairness and Efficiency' [2003] MLR 452

Mokal, R.J., *Corporate Insolvency Law: Theory and Application* (Oxford University Press, Oxford 2005)

Mokal, R.J., 'Contractarianism, Contractualism, and the Law of Corporate Insolvency' [2007] Singapore Journal of Legal Studies 51

Moore, S., 'Cenargo: A Tale of Two Courts, Comity and (Alleged!) Contempt!' January 2004 (available at: http://www.iiiglobal.org/downloads/country/USA/Articles/30-_cenargo.pdf)

Moore, S., 'Global Crossing versus Cenargo, The Right Way and the Wrong Way' *GLOBALTURNAROUND*, January 2004, issue 48, p. 8

Moss, G., 'Daisytek Followed in New German Case' (2004) 17(10) Insol. Int. 141

Moss, G., 'Creditors Voluntary Liquidation for Foreign Registered Companies' (2005) 18(1) Insol. Int. 12

Moss, G., 'Dismissal of Yucos Chapter 11 Proceedings' (2005) 18(5) Insol. Int. 77

Moss, G., 'Group Insolvency—Choice of Forum and Law: the European Experience under the Influence of English Pragmatism' (2007) 32 Brook. J. Int'l L. 1005

Moss, G., 'The Mystery of the Sphinx—COMI in the U.S.' (2007) 20(1) Insol. Int. 86

Moss, G. and Haravon, M., '"Building Europe"—the French Case Law on COMI' (2007) 20 Insol. Int. 20

Moss G. and Paulus, C.G., 'The European Insolvency Regulation—the Case for Urgent Reform' (2006) 19 Insolv. Int. 2

Moss, G., Fletcher, I.F., and Isaacs, S., (eds.), *The EC Regulation on Insolvency Proceedings: A Commentary and Annotated Guide* (Oxford University Press, Oxford 2002)

Muchlinski, P.T., 'Corporations in International Litigation: Problems of Jurisdiction and the United Kingdom Asbestos Cases' (2001) 50 ICLQ 1

Muchlinski, P.T., 'Holding Multinationals to Account: Recent Developments in English Litigation and the Company Law Review' (2002) 23(6) Comp. Law. 1

Muchlinski, P.T., *Multinational Enterprise and the Law*, 2nd edn (Oxford University Press, Oxford 2007)

Muscat, A., *The Liability of the Holding Company for the Debts of its Insolvent Subsidiary* (Dartmouth Publishing Group, Aldershot 1996)

Nakajima, C., 'Lifting The Veil' (1996) 17(6) Comp. Law. 187

New York Times, 'The Rise and Fall of Parma's First Family', 11 January 2004.

New York Times, 'Milan Prosecutors Try Again on Parmalat', 27 May 2004

New York Times, REUTERS, 'Judge Ready to Start Parmalat Hearings' 3 October 2004.

New York Times, The Associated Press, 'Ex-Parmalat CFO Reportedly Blames Tanzi', 3 October 2004

Nielsen, A. et al., 'The Cross-Border Insolvency Concordat: Principles to Facilitate the Resolution of International Insolvencies' (1996) 70 Am. Bankr. L.J. 533

Norley, L., 'INSOLVENCY: Tooled up' The Lawyer, 10 November 2003

Omar, P.J., 'The European Initiative on Wrongful Trading' (2003) 6 Insol. Law. 239

Organisation for Economic Co-operation and Development (OECD), The Responsibility of Parent Company for Their Subsidiaries (1980), 'Summary of Comparative Findings'

Organisation for Economic Co-operation and Development (OECD) (1981), 'International Investment and Multinational Enterprises: Recent International Direct Investment Trends'

Organisation for Economic Co-operation and Development (OECD), Guidelines for Multinational Enterprises 27 June 2000 (available at: http://www.oecd.org/dataoecd/56/36/1922428.pdf)

Pantaleo, P.V. et al, 'Rethinking the Role of Recourse in the Sale of Financial Assets' (1996) 52 Bus. Law. 159

Paulus, C.G., Zustandigkeitsfragen nach der Europaischen Insolvenzverodnung, International Insolvency Institute (available at: http://www.iiiglobal.org/downloads/country/Germany/Articles/12-_insolvenzverordnung.pdf)

Paulus, C.G., 'The Aftermath of "Eurofood"—BenQ holding BV and the Deficiencies of the ECJ Decision' (2007) 20(6) Insolv. Int. 85

Perkins, L., 'Note, A Defense of Pure Universalism in Cross-Border Corporate Insolvencies' (2000) 32 N.Y.U. J. Int'l L. & Pol. 787

Peter, H., 'Insolvency in a Group of Companies, Substantive and Procedural Consolidation: When and How?' in H. Peter, N. Jeandin and J. Kilborn (eds.), *The Challenges of Insolvency Law Reform in the 21st Century* (Verlag Schulthess, Zurich 2006) 199

Petkovic, D., '(Case Comment) Piercing the Corporate Veil in Capital Markets Transactions' (1996) 15(4) IBFL 41

Pettet, B., *Company Law*, 2nd edn (Pearson Longman, 2005)

Posner, R., 'The Legal Rights of Creditors of Affiliated Corporations: An Economic Approach' (1976) 43 U. Chi. L. Rev. 499

Pottow, J.A.E., 'Procedural Incrementalism: A Model for International Bankruptcy' (2005) 45(4) Virginia Journal of International Law 935

Pound, R., *The Spirit of the Common Law* (Marshall Jones Francestown NH, 1921)

Pound, R., *Jurisprudence* (Lawbook Exchange Ltd, 1959)

Prentice, D., 'A Survey of the Law Relating to Corporate Groups in the United Kingdom', in E. Wymeersch (ed.), *Groups of Companies in the EC* (De Gruyter, Berlin 1993)

Prentice, D., 'Corporate Personality, Limited Liability and the Protection of Creditors', in R. Grantham and C. Rickett (eds.), *Corporate Personality in the 20th Century* (Hart Publishing, Oxford 1998) 99

Principles and Guidelines for Creditor Rights and Insolvency Systems, based on The World Bank Principles and Guidelines for Effective Creditor Rights and Insolvency Systems and the UNCITRAL Legislative Guide on Insolvency Law (provisional text, January 2005, not yet published) (available at: http://web.worldbank.org/WBSITE/EXTERNAL/TOPICS/LAWANDJUSTICE/GILD/0,contentMDK:20196839~menuPK:146205~pagePK:64065425~piPK:162156~theSitePK:215006,00.html)

Proposal for a Council Regulation on the Statute for a European Private Company (COM(2008) 396/3) (available at: http://ec.europa.eu/internal_market/company/docs/epc/proposal_en.pdf)

Qi, L., 'The Rise of Pre-packaged Corporate Rescues on Both Sides of the Atlantic' (2007) 20(9) Insolv. Int. 129

Radin, M., 'The Endless Problem of Corporate Personality' (1932) 32 Colum. L. Rev. 643

Rajak, H., 'The Harmonisation of Insolvency Proceedings in the European Union' [2000] CFILR 180

Rajak, H., *Company Liquidations* (Sweet & Maxwell, London 2006)

Rajak, H., 'The Culture of Bankruptcy' in P. J. Omar, (ed.), *International Insolvency Law Themes and Perspectives* (Ashgate, Aldershot 2008) 3

Ramsay, I.M., 'Models of Corporate Regulation: The Mandatory/Enabling Debate' in R. Grantham and C. Rickett (eds.), *Corporate Personality in the 20th Century* (Hart Publishing, Oxford 1998) 215

Ramsay, I.M., 'Piercing the Corporate Veil in Australia' (2001) 19 Company and Securities Law Journal 250

Rapakko, T., *Unlimited Shareholder Liability in Multinationals* (Kluwer, The Hague 1997)

Rasmussen, R.K., 'Debtor's Choice: A Menu Approach to Corporate Bankruptcy' (1992) 71 Tex. L. Rev. 51

Rasmussen, R.K., 'A New Approach to Transnational Insolvencies' (1997) 19 Mich J. Int'l L. 1

Rasmussen, R.K., 'Resolving Transnational Insolvencies Through Private Ordering' (2000) 98 Mich L. Rev. 2252

Rasmussen, R.K., 'The Problem of Corporate Groups, a Comment on Professor Ziegel' (2002) 7 Fordham J. Corp. & Fin. L. 395

Rasmussen, R.K., 'Where are All the Transnational Bankruptcies?: The Puzzling Case for Universalism' (2007) 32 Brook. J. Int'l L. 983

Rawls, J., *A Theory of Justice* (Harvard University Press, Cambridge Mass. 1971)

Rawls, J., *Political Liberalism* (Columbia University Press, New York 1996)

Ribstein, L.E., 'Limited Liability and Theories of the Corporation' (1991) 50 Md. L. Rev. 80

Romano, R., 'Law as a Product: Some Pieces of the Incorporation Puzzle' (1985) 1 J. L. Econ. & Org. 225

Rosenn, K.S., 'Expropriation in Argentina and Brazil: Theory and Practice' (1975) 15 Va. J. Int'l L. 277

Ross, M., 'Tangled Webs: Unravelling the Strands after a Corporate Group Collapses' (1992) 3(11) ICCLR 385

Rothpletz, J.K., 'Ownership of a Subsidiary as a Basis for Jurisdiction' (1965) 20 New York University Intramural Law Review 127

Salafia, L., 'Cross-Border Insolvency Law in the United States and its Application to Multinational Corporate Groups' (2006) 21 Conn. J. Int'l L. 297

Schane, S.A., 'The Corporation is a Person: the Language of a Legal Fiction' (1987) 61 Tul. L. Rev. 563

Schlosser Report [1979] OJ C59/71

Schmitthoff, C.M., 'The Wholly Owned and the Controlled Subsidiary' [1978] JBL 218

Schmitthoff, C., 'Introduction', in C. M. Schmitthoff and F. Wooldridge (eds.), *Groups of Companies* (Sweet & Maxwell, London 1991) xiv

Schwartz, A., 'A Theory of Loan Priorities' (1989) 18 Journal of Legal Studies 209

Schwarcz, S., 'Structured Finance: The New Way to Securitize Assets' (1989) 11 Cardozo L.Rev. 607

Schwarcz, S., *Structured Finance: A Guide to the Principles of Asset Securitization*, 2nd edn (Practicing Law Institute, New York 1993)

Schwarcz, S., 'The Alchemy of Asset Securitization' (1994) 1 Stan. J. L. Bus. & Fin. 133

Schwarcz, S., 'Collapsing Corporate Structures: Resolving the Tension Between Form and Substance' [2004] The Business Lawyer 60

Schwarcz, S., 'Securitization Post-Enron' (2004) 25 Cardozo L. Rev. 1539

Scott, H.S., 'Supervision of International Banking Post-BCCI' (1992) 8 Ga. St. U. L. Rev. 487

Scott, H.S., 'Multinational Bank Insolvencies: The United States and BCCI', in J. S. Ziegel (ed.), *Current Developments in International and Comparative Insolvency Law* (Clarendon Press, Oxford 1994) 733

Shandro, S. and Tett, R., 'The Cenargo Case: A Tale of Conflict, Greed Contempt, Comity and Costs', Insol. World—Fourth Quarter 2003, p. 33

Shivji S.A., Smith, A., and Walters, A., 'The Cross-Border Insolvency Regulation 2006: An Emerging Jurisprudence' [2008] Am. Bankr. Inst. J. 40

Sigal, M., et al, 'The Law and Practice of International Insolvencies, Including A Draft Cross-Border Insolvency Concordat' (1994) 95 Ann. Surv. Bankr. L. 1

Silverman, R.J., 'Advances In Cross-Border Insolvency Cooperation: The UNCITRAL Model Law on Cross-Border Insolvency' (2000) 6 Ilsa J. Int'l & Comp. L. 265

Skeel, D.A., 'Rethinking the Line Between Corporate Law and Corporate Bankruptcy' (1994) 72 Tex. L. Rev. 471

Skeel, D.A., 'Creditors' Ball: The "New" New Corporate Governance in Chapter 11' (2003) 152 U. Pa. L. Rev. 917

Skeel, D.A., 'European Implication of Bankruptcy Venue Shopping in the U.S.' (2007) 54 Buff. L. Rev. 439

Skeel, D.A., 'Groups of Companies: Substantive Consolidation in the U.S.', in H. Peter, N. Jeandin and J. Kilborn (eds.), *The Challenges of Insolvency Law Reform in the 21st Century* (Verlag Schulthess, Zurich 2006) 229

Staehelin, D., 'No Substantive Consolidation in the Insolvency of Groups of Companies', in H. Peter, N. Jeandin and J. Kilborn (eds.), *The Challenges of Insolvency Law Reform in the 21st Century* (Verlag Schulthess, Zurich 2006) 213

Stein, 'Nineteenth Century English Company Law and Theories of Legal Personality' (1982–1983) 1 Quaderni Fiorentini 503

Strasser, K.A., 'Piercing the Veil in Corporate Groups' (2005) 37 Conn. L. Rev. 637

Sussman, O., 'The Economics of the EU's Corporate-Insolvency Law and the Quest for Harmonization by Market Forces' [2005], Oxford Financial Research Centre, Working Paper 2005-FE-16

Takeuchi, K., 'Issues in Concurrent Insolvency Jurisdiction: Comments on the Papers by Grierson and Flaschen-Silverman', in J. S. Ziegel (ed.), *Current Developments in International and Comparative Insolvency Law* (Clarendon Press, Oxford 1994) 647

Taylor, S., *GLOBALTURNAROUND*, 'DaisyTek Chain Reaction', July 2003, issue 42, p. 10

Tett, R. and Spence, N., 'COMI: Presumption, What Presumption' (2004) 17(9) Insolv. Int. 139

Teubner, G., 'Enterprise Corporatism: New Industrial Policy and the "Essence" of the Legal Person' (1988) 36 Am. J. Comp. L. 130

Teubner, G., 'Unitas Multiplex: Corporate Governance in Group Enterprises', in D. Sugarman and G. Teubner (eds.), *Regulating Corporate Groups in Europe* (Nomos, Baden-Baden 1990) 67

Teubner, G., 'Beyond Contract and Organisation? The External Liability of Franchising Systems in German Law', in C. Joerges (ed.), *Franchising and the Law: Theoretical and comparative Approaches in Europe and the United States* (Nomos, Baden-Baden 1992) 105

Teubner, G., *Law as an Autopoietic System* (Blackwell Publishers, Oxford 1993)

Teubner, G., 'The Many-headed Hydra: Networks as Higher Order Collective Actors', in J. McCahery, S. Picciotto and C. Scott (eds.), *Corporate Control and Accountability* (Clarendon Press, Oxford 1993) 41

Thompson, R.B., 'Piercing the Corporate Veil: An Empirical Study' (1991) 76 Cornell L.R. 1036

Thompson, R.B., 'Piercing the Veil within Corporate Groups: Corporate Shareholders as Mere Investors' (1999) 13 Conn. J. Int'l L. 379

Thompson, R.B., 'Piercing the Veil: is the Common Law the Problem?' (2005) Conn. L. Rev. 619

Tomasic, R., 'The Sociology of Legislation', in R. Tomasic (ed.), *Legislation and Society in Australia* (Allen & Unwin, Sydney 1980) 19

Tomasic, R., 'Creditor Participation in Insolvency Proceedings' EBRD Meeting held on 27–28 April 2006 (available at: http://www.oecd.org/dataoecd/41/44/38182698.pdf)

Torremans, P., 'Coming to Terms with the COMI Concept in the European Insolvency Regulation', in P. J. Omar (ed.), *International Insolvency Law Themes and Perspectives* (Ashgate, Aldershot 2008) 173

Trautman, D.T., et al, 'Four Models for International Bankruptcy' (1994) 41 Am. J. Comp. L. 573

Tugendhat, C., *The Multinationals* (Eyre and Spottiswoode, London 1971)

Tung, F., 'Skepticism about Universalism: International Bankruptcy and International Relations' (2 April 2002), Berkeley Program in Law & Economics, Working Paper Series, Paper 43. (Available at: http://repositories.cdlib.org/blewp/43/)

Turner, 'Conglomerate Mergers and Section 7 of the Clayton Act' (1965) 78 Harv. L. Rev. 1313

U.N. Comm'n on Int'l Trade Law (UNCITRAL), UNCITRAL Legislative Guide on Insolvency Law (2005) (available at: http://www.uncitral.org/pdf/english/texts/insolven/05-80722_Ebook.pdf)

U.N. Comm'n on Int'l Trade Law (UNCITRAL), UNCITRAL Legislative Guide on Secured Transactions (2008)

U.N. Comm'n on Int'l Trade Law (UNCITRAL), UNCITRAL Note by the Secretariat, Working Group V (Insolvency Law), 4 October 2006, A/CN.9/WG.V/WP.74/Add.1 (available at: http://www.uncitral.org/uncitral/en/commission/working_groups/5Insolvency.html)

U.N. Comm'n on Int'l Trade Law (UNCITRAL), UNCITRAL Note by the Secretariat, Working Group V (Insolvency Law), 4 October 2006, A/CN.9/WG.V/WP.74/Add.2 (available at: http://www.uncitral.org/uncitral/en/commission/working_groups/5Insolvency.html)

U.N. Comm'n on Int'l Trade Law (UNCITRAL), UNCITRAL Note by the Secretariat, Working Group V (Insolvency Law), 4 October 2006, A/CN.9/WG.V/WP.76/Add.2 (available at: http://www.uncitral.org/uncitral/en/commission/working_groups/5Insolvency.html)

U.N. Comm'n on Int'l Trade Law (UNCITRAL), UNCITRAL Note by the Secretariat, Working Group V (Insolvency Law), 31 December 2007, A/CN.9/WG.V/WP.80 (available at http://www.uncitral.org/uncitral/en/commission/working_groups/5Insolvency.html)

U.N. Comm'n on Int'l Trade Law (UNCITRAL), UNCITRAL Note by the Secretariat, Working Group V (Insolvency Law), 2 January 2008, A/CN.9/WG.V/WP.80/Add.1 (available at: http://www.uncitral.org/uncitral/en/commission/working_groups/5Insolvency.html)

U.N. Comm'n on Int'l Trade Law (UNCITRAL), UNCITRAL Note by the Secretariat, Working Group V (Insolvency Law), 1 September 2008, A/CN.9/WG.V/WP.82 (available at: http://www.uncitral.org/uncitral/en/commission/working_groups/5Insolvency.html)

U.N. Comm'n on Int'l Trade Law (UNCITRAL), UNCITRAL Note by the Secretariat, Working Group V (Insolvency Law), 2 September 2008, A/CN.9/WG.V/WP.82/Add.1 (available at: http://www.uncitral.org/uncitral/en/commission/working_groups/5Insolvency.html)

U.N. Comm'n on Int'l Trade Law (UNCITRAL), UNCITRAL Note by the Secretariat, Working Group V (Insolvency Law), 4 September 2008, A/CN.9/WG.V/WP.82/Add.2 (available at: http://www.uncitral.org/uncitral/en/commission/working_groups/5Insolvency.html)

U.N. Comm'n on Int'l Trade Law (UNCITRAL), UNCITRAL Note by the Secretariat, Working Group V (Insolvency Law), 4 September 2008, A/CN.9/WG.V/WP.82/

Add.3 (available at: http://www.uncitral.org/uncitral/en/commission/working_groups/5Insolvency.html)

U.N. Comm'n on Int'l Trade Law (UNCITRAL), UNCITRAL Note by the Secretariat, Working Group V (Insolvency Law), 10 September 2008, A/CN.9/WG.V/WP.82/Add.4 (available at: http://www.uncitral.org/uncitral/en/commission/working_groups/5Insolvency.html)

U.N. Comm'n on Int'l Trade Law (UNCITRAL), UNCITRAL Report of Working Group V (Insolvency Law) on the work of its thirty-first session, 8 January 2007, A/CN.9/618; (available at: http://www.uncitral.org/uncitral/en/commission/working_groups/5Insolvency.html)

U.N. Comm'n on Int'l Trade Law (UNCITRAL), UNCITRAL Report of Working Group V (Insolvency Law) on the work of its thirty-second session, 25 May 2007, A/CN.9/622 (available at http://www.uncitral.org/uncitral/en/commission/working_groups/5Insolvency.html)

U.N. Comm'n on Int'l Trade Law (UNCITRAL), UNCITRAL Report of Working Group V (Insolvency Law) on the work of its thirty-third session, 16 November 2007, A/CN.9/643 (available at: http://www.uncitral.org/uncitral/en/commission/working_groups/5Insolvency.html)

U.N. Comm'n on Int'l Trade Law (UNCITRAL), UNCITRAL Report of Working Group V (Insolvency Law) on the work of its thirty-fourth session, 14 March 2008, A/CN.9/647 (available at: http://www.uncitral.org/uncitral/en/commission/working_groups/5Insolvency.html)

U.N. Comm'n on Int'l Trade Law (UNCITRAL), UNCITRAL Draft report of Working Group V (Insolvency Law) on the work of its thirty-fifth session (Vienna, 17–21 November 2008) 17 November 2008, A/CN.9/WG.V/XXXV/CRP.1/Add.1

U.N. Comm'n on Int'l Trade Law (UNCITRAL), UNCITRAL Draft report of Working Group V (Insolvency Law) on the work of its thirty-fifth session (Vienna, 17–21 November 2008) 18 November 2008, A/CN.9/WG.V/XXXV/CRP.1/Add.2

UNCITRAL Notes on Cooperation, Communication and Coordination in Cross-Border Insolvency Proceedings, A/CN.9/WG.V/WP.83; available at: http://www.uncitral.org/uncitral/en/commission/working_groups/5Insolvency.html

UNCTAD, 2005 World Investment Report

United Nations (1978), Transnational Corporations in Development: a Re-examination. New York: UNCTNC

United Nations (1983), Transnational Corporations in World Development, 3rd Survey. New York: UNCTNC

United Nations (2006), A/CN.9/596, Insolvency Law: Possible Future Work, Note by the Secretariat (available at: http://daccessdds.un.org/doc/UNDOC/GEN/V06/517/90/PDF/V0651790.pdf?OpenElement)

United Nations General Assembly, Resolution 59/40

Unt, L., 'Note, International Relations and International Insolvency Cooperation: Liberalism, Institutionalism, and Transnational Legal Dialogue' (1997) 28 Law & Pol'y Int'l Bus. 1037

Van Galen, R., 'The European Insolvency Regulation and Groups of Companies', INSOL Europe Annual Congress, Cork, Ireland, 16–18 October 2003 (http://www.insol-europe.org)

Vernon, R., *Sovereignty at Bay: The Multinational Spread of U.S. Enterprises* (Longman, Harlow 1971)

Vernon, R., *The Economic and Political Consequences of Multinational Enterprise* (Harvard University Press, Cambridge MA 1973)

Vernon, R., 'The Product Cycle Hypothesis in a New International Environment' (1979) 41 Oxford Bull. Econ. Stat. 255

Verougstraete, I., *Manuel de la faillite et du concordat* (Kluwer Editions Jurdique Belgique, Waterloo 1998)

Vinogradoff, 'Juridical Persons' (1924) 24 Colum. L. Rev. 594

Virgos, M., 'The 1995 European Community Convention on Insolvency Proceedings: An Insider's View', in: Forum Internationale, no. 25, March 1998

Virgos, M., and Schmit, E., 'Report on the Convention on Insolvency Proceedings' (1996) 6500/1/96, REV1, DRS 8 (CFC)

Wallerstein, I., *The Modern World-System*, vols i and ii (Academic Press, New York 1974, 1980)

Warren, E., 'Bankruptcy Policy' (1987) 54 U. Chi. L. Rev. 775

Warren E. and Westbrook, J., 'Searching for Reorganization Realities' (1994) 72 Wash. Univ. L.Q. 1257

Warren E. and Westbrook J., 'Contracting Out of Bankruptcy: An Empirical Intervention' (2005) 118 Harv. L. Rev. 1197

Watson, 'Liability of a Company for the Debts of an Insolvent "Related Company"', (1983) J. Bus. L. 295

Webber, Eric A., 'Consensual Substantive Consolidation: Comments on the Working Papers of Professor Skeel and Dr. Staehelin', in H. Peter, N. Jeandin, and J. Kilborn (eds.), *The Challenges of Insolvency Law Reform in the 21st Century* (Verlag Schulthess, Zurich 2006) 235

Weidemann, H., 'The German Experience with the Law of Affiliated Enterprise', in K.J. Hopt (ed.), *Groups of Companies in European Laws, Legal and Economic Analyses on Multinational Enterprises*, vol. II (De Gruyter, Berlin 1982) 21

Weiss, 'The New Zealand Companies Amendment Act, 1980' (1981) 9 Austl. Bus. L. Rev. 290

Weissbrodt, A. J., 'Disproving the COMI presumption' (2008) *Eurofenix*, issue 32, 14

Wessels, B., 'Banks in Distress Under Rules of European Insolvency Law' (2006) 21(6) JIBLR 301

Wessels, B. 'The Changing Landscape of Cross-border Insolvency Law in Europe' (2007) 12(1) *Juridica International*, 116–24

Wessels, B., 'International Jurisdiction to Open Insolvency Proceedings in Europe, In Particular Against (Groups of) Companies' Working Papers Series, Institute for Law and Finance, Johann Wolfgang Goethe University (available at: http://www.iiiglobal. org/downloads/European%20Union/Articles/11-_InternJurisdictionCompanies.pdf)

Wessels, B., 'Cross-Border Insolvency Law in Europe: Present Status and Future Prospects' (2008) 1 PER, 1

Wessels, B., 'Principles of European Insolvency Law' International Insolvency Institute (available at: http://www.iiiglobal.org/downloads/European%20Union/Articles/21-_PEILABIjournal_appended.pdf)

Wessels, B., *International Insolvency Law* (Kluwer, Deventer 2006)

Westbrook, J.L., 'Choice of Avoidance Law in Global Insolvencies' (1991) 17 Brook. J. Int'l L. 499

Westbrook, J.L., 'Theory and Pragmatism in Global Insolvencies: Choice of Law and Choice of Forum' (1991) 65 Am. Bankr. L.J. 457

Westbrook, J.L., 'A Global Solution to Multinational Default' (2000) 98 Mich. L. Rev. 2276

Westbrook, J.L., 'Managing Defaulting Multinationals Within NAFTA', in I.F. Fletcher, L. Mistelis, and M. Cremona (eds.), *Foundations and Perspectives of International Trade Law* (Sweet & Maxwell, London 2001), ch. 30

Westbrook, J.L., 'Multinational Enterprises in General Default: Chapter 15, The ALI Principles, and The EU Insolvency Regulation' (2002) 76 Am. Bankr. L.J. 1

Westbrook, J.L., 'International Judicial Negotiations' (2003) 38 Tex. Int'l L.J. 567

Westbrook, J. L., 'Chapter 15 At Last' (2005) 79 Am. Bankr. L.J. 713

Westbrook, J. L., 'Universalism and Choice of Law' (2005) 23 Penn. St. Int'l L. Rev. 625.

Westbrook, J.L., 'Avoidance of Pre-Bankruptcy Transactions in Multinational Bankruptcy Cases' (2007) 42 Tex. Int'l. L.J. 899

Westbrook, J.L., 'Locating the Eye of the Financial Storm' (2007) 32 Brook. J. Int'l L. 1019

Westbrook, J.L., and Ziegel, J. S., 'NAFTA Insolvency Project' (1997) 23 Brook. J. Int'l L. 8

Wheeler, S., 'The Business Enterprise: A Socio-Legal Introduction', in S. Wheeler (ed.), *The Law of the Business Enterprise* (Oxford University Press, Oxford 1994) 39

White, M.J., 'Corporate Bankruptcy as a Filtering Device: Chapter 11 Reorganizations and Out-of-Court Debt Restructurings' (1994) 10 J. L. Econ. & Org. 268

White, M.J., 'The Costs of Corporate Bankruptcy: A US-European Comparison' in Bhandari, S. Jagdeep and A. Lawrence (eds.), *Corporate Bankruptcy: Legal and Economic Perspectives* (Cambridge University Press, Cambridge 1996) 467

Widen, W.H., 'Corporate Form and Substantive Consolidation' (2007) 75 Geo. Wash. L. Rev. 237

Widen, W.H., 'Report to the American Bankruptcy Institute: Prevalence of Substantive Consolidation in Large Public Company Bankruptcies from 2000 to 2005' [2008] 16(1) ABI L. Rev. 1

Wilkins, M., *The Emergence of Multinational Enterprises: American Business Abroad from the Colonial Era to 1914* (Harvard University Press, Cambridge MA 1970)

Wilkins, M., *The Maturing of Multinational Enterprise: American Business Abroad from 1914 to 1970* (Harvard University Press, Cambridge MA 1974)

Wilkinson, A., 'Piercing the Corporate Veil and the Insolvency Act 1986' (1987) 8 Co. Law. 124

Williamson, O.E., 'The Modern Corporation: Origins, Evolution, and Attributes' (1981) 19 J. Econ. Lit. 1537

Williamson, O.E., 'Organization Form, Residual Claimants and Corporate Control' (1983) 26 J. L. & Econ. O 351

Williamson O., and Masten, S., *Transaction Cost Economics* (Edward Elgar Publishing, Aldershot 1995)

Wolff, M. 'On the Nature of Legal Persons' (1938) 54 LQR 494

World Bank, 'Principles and Guidelines for Building Effective Insolvency Systems and Debtor-Creditor Regimes' (2001)

Yoshino, M.Y. and Srinivasa Rangan, U., *Strategic Alliances: An Entrepreneurial Approach to Globalization* (Harvard Business School Press, Cambridge MA 1995)

Ziegel, J.S., 'Corporate Groups and Crossborder Insolvencies: A Canada-United States Perspective' (2002) 7 Fordham J. Corp. & Fin. L. 367

Ziegel, J.S., 'Canada-United States Cross-Border Insolvency Relations and the UNCITRAL Model Law' (2007) 32 Brook. J. Int'l L. 1041

Index

Printed and bound by CPI Group (UK) Ltd, Croydon, CR0 4YY